ISAIAH II

(Chapters 36–66)

THE PREACHER'S OUTLINE & SERMON BIBLE®

ISAIAH II

(CHAPTERS 36-66)

THE PREACHER'S OUTLINE & SERMON BIBLE®

OLD TESTAMENT

KING JAMES VERSION

Leadership Ministries Worldwide
Chattanooga, TN

THE PREACHER'S OUTLINE & SERMON BIBLE® ISAIAH II

KING JAMES VERSION

Please address all requests for information or permission to:
Leadership Ministries Worldwide
Ph.# (800) 987-8790   E-Mail: info@lmw.org
Web: lmw.org

Library of Congress Catalog Card Number: 96-75921
International Standard Book Number: 978-1-57407-208-2

Printed in the United States of America

DEDICATED

To all the men and women of the world
who preach and teach the Gospel of
our Lord Jesus Christ and
to the Mercy and Grace of God

&

- Demonstrated to us in Christ Jesus our Lord.

  "In whom we have redemption through His blood, the forgiveness of sins, according to the riches of His grace." (Ep.1:7)

- Out of the mercy and grace of God, His Word has flowed. Let every person know that God will have mercy upon him, forgiving and using him to fulfill His glorious plan of salvation.

  "For God so loved the world, that he gave His only begotten Son, that whosoever believeth in Him should not perish, but have everlasting life. For God sent not his son into the world to condemn the world, but that the world through him might be saved." (Jn.3:16-17)

  "For this is good and acceptable in the sight of God our Saviour; who will have all men to be saved, and to come unto the knowledge of the truth." (1 Ti.2:3-4)

10/22

The Preacher's Outline & Sermon Bible®

is written for God's servants to use in their study, teaching, and preaching of God's Holy Word...

- to share the Word of God with the world.
- to help believers, both ministers and laypersons, in their understanding, preaching, and teaching of God's Word.
- to do everything we possibly can to lead men, women, boys, and girls to give their hearts and lives to Jesus Christ and to secure the eternal life that He offers.
- to do all we can to minister to the needy of the world.
- to give Jesus Christ His proper place, the place the Word gives Him. Therefore, no work of Leadership Ministries Worldwide will ever be personalized.

ACKNOWLEDGMENTS AND BIBLIOGRAPHY

Every child of God is precious to the Lord and deeply loved. And every child as a servant of the Lord touches the lives of those who come in contact with him or his ministry. The writing ministries of the following servants have touched this work, and we are grateful that God brought their writings our way. We hereby acknowledge their ministry to us, being fully aware that there are many others down through the years whose writings have touched our lives and who deserve mention, but whose names have faded from our memory. May our wonderful Lord continue to bless the ministries of these dear servants—and the ministries of us all—as we diligently labor to reach the world for Christ and to meet the desperate needs of those who suffer so much.

THE REFERENCE WORKS

Aharoni, Yohanan, Michael Avi-Yonah, Anson F. Rainey and Ze'ev Safrai, Editors. *The MacMillan Bible Atlas*, 3rd Ed. Jerusalem: Carta, The Israel Map and Publishing Company, 1993.

Albright, W.F. *History, Archaeology and Christian Humanism.* New York: McGraw Hill, 1964.

Archer, Gleason L. *A Survey of Old Testament Introduction.* Chicago, IL: Moody Bible Institute of Chicago, 1974.

———. *Encyclopedia of Bible Difficulties.* Grand Rapids, Michigan: Zondervan Publishing House, 1982.

Atlas of the World. Hammond Concise Edition. Maplewood, NJ: Hammond Inc., 1993.

Baker's Dictionary of Theology. Everett F. Harrison, Editor-in-Chief. Grand Rapids, MI: Baker Book House, 1960.

Barker, William P. *Everyone in the Bible.* Westwood, NJ: Fleming H. Revell Co., 1966.

Benware, Paul N. *Survey of the Old Testament.* "Everyman's Bible Commentary." Chicago, IL: Moody Bible Institute of Chicago, 1993.

Bromiley, Geoffrey W., Editor, et. al. *David.* "The International Standard Bible Encyclopedia." Grand Rapids, MI: Eerdmans Publishing Co., 1988.

Brown, Francis. *The New Brown-Driver-Briggs-Gesenius Hebrew-English Lexicon.* Peabody, MA: Hendrickson Publishers, 1979.

Cruden's Complete Concordance of the Old & New Testament. Philadelphia, PA: The John C. Winston Co., 1930.

Dake, Finis Jennings. *Dake's Annotated Reference Bible, The Holy Bible.* Lawrenceville, GA: Dake Bible Sales, Inc., 1963.

Douglas, J.D. Editor. *New Bible Dictionary.* Wheaton, IL: Tyndale House Publishers, Inc., 1982.

Easton's 1897 Bible Dictionary. Database NavPress Software, 1996.

Elwell, Walter A., Editor. *The Evangelical Dictionary of Theology.* Grand Rapids, MI: Baker Book House, 1984.

Enhanced Nave's Topics. Database NavPress Software, 1991, 1994.

Frank, Harry Thomas, ed. *Atlas of the Bible Lands.* Maplewood, NJ: Hammond Incorporated, 1977.

Freedman, David Noel, Editor, et. al. *The Anchor Bible Dictionary.* New York: Doubleday, 1992.

Funk & Wagnalls Standard Desk Dictionary. Lippincott & Crowell, Publishers, 1980, Vol.2.

Geisler, Norman. *A Popular Survey of the Old Testament.* Grand Rapids, MI: Baker Book House, 1977.

Gill, Dr. A.L., Compiler. *God's Promises For Your Every Need.* Dallas, TX: Word Publishing, 1995.

Good News Bible. Old Testament: © American Bible Society, 1976. New Testament: © American Bible Society, 1966, 1971, 1976. Collins World.

Good News for Modern Man, The New Testament. New York, NY: American Bible Society, 1971.

Goodrick, Edward W. and John R. Kohlenberger, III. *The NIV Exhaustive Concordance.* Grand Rapids, MI: Zondervan Publishing House, 1990.

Grun, Bernard. *The Timetables of History.* 3rd Edition. New York: Simon & Schuster, 1991.

Harrison, Roland Kenneth. *Introduction to the Old Testament.* Grand Rapids, MI: Eerdmans Publishing Co., 1969.

Holman Bible Dictionary. Nashville, TN: Broadman & Holman Publishers, 1991. Database NavPress Software.

Hooper, Jerry L., Editor. *The Holman Bible Atlas.* Philadelphia, PA: A.J. Holman Company, 1978.

ISBE. Grand Rapids, MI: Eerdmans Publishing Co., 1988.

Josephus, Flavius. *Complete Works.* Grand Rapids, MI: Kregel Publications, 1981.

Kaiser, Walter C. *A History of Israel.* Nashville, Tennessee: Broadman and Holman Publishers, 1998.

Kipfer, Barbara Ann, Ph.D. *Roget's 21st Century Thesaurus.* New York, NY: Dell Publishing, 1992.

Kohlenberger, John R. III. *The Interlinear NIV Hebrew-English Old Testament.* Grand Rapids, MI: Zondervan Publishing House, 1987.

Kouffman, Donald T. *The Dictionary of Religious Terms.* Westwood, NJ: Fleming H. Revell Co., 1967.

Life Application® Bible. Wheaton, IL: Tyndale House Publishers, Inc., 1991.

Life Application® Study Bible. New International Version. Tyndale House Publishers, Inc.: Wheaton, IL 1991, and Zondervan Publishing House: Grand Rapids, MI, 1984.

Lindsell, Harold and Woodbridge, Charles J. *A Handbook of Christian Truth.* Westwood, NJ: Fleming H. Revell Company, A Division of Baker Book House, 1953.

Living Quotations For Christians. Edited by Sherwood Eliot Wirt and Kersten Beckstrom. New York, NY: Harper & Row, Publishers, 1974.

Lockyer, Herbert. *All the Books and Chapters of the Bible.* Grand Rapids, MI: Zondervan Publishing House, 1966.

———. *All the Kings and Queens of the Bible.* Grand Rapids, MI: Zondervan Publishing House, 1961.

———. *All the Men of the Bible.* Grand Rapids, MI: Zondervan Publishing House, 1958.

———. *All the Miracles of the Bible.* Grand Rapids, MI: Zondervan Publishing House, 1961.

———. *All the Parables of the Bible.* Grand Rapids, MI: Zondervan Publishing House, 1963.

———. *The Women of the Bible.* Grand Rapids, MI: Zondervan Publishing House, 1967.

Luckenbill, Daniel David. *Ancient Records of Assyria and Babylonia*, 2 Vols. (ARAB) London: Histories and Mysteries of Man Ltd., 1989.

Martin, Alfred. *Survey of the Scriptures*, Part I, II, III. Chicago, IL: Moody Bible Institute of Chicago, 1961.

McDowell, Josh. *Evidence That Demands a Verdict*, Vol.1. San Bernardino, CA: Here's Life Publishers, Inc., 1979.

Miller, Madeleine S. & J. Lane. *Harper's Bible Dictionary*. New York, NY: Harper & Row Publishers, 1961.

Nave, Orville J. *Nave's Topical Bible*. Nashville, TN: The Southwestern Company. Copyright © by J.B. Henderson, 1921.

Nelson's Complete Book of Bible Maps & Charts. Nashville, TN: Thomas Nelson Publishers, Inc., 1996.

New American Standard Bible, Updated Edition. La Habra, CA: The Lockman Foundation, 1995.

New Bible Dictionary, 3rd Edition. Leicester, England: Universities & Colleges Christian Fellowship, 1996.

New Living Translation, Holy Bible. Wheaton, IL: Tyndale House Publishers, Inc., 1996.

NIV Thompson Student Bible. Jauchen, John S., Editor, et. al. Indianapolis, IN: Kirkbride Bible Company, 1999.

Orr, James, Editor. *The International Standard Bible Encyclopaedia*, Grand Rapids, MI: Eerdmans Publishing Co., 1939.

Orr, William. *How We May Know That God Is*. Wheaton, IL: Van Kampen Press, n.d.

Owens, John Joseph. *Analytical Key to the Old Testament*, Vols.1, 2, 3. Grand Rapids, MI: Baker Book House, 1989.

Payne, J. Barton. *Encyclopedia of Biblical Prophecy*. New York, NY: Harper & Row, Publishers, 1973.

Pilgrim Edition, Holy Bible. New York, NY: Oxford University Press, 1952.

Ridout, Samuel. *Lectures on the Tabernacle*. New York, NY: Loizeaux Brothers, Inc., 1914.

Silverman, David P. ed. *Ancient Egypt*. New York: Oxford University Press, 1997.

Smith, William. *Smith's Bible Dictionary*. Peabody, MA: Hendrickson Publishers, n.d.

Stone, Nathan J. *Names of God*. Chicago, IL: Moody Press, 1944.

Strong, James. *Strong's Exhaustive Concordance of the Bible*. Nashville, TN: Thomas Nelson, Inc., 1990.

_____. *The Tabernacle of Israel*. Grand Rapids, MI: Kregel Publications, 1987.

Strong's Greek and Hebrew Dictionary as compiled by iExalt Software. Database NavPress Software, 1990-1993.

The Amplified Bible. Scripture taken from THE AMPLIFIED BIBLE, Old Testament copyright © 1965, 1987 by the Zondervan Publishing House. The Amplified New Testament copyright © 1958, 1987 by The Lockman Foundation. Used by permission.

The Holy Bible in Four Translations. Minneapolis, MN: Worldwide Publications. Copyright © The Iversen-Norman Associates: New York, NY, 1972.

The Illustrated Bible Atlas, with Historical Notes by F. F. Bruce. Grand Rapids, MI: Kregel Publications, 1994.

The Interlinear Bible, Vols.1, 2, 3. Translated by Jay P. Green, Sr. Grand Rapids, MI: Baker Book House, 1976.

The Interpreter's Bible, 12 Vols. New York, NY: Abingdon Press, 1956.

The NASB Greek/Hebrew Dictionary and Concordance. La Habra, CA: The Lockman Foundation, 1988.

The Nelson Study Bible, New King James Version. Earl D. Radmacher, General Editor. Nashville, TN: Thomas Nelson Publishers, Inc., 1997.

The New Compact Bible Dictionary. Edited by T. Alton Bryant. Grand Rapids, MI: Zondervan Publishing House, 1967. Used by permission of Zondervan Publishing House.

The New Scofield Reference Bible. Edited by C.I. Scofield. New York, NY: Oxford University Press, 1967.

The New Testament-English, PI-RHO. "The Complete Biblical Library." Springfield, MO: World Library Press Inc, 1991.

The New Thompson Chain Reference Bible. Indianapolis, IN: B.B. Kirkbride Bible Co., Inc., 1964.

The New Unger's Bible Dictionary. Chicago, IL: Moody Press, 1998. Database NavPress Software, 1997.

The NIV Study Bible, New International Version. Grand Rapids, MI: Zondervan Publishing House, 1985.

The Old Testament Hebrew-English Dictionary, NUN—AYIN. "The Complete Biblical Library." Springfield, MO: World Library Press Inc., 1999.

The Open Bible. Nashville, TN: Thomas Nelson Publishers, 1977.

The Quest Study Bible. New International Version. Grand Rapids, MI: Zondervan Publishing House, 1994.

The Zondervan Pictorial Encyclopedia of the Bible, Vol.1. Merrill C. Tenney, Editor. Grand Rapids, MI: Zondervan Publishing House, 1982.

Theological Wordbook of the Old Testament. Edited by R. Laird Harris. Chicago, IL: Moody Bible Institute of Chicago, 1980.

Unger, Merrill F. & William White, Jr. *Nelson's Expository Dictionary of the Old Testament*. Nashville, TN: Thomas Nelson Publishers, 1980.

Vine, W.E., Merrill F. Unger, William White, Jr. *Vine's Complete Expository Dictionary of Old and New Testament Words*. Nashville, TN: Thomas Nelson Publishers, 1985.

Walton, John H. *Chronological and Background Charts of the Old Testament*. Grand Rapids, MI: Zondervan Publishing House, 1978.

Webster's Seventh New Collegiate Dictionary. Springfield, MA: G. & C. Merriam Company, Publishers, 1971.

Wilmington. Harold L. *The Outline Bible*. Wheaton, IL: Tyndale House Publishers, Inc., 1999.

Wilson, William. *Wilson's Old Testament Word Studies*. McLean, VA: MacDonald Publishing Company, n.d.

Wood, Leon. *A Survey of Israel's History*. Grand Rapids, MI: Zondervan Publishing House, 1982.

Young, Edward J. *An Introduction to the Old Testament*. Grand Rapids, MI: Eerdmans Publishing Co., 1964.

Young, Robert. *Young's Analytical Concordance to the Bible*. Grand Rapids, MI: Eerdmans Publishing Co., n.d.

Zodhiates, Spiros, Th.D., Executive Editor. *The Hebrew-Greek Key Study Bible, New International Version*. Chattanooga, TN: AMG Publishers, 1996.

Zondervan NIV Bible Library. Version 2.5. Grand Rapids, MI: Zondervan Publishing House.

ACKNOWLEDGMENTS AND BIBLIOGRAPHY

THE COMMENTARIES

Alexander, Joseph Addison. *The Prophecies of Isaiah.* "The Zondervan Commentary Series." Grand Rapids, MI: Zondervan Publishing House, 1981.

Bultema, Harry. *Isaiah.* Grand Rapids, MI: Kregel Publications, 1981.

Burroughs, P.E., D.D. *Old Testament Studies.* Nashville, TN: Sunday School Board, Southern Baptist Convention, 1915.

Clements, R.E. *Isaiah 1-39.* "The New Century Bible Commentary." Grand Rapids, MI: Eerdmans Publishing Co., 1980.

Criswell, W.A. *Isaiah an exposition.* Grand Rapids, MI: Zondervan Publishing House, 1977.

Dilday, Russell. *The Preacher's Commentary on 1, 2 Kings.* Dallas, TX: Word Publishing, 1987.

Elwell, Walter A., Editor. *Topical Analysis of the Bible.* (Grand Rapids, MI: Baker Book House, 1991.

Evans, Mary J. *1 and 2 Samuel.* "New International Biblical Commentary." Peabody, MA: Hendrickson Publishers, Inc., 2000.

Griffin, Gilbert L. *The Gospel in Isaiah.* Nashville, TN: Convention Press, 1968.

Grogan, G.W. *Isaiah.* "The Expositor's Bible Commentary," Vol.6. Grand Rapids, MI: Zondervan Publishing House, 1988.

Henry, Matthew. *Matthew Henry's Commentary*, 6 Vols. Old Tappan, NJ: Fleming H. Revell Co., n.d.

Heschel, Abraham J. *The Prophets.* Peabody, MA: Prince Press, 1962.

Holladay, William L. *Isaiah: Scroll of a Prophetic Heritage.* Grand Rapids, MI: Eerdmans Publishing Co., 1978.

Horton, Stanley M. *Isaiah.* "The Complete Biblical Library: The Old Testament," Vol.9. Springfield, MO: World Library Press Inc., 1995.

Ironside, H.A. *The Prophet Isaiah.* Neptune, NJ: Loizeaux Brothers, Inc., 1952.

Jennings, F.C. *Studies in Isaiah.* Neptune, NJ: Loizeaux Brothers, Inc., n.d.

Kaiser, Walter C., Jr. *A History of Israel.* Nashville, TN: Broadman & Holman Publishers, 1998.

Keil-Delitzsch. *Commentary on the Old Testament*, Vol.7. Grand Rapids, MI: Eerdmans Publishing Co., n.d.

Kirkpatrick, A.F., General Editor. *The Book of the Prophet Isaiah Chapters I-XXXIX.* "The Cambridge Bible for Schools and Colleges." New York, NY: Cambridge University Press, 1958.

———. *The Book of the Prophet Isaiah Chapters XL-LXVI.* "The Cambridge Bible for Schools and Colleges." New York, NY: Cambridge University Press, 1960.

Leupold, H.C. *Exposition of Isaiah,* Vol.1. Grand Rapids, MI: Baker Book House, 1968.

———. *Exposition of Isaiah,* Vol.2. Grand Rapids, MI: Baker Book House, 1972.

Maclaren, Alexander. *Expositions of Holy Scripture*, 11 Vols. Grand Rapids, MI: Eerdmans Publishing Co., 1952-59.

Martin, Alfred. *Isaiah, The Salvation of Jehovah.* "Everyman's Bible Commentary." Chicago, IL: Moody Bible Institute of Chicago, 1956.

McGee, J. Vernon. *Thru the Bible*, Vol.3. Nashville, TN: Thomas Nelson Publishers, 1982.

McKenna, David. *Isaiah 1-39.* "Mastering the Old Testament," Vol.16A. Dallas, TX: Word Publishing, 1994.

———. *Isaiah 40–66.* "Mastering the Old Testament." Dallas, TX: Word Publishing, 1994.

Morgan, G. Campbell. *Living Messages of the Books of the Bible*, Vol.1. Old Tappan, NJ: Fleming H. Revell, 1912.

Morris, Henry M. *The Genesis Record.* Grand Rapids, MI., 1996.

Motyer, J. Alec. *Isaiah.* "The Tyndale Old Testament Commentaries." Downers Grove, IL: Inter-Varsity Press, 1999.

———. *The Prophecy of Isaiah.* Downers Grove, IL: Inter-varsity Press, 1993.

Oswalt, John N. *Isaiah 1-39.* "The New International Commentary on the Old Testament." Grand Rapids, MI: Eerdmans Publishing Co. 1982.

———. *Isaiah 1-39.* "The New International Commentary on the Old Testament." Grand Rapids, MI: Eerdmans Publishing Co., 1998.

Poole, Matthew. *Matthew Poole's Commentary on the Holy Bible*, Vol.2. Peabody, MA: Hendrickson Publishers, n.d.

Rawlinson, George. *Isaiah.* "The Pulpit Commentary." Grand Rapids, MI: Eerdmans Publishing Co., 1950.

Redpath, Alan. *Victorious Christian Service.* Westwood, NJ: Fleming H. Revell Co., 1958.

Schulz, Samuel J. *The Old Testament Speaks*, 4th Edition. San Francisco, CA: Harper Collins Publishers, 1990.

Smith, James E. *What the Bible Teaches about the Promised Messiah.* Nashville, TN: Thomas Nelson Publishers, 1993.

Spurgeon, C.H. *Spurgeon's Sermon Notes. Genesis to Malachi.* Westwood, NJ: Fleming H. Revell Co., n.d.

The Pulpit Commentary. 23 Vols. Edited by H.D.M. Spence & Joseph S. Exell. Grand Rapids, MI: Eerdmans Publishing Co., 1950.

Walvoord, John F. and Roy B. Zuck, Editors. *The Bible Knowledge Commentary, Old Testament.* Colorado Springs, CO: Chariot Victor Publishing, 1985.

Whybray, R.N. *Isaiah 40-66.* "The New Century Bible Commentary." Grand Rapids, MI: Eerdmans Publishing Co., 1975.

Wiersbe, Warren W. *Be Comforted.* Wheaton, IL: Victor Books, 1992.

Willis, John T. *Isaiah.* "The Living Word Commentary on the Old Testament." Abilene, TX: ACU Press, 1984.

Wright, G. Ernest. *Isaiah.* "The Layman's Bible Commentary," Vol.11. Atlanta, GA: John Knox Press, 1964.

Young, Edward J. *The Book of Isaiah,* Vol.1. Grand Rapids, MI: Eerdmans Publishing Co., 1965.

———. *The Book of Isaiah,* Vol.2. Grand Rapids, MI: Eerdmans Publishing Co., 1969.

———. *The Book of Isaiah,* Vol.3. Grand Rapids, MI: Eerdmans Publishing Co., 1972.

THE ARTWORK

Isaiah. Art Resource. New York, NY. www.artres.com; The Jewish Museum, New York, NY.

ABBREVIATIONS

&	=	and
Bc.	=	because
Concl.	=	conclusion
Cp.	=	compare
Ct.	=	contrast
e.g.	=	for example
f.	=	following
Illust.	=	illustration
N.T.	=	New Testament

O.T.	=	Old Testament
p./pp.	=	page/pages
Pt.	=	point
Quest.	=	question
Rel.	=	religion
Rgt.	=	righteousness
Thru	=	through
v./vv.	=	verse/verses
vs.	=	versus

THE BOOKS OF THE OLD TESTAMENT

Book	Abbreviation	Chapters	Book	Abbreviation	Chapters
GENESIS	Gen. or Ge.	50	Ecclesiastes	Eccl. or Ec.	12
Exodus	Ex.	40	The Song of Solomon	S. of Sol. or Song	8
Leviticus	Lev. or Le.	27	Isaiah	Is.	66
Numbers	Num. or Nu.	36	Jeremiah	Jer. or Je.	52
Deuteronomy	Dt. or De.	34	Lamentations	Lam.	5
Joshua	Josh. or Jos.	24	Ezekiel	Ezk. or Eze.	48
Judges	Judg. or Jud.	21	Daniel	Dan. or Da.	12
Ruth	Ruth or Ru.	4	Hosea	Hos. or Ho.	14
1 Samuel	1 Sam. or 1 S.	31	Joel	Joel	3
2 Samuel	2 Sam. or 2 S.	24	Amos	Amos or Am.	9
1 Kings	1 Ki. or 1 K.	22	Obadiah	Obad. or Ob.	1
2 Kings	2 Ki. or 2 K.	25	Jonah	Jon. or Jona.	4
1 Chronicles	1 Chron. or 1 Chr.	29	Micah	Mic. or Mi.	7
2 Chronicles	2 Chron. or 2 Chr.	36	Nahum	Nah. or Na.	3
Ezra	Ezra or Ezr.	10	Habakkuk	Hab.	3
Nehemiah	Neh. or Ne.	13	Zephaniah	Zeph. or Zep.	3
Esther	Est.	10	Haggai	Hag.	2
Job	Job or Jb.	42	Zechariah	Zech. or Zec.	14
Psalms	Ps.	150	Malachi	Mal.	4
Proverbs	Pr.	31			

THE BOOKS OF THE NEW TESTAMENT

Book	Abbreviation	Chapters	Book	Abbreviation	Chapters
MATTHEW	Mt.	28	1 Timothy	1 Tim. or 1 Ti.	6
Mark	Mk.	16	2 Timothy	2 Tim. or 2 Ti.	4
Luke	Lk. or Lu.	24	Titus	Tit.	3
John	Jn.	21	Philemon	Phile. or Phm.	1
The Acts	Acts or Ac.	28	Hebrews	Heb. or He.	13
Romans	Ro.	16	James	Jas. or Js.	5
1 Corinthians	1 Cor. or 1 Co.	16	1 Peter	1 Pt. or 1 Pe.	5
2 Corinthians	2 Cor. or 2 Co.	13	2 Peter	2 Pt. or 2 Pe.	3
Galatians	Gal. or Ga.	6	1 John	1 Jn.	5
Ephesians	Eph. or Ep.	6	2 John	2 Jn.	1
Philippians	Ph.	4	3 John	3 Jn.	1
Colossians	Col.	4	Jude	Jude	1
1 Thessalonians	1 Th.	5	Revelation	Rev. or Re.	22
2 Thessalonians	2 Th.	3			

HOW TO USE
The Preacher's Outline & Sermon Bible®
Follow these easy steps to gain maximum benefit from The POSB.

① SUBJECT HEADING

② MAJOR POINTS

③ SUBPOINTS
&
SCRIPTURE

④ COMMENTARY

CHAPTER 13

D. The Most Excellent Quality of Life: Love, Not Gifts, 13:1-13[DS1]

1. The great importance of love
a. Verdict 1: Tongues without love are meaningless

b. Verdict 2: Gifts without love are nothing
1) Prophecy is nothing
2) Understanding all mysteries & knowledge are nothing
3) Faith is nothing
c. Verdict 3: Giving without love profits nothing
1) Giving one's goods
2) Giving one's life—martyrdom

2. The great acts of love

Though I speak with the tongues of men and of angels, and have not charity, I am become *as* sounding brass, or a tinkling cymbal.
2 And though I have *the gift of* prophecy, and understand all mysteries, and all knowledge; and though I have all faith, so that I could remove mountains, and have not charity, I am nothing.
3 And though I bestow all my goods to feed *the poor,* and though I give my body to be burned, and have not charity, it profiteth me nothing.
4 Charity suffereth long, *and* is kind; charity envieth not; charity vaunteth not itself, is not puffed up,
5 Doth not behave itself unseemly, seeketh not her own, is not easily provoked, thinketh no evil;

6 Rejoiceth not in iniquity, but rejoiceth in the truth;
7 Beareth all things, believeth all things, hopeth all things, endureth all things.
8 Charity never faileth: but whether *there be* prophecies, they shall fail; whether *there be* tongues, they shall cease; whether *there be* knowledge, it shall vanish away.
9 For we know in part, and we prophesy in part.
10 But when that which is perfect is come, then that which is in part shall be done away.
11 When I was a child, I spake as a child, I understood as a child, I thought as a child: but when I became a man, I put away childish things.
12 For now we see through a glass, darkly; but then face to face: now I know in part; but then shall I know even as also I am known.
13 And now abideth faith, hope, charity, these three; but the greatest of these *is* charity.

3. The great permanence of love
a. It never fails, never ceases, never vanishes

b. It is perfect & complete

c. It is maturity—mature behavior

d. It is the hope of being face-to-face with God—possessing perfect consciousness & knowledge

4. The great supremacy of love

DIVISION VII

THE QUESTIONS CONCERNING SPIRITUAL GIFTS, 12:1–14:40

D. The Most Excellent Quality of Life: Love, Not Gifts, 13:1-13

(13:1-13) **Introduction**: there is no question, what the world needs more than anything else is love. If people loved each other, really loved each other, there would be no more war, crime, abuse, injustice, poverty, hunger, starvation, homelessness, deprivation, or immorality. Love is the one ingredient that could revolutionize society. Love is the greatest quality of human life. Love is the supreme quality, the most excellent way for a man to live.
1. The great importance of love (vv.1-3).
2. The great acts of love (vv.4-7).
3. The great permanence of love (vv.8-12).
4. The great supremacy of love (v.13).

DEEPER STUDY # 1
(13:1-13) **Love**: throughout this passage, the word used for love or charity is the great word *agape*. (See DEEPER STUDY # 4, *Love*—Jn.21:15-17 for more discussion.) The meaning of *agape love* is more clearly seen by contrasting it with the various kinds of love. There are essentially four kinds of love. Whereas the English language has only the word *love* to describe all the affectionate experiences of men, the Greek language had a different word to describe each kind of love.
1. There is *passionate love* or *eros love*. This is the physical love between sexes; the patriotic love of a person for his nation; the ambition of a person for power, wealth, or fame. Briefly stated, *eros love* is the base love of a man that arises from his own inner passion. Sometimes *eros love* is focused upon good and other times it is focused upon bad. It should be noted that *eros love* is never used in the New Testament.
2. There is *affectionate love* or *storge love*. This is the kind of love that exists between parent and child and between loyal citizens and a trustworthy ruler. *Storge love* is also not used in the New Testament.
3. There is an *endearing love*, the love that cherishes. This is *phileo love*, the love of a husband and wife for each other, of a brother for a brother, of a friend for the dearest of friends. It is the love that cherishes, that holds someone or something ever so dear to one's heart.
4. There is *selfless and sacrificial love* or *agape love*. Agape love is the love of the mind, of the reason, of the will. It is the love that goes so far...
   • that it loves a person even if he does not deserve to be loved
   • that it actually loves the person who is utterly unworthy of being loved

---

① Glance at the **Subject Heading**. Think about it for a moment.

② Glance at the **Subject Heading** again, and then the **Major Points** (1, 2, 3, etc.). Do this several times, reviewing them together while quickly grasping the overall subject.

③ Glance at **both** the **Major Points** and **Subpoints** together while reading the **Scripture**. Do this slower than Step 2. Note how these points sit directly beside the related verse and simply restate what the Scripture is saying—in Outline form.

④ Next read the **Commentary**. Note that the *Major Point Numbers* in the Outline match those in the Commentary. A small raised number (**DS1**, **DS2, etc.**) at the end of a Subject Heading or Outline Point, directs you to a related **Deeper Study** in the Commentary.

Finally, read the **Thoughts** and **Support Scripture** (not shown).

As you read and re-read, pray that the Holy Spirit will bring to your attention exactly what you should preach and teach. May God bless you richly as you study and teach His Word.

The POSB contains everything you need for sermon preparation:

1. **The Subject Heading** describes the overall theme of the passage, and is located directly above the Scripture (keyed *alphabetically*).

2. **Major Points** are keyed with an outline *number* guiding you to related commentary. Note that the Commentary includes *"Thoughts"* (life application) and abundant Supporting Scriptures.

3. **Subpoints** explain and clarify the Scripture as needed.

4. **Commentary** is fully researched and developed for every point.

   • **Thoughts** (in bold) help apply the Scripture to real life.

   • **Deeper Studies** provide in-depth discussions of key words.

---

*"Woe is unto me, if I
preach not the gospel"*
(1 Co.9:16)

TABLE OF CONTENTS
ISAIAH ~ II
(CHAPTERS 36–66)

---

* A detailed listing of all the Prophets, their messages, and practical application can be found in the Resource Section of Isaiah Vol.1 and also as a separate supplement to *The Preacher's Outline and Sermon Bible*® entitled Old Testament Prophets, now available for a minimal cost.

THE BOOK OF

ISAIAH

AUTHOR: the very first words of this great book declare that Isaiah is the author. Almost the entire book consists of the visions and sermons of Isaiah the prophet, the son of Amoz. Such has been the clear position down through church history. During the eighteenth century, however, many liberal theories arose disputing the authorship. Nevertheless the following evidence strongly supports the position that Isaiah the prophet is the author:

1. The book of *Isaiah* states in the very first verse that the prophet Isaiah is the author.
2. The book of *Isaiah* was written from the perspective of a prophet. Set in the time after the fall of the Northern Kingdom, Isaiah preached for many years to the Southern Kingdom of Judah, warning them time and again to turn to the LORD for help. The author has one distinct purpose in mind: to declare, as his name reveals, that salvation is of the LORD and Him alone. Over and over Isaiah challenged Judah to be faithful in worshipping the only living and true God. These facts point to a prophet being the author of the great book of *Isaiah*.
3. The book of *Isaiah* was apparently written no later than 680 B.C., in keeping with the time of Isaiah's ministry.
4. The historical facts contained in the book were known to Isaiah personally.
5. Jewish and Christian tradition have always stated that Isaiah is the author of the book.
6. Throughout the book of *Isaiah*, the style, words, and thinking of the author match that of a prophet.

Although the evidence points strongly to the prophet Isaiah's being the author, it is far more important to know the Divine Author. The Holy Spirit of God *breathed* or *inspired* the great book of *Isaiah*. Through His inspiration, the Holy Spirit has given to the world a clear warning against sin and a graphic picture of the saving power of God. The inspiring prophecies in the book of *Isaiah* were written both as a warning and a promise to every reader.

DATE: completed no later than 680 B.C. and perhaps not long after 701 B.C. when the Assyrian army was destroyed. Since tradition strongly suggests that Isaiah was martyred by being sawed in two, it is reasonable to believe that he wrote down his messages *during* his ministry. The time of Isaiah's ministry was during the great Babylonian and Assyrian Empires, after the Northern Kingdom had fallen and gone into captivity. All that was left of the great kingdom of Israel was the small territory of Judah, which included only the tribes of Judah and Benjamin. These were desperate times, when God's people lived under the constant and threatening shadow of great foreign powers.

The Judean kings reigning during Isaiah's ministry were:
⟹ Uzziah (792–740 B.C.)
⟹ Jotham (750–731 B.C.)
⟹ Ahaz (735–715 B.C.)
⟹ Hezekiah (729–686 B.C.)

TO WHOM WRITTEN: the Southern Kingdom of Judah in particular and to the human race in general. The book of *Isaiah* was first written to the small nation of Judah:
⟹ to present God's wonderful salvation to all who would listen
⟹ to warn people of the penalty of sin if they continued to disobey and reject God
⟹ to comfort those who trusted in the LORD
⟹ to paint a graphic picture of the Messiah, both of His suffering for the sins of the world and of His coming reign over the world

PURPOSE:
1. The *Historical* Purpose:
   a. To record God's prophecies concerning Judah and Jerusalem (chs.1–12).
   b. To record God's judgment of the nations and His triumph over the world (chs.13–27).
   c. To record God's warnings to His people (chs.28–35).
   d. To document the reign of Hezekiah and his deliverance from Assyria, showing how his reign marked a shift from the threat of Assyria to the captivity of Judah by Babylon (chs.36–39).
   e. To record God's prophecies concerning Israel's deliverance, comfort, and glorious future (chs.40–64).
   f. To record God's prophecies that give a glimpse into the millennial reign of Christ on earth and the fulfillment of human history (chs.65–66).
2. The *Doctrinal* or *Spiritual* Purpose:
   a. To call God's people back to salvation and faithfulness (chs.1–6).
   b. To prophesy of the coming Messiah (chs.7–12).
   c. To warn other nations of the futility of trying to stand against the sovereign LORD (chs.13–35).
   d. To illustrate through the life of Hezekiah the tremendous delivering power of the LORD, no matter what the circumstances (chs.36-39).
   e. To give comfort to the people of God, assuring them that they will never be forgotten (chs.40–48).
   f. To paint a graphic picture of the Messiah, the Suffering Servant of the LORD (chs.49–53).
   g. To share the prophecies concerning the reign of Christ—His ability to avenge His people and restore all things (chs.54-66).
3. The *Christological* or *Christ-Centered* Purpose: prophecies concerning Christ are more clearly seen in the book of *Isaiah* than in any other Old Testament book except for *Psalms*. Isaiah foresaw at least twenty prophecies about the Messiah. (For a complete list of Old Testament prophecies fulfilled by Christ, see 52:13–53:12, DEEPER STUDY #1, p.204.)

The richest passage in Isaiah concerning Jesus Christ is 52:13–53:12, where Isaiah describes in detail the passion (sacrificial death) of the Savior. In this beloved section of Scripture, we see Christ fulfilling the sacrificial work of the Law on the cross. This is vitally important to Isaiah, because he understood that Christ would do more than *cover* sin—He would actually *cleanse* from sin all who would believe. Jesus Christ, the Savior of the world, came through David's family line (11:1) and died for the sins of the world, just as Isaiah foretold (53:4-5).

INTRODUCTION TO ISAIAH

SPECIAL FEATURES:

1. *Isaiah* is "The Great Book That Offers Hope to a Rebellious People" (1:1–5:30).
2. *Isaiah* is "The Great Book That Tells of the Great Vision of the LORD on His Throne" (6:1–7).
3. *Isaiah* is "The Great Book That Records the Call of Isaiah" (6:8–13).
4. *Isaiah* is "The Great Book That Warns of Coming Judgment but Promises a Wonderful Savior" (7:1–9:7).
5. *Isaiah* is "The Great Book That Warns That God Will Not Tolerate Pride" (9:8–10:34).
6. *Isaiah* is "The Great Book That Paints a Glorious Picture of the Coming Messiah, the Son of David" (11:1–12:6).
7. *Isaiah* is "The Great Book That Prophesies Judgment on the Heathen Nations" (13:1–24:23).
8. *Isaiah* is "The Great Book That Tells of God's Unswerving Faithfulness to His People and His Triumph Over the World" (25:1–27:13).
9. *Isaiah* is "The Great Book That Gives Prophecy After Prophecy of Judgment but Assures the Restoration of God's People" (28:1–35:10).
10. *Isaiah* is "The Great Book That Records God's Great Deliverances of King Hezekiah" (36:1–39:8).
11. *Isaiah* is "The Great Book That Promises Comfort and Deliverance to God's People" (40:1–48:22).
12. *Isaiah* is "The Great Book That Prophesies the Coming Messiah, the Suffering Servant Who Would Die for the Sins of the World" (49:1–53:12).
13. *Isaiah* is "The Great Book That Tells of the New Covenant to Come" (54:1–55:13).
14. *Isaiah* is "The Great Book That Warns of God's Judgment upon Idolators" (56:1–58:14).
15. *Isaiah* is "The Great Book That Assures the Restoration of Zion" (59:1–60:22).
16. *Isaiah* is "The Great Book That Prophesies Good News to Be Brought by the Messiah" (61:1–11).
17. *Isaiah* is "The Great Book That Tells of the Coming Salvation of Zion" (62:1–64:12).
18. *Isaiah* is "The Great Book That Predicts Time and Again the Coming Kingdom of the Messiah and the Consummation of Human History" (65:1–66:24).

AN EXTENSIVE HISTORICAL AND PRACTICAL BACKGROUND TO THE TIMES OF ISAIAH

THE FOUR KINGS WHO RULED DURING ISAIAH'S MINISTRY

The voice of one crying in the wilderness,
"Prepare ye the way of the Lord" (Is.40:3).

UZZIAH—792-740 B.C.

JOTHAM—750-731 B.C.

AHAZ—735-715 B.C.

HEZEKIAH—729-686 B.C.

Isaiah by Duccio di Buoninsegna (1308-1311)

An Extensive Historical and Practical Background to the Times of Isaiah

The Four Kings Who Ruled During Isaiah's Ministry

OVERVIEW: to gain a proper understanding of the book of *Isaiah*, a person should be aware of the historical background in which his prophecies were first preached. The most accurate history book in the world is, of course, the Bible. And there is a large section in the book of *Second Chronicles* revealing much of what happened during the reigns of the four kings to whom Isaiah ministered (Uzziah [*also called Azariah*], Jotham, Ahaz and Hezekiah).

Take a look at the outline below. As you glance at the practical outline points, you will immediately begin to see what a tremendous resource this overview can be. The reign of each king is outlined in detail including thoughts for application and deeper studies. The outlines in the following pages will be a great help to your study of the great book of *Isaiah* the prophet.

BACKGROUND TO ISAIAH'S DAY

I. **THE REIGN OF UZZIAH (AZARIAH): A CLEAR WARNING AGAINST PRIDE AND ARROGANCE, 2 CHR.26:1-23**

II. **THE REIGN OF JOTHAM: A PICTURE OF HOLDING FAST UNTIL THE END OF LIFE, 2 CHR.27:1-9**

III. **THE REIGN OF AHAZ: A PICTURE OF UTTER WICKEDNESS AND TOTAL DEPRAVITY, 2 CHR.28:1-27**

IV. **THE REIGN OF HEZEKIAH (PART 1)—THE CLEANSING OF THE TEMPLE FOR WORSHIP: A LESSON ON THE GREAT NEEDS OF THE CHURCH, 2 CHR.29:1-36**

V. **THE REIGN OF HEZEKIAH (PART 2)—A MEANINGFUL CELEBRATION OF THE PASSOVER: A PICTURE OF TRUE REVIVAL, 2 CHR.30:1-27**

VI. **THE REIGN OF HEZEKIAH (PART 3)—HIS RELIGIOUS REFORMS: THE PICTURE OF A REVIVED, ORDERLY CHURCH, 2 CHR.31:1-21**

VII. **THE REIGN OF HEZEKIAH (PART 4)—HIS DELIVERANCE FROM ASSYRIA, TERMINAL ILLNESS, AND DEATH: A PICTURE OF GOD'S UNLIMITED, SOVEREIGN POWER, 2 CHR.32:1-33**

(The Four Kings Who Ruled During Isaiah's Ministry)

I. THE REIGN OF UZZIAH (AZARIAH): A CLEAR WARNING AGAINST PRIDE AND ARROGANCE, 2 CHR.26:1-23

OUTLINE	SCRIPTURE	SCRIPTURE	OUTLINE

1. Uzziah's early years—his righteousness & achievements: Rewarded for seeking God
a. Uzziah's background
  1) He was crowned at age 16
  2) He was known for recapturing & rebuilding Elath, an important seaport at the eastern tip of the Red Sea
  3) He had a long reign as king: 52 years
  4) He was the son of Amaziah & Jecoliah
 	
  5) He had a strong spiritual life
   • Lived a righteous life, pleasing the LORD
   • Sought God & was instructed in the fear of God (His Word)—by a man named Zechariah
   • Was prosperous, successful as long as he sought God
b. Uzziah's important & far-reaching achievements
  1) He achieved success in battle
   • Warred against the Philistines, thereby extending Judah's territory
   • Warred against the Arabs & Meunites
 	
   • Warred against the Ammonites who paid him tribute
   • Became so powerful, his fame spread all the way to Egypt
  2) He achieved success in construction projects
   • Built fortress towers on the great wall surrounding Jerusalem
   • Built forts in the desert of southern Judah
   • Built cisterns to catch rain water
  3) He achieved success in ranching & agriculture
   • Had large livestock herds
   • Had many farms, vineyards, & workers
  4) He achieved success in building a strong, well-
	Then all the people of Judah took Uzziah, who *was* sixteen years old, and made him king in the room of his father Amaziah.
	2 He built Eloth, and restored it to Judah, after that the king slept with his fathers.
	3 Sixteen years old *was* Uzziah when he began to reign, and he reigned fifty and two years in Jerusalem. His mother's name also *was* Jecoliah of Jerusalem.
	4 And he did *that which was* right in the sight of the LORD, according to all that his father Amaziah did.
	5 And he sought God in the days of Zechariah, who had understanding in the visions of God: and as long as he sought the LORD, God made him to prosper.
	6 And he went forth and warred against the Philistines, and brake down the wall of Gath, and the wall of Jabneh, and the wall of Ashdod, and built cities about Ashdod, and among the Philistines.
	7 And God helped him against the Philistines, and against the Arabians that dwelt in Gur-baal, and the Mehunims.
	8 And the Ammonites gave gifts to Uzziah: and his name spread abroad *even* to the entering in of Egypt; for he strengthened *himself* exceedingly.
	9 Moreover Uzziah built towers in Jerusalem at the corner gate, and at the valley gate, and at the turning *of the wall,* and fortified them.
	10 Also he built towers in the desert, and digged many wells: for he had much cattle, both in the low country, and in the plains: husbandmen *also,* and vine dressers in the mountains, and in Carmel: for he loved husbandry.
	11 Moreover Uzziah had an host of fighting men, that
		went out to war by bands, according to the number of their account by the hand of Jeiel the scribe and Maaseiah the ruler, under the hand of Hananiah, *one* of the king's captains.
		12 The whole number of the chief of the fathers of the mighty men of valour *were* two thousand and six hundred.
		13 And under their hand *was* an army, three hundred thousand and seven thousand and five hundred, that made war with mighty power, to help the king against the enemy.
		14 And Uzziah prepared for them throughout all the host shields, and spears, and helmets, and habergeons, and bows, and slings *to cast* stones.
		15 And he made in Jerusalem engines, invented by cunning men, to be on the towers and upon the bulwarks, to shoot arrows and great stones withal. And his name spread far abroad; for he was marvellously helped, till he was strong.
		16 But when he was strong, his heart was lifted up to *his* destruction: for he transgressed against the LORD his God, and went into the temple of the LORD to burn incense upon the altar of incense.
		17 And Azariah the priest went in after him, and with him fourscore priests of the LORD, *that were* valiant men:
		18 And they withstood Uzziah the king, and said unto him, *It appertaineth* not unto thee, Uzziah, to burn incense unto the LORD, but to the priests the sons of Aaron, that are consecrated to burn incense: go out of the sanctuary; for thou hast trespassed; neither *shall it be* for thine honour from the LORD God.
		19 Then Uzziah was wroth, and *had* a censer in his hand
			trained military
			• Was organized by Jeiel, secretary of the army, & his assistant Maaseiah
			
			• Was led by 2,600 officers from the clan leaders of Judah
			
			• Was an elite force of 307,500 troops
			
			• Was well-equipped by the king
			
			• Developed a special machine that was placed on the corners of the wall of Jerusalem: Shot arrows & hurled stones like a catapult
			5) He achieved great fame & power through God's mighty hand
			2. Uzziah's latter years—his slide into sin & his fall: Judged for personal pride
			a. Uzziah's sin: Exalted himself & boldly burned incense in the temple
			
			  1) The High Priest & eighty other brave priests confronted the king in the temple
			
			   • They informed him of his lawless act: Burning incense was to be performed only by a priest, God's appointed intercessor (the priest was a type of Christ the High Priest, who alone could make prayer [incense] acceptable to God)
			   • They asked him to leave the sanctuary
			  2) The king reacted in anger & broke out in a verbal

OUTLINE	SCRIPTURE	SCRIPTURE	OUTLINE
rage against the priests: Refused to put down the censer b. Uzziah's judgment: Leprosy suddenly broke out on his forehead 　1) He was rushed out of the temple by the priests: A symbol of defilement, Le.22:2-6; Nu.12:10, 15 　2) He was afflicted by God 　3) He had leprosy until the day he died 　4) He lived in isolation,	to burn incense: and while he was wroth with the priests, the leprosy even rose up in his forehead before the priests in the house of the LORD, from beside the incense altar. 20 And Azariah the chief priest, and all the priests, looked upon him, and, behold, he *was* leprous in his forehead, and they thrust him out from thence; yea, himself hasted also to go out, because the LORD had smitten him. 21 And Uzziah the king was a leper unto the day of his	death, and dwelt in a several house, *being* a leper; for he was cut off from the house of the LORD: and Jotham his son *was* over the king's house, judging the people of the land. 22 Now the rest of the acts of Uzziah, first and last, did Isaiah the prophet, the son of Amoz, write. 23 So Uzziah slept with his fathers, and they buried him with his fathers in the field of the burial which *belonged* to the kings; for they said, He *is* a leper: and Jotham his son	Le.13:46; Nu.5:1-14; 12:15; 2 K.7:3 　5) He was excluded from the temple 　6) He put his son in charge of the government c. Uzziah's death & burial 　1) His achievements: Were recorded by the prophet Isaiah, Is.1:1; 6:1 　2) His death & burial: Was not buried with the kings due to his leprosy but was buried in a nearby field

(26:1-23) Introduction: pride is often thought of only in positive terms, not as a negative trait, and certainly not as a sin. People must have a healthy self-image and strong self-esteem in order to be successful in life. If all a person does is focus upon his weaknesses and lack of skills, he will never be successful or achieve anything of significance. It is absolutely essential to recognize our strengths and skills in order to plow through life capably and productively. We should take pride in who we are and in the abilities God has given us, acknowledging that it has all come from God and has been given to us to make a worthwhile contribution to society. This is an acceptable pride, a humble pride.

But pride becomes sinful when we exalt who we are and esteem our abilities over the abilities of others. When we use our appearance, authority, or skills to degrade, humiliate, shame, dominate, or enslave others—this kind of pride is evil. It is wicked arrogance and will cause us to face the terrifying judgment of God.

In the present Scripture, we first see King Uzziah as a man who achieved great success. But, tragically, when he looked at his achievements, he began to feel *overly* important, to become prideful, exalting himself before the LORD and over others. Just as his father Amaziah and his grandfather Josiah had experienced strong and righteous beginnings, so did Uzziah. But also like his father and grandfather, he had ended his life in a weak, sinful condition. Early in their reigns all three kings ruled over the Southern Kingdom in righteousness and justice, faithfully serving the LORD and the people. But in the end, all three kings failed both the LORD and the people.

In reading this account about Uzziah, the returning exiles under Ezra could see a clear warning. They must guard against pride and arrogance. The task laying out before them was enormous, the task of restoring *true worship* in the temple and of rebuilding their nation. Nevertheless, success was assured if they would seek the LORD and remain faithful to Him. As they went about their day-to-day duties, the LORD would give them confidence and support, enabling them to achieve their goals. But as God blessed them, they would need to guard against vanity and over-confidence, against thinking they were better than others because God was blessing them so much more than others. Being alert to the seduction of pride was the great lesson they needed to learn from the reign of Uzziah. And it is the much-needed lesson we too need to learn. This is, *The Reign of Uzziah (Azariah): A Clear Warning Against Pride and Arrogance*, 26:1-23.

　1. Uzziah's early years—his righteousness and achievements: rewarded for seeking God (vv.1-15).
　2. Uzziah's latter years—his slide into sin and his fall: judged for personal pride (vv.16-23).

1 **(26:1-15) Seeking, God, Example of—God, Seeking, Example of—Uzziah, King of Judah, Reign of—Kings, of the Southern Kingdom of Judah—Uzziah, Achievements of—Uzziah, Spiritual Life**: in the early years of Uzziah's reign, he lived a life of righteousness and made many significant contributions to the nation. Remember that Uzziah's father, King Amaziah, had left the city of Jerusalem in utter ruin (25:21-24). In a war he had launched against Israel, he was totally defeated and forced to surrender the capital city. In attacking Jerusalem, the forces of Israel had broken down a major section of the wall and looted the temple and palace. They also took as hostages many of the skilled and wealthy of the land and exiled them to Samaria. It was during this time, right after the exile of his father Amaziah, that Uzziah was crowned king. Throughout Scripture, Uzziah is also called "Azariah." Most likely "Azariah" was his personal name and "Uzziah" his throne name. Uzziah ruled over Judah at the same time that Jeroboam II ruled over the Northern Kingdom. Both of these kings had long, successful reigns, and they surprisingly were able to restore the boundaries of Israel to those achieved under David and Solomon (6-7; 2 K.14:25).

　a. The basic facts about Uzziah's background are given first (vv.1-5). Although he was only 16 years old, Uzziah was crowned king by the people right after his father Amaziah was taken captive and deported to Samaria, the capital of the Northern Kingdom (25:23-24). Thus he ruled in a co-regency with his father until his father's death. After Amaziah died, Uzziah recaptured and rebuilt Elath, an important seaport at the eastern tip of the Red Sea (v.2). Decades earlier it had been conquered by Solomon (8:17-18), but it was lost during the reign of Jehoram (21:8-10). Now, Elath is once again brought under the control of Judah, which gave the nation an important seaport for commerce and economic growth.

　Uzziah had a long reign as king, ruling for 52 years (v.3). Keep in mind that many of these years, from about 792 to 767, were spent in a co-regency with his father. Uzziah's mother's name was Jecoliah.

　Uzziah had a strong spiritual life, living righteously and pleasing the LORD (v.4). In the early days of his life, he was placed under the care of a man named Zechariah who instructed him in the *visions* or *fear* of God (v.5). Most likely, this means that he was instructed in the Word of God, taught the commandments of God as well as the duties of the king. As long as Uzziah sought the LORD, he was successful and prosperous.

b. The LORD blessed King Uzziah richly and enabled him to accomplish one thing after another. Five noteworthy and far-reaching achievements are given by Scripture (vv.6-15). Keep in mind that all these achievements were gifts of God, blessings poured out upon Uzziah because he was seeking the LORD.

1) Uzziah achieved success in war and in extending Judah's territory (vv.6-8). To secure peace in the west, he subdued the Philistines by conquering three of their major cities. He rebuilt these cities and some other towns and established fortresses throughout the conquered territory (vv.6-7). These cities included Gath, Jabneh, and Ashdod. After securing peace in the west, he marched southeastward in order to secure peace along the eastern border. The LORD enabled him to overpower the Arabs and the Meunites, most likely nomadic tribes who constantly raided Judean settlements along the eastern border of the nation.

Uzziah was also able to subject the Ammonites under his rule, for they paid an annual tribute or tax to the Southern Kingdom of Judah. Because of his military power and achievements, his fame spread throughout all the surrounding nations, including Egypt.

2) Uzziah achieved success in several major construction projects (vv.9-10). Remember that much of Jerusalem—including a large section of the wall—had been destroyed when Jehoash of Israel defeated Uzziah's father (25:23-24). Uzziah constructed not only the wall of Jerusalem but also built the towers on top of the wall and then fortified them all. In addition, he constructed forts in the desert of southern Judah and built many cisterns to catch rainwater for the great herds of livestock throughout the desert regions of the nation.

3) Uzziah achieved success in ranching and in agriculture, for he was a man who loved the soil (v.10). Without question he was unusually blessed by God. He owned large herds of livestock and a great number of farms. He also employed many workers to handle his various business enterprises.

4) Uzziah also achieved success in building a strong, well-trained military (v.11). It was organized by the secretary of the army Jeiel and his assistant Maaseiah and was led by 2,600 officers from the clan leaders of Judah (vv.11-12). Under their command was an elite force of 307,500 troops (v.13). These troops were well-equipped by the king with shields, spears, body armor, bows, and slings used to hurl stones. Interestingly, Uzziah developed a special machine that was placed on the corners of the wall of Jerusalem, a machine that shot arrows and hurled stones like a catapult (v.15).

5) Uzziah achieved great fame, a fame that spread far and wide (v.15). But it must be remembered, his fame and power were due to the help of the LORD.

Thought 1. In looking at the life of Uzziah, we must remember the crisis this young man faced. The very city in which he was living was destroyed in a major war. At only 16 years old. In addition, the young man witnessed thousands of people being killed, injured, and maimed, others being taken captive and exiled to a foreign land. He even witnessed his father being taken prisoner and exiled. Once his father was removed from power, the people obviously turned to the young man and crowned him king, laying the burden of the devastated city and nation upon his young shoulders. Having just experienced and witnessed so much, he was no doubt gripped with a spirit of apprehension and fear. The young man could do but one thing: seek the LORD for His help. And, thankfully, Uzziah did seek the LORD—a practice that became the dominant trait of his early life.

No matter what we may face in life, the answer is to do just what Uzziah did: seek the LORD. When we seek the LORD, He hears and answers our prayers. He meets our needs. He helps us wherever we need help. No matter what the problem may be—any hardship, trial, misfortune, temptation, seduction, enticement—the LORD will help us if we will only seek Him. Listen to what God says about seeking Him:

> "But seek ye first the kingdom of God, and his righteousness; and all these things shall be added unto you" (Mt.6:33).

> "Ask, and it shall be given you; seek, and ye shall find; knock, and it shall be opened unto you" (Mt.7:7).

> "For every one that asketh receiveth; and he that seeketh findeth; and to him that knocketh it shall be opened" (Lu.11:10).

> "And he spake a parable unto them *to this end,* that men ought always to pray, and not to faint" (Lu.18:1).

> "That they should seek the Lord, if haply they might feel after him, and find him, though he be not far from every one of us" (Ac.17:27).

> "Is any among you afflicted? let him pray. Is any merry? let him sing psalms. Is any sick among you? let him call for the elders of the church; and let them pray over him, anointing him with oil in the name of the Lord" (Js.5:13-14).

> "But if from thence thou shalt seek the LORD thy God, thou shalt find *him,* if thou seek him with all thy heart and with all thy soul" (De.4:29).

> "Seek the LORD and his strength, seek his face continually" (1 Chr.16:11).

> "This poor man cried, and the LORD heard *him,* and saved him out of all his troubles" (Ps.34:6).

> "This *is* the generation of them that seek him, that seek thy face, O Jacob. Selah" (Ps.24:6).

> "*When thou saidst,* Seek ye my face; my heart said unto thee, Thy face, LORD, will I seek" (Ps.27:8).

> "From the end of the earth will I cry unto thee, when my heart is overwhelmed: lead me to the rock *that* is higher than I" (Ps.61:2).

> "He shall call upon me, and I will answer him: I *will be* with him in trouble; I will deliver him, and honour him" (Ps.91:15).

> "Seek the LORD, and his strength: seek his face evermore" (Ps.105:4).

BACKGROUND TO ISAIAH'S DAY

(The Four Kings Who Ruled During Isaiah's Ministry)

"With my whole heart have I sought thee: O let me not wander from thy commandments" (Ps.119:10).

"Seek ye the LORD while he may be found, call ye upon him while he is near" (Is.55:6).

"And it shall come to pass, that before they call, I will answer; and while they are yet speaking, I will hear" (Is.65:24).

"And ye shall seek me, and find *me*, when ye shall search for me with all your heart" (Je.29:13).

"And I [Daniel] set my face unto the Lord God, to seek by prayer and supplications, with fasting, and sackcloth, and ashes" (Da.9:3).

"Sow to yourselves in righteousness, reap in mercy; break up your fallow ground: for *it is* time to seek the LORD, till he come and rain righteousness upon you" (Ho.10:12).

"For thus saith the LORD unto the house of Israel, Seek ye me, and ye shall live" (Am.5:4).

"Seek ye the LORD, all ye meek of the earth, which have wrought his judgment; seek righteousness, seek meekness: it may be ye shall be hid in the day of the LORD's anger" (Zep.2:3).

2 (26:16-23) **Pride, Example of—Self-Exaltation, Example of—Uzziah, Sin and Failure of—Judgment, Caused by, Sin**: in Uzziah's latter years, he slipped into sin and suffered the judgment of God. His sin was the fatal flaw of pride and self-exaltation. So far as is known, this was the only blot and blemish in the life of Uzziah. But as Matthew Henry says, it was a very serious blot and blemish. Other kings were guilty of sexual immorality, murder, oppression, persecution and idolatry.[1] Although Uzziah was not guilty of these gross sins, he was guilty of the horrible sin of pride and of exalting himself before the LORD and over others.

a. Uzziah became *puffed up* with pride and a sense of self-importance. Note exactly what Scripture says: it was when he had achieved so much, when he became so powerful, successful, prosperous, and famous—that he began to feel prideful. And his pride was to lead to his downfall. Exalting himself as a God-appointed priest, he actually entered the temple and burned incense before the LORD—a function that was to be performed only by the priest, God's appointed intercessor. Obviously, in his own eyes he had achieved great things for the LORD and was important to the LORD; therefore, he felt he could personally approach God without the help of the priest. But Uzziah was mistaken, for the LORD had long ago commanded that only the priest was to burn incense within the temple. When the priest burned the incense, he was symbolizing the need for an intercessor to stand between the LORD and His people and their prayers. This pointed to the Lord Jesus Christ as the Perfect Intercessor, the Mediator who alone could stand between God and His people. After the coming of Christ, people were to approach God through Christ, the Perfect Intercessor. Thereafter, prayer was to be offered through Christ, and people were to be accepted only through Christ. Down through history it was important for this symbolism to be protected and kept pure, for the burning of incense was symbolizing God's appointed intercessor who was yet to come, the Lord Jesus Christ. For this reason, Uzziah committed a horrible sin when he usurped the role of the priest in burning the incense.

Soon after Uzziah entered the temple, the High Priest and eighty other brave priests confronted the king to rebuke and stop him from committing this terrible violation. When they asked him to leave the sanctuary, he reacted in anger and broke out in a verbal rage against the priests.

b. Because of Uzziah's *puffed up* pride and self-exaltation, God chastised and disciplined him (vv.20-21). As soon as the king broke out in a verbal rage against the priests, he was instantly stricken with leprosy—even while he was standing there spouting out his rage. The priest immediately noticed the leprosy breaking out on Uzziah and rushed him out of the temple. Leprosy was a symbol of defilement; and no matter the consequences or cost to them personally, the priests had to protect the temple from becoming defiled (Le.22:2-6; Nu.12:10, 15). However, Uzziah was not about to retaliate against them, for he knew that the affliction was due to the LORD's hand of judgment against him. He was afflicted with leprosy because he had sinned. And note, he had leprosy until the day he died (v.21). Because of his affliction, he was forced to live in isolation and to step aside from public ruling (Le.13:46; Nu.5:1-14; 12:15; 2 K.7:3). He was also excluded from worshipping in the temple. Left with no choice, he put his son in charge of the government, allowing father and son to rule in a co-regency until Uzziah's death (v.21).

c. A summary of Uzziah's achievements and life were recorded by the prophet Isaiah (vv.22-23). But just where Isaiah recorded these is not known, for they are not included in the biblical book of *Isaiah*. The only information given in the biblical book *Isaiah* concerns Uzziah's death (Is.1:1; 6:1; 7:1). Thus, the information must have come from some other writing by the prophet Isaiah. After Uzziah's death and burial in Jerusalem, he was succeeded on the throne by his son Jotham. With the death of Uzziah, the Southern Kingdom experienced one of its last peaceful and prosperous periods. Although the people were unaware of the fact at the time, never again would they enjoy such success and prosperity as a nation. Other than for a few years during Josiah's reign (640–609 B.C.), they would always be suffering from the oppression of another nation or else facing the threat and pressure of being attacked. The Northern Kingdom of Israel would fall first, but soon thereafter the Southern Kingdom of Judah would follow and the people would be taken into exile by the Babylonians. The patience of the LORD would soon run out. The day of His longsuffering and mercy would soon be over. Judgment would soon come.

> **Thought 1**. Pride and self-exaltation are serious blemishes upon the life of any person. Personal pride exalts oneself over others and degrades them. Pride says, "I am better than someone else, more worthy of attention, recognition, and honor." A person who is prideful declares that he or she is more attractive or appealing, more knowledgeable or skillful, better able to do things. Of course, we must acknowledge and give thanks for who we are and for the knowledge and skills we do have. But we must never exalt our appearance, personality, position, wealth or abilities over others by degrading, shaming, embarrassing, or lording ourselves over them. Being attractive or talented or skillful is a blessing from God and must never be used to demean or degrade others. Listen to what God's Holy Word says about the terrible sins of pride and self-exaltation:

---

[1] Matthew Henry. *Matthew Henry's Commentary,* Vol.4. (Old Tappan, NJ: Fleming H. Revell Co., n.d.), p.988.

BACKGROUND TO ISAIAH'S DAY

(The Four Kings Who Ruled During Isaiah's Ministry)

"And whosoever shall exalt himself shall be abased; and he that shall humble himself shall be exalted" (Mt.23:12).

"Love not the world, neither the things *that are* in the world. If any man love the world, the love of the Father is not in him. For all that *is* in the world, the lust of the flesh, and the lust of the eyes, and the pride of life, is not of the Father, but is of the world" (1 Jn.2:15-16).

"The wicked in *his* pride doth persecute the poor: let them be taken in the devices that they have imagined" (Ps.10:2).

"Therefore pride compasseth them about as a chain; violence covereth them *as* a garment" (Ps.73:6).

"Thou hast rebuked the proud *that are* cursed, which do err from thy commandments" (Ps.119:21).

"Be not wise in thine own eyes: fear the LORD, and depart from evil" (Pr.3:7).

"The fear of the LORD *is* to hate evil: pride, and arrogancy, and the evil way, and the froward mouth, do I hate" (Pr.8:13).

"*When* pride cometh, then cometh shame: but with the lowly *is* wisdom" (Pr.11:2).

"Pride *goeth* before destruction, and an haughty spirit before a fall" (Pr.16:18).

"He loveth transgression that loveth strife: *and* he that exalteth his gate seeketh destruction" (Pr.17:19).

"An high look, and a proud heart, *and* the plowing of the wicked, *is* sin" (Pr.21:4).

"Seest thou a man wise in his own conceit? *there is* more hope of a fool than of him" (Pr.26:12).

"*As* a roaring lion, and a ranging bear; *so is* a wicked ruler over the poor people" (Pr.28:15).

"And I will punish the world for *their* evil, and the wicked for their iniquity; and I will cause the arrogancy of the proud to cease, and will lay low the haughtiness of the terrible" (Is.13:11).

"For thou hast said in thine heart, I will ascend into heaven, I will exalt my throne above the stars of God: I will sit also upon the mount of the congregation, in the sides of the north: I will ascend above the heights of the clouds; I will be like the most High. Yet thou shalt be brought down to hell, to the sides of the pit" (Is.14:13-15).

"Though thou exalt *thyself* as the eagle, and though thou set thy nest among the stars, thence will I bring thee down, saith the LORD" (Obad.4).

II. THE REIGN OF JOTHAM: A PICTURE OF HOLDING FAST UNTIL THE END OF LIFE, 2 CHR. 27:1-9

OUTLINE	SCRIPTURE	SCRIPTURE	OUTLINE
1. Jotham's very successful life: A godly, righteous walk that pleased the LORD a. His background 　1) He reigned 16 years 　2) He was the son of Jerusha b. His spiritual life 　1) He lived a righteous life 　2) He did not abuse the temple, exalt himself as his father had done 　3) He had little influence on the people: They continued in false worship c. His building projects 　1) He rebuilt the Upper Gate of the Temple 　2) He repaired part of the wall of Jerusalem 　3) He built towns, forts, & towers d. His war with Ammon 　1) He conquered the nation 　2) He forced them to pay an	Jotham *was* twenty and five years old when he began to reign, and he reigned sixteen years in Jerusalem. His mother's name also *was* Jerushah, the daughter of Zadok. 2 And he did *that which was* right in the sight of the LORD, according to all that his father Uzziah did: howbeit he entered not into the temple of the LORD. And the people did yet corruptly. 3 He built the high gate of the house of the LORD, and on the wall of Ophel he built much. 4 Moreover he built cities in the mountains of Judah, and in the forests he built castles and towers. 5 He fought also with the king of the Ammonites, and prevailed against them. And	the children of Ammon gave him the same year an hundred talents of silver, and ten thousand measures of wheat, and ten thousand of barley. So much did the children of Ammon pay unto him, both the second year, and the third. 6 So Jotham became mighty, because he prepared his ways before the LORD his God. 7 Now the rest of the acts of Jotham, and all his wars, and his ways, lo, they *are* written in the book of the kings of Israel and Judah. 8 He was five and twenty years old when he began to reign, and reigned sixteen years in Jerusalem. 9 And Jotham slept with his fathers, and they buried him in the city of David: and Ahaz his son reigned in his stead.	annual tribute for 3 years • 7,500 pounds of silver • 50,000 bushels of wheat • 50,000 bushels of barley **2. Jotham's very powerful reign: An obedient, steadfast rule that was blessed by the LORD** a. His achievements: Recorded in *The Book of the Kings of Israel & Judah* b. His reign: Was 25 years old when he was crowned & ruled for 16 years c. His death & burial: In Jerusalem d. His successor: Ahaz, his son

(27:1-9) Introduction: holding fast, persevering, being steadfast—these are traits that are lacking in so many lives today. Far too many people begin something—a project, a task, a program, a job, a relationship—and then never finish what they started. How many of us have begun projects and never finished them? Or have taken entirely too long to complete them? How many of us make promises and fail to keep them? How many children fail to do the tasks or chores assigned by parents? How many husbands and wives fail to keep their promise to be faithful to one another? How many workers fail to be diligent, loyal, and conscientious in their responsibilities? How many of us have made a commitment to the LORD and then slacked off, failing to be steadfast and dedicated? How many of us no longer hold fast to the profession of faith we have made?

The present Scripture is the story of King Jotham, a man who held fast to the end of his life. He persevered and followed the LORD through all the years of his life. When reading this account about Jotham, the returning exiles would have a dynamic example of the kind of life they needed to live. If they persevered in following the LORD, the LORD would bless them and help them to restore *true worship* to the temple and rebuild their nation. Just as the LORD had blessed King Jotham, so He would bless them if they continued to be faithful in following the LORD. This is, *The Reign of Jotham: A Picture of Holding Fast Until the End of Life*, 27:1-9.

1. Jotham's very successful life: a godly, righteous walk that pleased the LORD (vv.1-5).
2. Jotham's very powerful reign: an obedient, steadfast rule that was blessed by the LORD (vv.6-9).

1 **(27:1-5) Walk, Spiritual, Example of—Spiritual Walk, Example of—Righteous, Walk, Example of—Jotham, King of Judah, Reign of—Judah, Kingdom of, Kings**: Jotham, Uzziah's son, had a very successful life. He was greatly blessed because of his righteous walk before the LORD.

Jotham was only 25 years old when he was crowned king, and he reigned for 16 years, 11 of which were apparently spent as co-regent with his father Uzziah (26:21). Remember, his father had been stricken with leprosy because he failed to worship God as instructed. Because a person with leprosy was isolated, not able to carry on public functions, Jotham had to step in and rule with his father, managing the government while his father served behind the scenes. Jotham's mother was Jerusha, the daughter of the priest Zadok, which gives some indication that she lived a righteous life just as her husband King Uzziah had done prior to his downfall (26:4-5).

With a godly father and mother as examples, Jotham lived a righteous life before the LORD. He was strong and faithful in worship, proving to be even more faithful than his father. Uzziah had allowed his power to go to his head and committed the terrible sin of exalting himself before the LORD and over other people (the priests). But not Jotham. He always approached the LORD just as instructed. And he apparently always walked righteously before the LORD, executing true justice throughout the nation. However, his righteous reign seemed to have little influence on the people, for many of them continued to walk in their corrupt ways and to worship false gods. If he failed in any area, it was in this, that he failed to remove the high places of false worship. By not removing them, he became a stumbling block to the people, allowing them to continue to worship at the very site where false gods had formerly been worshipped. Down through the years, many of the people had allowed some of the false worship to seep into their worship of the LORD. As a result, much of the people's worship was now corrupted, nothing more than the worship of idols and false gods. Jotham allowed the people to continue their false worship at the high places. He failed to launch a reformation to turn the people back to the LORD. Thus Jotham stood guilty before the LORD and no doubt cut the heart of God. The *sins of omission* make a person just as guilty as the *sins of commission*. Therefore, failing to do right made Jotham just as guilty as the kings before him who had done wrong.

While serving as co-regent with his father Uzziah, Jotham continued the public works projects launched by his father. Then after his father's death, he completed several major building projects of his own. These included rebuilding the *upper gate* of the temple that stood near the palace. This was the major gate used by the king and his royal officials. He also repaired part of the wall of Jerusalem in addition to building towns, forts, and military lookout towers (vv.3-4). These were necessary for military defense and for storing food, supplies, and weapons. Maintaining a standing army and building fortresses and supply centers throughout the nation was an unending project for the kings of Judah (8:2, 4-6; 11:5-12; 14:6-8; 17:12-19; 26:9-15).

At some point during Jotham's reign, the Ammonites rebelled against Judah and refused to pay their annual tribute or tax. Losing this tax base would have seriously affected the economy of Judah. For this reason, Jotham was forced to march against the Ammonites, to conquer and reinstate the annual tax. The annual payments amounted to 7,500 pounds of silver, 50,000 bushels of wheat, and 50,000 bushels of barley. For a period of three years, the Ammonites faithfully paid the tribute, but the tribute then stopped, suggesting that the Ammonites were finally able to break free from Judean domination and gain their independence.

> **Thought 1**. A godly, righteous life pleases the LORD. If we follow the LORD day by day and keep His commandments, He promises to bless us. If we obey Him, He will be present with us, guiding and meeting our every need. God promises to look after and take care of the faithful, obedient believer. When we are faithful, God gives us the power to conquer all the trials and temptations of life. No matter what the hardship or misfortune, the seduction or enticement, God will give us the strength to triumphantly overcome the problem or to victoriously walk through it. Through the presence and power of Christ, we are given a victorious life. But to receive the presence and power of Christ we must live godly, righteous lives. We must obey the LORD, keep His holy commandments. Listen to what God's Holy Word says:

> "For I say unto you, That except your righteousness shall exceed *the righteousness* of the scribes and Pharisees, ye shall in no case enter into the kingdom of heaven" (Mt.5:20).
> "But seek ye first the kingdom of God, and his righteousness; and all these th *his* to your shame" (1 Co.15:34).
> "Wherefore take unto you the whole armour of God, that ye may be able to withstand in the evil day, and having done all, to stand. Stand therefore, having your loins girt about with truth, and having on the breastplate of righteousness" (Ep.6:13-14).
> "And this I pray, that your love may abound yet more and more in knowledge and *in* all judgment; That ye may approve things that are excellent; that ye may be sincere and without offence till the day of Christ; Being filled with the fruits of righteousness, which are by Jesus Christ, unto the glory and praise of God" (Ph.1:9-11).
> "I exhort therefore, that, first of all, supplications, prayers, intercessions, *and* giving of thanks, be made for all men; For kings, and *for* all that are in authority; that we may lead a quiet and peaceable life in all godliness and honesty" (1 Ti.2:1-2).
> "But refuse profane and old wives' fables, and exercise thyself *rather* unto godliness" (1 Ti.4:7).
> "For bodily exercise profiteth little: but godliness is profitable unto all things, having promise of the life that now is, and of that which is to come" (1 Ti.4:8).
> "But godliness with contentment is great gain" (1 Ti.6:6).
> "But thou, O man of God, flee these things; and follow after righteousness, godliness, faith, love, patience, meekness. Fight the good fight of faith, lay hold on eternal life, whereunto thou art also called, and hast professed a good profession before many witnesses" (1 Ti.6:11-12).
> "Teaching us that, denying ungodliness and worldly lusts, we should live soberly, righteously, and godly, in this present world; Looking for that blessed hope, and the glorious appearing of the great God and our Saviour Jesus Christ" (Tit.2:12-13).
> "*This is* a faithful saying, and these things I will that thou affirm constantly, that they which have believed in God might be careful to maintain good works. These things are good and profitable unto men" (Tit.3:8).
> "But whoso looketh into the perfect law of liberty, and continueth *therein*, he being not a forgetful hearer, but a doer of the work, this man shall be blessed in his deed" (Js.1:25).
> "But the day of the Lord will come as a thief in the night; in the which the heavens shall pass away with a great noise, and the elements shall melt with fervent heat, the earth also and the works that are therein shall be burned up. *Seeing* then *that* all these things shall be dissolved, what manner *of persons* ought ye to be in *all* holy conversation [behavior, conduct] and godliness, Looking for and hasting unto the coming of the day of God, wherein the heavens being on fire shall be dissolved, and the elements shall melt with fervent heat? Nevertheless we, according to his promise, look for new heavens and a new earth, wherein dwelleth righteousness. Wherefore, beloved, seeing that ye look for such things, be diligent that ye may be found of him in peace, without spot, and blameless" (2 Pe.3:10-14).
> "Blessed *are* they that do his commandments, that they may have right to the tree of life, and may enter in through the gates into the city" (Re.22:14).
> "Now therefore, if ye will obey my voice indeed, and keep my covenant, then ye shall be a peculiar treasure unto me above all people: for all the earth *is* mine" (Ex.19:5).

"Thou shalt keep therefore his statutes, and his commandments, which I command thee this day, that it may go well with thee, and with thy children after thee, and that thou mayest prolong *thy* days upon the earth, which the LORD thy God giveth thee, for ever" (De.4:40).

"Keep therefore the words of this covenant, and do them, that ye may prosper in all that ye do" (De.29:9).

"And if thou wilt walk in my ways, to keep my statutes and my commandments, as thy father David did walk, then I will lengthen thy days" (1 K.3:14).

"Then shalt thou prosper, if thou takest heed to fulfil the statutes and judgments which the LORD charged Moses with concerning Israel: be strong, and of good courage; dread not, nor be dismayed" (1 Chr.22:13).

"And he sought God in the days of Zechariah, who had understanding in the visions of God: and as long as he sought the LORD, God made him to prosper" (2 Chr.26:5).

"And in every work that he began in the service of the house of God, and in the law, and in the commandments, to seek his God, he did *it* with all his heart, and prospered" (2 Chr.31:21).

"Blessed *is* the man that walketh not in the counsel of the ungodly, nor standeth in the way of sinners, nor sitteth in the seat of the scornful. But his delight *is* in the law of the LORD; and in his law doth he meditate day and night. And he shall be like a tree planted by the rivers of water, that bringeth forth his fruit in his season; his leaf also shall not wither; and whatsoever he doeth shall prosper" (Ps.1:1-3).

"Though a sinner do evil an hundred times, and his *days* be prolonged, yet surely I know that it shall be well with them that fear God, which fear before him" (Ec.8:12).

"Say ye to the righteous, that *it shall be* well *with him:* for they shall eat the fruit of their doings" (Is.3:10).

"Sow to yourselves in righteousness, reap in mercy; break up your fallow ground: for *it is* time to seek the LORD, till he come and rain righteousness upon you" (Ho.10:12).

---

2 (27:6-9) **Obedience, Example of—Steadfastness, Example of—Jotham, Power of—Blessings, of God, Source of—Success, Source of—Obedience, Results of, God's Blessings—Steadfastness, Results of—Perseverance, Results of**: King Jotham was greatly blessed by God and grew more and more powerful throughout the years of his reign. God blessed him because he remained faithful to the LORD, obeying and keeping the LORD's commandments. He was steadfast in following the LORD, persevering to the very end of his life. Unlike so many in the past who had started out well but ended up forsaking the LORD, Jotham stayed true to the LORD all his days. He was faithful from beginning to end.

Jotham's life and achievements were recorded in *The Book of the Kings of Israel and Judah* (v.7). As mentioned earlier, he began to reign when he was 25 years old and ruled for 16 years (v.8). After his death, he was buried in Jerusalem and succeeded by his son Ahaz.

A significant fact needs to be noted about the people of Judah during these days. Under Uzziah's and Jotham's rule, Judah became very prosperous. The nation was strong both economically and militarily. The people became comfortable, so comfortable that they eventually became complacent and ignored the LORD and His commandments. In forgetting and neglecting the LORD, they set the stage for a king who would be utterly wicked and totally depraved. This man was to be the very next king, King Ahaz the son of Jotham. Just how complacent and wicked the people became is vividly described by the prophet Isaiah (see Isaiah chs.1–5). But for now, the lesson for us to note is the obedience and faithfulness of Jotham.

Thought 1. As believers, we are to obey the LORD, to be steadfast in following after Him. We are to persevere to the end, for all who persevere will be saved (Mt.10:22). Listen to what God's Holy Word says:
(1) We must obey the LORD.

"Not every one that saith unto me, Lord, Lord, shall enter into the kingdom of heaven; but he that doeth the will of my Father which is in heaven. Many will say to me in that day, Lord, Lord, have we not prophesied in thy name? and in thy name have cast out devils? and in thy name done many wonderful works? And then will I profess unto them, I never knew you: depart from me, ye that work iniquity" (Mt.7:21-23).

"Therefore whosoever heareth these sayings of mine, and doeth them, I will liken him unto a wise man, which built his house upon a rock: And the rain descended, and the floods came, and the winds blew, and beat upon that house; and it fell not: for it was founded upon a rock. And every one that heareth these sayings of mine, and doeth them not, shall be likened unto a foolish man, which built his house upon the sand: And the rain descended, and the floods came, and the winds blew, and beat upon that house; and it fell: and great was the fall of it" (Mt.7:24-27).

"Jesus answered and said unto him, If a man love me, he will keep my words: and my Father will love him, and we will come unto him, and make our abode with him" (Jn.14:23).

"If ye keep my commandments, ye shall abide in my love; even as I have kept my Father's commandments, and abide in his love" (Jn.15:10).

"Ye are my friends, if ye do whatsoever I command you" (Jn.15:14).

"Blessed *are* they that do his commandments, that they may have right to the tree of life, and may enter in through the gates into the city" (Re.22:14).

"Now therefore, if ye will obey my voice indeed, and keep my covenant, then ye shall be a peculiar treasure unto me above all people: for all the earth *is* mine" (Ex.19:5).

"Ye shall not tempt the LORD your God, as ye tempted *him* in Massah" (De.6:16).

"This book of the law shall not depart out of thy mouth; but thou shalt meditate therein day and night, that thou mayest observe to do according to all that is written therein: for then thou shalt make thy way prosperous, and then thou shalt have good success" (Jos.1:8).

"And Samuel said, Hath the LORD *as great* delight in burnt offerings and sacrifices, as in obeying the voice of the LORD? Behold, to obey *is* better than sacrifice, *and* to hearken than the fat of rams" (1 S.15:22).

(2) We must be faithful, steadfast, persevering to the very end.

"And ye shall be hated of all *men* for my name's sake: but he that endureth to the end shall be saved" (Mt.10:22).

"As the Father hath loved me, so have I loved you: continue ye in my love" (Jn.15:9).

"Therefore, my beloved brethren, be ye stedfast, unmovable, always abounding in the work of the Lord, forasmuch as ye know that your labour is not in vain in the Lord" (1 Co.15:58).

"Stand fast therefore in the liberty wherewith Christ hath made us free, and be not entangled again with the yoke of bondage" (Ga.5:1).

"And let us not be weary in well doing: for in due season we shall reap, if we faint not" (Ga.6:9).

"Only let your conversation [conduct, behavior] be as it becometh the gospel of Christ: that whether I come and see you, or else be absent, I may hear of your affairs, that ye stand fast in one spirit, with one mind striving together for the faith of the gospel" (Ph.1:27).

"Prove all things; hold fast that which is good. Abstain from all appearance of evil. And the very God of peace sanctify you wholly; and *I pray God* your whole spirit and soul and body be preserved blameless unto the coming of our Lord Jesus Christ" (1 Th.5:21-23).

"Seeing then that we have a great high priest, that is passed into the heavens, Jesus the Son of God, let us hold fast *our* profession" (He.4:14).

"Let us hold fast the profession of *our* faith without wavering; (for he is faithful that promised;)" (He.10:23).

"Wherefore seeing we also are compassed about with so great a cloud of witnesses, let us lay aside every weight, and the sin which doth *so* easily beset us, and let us run with patience the race that is set before us" (He.12:1).

"Blessed *is* the man that endureth temptation: for when he is tried, he shall receive the crown of life, which the Lord hath promised to them that love him" (Js.1:12).

"Behold, we count them happy which endure. Ye have heard of the patience of Job, and have seen the end of the Lord; that the Lord is very pitiful, and of tender mercy" (Js.5:11).

"Wherefore gird up the loins of your mind, be sober, and hope to the end for the grace that is to be brought unto you at the revelation of Jesus Christ" (1 Pe.1:13).

"Be sober, be vigilant; because your adversary the devil, as a roaring lion, walketh about, seeking whom he may devour: Whom resist stedfast in the faith, knowing that the same afflictions are accomplished in your brethren that are in the world" (1 Pe.5:8-9).

"Ye therefore, beloved, seeing ye know *these things* before, beware lest ye also, being led away with the error of the wicked, fall from your own stedfastness. But grow in grace, and *in* the knowledge of our Lord and Saviour Jesus Christ. To him *be* glory both now and for ever. Amen" (2 Pe.3:17-18).

"Remember therefore how thou hast received and heard, and hold fast, and repent. If therefore thou shalt not watch, I will come on thee as a thief, and thou shalt not know what hour I will come upon thee" (Re.3:3).

"Behold, I come quickly: hold that fast which thou hast, that no man take thy crown" (Re.3:11).

"But cleave unto the LORD your God, as ye have done unto this day" (Jos.23:8).

"If iniquity *be* in thine hand, put it far away, and let not wickedness dwell in thy tabernacles. For then shalt thou lift up thy face without spot; yea, thou shalt be stedfast, and shalt not fear" (Jb.11:14-15).

"The righteous also shall hold on his way, and he that hath clean hands shall be stronger and stronger" (Jb.17:9).

III. THE REIGN OF AHAZ: A PICTURE OF UTTER WICKEDNESS AND TOTAL DEPRAVITY, 2 CHR.28:1-27

OUTLINE	SCRIPTURE	SCRIPTURE	OUTLINE
1. Ahaz's shameful & devastating evil: The awful depth of wickedness & false worship a. He began to rule at age 20 & ruled for 16 years b. He was wicked: Did not live righteously as David had c. He followed the sinful ways of Israel's kings d. He promoted & led the people in false worship e. He committed the detestable sin of *human sacrifice*, even sacrificing his own sons f. He was totally committed to false worship **2. Ahaz's defeat by a Syrian & Israelite alliance (the Syro-Ephraimite War): A picture of God's justice & judgment** a. The defeat by Syria 1) The defeat was allowed by God 2) The defeat resulted in many prisoners' being exiled to Damascus b. The defeat by Israel 1) The Israelite king, Pekah, killed 120,000 soldiers in one day of the battle: Allowed by God as a just judgment for Judah's terrible evil 2) The Israelite warrior Zicri killed three royal officials • Maaseiah, the king's son • Azrikam, palace manager • Elkanah, second in command 3) The Israelites ransacked the cities of Judah • Exiled 200,000 women & children • Took a large amount of plunder c. The warning of God to victorious Israel: Sent by the prophet Obed 1) They were guilty of excessive cruelty • Had been allowed to de-	Ahaz *was* twenty years old when he began to reign, and he reigned sixteen years in Jerusalem: but he did not *that which was* right in the sight of the LORD, like David his father: 2 For he walked in the ways of the kings of Israel, and made also molten images for Baalim. 3 Moreover he burnt incense in the valley of the son of Hinnom, and burnt his children in the fire, after the abominations of the heathen whom the LORD had cast out before the children of Israel. 4 He sacrificed also and burnt incense in the high places, and on the hills, and under every green tree. 5 Wherefore the LORD his God delivered him into the hand of the king of Syria; and they smote him, and carried away a great multitude of them captives, and brought *them* to Damascus. And he was also delivered into the hand of the king of Israel, who smote him with a great slaughter. 6 For Pekah the son of Remaliah slew in Judah an hundred and twenty thousand in one day, *which were* all valiant men; because they had forsaken the LORD God of their fathers. 7 And Zichri, a mighty man of Ephraim, slew Maaseiah the king's son, and Azrikam the governor of the house, and Elkanah *that was* next to the king. 8 And the children of Israel carried away captive of their brethren two hundred thousand, women, sons, and daughters, and took also away much spoil from them, and brought the spoil to Samaria. 9 But a prophet of the LORD was there, whose name *was* Oded: and he went out before the host that came to Samaria, and said unto them, Behold, because the LORD God of	your fathers was wroth with Judah, he hath delivered them into your hand, and ye have slain them in a rage *that* reacheth up unto heaven. 10 And now ye purpose to keep under the children of Judah and Jerusalem for bondmen and bondwomen unto you: *but are there* not with you, even with you, sins against the LORD your God? 11 Now hear me therefore, and deliver the captives again, which ye have taken captive of your brethren: for the fierce wrath of the LORD *is* upon you. 12 Then certain of the heads of the children of Ephraim, Azariah the son of Johanan, Berechiah the son of Meshillemoth, and Jehizkiah the son of Shallum, and Amasa the son of Hadlai, stood up against them that came from the war, 13 And said unto them, Ye shall not bring in the captives hither: for whereas we have offended against the LORD *already,* ye intend to add *more* to our sins and to our trespass: for our trespass is great, and *there is* fierce wrath against Israel. 14 So the armed men left the captives and the spoil before the princes and all the congregation. 15 And the men which were expressed by name rose up, and took the captives, and with the spoil clothed all that were naked among them, and arrayed them, and shod them, and gave them to eat and to drink, and anointed them, and carried all the feeble of them upon asses, and brought them to Jericho, the city of palm trees, to their brethren: then they returned to Samaria. 16 At that time did king Ahaz send unto the kings of Assyria to help him. 17 For again the Edomites had come and smitten Judah, and carried away captives. 18 The Philistines also had	feat Judah because of God • Had gone too far in their cruelty: Their rage reached & disturbed all heaven 2) They were guilty of enslaving the men & women—guilty of sin against God, Le.25:39-46 3) They must return the slaves, for God's fierce wrath had turned against them (was ready to strike out with a just anger & judgment) d. The confrontation by some of Israel's leaders with the army 1) The leadership appointed a delegation of four to confront the army commanders 2) The delegation negotiated the release of the prisoners • Pointed out Israel's sin & guilt • Argued that God's fierce wrath had turned against them 3) The delegation convinced the army to turn over the prisoners & the plunder to them 4) The delegation ministered to the prisoners & personally escorted them back home to Judah • Clothed & fed them • Took care of the injured & wounded • Provided transportation for the weak • Escorted them back as far as Jericho **3. Ahaz's failed alliance with Assyria: A man who looked for a savior other than the LORD**[DS1] a. The reason for Ahaz's appeal for help from Assyria 1) Because of constant danger & the threat of raids &

OUTLINE	SCRIPTURE	SCRIPTURE	OUTLINE
attacks by surrounding nations • The Edomites on the east, 17 • The Philistines on the west & south 2) Because God was humbling (disciplining) Ahaz & Judah: Due to their sin & continued unfaithfulness b. The response of Tiglath-Pileser of Assyria: He oppressed Ahaz instead of helping him 1) Ahaz paid a large fee to secure the help of the Assyrians: Taken from the treasuries of the palace, the temple, & the leaders 2) Ahaz's bribe failed to help him **4. Ahaz's utter apostasy & his death: A total rejection of God** a. His apostasy, 2 K.16:10-18 1) He offered sacrifices to the Syrian false gods • The reason: He believed	invaded the cities of the low country, and of the south of Judah, and had taken Beth-shemesh, and Ajalon, and Gederoth, and Shocho with the villages thereof, and Timnah with the villages thereof, Gimzo also and the villages thereof: and they dwelt there. 19 For the LORD brought Judah low because of Ahaz king of Israel; for he made Judah naked, and transgressed sore against the LORD. 20 And Tilgath-pilneser king of Assyria came unto him, and distressed him, but strengthened him not. 21 For Ahaz took away a portion *out* of the house of the LORD, and *out* of the house of the king, and of the princes, and gave *it* unto the king of Assyria: but he helped him not. 22 And in the time of his distress did he trespass yet more against the LORD: this *is that* king Ahaz. 23 For he sacrificed unto the gods of Damascus, which smote him: and he said, Be-	cause the gods of the kings of Syria help them, *therefore* will I sacrifice to them, that they may help me. But they were the ruin of him, and of all Israel. 24 And Ahaz gathered together the vessels of the house of God, and cut in pieces the vessels of the house of God, and shut up the doors of the house of the LORD, and he made him altars in every corner of Jerusalem. 25 And in every several city of Judah he made high places to burn incense unto other gods, and provoked to anger the LORD God of his fathers. 26 Now the rest of his acts and of all his ways, first and last, behold, they *are* written in the book of the kings of Judah and Israel. 27 And Ahaz slept with his fathers, and they buried him in the city, *even* in Jerusalem: but they brought him not into the sepulchres of the kings of Israel: and Hezekiah his son reigned in his stead.	they had helped Syria defeat him: If he worshipped them, perhaps they would help him also • The result: Led to his downfall 2) He closed the temple • Plundered & destroyed the furnishings • Barricaded the doors 3) He set up altars for the worship of false gods at every street corner of Jerusalem 4) He built false worship centers in every town of Judah 5) He provoked, aroused the anger of God b. His reign & death 1) His reign was recorded in *The Book of the Kings of Judah & Israel* 2) His death & burial were in Jerusalem, but he was dishonored by the public who refused to bury him in the cemetery of the kings 3) His successor was Hezekiah, his son

(28:1-27) Introduction: one of the most *unpopular subjects* to discuss with people is the depravity of the human heart. The reason is that it is quite difficult for some to accept that the human heart is depraved, wicked. Within all of us there is some good. Every human being, no matter how wicked, will sometimes act kindly, helping other people and doing good deeds. But the truth is, no matter how good we may be, there are times when everyone of us acts selfishly or thinks evil thoughts, even times when we become unjustly upset or disturbed or angry with another person. None of us are without sin. As Scripture declares, "all have sinned and come short of the glory of God" (Ro.3:23). We are all short of God's perfection, of His perfect glory and holiness. Moreover, the light of God's glory and perfection shines forth so brilliantly that it will consume any imperfect thing that stands in His presence.

The present passage of Scripture paints the picture of a man who was utterly wicked and totally depraved. This man was Ahaz, a ruler who was to bring devastation upon the kingdom of Judah. In the history of the Southern Kingdom, no king had plunged the nation into the depths of depravity as much as King Ahaz.

In reading this account of King Ahaz's rule, the returning exiles under Ezra's leadership would see a strong warning against turning away from the LORD. When Ahaz assumed the throne, the nation of Judah had reached a summit of prosperity and success seldom experienced by any nation. Yet within just 16 years, Ahaz brought the nation to total ruin. He bankrupted the economy and decimated the military, causing indescribable suffering for the citizens of the nation. This is, *The Reign of Ahaz: A Picture of Utter Wickedness and Total Depravity*, 28:1-27.

1. Ahaz's shameful and devastating evil: the awful depth of wickedness and false worship (vv.1-4).
2. Ahaz's defeat by a Syrian and Israelite alliance (the Syro-Ephramite War): a picture of God's justice and judgment (vv.5-15).
3. Ahaz's failed alliance with Assyria: a man who looked for a savior other than the LORD (vv.16-21).
4. Ahaz's utter apostasy and his death: a total rejection of God (vv.22-27).

1 **(28:1-4) False Worship, Example of—Human Sacrifice, Example of—Wickedness, Depth of, Example—Worship, False, Example of—Ahaz, King, of Judah—Judah, Kings of—Evil, Depths of, Example**: now begins the reign of King Ahaz of Judah, a disgraceful reign, a reign of devastating evil. His appalling reign can be matched only by the evil reign of Jeroboam I in the Northern Kingdom (1 K.12:25–13:34). Ahaz set loose a stream of wickedness that rushed madly to its inevitable end, total destruction under the hand of God's judgment. Glance quickly at the outline, noting how the author simply introduces Ahaz and then immediately launches into a detailed record of his gross offenses within the nation (see outline and note—2 K.16:1-20 for more discussion).

BACKGROUND TO ISAIAH'S DAY

(The Four Kings Who Ruled During Isaiah's Ministry)

Ahaz began to rule at age 20 and ruled for 16 years (v.1). Based upon his age and the years of his rule, he must have served as co-regent with his father Jotham for some years.

Rejecting the righteous example of his father Jotham and his grandfather Uzziah, Ahaz instead followed the path of wickedness. He failed to walk in the righteous steps of his ancestor King David (v.1). Remember, David had a heart that was just like the heart of God (1 S.13:14). For this reason, he was held up as the ideal righteous king whose example was to be followed by all who succeeded him.

To his disgrace, Ahaz walked in the sinful ways of Israel's kings instead of following the righteous examples set by Judah's kings (v.2). And even more tragic, he promoted and led the people in the worship of the false god Baal. In the most revolting pagan practice imaginable, Ahaz committed the abominable sin of human sacrifice, even sacrificing his own sons to a false god. The false god was either Molech or another god associated with the Baal worship that was conducted in the valley of Ben Hinnom (2 K.23:10). By committing this atrocity, he was following a contemptible religious practice of the Canaanites, a people who had become so depraved that God had commanded their extermination, dooming them to eternal death (Le.18:28-30; 20:22-23; De.7:22-26; 12:2-4; 18:9-14).

Ahaz obviously became totally committed to idol worship at various high places throughout the nation (v.4). Note how Scripture describes his participation: as though he rushed from high place to high place, on the hilltops and under every spreading tree where an altar or worship center had been built. He was zealous—even fanatical—over the worship of false gods.

Thought 1. Sadly, far too many people today living in the depths of sin and false worship just as Ahaz did. Think of all those who commit repeated acts of lawlessness, violence, and immorality. How many are committing illicit acts of sex day after day, time after time, disobeying the clear commandment of God? How many people are lying and stealing over and over again? How many fail to be diligent, working hard at their employment, committing the sins of slothfulness, indulgence, and complacency? How many continue living in the sin of unbelief, either denying or refusing to accept the Lord Jesus Christ as the Savior of the world? No sin is any greater or more dangerous than the wickedness of unbelief. And tragically, most people have never trusted the Lord Jesus Christ as their Savior. As a result, most people are not worshipping the only living and true God but, rather, false gods. The living and true God is the Father of the Lord Jesus Christ, the Lord God who so loved the world that He gave His only Son to save the world. Listen to what God's Holy Word says:

(1) The human heart is corrupt, depraved, and most people are living in the depths of sin.

"For from within, out of the heart of men, proceed evil thoughts, adulteries, fornications, murders" (Mk.7:21).

"For the invisible things of him from the creation of the world are clearly seen, being understood by the things that are made, *even* his eternal power and Godhead; so that they are without excuse: Because that, when they knew God, they glorified *him* not as God, neither were thankful; but became vain in their imaginations, and their foolish heart was darkened. Professing themselves to be wise, they became fools, And changed the glory of the uncorruptible God into an image made like to corruptible man, and to birds, and fourfooted beasts, and creeping things. Wherefore God also gave them up to uncleanness through the lusts of their own hearts, to dishonour their own bodies between themselves: Who changed the truth of God into a lie, and worshipped and served the creature more than the Creator, who is blessed for ever. Amen" (Ro.1:20-25).

"This know also, that in the last days perilous times shall come. For men shall be lovers of their own selves, covetous, boasters, proud, blasphemers, disobedient to parents, unthankful, unholy, Without natural affection, trucebreakers, false accusers, incontinent, fierce, despisers of those that are good, Traitors, heady, highminded, lovers of pleasures more than lovers of God; Having a form of godliness, but denying the power thereof: from such turn away" (2 Ti.3:1-5).

"And God looked upon the earth, and, behold, it was corrupt; for all flesh had corrupted his way upon the earth" (Ge.6:12).

"They are all gone aside, they are *all* together become filthy: *there is* none that doeth good, no, not one" (Ps.14:3).

"And judgment is turned away backward, and justice standeth afar off: for truth is fallen in the street, and equity cannot enter" (Is.59:14).

"But we are all as an unclean *thing,* and all our righteousnesses *are* as filthy rags; and we all do fade as a leaf; and our iniquities, like the wind, have taken us away" (Is.64:6).

"The good *man* is perished out of the earth: and *there is* none upright among men: they all lie in wait for blood; they hunt every man his brother with a net" (Mi.7:2).

(2) The corruption and depravity of the human heart can be cleansed away through the shed blood of the Lord Jesus Christ.

"What then? are we better *than they?* No, in no wise: for we have before proved both Jews and Gentiles, that they are all under sin; As it is written, There is none righteous, no, not one: There is none that understandeth, there is none that seeketh after God. They are all gone out of the way, they are together become unprofitable; there is none that doeth good, no, not one. Their throat *is* an open sepulchre; with their tongues they have used deceit; the poison of asps *is* under their lips: Whose mouth *is* full of cursing and bitterness: Their feet *are* swift to shed blood: Destruction and misery *are* in their ways: And the way of peace have they not known: There is no fear of God before their eyes. Now we know that what things soever the law saith, it saith to them who are under the law: that every mouth may be stopped, and all the world may become guilty before God. Therefore by the deeds of the law

there shall no flesh be justified in his sight: for by the law *is* the knowledge of sin. But now the righteousness of God without the law is manifested, being witnessed by the law and the prophets; Even the righteousness of God *which is* by faith of Jesus Christ unto all and upon all them that believe: for there is no difference: For all have sinned, and come short of the glory of God; Being justified freely by his grace through the redemption that is in Christ Jesus: Whom God hath set forth *to be* a propitiation through faith in his blood, to declare his righteousness for the remission of sins that are past, through the forbearance of God; To declare, *I say,* at this time his righteousness: that he might be just, and the justifier of him which believeth in Jesus" (Ro.3:9-26).

"Much more then, being now justified by his blood, we shall be saved from wrath through him" (Ro.5:9).

"In whom we have redemption through his blood, the forgiveness of sins, according to the riches of his grace" (Ep.1:7).

"Neither by the blood of goats and calves, but by his own blood he entered in once into the holy place, having obtained eternal redemption *for us.* For if the blood of bulls and of goats, and the ashes of an heifer sprinkling the unclean, sanctifieth to the purifying of the flesh: How much more shall the blood of Christ, who through the eternal Spirit offered himself without spot to God, purge your conscience from dead works to serve the living God?" (He.9:12-14).

"Forasmuch as ye know that ye were not redeemed with corruptible things, *as* silver and gold, from your vain conversation *received* by tradition from your fathers; But with the precious blood of Christ, as of a lamb without blemish and without spot" (1 Pe.1:18-19).

"Who his own self bare our sins in his own body on the tree, that we, being dead to sins, should live unto righteousness: by whose stripes ye were healed" (1 Pe.2:24).

"For Christ also hath once suffered for sins, the just for the unjust, that he might bring us to God, being put to death in the flesh, but quickened by the Spirit" (1 Pe.3:18).

---

2 (28:5-15) **Judgment, Example of—God, Judgment of—Ahaz, Wars of—Judah, Wars of—Israel, Northern Kingdom of, Wars—Syro-Ephraimite War, Discussed—Syria, War Against Judah**: because of Ahaz's terrible evil, the LORD allowed him to be defeated in a war with the Syrians and Israelites. For some reason, Syria and Israel had formed an alliance and attacked the Southern Kingdom of Judah in what is known as the Syro-Ephraimite war. A detailed description of the bloody battle and the suffering brought upon the people of Judah is given by Scripture. Apparently, two campaigns or two different battalions, one under the command of Syria and the other under the command of Israel, were launched against Judah:

a. First, the Syrian attack against Judah was extremely successful (v.5). The LORD was using Syria and Israel to execute judgment against Judah because of Ahaz's and the people's sin. Defeating the Judean army, the Syrians captured and exiled large numbers of the soldiers and citizens of Judah, deporting them to Damascus.

b. Second, Israel's attack against Judah was also successful (vv.6-8). In just one day, Israel's King Pekah killed over 120,000 Judean soldiers. Scripture clearly says that behind the scenes God was executing a just judgment because of Judah's terrible evil of forsaking Him (v.6). Among the enormous number of casualties were three royal officials killed by a warrior named Zicri. These three officials included Maaseiah, the king's son, Azrikam, the palace manager, and Elkanah, second in command to the king (v.7). But the devastation of its army was not the only loss suffered by Judah. Marching throughout the countryside, Israel's army ransacked the cities of Judea, taking captive over 200,000 women and children and carrying them back to Samaria as exiles (v.8). In addition, they took a large amount of plunder from the towns and villages they had raided.

c. When Israel's army returned to Samaria, to their surprise they were immediately confronted by the prophet Oded who issued a strong warning to them (vv.9-11). His forceful warning included three points.

1) They were guilty of brutality, excessive cruelty (v.9). They were not victorious…
- because of their military power
- because of racial merit or value
- because they were more favored by God
- because they were more righteous and the Judeans more wicked

They were victorious because the LORD was executing justice upon Judah; for that reason, the LORD had allowed Israel to conquer King Ahaz and the Judean citizens. However, Israel's army had gone too far. They had used excessive force and given in to a spirit of brutality and cruelty. They had slaughtered the Judean army in a rage that had reached up and disturbed all of heaven. They had shown no mercy to the Judean soldiers, not even to those who had been captured.

2) The army had been guilty of enslaving the men and women, a serious violation of God's commandment. No Jew was allowed to enslave one of his fellow countrymen (Le.25:39-46). The victorious army of Israel needed to remember a fact: they themselves were guilty of sin before the LORD. Just as the LORD had executed judgment against Judah, so He would execute judgment against the Northern Kingdom unless they repented of their sins (v.10).

3) The leaders of Israel must return the Judean slaves, for God's fierce wrath had turned against them and was ready to strike in an act of *just* punishment (v.11). If they failed to show mercy, they would immediately face the judgment of God. But if they showed compassion and returned the slaves to their homeland, God would have compassion on them.

d. In response to the prophecy of Oded, a delegation of four political leaders confronted the military commanders (vv.12-15). They pointed out Israel's sin and guilt before the LORD and negotiated the release of the prisoners (v.13). Arguing that God's fierce wrath had turned against Israel, the delegation convinced the army to turn over the prisoners and return the plunder they had taken (v.14). In a remarkable demonstration of mercy, the army released the prisoners to the delegation. The delegation then immediately clothed and fed the prisoners, taking care of the injured and wounded (v.15). Finally, the delegation had the prisoners—all 200,000 women and children—taken back to their homeland. They even provided transportation for the weak and escorted some as far back as Jericho.

Thought 1. The very depth of wickedness and human depravity is seen in the life of Ahaz. He personally turned completely away from the LORD and then tragically led the people into false worship, even the atrocious practice of human sacrifice. His life stands as a strong warning to us: we must turn away from wickedness and false worship. If we continue to live sinful, wicked lives and reject the LORD, we will be doomed. God's judgment will fall upon us. Because God loves the world, He will not always tolerate behavior that causes suffering upon this earth. When we commit wickedness, we bring loss and suffering upon other people. When we steal, we cause a loss for one or more individuals; and if the theft involves a large item like an automobile or a huge sum of money, we can cause terrible suffering for those involved. Even if we shoplift, we cause loss for companies, who in turn have to raise their prices, which causes loss for all of us. Stated simply, all unrighteousness causes suffering and loss for someone.

So it is with false worship. None of us lives in isolation, which means that we all influence other people. Consequently, when we reject the LORD and participate in false worship—whether it is an actual idol or the idolization of fame, wealth, possessions, position, authority, sex, sports, television, a celebrity, or an any other physical token or ideal—we set a bad example for other people. We become stumbling blocks to our friends and to other children and adults, giving our stamp of approval to false worship. We mislead other people into idolatry and away from the LORD. All worship other than the worship of the LORD—the Father of the Lord Jesus Christ—is idolatry.

Again, committing wickedness and engaging in false worship will not always be tolerated by the LORD. God loves the world too much to allow the suffering to go on forever. If we mislead people and cause them to suffer, we will face the hand of God's judgment. Listen to what God's Holy Word says about His just and holy judgment:

> **"For the wrath of God is revealed from heaven against all ungodliness and unrighteousness of men, who hold the truth in unrighteousness....Being filled with all unrighteousness, fornication, wickedness, covetousness, maliciousness; full of envy, murder, debate, deceit, malignity; whisperers, Backbiters, haters of God, despiteful, proud, boasters, inventors of evil things, disobedient to parents, Without understanding, covenantbreakers, without natural affection, implacable, unmerciful: Who knowing the judgment of God, that they which commit such things are worthy of death, not only do the same, but have pleasure in them that do them" (Ro.1:18, 29-32).**

> **"Know ye not that the unrighteous shall not inherit the kingdom of God? Be not deceived: neither fornicators, nor idolaters, nor adulterers, nor effeminate, nor abusers of themselves with mankind, Nor thieves, nor covetous, nor drunkards, nor revilers, nor extortioners, shall inherit the kingdom of God" (1 Co.6:9-10).**

> **"Now the works of the flesh are manifest, which are *these;* Adultery, fornication, uncleanness, lasciviousness, Idolatry, witchcraft, hatred, variance, emulations, wrath, strife, seditions, heresies, Envyings, murders, drunkenness, revellings, and such like: of the which I tell you before, as I have also told *you* in time past, that they which do such things shall not inherit the kingdom of God" (Ga.5:19-21).**

> **"But fornication, and all uncleanness, or covetousness, let it not be once named among you, as becometh saints; Neither filthiness, nor foolish talking, nor jesting, which are not convenient: but rather giving of thanks. For this ye know, that no whoremonger, nor unclean person, nor covetous man, who is an idolater, hath any inheritance in the kingdom of Christ and of God. Let no man deceive you with vain words: for because of these things cometh the wrath of God upon the children of disobedience" (Ep.5:3-6).**

> **"But the fearful, and unbelieving, and the abominable, and murderers, and whoremongers, and sorcerers, and idolaters, and all liars, shall have their part in the lake which burneth with fire and brimstone: which is the second death" (Re.21:8).**

3 (28:16-21) **Salvation, Source, Example—Deliverance, Source, Example—Savior, False, Seeking—Deliverer, False, Seeking—Ahaz, Alliances of—Assyria, Alliance with Israel—Ahaz, Evil of**: right after his devastating defeat, Ahaz turned to Assyria for help (vv.17-19). With his nation torn apart and his army diminished, Ahaz and the Judeans were entirely helpless to defend themselves. Consequently, the cities and towns of the nation were under constant attack by the surrounding nations and marauders. Almost immediately the Edomites struck from the east, plundering and taking captives, while the Philistines raided various cities in the west and south (v.18). Having captured six cities, they then occupied them and added them to the territory of Philistia. No doubt these were dark, terrible days of suffering for the surviving Judeans. But remember why they were suffering so much: because God was humbling and disciplining them for their gross sins and continued unfaithfulness. King Ahaz had not only lived a life of wickedness before the nation, but he had also promoted wickedness among the people. And tragically, the people had followed in his footsteps, pursuing the path of unfaithfulness to the LORD.

When the Assyrian king Tiglath-Pileser received Ahaz's appeal for help, he did respond, but his actions ended up oppressing Ahaz instead of helping him (v.20). As the book of *Kings* explains, Assyria attacked Syria and conquered Damascus, the capital of Syria. This removed the Syrians as a threat. But this did not help Ahaz, for he was forced to pay a large fee to the Assyrians for their help. In doing so, Ahaz apparently bankrupted the nation by raiding the treasuries of the palace and temple and demanding huge sums of wealth from the princes of the nation. Obviously, there was little wealth left in the nation after his actions. King Ahaz had inherited a strong nation both economically and militarily, but he had foolishly brought defeat and devastation to the land. He had wrecked the economy and caused incomprehensible suffering for the people. By seeking help from the Assyrian king, a human savior, Ahaz was not helped but, rather, hurt (v.21).

BACKGROUND TO ISAIAH'S DAY

(The Four Kings Who Ruled During Isaiah's Ministry)

Thought 1. Ahaz was a man who looked for a savior other than the LORD. In seeking deliverance from trouble, he turned to a man, Tiglath-Pileser, not to God. But there is only one true Savior, the LORD Himself. And the LORD has proven His power to deliver His people down through the centuries. Still, Ahaz rejected the lessons of history and sought salvation in mortal man instead of turning to the eternal LORD.

However, Ahaz is not the only person to make this mistake. How many of us seek salvation in someone or some thing other than the Lord Jesus Christ? Only the Lord can save us. Only He has the power to deliver us from the sin and bondages of this life. When trials, temptations, hardships, misfortunes, or any other bitter enemy confronts us, there is only one living Savior—the Lord Jesus Christ Himself—who can deliver us. Only He has the power to carry us victoriously through this life and on into the eternity of heaven. Listen to what God's Holy Word says:

"**For God so loved the world, that he gave his only begotten Son, that whosoever believeth in him should not perish, but have everlasting life**" (Jn.3:16).

"**For the Son of man is come to seek and to save that which was lost**" (Lu.19:10).

"**Him hath God exalted with his right hand** *to be* **a Prince and a Saviour, for to give repentance to Israel, and forgiveness of sins**" (Ac.5:31).

"**There hath no temptation taken you but such as is common to man: but God** *is* **faithful, who will not suffer you to be tempted above that ye are able; but will with the temptation also make a way to escape, that ye may be able to bear** *it*" (1 Co.10:13).

"**Now unto him that is able to do exceeding abundantly above all that we ask or think, according to the power that worketh in us**" (Ep.3:20).

"**And the Lord shall deliver me from every evil work, and will preserve** *me* **unto his heavenly kingdom: to whom** *be* **glory for ever and ever. Amen**" (2 Ti.4:18).

"**Forasmuch then as the children are partakers of flesh and blood, he also himself likewise took part of the same; that through death he might destroy him that had the power of death, that is, the devil; And deliver them who through fear of death were all their lifetime subject to bondage**" (He.2:14-15).

"**For Christ also hath once suffered for sins, the just for the unjust, that he might bring us to God, being put to death in the flesh, but quickened by the Spirit**" (1 Pe.3:18).

"**The Lord knoweth how to deliver the godly out of temptations, and to reserve the unjust unto the day of judgment to be punished**" (2 Pe.2:9).

DEEPER STUDY #1

(2 Chr.28:16) **Assyria**: of all the enemies Israel faced, Assyria was the most terrifying. Assyria not only fought fiercely but also with unbelievable cruelty. The powerful enemy knew how to inflict shocking pain and horror. Their gruesome war tactics included such devices as placing an enemy on a sharp stake and flaying him alive and ripping open pregnant women with a sword. These devices were used to strike fear among the people and to force them into submission. Their lust for war and power knew no limits. There was simply nothing they would *not* do in their pursuit of victory and world domination.

Despite their brutality and savagery, the LORD used Assyria to punish Israel. Because the people of Israel and Judah insisted on committing idolatry, God allowed the Assyrians to conquer Israel. As a result, the people of Israel lived in fear and trepidation of Assyria from the 9th century B.C. until late in the 7th century B.C., when Assyria was finally conquered by the Scythians. In 722 B.C., the prophecy of judgment against Israel was fulfilled when Sargon II took Samaria. In that year, the Northern Kingdom fell, opening the way for more pressure on Jerusalem and the Southern Kingdom.

Foolishly, King Ahaz of Judah made an alliance with the Assyrian king Tiglath-Pileser, trusting in the former enemy to give him protection. The prophet Isaiah had clearly warned against forming a close agreement with such an evil nation, but King Ahaz would not listen. Soon Assyria demanded tribute from Judah. But even worse than that, Assyria insisted that Judah worship the false gods of Assyria. Out of fear, Ahaz had made the alliance. Now again out of fear, he was forced to agree to the tribute and to worship Assyria's false gods. In failing to fully trust in the LORD for protection, Judah's sin of idolatry led to a flood of terrible tragedy.

The teaching of Scripture is unmistakable: close alliances with unbelievers will result in tragedy. The believer simply cannot hold hands with the world and with God at the same time. We must trust in God and God alone for our needs. He is the only One who can provide for and protect us.

Note the kings of Assyria mentioned in the Bible:

⇒ Tiglath-Pil(n)eser III (or Pul) reigned from 745 to 727 B.C. (2 K.15:29; 16:7, 10). Tiglath-Pileser attacked Azariah in Judah and left behind a burning path of destruction. He easily smashed the fortified cities, just as a person would smash an ordinary dish (ARAB 1:770[2]). He forced the terrified King Ahaz and King Menahem to pay tribute to him (ARAB 1:815). Tiglath-Pileser also conquered city after city during the days of King Pekah of Israel (2 K.15:29). He was later hired by Ahaz, king of Judah, to attack the Northern Kingdom, which he did, assassinating King Rezin (2 K.16:7-10). During his invasion, he captured and deported many of the citizens to Assyria (1 Chr.5:26).

⇒ Shalmaneser V reigned from 727 to 722 B.C. (2 K.17:3; 18:9). He also expanded the Assyrian territory far beyond the kings who ruled Assyria before him (ARAB 1:830). When Hoshea, king of Israel, refused to pay the tribute demanded, Shalmaneser marched and set siege against Samaria for three years (2 K.17:5). Finally, after conquering the capital, he took all but a few people of the Northern Kingdom of Israel into exile (2 K.18:9-11).

---

2 Daniel David Luckenbill. *Ancient Records of Assyria and Babylonia*, 2 vols. (ARAB) (London: Histories and Mysteries of Man Ltd., 1989).

Background to Isaiah's Day

(The Four Kings Who Ruled During Isaiah's Ministry)

⇒ Sargon II reigned from 722 to 705 B.C. (Is.20:1) He took the control of Assyria away from Shalmaneser (ARAB 1:132). Sargon trampled across the land of Israel all the way to Ashdod, the Philistine coastal city. Iamani, the king of Ashdod, delayed paying tribute to Sargon. As a result, Sargon sent a field marshal to attack and capture the city. Iamani fled for his life, barely escaping by sea to Egypt, and leaving his family behind (ARAB 2:79, 92).

⇒ Sennacherib reigned from 705 to 681 B.C. (2 K.18:13; 19:16, 20, 36; 2 Chr.32:1-2, 9-10, 22; Is.36:1; 37:17, 21, 37). Sennacherib marched against Jerusalem but was unsuccessful. He recorded that he took away spoils of war; and, "like a caged bird, I shut up [Hezekiah] in Jerusalem, his royal city," and that "the terrifying splendor of my royalty overcame him" (ARAB 2:240, 312). But he did not record anything about the 185,000 soldiers being killed in one day by God. After this great miracle, Sennacherib was forced to lift the siege and withdraw from the city (2 K.19:35-36; 2 Chr.32:22). Sennacherib only wrote, "On Hezekiah [Judah's king], I laid my yoke" (ARAB 2:347), letting the reader assume that Sennacherib won the battle.

⇒ Esarhaddon reigned from 681 to 669 B.C. (2 K.19:37; Ezr.4:2; Is.37:38). He was the son of Sennacherib. Esarhaddon recorded that he summoned Manasseh, along with twenty-one other kings, and forced them into slave labor (ARAB 2:690).

---

4 (28:22-27) **Apostasy, Example of—Rejection, of God, Example—Turning Away, from God, Example—Forsaking, of God, Example—Ahaz, Rejection of God—Ahaz, Summary of His Reign**: Ahaz totally rejected God. He reached a depth of unfaithfulness seldom seen in men. When Ahaz was confronted by trouble, suffering or deep distress, he became even more unfaithful to the LORD. In the very times he should have been turning to the LORD, he turned elsewhere, seeking the help of men and of false gods. After his defeat by Syria, he even began to worship the gods of the Syrians. Foolishly, he held the belief that these false gods had helped Syria defeat him. He reasoned that if he worshipped these idols, perhaps the false gods would help him also (v.23). But the result was the exact opposite, for his idolatry and false worship led to the downfall of all Israel. Ahaz became totally immersed in false worship and idolatry. He even closed the doors of the temple to those who continued to worship the LORD. Plundering and destroying the temple's furnishings, he barricaded the doors and encouraged the people to worship the false gods he had adopted. He even set up altars for the worship of false gods on every street corner of Jerusalem and built false worship centers in every town of Judah. Steeped in wickedness and immersed in idol worship, he provoked and aroused the anger of the LORD (v.25).

Ahaz's life and reign were recorded in *The Book of the Kings of Judah and Israel* (v.26). After his death he was buried in Jerusalem. But he was dishonored by the public who refused to bury him in the cemetery of the kings. His successor was his son Hezekiah.

In evaluating his life and reign, it is evident that few men have lived such a wicked life and brought so much evil upon a nation and its people as did King Ahaz. In the midst of their suffering Ahaz sought a deliverer in mere man, King Tiglath-Pileser of Assyria. He placed his confidence in a human being, not in the LORD. Thus, he never received the help he needed, not the help of a permanent Savior and Deliverer. Neither he nor his people were rescued.

Thought 1. Ahaz forsook the LORD and fell into the depths of unbelief. The same is true with so many of us all around the world. Many of us have rejected the LORD either by denying Him or by refusing to accept Him as our personal Savior. The results of such a decision are, in this life, most tragic, for a person who rejects the LORD has only the arm of the flesh to help him. When a day of trouble or distress comes, God is not present to help or deliver, for unbelief and rejection pushes away the LORD and separates Him from us. Thus, when a severe accident or disease strikes, we are left all alone, in a state of separation. No help is available except what medicine and technology can give us. And as helpful as medicine and technology are, they are limited in what they can offer us. They can only delay death, not eliminate or erase it.

When the severe trials of life strike us and we need the LORD's help, He wants to help us. But if we continue in our unbelief and rejection, we cut ourselves off from His help. Yet in the midst of our hardships and misfortunes, if we will cry out for help, the LORD will hear and help us. This is His wonderful promise. But again, He cannot—nor will He—help us if we reject Him. Listen to what God says about unbelief and the rejection of Him:

"He came unto his own, and his own received him not. But as many as received him, to them gave he power to become the sons of God, *even* to them that believe on his name" (Jn.1:11-12).

"He that believeth on the Son hath everlasting life: and he that believeth not the Son shall not see life; but the wrath of God abideth on him" (Jn.3:36).

"I am come in my Father's name, and ye receive me not: if another shall come in his own name, him ye will receive" (Jn.5:43).

"I said therefore unto you, that ye shall die in your sins: for if ye believe not that I am *he,* ye shall die in your sins" (Jn.8:24).

"He that rejecteth me, and receiveth not my words, hath one that judgeth him: the word that I have spoken, the same shall judge him in the last day" (Jn.12:48).

"Now the Spirit speaketh expressly, that in the latter times some shall depart from the faith, giving heed to seducing spirits, and doctrines of devils" (1 Ti.4:1).

"For the time will come when they will not endure sound doctrine; but after their own lusts shall they heap to themselves teachers, having itching ears; And they shall turn away *their* ears from the truth, and shall be turned unto fables" (2 Ti.4:3-4).

"Harden not your hearts, as in the provocation, in the day of temptation in the wilderness: When your fathers tempted me, proved me, and saw my works forty years. Wherefore I was grieved with that generation, and said, They do alway err in *their* heart; and they have not known my ways. So I sware in my wrath, They shall not enter into my rest.) Take heed, brethren, lest there be in any of you an evil heart of unbelief, in departing from the living God" (He.3:8-12).

"Take heed, brethren, lest there be in any of you an evil heart of unbelief, in departing from the living God. But exhort one another daily, while it is called To day; lest any of you be hardened through the deceitfulness of sin. For we are made partakers of Christ, if we hold the beginning of our confidence stedfast unto the end; While it is said, To day if ye will hear his voice, harden not your hearts, as in the provocation. For some, when they had heard, did provoke: howbeit not all that came out of Egypt by Moses. But with whom was he grieved forty years? *was it* not with them that had sinned, whose carcases fell in the wilderness? And to whom sware he that they should not enter into his rest, but to them that believed not? So we see that they could not enter in because of unbelief" (He.3:12-19).

"Let us therefore fear, lest, a promise being left *us* of entering into his rest, any of you should seem to come short of it. For unto us was the gospel preached, as well as unto them: but the word preached did not profit them, not being mixed with faith in them that heard *it*. For we which have believed do enter into rest, as he said, As I have sworn in my wrath, if they shall enter into my rest: although the works were finished from the foundation of the world" (He.4:1-3).

"Let us labour therefore to enter into that rest, lest any man fall after the same example of unbelief" (He.4:11).

"I will therefore put you in remembrance, though ye once knew this, how that the Lord, having saved the people out of the land of Egypt, afterward destroyed them that believed not. And the angels which kept not their first estate, but left their own habitation, he hath reserved in everlasting chains under darkness unto the judgment of the great day. Even as Sodom and Gomorrha, and the cities about them in like manner, giving themselves over to fornication, and going after strange flesh, are set forth for an example, suffering the vengeance of eternal fire" (Jude 5-7).

"For my people have committed two evils; they have forsaken me the fountain of living waters, *and* hewed them out cisterns, broken cisterns, that can hold no water" (Je.2:13).

(The Four Kings Who Ruled During Isaiah's Ministry)

IV. THE REIGN OF HEZEKIAH (PART 1)— THE CLEANSING OF THE TEMPLE FOR WORSHIP: A LESSON ON THE GREAT NEEDS OF THE CHURCH, 2 CHR.29:1-36

OUTLINE	SCRIPTURE	SCRIPTURE	OUTLINE
1. Hezekiah's background: A godly, righteous man a. His reign: Began at age 25 b. His mother, Abijah, & grandfather, Zechariah: Were most likely believers c. His righteous life: Followed the godly example of David **2. Hezekiah's reformation, his cleansing of the temple: A need for ministers & churches to be holy, pure** a. The temple doors were quickly opened b. The religious leaders were all summoned to a meeting c. The order for much needed change was immediately given to the religious leaders: Must sanctify, cleanse themselves & the temple (church)—removing all rubbish & every defiling thing 1) Because they & their fathers had sinned & done evil, forsaking the Lord 2) Because they & their fathers had forsaken His temple (church) 3) Because they & their fathers had shut the doors of the temple (church): Had stopped the public worship services 4) Because God's anger & judgment had been aroused • He had given them up to trouble, horror, & ridicule, Je.19:8; 25:9, 18; 51:37 • He had given up their families to be conquered & exiled by Syria, Israel, Edom, & Philistia, 28:5-10, 17-18 d. The only answer to revival was clearly stated 1) The king & people must make a renewed covenant with the LORD 2) The priests & Levites must not neglect their	Hezekiah began to reign *when he was* five and twenty years old, and he reigned nine and twenty years in Jerusalem. And his mother's name *was* Abijah, the daughter of Zechariah. 2 And he did *that which was* right in the sight of the LORD, according to all that David his father had done. 3 He in the first year of his reign, in the first month, opened the doors of the house of the LORD, and repaired them. 4 And he brought in the priests and the Levites, and gathered them together into the east street, 5 And said unto them, Hear me, ye Levites, sanctify now yourselves, and sanctify the house of the LORD God of your fathers, and carry forth the filthiness out of the holy *place.* 6 For our fathers have trespassed, and done *that which was* evil in the eyes of the LORD our God, and have forsaken him, and have turned away their faces from the habitation of the LORD, and turned *their* backs. 7 Also they have shut up the doors of the porch, and put out the lamps, and have not burned incense nor offered burnt offerings in the holy *place* unto the God of Israel. 8 Wherefore the wrath of the LORD was upon Judah and Jerusalem, and he hath delivered them to trouble, to astonishment, and to hissing, as ye see with your eyes. 9 For, lo, our fathers have fallen by the sword, and our sons and our daughters and our wives are in captivity for this. 10 Now *it is* in mine heart to make a covenant with the LORD God of Israel, that his fierce wrath may turn away from us. 11 My sons, be not now negligent: for the LORD	hath chosen you to stand before him, to serve him, and that ye should minister unto him, and burn incense. 12 Then the Levites arose, Mahath the son of Amasai, and Joel the son of Azariah, of the sons of the Kohathites: and of the sons of Merari, Kish the son of Abdi, and Azariah the son of Jehalelel: and of the Gershonites; Joah the son of Zimmah, and Eden the son of Joah: 13 And of the sons of Elizaphan; Shimri, and Jeiel: and of the sons of Asaph; Zechariah, and Mattaniah: 14 And of the sons of Heman; Jehiel, and Shimei: and of the sons of Jeduthun; Shemaiah, and Uzziel. 15 And they gathered their brethren, and sanctified themselves, and came, according to the commandment of the king, by the words of the LORD, to cleanse the house of the LORD. 16 And the priests went into the inner part of the house of the LORD, to cleanse *it,* and brought out all the uncleanness that they found in the temple of the LORD into the court of the house of the LORD. And the Levites took *it,* to carry *it* out abroad into the brook Kidron. 17 Now they began on the first *day* of the first month to sanctify, and on the eighth day of the month came they to the porch of the LORD: so they sanctified the house of the LORD in eight days; and in the sixteenth day of the first month they made an end. 18 Then they went in to Hezekiah the king, and said, We have cleansed all the house of the LORD, and the altar of burnt offering, with all the vessels thereof, and the showbread table, with all the vessels thereof. 19 Moreover all the vessels, which king Ahaz in his reign	duties any longer • Must represent the LORD & serve Him • Must minister & burn incense (symbolized prayer) e. The obedience of the Levites & priests was immediate: They went to work as charged 1) The leaders of the Levites were appointed • Two leaders were appointed from each of the three major clans: Kohath, Merari, & Gershon • Two leaders were appointed from a fourth clan, Elizaphan • Other leaders were appointed from three clans of the Levitical musicians: Asaph, Zechariah, & Mattaniah 2) The Levites first sanctified themselves 3) The Levites then sanctified, cleansed the temple: Just as the king charged & as the LORD's Word instructed, 1 Chr.28:12, 19 • The priests removed all rubbish & every defiled thing from the sanctuary, taking them out to the courtyard • The Levites then carted out all the unclean items to the Kidron Valley • The cleansing took sixteen days: Eight days to clean the courts up to the portico or porch & then eight more days to cleanse the temple itself 4) The Levites & priests reported to the king • They had cleansed the entire temple, the altar, the table for sacred bread, & all the utensils • They had recovered & sanctified all the items

BACKGROUND TO ISAIAH'S DAY

(The Four Kings Who Ruled During Isaiah's Ministry)

OUTLINE	SCRIPTURE	SCRIPTURE	OUTLINE

& utensils taken by King Ahaz when he closed the temple
 	
3. Hezekiah's rededication of the temple: A new beginning in worship
  a. The civic leaders were summoned to attend
  1) The leaders brought animals to be sacrificed as a sin offering, Le.4:1–5:13
    • The purpose: To make atonement for the sins of the kingdom (royal court), the sanctuary (priest & Levites), & Judah (people)
 	
    • The priests offered the sacrifices to the LORD, sprinkling the blood on the altar: The blood of the bulls, rams, & lambs
 	
    • The king & the assembly (leaders) laid their hands on the goats (designated them as the substitute sacrifice for sin)
    • The priests then sacrificed the goats & sprinkled their blood on the altar: Was a sin offering to atone for *all Israel*, as was the burnt offering
 	
  2) The king stationed the Levite musicians in the temple for the dedication service
    • They were placed just as David, Gad the king's seer, & Nathan the prophet had instructed
    • They stood ready with their instruments
 	
  3) The king ordered the burnt offering to be sacrificed & presented to the LORD
    • The musicians sang & the instruments played throughout the sacrifice of the burnt offering
	did cast away in his transgression, have we prepared and sanctified, and, behold, they *are* before the altar of the LORD.
	20 Then Hezekiah the king rose early, and gathered the rulers of the city, and went up to the house of the LORD.
	21 And they brought seven bullocks, and seven rams, and seven lambs, and seven he goats, for a sin offering for the kingdom, and for the sanctuary, and for Judah. And he commanded the priests the sons of Aaron to offer *them* on the altar of the LORD.
	22 So they killed the bullocks, and the priests received the blood, and sprinkled *it* on the altar: likewise, when they had killed the rams, they sprinkled the blood upon the altar: they killed also the lambs, and they sprinkled the blood upon the altar.
	23 And they brought forth the he goats *for* the sin offering before the king and the congregation; and they laid their hands upon them:
	24 And the priests killed them, and they made reconciliation with their blood upon the altar, to make an atonement for all Israel: for the king commanded *that* the burnt offering and the sin offering *should be made* for all Israel.
	25 And he set the Levites in the house of the LORD with cymbals, with psalteries, and with harps, according to the commandment of David, and of Gad the king's seer, and Nathan the prophet: for *so was* the commandment of the LORD by his prophets.
	26 And the Levites stood with the instruments of David, and the priests with the trumpets.
	27 And Hezekiah commanded to offer the burnt offering upon the altar. And when the burnt offering began, the song of the LORD began *also* with the trumpets, and with the instruments *ordained* by David king of Israel.
		28 And all the congregation worshipped, and the singers sang, and the trumpeters sounded: *and* all *this continued* until the burnt offering was finished.
		29 And when they had made an end of offering, the king and all that were present with him bowed themselves, and worshipped.
		30 Moreover Hezekiah the king and the princes commanded the Levites to sing praise unto the LORD with the words of David, and of Asaph the seer. And they sang praises with gladness, and they bowed their heads and worshipped.
		31 Then Hezekiah answered and said, Now ye have consecrated yourselves unto the LORD, come near and bring sacrifices and thank offerings into the house of the LORD. And the congregation brought in sacrifices and thank offerings; and as many as were of a free heart burnt offerings.
		32 And the number of the burnt offerings, which the congregation brought, was threescore and ten bullocks, an hundred rams, *and* two hundred lambs: all these *were* for a burnt offering to the LORD.
		33 And the consecrated things *were* six hundred oxen and three thousand sheep.
		34 But the priests were too few, so that they could not flay all the burnt offerings: wherefore their brethren the Levites did help them, till the work was ended, and until the *other* priests had sanctified themselves: for the Levites *were* more upright in heart to sanctify themselves than the priests.
		35 And also the burnt offerings *were* in abundance, with the fat of the peace offerings, and the drink offerings for *every* burnt offering. So the service of the house of the LORD was set in order.
		36 And Hezekiah rejoiced, and all the people, that God had prepared the people: for the thing was *done* suddenly.
			• The whole assembly bowed & worshipped while the singers sang & the burnt offering was sacrificed
			
			  4) The king & everyone present knelt & worshipped after all the offerings had been presented
			
			  5) The king commanded the Levites to sing songs from the psalms of David & of Asaph the seer
			
			  b. The invitation was issued for the congregation to bring their individual offerings
			  1) The people's response was wholehearted
			    • Many brought their sacrifices & thanksgiving offerings
			    • Those with willing hearts brought burnt offerings
			
			  2) The offerings sacrificed were enormous in number
			    • The burnt offerings: 70 bulls, 100 rams, 200 male lambs
			
			    • The other offerings: 600 bulls & 3,000 sheep & goats
			  3) The priests were too few to handle all the work involved in the sacrificing of animals
			    • They were not yet sanctified, cleansed: Had been lax, slow to respond to the revival
			    • The Levites stepped in to help
			  4) The burnt offerings presented by the people were surprisingly numerous, as were the accompanying drink offerings & the large amount of fat from the fellowship offerings
			  c. The temple was restored for worship: The king & the people rejoiced over what God had done & done so quickly

BACKGROUND TO ISAIAH'S DAY

(The Four Kings Who Ruled During Isaiah's Ministry)

(29:1-36) Introduction: commitment, steadfastness, perseverance, endurance, holding fast, faithfulness—this is the great need of the church, not buildings and not money. A place for a body of believers to meet is essential. But the place can be a home, a hut, or out in the open air, as well as a magnificent structure.

Money is also essential to carry on the mission of the church, for the gospel of Christ must be carried not only to our own communities but also to the whole world. Therefore, the church is responsible not only to take the gospel to its own community and to meet the needs of its neighbors but also to meet the needs of everyone everywhere.

Yet as necessary as a meeting place and money are, these two resources are not the major needs of the church. The primary need is the resource of people, people who are wholeheartedly committed, dedicated, loyal, devoted, steadfast, persevering, enduring, and who are strong witnesses for Him. This is the greatest need of the church.

A *new reformation* is heralded, proclaimed in this present Scripture. After King Ahaz brought ruin upon Judah through war and the closing of the temple, the nation of Judah was in desperate need. Its economy was wrecked and its military was decimated. There was no courageous, godly leadership to restore the nation, not as long as King Ahaz lived and continued to reign. But God knew the catastrophic devastation that had swept over the nation, and even while Ahaz was still ruling, the LORD was preparing his son Hezekiah to take the throne and to restore the nation. The present passage covers the story of Hezekiah, a godly man who was to rule the nation in righteousness and justice. When he ascended to the throne, a renewed hope was aroused within the hearts of the people, a hope for the restoration of the nation to its former glory. Keep in mind that the Northern Kingdom of Israel had collapsed under the assault of Assyria during the reign of Ahaz, Hezekiah's father. The year of the Northern Kingdom's collapse and exile was 722 B.C. In His sovereignty, God knew that a strong and righteous king would need to be upon the throne of Judah following the fall of Israel. And though Hezekiah was reared in one of the most ungodly environments imaginable, he came to know the LORD in a very personal way, committing his life wholeheartedly to the LORD. His godly reign would not stop the tide of wickedness from flowing throughout Judah, but it would significantly delay the hand of God's judgment from falling upon the Southern Kingdom. Due much to Hezekiah's righteous reign, Judah would not fall to Babylon for over 100 years. Scripture records more on the history of Hezekiah than on any king other than David and Solomon.

In studying the history of Hezekiah, the returning exile would be aroused to recommit his life to the LORD and to make sure that the temple was kept pure for the worship of the LORD. Remember that the exiles were returning to Judah to achieve the very same goals that had challenged Hezekiah, those of restoring *true worship* in the temple and of rebuilding the nation. This is, *The Reign of Hezekiah (Part 1)—the Cleansing of the Temple for Worship: A Lesson on the Great Needs of the Church*, 29:1-36.

1. Hezekiah's background: a godly, righteous man (vv.1-2).
2. Hezekiah's reformation, his cleansing of the temple: a need for ministers and churches to be holy, pure (vv.3-19).
3. Hezekiah's rededication of the temple: a new beginning in worship (vv.20-36).

---

1 **(29:1-2) Godliness, Example of—Righteousness, Example of, Hezekiah—Character, Good, Example of—Commitment, Example of—Dedication, Example of—Devotion, to the LORD, Example of—Hezekiah, King of Judah—Kings, of the Southern Kingdom of Judah**: the major feature of Hezekiah's life and reign was his godly, righteous life before the LORD. He was totally devoted to God and committed to launching a reformation throughout the nation, a reformation that would reestablish *true worship* and rebuild the nation economically, politically, and militarily.

Hezekiah began his independent rule when he was 25 years old, and he reigned as an independent king for 29 years. Apparently, 14 years of his reign were spent serving as co-regent with his father Ahaz. Then he reigned 18 years alone and another 11 years as co-regent with his son Manasseh.[3] Considering that Hezekiah's father was Ahaz, one of history's most wicked kings, it is surprising that Hezekiah made a deep, genuine commitment to the LORD. Nevertheless, he did, and he had one of the most successful reigns among all the kings. His mother was Abijah, the daughter of a man named Zechariah. Perhaps Zechariah was the godly man who had advised King Uzziah (26:5) and served as a witness for the prophet Isaiah (8:2). If so, then Hezekiah's mother was probably a genuine believer who had a righteous influence upon him.

Whatever the case, at some point in his life, Hezekiah made a deep commitment to the LORD. He lived righteously, following the godly example of David (v.2).

Thought 1. Hezekiah's godliness and righteousness are dynamic examples for us. Against all odds, he chose to follow the LORD. With a father steeped in wickedness who had fallen into the very depths of depravity, Hezekiah stood little chance of ever making a commitment to the LORD. Nevertheless, he defied the odds, seeking to follow and to give his life over to the LORD. Likewise, no matter how bad or terrible our upbringing, we can break the cycle. We too can trust the LORD and become successful in life. Through the power of Christ, we can overcome the negative impact of alcoholic, abusive, or profane parents.

- If we were reared in a divisive, broken, or single-parent home, we can break the trend through the power of Christ.
- If we were reared in an uneducated or poverty-stricken environment, we can break the trend through the power of Christ.

Even an immoral, wicked, depraved, or corrupt environment can be overcome through the power of Christ. In Christ, God has given us the Savior, the Deliverer who can rescue us from bad parents, bad childhoods, and bad environments—no matter how dreadful or appalling they may be. In Christ, there is power to rise above the enslavements and bondages of our past. Therefore, if we reject Christ, it is *our* choice; we are without excuse. The power of Christ is available to all of us. Christ can enable us to live righteous and godly lives, lives free of all the bondages and enslavements of this life. Listen to what God's Holy Word says:

---

[3] John F. Walvoord and Roy B. Zuck, Editors. *The Bible Knowledge Commentary*. (Colorado Springs, CO: Chariot Victor Publishing, 1985), p.572.

"That it might be fulfilled which was spoken by Esaias the prophet, saying, Himself took our infirmities, and bare *our* sicknesses" (Mt.8:17).

"For God so loved the world, that he gave his only begotten Son, that whosoever believeth in him should not perish, but have everlasting life" (Jn.3:16).

"The thief cometh not, but for to steal, and to kill, and to destroy: I am come that they might have life, and that they might have *it* more abundantly" (Jn.10:10).

"Neither is there salvation in any other: for there is none other name under heaven given among men, whereby we must be saved" (Ac.4:12).

"For when we were yet without strength, in due time Christ died for the ungodly" (Ro.5:6).

"There hath no temptation taken you but such as is common to man: but God *is* faithful, who will not suffer you to be tempted above that ye are able; but will with the temptation also make a way to escape, that ye may be able to bear *it*" (1 Co.10:13).

"Awake to righteousness, and sin not; for some have not the knowledge of God: I speak *this* to your shame" (1 Co.15:34).

"[Christ] Who gave himself for our sins, that he might deliver us from this present evil world, according to the will of God and our Father" (Ga.1:4).

"Wherefore take unto you the whole armour of God, that ye may be able to withstand in the evil day, and having done all, to stand. Stand therefore, having your loins girt about with truth, and having on the breastplate of righteousness" (Ep.6:13-14).

"And this I pray, that your love may abound yet more and more in knowledge and *in* all judgment; That ye may approve things that are excellent; that ye may be sincere and without offence till the day of Christ; Being filled with the fruits of righteousness, which are by Jesus Christ, unto the glory and praise of God" (Ph.1:9-11).

"And the Lord shall deliver me from every evil work, and will preserve *me* unto his heavenly kingdom: to whom *be* glory for ever and ever. Amen" (2 Ti.4:18).

"Teaching us that, denying ungodliness and worldly lusts, we should live soberly, righteously, and godly, in this present world; Looking for that blessed hope, and the glorious appearing of the great God and our Saviour Jesus Christ" (Tit.2:12-13).

"Who gave himself for us, that he might redeem us from all iniquity, and purify unto himself a peculiar people, zealous of good works" (Tit.2:14).

"Forasmuch then as the children are partakers of flesh and blood, he also himself likewise took part of the same; that through death he might destroy him that had the power of death, that is, the devil; And deliver them who through fear of death were all their lifetime subject to bondage" (He.2:14-15).

"Who his own self bare our sins in his own body on the tree, that we, being dead to sins, should live unto righteousness: by whose stripes ye were healed" (1 Pe.2:24).

"The Lord knoweth how to deliver the godly out of temptations, and to reserve the unjust unto the day of judgment to be punished" (2 Pe.2:9).

"But the day of the Lord will come as a thief in the night; in the which the heavens shall pass away with a great noise, and the elements shall melt with fervent heat, the earth also and the works that are therein shall be burned up. *Seeing* then *that* all these things shall be dissolved, what manner *of persons* ought ye to be in *all* holy conversation [conduct, behavior] and godliness, Looking for and hasting unto the coming of the day of God, wherein the heavens being on fire shall be dissolved, and the elements shall melt with fervent heat? Nevertheless we, according to his promise, look for new heavens and a new earth, wherein dwelleth righteousness. Wherefore, beloved, seeing that ye look for such things, be diligent that ye may be found of him in peace, without spot, and blameless" (2 Pe.3:10-14).

"And he said, The LORD *is* my rock, and my fortress, and my deliverer" (2 S.22:2).

"But I *am* poor and needy; *yet* the Lord thinketh upon me: thou *art* my help and my deliverer; make no tarrying, O my God" (Ps.40:17).

"Surely he shall deliver thee from the snare of the fowler, *and* from the noisome pestilence" (Ps.91:3).

"They reel to and fro, and stagger like a drunken man, and are at their wit's end. Then they cry unto the LORD in their trouble, and he bringeth them out of their distresses. He maketh the storm a calm, so that the waves thereof are still. Then are they glad because they be quiet; so he bringeth them unto their desired haven. Oh that *men* would praise the LORD *for* his goodness, and *for* his wonderful works to the children of men!" (Ps.107:27-31).

"Fear not: for I have redeemed thee, I have called *thee* by thy name; thou *art* mine. When thou passest through the waters, I *will be* with thee; and through the rivers, they shall not overflow thee: when thou walkest through the fire, thou shalt not be burned; neither shall the flame kindle upon thee" (Is.43:1-2).

"Be not afraid of their faces: for I *am* with thee to deliver thee, saith the LORD" (Je.1:8).

"Sow to yourselves in righteousness, reap in mercy; break up your fallow ground: for *it is* time to seek the LORD, till he come and rain righteousness upon you" (Ho.10:12).

---

2 (29:3-19) **Churches, Needs of, to Be Pure—Ministers, Needs of, to Be Sanctified—Sanctification, Duty— Ministers, Duty—Churches, Duty—Hezekiah, Reformation of—Temple, Cleansing of, Example**: right after his father's death, in the very first month of his independent rule, Hezekiah launched a reformation throughout the nation. Under Ahaz's leadership, the nation had been devastated by war, resulting in a wrecked economy, military, and political administration.

BACKGROUND TO ISAIAH'S DAY

(The Four Kings Who Ruled During Isaiah's Ministry)

All three branches of government desperately needed to be strengthened. Thus, as soon as Hezekiah could fully take over the nation's command, he embarked on a strategy to rebuild the economy and the military and to strengthen the political base. But note this significant fact: the focus of the author is the *spiritual reformation* that Hezekiah initiated. He focused solely upon the basic need of the people, that of returning to the LORD and of serving Him. If the people would return to the LORD, they would have the blessings of God as they sought to rebuild the nation economically and militarily.

a. Hezekiah's very first act as sole ruler of Judah was to reopen the doors of the temple (v.3). His wicked father had closed the temple and barricaded the doors in an attempt to irradicate the worship of the LORD.

b. As soon as the doors were opened and repaired, Hezekiah summoned all the religious leaders of the nation to a meeting at the temple in Jerusalem. He then drew them together in the courtyard just east of the temple.

c. Once they were assembled, Hezekiah challenged the religious workers to sanctify and cleanse themselves as well as the temple of the LORD. He meant by this that they were to remove all sin from their lives and all rubbish from the temple (v.5). Both they and the temple needed to be sanctified, cleansed, and recommitted to the LORD. They needed to be totally set apart to His service. Four reasons were given for their sanctification.

1) First, they needed to be cleansed because they and their forefathers had sinned and done evil. They had forsaken the LORD (v.6). Note that Hezekiah does not say "my father" but "our fathers." It was not just Ahaz who had been guilty of forsaking the LORD but the entire nation. For that reason, Hezekiah laid the guilt of apostasy at the feet of all the people.

2) Second, they needed to be cleansed because they and their fathers had forsaken the LORD's temple, turning their backs upon Him and the worship of His Holy Name.

3) Third, they needed to be cleansed because they and their fathers had shut the doors of the temple and put out the lamps, plunging the temple into total darkness. They had disallowed any worship there. In addition, they had not burned incense to symbolize the offering up of prayers to the LORD, nor had they presented any burnt offerings at the sanctuary. Simply stated, they had failed to seek atonement and reconciliation with the LORD, failed to offer up public worship to Him.

4) Fourth, they needed to be cleansed because God's anger and judgment had been aroused. He had given them up to trouble, horror, and ridicule. He had given up their families to be conquered and exiled, enslaved by Syria, Samaria, Edom, and Philistia (28:5-10, 17-18).

d. There was only one answer for Judah: revival (vv.10-11). Hezekiah declared that he personally was going to make a renewed covenant, recommitment to the LORD. His purpose was to secure the favor of the LORD so the LORD would turn His fierce anger away from the nation.

After declaring his own intentions, Hezekiah with tenderness of heart addressed the religious workers as "my sons," calling upon them not to be negligent in their duty. They too needed to recommit their lives and renew their covenant with the LORD. As God's ministers, they represented Him and served Him. Therefore, they must sanctify and cleanse themselves in order to minister and burn incense before Him. Remember that incense symbolized prayer. It was necessary for the priests and Levites to be cleansed of all sin before they could pray and worship the LORD in purity of heart and life.

e. The Levites and priests immediately obeyed after Hezekiah's address. They went to work exactly as he had charged (vv.12-19).

1) The Levites appointed leaders to supervise their work (vv.12-14). Two leaders were appointed from each of the three major clans: Kohath, Merari, and Gershon. Two leaders were also appointed from a fourth clan, Elizaphan (v.13). Other leaders were appointed from three clans of the Levitical musicians, the clans of Asaph, Zechariah, and Mattaniah (vv.13-14).

2) After selecting their leadership, the Levites then sanctified themselves (v.15). This was a public service of sanctification, a service when they all assembled together as brothers, fellow servants of the LORD. Just picture the scene: a mass of priests and Levites gathered together in a service of recommitment to the LORD, sanctifying and setting themselves apart to serve the LORD with renewed devotion.

3) Once the Levites had personally recommitting their lives to the LORD, they then sanctified and cleansed the temple (vv.15-17). Just as the king had charged and as the LORD's Word instructed, they carried out their tasks (1 Chr.28:12, 19). The Levites removed all the rubbish and every defiled thing from the sanctuary and piled it all out in the courtyard. They then carted all the rubbish out through the Kidron Valley (v.16). The cleansing of the temple took sixteen days altogether (v.17). Eight days were needed to clean the courts up to the portico or porch, and then eight more days were needed to cleanse the temple itself.

4) After completing the cleansing of the temple, the Levites and priests went to the king and gave him their report (vv.18-19). They had cleansed the entire temple, the altar, the Table of Showbread, and all the utensils and articles used with each. Furthermore, they had recovered and sanctified (cleansed) all the items and utensils taken by King Ahaz when he closed the temple.

Thought 1. Ministers and churches have a responsibility to be holy and pure, for the LORD has set them apart to proclaim His Holy Word to the world and to minister to people. If the minister is slothful or living in sin, he becomes defiled and unclean before the LORD. As a result, the power of God does not rest upon his life, neither in preaching nor in ministering. He preaches and ministers without power, being empty and nothing more than sounding brass and tinkling cymbals (1 Co.13:1). As a poor, even bad, representative of the LORD, he is to face a far more severe judgment from the LORD. Why? Because the sinful, unclean, and defiled minister was given the unique privilege of proclaiming the unsearchable riches of Christ to a lost and dying world. For this reason, every minister of the gospel must be sanctified every day of his life, daily cleansed from sin and set apart anew to the LORD.

Similarly, the church must be sanctified, cleansed from all defilement and kept holy, set apart as a lighthouse for the LORD. Sitting on the streets of our cities and villages, the church building becomes a symbol of our need to worship and of the LORD's presence among us when we worship faithfully. For this reason, the church building is to be maintained and never abused. Unclean and shameful activities are not to be allowed in the church. Churches are not to be defiled by any behavior that dishonors or pollutes the air within the church or that damages the human body such as smoking, drinking alcoholic beverages, immoral or indecent activities, or any other pursuit that could arouse sinful behavior. The holy church is to be kept holy. It is to remain an atmosphere set apart for the worship of the LORD and the blessing of the people through the presence and health that God gives to his worshippers—both spiritual and physical health.

The sanctification or purity of the minister and of the church is an absolute essential. Listen to what God says about sanctification and holiness:

> "**Know ye not that ye are the temple of God, and *that* the Spirit of God dwelleth in you? If any man defile the temple of God, him shall God destroy; for the temple of God is holy, which *temple* ye are**" (1 Co.3:16-17).

> "**Know ye not that the unrighteous shall not inherit the kingdom of God? Be not deceived: neither fornicators, nor idolaters, nor adulterers, nor effeminate, nor abusers of themselves with mankind, Nor thieves, nor covetous, nor drunkards, nor revilers, nor extortioners, shall inherit the kingdom of God. And such were some of you: but ye are washed, but ye are sanctified, but ye are justified in the name of the Lord Jesus, and by the Spirit of our God**" (1 Co.6:9-11).

> "**What? know ye not that your body is the temple of the Holy Ghost *which is* in you, which ye have of God, and ye are not your own? For ye are bought with a price: therefore glorify God in your body, and in your spirit, which are God's**" (1 Co.6:19-20).

> "**Having therefore these promises, dearly beloved, let us cleanse ourselves from all filthiness of the flesh and spirit, perfecting holiness in the fear of God**" (2 Co.7:1).

> "**Husbands, love your wives, even as Christ also loved the church, and gave himself for it; That he might sanctify and cleanse it with the washing of water by the word, That he might present it to himself a glorious church, not having spot, or wrinkle, or any such thing; but that it should be holy and without blemish**" (Ep.5:25-27).

> "**For this is the will of God, *even* your sanctification, that ye should abstain from fornication**" (1 Th.4:3).

> "**And the very God of peace sanctify you wholly; and *I pray God* your whole spirit and soul and body be preserved blameless unto the coming of our Lord Jesus Christ**" (1 Th.5:23).

> "**Follow peace with all *men,* and holiness, without which no man shall see the Lord**" (He.12:14).

> "**But as he which hath called you is holy, so be ye holy in all manner of conversation; Because it is written, Be ye holy; for I am holy**" (1 Pe.1:15-16).

> "**And let the priests also, which come near to the LORD, sanctify themselves, lest the LORD break forth upon them**" (Ex.19:22).

> "**And ye shall be holy unto me: for I the LORD *am* holy, and have severed you from *other* people, that ye should be mine**" (Le.20:26).

> "**And said unto them, Hear me, ye Levites, sanctify now yourselves, and sanctify the house of the LORD God of your fathers, and carry forth the filthiness out of the holy *place***" (2 Chr.29:5).

> "**Wash you, make you clean; put away the evil of your doings from before mine eyes; cease to do evil**" (Is.1:16).

3 (29:20-36) **Beginning, New, Example of—Fresh Start, Example of—Worship, Duty, to Be Renewed—Rededication, of the Temple—Temple, Rededication of**: early in the morning on the day after receiving the report, Hezekiah led the people in a great rededication service for the newly sanctified temple. He and the people rededicated both their own lives and the temple to the LORD. No time was wasted in launching this new beginning, this fresh new start for worshiping of the LORD.

a. Rising earlier than usual, Hezekiah summoned all the city officials to join him in a rededication service in honor of the temple's being reopened and prepared for the worship of the LORD. Obviously, many of these officials had served in the evil and corrupt administration of King Ahaz. Therefore, they were just as guilty as Ahaz was of rejecting the LORD and misleading the people in the worship of idols. By summoning the officials to join him in a worship service of rededication, Hezekiah was taking a major stand for the LORD. He expected his officials to follow his example and to set a pattern for the people to follow. Also, by arising earlier than usual to summon the leaders, he demonstrated both excitement and devotion for the LORD, a fact that could not be missed by the royal officials.

1) Challenged by the example of their king, the leaders brought animals to be sacrificed as sin offerings to make atonement for their sins (see outline and notes—Le.4:1–5:13 for more discussion). Their purpose was to seek atonement…

- for the kingdom, which probably refers to the royal court, including the royal family and the royal officials of the nation
- for the sanctuary, which refers to the priests and Levites
- for Judah, which refers to the people or citizens of the nation

Seven of each kind of animal to be sacrificed were brought by the royal officials: seven bulls, seven rams, seven lambs, and seven male goats—all 28 animals to be presented as sin offerings for the personal sins of the officials as well as for the sins of the nation. Remember that the basic meaning of atonement is *covering* and *reconciliation*. By presenting these sin offerings to the LORD, the leaders were asking God to cover their sins and to reconcile them to the LORD through the substitute sacrifice of the animal. Also remember that the number seven symbolized perfection, completion. Thus, by bringing seven of each animal, the leaders were declaring a wholehearted, complete recommitment to the LORD.

Taking the animals, the priests offered the sacrifices to the LORD and sprinkled the blood on the altar (v.22). When the king and the leaders laid their hands on the goats, they identified them as the substitute sacrifice. By this act, they were declaring their faith in the LORD and in His promise to free them from sin through the substitute sacrifice. Of course, the substitute sacrifice was a type of the coming Savior and Messiah of the world, the Lord Jesus Christ Himself, who was the *Perfect Sacrifice* for sin. After sacrificing the goats, the priests sprinkled their blood on the altar. Thus, atonement was made for all Israel through the sin offering. Note also that sacrifices were made for the burnt offering, which was a symbol of reconciliation with God (v.24).

2) The king stationed the Levite musicians in the temple for the dedication service (v.25). They were placed there just as David, Gad the king's seer, and Nathan the prophet had instructed. And they stood ready to sing and play their instruments and trumpets at the appropriate time (v.26).

3) As soon as the king ordered the burnt offering to be sacrificed and presented to the LORD, the musicians began to sing and play their instruments. They continued with their music throughout the sacrifice of the burnt offering (vv.27-28). While the singers sang and the priests presented their offerings to the LORD, the entire assembly bowed and worshipped the LORD (v.28).

4) The king and all the royal officials also knelt and worshipped the LORD after the offerings were made (v.29). Just picture the scene, the mass of people seeking forgiveness for their sins and reconciliation with God—everyone kneeling and worshipping the LORD. They were seeking Him with all their hearts. Even the city officials who had been a stumbling block, guilty of trying to exterminate the true worship of the LORD, were now kneeling, asking for forgiveness and reconciliation with the LORD.

5) While the people were worshiping, the Levites were singing praises to the LORD. Note what they sang: the psalms of David and of Asaph the seer, the very same songs that we find in the Holy Bible (v.30).

b. After the leadership of the nation sought forgiveness and reconciliation with God, King Hezekiah invited the congregation to bring their sacrifices and thanksgiving offerings (see outline and notes—Le.3:1-17 for more discussion). The people needed to personally seek the LORD for forgiveness and reconciliation just as the leadership had individually sought the LORD.

1) Many people responded positively, bringing their sacrifices and thanksgiving offerings to the LORD. When making the thanksgiving offering, a person was allowed to eat some of the meat as a meal. However, some of the people—those with willing hearts—brought burnt offerings in which the entire animal was sacrificed. The person received none of the meat. The point being made is that some of the people—those who gave whole animals for the burnt offerings—were more willing to follow the LORD than others were. In other words, some were seeking forgiveness and reconciliation more wholeheartedly, completely, or sincerely than others.

2) The offerings sacrificed were enormous in number:
⇒ the burnt offerings numbered 70 bulls, 100 rams, and 200 male lambs
⇒ the other offerings totaled 600 bulls and 3,000 sheep and goats (v.33)

3) As the scores of people brought their offerings, the line began to back up and become congested. The number of priests was insufficient to handle all the work involved in sacrificing the animals (v.34). There were just too few priests who had responded to Hezekiah's challenge to sanctify and cleanse themselves. Sadly, too many of the priests had been lax, complacent, slow to respond to the revival. But not so with the Levites. Many more of them had been conscientious about sanctifying and purifying themselves. For this reason, they stepped in to help, taking the place of the priests and presenting the sacrifices to the LORD.

4) Hezekiah was very encouraged by the outcome of his restoration of the temple worship service. The burnt offerings presented by the people were surprisingly numerous, as were the accompanying drink offerings and the sizeable amount of fat offered from the fellowship offerings (v.35). The large number of offerings indicated a tremendous response to the reopening of the temple, and a wonderful spirit of revival broke out among the people.

c. Within the very first month of Hezekiah's reign, he restored the temple and swung its doors wide open for worship. In concluding their first worship service in the newly restored temple, the king and the people rejoiced over what God had done—rejoicing especially because it had been accomplished so quickly (v.36).

Thought 1. The lesson for us is most challenging, that of getting a *new beginning in worship*. How many of us need a fresh start, a revitalization of our worship? For many of us, worship has become dull, uninteresting, irrelevant, impractical, having little to do with day-to-day life. Perhaps, the lessons and sermons come across as little more than stories about ancient history or as typical self-esteem, ego-boosting seminars or speeches. Maybe little is said or done that seems to make a difference in life. Many of us get little or nothing out of worship, little motivation or enthusiasm, guidance or direction, provision or supply, assurance or security. There appears to be a lack of true godly power—the power of salvation and deliverance—in the worship so many of us participate in, as well as our own personal worship.

A new beginning, a fresh start is desperately needed in our worship. We must take two steps to renew it, the very same steps taken by Hezekiah and the people of his day:

(1) First, the leaders of God's people must approach the LORD through the *substitute sacrifice* of the Lord Jesus Christ, the only Perfect Sacrifice that is acceptable to God. This was exactly what Hezekiah led his people to do. They first sought forgiveness of sins and reconciliation with God. And they sought forgiveness and reconciliation through the *substitute sacrifice* (vv.21-30).

(2) Second, after the leaders have recommitted their lives to the LORD, the invitation must be extended to the congregation to approach the LORD through the *substitute sacrifice* of the Lord Jesus Christ (vv.31-36). Approaching God

through the Lord Jesus Christ will bring forgiveness of sins and reconciliation, for God forgives the sins of all who come to Him through the death of His Son. And when a person comes, God reconciles that person to Himself.

Reemphasizing the fact, a new beginning in worship can be achieved if, first, the leadership of God's people will recommit their lives to the LORD and, second, the people will follow the example of the leadership in recommitting their lives to the LORD. When we seek the LORD through Christ, the substitute sacrifice, God guarantees a new beginning in worship—whether corporately as a church body or individually. Listen to what God's Holy Word says:

"And that repentance and remission of sins should be preached in his name among all nations, beginning at Jerusalem" (Lu.24:47).

"God *is* a Spirit: and they that worship him must worship *him* in spirit and in truth" (Jn.4:24).

"Jesus saith unto him, I am the way, the truth, and the life: no man cometh unto the Father, but by me" (Jn.14:6).

"I beseech you therefore, brethren, by the mercies of God, that ye present your bodies a living sacrifice, holy, acceptable unto God, *which is* your reasonable service. And be not conformed to this world: but be ye transformed by the renewing of your mind, that ye may prove what is that good, and acceptable, and perfect, will of God" (Ro.12:1-2).

"For it is written, *As* I live, saith the Lord, every knee shall bow to me, and every tongue shall confess to God" (Ro.14:11).

"To wit, that God was in Christ, reconciling the world unto himself, not imputing their trespasses unto them; and hath committed unto us the word of reconciliation. Now then we are ambassadors for Christ, as though God did beseech *you* by us: we pray *you* in Christ's stead, be ye reconciled to God" (2 Co.5:19-20).

"And walk in love, as Christ also hath loved us, and hath given himself for us an offering and a sacrifice to God for a sweetsmelling savour" (Ep.5:2).

"Wherefore God also hath highly exalted him, and given him a name which is above every name: That at the name of Jesus every knee should bow, of *things* in heaven, and *things* in earth, and *things* under the earth; And *that* every tongue should confess that Jesus Christ *is* Lord, to the glory of God the Father" (Ph.2:9-11).

"Who gave himself for us, that he might redeem us from all iniquity, and purify unto himself a peculiar people, zealous of good works" (Tit.2:14).

"Who his own self bare our sins in his own body on the tree, that we, being dead to sins, should live unto righteousness: by whose stripes ye were healed" (1 Pe.2:24).

"For Christ also hath once suffered for sins, the just for the unjust, that he might bring us to God, being put to death in the flesh, but quickened by the Spirit" (1 Pe.3:18).

"That which we have seen and heard declare we unto you, that ye also may have fellowship with us: and truly our fellowship *is* with the Father, and with his Son Jesus Christ" (1 Jn.1:3).

"And they sing the song of Moses the servant of God, and the song of the Lamb, saying, Great and marvellous *are* thy works, Lord God Almighty; just and true *are* thy ways, thou King of saints" (Re.15:3).

"Look unto me, and be ye saved, all the ends of the earth: for I *am* God, and *there is* none else. I have sworn by myself, the word is gone out of my mouth *in* righteousness, and shall not return, That unto me every knee shall bow, every tongue shall swear" (Is.45:22-23).

BACKGROUND TO ISAIAH'S DAY

(The Four Kings Who Ruled During Isaiah's Ministry)

V. THE REIGN OF HEZEKIAH (PART 2)—A MEANINGFUL CELEBRATION OF THE PASSOVER: A PICTURE OF TRUE REVIVAL, 2 CHR.30:1-27

OUTLINE	SCRIPTURE	SCRIPTURE	OUTLINE
1. The plans for a great Passover Feast: A picture of witnessing, inviting people to Christ, the Lamb of God a. The decision to celebrate the Passover 1) The invitation was sent to *all Israel* & Judah 2) The decision was made to celebrate the Passover in the second month, not as it usually was in the first month, Ex.12:1-2 • Due to the priests: Not enough of them had yet turned back—consecrated themselves—to the LORD • Due to the people: They had not had time to travel to Jerusalem 3) The king & his officials were pleased & in agreement about the decision b. The invitation to attend the Passover proclaimed throughout the entire nation 1) The proclamation was sent from Beersheba to Dan: The farthest cities in the Southern & Northern Kingdoms 2) The Passover had been neglected for a long time: Not many had observed it c. The message of the invitation, the proclamation, 2 Chr.7:14; 29:6-9; Zec.1:2-6 1) Return to the LORD • The LORD identified: The God of Abraham, Isaac, & Israel (Jacob) • The promise made: He will return to you who have escaped death & exile 2) Do not follow the sinful examples of your fathers & brothers • They forsook the LORD • God judged them, gave them up to desolation 3) Do not be stubborn, unresponsive to God: Submit to Him 4) Come to the temple (church) • The place God has sanctified (set apart, made holy) forever • The reason: God will turn His anger away	And Hezekiah sent to all Israel and Judah, and wrote letters also to Ephraim and Manasseh, that they should come to the house of the LORD at Jerusalem, to keep the passover unto the LORD God of Israel. 2 For the king had taken counsel, and his princes, and all the congregation in Jerusalem, to keep the passover in the second month. 3 For they could not keep it at that time, because the priests had not sanctified themselves sufficiently, neither had the people gathered themselves together to Jerusalem. 4 And the thing pleased the king and all the congregation. 5 So they established a decree to make proclamation throughout all Israel, from Beer-sheba even to Dan, that they should come to keep the passover unto the LORD God of Israel at Jerusalem: for they had not done *it* of a long time *in such sort* as it was written. 6 So the posts went with the letters from the king and his princes throughout all Israel and Judah, and according to the commandment of the king, saying, Ye children of Israel, turn again unto the LORD God of Abraham, Isaac, and Israel, and he will return to the remnant of you, that are escaped out of the hand of the kings of Assyria. 7 And be not ye like your fathers, and like your brethren, which trespassed against the LORD God of their fathers, *who* therefore gave them up to desolation, as ye see. 8 Now be ye not stiffnecked, as your fathers *were, but* yield yourselves unto the LORD, and enter into his sanctuary, which he hath sanctified for ever: and serve the LORD your God, that the fierceness of his wrath may turn away from you.	9 For if ye turn again unto the LORD, your brethren and your children *shall find* compassion before them that lead them captive, so that they shall come again into this land: for the LORD your God *is* gracious and merciful, and will not turn away *his* face from you, if ye return unto him. 10 So the posts passed from city to city through the country of Ephraim and Manasseh even unto Zebulun: but they laughed them to scorn, and mocked them. 11 Nevertheless divers of Asher and Manasseh and of Zebulun humbled themselves, and came to Jerusalem. 12 Also in Judah the hand of God was to give them one heart to do the commandment of the king and of the princes, by the word of the LORD. 13 And there assembled at Jerusalem much people to keep the feast of unleavened bread in the second month, a very great congregation. 14 And they arose and took away the altars that *were* in Jerusalem, and all the altars for incense took they away, and cast *them* into the brook Kidron. 15 Then they killed the passover on the fourteenth *day* of the second month: and the priests and the Levites were ashamed, and sanctified themselves, and brought in the burnt offerings into the house of the LORD. 16 And they stood in their place after their manner, according to the law of Moses the man of God: the priests sprinkled the blood, *which* they received of the hand of the Levites. 17 For *there were* many in the congregation that were not sanctified: therefore the Levites had the charge of the killing of the passovers for every one *that was* not clean,	from you 5) Repent & God will have compassion upon you • He will move the captors to release your families to return home • The reason: He is gracious & compassionate • The condition: He will not turn His face from you—if you repent d. The response to the invitation 1) The vast majority of the Northern Kingdom scorned & ridiculed the messengers & the invitation 2) Some men from three tribes did humble themselves & make the pilgrimage: Asher, Manasseh, & Zebulun 3) Judah responded very favorably: Was stirred by the hand of God to obey the Word of God & to keep the Passover **2. The celebration of the Passover: A picture of genuine revival** a. The people assembled b. The people turned away from false worship: They arose & destroyed all the altars to false gods, throwing them into the Kidron Valley, 28:24 c. The people believed God's promise of salvation through the substitute sacrifice: They slaughtered the Passover lambs d. The religious workers consecrated themselves anew: They were shamed & stirred by the people's zeal 1) They brought burnt offerings 2) They then took their places at the temple & began to serve as God's law instructs • They sprinkled the blood on the altar • They helped the worshippers who were not ritually, ceremonially clean: Killed & sanctified the lambs, set them apart for the LORD

30

OUTLINE	SCRIPTURE	SCRIPTURE	OUTLINE
	to sanctify *them* unto the LORD.	confession to the LORD God of their fathers.	lowship offerings & confessing their sins
e. The priests & Levites judged people by the intent of their hearts, not by ritual & ceremony	18 For a multitude of the people, *even* many of Ephraim, and Manasseh, Issachar, and Zebulun, had not cleansed themselves,	23 And the whole assembly took counsel to keep other seven days: and they kept *other* seven days with gladness.	g. The people decided to continue the festival for seven additional days
1) Most of the people from the Northern Kingdom were not supposed to eat the Passover meal: Because they were unfit, had not gone through the required ritual, Ex.12:43-49	yet did they eat the passover otherwise than it waswritten. But Hezekiah prayed for them, saying, The good LORD pardon every one	24 For Hezekiah king of Judah did give to the congregation a thousand bullocks and seven thousand sheep; and the princes gave to the congregation a thousand bullocks and ten thousand sheep: and a great number of priests sanctified themselves.	1) The king provided 1,000 bulls & 7,000 sheep & goats for sacrifice 2) The royal officials donated 1,000 bulls & 10,000 sheep & goats
2) Hezekiah prayed for them: Asked God to forgive & accept them	19 *That* prepareth his heart to seek God, the LORD God of his fathers, though *he be* not *cleansed* according to the purification of the sanctuary.		3) The priests—a great number—renewed their commitment & returned to the ministry, 3
3) The LORD heard Hezekiah's prayer & healed them: Forgave & accepted them	20 And the LORD hearkened to Hezekiah, and healed the people.	25 And all the congregation of Judah, with the priests and the Levites, and all the congregation that came out of Israel, and the strangers that came out of the land of Israel, and that dwelt in Judah, rejoiced.	4) The people & religious workers—including the foreigners—rejoiced greatly in the LORD
f. The people were filled with joyful praise	21 And the children of Israel that were present at Jerusalem kept the feast of unleavened bread seven days with great gladness: and the Levites and the priests praised the LORD day by day, *singing* with loud instruments unto the LORD.	26 So there was great joy in Jerusalem: for since the time of Solomon the son of David king of Israel *there was* not the like in Jerusalem.	
1) The people celebrated the Feast of Unleavened Bread for seven days: A symbol of the need & urgency to leave Egypt (the world) 2) The musicians sang & played music every day 3) The king encouraged the religious workers daily	22 And Hezekiah spake comfortably unto all the Levites that taught the good knowledge of the LORD: and they did eat throughout the	27 Then the priests the Levites arose and blessed the people: and their voice was heard, and their prayer came	5) The rejoicing was greater than any since the days of Solomon & David
4) The people continued the feast for seven days, sacrificing their peace or fellowship offerings	feast seven days, offering peace offerings, and making	*up* to his holy dwelling place, *even* unto heaven.	h. The priests & Levites prayed for the people, & their prayers were heard by God, 7:12

(30:1-27) **Introduction**: in observing people today, we see that far too many are lax, complacent, slothful, self-satisfied, overly comfortable, and too easygoing. There is a lack of ambition and diligence, an inner motivation that drives a person to do a good job, to complete the task, to succeed and to achieve. Far too many people are indulging themselves, living lives of extravagance, hoarding wealth instead of giving to meet the needs of the world. In addition, wickedness, immorality and violence are sweeping the earth. Righteousness and godliness seem to be on the decline.

If there has ever been a day when revival—a renewed spirit of righteousness and godliness is needed, it is today. A true revival is the subject of the present Scripture. As soon as King Hezekiah assumed the throne of Judah, he did all he could to launch a spiritual revival throughout the nation. For years the temple had been shut down and its doors barricaded there in an attempt to eliminate the worship of the LORD from the land. But within a period of one month, King Hezekiah had reestablished worship within the temple and the people experienced the first taste of genuine revival. Longing to see the revival continue, Hezekiah called the leadership of the nation together to discuss ways to strengthen the people's recommitment to the LORD.

In reading this account, the exiles returning with Ezra would be stirred to seek true revival among themselves. As they sought to restore *true worship* in the temple and to rebuild their nation, they desperately needed a continued spirit of renewal and new life filling their hearts and flowing among them. This is, *The Reign of Hezekiah (Part 2)—a Meaningful Celebration of the Passover: A Picture of True Revival*, 30:1-27.

    1. The plans for a great Passover Feast: a picture of witnessing, inviting people to Christ, the Lamb of God (vv.1-12).

    2. The celebration of the Passover: a picture of genuine revival (vv.13-27).

1 (30:1-12) **Witnessing, Example of—Passover, Celebration of—Hezekiah, Reformation of—Hezekiah, Attempt to Reunite Israel and Judah**: longing to keep the fires of revival burning within the hearts of his people, Hezekiah laid the plans for a great Passover Feast. The temple had been closed for years and no worship allowed within its sacred walls. But now the temple was restored and a great worship service had been held to celebrate its restoration. Many of the people had made recommitments to the LORD and their commitments needed to be strengthened, reinforced so they would remain faithful to the LORD. It was the season for the Passover, the most meaningful feast or festival of the Jews, for it celebrated their liberation from Egyptian slavery and the wonderful hope of the promised land. Hezekiah saw in this the opportunity to use the Passover to strengthen the recommitment of the people and also to reinstate the annual celebration of this important feast. Scripture gives the details of the plans laid out by Hezekiah:

a. Once the decision to celebrate the Passover was made, the invitation to attend was sent to *all Israel* as well as to Judah (v.1, 5). In celebrating the Passover, Hezekiah saw the opportunity to reach out in an attempt to reunite "*all Israel.*" Remember that the Northern Kingdom had earlier been conquered by the Assyrians and most of the people exiled and taken to Assyria as slaves (see outline and note—2 K.17:1-41 for more discussion). In ancient times, when a ruler conquered a nation and then deported its citizens, he left a few citizens behind to maintain the land and to provide some tribute to the conquering nation. In addition, the ruler usually replaced the conquered population with refugees from other nations. When the Assyrians conquered the northern kingdom of Israel, they did just this: they left a few Israelites behind and transported foreign refugees to Israel to maintain the land as a vassal state of Assyria. Thus Hezekiah saw an opportunity to reach out to the people of the Northern Kingdom. The potential for spiritually reuniting *all Israel* now existed. The Passover celebration could be used to call *all Israel* together in the worship of the LORD. If spiritual unity could be achieved and the people of both the Northern and Southern Kingdoms would recommit their lives to the LORD, perhaps the LORD would bless, reuniting and restoring the entire nation of Israel.

Hezekiah involved all the royal officials in the decision to celebrate the Passover (vv.2-3). Together they decided to celebrate it in the second month, not as it usually was in the first month (Ex.12:1-2; De.16:1-8). Bear in mind that Hezekiah had assumed the throne in the first month of the year and that he had immediately ordered the temple to be reopened and restored for worship. The Passover was ordinarily celebrated in the first month of the year, but preparing the temple for worship had taken sixteen days (29:17). This meant that Hezekiah would have to wait another year to celebrate the Passover or else make the decision to celebrate it in the second month. God's law did make allowances for the celebration date to be changed, in particular for people who were ritually defiled or absent due to being out of town traveling (Nu.9:9-14). Two reasons are given for Hezekiah's delaying the Passover:

⇒ The Passover needed to be delayed due to the priests. Not enough of them had yet been recruited, contacted, and challenged to recommit themselves to the LORD (v.3). More time was needed to spread the word of the restored temple to the priests throughout the nation. Once they heard and were challenged to sanctify themselves, many of them would respond.

⇒ Second, the Passover needed to be delayed in order to give people time to travel to Jerusalem. Delaying the Passover one month satisfied both the king and his officials (v.4). They were all in full agreement about the decision they were making.

b. Once the decision had been made to delay the feast, the invitation to attend the Passover was proclaimed throughout the entire nation (v.5). A proclamation was sent from Beersheba to Dan, which represented the farthest cities in the Southern and Northern Kingdoms. For over 200 years, since the days of Solomon, the Passover had been neglected as a national celebration at the temple (v.5). Very few of the people had been faithful in celebrating it.

c. Hezekiah sent letters of invitation and proclamation to all the people throughout both Judah and Israel (vv.6-9). In reality, the proclamation was a written sermon that included five points.

1) First, Hezekiah called upon the people to return to the LORD (v.6). He unmistakably identified the LORD as the true God in contrast to the false gods being worshipped by so many of the people. They must return to the God of Abraham, Isaac and Israel (Jacob). Note that Hezekiah was basing his call to the people upon the Abrahamic covenant, (see outline and note—Ge.12:1-3 for more discussion). It was in the Abrahamic covenant that the LORD had given the wonderful promise of the *promised land*. Because of the terrible oppression by the Assyrians, the people would have their hearts stirred with renewed hope when they were reminded of God's promises. Obviously Hezekiah mentioned Abraham for this very purpose, to arouse the people's hope for the restoration and reunification of the nation (promised land). In fact, Hezekiah declared that the LORD would return to all who had escaped death and exile at the hand of the Assyrians, if the people would just return to the LORD.

2) Second, Hezekiah warned the people: they must not follow the sinful example of their fathers and brothers (v.7). Their forefathers forsook the LORD, and the LORD judged them by allowing various nations to conquer and exile them, devastating the land and enslaving many of the people (28:5-10, 17-18; 2 K.17:1-41).

3) Third, Hezekiah challenged the people not to be stubborn, unresponsive to God (v.8). They must not continue to be stiff-necked, rejecting the LORD and refusing to obey His commandments. They must submit, yield to Him.

4) Fourth, Hezekiah challenged the people to come to the temple, the very place God had sanctified, set apart, and made holy forever (v.8). Note the wonderful hope Hezekiah held out for the people: if they would return to the LORD, worshipping and serving Him, God would turn His anger away from them. The implication is that He would restore and reunify them as a people as well as their nation, the promised land.

5) Fifth, Hezekiah challenged the people to repent, to turn away from their sin and return to the LORD (v.9). If they returned to Him, God would have compassion upon them. He would move upon the captors to release their families to return home to the promised land. God would do this because He is gracious and compassionate. But note, there was a condition: repentance. If they repented, He would not turn His face from them.

d. The response to the couriers' proclamation to the people was mixed (vv.10-12). The vast majority of the Northern Kingdom scorned and ridiculed the messengers and the invitation (v.10). However, some of the people from three tribes did humble themselves and make the pilgrimage to the temple in Jerusalem (v.11). Those who responded favorably were from the northern tribes of Asher, Manasseh, and Zebulun.

In the Southern Kingdom of Judah, the hand of the LORD was moving mightily upon the people, so a great number of them responded very positively (v.12). They obeyed the Word of the LORD and made the pilgrimage to keep the Passover.

Thought 1. This is a vivid picture of witnessing and of bearing strong testimony for the LORD, inviting people to Christ, the Lamb of God. If the world has ever needed to hear the message of the *Lamb* of God, it is today. Never has the gospel of Christ been so desperately needed. Witnesses for Christ—dynamic witnesses—are needed. If we are followers of Christ, we need to be proclaiming the wonderful salvation He has provided for people, for He is the Perfect *Lamb* of God. By His sacrificial death upon the cross, He bore the judgment of God against all hatred, brutality, savagery, enslavement, murder, rape, sexual abuse—all the sins of violence, lawlessness, and immorality. The Perfect *Lamb* of God—the Lord Jesus Christ—bore the penalty of death for our sins. He died for you and for me. Therefore, if we ask God to allow the death, the blood of Christ, to cover us, God's judgment will *pass over* us. God's judgment will never fall upon us, for Christ covered and bore our sins for us. This is the meaning of the *Passover*. If we trust Christ as our personal Savior to save us from sin through His death on the cross, we are spared from God's hand of judgment. It *passes over* us. His death, His blood covers our sins.

This wonderful, glorious message of salvation and deliverance must be proclaimed to the world. Listen to what God's Holy Word says:

(1) Jesus Christ is the Perfect Lamb of God. His blood cleanses us from all sin and removes the judgment of God from us.

> "The next day John seeth Jesus coming unto him, and saith, Behold the Lamb of God, which taketh away the sin of the world" (Jn.1:29).
>
> "For this is my blood of the new testament, which is shed for many for the remission of sins" (Mt.26:28).
>
> "Take heed therefore unto yourselves, and to all the flock, over the which the Holy Ghost hath made you overseers, to feed the church of God, which he hath purchased with his own blood" (Ac.20:28).
>
> "Much more then, being now justified by his blood, we shall be saved from wrath through him" (Ro.5:9).
>
> "Purge out therefore the old leaven, that ye may be a new lump, as ye are unleavened. For even Christ our passover is sacrificed for us" (1 Co.5:7).
>
> "How much more shall the blood of Christ, who through the eternal Spirit offered himself without spot to God, purge your conscience from dead works to serve the living God?" (He.9:14).
>
> "Forasmuch as ye know that ye were not redeemed with corruptible things, *as* silver and gold, from your vain conversation [conduct, behavior] *received* by tradition from your fathers; But with the precious blood of Christ, as of a lamb without blemish and without spot" (1 Pe.1:18-19).
>
> "But if we walk in the light, as he is in the light, we have fellowship one with another, and the blood of Jesus Christ his Son cleanseth us from all sin" (1 Jn.1:7).
>
> "And from Jesus Christ, *who is* the faithful witness, *and* the first begotten of the dead, and the prince of the kings of the earth. Unto him that loved us, and washed us from our sins in his own blood" (Re.1:5).
>
> "He was oppressed, and he was afflicted, yet he opened not his mouth: he is brought as a lamb to the slaughter, and as a sheep before her shearers is dumb, so he openeth not his mouth" (Is.53:7).

(2) We must bear strong witness and testimony to the Lamb of God, the Lord Jesus Christ.

> "Whosoever therefore shall confess me before men, him will I confess also before my Father which is in heaven. But whosoever shall deny me before men, him will I also deny before my Father which is in heaven" (Mt.10:32-33).
>
> "Go ye therefore, and teach all nations, baptizing them in the name of the Father, and of the Son, and of the Holy Ghost: Teaching them to observe all things whatsoever I have commanded you: and, lo, I am with you alway, *even* unto the end of the world. Amen" (Mt.28:19-20).
>
> "And he said unto them, Go ye into all the world, and preach the gospel to every creature" (Mk.16:15).
>
> "Also I say unto you, Whosoever shall confess me before men, him shall the Son of man also confess before the angels of God: But he that denieth me before men shall be denied before the angels of God" (Lu.12:8-9).
>
> "And ye also shall bear witness, because ye have been with me from the beginning" (Jn.15:27).
>
> "Then said Jesus to them again, Peace *be* unto you: as *my* Father hath sent me, even so send I you" (Jn.20:21).
>
> "But ye shall receive power, after that the Holy Ghost is come upon you: and ye shall be witnesses unto me both in Jerusalem, and in all Judaea, and in Samaria, and unto the uttermost part of the earth" (Ac.1:8).
>
> "And they were all filled with the Holy Ghost, and began to speak with other tongues, as the Spirit gave them utterance" (Ac.2:4).
>
> "For we cannot but speak the things which we have seen and heard" (Ac.4:20).
>
> "Go, stand and speak in the temple to the people all the words of this life. And when they heard *that*, they entered into the temple early in the morning, and taught. But the high priest came, and they that were with him, and called the council together, and all the senate of the children of Israel and sent to the prison to have them brought" (Ac.5:20-21).
>
> "For thou shalt be his witness unto all men of what thou hast seen and heard" (Ac.22:15).
>
> "We having the same spirit of faith, according as it is written, I believed, and therefore have I spoken; we also believe, and therefore speak" (2 Co.4:13).
>
> "Be not thou therefore ashamed of the testimony of our Lord, nor of me his prisoner: but be thou partaker of the afflictions of the gospel according to the power of God" (2 Ti.1:8).
>
> "These things speak, and exhort, and rebuke with all authority. Let no man despise thee" (Tit.2:15).

"But sanctify the Lord God in your hearts: and *be* ready always to *give* an answer to every man that asketh you a reason of the hope that is in you with meekness and fear" (1 Pe.3:15).

"Come *and* hear, all ye that fear God, and I will declare what he hath done for my soul" (Ps.66:16).

"I will mention the lovingkindnesses of the LORD, *and* the praises of the LORD, according to all that the LORD hath bestowed on us, and the great goodness toward the house of Israel, which he hath bestowed on them according to his mercies, and according to the multitude of his lovingkindnesses" (Is.63:7).

"Then they that feared the LORD spake often one to another: and the LORD hearkened, and heard *it,* and a book of remembrance was written before him for them that feared the LORD, and that thought upon his name" (Mal.3:16).

---

2 (30:13-27) **Revival, Example of—Renewal, Spiritual, Example of—Reawakening, Example of—Passover, Celebration**: at last, the long-awaited day arrived for the celebration of the Passover. And following immediately upon the heels of the Passover was the Feast of Unleavened Bread. Remember that the Festival of Unleavened Bread was tied to the Passover and that it was celebrated for seven full days. The Festival of Unleavened Bread symbolized the sudden and hasty flight of Israel from Egyptian slavery and their need to be *spiritually separated* from Egypt, a symbol of the world (see outline and note—Le.23:4-14, pt.2 for more discussion). Scripture paints an exciting picture of the joyful occasion:

a. People flooded into Jerusalem from all over the Northern and Southern Kingdoms, from both Israel and Judah. Those from the Northern Kingdom of Israel came primarily from the three tribes mentioned above, Asher, Manasseh, and Zebulun (v.11). People from Judah flooded in from all over the nation, being moved by the Spirit of God to respond favorably to Hezekiah's proclamation (v.13). Moreover, many of the people from Jerusalem and the surrounding villages had still recommitted their lives to the LORD and were already gripped by a spirit of revival.

b. In preparation for the Passover, the people continued their spiritual reformation. Before celebrating the Passover, they tore down and removed the altars in Jerusalem that had been set up by the wicked King Ahaz (28:24). They took the altars that had been built to the false gods, destroyed them, and threw them into the Kidron Valley. By destroying all the altars of the false gods, the people demonstrated the sincerity of their hearts in seeking the LORD, Him and Him alone.

c. The people were now ready to celebrate the Passover Feast with their hearts fully prepared (v.15). Believing God's promise of salvation through the *substitute sacrifice,* they slaughtered the Passover lambs (v.15).

d. Interestingly, the religious workers—priests and Levites—were put to shame by the renewed dedication and zeal of the laypersons. Keep in mind that many of the religious workers had been slow to respond to Hezekiah's call for spiritual renewal (v.3; 29:34). They had been lax and complacent in responding to the revival that was sweeping the nation, in particular among the laypersons. But when they witnessed the spirit of revival, the zeal that was gripping the laypeople, they obviously began to sense guilt and to be convicted by God's Spirit. They began to feel uneasy, embarrassed, and were aroused to recommit themselves anew to the LORD. Bringing their burnt offerings to the temple, the priests and Levites confessed their sins and approached the LORD through the *substitute sacrifice.* Now cleansed from their sins and consecrated before the LORD, they took their places at the temple and began to serve the people as they brought their sacrifices to be offered to the LORD. The priests sprinkled the blood of the sacrifice on the altar, just as God's law had instructed. Both the priests and Levites helped the worshippers who were not ritually, ceremonially clean (v.17). According to the law, it was the duty of family heads to kill the Passover lamb. But so many family heads had forsaken the LORD for so long, they also were not spiritually clean. For this reason, the Levites had to step in to kill the lambs for the family heads, sanctifying and setting them apart for the LORD.

e. Because such a large number of the people were spiritually unclean, the priests and Levites began to judge people by the intent of their heart, not by ritual and ceremony (vv.18-20). Most of the people from the Northern Kingdom were not supposed to eat the Passover meal because they were unfit; that is, they had not gone through the required ritual of cleansing (Ex.12:43-49). Remember that the Passover itself lasted only one day. Apparently, there were far too many people for the priests to handle within the time frame allowed. Therefore, Hezekiah and the priests allowed these people to participate in the *Passover meal.* Offering a special prayer in their behalf, Hezekiah asked God to forgive them for not following the strict *letter of the law,* beseeching the LORD to accept them because their hearts were set on seeking God (v.19). Scripture clearly states that the LORD heard Hezekiah's prayer and healed the people. That is, the LORD forgave and accepted them.

f. After offering the Passover sacrifice to the LORD, the people were filled with joyful praise and celebrated the Feast of Unleavened Bread for seven days (vv.21-22). Each day was filled with music as the musicians sang and played their instruments. Meanwhile the king encouraged the religious workers, in particular the Levites. For seven wonderful days the people continued to celebrate the festival. They sacrificed their peace or fellowship offerings and confessed their sins.

g. So great was the spirit of revival that swept over the people, they decided to continue the festival for seven additional days (vv.23-26). Due to the multitude of people seeking the LORD, there were not enough sacrificial animals available to meet the need. As a result, the king himself provided 1,000 bulls and 7,000 sheep and goats for sacrifice during this second week of services (v.24). Even the royal officials generously donated 1,000 bulls and 10,000 sheep and goats.

The spirit of revival sweeping across the land was so great that a large number of priests had renewed their commitment to the LORD and returned to the ministry (v.3, 15). Thus, all the people from both Judah and Israel, and all the priests and Levites, and all the foreigners who attended the festival rejoiced enthusiastically in the LORD (v.25). Not since the days of Solomon and David had there been such joy and rejoicing (v.26).

h. As the people came, either to make their sacrifices or for other reasons, the priests and Levites blessed and prayed for them (v.27). And their prayers reached up to heaven, the holy dwelling place of God Himself. Their prayers was heard by the LORD (7:12).

Thought 1. What a picture of genuine revival! A picture that shows us just how critically important it is today. God's church and people need to be renewed and revitalized. Revival must sweep this earth, revival that sees multitudes of believers recommitting their lives and unbelievers turning to the Lord Jesus Christ for salvation. Too many believers are lax, complacent, and comfortable, being *at ease in Zion*. Far too many have become worldly, fleshly, lusting after the pleasures and possessions of this world. Many have given in to the enticements of immorality, greed, fortune, and fame. Too few of us are obeying the commandment of God to assemble ourselves together in worship. Too few of us are living righteous and holy lives, bearing strong witness and testimony for the LORD. Only some of us are even trying to turn others to Christ or are faithful to the church, supporting it through our tithes and service.

And yet revival is necessary not only among the laypersons but also among the ministers of the church. Far too many ministers are living complacent, indulgent, worldly, and carnal lives. Many have given themselves over to lives of comfort and ease and to all the other sins listed in God's Holy Word, sins too terrible to mention when dealing with ministers of the gospel.

Wherever we look today, revival is needed. Every nation, as well as every community and church, need to be revived and led to make recommitments to the LORD. For this reason, God's people must be about the business of the LORD, working to bring about revival and renewal. Listen to what God's Holy Word says:

"For as the Father raiseth up the dead, and quickeneth *them;* even so the Son quickeneth whom he will" (Jn.5:21).

"It is the spirit that quickeneth; the flesh profiteth nothing: the words that I speak unto you, *they* are spirit, and *they* are life" (Jn.6:63).

"Then they that gladly received his word were baptized: and the same day there were added *unto them* about three thousand souls" (Ac.2:41).

"And the people with one accord gave heed unto those things which Philip spake, hearing and seeing the miracles which he did" (Ac.8:6).

"And all that dwelt at Lydda and Saron saw him, and turned to the Lord" (Ac.9:35).

"And the hand of the Lord was with them: and a great number believed, and turned unto the Lord" (Ac.11:21).

"I beseech you therefore, brethren, by the mercies of God, that ye present your bodies a living sacrifice, holy, acceptable unto God, *which is* your reasonable service. And be not conformed to this world: but be ye transformed by the renewing of your mind, that ye may prove what is that good, and acceptable, and perfect, will of God" (Ro.12:1-2).

"For which cause we faint not; but though our outward man perish, yet the inward *man* is renewed day by day. For our light affliction, which is but for a moment, worketh for us a far more exceeding *and* eternal weight of glory; While we look not at the things which are seen, but at the things which are not seen: for the things which are seen *are* temporal; but the things which are not seen *are* eternal" (2 Co.4:16-18).

"For godly sorrow worketh repentance to salvation not to be repented of: but the sorrow of the world worketh death" (2 Co.7:10).

"That ye put off concerning the former conversation [conduct, behavior] the old man, which is corrupt according to the deceitful lusts; And be renewed in the spirit of your mind; And that ye put on the new man, which after God is created in righteousness and true holiness" (Ep.4:22-24).

"And have put on the new *man,* which is renewed in knowledge after the image of him that created him" (Col.3:10).

"Not by works of righteousness which we have done, but according to his mercy he saved us, by the washing of regeneration, and renewing of the Holy Ghost" (Tit.3:5).

"Then the children of Israel did put away Baalim and Ashtaroth, and served the LORD only" (1 S.7:4).

"The LORD *is* nigh unto them that are of a broken heart; and saveth such as be of a contrite spirit" (Ps.34:18).

"Create in me a clean heart, O God; and renew a right spirit within me" (Ps.51:10).

"Restore unto me the joy of thy salvation; and uphold me *with thy* free spirit. *Then* will I teach transgressors thy ways; and sinners shall be converted unto thee" (Ps.51:12-13).

"The sacrifices of God *are* a broken spirit: a broken and a contrite heart, O God, thou wilt not despise" (Ps.51:17).

"Turn us again, O God of hosts, and cause thy face to shine; and we shall be saved" (Ps.80:7).

"So will not we go back from thee: quicken us, and we will call upon thy name" (Ps.80:18).

"Wilt thou not revive us again: that thy people may rejoice in thee?" (Ps.85:6).

"My soul cleaveth unto the dust: quicken thou me according to thy word" (Ps.119:25).

"Behold, I have longed after thy precepts: quicken me in thy righteousness" (Ps.119:40).

"Quicken me, O LORD, for thy name's sake: for thy righteousness' sake bring my soul out of trouble" (Ps.143:11).

"Until the spirit be poured upon us from on high, and the wilderness be a fruitful field, and the fruitful field be counted for a forest. Then judgment shall dwell in the wilderness, and righteousness remain in the fruitful field. And the work of righteousness shall be peace; and the effect of righteousness quietness and assurance for ever" (Is.32:15-17).

"But they that wait upon the LORD shall renew *their* strength; they shall mount up with wings as eagles; they shall run, and not be weary; *and* they shall walk, and not faint" (Is.40:31).

"Blessed *is* the man *that* doeth this, and the son of man *that* layeth hold on it; that keepeth the sabbath from polluting it, and keepeth his hand from doing any evil" (Is.56:2).

BACKGROUND TO ISAIAH'S DAY

(The Four Kings Who Ruled During Isaiah's Ministry)

"A new heart also will I give you, and a new spirit will I put within you: and I will take away the stony heart out of your flesh, and I will give you an heart of flesh" (Eze.36:26).

"And rend your heart, and not your garments, and turn unto the LORD your God: for he *is* gracious and merciful, slow to anger, and of great kindness, and repenteth him of the evil" (Joel 2:13).

"O LORD, I have heard thy speech, *and* was afraid: O LORD, revive thy work in the midst of the years, in the midst of the years make known; in wrath remember mercy" (Hab.3:2).

VI. THE REIGN OF HEZEKIAH (PART 3)—HIS RELIGIOUS REFORMS: THE PICTURE OF A REVIVED, ORDERLY CHURCH, 2 CHR.31:1-21

OUTLINE	SCRIPTURE	SCRIPTURE	OUTLINE
1. The people rejected false worship: Realizing the powerlessness & hopelessness of false worship a. They destroyed the false worship centers throughout Judah when they left the Passover: Destroyed both the idols & the sites (high places) throughout Judah, Benjamin, Ephraim, & Manasseh b. They were totally committed: Would not return home until all gods & sites were destroyed **2. The king reestablished regular worship services: Worshipping the LORD** a. Hezekiah reorganized the priests & Levites into divisions: Based upon their duties, 1 Chr.23:1–26:28 1) To present the offerings 2) To minister & serve 3) To give thanks & praise b. Hezekiah personally provided for the temple from his own wealth: Gave the burnt offerings for the regular worship services **3. The king commanded the people to support the religious workers: Giving to support the LORD's work** a. The purpose: So the workers could devote themselves to God's Word b. The response of the people 1) The people gave • Gave the firstfruits (very first) of their produce • Gave a tithe of their livestock • Gave over a period of five months	Now when all this was finished, all Israel that were present went out to the cities of Judah, and brake the images in pieces, and cut down the groves, and threw down the high places and the altars out of all Judah and Benjamin, in Ephraim also and Manasseh, until they had utterly destroyed them all. Then all the children of Israel returned, every man to his possession, into their own cities. 2 And Hezekiah appointed the courses of the priests and the Levites after their courses, every man according to his service, the priests and Levites for burnt offerings and for peace offerings, to minister, and to give thanks, and to praise in the gates of the tents of the LORD. 3 *He appointed* also the king's portion of his substance for the burnt offerings, *to wit,* for the morning and evening burnt offerings, and the burnt offerings for the sabbaths, and for the new moons, and for the set feasts, as *it is* written in the law of the LORD. 4 Moreover he commanded the people that dwelt in Jerusalem to give the portion of the priests and the Levites, that they might be encouraged in the law of the LORD. 5 And as soon as the commandment came abroad, the children of Israel brought in abundance the firstfruits of corn, wine, and oil, and honey, and of all the increase of the field; and the tithe of all *things* brought they in abundantly. 6 And *concerning* the children of Israel and Judah, that dwelt in the cities of Judah, they also brought in the tithe of oxen and sheep, and the tithe of holy things which were consecrated unto the LORD their God, and laid *them* by heaps. 7 In the third month they began to lay the foundation of	the heaps, and finished *them* in the seventh month. 8 And when Hezekiah and the princes came and saw the heaps, they blessed the LORD, and his people Israel. 9 Then Hezekiah questioned with the priests and the Levites concerning the heaps. 10 And Azariah the chief priest of the house of Zadok answered him, and said, Since *the people* began to bring the offerings into the house of the LORD, we have had enough to eat, and have left plenty: for the LORD hath blessed his people; and that which is left *is* this great store. 11 Then Hezekiah commanded to prepare chambers in the house of the LORD; and they prepared *them,* 12 And brought in the offerings and the tithes and the dedicated *things* faithfully: over which Cononiah the Levite *was* ruler, and Shimei his brother *was* the next. 13 And Jehiel, and Azaziah, and Nahath, and Asahel, and Jerimoth, and Jozabad, and Eliel, and Ismachiah, and Mahath, and Benaiah, *were* overseers under the hand of Cononiah and Shimei his brother, at the commandment of Hezekiah the king, and Azariah the ruler of the house of God. 14 And Kore the son of Imnah the Levite, the porter toward the east, *was* over the freewill offerings of God, to distribute the oblations of the LORD, and the most holy things. 15 And next him *were* Eden, and Miniamin, and Jeshua, and Shemaiah, Amariah, and Shecaniah, in the cities of the priests, in *their* set office, to give to their brethren by courses, as well to the great as to the small: 16 Beside their genealogy of males, from three years old and upward, *even* unto every one that entereth into the	2) The king & his officials visited the High Priest to get a report on the offerings • Saw huge piles of gifts & praised the LORD • Asked the High Priest for a report on the offerings 3) The High Priest Azariah gave a wonderful report to the king & his officials • The religious workers had plenty to eat & to spare since the people began to bring their offerings • The balance—what was left over—was lying there in huge piles 4) The king, after hearing the report, immediately issued an order for the temple storerooms to be prepared 5) The offerings & gifts were then locked in the storerooms—faithfully c. The assignment of supervisors to oversee the collection & distribution of the offerings 1) The chief supervisor was Conaniah, & his brother Shimei was his assistant: Ten other deputy supervisors served under them 2) The chief supervisor of the freewill offerings & their distribution was Kore: He was assisted by six deputy Levites • They distributed the offerings to the priests who lived outside of Jerusalem, Jos.21:18-19 • They distributed to all males three years old & older who had been dedicated to the

OUTLINE	SCRIPTURE	SCRIPTURE	OUTLINE
ministry & the temple by their parents	house of the LORD, his daily portion for their service in their charges according to their courses;	fields of the suburbs of their cities, in every several city, the men that were expressed by name, to give portions to	Certain men were appointed to deliver adequate portions to them
• They distributed to all priests who were listed in the genealogical records by families & to all who were 21 years old & older	17 Both to the genealogy of the priests by the house of their fathers, and the Levites from twenty years old and upward, in their charges by their courses;	all the males among the priests, and to all that were reckoned by genealogies among the Levites. 20 And thus did Hezekiah throughout all Judah, and	4. **The king served the LORD faithfully: Being totally committed**
• They did not neglect the families: They distributed to the families of all the priests	18 And to the genealogy of all their little ones, their wives, and their sons, and their daughters, through all the congregation: for in their set office they sanctified themselves in holiness:	wrought *that which was* good and right and truth before the LORD his God. 21 And in every work that he began in the service of the house of God, and in the law,	a. He did what was good & right before God b. He sought God wholeheartedly in everything 1) In the service of God's house
• They did not forget the priest in rural areas:	19 Also of the sons of Aaron the priests, *which were* in the	and in the commandments, to seek his God, he did *it* with all his heart, and prospered.	2) In obedience to God's Word & commandments

(31:1-21) **Introduction**: despite the wretched state that the world is in, the tragic condition and the outright wickedness and immorality, the church today seems lethargic, sluggish, apathetic, somewhat drowsy and sleepy-eyed. A spirit of slumber, unconcern, and inactivity has crept into the lives of countless believers. Many have become indifferent, forgetting the mission of the LORD to reach the world for Christ. Too few are witnessing and sharing the gospel of Christ. Many believers have even forsaken the church, failing to consistently worship the LORD, the LORD whom they profess has saved them. A concern for lost family members is lacking in the hearts of many believers. Far too many have made promises to serve the LORD and His church, but they have broken their promises. Many believers served in the past, but now they have resigned their positions of service and are inactive.

Even more tragic is the apostasy being committed by so-called believers. Untold numbers have turned away from the LORD. They no longer follow Him. They have turned to sin and wickedness. Slipping into immorality, lawlessness, and sometimes violence, believers are dishonoring the LORD. The very name of God is discredited and shamed when a believer…

- looks at pornography
- curses or uses profanity
- tells off-colored jokes
- becomes intoxicated
- commits immorality

- abuses a spouse or child verbally, mentally, or physically
- becomes bitter or vengeful
- gives in to covetousness or greed
- fails to study the Scripture and pray
- fails to worship and bear witness for the LORD

If there has ever been a day when revival within the church is needed, it is today. God's people need to be broken over their sins. They need to confess and repent by turning from their wicked ways and coming back to the LORD. A spirit of revival needs to flood the hearts of God's people and sweep throughout the church and the world.

God's people in both Judah and Israel had just experienced a marvelous revival. A summons had been sent throughout all the land by King Hezekiah, inviting the people to celebrate the Passover and the Festival of Unleavened Bread. In response, thousands of people had flooded to the temple in Jerusalem to seek the LORD with renewed hearts and to celebrate the Passover festival. As soon as the celebration began, God poured out a spirit of revival upon the people. A desire to reform the nation, to turn the nation back to the LORD, filled the hearts of both Hezekiah and the people. As a result, a number of major reforms were launched. Several of these are discussed in the present Scripture. In reading about these reforms, the returning exiles under Ezra would be encouraged to reinstitute the very same changes and improvements. For just as the LORD blessed Hezekiah and his people in carrying out their reforms, so the LORD would bless the exiles as they sought to reinstitute *true worship* within the temple and rebuild their nation. And just as it took both clergy and laypersons during the days of Hezekiah, so the returning exiles needed everyone helping them in their restoration task. This is, *The Reign of Hezekiah (Part 3)—His Religious Reforms: The Picture of a Revived, Orderly Church*, 31:1-21.

1. The people rejected false worship: realizing the powerlessness and hopelessness of false worship (v.1).
2. The king reestablished regular worship services: worshipping the LORD (vv.2-3).
3. The king commanded the people to support the religious workers: giving to support the LORD'S work (vv.4-19).
4. The king served the LORD faithfully: being totally committed (vv.20-21).

1 (31:1) **Idolatry, Rejection of, Example—Worship, False, Rejection of—Idols, Powerlessness and Hopelessness of—Powerlessness, of Idols, Example of—Hopelessness, of False Worship, Example—Hezekiah, Reformation of—Revival, Results of—Reformation, Results of**: continuing his religious reform, Hezekiah led the people to reject false worship, for he knew the powerlessness and hopelessness of worshipping false gods.

For fourteen days the people had been celebrating the Passover and the Festival of Unleavened Bread. A powerful spirit of revival now gripped their hearts. Prior to leaving Jerusalem, the people apparently made the decision to destroy all their idols and false worship centers when they got back home. Therefore, while traveling and as the caravans of pilgrims reached one city after another, the people would join together to destroy the idols and false worship centers of that particular city. They destroyed all the sites of false worship throughout Judah and Benjamin and in the former Northern Kingdom, particularly in

Ephraim and Manasseh. The people had been genuinely revived, making renewed commitments to the LORD. A righteous anger against sin and a holy zeal for the LORD were flooding their hearts. The LORD and the LORD alone is the only living and true God. Thus He and He alone is to be worshipped. All other gods are nothing more than the creation of man's mind. They are false gods, powerless to help people in the hour of their need. False gods leave people hopeless, without any possibility of help whatsoever. Consequently, all the images of false gods and all the sites of false worship were to be utterly destroyed. None were to be spared. No matter how ancient the false religion was, or how costly, attractive, or popular, the false worship centers were, they were all to be destroyed.

Note the depth of the people's revived spirit, the sincerity of their renewed commitment. They would not return home until all false worship centers were destroyed. They were totally devoted to the worship of the LORD, to worshipping Him and Him alone.

Thought 1. False worship is to be deliberately and totally rejected, for it dooms a person to a tragic end. First, if we engage in false worship, our spirits become helpless, powerless. The living and true LORD is not with us if we are worshipping false gods. His presence and power are not available to help us when we face the crises, trials, and temptations of life. We are left to ourselves and to what help other people can give us. Why? Because false gods are nothing more than the creation of people's thoughts and ideas, nothing more than what a person imagines god to be.

Second, false gods doom us to an eternity of hopelessness. Only the living and true God can deliver us from death and give us eternal life. And, as important, only He can deliver us from the judgment and hell that God's Holy Word says are coming. False gods are empty, vacant, blank. Therefore if our hope is in false gods, then our hope is false, misplaced, and empty. For a false god is not living and is utterly helpless to give us hope. A non-existent god has no power to impart hope or anything else to us.

Again, false gods are non-existent; they are powerless and helpless. Consequently, worshipping false gods leaves us powerless to conquer the trials and temptations of this life. Worshipping false gods also leaves us powerless to conquer death and to be delivered from the judgment and hell to come. Listen to what God says about idolatry and false worship:

> **"Forasmuch then as we are the offspring of God, we ought not to think that the Godhead is like unto gold, or silver, or stone, graven by art and man's device" (Ac.17:29).**

> **"For the wrath of God is revealed from heaven against all ungodliness and unrighteousness of men, who hold the truth in unrighteousness; Because that which may be known of God is manifest in them; for God hath showed *it* unto them. For the invisible things of him from the creation of the world are clearly seen, being understood by the things that are made, *even* his eternal power and Godhead; so that they are without excuse: Because that, when they knew God, they glorified *him* not as God, neither were thankful; but became vain in their imaginations, and their foolish heart was darkened. Professing themselves to be wise, they became fools, And changed the glory of the uncorruptible God into an image made like to corruptible man, and to birds, and fourfooted beasts, and creeping things. Wherefore God also gave them up to uncleanness through the lusts of their own hearts, to dishonour their own bodies between themselves: Who changed the truth of God into a lie, and worshipped and served the creature more than the Creator, who is blessed for ever. Amen" (Ro.1:18-25).**

> **"As concerning therefore the eating of those things that are offered in sacrifice unto idols, we know that an idol *is* nothing in the world, and that *there is* none other God but one. For though there be that are called gods, whether in heaven or in earth, (as there be gods many, and lords many,) But to us *there is but* one God, the Father, of whom *are* all things, and we in him; and one Lord Jesus Christ, by whom *are* all things, and we by him" (1 Co.8:4-6).**

> **"Ye know that ye were Gentiles, carried away unto these dumb idols, even as ye were led" (1 Co.12:2).**

> **"Little children, keep yourselves from idols. Amen" (1 Jn.5:21).**

> **"Thou shalt have no other gods before me. Thou shalt not make unto thee any graven image, or any likeness *of any thing* that *is* in heaven above, or that *is* in the earth beneath, or that *is* in the water under the earth: Thou shalt not bow down thyself to them, nor serve them: for I the LORD thy God *am* a jealous God, visiting the iniquity of the fathers upon the children unto the third and fourth *generation* of them that hate me" (Ex.20:3-5).**

> **"Ye shall make you no idols nor graven image, neither rear you up a standing image, neither shall ye set up *any* image of stone in your land, to bow down unto it: for I *am* the LORD your God" (Le.26:1).**

> **"The graven images of their gods shall ye burn with fire: thou shalt not desire the silver or gold *that is* on them, nor take *it* unto thee, lest thou be snared therein: for it *is* an abomination to the LORD thy God" (De.7:25).**

> **"Take heed to yourselves, that your heart be not deceived, and ye turn aside, and serve other gods, and worship them" (De.11:16).**

> **"There shall no strange god be in thee; neither shalt thou worship any strange god" (Ps.81:9).**

> **"Not unto us, O LORD, not unto us, but unto thy name give glory, for thy mercy, *and* for thy truth's sake. Wherefore should the heathen say, Where *is* now their God? But our God *is* in the heavens: he hath done whatsoever he hath pleased. Their idols *are* silver and gold, the work of men's hands. They have mouths, but they speak not: eyes have they, but they see not: They have ears, but they hear not: noses have they, but they smell not: They have hands, but they handle not: feet have they, but they walk not: neither speak they through their throat. They that make them are like unto them; *so is* every one that trusteth in them" (Ps.115:1-8).**

BACKGROUND TO ISAIAH'S DAY

(The Four Kings Who Ruled During Isaiah's Ministry)

"To whom then will ye liken God? or what likeness will ye compare unto him? The workman melteth a graven image, and the goldsmith spreadeth it over with gold, and casteth silver chains. He that *is* so impoverished that he hath no oblation chooseth a tree *that* will not rot; he seeketh unto him a cunning workman to prepare a graven image, *that* shall not be moved. Have ye not known? have ye not heard? hath it not been told you from the beginning? have ye not understood from the foundations of the earth? *It is* he that sitteth upon the circle of the earth, and the inhabitants thereof *are* as grasshoppers; that stretcheth out the heavens as a curtain, and spreadeth them out as a tent to dwell in: That bringeth the princes to nothing; he maketh the judges of the earth as vanity. Yea, they shall not be planted; yea, they shall not be sown: yea, their stock shall not take root in the earth: and he shall also blow upon them, and they shall wither, and the whirlwind shall take them away as stubble. To whom then will ye liken me, or shall I be equal? saith the Holy One. Lift up your eyes on high, and behold who hath created these *things*, that bringeth out their host by number: he calleth them all by names by the greatness of his might, for that *he is* strong in power; not one faileth. Why sayest thou, O Jacob, and speakest, O Israel, My way is hid from the LORD, and my judgment is passed over from my God? Hast thou not known? hast thou not heard, *that* the everlasting God, the LORD, the Creator of the ends of the earth, fainteth not, neither is weary? *there is* no searching of his understanding. He giveth power to the faint; and to *them that have* no might he increaseth strength. Even the youths shall faint and be weary, and the young men shall utterly fall: But they that wait upon the LORD shall renew *their* strength; they shall mount up with wings as eagles; they shall run, and not be weary; *and* they shall walk, and not faint" (Is.40:18-31).

"I *am* the LORD: that *is* my name: and my glory will I not give to another, neither my praise to graven images" (Is.42:8).

"Assemble yourselves and come; draw near together, ye *that are* escaped of the nations: they have no knowledge that set up the wood of their graven image, and pray unto a god *that* cannot save" (Is.45:20).

"They *are* upright as the palm tree, but speak not: they must needs be borne, because they cannot go. Be not afraid of them; for they cannot do evil, neither also *is it* in them to do good" (Je.10:5).

---

2 (31:2-3) **Worship, Duty—Ministers, Duty—Priests, Duty—Levites, Duty—Worship, Services of, Organized—Hezekiah, Religious Reforms—Reformation, Religious, of Hezekiah**: right after celebrating the Passover, Hezekiah reestablished regular worship services within the temple. To do this he had to reorganize the priests and Levites, reassigning them to their tasks (1 Chr.23:1-26:28). Remember, his father had closed the temple, barricading the doors in an attempt to eliminate the worship of the LORD throughout the land. As a result, the various responsibilities of the religious workers and of worship itself had fallen into utter chaos. In reestablishing regular worship within the temple, Hezekiah needed to reassign the priests and Levites to their various divisions of service and to spell out their duties. Their duties were threefold:

⇒ to present the burnt offerings daily to the LORD as well as the special offerings brought by the people
⇒ to serve and minister to both the LORD and the people
⇒ to offer thanksgiving and praise to the LORD within the gates of the temple

As David and Solomon had been faithful in worship and in supporting the temple and Hezekiah followed their example (1 Chr.29:1-5; 2 Chr.9:10-11). He set a dynamic example of personal worship and of supporting the temple from his own wealth (v.3). He personally gave all the animals for both the morning and evening burnt offerings as well as for the burnt offerings on the Sabbath, special holidays, and festivals.

Thought 1. Hezekiah is a dynamic example for us. He established regular worship services for the people and was personally faithful in worshipping the LORD, likewise must we be. Worship is due the LORD. He is the Creator and Sustainer of the universe, the Maker of heaven and earth and all that is therein. He is the Sovereign LORD, having established and overseen all the laws that control the universe and human life. All glory and majesty belong to Him, and all dominion and power are His forever and ever.

Who the LORD is—His person, His being—demands that we worship Him. In addition, what the LORD has done demands that we worship Him. The LORD has not only given us life upon this earth, but He has also provided salvation for us. And no greater provision could be given us than to be saved from sin with all its bondages; from death with all its apprehension, dread, and fear; and from hell with all its torment and horror. Salvation from sin, death, and hell—no greater gift could ever be granted us. This is what the LORD has done for us: redeemed us from all the entrapments of this life. Through His salvation we can live victoriously, conquering all the crises and temptations that confront us. Furthermore, the LORD has made it possible for us never to experience death but instead to live with Him eternally.

Because of who the LORD is and what He has done for us, He is to be worshipped. Listen to what God's Holy Word says about worship:

"Then saith Jesus unto him, Get thee hence, Satan: for it is written, Thou shalt worship the Lord thy God, and him only shalt thou serve" (Mt.4:10).
"Let your light so shine before men, that they may see your good works, and glorify your Father which is in heaven" (Mt.5:16).
"And he came to Nazareth, where he had been brought up: and, as his custom was, he went into the synagogue on the sabbath day, and stood up for to read" (Lu.4:16).
"And they worshipped him, and returned to Jerusalem with great joy: And were continually in the temple, praising and blessing God. Amen" (Lu.24:52-53).

"And they, continuing daily with one accord in the temple, and breaking bread from house to house, did eat their meat with gladness and singleness of heart, Praising God, and having favour with all the people. And the Lord added to the church daily such as should be saved" (Ac.2:46-47).

"Now the God of patience and consolation grant you to be likeminded one toward another according to Christ Jesus: That ye may with one mind *and* one mouth glorify God, even the Father of our Lord Jesus Christ" (Ro.15:5-6).

"What? know ye not that your body is the temple of the Holy Ghost *which is* in you, which ye have of God, and ye are not your own? For ye are bought with a price: therefore glorify God in your body, and in your spirit, which are God's" (1 Co.6:19-20).

"Giving thanks unto the Father, which hath made us meet to be partakers of the inheritance of the saints in light" (Col.1:12).

"In every thing give thanks: for this is the will of God in Christ Jesus concerning you" (1 Th.5:18).

"*Let your* conversation *be* without covetousness; *and be* content with such things as ye have: for he hath said, I will never leave thee, nor forsake thee" (He.13:5).

"But ye *are* a chosen generation, a royal priesthood, an holy nation, a peculiar people; that ye should show forth the praises of him who hath called you out of darkness into his marvellous light" (1 Pe.2:9).

"Fear God, and give glory to him; for the hour of his judgment is come: and worship him that made heaven, and earth, and the sea, and the fountains of waters" (Re.14:7).

"Then saith he unto me, See *thou do it* not: for I am thy fellowservant, and of thy brethren the prophets, and of them which keep the sayings of this book: worship God" (Re.22:9).

"But unto the place which the LORD your God shall choose out of all your tribes to put his name there, *even* unto his habitation shall ye seek, and thither thou shalt come" (De.12:5).

"Sing praises to the LORD, which dwelleth in Zion: declare among the people his doings" (Ps.9:11).

"LORD, I have loved the habitation of thy house, and the place where thine honour dwelleth" (Ps.26:8).

"One *thing* have I desired of the LORD, that will I seek after; that I may dwell in the house of the LORD all the days of my life, to behold the beauty of the LORD, and to enquire in his temple" (Ps.27:4).

"Praise the LORD with harp: sing unto him with the psaltery *and* an instrument of ten strings" (Ps.33:2).

"And my tongue shall speak of thy righteousness *and* of thy praise all the day long" (Ps.35:28).

"Let the people praise thee, O God; let all the people praise thee" (Ps.67:3).

"Blessed *are* they that dwell in thy house: they will be still praising thee. Selah" (Ps.84:4).

"For a day in thy courts *is* better than a thousand. I had rather be a doorkeeper in the house of my God, than to dwell in the tents of wickedness" (Ps.84:10).

"O come, let us worship and bow down: let us kneel before the LORD our maker" (Ps.95:6).

"O worship the LORD in the beauty of holiness: fear before him, all the earth" (Ps.96:9).

"Enter into his gates with thanksgiving, *and* into his courts with praise: be thankful unto him, *and* bless his name" (Ps.100:4).

"Seven times a day do I praise thee because of thy righteous judgments" (Ps.119:164).

"I was glad when they said unto me, Let us go into the house of the LORD" (Ps.122:1).

"Let them give glory unto the LORD, and declare his praise in the islands" (Is.42:12).

---

3 (31:4-19) **Support, of the Church—Support, of the LORD's Work—Stewardship, Duty—Giving, to the Church, Example of—Reformation, of Stewardship—Hezekiah, Reforms of, Stewardship—Ministers, Duty, to Study and Administer God's Word**: Hezekiah's reformation also restored the offerings that supported the priests and Levites (see outline and notes—Le.6:8–7:38; Nu.18:8-32; De.14:22-29; 18:1-8; 26:1-11). The offerings had long been neglected, especially during the years when the worship services were stopped by King Ahaz (28:24). Without support, the priests and Levites would not have time to conduct the worship services and minister to the people. They would have to be out working at secular employment. Thus, reinstating the offerings to support the LORD's work was an absolute essential.

a. The purpose for reinstating the offerings is stated in a very clear and straightforward manner: the priests and their associates needed to devote themselves to God's law, His Holy Word (v.4). If they had to be out working for a livelihood, they would not have the time to prepare and conduct the worship services nor to minister to the people. Support was an absolute essential for them to fulfill their calling and responsibilities.

b. As soon as King Hezekiah's decree was circulated among the citizens of the nation, the people immediately responded with willing, overflowing hearts (vv.5-12). Generously, even excitedly, they gave abundant offerings to the priests and Levites who had recommitted their lives to serve the LORD and His people (vv.5-7):

⇒ They gave the first fruits (very first) of their produce, freely giving large amounts of grain, wine, oil, honey, and all their other produce.

⇒ They also gave a tithe of their livestock, bringing large herds to the priests and Levites (v.6).

⇒ They continued to give liberally for a period of five months (v.7). Remember that the first month of Hezekiah's reign had been spent in preparing the temple for worship. The second month had been spent in a special worship service and in celebrating the Passover and the Festival of Unleavened Bread. It was in the third month that Hezekiah issued his decree that reinstituted the offerings. Thus, the people began tithing in the third month and continued to bring an abundance of offerings until the seventh month.

At the end of the seventh month, the king and his officials visited the High Priest to secure reports on the offerings (v.8). When they arrived, they saw huge piles of gifts, whereupon Hezekiah immediately praised the LORD and pronounced a blessing upon His people.

BACKGROUND TO ISAIAH'S DAY

(The Four Kings Who Ruled During Isaiah's Ministry)

In response to the king's request for a report on the offerings, the High Priest Azariah gave an astounding and marvelous account (v.10). Demonstrating a true spirit of revival, the people had willingly and generously responded. They had brought more than enough food and money to take care of the priests and Levites and their families. Thus the piles of supplies now being seen by the king were the remainder, what was left over from the offering.

After hearing the report and seeing the piles heaped up, Hezekiah immediately issued an order for the temple storerooms to be prepared and for the offerings to be faithfully locked in the storerooms (vv.11-12).

c. With such huge offerings being brought to the temple, it became necessary for Hezekiah to appoint supervisors to oversee the collection and distribution of the gifts (vv.12-19). If the overseers left the grain and other perishable gifts exposed, they were apt to rot or be wasted or stolen. For this reason, it was absolutely essential for storage rooms to be prepared and for supervisors to watch over and manage all the contributions.

1) The chief supervisor was Conaniah. His brother Shimei was his assistant (vv.12-13). Ten other deputy supervisors were appointed to serve under them. Note that these twelve men were in charge of supervising the offerings within the temple itself.

2) Another chief supervisor was appointed to oversee the freewill or volunteer offerings (Le.7:11-21). His name was Kore, and he had six deputy Levites to assist him (vv.14-19). Their particular responsibility was to distribute the offerings to the priests who lived outside of Jerusalem (Jos.21:18-19). Even young boys three years old received a distribution of the offerings, for they had been dedicated to the ministry and the temple by their parents. Some day they would become the priests ministering in the temple, serving the LORD and the people (v.16).

All priests listed in the genealogical records of priests shared in the distribution of the offerings (v.17). The genealogical records of Levites were also used for their distribution.

No family listed in the genealogical records of the priests and Levites was neglected. All the little babies, the wives, the sons and daughters—all received their share of the offerings. They had been faithful in recommitting their lives to the LORD, setting themselves apart to live holy and righteous lives and to faithfully serving Him. Even the priests—the descendants of Aaron—who lived on distant farms in distant towns received their portion of the offerings; certain men were appointed to deliver the offerings throughout the entire nation. All who were recorded in the genealogies, no matter where they lived, were to receive their portion.

Thought 1. Supporting the church and the ministers of the gospel is an absolute essential, for the laborer deserves wages. When the minister is serving the LORD and His people, he deserves to be compensated. Think for a moment about the work of the minister:

⇒ preaching and teaching an average of three or more times every week: reading, studying, preparing, and praying
⇒ visiting not only church members in the hospital but also relatives and friends of church members
⇒ visiting and ministering to church members when serious problems arise
⇒ counseling church members and occasionally non-church members
⇒ visiting and comforting family members when a death occurs, conduct funerals
⇒ marriage counseling and conducting marriage ceremonies
⇒ meeting with major committees
⇒ planning and managing the ministry of the church including its employees, business, missions, work, committees, schedules, finances, building programs, outreach program, and whatever else may come up—along with all the unique problems that come with each.
⇒ visiting and reaching new people for the LORD and the church.
⇒ constantly facing the scrutiny of church members and handling any and all criticisms, grumblings, and divisions that arise.

Imagine all the duties listed above and then picture this: at the top of the list is the primary responsibility of preparing at least three sermons or lessons—challenging, interesting, and new lessons—every week, week after week and year after year. How can a person conceivably carry out all these duties? Only by the strength and empowering of the Lord Jesus Christ Himself. So when a person serves the Lord and His church, he deserves to be compensated for his work and ministry.

In addition, the church must be supported financially, for the church has been given the greatest mission in all the world, that of proclaiming the good news of God's very own Son. Through the Lord Jesus Christ and Him alone, the world can be saved from sin, death, and judgment to come. Without Christ, people will die and face the judgment of God. They will be eternally separated from God and destined to live forever in a place Jesus Christ called *hell*, a place that He says is filled with torment and anguish.

The gospel cannot be carried to the world without finances. Without the necessary funds, missionaries, evangelists, and ministers cannot be sent around the world to proclaim the gospel. We must give sacrificially to take the gospel around the world and to meet the desperate needs of people who are crying for help. Listen to what God's Holy Word says about giving in order to support His church and work around the world:

"Give, and it shall be given unto you; good measure, pressed down, and shaken together, and running over, shall men give into your bosom. For with the same measure that ye mete withal it shall be measured to you again" (Lu.6:38).

"And he looked up, and saw the rich men casting their gifts into the treasury. And he saw also a certain poor widow casting in thither two mites. And he said, Of a truth I say unto you, that this poor widow hath cast in more than they all: For all these have of their abundance cast in unto the offerings of God: but she of her penury hath cast in all the living that she had" (Lu.21:1-4).

"Neither was there any among them that lacked: for as many as were possessors of lands or houses sold them, and brought the prices of the things that were sold, And laid *them* down at the apostles' feet: and distribution was made unto every man according as he had need" (Ac.4:34-35).

"Then the disciples, every man according to his ability, determined to send relief unto the brethren which dwelt in Judaea" (Ac.11:29).

"Upon the first *day* of the week let every one of you lay by him in store, as *God* hath prospered him, that there be no gatherings when I come" (1 Co.16:2).

"How that in a great trial of affliction the abundance of their joy and their deep poverty abounded unto the riches of their liberality" (2 Co.8:2).

"For if there be first a willing mind, *it is* accepted according to that a man hath, *and* not according to that he hath not" (2 Co.8:12).

"But this *I say,* He which soweth sparingly shall reap also sparingly; and he which soweth bountifully shall reap also bountifully. Every man according as he purposeth in his heart, *so let him give;* not grudgingly, or of necessity: for God loveth a cheerful giver" (2 Co.9:6-7).

"For even in Thessalonica ye sent once and again unto my necessity" (Ph.4:16).

"And they came, both men and women, as many as were willing hearted, *and* brought bracelets, and earrings, and rings, and tablets, all jewels of gold: and every man that offered *offered* an offering of gold unto the LORD" (Ex.35:22).

"And they spake unto Moses, saying, The people bring much more than enough for the service of the work, which the LORD commanded to make" (Ex.36:5).

"And all the tithe of the land, *whether* of the seed of the land, *or* of the fruit of the tree, *is* the LORD's: *it is* holy unto the LORD" (Le.27:30).

"Every man *shall give* as he is able, according to the blessing of the LORD thy God which he hath given thee" (De.16:17).

"Blessed *is* he that considereth the poor: the LORD will deliver him in time of trouble" (Ps.41:1).

"Honour the LORD with thy substance, and with the firstfruits of all thine increase: So shall thy barns be filled with plenty, and thy presses shall burst out with new wine" (Pr.3:9-10).

"The liberal soul shall be made fat: and he that watereth shall be watered also himself" (Pr.11:25).

"He that hath a bountiful eye shall be blessed; for he giveth of his bread to the poor" (Pr.22:9).

"And *if* thou draw out thy soul to the hungry, and satisfy the afflicted soul; then shall thy light rise in obscurity, and thy darkness *be* as the noonday" (Is.58:10).

"Bring ye all the tithes into the storehouse, that there may be meat in mine house, and prove me now herewith, saith the LORD of hosts, if I will not open you the windows of heaven, and pour you out a blessing, that *there shall* not *be room* enough *to receive it*" (Mal.3:10).

4 (31:20-21) **Commitment, Example of—Dedication, Example of—Wholehearted, Example of—Faithful, Example of—Hezekiah, Example of, Wholehearted Commitment**: in everything Hezekiah did, he was faithful to the LORD. He was committed wholeheartedly. Hezekiah reformed the temple and reestablished regular worship services for the people. But he was also personally faithful in worshipping the LORD and in obeying the commandments of the LORD. As a result, the LORD made him successful and gave him prosperity.

Thought 1. Once we have made a commitment to the LORD, we must be true to that commitment. Whether the commitment is a profession of faith or a commitment to serve the LORD in some capacity, God expects us to be faithful. Scripture says "a double-minded man is unstable in all his ways" (Js.1:8). Only the person who perseveres, who follows through with his commitment will be saved and receive the reward. A lukewarm, halfhearted commitment is like water that is neither hot nor cold and is spewed out of God's mouth (Re.3:15-16). Success and prosperity can only be achieved through wholehearted commitment and diligent labor. Conquering or overcoming the trials and temptations of this life with all their pitfalls can be achieved only if we are totally committed to the LORD. Only the committed receive the conquering power of Christ. If we are fully devoted to the LORD, He gives us the power to overcome any obstacle that confronts us, no matter the severity of the problem or situation. Christ's power is available to any person who is totally dedicated to Him. A heart that is wholly devoted to the LORD will be blessed by the LORD. Listen to what God says about total commitment to Him:

"Jesus said unto him, If thou wilt be perfect, go *and* sell that thou hast, and give to the poor, and thou shalt have treasure in heaven: and come *and* follow me" (Mt.19:21).

"Jesus said unto him, Thou shalt love the Lord thy God with all thy heart, and with all thy soul, and with all thy mind. This is the first and great commandment" (Mt.22:37-38).

"Then Peter began to say unto him, Lo, we have left all, and have followed thee" (Mk.10:28).

"And after these things he went forth, and saw a publican, named Levi, sitting at the receipt of custom: and he said unto him, Follow me. And he left all, rose up, and followed him" (Lu.5:27-28).

"And he said to *them* all, If any *man* will come after me, let him deny himself, and take up his cross daily, and follow me" (Lu.9:23).

"So likewise, whosoever he be of you that forsaketh not all that he hath, he cannot be my disciple" (Lu.14:33).

"And he said unto them, Verily I say unto you, There is no man that hath left house, or parents, or brethren, or wife, or children, for the kingdom of God's sake, Who shall not receive manifold more in this present time, and in the world to come life everlasting" (Lu.18:29-30).

"For if ye live after the flesh, ye shall die: but if ye through the Spirit do mortify the deeds of the body, ye shall live" (Ro.8:13).

"I beseech you therefore, brethren, by the mercies of God, that ye present your bodies a living sacrifice, holy, acceptable unto God, *which is* your reasonable service. And be not conformed to this world: but be ye transformed by the renewing of your mind, that ye may prove what *is* that good, and acceptable, and perfect, will of God" (Ro.12:1-2).

"But I keep under my body, and bring *it* into subjection: lest that by any means, when I have preached to others, I myself should be a castaway" (1 Co.9:27).

"I am crucified with Christ: nevertheless I live; yet not I, but Christ liveth in me: and the life which I now live in the flesh I live by the faith of the Son of God, who loved me, and gave himself for me" (Ga.2:20).

"And they that are Christ's have crucified the flesh with the affections and lusts" (Ga.5:24).

"But what things were gain to me, those I counted loss for Christ. Yea doubtless, and I count all things *but* loss for the excellency of the knowledge of Christ Jesus my Lord: for whom I have suffered the loss of all things, and do count them *but* dung, that I may win Christ, And be found in him, not having mine own righteousness, which is of the law, but that which is through the faith of Christ, the righteousness which is of God by faith: That I may know him, and the power of his resurrection, and the fellowship of his sufferings, being made conformable unto his death; If by any means I might attain unto the resurrection of the dead" (Ph.3:7-11).

"Nevertheless the foundation of God standeth sure, having this seal, The Lord knoweth them that are his. And, Let every one that nameth the name of Christ depart from iniquity. But in a great house there are not only vessels of gold and of silver, but also of wood and of earth; and some to honour, and some to dishonour. If a man therefore purge himself from these, he shall be a vessel unto honour, sanctified, and meet for the master's use, *and* prepared unto every good work" (2 Ti.2:19-21).

"For Moses had said, Consecrate yourselves to day to the LORD, even every man upon his son, and upon his brother; that he may bestow upon you a blessing this day" (Ex.32:29).

"And thou shalt love the LORD thy God with all thine heart, and with all thy soul, and with all thy might. And these words, which I command thee this day, shall be in thine heart: And thou shalt teach them diligently unto thy children, and shalt talk of them when thou sittest in thine house, and when thou walkest by the way, and when thou liest down, and when thou risest up. And thou shalt bind them for a sign upon thine hand, and they shall be as frontlets between thine eyes. And thou shalt write them upon the posts of thy house, and on thy gates" (De.6:5-9).

"Blessed *are* they that keep his testimonies, *and that* seek him with the whole heart" (Ps.119:2).

"Trust in the LORD with all thine heart; and lean not unto thine own understanding. In all thy ways acknowledge him, and he shall direct thy paths" (Pr.3:5-6).

"My son, give me thine heart, and let thine eyes observe my ways" (Pr.23:26).

"And ye shall seek me, and find *me,* when ye shall search for me with all your heart" (Je.29:13).

"Therefore also now, saith the LORD, turn ye *even* to me with all your heart, and with fasting, and with weeping, and with mourning" (Joel 2:12).

(The Four Kings Who Ruled During Isaiah's Ministry)

VII. THE REIGN OF HEZEKIAH (PART 4)—HIS DELIVERANCE FROM ASSYRIA, TERMINAL ILLNESS, AND DEATH: A PICTURE OF GOD'S UNLIMITED, SOVEREIGN POWER, 2 CHR.32:1-33

OUTLINE	SCRIPTURE	SCRIPTURE	OUTLINE
1. Hezekiah's deliverance from the Assyrian invasion: God's power to deliver His people a. The invasion by Assyria's king Sennacherib: He laid siege to the fortified cities of Judah b. The preparations for war by Hezekiah 1) He stopped up the springs outside the city: To block or conceal the water supply from the Assyrians • The project took a large force of men • The project included blocking all the springs & stopping the major stream flowing through the land 2) He reinforced the city's fortifications • Repaired the city's wall • Built additional towers • Built a second wall at strategic locations • Reinforced the Millo, the supporting terraces 3) He made more weapons for the army 4) He organized the citizens into an army & appointed officers over them 5) He assembled the people & encouraged them • They must be strong & courageous • They must not fear nor be discouraged by the huge army of the Assyrians • They must know this one fact: They have a greater power, for the Assyrians have only men—only the arm of the flesh • They must trust the LORD to help & to fight their battles for them c. The threat by the Assyrian king & his demand for Hezekiah to surrender: The Assyrian king sent a large ar-	After these things, and the establishment thereof, Sennacherib king of Assyria came, and entered into Judah, and encamped against the fenced cities, and thought to win them for himself. 2 And when Hezekiah saw that Sennacherib was come, and that he was purposed to fight against Jerusalem, 3 He took counsel with his princes and his mighty men to stop the waters of the fountains which *were* without the city: and they did help him. 4 So there was gathered much people together, who stopped all the fountains, and the brook that ran through the midst of the land, saying, Why should the kings of Assyria come, and find much water? 5 Also he strengthened himself, and built up all the wall that was broken, and raised *it* up to the towers, and another wall without, and repaired Millo *in* the city of David, and made darts and shields in abundance. 6 And he set captains of war over the people, and gathered them together to him in the street of the gate of the city, and spake comfortably to them, saying, 7 Be strong and courageous, be not afraid nor dismayed for the king of Assyria, nor for all the multitude that *is* with him: for *there be* more with us than with him: 8 With him *is* an arm of flesh; but with us *is* the LORD our God to help us, and to fight our battles. And the people rested themselves upon the words of Hezekiah king of Judah. 9 After this did Sennacherib king of Assyria send his servants to Jerusalem, (but he *himself laid siege* against	Lachish, and all his power with him,) unto Hezekiah king of Judah, and unto all Judah that *were* at Jerusalem, saying, 10 Thus saith Sennacherib king of Assyria, Whereon do ye trust, that ye abide in the siege in Jerusalem? 11 Doth not Hezekiah persuade you to give over yourselves to die by famine and by thirst, saying, The LORD our God shall deliver us out of the hand of the king of Assyria? 12 Hath not the same Hezekiah taken away his high places and his altars, and commanded Judah and Jerusalem, saying, Ye shall worship before one altar, and burn incense upon it? 13 Know ye not what I and my fathers have done unto all the people of *other* lands? were the gods of the nations of those lands any ways able to deliver their lands out of mine hand? 14 Who *was there* among all the gods of those nations that my fathers utterly destroyed, that could deliver his people out of mine hand, that your God should be able to deliver you out of mine hand? 15 Now therefore let not Hezekiah deceive you, nor persuade you on this manner, neither yet believe him: for no god of any nation or kingdom was able to deliver his people out of mine hand, and out of the hand of my fathers: how much less shall your God deliver you out of mine hand? 16 And his servants spake yet *more* against the LORD God, and against his servant Hezekiah. 17 He wrote also letters to rail on the LORD God of Israel, and to speak against him, saying, As the gods of the nations of *other* lands have not delivered their people out of	my to Jerusalem to intimidate Hezekiah & to demand his surrender, 2 K.18:17-18 d. The Assyrian officer's address to Jerusalem's officials & the citizens standing near the wall: He questioned their confidence in the tactics of Hezekiah 1) He declared that Hezekiah was only deceiving them by persuading them to trust the LORD: They would die of hunger & thirst due to the Assyrian siege 2) He charged Hezekiah with displeasing the LORD by destroying the high places & altars of worship (a misunderstanding of God & idolatry) 3) He sought to intimidate the people through propaganda: Threatened them with the power of Assyria • No nation had ever been delivered from Assyria, not by any god • No people had ever been saved from the Assyrians by any god • Their God would be powerless against Assyria: Equated the LORD with false gods 4) He again charged Hezekiah with deceiving the people: Claimed the evidence was clear • No god of any nation had been able to save its people from Assyria • How much less would their God be able to deliver them? He would be powerless against Assyria 5) He continued on & on in his propaganda, speaking against the LORD & Hezekiah • He presented letters from the Assyrian king scorning & denying the power of the LORD to rescue His people

OUTLINE	SCRIPTURE	SCRIPTURE	OUTLINE
• He spoke loudly in Hebrew to strike terror in the hearts of the people standing on the wall of Jerusalem e. The fallacy of the Assyrian argument: Did not understand the difference between the LORD & false gods that were only creations of people's minds, the works of their hands f. The wonderful deliverance by God's mighty power 1) The king & Isaiah cried out to God in prayer 2) The LORD sent an angel who utterly annihilated the Assyrian army: Executed 185,000 soldiers during the night, 2 K.19:35 3) The Assyrian king Sennacherib withdrew his army: He was later assassinated by his sons g. The continued deliverance & blessings of God 1) The LORD saved Hezekiah & the people from Assyria & from all others, giving them peace 2) The people expressed their appreciation by bringing gifts both to the LORD & to King Hezekiah 3) The surrounding nations highly esteemed Hezekiah after the Assyrian victory **2. Hezekiah's terminal illness & prosperity: God's power to answer prayer & to heal** a. Hezekiah's fatal illness: God healed him in answer to prayer b. Hezekiah's pride: His heart was lifted up & he did not acknowledge the LORD as he should have 1) The LORD's wrath began to loom over & convict him	mine hand, so shall not the God of Hezekiah deliver his people out of mine hand. 18 Then they cried with a loud voice in the Jews' speech unto the people of Jerusalem that *were* on the wall, to affright them, and to trouble them; that they might take the city. 19 And they spake against the God of Jerusalem, as against the gods of the people of the earth, *which were* the work of the hands of man. 20 And for this *cause* Hezekiah the king, and the prophet Isaiah the son of Amoz, prayed and cried to heaven. 21 And the LORD sent an angel, which cut off all the mighty men of valour, and the leaders and captains in the camp of the king of Assyria. So he returned with shame of face to his own land. And when he was come into the house of his god, they that came forth of his own bowels slew him there with the sword. 22 Thus the LORD saved Hezekiah and the inhabitants of Jerusalem from the hand of Sennacherib the king of Assyria, and from the hand of all *other,* and guided them on every side. 23 And many brought gifts unto the LORD to Jerusalem, and presents to Hezekiah king of Judah: so that he was magnified in the sight of all nations from thenceforth. 24 In those days Hezekiah was sick to the death, and prayed unto the LORD: and he spake unto him, and he gave him a sign. 25 But Hezekiah rendered not again according to the benefit *done* unto him; for his heart was lifted up: therefore there was wrath upon him, and upon Judah and Jerusalem.	26 Notwithstanding Hezekiah humbled himself for the pride of his heart, *both* he and the inhabitants of Jerusalem, so that the wrath of the LORD came not upon them in the days of Hezekiah. 27 And Hezekiah had exceeding much riches and honour: and he made himself treasuries for silver, and for gold, and for precious stones, and for spices, and for shields, and for all manner of pleasant jewels; 28 Storehouses also for the increase of corn, and wine, and oil; and stalls for all manner of beasts, and cotes for flocks. 29 Moreover he provided him cities, and possessions of flocks and herds in abundance: for God had given him substance very much. 30 This same Hezekiah also stopped the upper watercourse of Gihon, and brought it straight down to the west side of the city of David. And Hezekiah prospered in all his works. 31 Howbeit in *the business of* the ambassadors of the princes of Babylon, who sent unto him to enquire of the wonder that was *done* in the land, God left him, to try him, that he might know all *that was* in his heart. 32 Now the rest of the acts of Hezekiah, and his goodness, behold, they *are* written in the vision of Isaiah the prophet, the son of Amoz, *and* in the book of the kings of Judah and Israel. 33 And Hezekiah slept with his fathers, and they buried him in the chiefest of the sepulchres of the sons of David: and all Judah and the inhabitants of Jerusalem did him honour at his death. And Manasseh his son reigned in his stead.	2) The king repented of his pride & the people humbled themselves 3) The LORD delayed His hand of judgment against Judah during Hezekiah's lifetime c. Hezekiah's prosperity 1) He built treasuries to store his wealth 2) He built storage buildings for his farms 3) He built stalls for his livestock 4) He built towns for the nation 5) He acquired vast flocks & herds with the great wealth given by God d. Hezekiah's major building project: The construction of a water tunnel for Jerusalem, 2 K.20:20 e. Hezekiah's test by God 1) The Babylonian ruler sent envoys to ask about his healing by God[DS1] 2) The LORD tested Hezekiah: To expose what was in his heart (vv.24-26). f. Hezekiah's reign & acts of devotion: Recorded in *The Vision of the Prophet Isaiah Son of Amoz*—included in *The Book of the Kings of Judah & Israel* g. Hezekiah's death & burial in Jerusalem 1) He was greatly honored by the people 2) He was succeeded by his son Manasseh

(32:1-33) Introduction: at any given time within any country, government, or ruling body, a crisis can arise, a critical situation that has to be handled. The crisis can be the threat of war or war itself, a broken treaty, terrorist actions, an uprising, or a natural disasters such as an earthquake, a hurricane, a forest fire, or a flash flood.

On a personal level, every one of us also faces crises in life, critical situations such as: serious illness, disease, accidents, financial difficulties, loss of a job, divisive relationships, and a host of other potentially serious problems.

But no matter what confronts us, there is wonderful news. Unlimited, sovereign power is available to *carry us through* the crisis. That power is the power of God Himself. We are the creation of God's hand; therefore, God loves us and cares about what happens to us. Thus He makes His power available to us, a power that has the strength to *carry us through* any crisis.

God's unlimited, sovereign power is the subject of this Scripture. God's power delivered Hezekiah from an invasion by the oppressive Assyrians, who were the terror and scourge of the world during that particular period of history. In reading this account, the returning exiles would learn that God could also deliver them through any crisis, no matter how critical the situation. The same power that God had used to deliver Hezekiah and the people of his day was available to deliver the returning exiles if they remained faithful. This is, *The Reign of Hezekiah (Part 4)—His Deliverance from Assyria, Terminal Illness, and Death: A Picture of God's Unlimited, Sovereign Power*, 32:1-33.

1. Hezekiah's deliverance from the Assyrian invasion: God's power to deliver His people (vv.1-23).
2. Hezekiah's terminal illness and prosperity: God's power to answer prayer and to heal (vv.24-33).

1 (32:1-23) **Power, of God, Example of—Deliverance, Source, God's Power—Assyria, Wars of, Against Judah—Judah, Wars of, Invaded by Assyria—Hezekiah, Wars of, Invaded by Assyria**: Hezekiah was mightily delivered from an Assyrian invasion, the superpower of that day. Assyria was a terrifying and bothersome nuisance to her neighbors in the world, but God's mighty power would deliver His people. Earlier, Hezekiah's father Ahaz had willingly subjected Judah to Assyria, which meant that they were paying a heavy annual tribute or tax to the domineering nation (28:16-21). Nevertheless, the LORD filled Hezekiah with inner strength, giving him the courage to resist the oppression of the Assyrians. Rebelling against the king of Assyria and refusing to pay the tax took enormous courage. But God filled Hezekiah's heart with an inner strength, a strength seldom seen in rulers. As a result, Hezekiah broke the heavy yoke of Assyrian oppression.

However, Hezekiah went on to make a very unwise decision. Rejecting the warning of the LORD through His prophet Isaiah, Hezekiah formed an alliance with Egypt, and together they marched against the Philistines and others who were *vassal states* of Assyria (Is.30:1-5; 31:1-3). In battle after battle, the coalition defeated the Philistines as far as Gaza and its territory (2 K.18:7-8). It was these two reasons that aroused the Assyrian King Sennacherib to invade Judah.

a. The invasion by Assyria took place in the fourteenth year of Hezekiah's reign. Seeking to subject Hezekiah under Assyria's yoke again, Sennacherib launched a major military campaign by laying siege to all the fortified cities of Judah (v.1).

b. Knowing that Assyria would soon be attacking Jerusalem, Hezekiah began to make preparations for the expected battle (vv.2-8). Five major preparations were made:

1) First, Hezekiah had the military block off and conceal all the streams, that is, the water supply, outside the city (vv.3-4). A large force of men was needed for this defensive measure, for there were apparently a large number of springs surrounding the city. No doubt working at a feverish pace, they quickly concealed the springs and somehow cut off the major spring that ran through the land. By doing this, water would not be available for the Assyrian troops.

2) Second, Hezekiah reinforced the city's fortifications (v.5). These construction projects included...
   - repairing the city's wall
   - building additional towers on the wall
   - building a second wall outside the main wall at strategic locations
   - reinforcing the millo, that is, the supporting terraces

3) Third, Hezekiah had a substantial number of additional weapons manufactured for the army (v.5).
4) Fourth, Hezekiah organized the citizens into an army and appointed officers over them (v.6).
5) Fifth, Hezekiah assembled the people in the square at the city gate and encouraged them in the LORD. The LORD was to be their only hope of deliverance against the cruel Assyrian army (vv.6-8). Drawing on the great strength and courage that God had instilled within him, Hezekiah shouted out four exhortations to his people:
   ⇒ They must be strong and courageous, rejecting any thought of surrendering the city. They must be resolved, determined to stand against the enemy to the last person, standing boldly and bravely, side by side, holding their posts and not giving a foothold to the enemy (v.7).
   ⇒ They must not fear nor be discouraged by the massive size or might of the well-equipped Assyrian forces (v.7).
   ⇒ They, God's people, must know this one fact: they had a greater power than the Assyrians. The Assyrians had only men—only the arm of the flesh—but God's people had the LORD (vv.7-8). His unlimited power would protect His people and conquer any enemy who attacked them.
   ⇒ They must, therefore, trust the LORD to help fight their battles for them (v.8). Not only would the LORD help them in their conflict, but He would also actually fight the battle for them.

c. Sometime later, the Assyrian king sent an envoy and a large army to Jerusalem to intimidate Hezekiah and to demand his surrender (v.9; 2 K.18:17-18). *Second Kings* tells us that a large number of Assyrian troops laid siege to Jerusalem (2 K.18:17). With this action, the Assyrian king was launching a propaganda war of intimidation, threatening and demanding that Hezekiah surrender Jerusalem to the Assyrians.

d. After the officials set up siege around the capital, the Assyrian officer appointed by King Sennacherib approached the city. He addressed Jerusalem's officials and the citizens standing nearby on the wall (vv.10-18). Shouting out, he questioned their confidence in Hezekiah and in his tactics.

1) He declared that Hezekiah was only misleading them by persuading them to trust the LORD (v.11). If they continued to listen to the deception of Hezekiah, they would die of hunger and thirst due to the Assyrian siege.
2) The Assyrian spokesman charged Hezekiah with displeasing the LORD by destroying the high places and altars of the gods (v.12). Note that he put his charge in the form of a question, attempting to arouse the people to question Hezekiah's dependence on the LORD. How could the LORD bless Hezekiah since the king had destroyed the worship centers of the gods? Of course, this was a complete misunderstanding of the LORD since He is the only living and true God and all other gods are false.

3) The Assyrian spokesman then sought to intimidate the Judean officials and people who were standing on the walls listening to the negotiations. Being a skilled negotiator, the Assyrian spokesman continued to argue his case in the form of questions. He aroused the Judeans to think about the power of Assyria, arguing…
   - that no nation had ever been delivered from Assyria, not by any god (v.13)
   - that no people had ever been saved from the Assyrians by any god (v.14)
   - that the Judean God would be powerless against Assyria (v.14)

   Note how he equated the LORD with false gods, which was the fallacy of his argument. The LORD is not just one god among many. He is the only living and true God.

4) Again, the Assyrian spokesman charged Hezekiah with deceiving the people. Moreover any thinking people could easily recognize the deception (v.15). No god of any nation had been able to save its people from Assyria. How much less would the Judean God be able to deliver them? The Judean god would be powerless against Assyria.

5) Continuing on in his propaganda, the Assyrian commander railed against the LORD and Hezekiah (vv.16-18). Remember that Sennacherib had remained behind in Lachish (v.9), but he sent letters that were to be presented to Hezekiah (v.17). These letters scorned and denied the power of the LORD to rescue His people. Shouting out as loudly as he could, the spokesman shared the letters in Hebrew in order to strike terror in the hearts of the people standing on the wall of Jerusalem (v.18).

e. But there was a fallacy, a serious illusion, a fatal misconception (19). There is only one true and living God, the LORD Himself. All other gods are false, the fabrication of people's overactive imaginations, the busywork of people's hands.

f. Facing the fierce, overwhelming Assyrians, Hezekiah and Isaiah did the only thing they could do: they cried out to the LORD in prayer (vv.20-21). That very night the hand of God's mighty power and judgment fell upon the Assyrian invaders. The LORD sent an angel into the Assyrian camp sometime during the night, and the angel executed 185,000 soldiers (v.21; 2 K.19:35-37). Stunned, horrified, dismayed, and confused about what had happened, the Assyrian survivors broke camp and withdrew, returning to Ninevah. And in disgrace they remained there. Soon thereafter, Assyria's King Sennacherib was assassinated by his own son as he went into the temple of his false god to worship.

g. As a result of this great and miraculous deliverance, Hezekiah and his people had a long period of peace (vv.22-23). Other nations were now obviously afraid to attack Judah, for the LORD was protecting His people on every side, giving them peace throughout the land.

In an expression of appreciation, the people brought offerings for the LORD and valuable gifts for Hezekiah. Hezekiah was even highly respected by all the surrounding nations after the victory over Assyria.

Thought 1. God has the power to deliver His people. No matter what we may be facing…

• disappointment	• purposelessness	• unfaithfulness
• discouragement	• disease	• tragedy
• depression	• accident	• the loss of a loved one
• loneliness	• financial difficulty	• unemployment
• emptiness	• broken relationships	

The Lord's power is more than sufficient to meet our every need. God's power is always available to…

• deliver us	• provide for us	• love us
• set us free	• lift us up	• watch over us
• rescue us	• walk with us	• protect us
• save us	• carry us	• shield us
• strengthen us	• care for us	• comfort us

Even in death, God delivers us. So that we never have to taste or experience death, He transfers us immediately—quicker than the eye can blink—into the spiritual world or dimension of being. And there we live forever in the LORD's presence.

If we will trust the LORD in all that we do, crying out to Him for deliverance, nothing will ever be able to conquer or defeat us. The LORD will empower us to stand up and *walk through* any trial or temptation, no matter how terrifying or seductive. Listen to what God's Holy Word says:

"Who shall separate us from the love of Christ? *shall* tribulation, or distress, or persecution, or famine, or nakedness, or peril, or sword?…Nay, in all these things we are more than conquerors through him that loved us. For I am persuaded, that neither death, nor life, nor angels, nor principalities, nor powers, nor things present, nor things to come, Nor height, nor depth, nor any other creature, shall be able to separate us from the love of God, which is in Christ Jesus our Lord" (Ro.8:35, 37-39).

"There hath no temptation taken you but such as is common to man: but God *is* faithful, who will not suffer you to be tempted above that ye are able; but will with the temptation also make a way to escape, that ye may be able to bear *it*" (1 Co.10:13).

"For we would not, brethren, have you ignorant of our trouble which came to us in Asia, that we were pressed out of measure, above strength, insomuch that we despaired even of life: But we had the sentence of death in ourselves, that we should not trust in ourselves, but in God which raiseth the dead: Who delivered us from so great a death, and doth deliver: in whom we trust that he will yet deliver *us*" (2 Co.1:8-10).

"And he said unto me, My grace is sufficient for thee: for my strength is made perfect in weakness. Most gladly therefore will I rather glory in my infirmities, that the power of Christ may rest upon me. Therefore I take pleasure in infirmities, in reproaches, in necessities, in persecutions, in distresses for Christ's sake: for when I am weak, then am I strong" (2 Co.12:9-10).

"That he would grant you, according to the riches of his glory, to be strengthened with might by his Spirit in the inner man" (Ep.3:16).

"Now unto him that is able to do exceeding abundantly above all that we ask or think, according to the power that worketh in us" (Ep.3:20).

"Henceforth there is laid up for me a crown of righteousness, which the Lord, the righteous judge, shall give me at that day: and not to me only, but unto all them also that love his appearing" (2 Ti.4:8).

"Forasmuch then as the children are partakers of flesh and blood, he also himself likewise took part of the same; that through death he might destroy him that had the power of death, that is, the devil; And deliver them who through fear of death were all their lifetime subject to bondage" (He.2:14-15).

"Who through faith subdued kingdoms, wrought righteousness, obtained promises, stopped the mouths of lions, Quenched the violence of fire, escaped the edge of the sword, out of weakness were made strong, waxed valiant in fight, turned to flight the armies of the aliens" (He.11:33-34).

"So that we may boldly say, The Lord is my helper, and I will not fear what man shall do unto me" (He.13:6).

"The Lord knoweth how to deliver the godly out of temptations, and to reserve the unjust unto the day of judgment to be punished" (2 Pe.2:9).

"For whatsoever is born of God overcometh the world: and this is the victory that overcometh the world, even our faith. Who is he that overcometh the world, but he that believeth that Jesus is the Son of God?" (1 Jn.5:4-5).

"And he said, The LORD is my rock, and my fortress, and my deliverer" (2 S.22:2).

"For thou hast girded me with strength to battle: them that rose up against me hast thou subdued under me" (2 S.22:40).

"He shall deliver thee in six troubles: yea, in seven there shall no evil touch thee" (Jb.5:19).

"The LORD is my strength and my shield; my heart trusted in him, and I am helped: therefore my heart greatly rejoiceth; and with my song will I praise him" (Ps.28:7).

"But I am poor and needy; yet the Lord thinketh upon me: thou art my help and my deliverer; make no tarrying, O my God" (Ps.40:17).

"Through thee will we push down our enemies: through thy name will we tread them under that rise up against us" (Ps.44:5).

"Surely he shall deliver thee from the snare of the fowler, and from the noisome pestilence" (Ps.91:3).

"They reel to and fro, and stagger like a drunken man, and are at their wit's end. Then they cry unto the LORD in their trouble, and he bringeth them out of their distresses. He maketh the storm a calm, so that the waves thereof are still. Then are they glad because they be quiet; so he bringeth them unto their desired haven. Oh that men would praise the LORD for his goodness, and for his wonderful works to the children of men!" (Ps.107:27-31).

"But they that wait upon the LORD shall renew their strength; they shall mount up with wings as eagles; they shall run, and not be weary; and they shall walk, and not faint" (Is.40:31).

"Fear thou not; for I am with thee: be not dismayed; for I am thy God: I will strengthen thee; yea, I will help thee; yea, I will uphold thee with the right hand of my righteousness" (Is.41:10).

"Fear not: for I have redeemed thee, I have called thee by thy name; thou art mine. When thou passest through the waters, I will be with thee; and through the rivers, they shall not overflow thee: when thou walkest through the fire, thou shalt not be burned; neither shall the flame kindle upon thee" (Is.43:1-2).

"And even to your old age I am he; and even to hoar [gray] hairs will I carry you: I have made, and I will bear; even I will carry, and will deliver you" (Is.46:4).

"Be not afraid of their faces: for I am with thee to deliver thee, saith the LORD" (Je.1:8).

"He delivereth and rescueth, and he worketh signs and wonders in heaven and in earth, who hath delivered Daniel from the power of the lions" (Da.6:27).

---

2 (32:24-33) **Prayer, Power of—Power, of Prayer—Sickness, Healed by—Illness, Healed by—Disease, Healed by—Healing, Source of, Prayer—Hezekiah, Terminal Illness of—Prosperity, Example of—Hezekiah, Prosperity of—Tests - Testing, of God, Example of**: in closing out Hezekiah's reign, the author discusses the king's terminal illness and his prosperity. The account given here is more abbreviated than the story given in *Second Kings* (2 K.20:1-21).

a. Shockingly, right after the deliverance of Jerusalem from the Assyrian threat, Hezekiah became deathly sick and was soon to die. Yet in faith he prayed to the LORD. The LORD, out of compassion, immediately answered the king's prayer and miraculously healed him.

b. After Hezekiah's healing, he let pride fill his heart and did not acknowledge the LORD as he should have (vv.25-26). As a result, God pronounced judgment upon Hezekiah and the nation. But during the pronouncement, Hezekiah repented of his pride. Both he and the people humbled themselves before the LORD. Because of their sincere repentance and humility, the LORD delayed His hand of judgment during Hezekiah's lifetime (v.26).

But what had stirred pride within his heart? When the crown prince of Babylon heard about the miraculous healing of Hezekiah, his curiosity was aroused (v.31; 2 K.20:12). So he sent several envoys to inquire about the healing. While entertaining the ambassadors, Hezekiah pridefully showed them his vast wealth (2 K.20:12-21). Obviously, this included the strength of his military as well as the wealth found in the palace, the temple treasuries, and the storage cities throughout the nation. Immediately, the LORD sent the prophet Isaiah to rebuke the king. With the authority of God Himself, Isaiah pronounced God's judgment upon Hezekiah and Judah due to the king's pride and the people's sins down through the centuries (1 K.16–18). Some day in the near future, Babylon would conquer Judah and carry off all the wealth of the nation, the very wealth Hezekiah had so readily shown to the Babylonian ambassadors. Unsurprisingly, the ambassadors would not forget what they had seen. Future leaders of Babylon would covet the wealth, all because of Hezekiah's self-exaltation and vanity.

c. In summarizing Hezekiah's reign, the author tells of the LORD's great blessings upon his life. He gave him great wealth and prosperity. So much wealth was accumulated that he had to build several treasury buildings to store his silver, precious stones, spices, shields, and all the other valuable items (v.27).

Hezekiah also built storage buildings to harvest the grain, wine, and oil from his farms (v.28). He had barns, stalls, and pens erected for his livestock. In addition, he built a large number of towns throughout the nation as well as acquiring a vast number of flocks and herds. All this was a sign of God's blessing upon Hezekiah.

d. Hezekiah's major building project was the construction of a water tunnel for Jerusalem (2 K.20:20). Cutting a tunnel beneath Jerusalem, he was able to provide a permanent water supply for the capital city. As Scripture says, Hezekiah succeeded and prospered in all the works he undertook.

e. In the midst of God's blessings upon his life, the LORD tested Hezekiah (v.31). The LORD had used the ambassadors sent by the Babylonian ruler to test the heart of the king. Knowing that Hezekiah was taking personal pride in his wealth, the LORD sought to expose the arrogance of his heart. As noted above, Hezekiah repented of his pride and the LORD delayed the pronounced judgment upon him and the nation.

e. A summary of Hezekiah's righteous reign and his acts of devotion were recorded in *The Vision of the Prophet Isaiah Son of Amoz*. Note that this particular writing of Isaiah was included in *The Book of the Kings of Judah and Israel* (v.32).

f. After Hezekiah's death, he was buried in Jerusalem and greatly honored by the people (v.33). His successor was his son Manasseh.

Thought 1. The power of prayer is indescribable and too wonderful for words. Why? Because there is no limit to God's power. God is omnipotent, all-powerful, possessing perfect and unlimited power to do anything He desires. And yet, God is not only omnipotent but also omniscient, knowing all things. Nothing is hid from God nor out of His sight. God sees and knows all things. The fact of God's omnipotence and omniscience is the most glorious news, for God knows when a serious illness strikes us or a crisis confronts us. God then has the power to handle our serious illness or the severe crisis. When we face these seemingly insurmountable problems, our responsibility is to pray, turning our face toward the LORD and crying out to Him. If we are sincere and willing to turn our lives totally over to Him, God will hear and answer our prayer. In some cases, He will miraculously heal us. In other cases, He will give us the strength to *walk through* the illness or crisis victoriously, even conquering death itself. Through prayer, there is nothing, absolutely nothing, that can conquer and overcome us, for God knows the very number of hairs on our head—everything about us—and God has the power to help us. Listen to what God's Word says about the *power of prayer*.

"**Ask, and it shall be given you; seek, and ye shall find; knock, and it shall be opened unto you**" (Mt.7:7).

"**Therefore I say unto you, What things soever ye desire, when ye pray, believe that ye receive *them*, and ye shall have *them***" (Mk.11:24).

"**If ye abide in me, and my words abide in you, ye shall ask what ye will, and it shall be done unto you**" (Jn.15:7).

"**Hitherto have ye asked nothing in my name: ask, and ye shall receive, that your joy may be full**" (Jn.16:24).

"**For this thing I besought the Lord thrice, that it might depart from me. And he said unto me, My grace is sufficient for thee: for my strength is made perfect in weakness. Most gladly therefore will I rather glory in my infirmities, that the power of Christ may rest upon me. Therefore I take pleasure in infirmities, in reproaches, in necessities, in persecutions, in distresses for Christ's sake: for when I am weak, then am I strong**" (2 Co.12:8-10).

"**Now unto him that is able to do exceeding abundantly above all that we ask or think, according to the power that worketh in us**" (Ep.3:20).

"**And the prayer of faith shall save the sick, and the Lord shall raise him up; and if he have committed sins, they shall be forgiven him. Confess *your* faults one to another, and pray one for another, that ye may be healed. The effectual fervent prayer of a righteous man availeth much. Elias was a man subject to like passions as we are, and he prayed earnestly that it might not rain: and it rained not on the earth by the space of three years and six months. And he prayed again, and the heaven gave rain, and the earth brought forth her fruit**" (Js.5:15-18).

"**And whatsoever we ask, we receive of him, because we keep his commandments, and do those things that are pleasing in his sight**" (1 Jn.3:22).

"**Call unto me, and I will answer thee, and show thee great and mighty things, which thou knowest not**" (Je.33:3).

BACKGROUND TO ISAIAH'S DAY

(The Four Kings Who Ruled During Isaiah's Ministry)

DEEPER STUDY #1

(2 Chr.32:31) **Babel/Babylon**: the capital city of Babylon was 80km or 50 miles south of the modern Baghdad, the capital of Iraq.[4] Babylon was also southeast of and right next to Assyria. Although Assyria became the dominant world power of its time and Babylon was not far away, Assyria could never keep Babylon completely subject to them. Eventually, Babylon became the strongest power in the world.

In the Old Testament, Babylon is a name that refers to several different categories: a city, a nation, a people and, symbolically, a civilization or society that man builds in defiance of God. From the beginning of human history, ever since the Tower of Babel (Ge.11:9), Babylon has represented a civilization that is devoted to materialism and sensual pleasure. In addition, the wicked, oppressive, rebellious pride of governments and nations—the very worst of human government—is symbolized in the name Babylon. Babylon further represents the power of darkness that seeks to enslave and oppress people. Therefore, any world power that rises up in willful rebellion against God—against establishing a truly free, just, and righteous society—is following in the footsteps of Babylon. The notorious city of Babylon was characterized by its self-inflating, hostile defiance toward God and its brutal oppression of all other peoples. Even when the end time comes and Babylon is once again rebuilt, it will stand as a symbol of rebellion and enmity against the LORD. Babylon will be the capital of an apostate civilization that rebels against the LORD (see outline and notes—Re.14:8; 17:1–18:24 for more discussion).

The Hebrew word for Babel and Babylon is the same. And just as pride and wickedness were in the hearts of the people who tried to build the Tower of Babel (Ge.11:4), great pride and wickedness were in the people of Babylon—so much so that the final empire that will take its stand against God will also be called Babylon (Re.16:19). In the same way that the people of Babel stood together against God, so it will be in the last days of world history. The ungodly and greedy of this world will unite, believing that nothing and no one will be able to tear apart their united political system.

A less talked about but equally significant fact to note about Babylon is this: while the Bible paints the picture of pride in the Babylonians of Old Testament times, we also see that God used the Babylonians to execute judgment against other wicked nations of that day and to discipline the people of Judah for their idolatry. Nebuchadnezzar conquered Jerusalem and led away all but a few of the people of Judah (2 K.24:11-16). Additionally, he took the temple treasures and put them in his own palace (2 Chr.36:7), but he did not recognize the one true God as the source of his success. Instead, Nebuchadnezzar became so full of pride that he claimed all credit for what he had done in life, giving no honor the LORD at all. But note carefully what happened to Nebuchadnezzar, who was considered at that time the most powerful man in the world:

> **"The king spake, and said, Is not this great Babylon, that I have built for the house of the kingdom by the might of my power, and for the honour of my majesty? While the word *was* in the king's mouth, there fell a voice from heaven, *saying*, O king Nebuchadnezzar, to thee it is spoken; The kingdom is departed from thee. And they shall drive thee from men, and thy dwelling *shall be* with the beasts of the field: they shall make thee to eat grass as oxen, and seven times shall pass over thee, until thou know that the most High ruleth in the kingdom of men, and giveth it to whomsoever he will. The same hour was the thing fulfilled upon Nebuchadnezzar: and he was driven from men, and did eat grass as oxen, and his body was wet with the dew of heaven, till his hairs were grown like eagles' *feathers*, and his nails like birds' *claws*." (Da.4:30-33).**

Nebuchadnezzar was not restored to his right mind or his throne until he gave all honor and glory to the LORD. Despite Nebuchadnezzar's experience, his grandson Belshazzar desecrated the vessels from the temple of the LORD by using them in a pagan feast. Belshazzar and the Babylonian leaders could not have been more arrogant against the living God! For this awful pride, Belshazzar and the nation suffered the terrifying judgment of God. God Himself wrote on the wall of the palace, declaring the immediate defeat and death of Belshazzar and the end of the Babylonian kingdom once and for all (Da.5:5-6, 18-30). God brought them down as He did Sodom and Gomorrah (Is.13:19). There was nothing left of the once mighty Babylonian empire.

The lesson for us today is clear: God judges individuals as well as nations. God will not put up with pride, not for long. If we do not put away pride and walk humbly before the LORD, judgment will come. No one can be prideful in the face of God, proclaiming his own greatness. No one...

- no matter who he is
- no matter how much power or wealth he has
- no matter what position or authority he has
- no matter what others think of him
- no matter how feared or respected he is

The world is going to face a day of final judgment. All the nations, governments, civilizations, cultures, societies, cities, and communities will stand before God to give an account for what they have done. God is going to execute perfect justice upon this earth, correcting all the wrongs that have ever been done. No mistreatment of other people has ever escaped the eye of God. Every act, including every word and thought, has been seen and heard by the Sovereign LORD and Majesty of the universe. Scripture even declares that a record is being kept of every word and thought ever conceived or spoken by a person (Mt.12:36; 2 Co.10:3-5). Everything we have ever done, whether inside or outside of our bodies, will face the judgment of God. There is to be a final day of judgment upon this earth, a day when all injustices and evil deeds will be corrected. Exactly as God's predicted, judgment fell upon Babylon. Likewise, it will fall upon this earth and upon every human being who has lived on this earth. The hand of God will bring down the prideful. Judgment is certain. Babylon is a clear picture of pride and the need for every person to repent.

> **"Pride goeth before destruction, and an haughty spirit before a fall" (Pr.16:18).**
>
> **"Alas, alas, that great city Babylon, that mighty city! for in one hour is thy judgment come" (Re.18:10).**
>
> **"And I will break the pride of your power; and I will make your heaven as iron, and your earth as brass" (Le.26:19).**

---

4 J.D. Douglas, Editor. *New Bible Dictionary*. (Wheaton, IL: Tyndale House Publishers, Inc., 1982), p. 111.

TIMELINE OF KINGS, PROPHETS AND HISTORY*

THE UNITED KINGDOM

BIBLE REF.	KINGS (YEARS REIGNED)	PROPHETS
1 S.16:1–1 K.2:11; 1 Chr.11:1–30	David (40) (1011–971)	Samuel (1095–1015), Gad (1015–950), Asaph (1004), Nathan (1003–931), Heman (971)
1 K.2:12–11:43; 1 Chr.28:1–2 Chr.9:31	Solomon (40) (971–931)	

DATE / FOREIGN KINGS / HISTORY

DATE BC	FOREIGN KINGS	WORLD EVENTS (HISTORY)
1000	Ashur-Rabi II (1010–970) *(Assyria)*; Hiram (1003–966) *(Tyre)*; Tiglath-Pileser II (960–935) *(Assyria)*	David captures Jerusalem (1004)
950		Foundation for the Temple (966); 22nd Egyptian Dynasty (945)
930	Shishak I (945–924) *(Egypt)*	Kingdom Divided (930)
900	Ben-Hadad I (900) *(Syria)*; Eth-Baal (887–856) *(Sidon)*	Assyria makes peace with Babylon (915)
850	Hazael (840) *(Syria)*	Jehoshaphat leads a revival (865); Elijah's contest with prophets of Baal (857); Elijah's mantle passed to Elisha (845)
800	Ben-Hadad II (798) *(Syria)*	Carthage established (814); Joash repairs Temple (812); 23rd Egyptian dynasty (800)
750	Ben-Hadad III (773) *(Syria)*; Rezin (750) *(Syria)*	Olympic games begin (776); Rome founded (753); Babylonian and Chinese calendar (750)

THE DIVIDED KINGDOM — NORTHERN KINGDOM OF ISRAEL

BIBLE REF.	KINGS (YEARS REIGNED)	PROPHETS
1 K.12:1–24; 12:25–14:20; 2 Chr.10:1–16	Jeroboam I (22) (931–910)	Ahijah (931–910); Man from Judah (930); Shemaiah (927)
1 K.15:25–31	Nadab (2) (910–909)	
1 K.15:16–16:7; 2 Chr.16:1–6	Baasha (24) (909–886)	Jehu (886)
1 K.16:6–14	Elah (2) (886–885)	
1 K.16:9–20	Zimri (7 days) (885)	
1 K.16:21–28	Omri (12) (885–874)	Hanani (870)
1 K.16:28–22:40; 2 Chr.18:1–34	Ahab (22) (874–853)	Elijah (860–845)
1 K.22:49–51; 2 K.1:1–18; 2 Chr.20:35–37; 22:1–11	Ahaziah (2) (853–852); Joram/Jehoram (12) (852–841)	Micaiah (853); Elisha (850–795); Eliezer (849–48)
2 K.1:17; 3:1–8:15		
2 K.9:1–10:36; 2 Chr.22:7–9	Jehu (28)	
2 K.13:1–9	Jehoahaz (17) (814–798)	
2 K.13:9–25; 14:8–16	Jehoash (16) (798–782)	Zechariah (797)
2 K.14:23–29	Jeroboam II (41) (793–753)	Jonah (780–765)
2 K.15:8–12	Zechariah (6 mos) (753)	Amos (750)
2 K.15:13–15	Shallum (1 mo) (752)	
2 K.15:16–22	Menahem (10) (752–742)	

THE DIVIDED KINGDOM — SOUTHERN KINGDOM OF JUDAH

BIBLE REF.	KINGS (YEARS REIGNED)	PROPHETS
1 K.12:1–24; 14:21–31; 2 Chr.9:31–12:16	Rehoboam (17) (931–913)	
1 K.15:1–8; 2 Chr.12:16–14:1	Abijah (3) (913–911)	
1 K.15:9–24; 2 Chr.14:1–16:14	Asa (911–870)	Iddo (910); Azariah (896)
1 K.22:41–50; 2 K.3:6–14; 2 Chr.17:1–21:1	Jehoshaphat (25) (873–848)	
2 K.8:16–24; 2 Chr.21:1–20	Jehoram (8) (853–841)	
2 K.8:25–29; 9:27–29; 2 Chr.22:1–10	Ahaziah (2) (841)	Obadiah (845)
2 K.11:1–16; 2 Chr.22:10–23:21	Athaliah (7) (841–835)	
2 K.11:17–12:21; 2 Chr.22:11–12; 24:1–27	Joash/Jehoash (40) (835–796)	Joel (830)
2 K.14:1–20; 2 Chr.24:27–25:28	Amaziah (29) (796–767)	
2 K.14:21–22; 15:1–7; 2 Chr.26:1–23	Azariah/Uzziah (52) (792–740)	Hosea (788–723); Jonah (780–765)
2 K.15:32–38; 2 Chr.26:23–27:9	Jotham (16) (750–731)	

THE DIVIDED KINGDOM

SOUTHERN KINGDOM OF JUDAH			NORTHERN KINGDOM OF ISRAEL			DATE BC	HISTORY	
BIBLE REF.	KINGS (YEARS REIGNED)	PROPHETS	PROPHETS	KINGS (YEARS REIGNED)	BIBLE REF.		FOREIGN KINGS	WORLD EVENTS
				Pekahiah (2) (742–740)	2 K.15:23-26		Tiglath-Pil[n]eser III [or Pul] (745–727) (Assyria)	Assyria takes control of Northern Kingdom (745–627)
2 K.15:38-16:20; 2 Chr.27:9-27; Is.7:1-9:1	Ahaz (16) (735–715)	Isaiah (740–690)		Pekah (20) (752–732) (ruled only in Gilead) (740–732) (ruled in Samaria)	2 K.15:27-31		Shalmaneser V (727–722) (Assyria)	Assyria invades Northern Israel (732)
		Micah (735–725) Oded (733)		Hoshea (9) (732–722)	2 K.17:1-23		So (727–716) (Egypt) Sargon II (710–705) (Assyria)	Fall of Northern Kingdom (722)
2 K.18:1-20:21; 2 Chr.28:27-32:33; Pr.25:1. Is.36:1-39:8	Hezekiah (29) (729–686)					700	Sennacherib (705–681) (Assyria) Merodach-Baladan (721–710, 705–704) (Assyria)	Sennacherib defeats Egypt (701) Hezekiah's tunnel (701)
							Tirhakah (690–664) (Egypt)	185,000 Assyrians killed by God (701)
2 K.20:21-21:18; 2 Chr.32:33-33:20	Manasseh (55) (696–642)	Nahum (663–612)				650	Esarhaddon (681–669) (Assyria)	Sennacherib destroys Babylon (689)
2 K.21:18-26; 2 Chr.33:20-25	Amon (2) (642–640)	Zephaniah (640–609)					Nabopolassar (626–605) (Assyria)	Josiah's reform (621) Nineveh destroyed (612)
2 K.21:26-23:30; 2 Chr.33:25-35:27	Josiah (31) (640–609)	Jeremiah (627–562)					Neco (610–595) (Egypt)	Battle of Carchemish (605) 1st group of exiles from Judah taken to Babylon (605)
2 K.23:31-33; 2 Chr.36:1-4	Jehoaz/Jehoahaz (3 mos) (609)	Habakkuk (615–598)				600	Nebuchadnezzar II (605–562) (Babylon)	2nd group of exiles from Judah taken to Babylon (597)
2 K.23:34-24:7; 2 Chr.36:5-8	Jehoiakim (11) (608–598)	Daniel (605–535)						Fall of Judah—Third group of exiles from Judah taken to Babylon (586)
2 K.24:8-17; 25:27-30; 2 Chr.36:8-10;	Jehoiachin (3 mos) (598–597)	Ezekiel (593–571)						
2 K.24:18-25:21; 2 Chr.36:10-14; Je.21:1-52:11	Zedekiah/Mattaniah (11) (597–586)					550	Evil-Merodach (562–560) (Babylon)	Fall of Babylon to Medo-Persian Empire (539)
2 K.25:22-26; Je.40:5-41:18	Gedaliah (2 mos) (Appointed by Nebuchadnezzar) (586)						Cyrus II (559–530) (Medo-Persia)	
		Haggai (520) Zechariah (520–518)					Belshazzar (552–539) (Babylon)	Cyrus II decrees that the Jews may return to the Holy Land (538) 1st exiles return to Holy Land with Zerubbabel (537)
						500	Darius I (521–486) (Medo-Persia)	1st Temple foundation laid (536) 2nd Temple foundation laid (520) Temple completed (516) Republic of Rome est. (509) 2nd return under Ezra (458)
		Malachi (430)				450	Artaxerxes (465–425) (Persia)	3rd return under Nehemiah (445)

*Some dates are approximate.

The resources used for the timeline are as follows:

1 The Bible
2 Archer, Gleason L. Encyclopedia of Bible Difficulties. (Grand Rapids, Michigan: Zondervan Publishing House), 1982.
3 Freedman, David Noel, ed., et. al. The Anchor Bible Dictionary. (New York: Doubleday), 1992.
4 Grun, Bernard. The Timetables of History. 3rd ed. (New York: Simon & Schuster), 1991.
5 Kaiser, Walter C. A History of Israel. (Nashville, Tennessee: Broadman & Holman Publishers), 1998.
6 Silverman, David P., ed. Ancient Egypt. (New York: Oxford University Press), 1997.

OUTLINE OF ISAIAH

THE PREACHER'S OUTLINE AND SERMON BIBLE® is *unique*. It differs from all other Study Bibles and Sermon Resource Materials in that every Passage and Subject is outlined right beside the Scripture. When you choose any *Subject* below and turn to the reference, you have not only the Scripture but also an outline of the Scripture and Subject *already prepared for you—verse by verse*.

For a quick example, choose one of the subjects below and turn over to the Scripture; you will find this to be a marvelous help for more organized and streamlined study.

In addition, every point of the Scripture and Subject is *fully developed in a Commentary with supporting Scripture* at the end of each point. Again, this arrangement makes sermon preparation much simpler and more efficient.

Note something else: the Subjects of *Isaiah* have titles that are both Biblical and *practical*. The practical titles are often more appealing to people. This *benefit* is clearly seen for use on billboards, bulletins, church newsletters, etc.

A suggestion: for the *quickest* overview of *Isaiah,* first read *all the Division titles* (I, II, III, etc.), then come back and read the individual outline titles.

OUTLINE OF ISAIAH

PART II—THE HISTORICAL SECTION, 36:1–39:8

IV.   THE TURNING POINT OF HEZEKIAH'S REIGN: A SHIFT FROM THE THREAT OF ASSYRIA TO THE CAPTIVITY OF JUDAH BY BABYLON, 36:1–39:8
  A.   The End of the Assyrian Threat: God's Power to Deliver His People, 36:1–37:38
  B.   The Stage Set for the Coming Captivity of Judah by Babylon: The Power of Prayer and the Danger of Sinful Pride, 38:1–39:8

PART III: THE PROPHECIES OF COMFORT, 40:1–66:24

V.   THE PROPHECIES OF COMFORT AND FREEDOM: A PICTURE OF BELIEVERS BEING SET FREE FROM THE CAPTIVITY OF SIN AND DEATH, 40:1–48:22
  A.   Set Free Through God's Salvation and Greatness, 40:1-31
  B.   Set Free Through God's Power to Control Human History, the Very Deeds of People, 41:1-29
  C.   Set Free Through God's Perfect Servant, the Messiah, the Lord Jesus Christ (The First of Four "Servant Songs"), 42:1-25
  D.   Set Free Through the Redeemer, the LORD, Your God: A Study of Redemption, 43:1-28
  E.   Set Free By the LORD, the Only Living and True God, 44:1-28
  F.   Set Free By God's Power to Work Through People and Nations: A Look at God's Enormous Power, 45:1-25
  G.   Set Free by Turning Away from Idolatry: A Study of Idolatry, 46:1-13
  H.   Set Free by God's Judgment of the Oppressor, Babylon: A Warning to All Who Oppress Others, 47:1-15
  I.   Set Free by God's Plan of Redemption: The Hope of Being Delivered from God's Judgment and Wrath, 48:1-22

VI. **THE PROPHECIES OF THE GREAT DELIVERER: THE SUFFERING SERVANT OF GOD, THE SAVIOR OF THE WORLD, 49:1–57:21**

    A. The Savior's Mission to the World: Being Eternally Called to Reach the Earth for God, 49:1–50:11

    B. The Savior's Cry of Salvation: Listen! Wake Up! Depart! 51:1–52:12

    C. The Savior's Suffering, His Atoning Death, 52:13–53:12

    D. The Savior's Great Promises to Israel—Restoration: Repentant Backsliders Will Return to Him, 54:1-17

    E. The Savior's Great Invitation to the World, 55:1–56:8

    F. The Savior's Message to Leaders and Idolaters and to the Prideful and Greedy, 56:9–57:21

    G. The Savior's Message to the Hypocrites: Guilty of Deceptive, Phony Behavior, 58:1-14

    H. The Savior's Message to the Wicked: Guilty of Sin and Separated from God, 59:1-21

VII. **THE PROPHECIES OF A GREAT AND GLORIOUS FUTURE: 60:1–66:24**

    A. The Future Glory of Jerusalem: A Picture of the Holy City During the Messiah's Kingdom on Earth—the Millennium, 60:1-22

    B. The Gift of Salvation Through the Coming Savior, 61:1–62:12

    C. The Great Day of God's Vengeance and Mercy: A Picture of Armageddon, 63:1–64:12

    D. The Last Days of Human History (Part 1), 65:1-25

    E. The Last Days of Human History (Part 2), 66:1-24

DIVISION IV

THE TURNING POINT OF HEZEKIAH'S REIGN: A SHIFT FROM THE THREAT OF ASSYRIA TO THE CAPTIVITY OF JUDAH BY BABYLON, 36:1–39:8

PART II—THE HISTORICAL SECTION, 36:1–39:8

(1:1–12:6) **DIVISION OVERVIEW**: a turning point now takes place in the great book of *Isaiah*. A shift occurs from Assyria's threat to Judah over to the captivity of Judah by Babylon. The shift takes place during the strong, godly reign of King Hezekiah of Judah. This division of the book of *Isaiah* opens with a scene of terror—the siege of Jerusalem by the Assyrians. Doom hung heavily in the air. Hezekiah's response to the impossible situation is to turn to the LORD and cry out for divine help. In doing so, Hezekiah moved the heart of God and we see a gripping picture of God's power to deliver His people from any circumstance. God promised and carried out the deliverance of His people. Overnight, 185,000 Assyrians were slaughtered by the Angel of the Lord and the threat of Assyria was eliminated.

However, immediately after Judah's deliverance from Assyria, another crisis struck. King Hezekiah was smitten with a deadly illness and his days were numbered. Once again, Hezekiah responded by seeking the LORD, and the Lord again responded in compassion, delivering Hezekiah from certain doom. The king was healed completely and given fifteen more years to live. But what happened next would change the history of Judah forever and mark the beginning of its fall.

After God's great deliverances, Hezekiah became filled with pride and a false sense of security. When ambassadors from Babylon came to seek Judah as an ally, Hezekiah foolishly showed the foreigners all the national treasures. Immediately afterward, Isaiah prophesied the future invasion of the nation by Babylon and the subsequent fall of both Judah and its beloved capital, Jerusalem. Some generations later, the prophecy was completely fulfilled: Babylon conquered Judah, plundered the treasury, and took the survivors captive, scattering the exiles throughout the Babylonian Empire.

Although Hezekiah was a righteous ruler and a committed follower of the Lord, his prideful actions would contribute significantly to the downfall of the nation and change its destiny forever. Total destruction and captivity would now hang over the nation and its people like a dark, heavy cloud.

THE TURNING POINT OF HEZEKIAH'S REIGN: A SHIFT FROM THE THREAT OF ASSYRIA TO THE CAPTIVITY OF JUDAH BY BABYLON, 36:1–39:8

A. The End of the Assyrian Threat: God's Power to Deliver His People, 36:1–37:38

B. The Stage Set for the Coming Captivity of Judah by Babylon: The Power of Prayer and the Danger of Sinful Pride, 38:1–39:8

CHAPTER 36

PART II—THE HISTORICAL SECTION, 36:1–39:8

IV. THE TURNING POINT OF HEZEKIAH'S REIGN: A SHIFT FROM THE THREAT OF ASSYRIA TO THE CAPTIVITY OF JUDAH BY BABYLON, 36:1–39:8

A. The End of the Assyrian Threat: God's Power to Deliver His People, 36:1–37:38

36:1-22; see 2 K 18:17-35; 2 Chr.32:9-19 37:1-38; see 2 K.19:1-37

1. **The Assyrian invasion of Judah by King Sennacherib: A decision demanded—trust the power of man or of God**
   a. The king's easy conquest of all the fortified cities
   b. The Assyrian's siege of Jerusalem & the demand for surrender
      1) They camped at the city's water source
      2) They summoned Hezekiah for negotiations, but he sent three court officials instead
      3) The Assyrian field commander—as spokesman for the "great king" of Assyria—questioned Hezekiah's tactics of & why he was so confident
         • Questioned Hezekiah's claim of military strength: His claim was empty, his army weak
         • Questioned Hezekiah's dependence on Egypt: In war, Egypt would splinter like a reed & cause the destruction of any ally leaning upon it
         • Questioned Hezekiah's dependence on the LORD: Claimed must have displeased the LORD by destroying the high places & altars of worship (a misunderstanding of God & idolatry)
      4) The field commander demanded Hezekiah's surrender
         • Because of the weakness of Judah's army: Had

Now it came to pass in the fourteenth year of king Hezekiah, *that* Sennacherib king of Assyria came up against all the defenced cities of Judah, and took them.
2 And the king of Assyria sent Rabshakeh from Lachish to Jerusalem unto king Hezekiah with a great army. And he stood by the conduit of the upper pool in the highway of the fuller's field.
3 Then came forth unto him Eliakim, Hilkiah's son, which was over the house, and Shebna the scribe, and Joah, Asaph's son, the recorder.
4 And Rabshakeh said unto them, Say ye now to Hezekiah, Thus saith the great king, the king of Assyria, What confidence is this wherein thou trustest?
5 I say, *sayest thou,* (but *they are but* vain words) *I have* counsel and strength for war: now on whom dost thou trust, that thou rebellest against me?
6 Lo, thou trustest in the staff of this broken reed, on Egypt; whereon if a man lean, it will go into his hand, and pierce it: so *is* Pharaoh king of Egypt to all that trust in him.
7 But if thou say to me, We trust in the LORD our God: *is it* not he, whose high places and whose altars Hezekiah hath taken away, and said to Judah and to Jerusalem, Ye shall worship before this altar?
8 Now therefore give pledges, I pray thee, to my master the king of Assyria, and I will give thee two thousand horses, if thou be able

on thy part to set riders upon them.
9 How then wilt thou turn away the face of one captain of the least of my master's servants, and put thy trust on Egypt for chariots and for horsemen?
10 And am I now come up without the LORD against this land to destroy it? the LORD said unto me, Go up against this land, and destroy it.
11 Then said Eliakim and Shebna and Joah unto Rabshakeh, Speak, I pray thee, unto thy servants in the Syrian language; for we understand *it:* and speak not to us in the Jews' language, in the ears of the people that *are* on the wall.
12 But Rabshakeh said, Hath my master sent me to thy master and to thee to speak these words? *hath he* not *sent me* to the men that sit upon the wall, that they may eat their own dung, and drink their own piss with you?
13 Then Rabshakeh stood, and cried with a loud voice in the Jews' language, and said, Hear ye the words of the great king, the king of Assyria.
14 Thus saith the king, Let not Hezekiah deceive you: for he shall not be able to deliver you.
15 Neither let Hezekiah make you trust in the LORD, saying, The LORD will surely deliver us: this city shall not be delivered into the hand of the king of Assyria.
16 Hearken not to Hezekiah: for thus saith the king of Assyria, Make *an agreement* with me *by* a present, and come out to me: and eat ye every one of his vine, and every one of his fig tree, and drink ye every one the waters of his own cistern;
17 Until I come and take you away to a land like your own land, a land of corn and wine, a land of bread and vineyards.
18 *Beware* lest Hezekiah persuade you, saying, The LORD will deliver us. Hath any of the gods of the nations delivered his land out of the hand of the king of Assyria?
19 Where *are* the gods of

few horses & horsemen

   • Because the whole army of Judah could not stand against one of Assyria's least ranking officers
   • Because Judah could not depend upon Egypt
   • Because even the LORD Himself was now against Judah: The LORD had instructed Assyria's king to attack & destroy the nation
   c. The Judean official's request for the Assyrian envoys to speak in Aramaic, not Hebrew: Feared that despair would grip the heart of the crowd who were standing on the wall listening to the negotiations

      1) The commander refused: Realized the importance of propaganda in destroying the people's confidence
      2) The commander stated that his message was for all the people, not just the leaders: The people would suffer the most if Assyria attacked
   d. The commander's second speech: Addressed more to the crowd standing nearby
      1) He appealed for them to hear the "great king"

      2) He encouraged them to oppose Hezekiah
         • Hezekiah could not deliver them
         • Hezekiah was only deceiving them by persuading them to trust the LORD: The LORD *would not* deliver them

      3) He challenged them to surrender & make peace: Because life would be far better under Assyrian rule
         • They would have plenty to eat & drink (not dung & urine as they would under a siege)

         • They would be transported to a fruitful land just like their own

      4) He challenged them to choose life, not death
         • They must not listen to Hezekiah
         • They were being misled by his promise of the LORD's deliverance
      5) He threatened the people

with the power of Assyria
- No nation had ever been delivered from Assyria, not by any god
- Not even the LORD would be able to deliver Jerusalem (or Judah) from an Assyrian attack

e. The response to the Assyrian threats
  1) The people kept silent

  2) The royal officials carried their report to Hezekiah: Approached him with torn clothes, a sign of distress & grief

2. The LORD's assurance of deliverance: God's promise to the believer
a. The distress of Hezekiah over the report, 36:22

b. The appeal of Hezekiah to the prophet Isaiah
  1) He sent a delegation to Isaiah, seeking prayer & some word from the LORD

  2) He sent this message
  - That this was a black day of trouble, rebuke, & disgrace for Judah (due to their sins)

  - That perhaps the LORD had heard the Assyrian king ridicule & defy the name of the living God

  - That Isaiah needed to pray for those still surviving

c. The concise & comforting prediction by Isaiah: Proclaimed the promise of God, a message of hope
  1) The people & Hezekiah were not to fear the threats & blasphemous words of Assyria's king

  2) The LORD would cause Sennacherib to return home: Once there, he would face a violent death by being

Hamath and Arphad? where *are* the gods of Sepharvaim? and have they delivered Samaria out of my hand?
20 Who *are they* among all the gods of these lands, that have delivered their land out of my hand, that the LORD should deliver Jerusalem out of my hand?
21 But they held their peace, and answered him not a word: for the king's commandment was, saying, Answer him not.
22 Then came Eliakim, the son of Hilkiah, that *was* over the household, and Shebna the scribe, and Joah, the son of Asaph, the recorder, to Hezekiah with *their* clothes rent, and told him the words of Rabshakeh.

CHAPTER 37

And it came to pass, when king Hezekiah heard *it,* that he rent his clothes, and covered himself with sackcloth, and went into the house of the LORD.
2 And he sent Eliakim, who *was* over the household, and Shebna the scribe, and the elders of the priests covered with sackcloth, unto Isaiah the prophet the son of Amoz.
3 And they said unto him, Thus saith Hezekiah, This day *is* a day of trouble, and of rebuke, and of blasphemy: for the children are come to the birth, and *there is* not strength to bring forth.
4 It may be the LORD thy God will hear the words of Rabshakeh, whom the king of Assyria his master hath sent to reproach the living God, and will reprove the words which the LORD thy God hath heard: wherefore lift up *thy* prayer for the remnant that is left.
5 So the servants of king Hezekiah came to Isaiah.
6 And Isaiah said unto them, Thus shall ye say unto your master, Thus saith the LORD, Be not afraid of the words that thou hast heard, wherewith the servants of the king of Assyria have blasphemed me.
7 Behold, I will send a blast upon him, and he shall hear a rumour, and return to his own land; and I will cause

him to fall by the sword in his own land.
8 So Rabshakeh returned, and found the king of Assyria warring against Libnah: for he had heard that he was departed from Lachish.
9 And he heard say concerning Tirhakah king of Ethiopia, He is come forth to make war with thee. And when he heard *it,* he sent messengers to Hezekiah, saying,
10 Thus shall ye speak to Hezekiah king of Judah, saying, Let not thy God, in whom thou trustest, deceive thee, saying, Jerusalem shall not be given into the hand of the king of Assyria.
11 Behold, thou hast heard what the kings of Assyria have done to all lands by destroying them utterly; and shalt thou be delivered?
12 Have the gods of the nations delivered them which my fathers have destroyed, *as* Gozan, and Haran, and Rezeph, and the children of Eden which *were* in Telassar?
13 Where *is* the king of Hamath, and the king of Arphad, and the king of the city of Sepharvaim, Hena, and Ivah?
14 And Hezekiah received the letter from the hand of the messengers, and read it: and Hezekiah went up unto the house of the LORD, and spread it before the LORD.
15 And Hezekiah prayed unto the LORD, saying,
16 O LORD of hosts, God of Israel, that dwellest *between* the cherubims, thou *art* the God, *even* thou alone, of all the kingdoms of the earth: thou hast made heaven and earth.
17 Incline thine ear, O LORD, and hear; open thine eyes, O LORD, and see: and hear all the words of Sennacherib, which hath sent to reproach the living God.
18 Of a truth, LORD, the kings of Assyria have laid waste all the nations, and their countries,
19 And have cast their gods into the fire: for they *were* no gods, but the work of men's hands, wood and stone: therefore they have destroyed them.

cut down with a sword

d. The beginning of Isaiah's prophecy: Began to take shape
  1) The Assyrian commander withdrew to help his king fight against Libnah
  2) The Assyrian king had received a report that Egypt was rapidly marching to fight against him

e. The Assyrian king's second message sent to Hezekiah

  1) He stressed the absurdity of Hezekiah's trust in his God to deliver Jerusalem

  2) He scoffed at Hezekiah
  - Reminded him what Assyria had done to all the countries they had attacked
  - Asked why Judah was different: Declared no god had delivered any nation from the power of Assyria

  3) He threatened Hezekiah personally: Asked where the kings of the conquered nations were

3. Hezekiah's desperate prayer for deliverance: Seeking the LORD for help
a. He spread the letter out before the LORD in the temple: A threefold prayer
b. He declared God's greatness

  1) He is the LORD, the God of Israel
  2) He alone is God over all kingdoms
  3) He is the Creator

c. He explained the problem
  1) He pleaded for the LORD to notice how Sennacherib had insulted the living God

  2) He acknowledged the power & conquests of Assyria

  3) He declared that the false gods of the conquered nations could not have saved them: They were only lifeless & powerless idols made by men's hands

d. He cried for deliverance & expressed his major concern: That all nations know that the LORD alone is God

4. The rescue of Judah from the Assyrian threat: God's wonderful deliverance

a. The message of judgment against King Sennacherib

   1) He would flee Jerusalem, the Virgin Daughter (not violate, rape the city)

   2) He would be mocked by the Virgin Daughter as he fled

b. The reason for the judgment upon Sennacherib

   1) He had ridiculed & blasphemed the Holy One of Israel

   2) He had heaped insults on the LORD

   3) He thought himself above all men, boasting in his military power
- To conquer all mountains: Nations
- To cut down the tallest trees: Leaders
- To reach the farthest parts of the earth

- To dig wells & drink fresh water of foreign lands
- To dry up the rivers of Egypt when he set foot in the country

c. The basic truth not yet learned by the Assyrian king: God is sovereign over all men & nations

   1) God Himself had ordained Assyria's conquests & rise to superpower status

   2) God had weakened the people conquered by Assyria: Used Assyria to judge—discipline & correct—Israel & other nations

   3) God knew every movement of Sennacherib & his rage against the LORD

---

20 Now therefore, O LORD our God, save us from his hand, that all the kingdoms of the earth may know that thou *art* the LORD, *even* thou only. 21 Then Isaiah the son of Amoz sent unto Hezekiah, saying, Thus saith the LORD God of Israel, Whereas thou hast prayed to me against Sennacherib king of Assyria: 22 This *is* the word which the LORD hath spoken concerning him; The virgin, the daughter of Zion, hath despised thee, *and* laughed thee to scorn; the daughter of Jerusalem hath shaken her head at thee. 23 Whom hast thou reproached and blasphemed? and against whom hast thou exalted *thy* voice, and lifted up thine eyes on high? *even* against the Holy One of Israel. 24 By thy servants hast thou reproached the Lord, and hast said, By the multitude of my chariots am I come up to the height of the mountains, to the sides of Lebanon; and I will cut down the tall cedars thereof, *and* the choice fir trees thereof: and I will enter into the height of his border, *and* the forest of his Carmel. 25 I have digged, and drunk water; and with the sole of my feet have I dried up all the rivers of the besieged places. 26 Hast thou not heard long ago, *how* I have done it; *and* of ancient times, that I have formed it? now have I brought it to pass, that thou shouldest be to lay waste defenced cities *into* ruinous heaps. 27 Therefore their inhabitants *were* of small power, they were dismayed and confounded: they were *as* the grass of the field, and *as* the green herb, *as* the grass on the housetops, and *as corn* blasted before it be grown up. 28 But I know thy abode, and thy going out, and thy coming in, and thy rage against me.

---

29 Because thy rage against me, and thy tumult, is come up into mine ears, therefore will I put my hook in thy nose, and my bridle in thy lips, and I will turn thee back by the way by which thou camest. 30 And this *shall be* a sign unto thee, Ye shall eat *this* year such as groweth of itself; and the second year that which springeth of the same: and in the third year sow ye, and reap, and plant vineyards, and eat the fruit thereof. 31 And the remnant that is escaped of the house of Judah shall again take root downward, and bear fruit upward: 32 For out of Jerusalem shall go forth a remnant, and they that escape out of mount Zion: the zeal of the LORD of hosts shall do this. 33 Therefore thus saith the LORD concerning the king of Assyria, He shall not come into this city, nor shoot an arrow there nor come before it with shields, nor cast a bank against it. 34 By the way that he came, by the same shall he return, and shall not come into this city, saith the LORD. 35 For I will defend this city to save it for mine own sake, and for my servant David's sake. 36 Then the angel of the LORD went forth, and smote in the camp of the Assyrians a hundred and fourscore and five thousand: and when they arose early in the morning, behold, they *were* all dead corpses. 37 So Sennacherib king of Assyria departed, and went and returned, and dwelt at Nineveh. 38 And it came to pass, as he was worshipping in the house of Nisroch his god, that Adrammelech and Sharezer his sons smote him with the sword; and they escaped into the land of Armenia: and Esar-haddon his son reigned in his stead.

---

d. The LORD's judgment pronounced upon Sennacherib
   1) He would be defeated, subdued like an animal, & returned to his own land
   2) The reason: His rage & arrogance toward God

e. The LORD's sign of assurance given to Hezekiah
   1) Judah would recover from the invasion after two years: Would sow & reap in the third year

   2) Judah would be left with a remnant, survivors who would experience a miraculous growth in population

- God would give a remnant out of Jerusalem, Is.10:20-23 (refers both to that day & to the day of the Messiah, Ro.11:5)
- God's zeal would do this

f. The clear, unmistakable declaration of God: The Assyrian king would not conquer Jerusalem
   1) Would not enter the city, attack, shoot an arrow, nor lay a siege ramp
   2) Would return to his own land
   3) Would not enter Jerusalem: A strong reemphasis
   4) The reason: The city would be defended by God Himself—for His own honor & for the sake of David

g. The judgment of God against Assyria & Sennacherib: The prophecy of Isaiah fulfilled
   1) The angel of the LORD went into the Assyrian camp & executed 185,000 soldiers during the night
   2) The Assyrian survivors— stunned, perplexed— broke camp & withdrew, then returned to Nineveh & stayed there
   3) The Assyrian king Sennacherib was later assassinated while worshipping his false god
- Was killed by his two sons, Adrammelech & Sharezer
- Was succeeded by his son Esarhaddon

DIVISION IV

THE TURNING POINT OF HEZEKIAH'S REIGN: A SHIFT FROM THE THREAT OF ASSYRIA TO THE CAPTIVITY OF JUDAH BY BABYLON, 36:1–39:8

A. The End of the Assyrian Threat: God's Power to Deliver His People, 36:1–37:38

(36:1–37:38) **Introduction**: When facing a serious trial, how often has fear gripped your heart, buckled your knees, and dissolved your courage? How often have you been gripped with despair or felt utter discouragement? And when facing a temptation, has your will to withstand ever collapsed? Have you given in to seduction when the appeal was just too enticing? Have you allowed your flesh to be aroused, your passion to run wild to the point that you could no longer resist or refuse?

Standing tall and holding fast for the LORD—being a real man or woman—is the great practical lesson of this Scripture. This is the story of Hezekiah, perhaps the greatest king who ever ruled the Southern Kingdom of Judah. In God's sovereignty, He knew that a strong, righteous king would need to be upon the throne of Judah right after the fall of Israel, the Northern Kingdom, under the assault of Assyria. Thus, God moved to turn the heart of a young man to the LORD, a young man who was reared in one of the most ungodly environments imaginable. Although the godly reign of Hezekiah would not stop the tide of wickedness from flowing throughout Judah, it would significantly delay the hand of God's judgment from falling upon them. The Southern Kingdom of Judah would not fall to Babylon for over 100 years. Note this fact: after the fall of the Northern Kingdom, the Southern Kingdom of Judah is often given the ancient name of Israel. This fact needs to be kept in mind as the remaining kings are studied. This is, *The End of the Assyrian Threat: God's Power to Deliver His People*, 36:1–37:38.

1. The Assyrian invasion of Judah by King Sennacherib: a decision demanded—trust the power of man or of God (36:1-22).
2. The LORD's assurance of deliverance: God's promise to the believer (37:1-13).
3. Hezekiah's desperate prayer for deliverance: seeking the LORD for help (37:14-20).
4. The rescue of Judah from the Assyrian threat: God's wonderful deliverance (37:21-38).

---

1 (36:1-22) **Persecution, by Whom, Enemies—Oppression, by Whom, Spiritual Enemies—Enemies, Works of, Threats and Oppression—Judah, Wars of, Against Assyria—Assyria, Invasion of Judah**: because of Hezekiah's rebellion against Assyria and his military moves against the Philistines, the Assyrians eventually turned their attention to Hezekiah, king of the Southern Kingdom of Judah. Having conquered all of the Northern Kingdom, the Assyrians now invaded Judah. The invasion took place in the fourteenth year of King Hezekiah's reign, but note: Hezekiah had expected the invasion by the Assyrians. He had prepared Jerusalem by fortifying the capital, by making more weapons for the army, and by organizing the citizens' army. He went so far as to stop up the springs outside the city in order to block or conceal the water supply from the Assyrians (2 Chr.32:1-6). A dramatic, suspenseful account of Assyria's invasion and threats against Judah is pictured:

OUTLINE	SCRIPTURE	SCRIPTURE	OUTLINE
1. The Assyrian invasion of Judah by King Sennacherib: A decision demanded—trust the power of man or of God	Now it came to pass in the fourteenth year of king Hezekiah, *that* Sennacherib king of Assyria came up against all the defenced cities of Judah, and took them.	*they are but* vain words) *I have* counsel and strength for war: now on whom dost thou trust, that thou rebellest against me?	claim of military strength: His claim was empty, his army weak
a. The king's easy conquest of all the fortified cities			
b. The Assyrian's siege of Jerusalem & the demand for surrender	2 And the king of Assyria sent Rabshakeh from Lachish to Jerusalem unto king Hezekiah with a great army. And he stood by the conduit of the upper pool in the highway of the fuller's field.	6 Lo, thou trustest in the staff of this broken reed, on Egypt; whereon if a man lean, it will go into his hand, and pierce it: so *is* Pharaoh king of Egypt to all that trust in him.	• Questioned Hezekiah's dependence on Egypt: In war, Egypt would splinter like a reed & cause the destruction of any ally leaning upon it
1) They camped at the city's water source			
2) They summoned Hezekiah for negotiations, but he sent three court officials instead	3 Then came forth unto him Eliakim, Hilkiah's son, which was over the house, and Shebna the scribe, and Joah, Asaph's son, the recorder.	7 But if thou say to me, We trust in the LORD our God: *is it* not he, whose high places and whose altars Hezekiah hath taken away, and said to Judah and to Jerusalem, Ye shall worship before this altar?	• Questioned Hezekiah's dependence on the LORD: Claimed must have displeased the LORD by destroying the high places & altars of worship (a misunderstanding of God & idolatry)
3) The Assyrian field commander—as spokesman for the "great king" of Assyria—questioned Hezekiah's tactics of & why he was so confident	4 And Rabshakeh said unto them, Say ye now to Hezekiah, Thus saith the great king, the king of Assyria, What confidence is this wherein thou trustest?	8 Now therefore give pledges, I pray thee, to my master the king of Assyria, and I will give thee two thousand horses, if thou be able	4) The field commander demanded Hezekiah's surrender
• Questioned Hezekiah's	5 I say, *sayest thou*, (but		• Because of the weakness of Judah's army: Had

OUTLINE	SCRIPTURE	SCRIPTURE	OUTLINE
few horses & horsemen • Because the whole army of Judah could not stand against one of Assyria's least ranking officers • Because Judah could not depend upon Egypt • Because even the LORD Himself was now against Judah: The Lord had instructed Assyria's king to attack & destroy the nation c. The Judean official's request for the Assyrian envoys to speak in Aramaic, not Hebrew: Feared that despair would grip the heart of the crowd who were standing on the wall listening to the negotiations 1) The commander refused: Realized the importance of propaganda in destroying the people's confidence 2) The commander stated that his message was for all the people, not just the leaders: The people would suffer the most if Assyria attacked d. The commander's second speech: Addressed more to the crowd standing nearby 1) He appealed for them to hear the "great king" 2) He encouraged them to oppose Hezekiah • Hezekiah could not deliver them • Hezekiah was only deceiving them by persuading them to trust the LORD: The LORD	on thy part to set riders upon them. 9 How then wilt thou turn away the face of one captain of the least of my master's servants, and put thy trust on Egypt for chariots and for horsemen? 10 And am I now come up without the LORD against this land to destroy it? the LORD said unto me, Go up against this land, and destroy it. 11 Then said Eliakim and Shebna and Joah unto Rabshakeh, Speak, I pray thee, unto thy servants in the Syrian language; for we understand it: and speak not to us in the Jews' language, in the ears of the people that are on the wall. 12 But Rabshakeh said, Hath my master sent me to thy master and to thee to speak these words? hath he not sent me to the men that sit upon the wall, that they may eat their own dung, and drink their own piss with you? 13 Then Rabshakeh stood, and cried with a loud voice in the Jews' language, and said, Hear ye the words of the great king, the king of Assyria. 14 Thus saith the king, Let not Hezekiah deceive you: for he shall not be able to deliver you. 15 Neither let Hezekiah make you trust in the LORD, saying, The LORD will surely deliver us: this city shall not be delivered into the hand of	the king of Assyria. 16 Hearken not to Hezekiah: for thus saith the king of Assyria, Make *an agreement* with me *by* a present, and come out to me: and eat ye every one of his vine, and every one of his fig tree, and drink ye every one the waters of his own cistern; 17 Until I come and take you away to a land like your own land, a land of corn and wine, a land of bread and vineyards. 18 *Beware* lest Hezekiah persuade you, saying, The LORD will deliver us. Hath any of the gods of the nations delivered his land out of the hand of the king of Assyria? 19 Where *are* the gods of Hamath and Arphad? where *are* the gods of Sepharvaim? and have they delivered Samaria out of my hand? 20 Who *are they* among all the gods of these lands, that have delivered their land out of my hand, that the LORD should deliver Jerusalem out of my hand? 21 But they held their peace, and answered him not a word: for the king's commandment was, saying, Answer him not. 22 Then came Eliakim, the son of Hilkiah, that *was* over the household, and Shebna the scribe, and Joah, the son of Asaph, the recorder, to Hezekiah with *their* clothes rent, and told him the words of Rabshakeh.	*would not* deliver them 3) He challenged them to surrender & make peace: Because life would be far better under Assyrian rule • They would have plenty to eat & drink (not dung & urine as they would under a siege) • They would be transported to a fruitful land just like their own 4) He challenged them to choose life, not death • They must not listen to Hezekiah • They were being misled by his promise of the LORD's deliverance 5) He threatened the people with the power of Assyria • No nation had ever been delivered from Assyria, not by any god • Not even the LORD would be able to deliver Jerusalem (or Judah) from an Assyrian attack e. The response to the Assyrian threats 1) The people kept silent 2) The royal officials carried their report to Hezekiah: Approached him with torn clothes, a sign of distress & grief

a. The military campaign launched by Assyria against the western world of that time was huge. Thus, they easily conquered all the fortified cities of Judah (36:1). According to the historical records of Sennacherib, he captured 46 fortified cities, numerous small towns or villages; captured over 200,000 people; and, through his siege, trapped Hezekiah in Jerusalem just "like a caged bird."[1]

b. Remaining behind at Lachish with the main army, Sennacherib sent an envoy with a large number of troops to position a blockade around Jerusalem (vv.2-10). With this action, the Assyrian king was initiating a propaganda war of intimidation, threatening and demanding that Hezekiah surrender Jerusalem to the Assyrians. After setting up the siege around the capital, the three officials sent by Sennacherib approached the city and stopped at the aqueduct of the upper pool (v.2). Note that the location of the canal or aqueduct was called the *Washerman's Field*, which means that it was a popular place for residents to wash their clothes. Obviously, this spot was within earshot of the city walls, for the Assyrian officials called out and summoned Hezekiah to join them in negotiations for surrender. But instead of joining the negotiations himself, Hezekiah sent three royal officials whose positions would match those of the Assyrian officials. By this action, Hezekiah was insisting on being treated as an equal to the Assyrian king. Had the king of Assyria himself come for negotiations, Hezekiah no doubt would have carried out the negotiations personally, king to king.

Standing face-to-face with the Judean negotiators, the Assyrian commander challenged the tactics of Hezekiah and asked why he was so confident (vv.4-7). Claiming that he was the personal spokesman for the *great king* of Assyria, he questioned three of Hezekiah's actions:

---

[1] Daniel David Luckenbill. *Ancient Records of Assyria and Babylonia,* Vol.2. (London, ENG: Histories & Mysteries of Man Ltd., 1989), p.120.

⇒ He cast doubt on Hezekiah's claim of military strength, alleging that Hezekiah's words were empty and the Judean army was weak (v.4).

⇒ He also scoffed at Hezekiah's dependence upon Egypt, claiming that in an actual war, Egypt would splinter like a reed and cause the defeat of any ally who was leaning upon it (v.6).

⇒ Continuing to belittle Hezekiah, the Assyrian spokesman questioned Hezekiah's dependence on the LORD (v.7). But note that he showed a complete misunderstanding of God and of idolatry, for he claimed that Hezekiah had displeased the LORD by destroying the high places and altars of worship throughout Judah and Jerusalem.

Having questioned Hezekiah's military strength, his alliance with Egypt, and his dependence on the LORD, the Assyrian commander then demanded that Hezekiah surrender (vv.8-10). Obviously a skilled negotiator, the commander gave four strong reasons why Judah's king should concede defeat:

⇒ Hezekiah should surrender because of the weakness of Judah's army. Ridiculing the fact that Judah had few horses and horsemen, the commander declared that he would give 2,000 horses to Judah if they could put riders on them.

⇒ Hezekiah should surrender because the whole army of Judah could not defend itself against one of Assyria's least ranking officers (v.9).

⇒ Hezekiah should surrender because Judah could not depend upon Egypt.

⇒ Hezekiah should surrender because even the LORD Himself was now against Judah (v.10).

Note that the commander declared that the LORD had actually instructed Assyria's king to attack Judah and destroy the nation. No doubt this struck fear in those who overheard the claim. Keep in mind that the Northern Kingdom of Israel had already fallen to Assyria. Could God actually be behind the Assyrian invasion, using the Assyrians as an instrument of His judgment?

c. When it was time for the Judean officials to speak, they surprisingly requested that the Assyrian envoy speak in Aramaic, not in Hebrew (vv.11-12). There was a twofold reason for this:

⇒ Aramaic was the international language for diplomacy and commercial transactions throughout western Asia.

⇒ The Judean people standing on the wall could overhear the negotiations.[2] By overhearing the threats of the Assyrian envoys spoken in their own Hebrew language, there was the danger that the crowd would be gripped with fear and despair.

But the Assyrian commander refused, for he realized the importance of propaganda, of destroying the people's confidence. Even in responding to the Judean officials he sought to turn the hearts of the people on the wall. He stated that his message was for all the people and not just for leaders because the people themselves would suffer the most if Assyria attacked. What a skillful negotiator the Assyrians had!

d. Still the commander was not through with his propaganda: launching a second major speech, he addressed his words more to the crowd standing nearby than to the Judean officials (vv.13-20). Shouting an appeal for them to hear the *great king*, he encouraged the people to oppose Hezekiah, to actually instigate a revolt against him. He declared that Hezekiah could not deliver them from the Assyrian forces, that the king was only deceiving them by persuading them to trust the LORD, for the LORD would not deliver them (vv.13-15).

Still shouting out to the crowd on the wall, he challenged them to surrender and make a peace treaty. He claimed life would be far better for them under Assyrian rule (vv.16-17). Under the Assyrians they would have plenty to eat and drink; whereas if they continued their opposition, they would end up eating their own filth and drinking their own urine (v.12). If they surrendered, though, they would be transplanted to another fruitful land, a land just like their own there in Judah.

Finally, the commander challenged the people to make a decision: to choose life, not death (v.18). To choose life, they must not listen to Hezekiah, for he was misleading them by his promise of the LORD's deliverance.

In closing his second speech he threatened the people with the power of Assyria (vv.19-20). He bombarded them with provoking thoughts, laying out three disturbing scenarios:

⇒ No nation had ever been delivered from Assyria, not by any god.

⇒ No god was able to deliver Samaria, that is, the Northern Kingdom of Israel.

⇒ How, then, could the LORD deliver Jerusalem from the hand of the Assyrians?

e. Note the response of the people to the Assyrian threats: they kept silent (vv.21-22). Concluding the negotiations, the royal officials of Judah carried their report to Hezekiah. But note how they approached him: with torn clothes, a sign of distress and grief.

Thought 1. Hezekiah stood fast for the LORD, stood fast against a brutal and murderous enemy. And just think: the enemy was the superpower of that day with a far superior military force. Sweeping all across much of the known world, the Assyrians had already conquered and subjected nation after nation under their rule. Their conquest had even included the Northern Kingdom of Israel and all the cities of Judah except Jerusalem itself. Now the Assyrians were standing at the gates of Jerusalem, threatening to totally destroy the capital and to exile all its citizens, scattering them all over the world. But even with the enemy at the gate threatening utter destruction, Hezekiah held fast to his faith in the LORD and stood strongly against the enemies of God and God's people.

What a living, dynamic example for us! No matter what may confront us—no matter how terrible the trial or temptation, the pressure or distress, the threat or ridicule, the persecution or abuse, we must stand fast for the LORD. Standing up, standing tall, being a real man or woman for the LORD is one of the great needs of our day. We are not to be weaklings. Our knees are not to buckle. Our courage is not to collapse. Our hearts are not to shrink back. We are to persevere, endure, stand fast for the LORD, trusting His Spirit to empower us.

---

2 Russell Dilday. *1, 2 Kings*. "Mastering the Old Testament," Vol.9. (Dallas, TX: Word Publishing, 1987), p.437.

"And ye shall be hated of all *men* for my name's sake: but he that endureth to the end shall be saved" (Mt.10:22).

"Therefore, my beloved brethren, be ye stedfast, unmovable, always abounding in the work of the Lord, forasmuch as ye know that your labour is not in vain in the Lord" (1 Co.15:58).

"Stand fast therefore in the liberty wherewith Christ hath made us free, and be not entangled again with the yoke of bondage" (Ga.5:1).

"And let us not be weary in well doing: for in due season we shall reap, if we faint not" (Ga.6:9).

"Only let your conversation [behavior, conduct] be as it becometh the gospel of Christ: that whether I come and see you, or else be absent, I may hear of your affairs, that ye stand fast in one spirit, with one mind striving together for the faith of the gospel" (Ph.1:27).

"Prove all things; hold fast that which is good. Abstain from all appearance of evil. And the very God of peace sanctify you wholly; and *I pray God* your whole spirit and soul and body be preserved blameless unto the coming of our Lord Jesus Christ" (1 Th.5:21-23).

"Seeing then that we have a great high priest, that is passed into the heavens, Jesus the Son of God, let us hold fast *our* profession" (He.4:14).

"Let us hold fast the profession of *our* faith without wavering; (for he *is* faithful that promised;)" (He.10:23).

"Wherefore seeing we also are compassed about with so great a cloud of witnesses, let us lay aside every weight, and the sin which doth so easily beset *us,* and let us run with patience the race that is set before us" (He.12:1).

"Wherefore gird up the loins of your mind, be sober, and hope to the end for the grace that is to be brought unto you at the revelation of Jesus Christ" (1 Pe.1:13).

"Be sober, be vigilant; because your adversary the devil, as a roaring lion, walketh about, seeking whom he may devour: Whom resist stedfast in the faith, knowing that the same afflictions are accomplished in your brethren that are in the world" (1 Pe.5:8-9).

"Ye therefore, beloved, seeing ye know *these things* before, beware lest ye also, being led away with the error of the wicked, fall from your own stedfastness. But grow in grace, and *in* the knowledge of our Lord and Saviour Jesus Christ. To him *be* glory both now and for ever. Amen" (2 Pe.3:17-18).

"Remember therefore how thou hast received and heard, and hold fast, and repent. If therefore thou shalt not watch, I will come on thee as a thief, and thou shalt not know what hour I will come upon thee" (Re.3:3).

"Behold, I come quickly: hold that fast which thou hast, that no man take thy crown" (Re.3:11).

"But cleave unto the LORD your God, as ye have done unto this day" (Jos.23:8).

"If iniquity *be* in thine hand, put it far away, and let not wickedness dwell in thy tabernacles. For then shalt thou lift up thy face without spot; yea, thou shalt be stedfast, and shalt not fear" (Jb.11:14-15).

---

2 (37:1-13) **Assurance, of Deliverance, Example of—Promises, of God, Deliverance, Example of—God, Deliverance of—Hezekiah, Deliverance from Assyria, Promised**: the LORD gave a wonderful assurance to Hezekiah, the assurance that the king and his people would be delivered from the invading Assyrians. Remember what had happened years earlier: Hezekiah's father Ahaz had surrendered to Assyria, subjugating the nation as a *vassal state* under the Assyrian government. This meant that Ahaz was able to remain on king of Judah and that the people were allowed to keep their properties, but they were forced to pay a large tribute or tax to Assyria (see outline and note—2 K.16:1-20 for more discussion). Once Hezekiah became king, and because of his commitment to the LORD, he revolted against the oppressive domination of the Assyrians. This is what had aroused King Sennacherib of Assyria to invade Judah and to lay siege to the capital Jerusalem (36:1-22). Envoys from the Assyrian king had just confronted representatives sent by Hezekiah, demanding that Hezekiah unconditionally surrender to the Assyrian forces. Using every intimidating threat known to negotiators, the Assyrian envoy demanded that Hezekiah either choose death or surrender (36:18-20). While his own royal officials were carrying on the negotiations, King Hezekiah was anxiously waiting back in the palace for their return. With this background, note what happened:

OUTLINE	SCRIPTURE	SCRIPTURE	OUTLINE
2. The LORD's assurance of deliverance: God's promise to the believer	And it came to pass, when king Hezekiah heard *it,* that he rent his clothes, and covered himself with sackcloth, and went into the house of the LORD.	Thus saith Hezekiah, This day *is* a day of trouble, and of rebuke, and of blasphemy: for the children are come to the birth, and *there is* not strength to bring forth.	• That this was a black day of trouble, rebuke, & disgrace for Judah (due to their sins)
a. The distress of Hezekiah over the report, 36:22			
b. The appeal of Hezekiah to the prophet Isaiah	2 And he sent Eliakim, who *was* over the household, and Shebna the scribe, and the elders of the priests covered with sackcloth, unto Isaiah the prophet the son of Amoz.	4 It may be the LORD thy God will hear the words of Rabshakeh, whom the king of Assyria his master hath sent to reproach the living God, and will reprove the words	• That perhaps the LORD had heard the Assyrian king ridicule & defy the name of the living God
1) He sent a delegation to Isaiah, seeking prayer & some word from the LORD			
2) He sent this message	3 And they said unto him,	which the LORD thy God hath	• That Isaiah needed to

OUTLINE	SCRIPTURE	SCRIPTURE	OUTLINE
pray for those still surviving c. The concise & comforting prediction by Isaiah: Proclaimed the promise of God, a message of hope 1) The people & Hezekiah were not to fear the threats & blasphemous words of Assyria's king 2) The LORD would cause Sennacherib to return home: Once there, he would face a violent death by being cut down with a sword d. The beginning of Isaiah's prophecy: Began to take shape 1) The Assyrian commander withdrew to help his king fight against Libnah 2) The Assyrian king had received a report that Egypt was rapidly march-	heard: wherefore lift up *thy* prayer for the remnant that is left. 5 So the servants of king Hezekiah came to Isaiah. 6 And Isaiah said unto them, Thus shall ye say unto your master, Thus saith the LORD, Be not afraid of the words that thou hast heard, wherewith the servants of the king of Assyria have blasphemed me. 7 Behold, I will send a blast upon him, and he shall hear a rumour, and return to his own land; and I will cause him to fall by the sword in his own land. 8 So Rabshakeh returned, and found the king of Assyria warring against Libnah: for he had heard that he was departed from Lachish. 9 And he heard say concerning Tirhakah king of Ethiopia, He is come forth to	make war with thee. And when he heard *it,* he sent messengers to Hezekiah, saying, 10 Thus shall ye speak to Hezekiah king of Judah, saying, Let not thy God, in whom thou trustest, deceive thee, saying, Jerusalem shall not be given into the hand of the king of Assyria. 11 Behold, thou hast heard what the kings of Assyria have done to all lands by destroying them utterly; and shalt thou be delivered? 12 Have the gods of the nations delivered them which my fathers have destroyed, *as* Gozan, and Haran, and Rezeph, and the children of Eden which *were* in Telassar? 13 Where *is* the king of Hamath, and the king of Arphad, and the king of the city of Sepharvaim, Hena, and Ivah?	ing to fight against him e. The Assyrian king's second message sent to Hezekiah 1) He stressed the absurdity of Hezekiah's trust in his God to deliver Jerusalem 2) He scoffed at Hezekiah • Reminded him what Assyria had done to all the countries they had attacked • Asked why Judah was different: Declared no god had delivered any nation from the power of Assyria 3) He threatened Hezekiah personally: Asked where the kings of the conquered nations were

a. When Hezekiah's negotiators returned and gave their report on the Assyrian threats and their ridicule of the LORD, Hezekiah was filled with deep distress. Tearing his clothes and putting on sackcloth as symbols of repentance and grief, Hezekiah went into the temple to seek the face of the LORD (37:1). Knowing that the troops within Jerusalem could not stand against the mighty army of Assyria, he recognized there was nothing in his power he could do to save the people. Thus, he took the only step that could save them: he turned to the LORD for help.

b. But before entering the temple, Hezekiah sent a delegation to make an appeal to the prophet Isaiah, seeking prayer and some word from the LORD (vv.2-4). Three points were included in the message sent by the king to the prophet:

⇒ He stated that this was a black day for Judah, a day of trouble, rebuke, and disgrace. The LORD was obviously chastising and correcting them for their sins (v.3; He.12:9-15). Note the illustration used by Hezekiah to describe his inability to deliver the people: just as mothers at times do not have the strength to deliver their children, so he and Jerusalem did not have the power to deliver themselves from Assyria.

⇒ He said that perhaps the LORD had heard the Assyrian king ridicule and defy the name of the living God (v.4).

⇒ He appealed to Isaiah for prayer, prayer for all who still survived.

c. Responding to the king's appeal, Isaiah sent back a concise and comforting prediction from God, a wonderful promise and message of hope (vv.5-7). The people and Hezekiah were not to fear the threats and blasphemous words of Assyria's king. The LORD Himself had indeed heard the commander's threats against Jerusalem and his blasphemy against the Name of the LORD. The LORD Himself would call Sennacherib to return home to his own country, and once there he would face a violent death by being cut down with a sword (v.7).

d. Immediately after the prediction by Isaiah, God's promise to His people began to take shape (vv.8-9). The Assyrian commander, after hearing that Sennacherib had left Lachish to join the fighting against Libnah, left Jerusalem to give his report. But when he reached Sennacherib, he discovered that the Assyrian king had received a disturbing report from elsewhere. Supposedly, Egypt was rapidly marching up the Philistine coast to join in the fight against the Assyrians.

e. To prevent Judah from joining the forces that were mobilizing against him, the Assyrian king quickly sent a second message to Hezekiah (vv.9-13). His message stressed the absurdity of Hezekiah's trust in God to deliver Jerusalem. Again threatening Hezekiah, he reminded the king what Assyria had done to all the countries they had attacked. Then he asked why Hezekiah thought Judah would be any different, declaring that no god had delivered any nation from the power of Assyria (vv.11-12). Finally, he threatened Hezekiah personally, asking where all the kings of the conquered nations were (v.13). The implication was clear: all of the kings who had opposed Assyria had died violent deaths.

Thought 1. Think of the wonderful assurance God gave to Hezekiah. Facing impossible odds and a hopeless situation, the king was utterly helpless to deliver himself or his people. But God stepped forth in the person of His prophet Isaiah and gave Hezekiah the promise of deliverance.

Nothing compares to the assurance that God gives us—His people—in times of need. Above all else, when the crises of life confront us, the thing most needed is the comfort and reassurance that only God can give. God's assurance builds confidence, courage, and security within us. And when God assures us of His presence and promises, our hearts are encouraged, inspired, persuaded, and fulfilled. Listen to some of the great assurances of God:

"Being confident of this very thing, that he which hath begun a good work in you will perform *it* until the day of Jesus Christ" (Ph.1:6).

"That their hearts might be comforted, being knit together in love, and unto all riches of the full assurance of understanding, to the acknowledgement of the mystery of God, and of the Father, and of Christ" (Col.2:2).

"For our gospel came not unto you in word only, but also in power, and in the Holy Ghost, and in much assurance; as ye know what manner of men we were among you for your sake" (1 Th.1:5).

"For the which cause I also suffer these things: nevertheless I am not ashamed: for I know whom I have believed, and am persuaded that he is able to keep that which I have committed unto him against that day" (2 Ti.1:12).

"And the Lord shall deliver me from every evil work, and will preserve *me* unto his heavenly kingdom: to whom *be* glory for ever and ever. Amen" (2 Ti.4:18).

"Let us draw near with a true heart in full assurance of faith, having our hearts sprinkled from an evil conscience, and our bodies washed with pure water" (He.10:22).

"And hereby we do know that we know him, if we keep his commandments" (1 Jn.2:3).

"And hereby we know that we are of the truth, and shall assure our hearts before him" (1 Jn.3:19).

"Hereby know we that we dwell in him, and he in us, because he hath given us of his Spirit" (1 Jn.4:13).

"And this is the record, that God hath given to us eternal life, and this life is in his Son. He that hath the Son hath life; *and* he that hath not the Son of God hath not life. These things have I written unto you that believe on the name of the Son of God; that ye may know that ye have eternal life, and that ye may believe on the name of the Son of God" (1 Jn.5:11-13).

"Now unto him that is able to keep you from falling, and to present *you* faultless before the presence of his glory with exceeding joy, To the only wise God our Saviour, *be* glory and majesty, dominion and power, both now and ever. Amen" (Jude 24-25).

3 (37:14-20) **Seeking, for Deliverance—Deliverance, Seeking, Example of—Prayer, for Deliverance, Example of—Desperation, Answer to, Prayer, Example of—Distress, Answer to, Prayer—Grief, Answer to, Prayer—Hezekiah, Prayer of, for Deliverance**: in response to the second message from the Assyrian king, Hezekiah again took his desperate situation to the LORD in prayer. But this time he did not seek the LORD's word through Isaiah the prophet. Under intense pressure and strain, he went directly to the LORD in prayer.

OUTLINE	SCRIPTURE	SCRIPTURE	OUTLINE
3. Hezekiah's desperate prayer for deliverance: Seeking the LORD for help	14 And Hezekiah received the letter from the hand of the messengers, and read it: and Hezekiah went up unto the house of the LORD, and spread it before the LORD.	the words of Sennacherib, which hath sent to reproach the living God.	ib had insulted the living God
a. He spread the letter out before the LORD in the temple: A threefold prayer		18 Of a truth, LORD, the kings of Assyria have laid waste all the nations, and their countries,	2) He acknowledged the power & conquests of Assyria
b. He declared God's greatness	15 And Hezekiah prayed unto the LORD, saying,	19 And have cast their gods into the fire: for they *were* no gods, but the work of men's hands, wood and stone: therefore they have destroyed them.	3) He declared that the false gods of the conquered nations could not have saved them: They were only lifeless & powerless idols made by men's hands
1) He is the LORD, the God of Israel	16 O LORD of hosts, God of Israel, that dwellest *between* the cherubims, thou *art* the God, *even* thou alone, of all the kingdoms of the earth: thou hast made heaven and earth.		
2) He alone is God over all kingdoms			
3) He is the Creator			
c. He explained the problem	17 Incline thine ear, O LORD, and hear; open thine eyes, O LORD, and see: and hear all	20 Now therefore, O LORD our God, save us from his hand, that all the kingdoms of the earth may know that thou *art* the LORD, *even* thou only.	d. He cried for deliverance & expressed his major concern: That all nations know that the LORD alone is God
1) He pleaded for the LORD to notice how Sennacher-			

a. Once again, Hezekiah went up to the temple and humbled himself as a child before the LORD (v.14). Spreading out the letter from the Assyrian king, he laid it before the LORD and began to pour out his soul, crying for deliverance. Note that he offered up a threefold prayer.

b. First, Hezekiah declared God's greatness (v.16). Addressing the LORD as the God of Israel who is enthroned between the cherubim of the Ark, Hezekiah acknowledged that the LORD alone is God over all the kingdoms of the earth. He alone is the Supreme Creator who has made heaven and earth.

c. Second, Hezekiah explained the problem confronting him and the Judeans (vv.17-19). Yet note Hezekiah's major concern, what he stressed first: the insults launched against the LORD by the Assyrians. He pleaded for the LORD to open His eyes, to notice how the Assyrian king Sennacherib had insulted the living God. He then acknowledged the power and conquests of Assyria, how they had destroyed nation after nation. Hezekiah next declared a significant truth: the false gods of the conquered nations could not have saved them, for they were only lifeless, powerless idols made by men's hands (v.19).

d. Third, Hezekiah cried out for the LORD God to deliver him and his people from the hand of the Assyrians. But note why: that all the kingdoms of the earth may know that the LORD alone is God (v.20).

Thought 1. When crises confront us—unexpected, desperate, traumatic, or tragic situations—we have at our disposal a powerful resource: prayer. We have access into the very presence of the living God Himself. The door into God's presence is always open, and God is always available to help us—whether by miraculous deliverance or an infusion of strength to walk through the crisis. He will lead, guide, and strengthen us to deal with any difficult problem, even through the crisis of death itself. Prayer, seeking and calling upon the Name of the LORD, is always available to us. This is the reason the LORD has established prayer as the most powerful law throughout the universe. Through the *law of prayer,* God operates and moves to meet the needs of His people. Listen to what the Word of God says about prayer and seeking His face for help:

"Therefore I say unto you, What things soever ye desire, when ye pray, believe that ye receive *them,* and ye shall have *them*" (Mk.11:24).

"For every one that asketh receiveth; and he that seeketh findeth; and to him that knocketh it shall be opened" (Lu.11:10).

"If ye abide in me, and my words abide in you, ye shall ask what ye will, and it shall be done unto you" (Jn.15:7).

"Hitherto have ye asked nothing in my name: ask, and ye shall receive, that your joy may be full" (Jn.16:24).

"Is any among you afflicted? let him pray. Is any merry? let him sing psalms. Is any sick among you? let him call for the elders of the church; and let them pray over him, anointing him with oil in the name of the Lord" (Js.5:13-14).

"And whatsoever we ask, we receive of him, because we keep his commandments, and do those things that are pleasing in his sight" (1 Jn.3:22).

"But if from thence thou shalt seek the LORD thy God, thou shalt find *him,* if thou seek him with all thy heart and with all thy soul" (De.4:29).

"Seek the LORD and his strength, seek his face continually" (1 Chr.16:11).

"If my people, which are called by my name, shall humble themselves, and pray, and seek my face, and turn from their wicked ways; then will I hear from heaven, and will forgive their sin, and will heal their land" (2 Chr.7:14).

"Thou shalt not be afraid for the terror by night; *nor* for the arrow *that* flieth by day" (Ps.91:5).

"Seek the LORD, and his strength: seek his face evermore" (Ps.105:4).

"Seek ye the LORD while he may be found, call ye upon him while he is near" (Is.55:6).

"And it shall come to pass, that before they call, I will answer; and while they are yet speaking, I will hear" (Is.65:24).

"And ye shall seek me, and find *me,* when ye shall search for me with all your heart" (Je.29:13).

"For thus saith the LORD unto the house of Israel, Seek ye me, and ye shall live" (Am.5:4).

"Seek ye the LORD, all ye meek of the earth, which have wrought his judgment; seek righteousness, seek meekness: it may be ye shall be hid in the day of the LORD'S anger" (Zep.2:3).

4 (37:21-38) **Deliverance, Promised, Example of—Promise, of Deliverance, Example of—Deliverance, of Judah, from the Assyrians—Hezekiah, Deliverance from, the Assyrians—Prayer, Answered, Example**: the LORD reinforced the wonderful promise he had given earlier to Hezekiah. The king and his people would be delivered from the Assyrian threat. Even while Hezekiah was in the temple praying, the LORD was giving a message to Isaiah to take to the king. Isaiah brought God's message—14 verses long—in the form of a poem or song, a *song of judgment* against the Assyrian king Sennacherib (vv.22-35). Then in the final three verses of the chapter, we see the judgment of God against King Sennacherib taking place just as the prophet Isaiah predicted (vv.36-38).

OUTLINE	SCRIPTURE	SCRIPTURE	OUTLINE
4. The rescue of Judah from the Assyrian threat: God's wonderful deliverance a. The message of judgment against King Sennacherib 1) He would flee Jerusalem, the Virgin Daughter (not violate, rape the city) 2) He would be mocked by the Virgin Daughter as he fled b. The reason for the judgment upon Sennacherib 1) He had ridiculed & blasphemed the Holy One of Israel	21 Then Isaiah the son of Amoz sent unto Hezekiah, saying, Thus saith the LORD God of Israel, Whereas thou hast prayed to me against Sennacherib king of Assyria: 22 This *is* the word which the LORD hath spoken concerning him; The virgin, the daughter of Zion, hath despised thee, *and* laughed thee to scorn; the daughter of Jerusalem hath shaken her head at thee. 23 Whom hast thou reproached and blasphemed? and against whom hast thou exalted *thy* voice, and lifted up thine eyes on high? *even*	against the Holy One of Israel. 24 By thy servants hast thou reproached the Lord, and hast said, By the multitude of my chariots am I come up to the height of the mountains, to the sides of Lebanon; and I will cut down the tall cedars thereof, *and* the choice fir trees thereof: and I will enter into the height of his border, *and* the forest of his Carmel. 25 I have digged, and drunk water; and with the sole of my feet have I dried up all the rivers of the besieged places. 26 Hast thou not heard long	 2) He had heaped insults on the LORD 3) He thought himself above all men, boasting in his military power • To conquer all mountains: Nations • To cut down the tallest trees: Leaders • To reach the farthest parts of the earth • To dig wells & drink fresh water of foreign lands • To dry up the rivers of Egypt when he set foot in the country

OUTLINE	SCRIPTURE	SCRIPTURE	OUTLINE

c. The basic truth not yet learned by the Assyrian king: God is sovereign over all men & nations
  1) God Himself had ordained Assyria's conquests & rise to superpower status
  2) God had weakened the people conquered by Assyria: Used Assyria to judge—discipline & correct—Israel & other nations
 	
  3) God knew every movement of Sennacherib & his rage against the LORD
 	
d. The LORD's judgment pronounced upon Sennacherib
  1) He would be defeated, subdued like an animal, & returned to his own land
  2) The reason: His rage & arrogance toward God
e. The LORD's sign of assurance given to Hezekiah
  1) Judah would recover from the invasion after two years: Would sow & reap in the third year
 	
  2) Judah would be left with a remnant, survivors who would experience a miraculous growth in population
  • God would give a rem-
	ago, *how* I have done it; *and* of ancient times, that I have formed it? now have I brought it to pass, that thou shouldest be to lay waste defenced cities *into* ruinous heaps.
	27 Therefore their inhabitants *were* of small power, they were dismayed and confounded: they were *as* the grass of the field, and *as* the green herb, *as* the grass on the housetops, and *as corn* blasted before it be grown up.
	28 But I know thy abode, and thy going out, and thy coming in, and thy rage against me.
	29 Because thy rage against me, and thy tumult, is come up into mine ears, therefore will I put my hook in thy nose, and my bridle in thy lips, and I will turn thee back by the way by which thou camest.
	30 And this *shall be* a sign unto thee, Ye shall eat *this* year such as groweth of itself; and the second year that which springeth of the same: and in the third year sow ye, and reap, and plant vineyards, and eat the fruit thereof.
	31 And the remnant that is escaped of the house of Judah shall again take root downward, and bear fruit upward:
		32 For out of Jerusalem shall go forth a remnant, and they that escape out of mount Zion: the zeal of the LORD of hosts shall do this.
		33 Therefore thus saith the LORD concerning the king of Assyria, He shall not come into this city, nor shoot an arrow there nor come before it with shields, nor cast a bank against it.
		34 By the way that he came, by the same shall he return, and shall not come into this city, saith the LORD.
		35 For I will defend this city to save it for mine own sake, and for my servant David's sake.
		36 Then the angel of the LORD went forth, and smote in the camp of the Assyrians a hundred and fourscore and five thousand: and when they arose early in the morning, behold, they *were* all dead corpses.
		37 So Sennacherib king of Assyria departed, and went and returned, and dwelt at Nineveh.
		38 And it came to pass, as he was worshipping in the house of Nisroch his god, that Adrammelech and Sharezer his sons smote him with the sword; and they escaped into the land of Armenia: and Esar-haddon his son reigned in his stead.
			nant out of Jerusalem, Is.10:20-23 (refers both to that day & to the day of the Messiah, Ro.11:5)
			  • God's zeal would do this
			f. The clear, unmistakable declaration of God: The Assyrian king would not conquer Jerusalem
			  1) Would not enter the city, attack, shoot an arrow, nor lay a siege ramp
			  2) Would return to his own land
			  3) Would not enter Jerusalem: A strong re-emphasis
			  4) The reason: The city would be defended by God Himself—for His own honor & for the sake of David
			g. The judgment of God against Assyria & Sennacherib: The prophecy of Isaiah fulfilled
			  1) The angel of the LORD went into the Assyrian camp & executed 185,000 soldiers during the night
			  2) The Assyrian survivors—stunned, perplexed—broke camp & withdrew, then returned to Nineveh & stayed there
			  3) The Assyrian king Sennacherib was later assassinated while worshipping his false god
			  • Was killed by his two sons, Adrammelech & Sharezer
			  • Was succeeded by his son Esarhaddon

a. Conveying God's message to Hezekiah, Isaiah declared the judgment of God against King Sennacherib (vv.21-22). The Assyrian king would flee Jerusalem; and as he fled, he would be mocked by the people. Note that Jerusalem is referred to as *The Virgin Daughter of Zion*, which simply means that no enemy had ever conquered or defiled the city, not since it had been made the capital of Israel by King David.

b. After giving the details of the judgment, Isaiah stated why Sennacherib was to be severely punished (vv.23-25). First, he had ridiculed and blasphemed the Holy One of Israel, the LORD God of the universe Himself. Second, he had heaped insults on the LORD, on the God who would not tolerate insults or rejection. Third, the king had considered himself above all men and gods, boasting in his military power (vv.24-25). He had taken great pride in himself, bragging…

- that he could conquer all mountains or nations
- that he could cut down the tallest trees, that is, leaders
- that he could reach the farthest parts of the earth
- that he could dig wells and drink the fresh water of foreign lands
- that he had the power to dry up the rivers of Egypt, that is, their defenses

c. God then charged the Assyrian king with being ignorant of a very basic truth. What was this truth? That the LORD Himself was sovereign over all men and nations (vv.26-28). It was God Himself who had ordained the rise and superpower status of Assyria. The LORD had used Assyria as an instrument to weaken, discipline, and correct other nations. Therefore, it was because of God alone that Assyria had been raised up by the LORD to become a world power. Judgment, discipline, and correction had to be carried out upon the nations of the world to stir them to turn and cry out to the LORD.

Furthermore, God was not only sovereign over Assyria and the other nations of the world, He also knew every movement of the Assyrian king and his rage against the LORD (v.28).

d. After pronouncing the LORD's judgment upon King Sennacherib and Assyria, Isaiah declared that the king would be defeated, subdued like an animal, and returned to his own land (v.29). Sennacherib's rage and arrogance against the LORD were the reasons he was to suffer the LORD's judgment. Note the reference to a hook being put in the king's nose and a bit in his mouth. The hook and bit were generally used to control animals, but it was the practice of the Assyrians to use hooks and bits to control their prisoners.

e. Turning to Hezekiah, Isaiah gave a sign that assured the king of God's wonderful provision (vv.30-32). All that had been invaded and defeated by Assyria, which was everything except Jerusalem, would recover from the invasion after two years. The people would be able to sow and reap in the third year. Note how this wonderful promise is broken down year by year. In the first year, the year of the invasion, the people had not been able to plant their crops. But there would already be enough food growing in the fields to feed the population that had survived. During the second year there would still be enough food sprouting from what had spilled upon the ground. In the third year, the people would be able to cultivate the land and reap the harvest.

Still the wonderful assurance of food was not all that God was promising. Judah would also be left with a remnant, survivors who would experience a miraculous growth in population (also see Is.10:20-23). In His zeal, the LORD of Hosts would fulfill this promise. Note how the remnant referred to in these verses applies both to that day and to the day of the Messiah (Ro.11:5).

f. In closing, Isaiah shared the clear, unmistakable assurance of God: the Assyrian king would not conquer Jerusalem (vv.33-35).

⇒ The Assyrian king would not enter the city, attack, shoot an arrow, nor lay a siege ramp against Jerusalem (see note—2 K.25:1-21 for an excellent description of siege warfare by Russell Dilday).
⇒ The Assyrian king would quickly return to his own land, going back by the quickest route he knew.
⇒ The Assyrian king would definitely not enter the city of Jerusalem.
⇒ The city would be defended by God Himself, defended for God's own honor and for the sake of David.

g. That very night the judgment of God against Assyria and King Sennacherib fell. The prophecy of Isaiah came true, and the promise of God was fulfilled (vv.36-38). During the night, the Angel of the LORD went into the Assyrian camp and executed 185,000 soldiers. Utterly shocked and not understanding what had happened, the Assyrian survivors broke camp and withdrew, returning to Nineveh. And note, the Assyrian army remained in Ninevah and lived there. Sometime after returning, King Sennacherib was assassinated while worshipping in the temple of his false god Nishroch (v.38). He was killed by two of his own sons, Adrammelech and Sharezer. Right after his death he was succeeded by another son, Esarhaddon.

Thought 1. *Deliverance* is one of the great promises of God. When we call upon God for deliverance, one of two things happens: either God miraculously delivers us, or else He gives us the power to walk through the obstacle standing in our way. Even in facing the obstacle of death, power is available to the believer. Quicker than the eye can blink, the power of God transfers the believer from this physical earth into the spiritual world. Death is conquered, triumphed over. And the believer lives forever in God's presence.

No matter what confronts us—disease, accident, financial difficulty, divorce, or any other trial or hardship—God promises to deliver us. If we will turn to the LORD for deliverance, cry out to Him in prayer, genuinely trust Him to deliver, He will give us the power to overcome the hindrance or to walk through it victoriously. Listen to the wonderful promises of God's deliverance:

"Who shall separate us from the love of Christ? *shall* tribulation, or distress, or persecution, or famine, or nakedness, or peril, or sword?...Nay, in all these things we are more than conquerors through him that loved us. For I am persuaded, that neither death, nor life, nor angels, nor principalities, nor powers, nor things present, nor things to come, Nor height, nor depth, nor any other creature, shall be able to separate us from the love of God, which is in Christ Jesus our Lord" (Ro.8:35, 37-39).

"There hath no temptation taken you but such as is common to man: but God *is* faithful, who will not suffer you to be tempted above that ye are able; but will with the temptation also make a way to escape, that ye may be able to bear *it*" (1 Co.10:13).

"Now unto him that is able to do exceeding abundantly above all that we ask or think, according to the power that worketh in us" (Ep.3:20).

"For we would not, brethren, have you ignorant of our trouble which came to us in Asia, that we were pressed out of measure, above strength, insomuch that we despaired even of life: But we had the sentence of death in ourselves, that we should not trust in ourselves, but in God which raiseth the dead: Who delivered us from so great a death, and doth deliver: in whom we trust that he will yet deliver *us*" (2 Co.1:8-10).

"And the Lord shall deliver me from every evil work, and will preserve *me* unto his heavenly kingdom: to whom *be* glory for ever and ever. Amen" (2 Ti.4:18).

"Forasmuch then as the children are partakers of flesh and blood, he also himself likewise took part of the same; that through death he might destroy him that had the power of death, that is, the devil; And deliver them who through fear of death were all their lifetime subject to bondage" (He.2:14-15).

"The Lord knoweth how to deliver the godly out of temptations, and to reserve the unjust unto the day of judgment to be punished" (2 Pe.2:9).

"For whatsoever is born of God overcometh the world: and this is the victory that overcometh the world, *even* our faith. Who is he that overcometh the world, but he that believeth that Jesus is the Son of God?" (1 Jn.5:4-5).

"He shall deliver thee in six troubles: yea, in seven [the full number of trials] there shall no evil touch thee" (Jb.5:19).

"Through thee will we push down our enemies: through thy name will we tread them under that rise up against us" (Ps.44:5).

"And *even* to *your* old age I *am* he; and *even* to hoar [gray] hairs will I carry *you:* I have made, and I will bear; even I will carry, and will deliver *you*" (Is.46:4).

"Be not afraid of their faces: for I *am* with thee to deliver thee, saith the LORD" (Je.1:8).

"He delivereth and rescueth, and he worketh signs and wonders in heaven and in earth, who hath delivered Daniel from the power of the lions" (Da.6:27).

CHAPTER 38

B. The Stage Set for the Coming Captivity of Judah by Babylon: The Power of Prayer & the Danger of Sinful Pride, 38:1–39:8

38:1-8; see 20:1-11; 2 Chr.32:24-26
39:1-8; see 2 K.20:12-19

1. Hezekiah's crisis with a terminal illness: The power of prayer

a. Isaiah's visit to Hezekiah & the LORD's message
1) Hezekiah was to put his affairs in order
2) Hezekiah was to die, not recover

b. Hezekiah's earnest prayer
1) He turned his face to the wall & prayed
2) He reminded God of three facts
- His faithful walk
- His loyal heart
- His righteous behavior
3) He wept bitterly: Submitted his life to God's will

c. God's immediate answer to Hezekiah's prayer: Before Isaiah left the palace courtyard, 2 K.20:4
1) The LORD sent Isaiah back to Hezekiah with a second message
- God would heal him: Add 15 years to his life
- God would deliver him & Jerusalem from Assyria: For God's honor & for David's sake
2) The LORD would give the king a sign, 22

- The shadow on a sundial would move ten degrees backward
- The sign fulfilled: The shadow actually moved back ten degrees

2. Hezekiah's testimony concerning his terminal illness: The power of God to heal

a. Hezekiah had been depressed
1) He knew he was in the prime of life & was being robbed of years
2) He knew he would soon die & never again enjoy wonderful experiences of life
- Worship of the LORD
- Fellowship with others
3) He felt his life was being

In those days was Hezekiah sick unto death. And Isaiah the prophet the son of Amoz came unto him, and said unto him, Thus saith the LORD, Set thine house in order: for thou shalt die, and not live.

2 Then Hezekiah turned his face toward the wall, and prayed unto the LORD,

3 And said, Remember now, O LORD, I beseech thee, how I have walked before thee in truth and with a perfect heart, and have done *that which is* good in thy sight. And Hezekiah wept sore.

4 Then came the word of the LORD to Isaiah, saying,

5 Go, and say to Hezekiah, Thus saith the LORD, the God of David thy father, I have heard thy prayer, I have seen thy tears: behold, I will add unto thy days fifteen years.

6 And I will deliver thee and this city out of the hand of the king of Assyria: and I will defend this city.

7 And this *shall be* a sign unto thee from the LORD, that the LORD will do this thing that he hath spoken;

8 Behold, I will bring again the shadow of the degrees, which is gone down in the sun dial of Ahaz, ten degrees backward. So the sun returned ten degrees, by which degrees it was gone down.

9 The writing of Hezekiah king of Judah, when he had been sick, and was recovered of his sickness:

10 I said in the cutting off of my days, I shall go to the gates of the grave: I am deprived of the residue of my years.

11 I said, I shall not see the LORD, *even* the LORD, in the land of the living: I shall behold man no more with the inhabitants of the world.

12 Mine age is departed, and

is removed from me as a shepherd's tent: I have cut off like a weaver my life: he will cut me off with pining sickness: from day *even* to night wilt thou make an end of me.

13 I reckoned till morning, *that,* as a lion, so will he break all my bones: from day *even* to night wilt thou make an end of me.

14 Like a crane *or* a swallow, so did I chatter: I did mourn as a dove: mine eyes fail *with looking* upward: O LORD, I am oppressed; undertake for me.

15 What shall I say? he hath both spoken unto me, and himself hath done *it:* I shall go softly all my years in the bitterness of my soul.

16 O Lord, by these *things men* live, and in all these *things is* the life of my spirit: so wilt thou recover me, and make me to live.

17 Behold, for peace I had great bitterness: but thou hast in love to my soul *delivered it* from the pit of corruption: for thou hast cast all my sins behind thy back.

18 For the grave cannot praise thee, death can *not* celebrate thee: they that go down into the pit cannot hope for thy truth.

19 The living, the living, he shall praise thee, as I *do* this day: the father to the children shall make known thy truth.

20 The LORD *was ready* to save me: therefore we will sing my songs to the stringed instruments all the days of our life in the house of the LORD.

21 For Isaiah had said, Let them take a lump of figs, and lay *it* for a plaster upon the boil, and he shall recover.

22 Hezekiah also had said, What *is* the sign that I shall go up to the house of the LORD?

CHAPTER 39

At that time Merodachbaladan, the son of Baladan, king of Babylon, sent letters and a present to Hezekiah: for he had heard that he had been sick, and was recovered.

2 And Hezekiah was glad of them, and showed them the house of his precious

snatched from him
- Like a tent being taken down & moved elsewhere
- Like a piece of cloth being cut away

4) He was broken in both body & spirit: He felt the pain day & night

b. Hezekiah had cried out to the LORD in prayer
1) He pleaded & moaned
2) He prayed so much his eyes became weary

c. Hezekiah had made a renewed commitment to the LORD
1) To walk humbly before the LORD
- Because humility was the answer to his anguish
- Because humility stirs God to give people life
2) To declare the LORD's healing power

3) To acknowledge the LORD's love
- In allowing him to grow through suffering
- In delivering him
- In forgiving his sins
4) To praise the LORD: Because the dead cannot praise Him, only the living
5) To hope in God's faithfulness
6) To bear strong witness about the LORD
- To share God's faithfulness with his children
- To proclaim God's salvation
7) To worship faithfully in the temple (church) of the LORD

d. Hezekiah had been healed through a treatment prescribed by God's prophet: An ointment of figs

e. Hezekiah had prayed for a special sign to assure he would be healed, would again worship in the temple, 7-8

3. Hezekiah's unwise entertainment of ambassadors from Babylon: A picture of pride, 2 Chr.32:25

a. The crown prince's concern over Hezekiah's illness

b. Hezekiah's warm reception of & prideful entertainment of the Babylonian representatives

1) He obviously shared the story of his healing 2) He foolishly showed the Babylonians his vast wealth in the palace treasury & throughout the kingdom c. The LORD's rebuke of Hezekiah through His prophet Isaiah 1) Isaiah confronted & questioned Hezekiah about his unwise entertainment of the ambassadors 2) Hezekiah made no attempt to hide his actions, but freely shared what he had done: He had shown the representatives all the wealth & treasuries of the	things, the silver, and the gold, and the spices, and the precious ointment, and all the house of his armour, and all that was found in his treasures: there was nothing in his house, nor in all his dominion, that Hezekiah showed them not. 3 Then came Isaiah the prophet unto king Hezekiah, and said unto him, What said these men? and from whence came they unto thee? And Hezekiah said, They are come from a far country unto me, *even* from Babylon. 4 Then said he, What have they seen in thine house? And Hezekiah answered, All that *is* in mine house have they seen: there is nothing among my treasures that I	have not showed them. 5 Then said Isaiah to Hezekiah, Hear the word of the LORD of hosts: 6 Behold, the days come, that all that *is* in thine house, and *that* which thy fathers have laid up in store until this day, shall be carried to Babylon: nothing shall be left, saith the LORD. 7 And of thy sons that shall issue from thee, which thou shalt beget, shall they take away; and they shall be eunuchs in the palace of the king of Babylon. 8 Then said Hezekiah to Isaiah, Good *is* the word of the LORD which thou hast spoken. He said moreover, For there shall be peace and truth in my days.	nation d. God's judgment pronounced upon Hezekiah & Judah: Due to Hezekiah's pride & the sins of the nation down through the centuries 1) One day Babylon would conquer Judah & carry off all the wealth of the nation 2) Some of Hezekiah's descendants would be exiled to Babylon e. Hezekiah's repentance 1) He humbly accepted God's judgment 2) He questioned if he would finish his days in peace & security

DIVISION IV

THE TURNING POINT OF HEZEKIAH'S REIGN: A SHIFT FROM THE THREAT OF ASSYRIA TO THE CAPTIVITY OF JUDAH BY BABYLON, 36:1–39:8

B. The Stage Set for the Coming Captivity of Judah by Babylon: The Power of Prayer and the Danger of Sinful Pride, 38:1–39:8

(38:1–39:8) **Introduction**: in looking at ourselves as human beings, we realize that we are mere creatures of flesh and bone, made of decaying matter. In addition, our flesh is subject to numerous illnesses and injuries, many of which can severely cripple or shorten our lives. When we consider that we live in bodies of flesh and also in a corruptible world, a great need is immediately apparent. What is this need? The need to be delivered from this corruptible flesh and from all the diseases, accidents, trials, and temptations that happen to us in life. When illness strikes or misfortune happens, we need a deliverer, a rescuer, a savior.

In such times, God's Holy Word gives us wonderful news: the LORD is available to help us. The LORD will rescue and deliver us from this corruptible flesh and through all the diseases and injuries that befall us. *Through* our prayers—our calling out to God for help—and *because* of our prayers, God says He will deliver us. The importance of prayer is one of the great lessons taught in this present passage of Scripture.

But there is also a severe warning about the danger of pride. Nothing will condemn our souls before God quicker than the sin of pride. These two powerful messages are clearly demonstrated in the life of King Hezekiah, the subject of the present Scripture. Keep in mind that Hezekiah's terminal illness took place with the threat of Assyria's returning to invade Judah lying right over the horizon. Humanly speaking, Hezekiah's situation was gloomy, but if he died, there would be no hope whatsoever—not in the minds of the people. This is, *The Stage Set for the Coming Captivity of Judah by Babylon: The Power of Prayer and the Danger of Sinful Pride*, 38:1–39:8.

1. Hezekiah's crisis terminal illness: the power of prayer (38:1-8).
2. Hezekiah's testimony concerning his terminal illness: the power of God to heal (38:9-22).
3. Hezekiah's unwise entertainment of ambassadors from Babylon: a picture of pride (39:1-8).

1 (38:1-8) **Prayer, Power of—Sickness, Healed by—Illness, Healed by—Disease, Healed by—Healing, Source of, Prayer—Hezekiah, Terminal Illness of**: shockingly, right after the deliverance of Jerusalem from the Assyrian threat, Hezekiah became deathly sick and was soon to die. The actual date of Hezekiah's death was in 686 B.C. Given that God extended his life for 15 years after his initial diagnosis, this means that his illness took place somewhere around 701 B.C., in the very year of Assyria's invasion (see Is.36:1–37:38).[1] In facing his illness, Hezekiah shows us the power of prayer:

[1] John F. Walvoord and Roy B. Zuck, Editors. *The Bible Knowledge Commentary, Old Testament*. (Colorado Springs, CO: Chariot Victor Publishing, 1985), p.578.

OUTLINE	SCRIPTURE	SCRIPTURE	OUTLINE
1. Hezekiah's crisis with a terminal illness: The power of prayer a. Isaiah's visit to Hezekiah & the LORD's message 　1) Hezekiah was to put his affairs in order 　2) Hezekiah was to die, not recover b. Hezekiah's earnest prayer 　1) He turned his face to the wall & prayed 　2) He reminded God of three facts 　• His faithful walk 　• His loyal heart 　• His righteous behavior 　3) He wept bitterly: Submitted his life to God's will c. God's immediate answer to Hezekiah's prayer: Before Isaiah left the palace court-	In those days was Hezekiah sick unto death. And Isaiah the prophet the son of Amoz came unto him, and said unto him, Thus saith the LORD, Set thine house in order: for thou shalt die, and not live. 2　Then Hezekiah turned his face toward the wall, and prayed unto the LORD, 3　And said, Remember now, O LORD, I beseech thee, how I have walked before thee in truth and with a perfect heart, and have done *that which is* good in thy sight. And Hezekiah wept sore. 4　Then came the word of the LORD to Isaiah, saying, 5　Go, and say to Hezekiah,	Thus saith the LORD, the God of David thy father, I have heard thy prayer, I have seen thy tears: behold, I will add unto thy days fifteen years. 6　And I will deliver thee and this city out of the hand of the king of Assyria: and I will defend this city. 7　And this *shall be* a sign unto thee from the LORD, that the LORD will do this thing that he hath spoken; 8　Behold, I will bring again the shadow of the degrees, which is gone down in the sun dial of Ahaz, ten degrees backward. So the sun returned ten degrees, by which degrees it was gone down.	yard, 2 K.20:4 1) The LORD sent Isaiah back to Hezekiah with a second message 　• God would heal him: Add 15 years to his life 　• God would deliver him & Jerusalem from Assyria: For God's honor & for David's sake 2) The LORD would give the king a sign, 22 　• The shadow on a sundial would move ten degrees backward 　• The sign fulfilled: The shadow actually moved back ten degrees

a. When Hezekiah was on his deathbed, the LORD sent Isaiah to the king with the message that he was to put his affairs in order. He was soon to die (v.1).

b. But note how Hezekiah received the fatal news: he immediately turned his face to the wall away from Isaiah and began to pray to the LORD (vv.2-3). He reminded the LORD of three facts:
⇒ He was faithful in following the LORD.
⇒ He was loyal and wholly devoted to the LORD.
⇒ He had behaved righteously before the LORD.

Then Hezekiah began to weep bitterly (v.3). By weeping, he was indicating that his heart was broken, that he was submitting his life to the LORD's will.

c. In compassion, the LORD immediately answered King Hezekiah's prayer (vv.4-7). Isaiah had obviously already left the room and was heading for home when the king began to pray, for before Isaiah even left the palace courtyard, a message came to him from the LORD (vv.4-7). Isaiah was to return immediately to Hezekiah with a second message. God had heard his prayer and seen his brokenness; therefore the LORD would heal him. On the third day he would arise, go up to the temple, and worship the LORD. In fact, the LORD would add 15 years to his life and would deliver him and Jerusalem from Assyria (v.6). For God's honor and for David's sake, the LORD would defend the capital and not allow it to fall to the Assyrians. Note how this promise suggests that Hezekiah was struck with the terminal illness during the actual siege of Jerusalem by the Assyrians.

Turning to the servants, Isaiah instructed them to prepare an ointment of fig leaves to place upon the king. In obedience to the prophet, they nursed the king and he soon recovered.

d. Hezekiah, needing assurance from the LORD, requested a sign from Isaiah that he would recover and worship in the temple on the third day (vv.7-8, 22; 2 K.20:8-11). The LORD proved His promise and granted the request of the sick king. He gave Hezekiah a choice that involved moving the sun's shadow on the king's sundial either 10 degrees backward or 10 degrees forward. Choosing the more difficult miracle, Hezekiah asked for the shadow to move backward 10 degrees. As requested, the prophet Isaiah called upon the LORD and the miracle occurred. The shadow of the sundial actually moved back 10 degrees (see 2 K.20:8-11 for the details of the miracle).

Thought 1. There is no limit to the power of prayer, for there is no limit to God's power. God is omnipotent, all-powerful, possessing perfect and boundless power to do anything He desires. But God is not only omnipotent, He is also omniscient, knowing all things. Nothing is hidden from God. God sees and knows all.

This message of God's omnipotence and omniscience is wonderful news, for God knows when serious illnesses strike us or crises confront us. And God has the power to handle whatever we may face, no matter how severe or painful. When we face these mammoth problems, our responsibility is to pray, turning toward the LORD and crying out to Him. If we are sincere and willing to turn our lives totally over to Him, God will hear and answer our prayers. In some cases, He will miraculously heal us. In other cases, He will give us the strength to walk through the illness or crisis victoriously. Through prayer there is nothing—absolutely nothing—that can defeat or overcome us, not even death itself. God's knowledge is infinite. He knows everything about us, even the very number of hairs upon our head. Along with that God has the power to help us. Listen to what God's Word says about the *power of prayer*.

"**Ask, and it shall be given you; seek, and ye shall find; knock, and it shall be opened unto you**" (Mt.7:7).

"**Therefore I say unto you, What things soever ye desire, when ye pray, believe that ye receive** *them,* **and ye shall have** *them*" (Mk.11:24).

"If ye abide in me, and my words abide in you, ye shall ask what ye will, and it shall be done unto you" (Jn.15:7).

"Hitherto have ye asked nothing in my name: ask, and ye shall receive, that your joy may be full" (Jn.16:24).

"For this thing I besought the Lord thrice, that it might depart from me. And he said unto me, My grace is sufficient for thee: for my strength is made perfect in weakness. Most gladly therefore will I rather glory in my infirmities, that the power of Christ may rest upon me. Therefore I take pleasure in infirmities, in reproaches, in necessities, in persecutions, in distresses for Christ's sake: for when I am weak, then am I strong" (2 Co.12:8-10).

"Now unto him that is able to do exceeding abundantly above all that we ask or think, according to the power that worketh in us" (Ep.3:20).

"And the prayer of faith shall save the sick, and the Lord shall raise him up; and if he have committed sins, they shall be forgiven him. Confess *your* faults one to another, and pray one for another, that ye may be healed. The effectual fervent prayer of a righteous man availeth much. Elias was a man subject to like passions as we are, and he prayed earnestly that it might not rain: and it rained not on the earth by the space of three years and six months. And he prayed again, and the heaven gave rain, and the earth brought forth her fruit" (Js.5:15-18).

"And whatsoever we ask, we receive of him, because we keep his commandments, and do those things that are pleasing in his sight" (1 Jn.3:22).

"Call unto me, and I will answer thee, and show thee great and mighty things, which thou knowest not" (Je.33:3).

---

2 **(38:9-22) Healing, Testimony of, Hezekiah—Healing Power of, God—Hezekiah, Healing of—Recommitment, Stirred by, Trials—Trials, Results of, Stirs Recommitment—Illness – Sickness, Results of, Stirs Recommitment**: after God's miraculous healing of Hezekiah's terminal illness, the king was filled with praise and thanksgiving to God. As a witness to the LORD he sat down and wrote the following testimony of his experience. There is a possibility that he summoned close friends or leaders of the nation to a special meeting at which he shared his healing experience with them. Whatever the case, the LORD preserved Hezekiah's testimony in His Holy Word, so that all succeeding generations may know the power of God to heal His people.

OUTLINE	SCRIPTURE	SCRIPTURE	OUTLINE

2. Hezekiah's testimony concerning his terminal illness: The power of God to heal
 	
a. Hezekiah had been depressed
  1) He knew he was in the prime of life & was being robbed of years
  2) He knew he would soon die & never again enjoy wonderful experiences of life
  • Worship of the LORD
  • Fellowship with others
  3) He felt his life was being snatched from him
  • Like a tent being taken down & moved elsewhere
  • Like a piece of cloth being cut away
  4) He was broken in both body & spirit: He felt the pain day & night
 	
b. Hezekiah had cried out to the LORD in prayer
  1) He pleaded & moaned
  2) He prayed so much his eyes became weary
 	
c. Hezekiah had made a renewed commitment to the LORD
  1) To walk humbly before
	9 The writing of Hezekiah king of Judah, when he had been sick, and was recovered of his sickness:
	10 I said in the cutting off of my days, I shall go to the gates of the grave: I am deprived of the residue of my years.
	11 I said, I shall not see the LORD, *even* the LORD, in the land of the living: I shall behold man no more with the inhabitants of the world.
	12 Mine age is departed, and is removed from me as a shepherd's tent: I have cut off like a weaver my life: he will cut me off with pining sickness: from day *even* to night wilt thou make an end of me.
	13 I reckoned till morning, *that,* as a lion, so will he break all my bones: from day *even* to night wilt thou make an end of me.
	14 Like a crane *or* a swallow, so did I chatter: I did mourn as a dove: mine eyes fail *with looking* upward: O LORD, I am oppressed; undertake for me.
	15 What shall I say? he hath both spoken unto me, and himself hath done *it:* I shall go softly all my years
		in the bitterness of my soul.
		16 O Lord, by these *things men* live, and in all these *things is* the life of my spirit: so wilt thou recover me, and make me to live.
		17 Behold, for peace I had great bitterness: but thou hast in love to my soul *delivered it* from the pit of corruption: for thou hast cast all my sins behind thy back.
		18 For the grave cannot praise thee, death can *not* celebrate thee: they that go down into the pit cannot hope for thy truth.
		19 The living, the living, he shall praise thee, as I *do* this day: the father to the children shall make known thy truth.
		20 The LORD *was ready* to save me: therefore we will sing my songs to the stringed instruments all the days of our life in the house of the LORD.
		21 For Isaiah had said, Let them take a lump of figs, and lay *it* for a plaster upon the boil, and he shall recover.
		22 Hezekiah also had said, What *is* the sign that I shall go up to the house of the LORD?
			the LORD
			  • Because humility was the answer to his anguish
			  • Because humility stirs God to give people life
			  2) To declare the LORD's healing power
			
			  3) To acknowledge the LORD's love
			  • In allowing him to grow through suffering
			  • In delivering him
			  • In forgiving his sins
			  4) To praise the LORD: Because the dead cannot praise Him, only the living
			  5) To hope in God's faithfulness
			  6) To bear strong witness about the LORD
			  • To share God's faithfulness with his children
			
			  • To proclaim God's salvation
			  7) To worship faithfully in the temple (church) of the LORD
			
			d. Hezekiah had been healed through a treatment prescribed by God's prophet: An ointment of figs
			e. Hezekiah had prayed for a special sign to assure he would be healed, would

a. When Hezekiah was stricken with a deadly illness, he became deeply depressed (vv.10-13). He was in the prime of life and felt as though he was being robbed of years. Although he had achieved much for the nation, he felt he had so much more to do. But the *gates of death* were swung wide open and he lay ready to leave this world and enter those gates. Grief and disappointment overwhelmed his soul. He knew he would never again enjoy the wonderful experiences of life…

- never again see or commune with the LORD in worship
- never again fellowship or enjoy the company of others (v.11)

Sensing his imminent death, Hezekiah compared his house or body to a tent that was being quickly taken down and moved elsewhere (v.12). He believed his life was being cut off as quickly as a weaver snips a piece of cloth from the loom. Death was so close, Hezekiah expected the LORD to end his life before the night turned to day. As he waited patiently for the dawn to break, he was broken in both body and spirit. Day and night he suffered agonizing, unbearable pain, as if a lion had attacked and broken all his bones (vv.12-13).

b. Knowing that his only hope lay in the LORD, Hezekiah cried out in prayer (v.14). His continuous low moaning sounded like that of a grieving dove. But in all his groaning and agonizing pain, he knew that God was there with him. Weeping in prayer, he cried out to the LORD for help.

c. During three days of his agonizing pain and illness (2 K.20:5), Hezekiah did what so many do when facing a dire circumstance. He made a renewed commitment to the LORD (vv.15-20). If God would heal him, he promised to do seven things:

1) He would walk humbly before the LORD (v.15). Humbling himself was the answer to his anguish of soul, for the LORD hears the prayers of the humble and exalts them. He revives the spirit of the humble and contrite. But He lowers or puts down the proud and shuts His ears to their prayers.

> **"And whosoever shall exalt himself shall be abased; and he that shall humble himself shall be exalted" (Mt.23:12).**
> **"For thus saith the high and lofty One that inhabiteth eternity, whose name *is* Holy; I dwell in the high and holy *place,* with him also *that is* of a contrite and humble spirit, to revive the spirit of the humble, and to revive the heart of the contrite ones" (Is.57:15).**

2) Hezekiah promised to bear strong witness to the LORD'S healing power (v.16). Through the experience of suffering he had leaned a wonderful truth: God's discipline—the discipline of suffering—is good. It aroused his spirit to seek the LORD, to live in prayer, to commune and fellowship with the LORD. Through his suffering he was discovering *true life,* a true and deep relationship with the LORD. And when he drew close to the LORD, the LORD healed him, allowing him to live another fifteen years (2 K.20:6).

> **"For with God nothing shall be impossible" (Lu.1:37).**
> **"Is any sick among you? let him call for the elders of the church; and let them pray over him, anointing him with oil in the name of the Lord: And the prayer of faith shall save the sick, and the Lord shall raise him up; and if he have committed sins, they shall be forgiven him" (Js.5:14-15).**
> **"But he *was* wounded for our transgressions, *he was* bruised for our iniquities: the chastisement of our peace *was* upon him; and with his stripes we are healed" (Is.53:5).**

3) Hezekiah promised to acknowledge the LORD's love (v.17). He actually said that his terminal illness was for *his own good.* It was for a positive and beneficial purpose. Three purposes are spelled out!
⇒ His suffering stirred him to grow more mature spiritually, bringing him far closer to the LORD.
⇒ His suffering taught him a great deal about the love of God, about how the LORD longs to deliver His people from their trials.
⇒ His suffering led to the forgiveness of his sins, rousing him to correct his misbehavior and turn back to the LORD.

> **"For God so loved the world, that he gave his only begotten Son, that whosoever believeth in him should not perish, but have everlasting life" (Jn.3:16).**
> **"But God commendeth his love toward us, in that, while we were yet sinners, Christ died for us" (Ro.5:8).**
> **"But God, who is rich in mercy, for his great love wherewith he loved us, Even when we were dead in sins, hath quickened us together with Christ, (by grace ye are saved;)" (Ep.2:4-5).**
> **"Behold, what manner of love the Father hath bestowed upon us, that we should be called the sons of God: therefore the world knoweth us not, because it knew him not" (1 Jn.3:1).**
> **"The LORD hath appeared of old unto me, *saying,* Yea, I have loved thee with an everlasting love: therefore with lovingkindness have I drawn thee" (Je.31:3).**

4) Hezekiah promised to praise the LORD among people as long as he lived (v.18). Of course after he died, Hezekiah could no longer praise God for what He had done for him. The dead are gone, unable to sing God's praise among the living.

> **"By him therefore let us offer the sacrifice of praise to God continually, that is, the fruit of *our* lips giving thanks to his name" (He.13:15).**

"But ye *are* a chosen generation, a royal priesthood, an holy nation, a peculiar people; that ye should show forth the praises of him who hath called you out of darkness into his marvellous light" (1 Pe.2:9).

"Sing praises to the LORD, which dwelleth in Zion: declare among the people his doings" (Ps.9:11).

"Let the people praise thee, O God; let all the people praise thee" (Ps.67:3).

5) Hezekiah promised to hope in God's truth, His faithfulness (v.18). If God would heal him, the king promised to place his hope in the promises of God and in God's faithfulness to fulfill His promises.

"God *is* faithful, by whom ye were called unto the fellowship of his Son Jesus Christ our Lord" (1 Co.1:9).

"Wherefore let them that suffer according to the will of God commit the keeping of their souls *to him* in well doing, as unto a faithful Creator" (1 Pe.4:19).

"Know therefore that the LORD thy God, he *is* God, the faithful God, which keepeth covenant and mercy with them that love him and keep his commandments to a thousand generations" (De.7:9).

"Blessed *be* the LORD, that hath given rest unto his people Israel, according to all that he promised: there hath not failed one word of all his good promise, which he promised by the hand of Moses his servant" (1 K.8:56).

"I will sing of the mercies of the LORD for ever: with my mouth will I make known thy faithfulness to all generations" (Ps.89:1).

6) Hezekiah promised to bear strong witness to the LORD (vv.19-20). If God allowed him to live, he would share the truth with his children. He would make sure his children heard the promises of God and the wonderful truth that God is faithful, that He will fulfill His promises. He would also proclaim God's salvation, the glorious reality that the LORD had saved him.

"And he said unto them, Go ye into all the world, and preach the gospel to every creature" (Mk.16:15).

"For we cannot but speak the things which we have seen and heard" (Ac.4:20).

"Come *and* hear, all ye that fear God, and I will declare what he hath done for my soul" (Ps.66:16).

"I will mention the lovingkindnesses of the LORD, *and* the praises of the LORD, according to all that the LORD hath bestowed on us, and the great goodness toward the house of Israel, which he hath bestowed on them according to his mercies, and according to the multitude of his lovingkindnesses" (Is.63:7).

7) Hezekiah promised to worship faithfully in the temple (church) of the LORD (v.20). If God would heal him, he would be dedicated and dependable, faithful in his public worship all the days of his life. He would not neglect meeting with others to worship the LORD.

"And they went into Capernaum; and straightway on the sabbath day he entered into the synagogue, and taught" (Mk.1:21).

"And he came to Nazareth, where he had been brought up: and, as his custom was, he went into the synagogue on the sabbath day, and stood up for to read" (Lu.4:16).

"And they worshipped him, and returned to Jerusalem with great joy: And were continually in the temple, praising and blessing God. Amen" (Lu.24:52-53).

"And they, continuing daily with one accord in the temple, and breaking bread from house to house, did eat their meat with gladness and singleness of heart, Praising God, and having favour with all the people. And the Lord added to the church daily such as should be saved" (Ac.2:46-47).

"Not forsaking the assembling of ourselves together, as the manner of some *is;* but exhorting *one another:* and so much the more, as ye see the day approaching" (He.10:25).

"But unto the place which the LORD your God shall choose out of all your tribes to put his name there, *even* unto his habitation shall ye seek, and thither thou shalt come" (De.12:5).

"Blessed *are* they that dwell in thy house: they will be still praising thee. Selah" (Ps.84:4).

d. Hezekiah was healed through a treatment prescribed by the prophet Isaiah (v.21). Isaiah instructed the king's servants to prepare an ointment of fig leaves to place on the king. Three days later the king was restored to health, recovered completely.

e. Before he was healed, Hezekiah needed further assurance from the LORD, a sign that he would recover and be able to worship in the temple on the third day (v.22). As seen above in verses seven and eight, the LORD gave Hezekiah the sign of the shadow on a sun dial.

3 (39:1-8) **Pride, Example of—Arrogance, Example of—Self-Exaltation, Example of—Hezekiah, Pride of:** although Hezekiah was righteous and totally committed to the LORD, he was not perfect. Soon after his illness, he unwisely entertained some ambassadors from Babylon, and in his entertaining he exposed a heart of pride and self-exaltation. Because of his pride, the judgment of God was pronounced upon him and a prediction made concerning the future destiny of the nation. In a very straightforward manner, Scripture shares the story of the king's pride.

OUTLINE	SCRIPTURE	SCRIPTURE	OUTLINE
	CHAPTER 39	they seen in thine house? And Hezekiah answered, All that *is* in mine house have they seen: there is nothing among my treasures that I have not showed them.	tempt to hide his actions, but freely shared what he had done: He had shown the representatives all the wealth & treasuries of the nation

3. Hezekiah's unwise entertainment of ambassadors from Babylon: A picture of pride, 2 Chr.32:25
  a. The crown prince's concern over Hezekiah's illness
  b. Hezekiah's warm reception of & prideful entertainment of the Babylonian representatives
    1) He obviously shared the story of his healing
    2) He foolishly showed the Babylonians his vast wealth in the palace treasury & throughout the kingdom
	At that time Merodach-baladan, the son of Baladan, king of Babylon, sent letters and a present to Hezekiah: for he had heard that he had been sick, and was recovered.
	2 And Hezekiah was glad of them, and showed them the house of his precious things, the silver, and the gold, and the spices, and the precious ointment, and all the house of his armour, and all that was found in his treasures: there was nothing in his house, nor in all his dominion, that Hezekiah showed them not.
		5 Then said Isaiah to Hezekiah, Hear the word of the LORD of hosts:
		6 Behold, the days come, that all that *is* in thine house, and *that* which thy fathers have laid up in store until this day, shall be carried to Babylon: nothing shall be left, saith the LORD.
		7 And of thy sons that shall issue from thee, which thou shalt beget, shall they take away; and they shall be eunuchs in the palace of the king of Babylon.
			d. God's judgment pronounced upon Hezekiah & Judah: Due to Hezekiah's pride & the sins of the nation down through the centuries
			  1) One day Babylon would conquer Judah & carry off all the wealth of the nation
			
			  2) Some of Hezekiah's descendants would be exiled to Babylon

c. The LORD's rebuke of Hezekiah through His prophet Isaiah
    1) Isaiah confronted & questioned Hezekiah about his unwise entertainment of the ambassadors
    2) Hezekiah made no at-
	3 Then came Isaiah the prophet unto king Hezekiah, and said unto him, What said these men? and from whence came they unto thee? And Hezekiah said, They are come from a far country unto me, *even* from Babylon.
	4 Then said he, What have
		8 Then said Hezekiah to Isaiah, Good *is* the word of the LORD which thou hast spoken. He said moreover, For there shall be peace and truth in my days.	e. Hezekiah's repentance
			  1) He humbly accepted God's judgment
			  2) He questioned if he would finish his days in peace & security

a. Hearing about Hezekiah's deathly illness, the crown prince of Babylon, Merodach-Baladan, sent a letter and some gifts to Hezekiah as an expression of his concern (v.1). Why would the crown prince of Babylon, the soon to be superpower of the world, want to express his concern for Hezekiah? *Second Chronicles* tells us that his curiosity was aroused when he heard about the miraculous healing of Hezekiah and the movement of the sundial (2 Chr.32:31). But additional information is supplied by the Jewish historian Josephus. He says that the king of Babylon sought Hezekiah as a friend and ally.[2]

b. Whatever Merodach-Baladan's purpose, Hezekiah gave the ambassadors a warm reception (v.2). With pride swelling up in his heart, Hezekiah entertained the envoys by sharing the story of his healing and then foolishly, showing them his vast wealth. There was nothing in his palace or throughout the kingdom that he failed to show them. Obviously, this included the strength of his military as well as the wealth found in the palace and temple treasuries.

c. As would be expected, the LORD immediately rebuked Hezekiah through the prophet Isaiah (vv.3-4). Isaiah confronted the king and questioned him about his entertainment of the ambassadors. Making no attempt to hide his actions, Hezekiah freely shared what he had done. He had shown them the wealth, the treasuries of the nation.

d. No doubt heavy-hearted, but with the authority of God Himself, the prophet Isaiah pronounced God's judgment upon Hezekiah and Judah. Due to Hezekiah's pride and the sins of the nation down through the centuries, Judah would face God's condemnation (vv.5-7). One day in the near future, Babylon would conquer Judah and carry off all the wealth of the nation. What the Babylonian ambassadors had seen—all the treasures of the king as well as those of the nation—would not be forgotten. Future leaders of Babylon would covet the wealth shown by Hezekiah in his moment of self-exaltation and pride. Moreover, some of Hezekiah's descendents would be exiled to Babylon and be forced to serve as eunuchs (devoted slaves) in the palace of Babylon's king.

e. In a spirit of repentance, Hezekiah humbly accepted God's judgment (v.8). But in his private thoughts, he was wondering and asking himself if he would finish out his days in peace and security.

Thought 1. Pride is a terrible evil. When a person begins to look upon himself as being superior to or better than others, he…
- exalts himself over others, applauding his own efforts
- feels that he should be preferred over others
- considers himself to be more valuable than others

A person who is full of pride and self-exaltation is often arrogant, overbearing, and disrespectful. He frequently puts other people down, degrades, shames, embarrasses, stifles, harms, subjects, and in some cases even enslaves others. For this reason, God strongly condemns pride and the exalting of ourselves above others:

"And whosoever shall exalt himself shall be abased; and he that shall humble himself shall be exalted" (Mt.23:12).

"*Be* of the same mind one toward another. Mind not high things, but condescend to men of low estate. Be not wise in your own conceits" (Ro.12:16).

---

2 Flavius Josephus. *Complete Works. Antiquities of the Jews.* (Grand Rapids, MI: Kregel Publications, 1981), Book 10, Ch.2, p.214.

"And if any man think that he knoweth any thing, he knoweth nothing yet as he ought to know" (1 Co.8:2).

"For if a man think himself to be something, when he is nothing, he deceiveth himself" (Ga.6:3).

"But he giveth more grace. Wherefore he saith, God resisteth the proud, but giveth grace unto the humble" (Js.4:6).

"For all that *is* in the world, the lust of the flesh, and the lust of the eyes, and the pride of life, is not of the Father, but is of the world" (1 Jn.2:16).

"The wicked in *his* pride doth persecute the poor: let them be taken in the devices that they have imagined" (Ps.10:2).

"They that trust in their wealth, and boast themselves in the multitude of their riches; None *of them* can by any means redeem his brother, nor give to God a ransom for him" (Ps.49:6-7).

"Thou hast rebuked the proud *that are* cursed, which do err from thy commandments" (Ps.119:21).

"Be not wise in thine own eyes: fear the LORD, and depart from evil" (Pr.3:7).

"These six *things* doth the LORD hate: yea, seven *are* an abomination unto him: A proud look, a lying tongue, and hands that shed innocent blood, An heart that deviseth wicked imaginations, feet that be swift in running to mischief, A false witness *that* speaketh lies, and he that soweth discord among brethren" (Pr.6:16-19).

"*When* pride cometh, then cometh shame: but with the lowly *is* wisdom" (Pr.11:2).

"An high look, and a proud heart, *and* the plowing of the wicked, *is* sin" (Pr.21:4).

"Seest thou a man wise in his own conceit? *there is* more hope of a fool than of him" (Pr.26:12).

"He that is of a proud heart stirreth up strife: but he that putteth his trust in the LORD shall be made fat" (Pr.28:25).

"A man's pride shall bring him low: but honour shall uphold the humble in spirit" (Pr.29:23).

"Woe unto *them that are* wise in their own eyes, and prudent in their own sight!" (Is.5:21).

"For thou hast said in thine heart, I will ascend into heaven, I will exalt my throne above the stars of God: I will sit also upon the mount of the congregation, in the sides of the north: I will ascend above the heights of the clouds; I will be like the most High. Yet thou shalt be brought down to hell, to the sides of the pit" (Is.14:13-15).

"Son of man, say unto the prince of Tyrus, Thus saith the Lord GOD; Because thine heart *is* lifted up, and thou hast said, I *am* a God, I sit *in* the seat of God, in the midst of the seas; yet thou *art* a man, and not God, though thou set thine heart as the heart of God: Behold, thou *art* wiser than Daniel; there is no secret that they can hide from thee: With thy wisdom and with thine understanding thou hast gotten thee riches, and hast gotten gold and silver into thy treasures: By thy great wisdom *and* by thy traffick hast thou increased thy riches, and thine heart is lifted up because of thy riches: Therefore thus saith the Lord GOD; Because thou hast set thine heart as the heart of God; Behold, therefore I will bring strangers upon thee, the terrible of the nations: and they shall draw their swords against the beauty of thy wisdom, and they shall defile thy brightness. They shall bring thee down to the pit, and thou shalt die the deaths of *them that are* slain in the midst of the seas" (Eze.28:2-8).

"Though thou exalt *thyself* as the eagle, and though thou set thy nest among the stars, thence will I bring thee down, saith the LORD" (Obad.4).

DIVISION V

THE PROPHECIES OF COMFORT AND FREEDOM: A PICTURE OF BELIEVERS BEING SET FREE FROM THE CAPTIVITY OF SIN AND DEATH, 40:1–48:22

PART III: THE PROPHECIES OF COMFORT, 40:1–66:24

(40:1–48:22) **DIVISION OVERVIEW**: the prophecies and messages of Isaiah now shift many years into the future. Someday in the distant future, Judah and its beloved capital, Jerusalem, would fall to Babylon. Tragically, the citizens would suffer the horrors of defeat and slavery. Most of the survivors would be deported and exiled, scattered throughout the Babylonian Empire. The people of Judah would lose everything: their homes, property, wealth, communities, cities, nation, worship centers, and their beloved temple in Jerusalem. And they would be gripped by piercing grief, because many of their husbands and sons would be slaughtered by the invading army. Everyone would be destitute, and a spirit of hopelessness and despair would continually flood their hearts.

But in the midst of the Jews' hardship and sorrow, the LORD gave them a wonderful promise. The day was coming when they would be *comforted* and *set free* from their captivity to Babylon and from sin and death. In the nine messages of this division, the herald of God proclaims God's wonderful promise of comfort and freedom. And he proclaims this message just as loudly as he had the messages of condemnation and judgment. Judgment was coming upon Judah, but it is also coming upon all the other nations of the world. Nevertheless, God had made a promise to save His people, and He would keep it. Through His power and the promised Messiah, God's prophecy of *comfort* and *freedom* would be fulfilled. His people would be set free from their captivity to Babylon and from their enslavement to sin and death.

Several years passed since the reign of Hezekiah. The Jews were now in captivity in Babylon, but Isaiah was prophesying comfort and freedom to them. In these prophecies of Isaiah, God's great redeeming power is clearly pictured. If the exiles would repent of their idolatry and wicked ways, the Lord would deliver them from captivity in Babylon.

THE PROPHECIES OF COMFORT AND FREEDOM: A PICTURE OF BELIEVERS BEING SET FREE FROM THE CAPTIVITY OF SIN AND DEATH, 40:1–48:22

A. Set Free Through God's Salvation and Greatness, 40:1-31

B. Set Free Through God's Power to Control Human History, the Very Deeds of People, 41:1-29

C. Set Free Through God's Perfect Servant, the Messiah, the Lord Jesus Christ (The First of Four "Servant Songs"), 42:1-25

D. Set Free Through the Redeemer, the Lord, Your God: A Study of Redemption, 43:1-28

E. Set Free By the Lord, the Only Living and True God, 44:1-28

F. Set Free By God's Power to Work Through People and Nations: A Look at God's Enormous Power, 45:1-25

G. Set Free by Turning Away from Idolatry: A Study of Idolatry, 46:1-13

H. Set Free by God's Judgment of the Oppressor, Babylon: A Warning to All Who Oppress Others, 47:1-15

I. Set Free by God's Plan of Redemption: The Hope of Being Delivered from God's Judgment and Wrath, 48:1-22

CHAPTER 40

PART III: THE PROPHECIES OF COMFORT, 40:1–66:24

V. THE PROPHECIES OF COMFORT & FREEDOM: A PICTURE OF BELIEVERS BEING SET FREE FROM THE CAPTIVITY OF SIN & DEATH, 40:1–48:22

A. Set Free Through God's Salvation & Greatness, 40:1-31

1. God's salvation proclaimed
a. Voice 1: Comfort God's people
   1) Their captivity—warfare, hardship—is over: A prediction of God's deliverance from the Babylonian captivity
   2) Their sins are paid for, pardoned: Because they had obviously repented
b. Voice 2: Prepare the way for the LORD—repent
   1) The preparation
      • Build a straight highway for the LORD's army
      • Remove all obstacles

   2) The result
      • God's glory will be revealed
      • All mankind will see God's glory
c. Voice 3: Recognize the contrast between people & God
   1) People & their glory fade away—just as grass withers & flowers fall: Because God has power over all

   2) God & His Word stand forever: He will fulfill His promises

d. Voice 4: Proclaim the "Good News" of God's deliverance
   1) Fearlessly proclaim God's coming to rescue His people

   2) Fearlessly proclaim God's coming in power
      • to rule
      • to reward people

Comfort ye, comfort ye my people, saith your God.
2 Speak ye comfortably to Jerusalem, and cry unto her, that her warfare is accomplished, that her iniquity is pardoned: for she hath received of the LORD's hand double for all her sins.
3 The voice of him that crieth in the wilderness, Prepare ye the way of the LORD, make straight in the desert a highway for our God.
4 Every valley shall be exalted, and every mountain and hill shall be made low: and the crooked shall be made straight, and the rough places plain:
5 And the glory of the LORD shall be revealed, and all flesh shall see it together: for the mouth of the LORD hath spoken it.
6 The voice said, Cry. And he said, What shall I cry? All flesh is grass, and all the goodliness thereof is as the flower of the field:
7 The grass withereth, the flower fadeth: because the spirit of the LORD bloweth upon it: surely the people is grass.
8 The grass withereth, the flower fadeth: but the word of our God shall stand for ever.
9 O Zion, that bringest good tidings, get thee up into the high mountain; O Jerusalem, that bringest good tidings, lift up thy voice with strength; lift it up, be not afraid; say unto the cities of Judah, Behold your God!
10 Behold, the Lord GOD will come with strong hand, and his arm shall rule for him: behold, his reward is with him, and his work before him.
11 He shall feed his flock like a shepherd: he shall gather the lambs with his arm, and carry them in his bosom, and shall gently lead those that are with young.
12 Who hath measured the waters in the hollow of his hand, and meted out heaven with the span, and comprehended the dust of the earth in a measure, and weighed the mountains in scales, and the hills in a balance?
13 Who hath directed the Spirit of the LORD, or being his counsellor hath taught him?
14 With whom took he counsel, and who instructed him, and taught him in the path of judgment, and taught him knowledge, and showed to him the way of understanding?
15 Behold, the nations are as a drop of a bucket, and are counted as the small dust of the balance: behold, he taketh up the isles as a very little thing.
16 And Lebanon is not sufficient to burn, nor the beasts thereof sufficient for a burnt offering.
17 All nations before him are as nothing; and they are counted to him less than nothing, and vanity.
18 To whom then will ye liken God? or what likeness will ye compare unto him?
19 The workman melteth a graven image, and the goldsmith spreadeth it over with gold, and casteth silver chains.
20 He that is so impoverished that he hath no oblation chooseth a tree that will not rot; he seeketh unto him a cunning workman to prepare a graven image, that shall not be moved.
21 Have ye not known? have ye not heard? hath it not been told you from the beginning? have ye not understood from the foundations of the earth?
22 It is he that sitteth upon the circle of the earth, and the inhabitants thereof are as grasshoppers; that stretcheth out the heavens as a curtain, and spreadeth them out as a tent to dwell in:

   3) Fearlessly proclaim God's tender care for His people
      • He feeds them
      • He leads them

2. God's greatness proclaimed
a. The LORD is greater than the universe He has created

b. The LORD is greater than any counselor or teacher
   1) He needs no counselor or advice
   2) He needs no one to teach Him the path of justice
   3) He needs no one to impart knowledge or understanding to Him

c. The LORD is greater than all the nations of the earth—in all their power & glory
   1) Their existence is as a tiny drop in a large bucket, as mere dust on a set of scales
   2) Their forests & animals are not enough to make a sacrifice worthy of God
   3) Their significance is worthless, less than nothing before God

d. The LORD is greater than all the images & false gods of this world
   1) The idols & false gods are made by man
      • The skilled craftsman uses metal, gold, & silver
      • The skilled craftsman uses a non-rotting wood for the poor

   2) The people are questioned about their false worship
      • Why do they not know?
      • Have they not heard the truth, that God alone is the Creator?
e. The LORD is greater than all the people of the earth
   1) He sits enthroned above the earth: Its people are as grasshoppers before Him
   2) He created & uses the heavens like a tent

3) He removes the rulers & judges of this earth
- Makes them useless
- Blasts them with the fury of His breath: Causes them to wither away like a plant or to be swept away like chaff by a whirlwind

f. The LORD is greater than any being in the entire universe
1) He alone is the "Holy One"
2) He alone created all the heavens
- He causes the starry host to shine
- He calls all the stars by name
- He uses His power to keep the stars in place
g. The LORD is more powerful than any trial or temptation

23 That bringeth the princes to nothing; he maketh the judges of the earth as vanity. 24 Yea, they shall not be planted; yea, they shall not be sown: yea, their stock shall not take root in the earth: and he shall also blow upon them, and they shall wither, and the whirlwind shall take them away as stubble. 25 To whom then will ye liken me, or shall I be equal? saith the Holy One. 26 Lift up your eyes on high, and behold who hath created these *things,* that bringeth out their host by number: he calleth them all by names by the greatness of his might, for that *he is* strong in power; not one faileth. 27 Why sayest thou, O Jacob, and speakest, O Israel,

My way is hid from the LORD, and my judgment is passed over from my God? 28 Hast thou not known? hast thou not heard, *that* the everlasting God, the LORD, the Creator of the ends of the earth, fainteth not, neither is weary? *there is* no searching of his understanding. 29 He giveth power to the faint; and to *them that have* no might he increaseth strength. 30 Even the youths shall faint and be weary, and the young men shall utterly fall: 31 But they that wait upon the LORD shall renew *their* strength; they shall mount up with wings as eagles; they shall run, and not be weary; *and* they shall walk, and not faint.

1) The complaint: God is far away, unconcerned, or does not know about my problem
2) The answer of God
- He is the everlasting God, the Creator of the whole earth
- He never faints or becomes weary

- He strengthens the weary & weak

- He renews the strength of those who hope in the LORD: Strengthens them with far more strength than even young men have

DIVISION V

THE PROPHECIES OF COMFORT AND FREEDOM: A PICTURE OF BELIEVERS BEING SET FREE FROM THE CAPTIVITY OF SIN AND DEATH, 40:1–48:22

A. Set Free Through God's Salvation and Greatness, 40:1-31

(40:1-31) **Introduction**: all of us go through difficult times in our lives. For some of us the instances are few and far between, and the issues are not that serious. But for others of us the difficulties are almost constant and their nature is very serious, sometimes even life-threatening. When circumstances are overwhelming and the outlook is totally bleak, what can we do? To whom can we turn? Is there any hope? The resounding answer is "Yes!"

In God's Word we find the most wonderful and encouraging news: God promises to set His people free from their world of hardships and heavy burdens, from their captivity and enslavements by the wicked of this world. He also promises to walk with true believers through every trial and misfortune they experience. But He not only walks with His people through their trials, He also brings them through victoriously. So no matter what grips a person's life, he or she can be liberated by God's salvation. God will rescue or deliver His people from whatever forces hold them in bondage or hold them down. This is the wonderful message of the present Scripture.

At the time Isaiah wrote this wonderful message of salvation, he knew that the Jews were facing 160 plus very difficult years. For about 93 years they would witness a stream of unparalleled wickedness flow through their nation, a stream that would gain momentum and rush madly to its inevitable end, the fall of their nation to Babylon. They would then be deported and spend 70 long years scattered throughout the Babylon Empire. They were to suffer the unbearable discrimination and hardship of a subjected, enslaved people.

Thus, encouragement—a deep sense of God's care and comfort—would be desperately needed during these long, difficult years. The people needed to trust God, to believe in His glorious promise of deliverance. They needed to live righteously and godly as they looked forward to the day of their redemption by the Savior. Within their hearts they needed to keep alive the hope of God's salvation, the hope that He would deliver them from their captivity and lead them back to Judah, the promised land of God. To keep their hope alive, the LORD stirred Isaiah to preach this much-needed message: this is, *Set Free Through God's Salvation and Greatness,* 40:1-31.

1. God's salvation proclaimed (vv.1-11).
2. God's greatness proclaimed (vv.12-31).

1 (40:1-11) **Comfort, to Proclaim—Salvation, Duty to Proclaim—Repentance, Duty, to Proclaim—Man, Compared with God, Temporal Versus Eternal—Life, Brevity of—Word of God, Duration of, Eternal—Way of the LORD, Duty, to Prepare—Good News, Duty, to Proclaim—Witness – Witnessing, Duty, to Proclaim Good Tidings**: God's people are set free through the proclamation of His salvation. God will deliver His people from captivity. No matter what enemy holds them in bondage, He will set them free. Salvation is the wonderful message now being proclaimed by God Himself. And note this fact: four voices altogether proclaim the message of God's salvation. A wonderful hope is being offered to those who are facing terrible trials and who are being held captive by cruel enemies. Note the four voices and the message each proclaims:

OUTLINE	SCRIPTURE	SCRIPTURE	OUTLINE

1. God's salvation proclaimed
  a. Voice 1: Comfort God's people
    1) Their captivity—warfare, hardship—is over: A prediction of God's deliverance from the Babylonian captivity
    2) Their sins are paid for, pardoned: Because they had obviously repented
  b. Voice 2: Prepare the way for the LORD—repent
    1) The preparation
     • Build a straight highway for the LORD's army
     • Remove all obstacles
 	
    2) The result
     • God's glory will be revealed
     • All mankind will see God's glory
  c. Voice 3: Recognize the contrast between people & God
    1) People & their glory fade
	Comfort ye, comfort ye my people, saith your God.
	2 Speak ye comfortably to Jerusalem, and cry unto her, that her warfare is accomplished, that her iniquity is pardoned: for she hath received of the LORD'S hand double for all her sins.
	3 The voice of him that crieth in the wilderness, Prepare ye the way of the LORD, make straight in the desert a highway for our God.
	4 Every valley shall be exalted, and every mountain and hill shall be made low: and the crooked shall be made straight, and the rough places plain:
	5 And the glory of the LORD shall be revealed, and all flesh shall see *it* together: for the mouth of the LORD hath spoken *it.*
	6 The voice said, Cry. And he said, What shall I cry? All flesh *is* grass, and all the
		goodliness thereof *is* as the flower of the field:
		7 The grass withereth, the flower fadeth: because the spirit of the LORD bloweth upon it: surely the people *is* grass.
		8 The grass withereth, the flower fadeth: but the word of our God shall stand for ever.
		9 O Zion, that bringest good tidings, get thee up into the high mountain; O Jerusalem, that bringest good tidings, lift up thy voice with strength; lift *it* up, be not afraid; say unto the cities of Judah, Behold your God!
		10 Behold, the Lord GOD will come with strong *hand,* and his arm shall rule for him: behold, his reward *is* with him, and his work before him.
		11 He shall feed his flock like a shepherd: he shall gather the lambs with his arm, and carry *them* in his bosom, *and* shall gently lead those that are with young.
			away—just as grass withers & flowers fall: Because God has power over all
			
			    2) God & His Word stand forever: He will fulfill His promises
			  d. Voice 4: Proclaim the "Good News" of God's deliverance
			    1) Fearlessly proclaim God's coming to rescue His people
			
			    2) Fearlessly proclaim God's coming in power
			     • to rule
			     • to reward people
			
			    3) Fearlessly proclaim God's tender care for His people
			     • He feeds them
			     • He leads them

a. The first voice is that of God. He cries out, "Comfort, comfort my people" (v.1). As His people walked through the coming hardships and captivity, the LORD wanted them to be comforted. He loved them from the depths of His being, so He reached out to them in empathy, with intense compassion. He wanted His people aroused to trust Him, confessing their sins and casting their lives totally upon Him. He wanted them to worship, obey, and walk in fellowship with Him throughout their lives. True *comfort of soul* comes only from the LORD. This comfort includes deep spiritual rest, a rest of assurance that one's life is in God's hands. To the righteous believer God will give strength and courage to bear whatever lies ahead, working all things out for good (Ro.8:28). Even if the righteous believer dies due to the trial confronting him, he knows (has assurance) that God will immediately transfer him into His presence—quicker than the eye can blink.

The Jews would desperately need this deep-seated comfort of soul in the coming years. Their suffering would at times be almost unbearable. Every discouraging thought and emotion that a person could experience would hit them. Imagine what it would be like to see the military defenses of one's nation wiped out and all the major cities and land utterly devastated, as well as multiplied thousands of citizens abused, raped, and slaughtered. In addition to this horrifying sight, the Jewish survivors were to be taken captive and deported to other nations throughout the Babylonian empire. This was the terrible trial Isaiah foresaw lying ahead for the Jews. Understandably, facing such a dismal future would cause many to become deeply distressed and discouraged. They would lose all hope for the future. Even some righteous believers would question God, wondering why He would allow them to suffer so much. Some would even be tempted to distrust the LORD's promises and give up their faith.

Thus, to prepare His people for the coming trials, God cried out, "Comfort, comfort my people." The double *comfort* stresses the importance and urgency of getting the message out, for the people would be desperate, suffering indescribable and terrifying trials.

In proclaiming the comfort of God, the prophets were to "speak tenderly to Jerusalem," demonstrating God's compassion and kindness. God's heart reached out with tender feelings for His people. *To speak tenderly* means to speak to the hearts of the people, to place God's comfort right next to the hearts of the people who suffer. Two words of *comfort* were to be shared with the people.

  1) Their *warfare*—hardship and demanding circumstances—was complete (v.2). The Hebrew literally reads *warfare,* which refers to the difficult trials the Jews suffered during their captivity. In predicting that the *warfare* was over, the LORD was promising the release of the Jews and their return to the promised land of Judah. Through Isaiah the LORD predicted that the harsh rigors of the Jews' captivity would soon be over. Just imagine what comfort this would be to the righteous believers who lived during the Babylonian captivity. Their struggle against the cruel Babylonians would come to an end. The day of their deliverance was at hand. God Himself gave them this assurance. They could rest in His Word, be comforted in this wonderful promise.

  2) Their sins were pardoned, forgiven. What a glorious assurance for God's people! Down through the centuries the Israelites had committed terrible sins against the LORD. The *cup of their iniquity* was full, overflowing with horrible evil, the evil of...

- immorality
- drunkenness
- pride
- abuse

- lawlessness
- violence
- idolatry
- hypocrisy

- empty formal worship (1:11-15)
- unbelief and distrust
- ridicule of God's Word
- mockery and persecution of God's people

Since the days of Moses, God's prophets had warned the people: if they turned against the LORD and walked in unrighteousness, they would face His judgment (see outlines and notes—Le.26:14-39, esp.31-39; De.28:15-68 for more discussion). God allowed the collapse of Judah and the Babylonian captivity as a means of judgment to *arouse* the Jews to repent. Isaiah was predicting that their suffering *would stir* some of the people to turn back to God, to cry out for His help. These would repent of their sins, and God would forgive them.

In the future, when the Jews found themselves in the midst of the captivity, they could remember the prophecy of Isaiah. They could take great hope in the promise of God: their captivity—warfare, hard service in Babylon—would end, and their sins would be forgiven. Of course, it was understood that repentance, turning back to God, was the prerequisite for forgiveness (Le.26:40-42; Is.55:7; Eze.18:21).

"Jesus answered them, Verily, verily, I say unto you, Whosoever committeth sin is the servant of sin. And the servant abideth not in the house for ever: *but* the Son abideth ever. If the Son therefore shall make you free, ye shall be free indeed" (Jn.8:34-36).

"Know ye not, that to whom ye yield yourselves servants to obey, his servants ye are to whom ye obey; whether of sin unto death, or of obedience unto righteousness? But God be thanked, that ye were the servants of sin, but ye have obeyed from the heart that form of doctrine which was delivered you. Being then made free from sin, ye became the servants of righteousness" (Ro.6:16-18).

"For when ye were the servants of sin, ye were free from righteousness. What fruit had ye then in those things whereof ye are now ashamed? for the end of those things *is* death. But now being made free from sin, and become servants to God, ye have your fruit unto holiness, and the end everlasting life. For the wages of sin *is* death; but the gift of God *is* eternal life through Jesus Christ our Lord" (Ro.6:20-23).

"But I see another law in my members, warring against the law of my mind, and bringing me into captivity to the law of sin which is in my members. O wretched man that I am! who shall deliver me from the body of this death? I thank God through Jesus Christ our Lord. So then with the mind I myself serve the law of God; but with the flesh the law of sin" (Ro.7:23-25).

"In whom we have redemption through his blood, the forgiveness of sins, according to the riches of his grace" (Ep.1:7).

"And the servant of the Lord must not strive; but be gentle unto all *men*, apt to teach, patient, In meekness instructing those that oppose themselves; if God peradventure will give them repentance to the acknowledging of the truth; And *that* they may recover themselves out of the snare of the devil, who are taken captive by him at his will" (2 Ti.2:24-26).

"If we confess our sins, he is faithful and just to forgive us *our* sins, and to cleanse us from all unrighteousness" (1 Jn.1:9).

"I, *even* I, *am* he that blotteth out thy transgressions for mine own sake, and will not remember thy sins" (Is.43:25).

"I have blotted out, as a thick cloud, thy transgressions, and, as a cloud, thy sins: return unto me; for I have redeemed thee" (Is.44:22).

"Who *is* a God like unto thee, that pardoneth iniquity, and passeth by the transgression of the remnant of his heritage? he retaineth not his anger for ever, because he delighteth *in* mercy" (Mi.7:18).

b. The second voice is human, probably the prophet Isaiah himself (vv.3-5). The cry of this voice is wonderful news: prepare the way for the LORD, for He is soon coming. This is a picture of the Near East custom of sending ambassadors ahead of a king to announce His coming. A king's visit to an area was a cause for great celebration. Enormous preparations would be made. Either a special road would be built or an existing roadway upgraded and readied for the monarch's appearance. Preparations always included leveling the roadway by filling in the valleys, lowering the hills, and straightening out the crooked sections. All obstacles that lay in the roadway would be removed.

With the LORD's announced coming, the people were to make the most careful preparations. Specifically what?

⇒ They were to straighten out their lives and remove all crooked, unrighteous behavior.

"Teaching us that, denying ungodliness and worldly lusts, we should live soberly, righteously, and godly, in this present world; Looking for that blessed hope, and the glorious appearing of the great God and our Saviour Jesus Christ" (Tit.2:12-13).

⇒ They were to level out the paths of their lives: be faithful and consistent, riding smoothly over all the valleys and mountains, the ups and downs of life, with confident and righteous behavior.

"Wherefore lift up the hands which hang down, and the feeble knees; And make straight paths for your feet, lest that which is lame be turned out of the way; but let it rather be healed. Follow peace with all *men*, and holiness, without which no man shall see the Lord: Looking diligently lest any man fail of the grace of God; lest any root of bitterness springing up trouble *you*, and thereby many be defiled; Lest there *be* any fornicator, or profane person, as Esau, who for one morsel of meat sold his birthright. For ye know how that afterward, when he would have inherited the blessing, he was rejected: for he found no place of repentance, though he sought it carefully with tears" (He.12:12-17).

A wonderful promise was given to those who prepared for the LORD's coming: God's glory would be revealed to them (v.5). All mankind would see His glory. Scripture applies this passage to the ministry of John the Baptist, saying that he is the *forerunner* of the Lord Jesus Christ. John is the one who prepared the way for the Messiah's coming to earth (Jn.1:19-34). But in reality the prophecy applies to every human being of every generation. We all must prepare for the coming of the LORD. In Isaiah's day the Jews needed to prepare for the LORD's coming to deliver them from Babylonian captivity. Whereas in John's day the people needed to prepare by doing exactly what he preached: repent and be baptized, for the Lamb of God who takes away the sins of the world was soon coming. Today, people need to prepare by staying alert and watching for the Lord's return. We must be thoughtful, living righteous, godly lives, looking for the blessed hope and the glorious appearing of the great God and Savior, the Lord Jesus Christ (Tit.2:12-13).

"And he came into all the country about Jordan, preaching the baptism of repentance for the remission of sins" (Lu.3:3).

"I tell you, Nay: but, except ye repent, ye shall all likewise perish" (Lu.13:3).

"And said unto them, Thus it is written, and thus it behoved Christ to suffer, and to rise from the dead the third day: And that repentance and remission of sins should be preached in his name among all nations, beginning at Jerusalem" (Lu.24:46-47).

"Then Peter said unto them, Repent, and be baptized every one of you in the name of Jesus Christ for the remission of sins, and ye shall receive the gift of the Holy Ghost" (Ac.2:38).

"Repent ye therefore, and be converted, that your sins may be blotted out, when the times of refreshing shall come from the presence of the Lord" (Ac.3:19).

"If my people, which are called by my name, shall humble themselves, and pray, and seek my face, and turn from their wicked ways; then will I hear from heaven, and will forgive their sin, and will heal their land" (2 Chr.7:14).

"Let the wicked forsake his way, and the unrighteous man his thoughts: and let him return unto the LORD, and he will have mercy upon him; and to our God, for he will abundantly pardon" (Is.55:7).

"But if the wicked will turn from all his sins that he hath committed, and keep all my statutes, and do that which is lawful and right, he shall surely live, he shall not die" (Eze.18:21).

c. The third voice is God speaking to Isaiah directly, instructing the prophet to simply *cry out* (vv.6-8). Somewhat puzzled, Isaiah asked what message he was to proclaim. In response the LORD instructed him to contrast the difference between people and God. Isaiah was to proclaim...
* that people and their glory, like grass and beautiful flowers, wither and fade away quickly
* that God and His Word are eternal, strong and unfailing

With so many problems confronting the people of Isaiah's day, the future looked bleak and hopeless. No person or body of leaders had the strength to save them from their enemies. But God could. All He had to do was speak the word of judgment and the very breath of His Word would blow away His people's oppressive enemies.

Whereas human life is ever so short compared to eternity, God and His Word stand forever (vv.7-8). People age, deteriorate, fail, and die, but God's promises are eternal: sure, enduring, lasting forever. God's Word is imperishable, never withering. God's Word will be fulfilled, proven, verified through all the years of time, and also of eternity. Consequently, God's people can trust God's Word. Far from being hopeless, they can have great hope in the future, for God will fulfill His wonderful promises. He will deliver His people from their captivity, their oppressors, and their hardships. The great day is coming when God's people will be set free. No matter what they are facing, God's people—those who truly trust Him and His Word—will be set free to return and live in the promised land of God.

"For verily I say unto you, Till heaven and earth pass, one jot or one tittle shall in no wise pass from the law, till all be fulfilled" (Mt.5:18).

"Heaven and earth shall pass away: but my words shall not pass away" (Lu.21:33).

"God *is* faithful, by whom ye were called unto the fellowship of his Son Jesus Christ our Lord" (1 Co.1:9).

"But the rich, in that he is made low: because as the flower of the grass he shall pass away" (Js.1:10).

"For all flesh *is* as grass, and all the glory of man as the flower of grass. The grass withereth, and the flower thereof falleth away" (1 Pe.1:24).

"Know therefore that the LORD thy God, he *is* God, the faithful God, which keepeth covenant and mercy with them that love him and keep his commandments to a thousand generations" (De.7:9).

"Blessed *be* the LORD, that hath given rest unto his people Israel, according to all that he promised: there hath not failed one word of all his good promise, which he promised by the hand of Moses his servant" (1 K.8:56).

"For he remembered that they *were but* flesh; a wind that passeth away, and cometh not again" (Ps.78:39).

"Thou carriest them away as with a flood; they are *as* a sleep: in the morning *they are* like grass *which* groweth up. In the morning it flourisheth, and groweth up; in the evening it is cut down, and withereth" (Ps.90:5-6).

"Thy testimonies are very sure: holiness becometh thine house, O LORD, for ever" (Ps.93:5).

"*As for* man, his days *are* as grass: as a flower of the field, so he flourisheth. For the wind passeth over it, and it is gone; and the place thereof shall know it no more" (Ps.103:15-16).

"The works of his hands *are* verity and judgment; all his commandments *are* sure" (Ps.111:7).

"I, *even* I, *am* he that comforteth you: who *art* thou, that thou shouldest be afraid of a man *that* shall die, and of the son of man *which* shall be made as grass" (Is.51:12).

"But we are all as an unclean *thing,* and all our righteousnesses *are* as filthy rags; and we all do fade as a leaf; and our iniquities, like the wind, have taken us away" (Is.64:6).

"For I *am* the LORD: I will speak, and the word that I shall speak shall come to pass; it shall be no more prolonged: for in your days, O rebellious house, will I say the word, and will perform it, saith the Lord GOD" (Eze.12:25).

d. The fourth voice is that of righteous believers, all within Jerusalem (Zion) who truly believe and follow the LORD. They are to proclaim the *good news* of God's salvation, His deliverance (vv.9-11). The message is so important that it must be shared with everyone. True believers must climb the mountains so their voices will be carried far and wide as they proclaim the *good news*. And they must not fear rejection of the message or persecution.

⇒ They must not be cowardly by shrinking back from proclaiming the *good news*.

⇒ They must not tone down or soften the demand of God for true belief and repentance in order to be saved and rescued by Him.

The *good news* is not to be twisted into a lie, making everyone acceptable to God. God declares that only those who genuinely believe and follow Him will be saved. Three facts about God are to be loudly proclaimed.

1) The righteous believer is to fearlessly proclaim the coming of God to save His people from their captivity (v.9). In Isaiah's day the LORD had come to His people in a marvelous way, rescuing them from the terrifying threat of the Assyrians (36:1–37:38). But here Isaiah is giving a wonderful promise to all of God's people. In the future, when they are held captive by oppressive enemies, the LORD will come to the rescue. He will step forth, appear in their midst, and deliver them. Based upon Scripture, Isaiah's prophecy has a fourfold application.

First, the LORD was promising to come to deliver the Jewish believers from the Babylonian captivity. Although this event lay out in the future, Isaiah foresaw God's wonderful deliverance of His people from their bondage (Is.52:7-11; 2 Co.6:17-18).

Second, the LORD was promising to come in the person of the Messiah, the Lord Jesus Christ. Through Christ, God promised to rescue His people from Satan, setting them free from sin, death, and hell. Isaiah foresaw the salvation of God coming in the person of the Lord Jesus Christ (Is.9:6-7).

Third, the coming of the Lord also refers to the second coming of Christ, the time when He will return to set up God's kingdom on earth. In that day the Lord will establish righteousness and justice on the earth. He will deliver His people from all the wickedness and injustices of evil people and nations (Is.11:1-5; 16:5; Ps.67:4).

Fourth, the LORD was promising to come to rescue His people when they face a trial or threat from any enemy. His presence will guide His people through the trial, and His strength will empower them to withstand all hardships. God also assures His people of victory. He will make them *more than conquerors.* They will be triumphant, even over death itself (Ps.44:5; Ro.8:35; 8:37; 1 Jn.5:4-5; He.2:14-15).

2) The righteous believer is to be fearless in proclaiming not only that the LORD is coming, but also that the LORD is coming in power. The LORD will raise His arm in a symbol of glorious power and strike down all the enemies who defy God and oppose His people. God's mighty power will rescue the people who truly believe and follow Him. As a mighty conqueror, the LORD will use His power to redeem His people. Most likely this is a picture of the future Messianic kingdom, the time when the Lord Jesus Christ will return to set up the kingdom of God on earth. In that day He will defeat all the enemies who stand opposed to God and His people. Through the exercise of His mighty power, the LORD will remove all unbelievers from the face of the earth. Only the righteous will be left as citizens of God's kingdom. The LORD will reward all His people with the blessings of God's kingdom. But the wicked will be rewarded with judgment (Is.43:10; 62:6; 63:7; 2 Ti.1:7-10).

3) The righteous believer is to fearlessly proclaim God's tender care for His people (v.11). God is the shepherd of all who belong to Him (Ps.80:1). And Jesus Christ is the good shepherd (Jn.10:11).[1] The LORD is not only the God of justice and judgment, but He is also the God of love, compassion, and mercy. As a shepherd cares for the sheep of His flock, so the LORD cares for His people. He gathers them in His arms and holds them close to His heart. He feeds them, providing nourishment and growth. And He leads them, protecting and showing them the way to go.

"And ye also shall bear witness, because ye have been with me from the beginning" (Jn.15:27).

"For we cannot but speak the things which we have seen and heard" (Ac.4:20).

"Go, stand and speak in the temple to the people all the words of this life. And when they heard *that,* they entered into the temple early in the morning, and taught. But the high priest came, and they that were with him, and called the council together, and all the senate of the children of Israel and sent to the prison to have them brought" (Ac.5:20-21).

"And we are his witnesses of these things; and *so is* also the Holy Ghost, whom God hath given to them that obey him" (Ac.5:32).

"And he said, The God of our fathers hath chosen thee, that thou shouldest know his will, and see that Just One, and shouldest hear the voice of his mouth. For thou shalt be his witness unto all men of what thou hast seen and heard" (Ac.22:14-15).

"We having the same spirit of faith, according as it is written, I believed, and therefore have I spoken; we also believe, and therefore speak" (2 Co.4:13).

"Be not thou therefore ashamed of the testimony of our Lord, nor of me his prisoner: but be thou partaker of the afflictions of the gospel according to the power of God" (2 Ti.1:8).

---

[1] Matthew Henry. *Matthew Henry's Commentary,* Vol.4. (Old Tappan, NJ: Fleming H. Revell Co., n.d.), p.214

"These things speak, and exhort, and rebuke with all authority. Let no man despise thee" (Tit.2:15).

"Ye *are* my witnesses, saith the LORD, and my servant whom I have chosen: that ye may know and believe me, and understand that I *am* he: before me there was no God formed, neither shall there be after me" (Is.43:10).

"I will mention the lovingkindnesses of the LORD, *and* the praises of the LORD, according to all that the LORD hath bestowed on us, and the great goodness toward the house of Israel, which he hath bestowed on them according to his mercies, and according to the multitude of his lovingkindnesses" (Is.63:7).

[2] (40:12-31) **Greatness, of God, Greater than Seven Things—Universe, Facts Concerning, God Is Greater—Teachers, Facts Concerning, God Is Greater—Counselors, Facts Concerning, God Is Greater—Nations, Facts Concerning, God Is Greater—Nations, Power of, God's Power Greater—Idolatry, Weakness of, No Comparison with God—Gods, False, Inadequacy of, Made by Man—Man, Compared with God, God Is Greater—Women, Compared with God, God Is Greater—Heavenly or Spiritual Beings, Compared with God, God Is Greater—Temptations, Facts Concerning, God Is Greater—Trials, Facts Concerning, God Is Greater**: God's people are set free through the proclamation of His greatness. How could the Jews know that God would set them free from oppressive enemies such as Assyria, Babylon, and Persia? How could they know that God would fulfill His promise of restoration, freeing them from the Babylonian captivity and returning them to the promised land? How can any people know that God will rescue them from the bondages and enslavements of this life? from the captivity of sin, death, Satan, and hell? Isaiah answered these questions. Remembering who God is—keeping in mind His *awesome greatness*—will give assurance. God is *omnipotent,* which means all-powerful. He is also *omniscient,* which means knowing all things, including the needs of His people and what must be done to meet those needs. And God is *omnipresent,* which means He is present everywhere. Possessing all power and knowledge and being present everywhere means that God can literally do anything, meeting every need of every person who truly follows Him. He can fulfill what He has promised. He can set His people free.

To assure God's people that God will fulfill His promises, Isaiah declares that God is greater than anything on earth or anything scattered throughout the universe or even beyond. Seven comparisons are made:

OUTLINE	SCRIPTURE	SCRIPTURE	OUTLINE
2. God's greatness proclaimed a. The LORD is greater than the universe He has created	12 Who hath measured the waters in the hollow of his hand, and meted out heaven with the span, and comprehended the dust of the earth in a measure, and weighed the mountains in scales, and the hills in a balance?	smith spreadeth it over with gold, and casteth silver chains. 20 He that *is* so impoverished that he hath no oblation chooseth a tree *that* will not rot; he seeketh unto him a cunning workman to prepare a graven image, *that* shall not be moved.	• The skilled craftsman uses metal, gold, & silver • The skilled craftsman uses a non-rotting wood for the poor
b. The LORD is greater than any counselor or teacher 1) He needs no counselor or advice 2) He needs no one to teach Him the path of justice 3) He needs no one to impart knowledge or understanding to Him	13 Who hath directed the Spirit of the LORD, or *being* his counsellor hath taught him? 14 With whom took he counsel, and *who* instructed him, and taught him in the path of judgment, and taught him knowledge, and showed to him the way of understanding?	21 Have ye not known? have ye not heard? hath it not been told you from the beginning? have ye not understood from the foundations of the earth? 22 *It is* he that sitteth upon the circle of the earth, and the inhabitants thereof *are* as	2) The people are questioned about their false worship • Why do they not know? • Have they not heard the truth, that God alone is the Creator?
c. The LORD is greater than all the nations of the earth—in all their power & glory 1) Their existence is as a tiny drop in a large bucket, as mere dust on a set of scales 2) Their forests & animals are not enough to make a sacrifice worthy of God 3) Their significance is worthless, less than nothing before God	15 Behold, the nations *are* as a drop of a bucket, and are counted as the small dust of the balance: behold, he taketh up the isles as a very little thing. 16 And Lebanon *is* not sufficient to burn, nor the beasts thereof sufficient for a burnt offering. 17 All nations before him *are* as nothing; and they are counted to him less than nothing, and vanity.	grasshoppers; that stretcheth out the heavens as a curtain, and spreadeth them out as a tent to dwell in: 23 That bringeth the princes to nothing; he maketh the judges of the earth as vanity. 24 Yea, they shall not be planted; yea, they shall not be sown: yea, their stock shall not take root in the earth: and he shall also blow upon them, and they shall wither, and the whirlwind shall take them away as stubble.	e. The LORD is greater than all the people of the earth 1) He sits enthroned above the earth: Its people are as grasshoppers before Him 2) He created & uses the heavens like a tent 3) He removes the rulers & judges of this earth • Makes them useless • Blasts them with the fury of His breath: Causes them to wither away like a plant or to be swept away like chaff by a whirlwind
d. The LORD is greater than all the images & false gods of this world 1) The idols & false gods are made by man	18 To whom then will ye liken God? or what likeness will ye compare unto him? 19 The workman melteth a graven image, and the gold-	25 To whom then will ye liken me, or shall I be equal? saith the Holy One. 26 Lift up your eyes on high,	f. The LORD is greater than any being in the entire universe 1) He alone is the "Holy One" 2) He alone created all the

OUTLINE	SCRIPTURE	SCRIPTURE	OUTLINE

heavens
• He causes the starry host to shine
• He calls all the stars by name
• He uses His power to keep the stars in place
g. The LORD is more powerful than any trial or temptation
  1) The complaint: God is far away, unconcerned, or does not know about my problem
  2) The answer of God
    • He is the everlasting God, the Creator of the
	and behold who hath created these *things*, that bringeth out their host by number: he calleth them all by names by the greatness of his might, for that *he is* strong in power; not one faileth.
	27 Why sayest thou, O Jacob, and speakest, O Israel, My way is hid from the LORD, and my judgment is passed over from my God?
	28 Hast thou not known? hast thou not heard, *that* the everlasting God, the LORD, the Creator of the ends of the
		earth, fainteth not, neither is weary? *there is* no searching of his understanding.
		29 He giveth power to the faint; and to *them that have* no might he increaseth strength.
		30 Even the youths shall faint and be weary, and the young men shall utterly fall:
		31 But they that wait upon the LORD shall renew *their* strength; they shall mount up with wings as eagles; they shall run, and not be weary; *and* they shall walk, and not faint.
			whole earth
			• He never faints or becomes weary
			
			• He strengthens the weary & weak
			
			• He renews the strength of those who hope in the LORD: Strengthens them with far more strength than even young men have

a. The LORD is greater than the universe He has created (v.12). Note the descriptive pictures that show just how great God is:
   ⇒ all the waters of the earth are nothing more than a drop of water in the palm of God's hand
   ⇒ all the heavens—the stars, sun, moon, planets, the entire universe—measure no more than the width of God's hand
   ⇒ the weight of the earth—its dust, mountains, and hills—is known by the LORD and the LORD alone

The point being made is that God is the great Creator. He and He alone created the universe. He is *far greater* than the universe itself. The universe with its multiplied billions of heavenly bodies were created by the LORD. He is omniscient and omnipotent, possessing the knowledge and power to do anything. And He used His knowledge and power to create the entire universe. This fact means…
  • that God is *far greater* than the universe He has created
  • that atheism and agnosticism are baseless beliefs upon which to build one's life
  • that unbelief is a dangerous position to take against the Creator of the universe

> **"Who being the brightness of *his* glory, and the express image of his person, and upholding all things by the word of his power, when he had by himself purged our sins, sat down on the right hand of the Majesty on high" (He.1:3).**
> **"In the beginning God created the heaven and the earth" (Ge.1:1).**
> **"Thou, *even* thou, *art* LORD alone; thou hast made heaven, the heaven of heavens, with all their host, the earth, and all *things* that *are* therein, the seas, and all that *is* therein, and thou preservest them all; and the host of heaven worshippeth thee" (Ne.9:6).**
> **"Of old hast thou laid the foundation of the earth: and the heavens *are* the work of thy hands" (Ps.102:25).**

b. The LORD is greater than any counselor or teacher (vv.13-14). God's knowledge, understanding, and justice are infinite. Therefore, He has no need for a counselor or advisor, since there is no being anywhere in the entire universe who can add to His knowledge, understanding, or spirit of justice. God is totally self-sufficient:
   ⇒ He needs no counselor to advise or instruct Him about what to do (v.13).
   ⇒ He needs no one to enlighten Him or to teach Him the path of justice or to show Him what to do (v.14).
   ⇒ He needs no one to impart knowledge or understanding to Him.

The LORD is greater than all counselors or teachers combined throughout all generations of human history. The LORD is totally self-sufficient, knowing exactly what to do, how to do it, and when to do it.[2]

> **"O the depth of the riches both of the wisdom and knowledge of God! how unsearchable *are* his judgments, and his ways past finding out! For who hath known the mind of the Lord? or who hath been his counsellor? Or who hath first given to him, and it shall be recompensed unto him again? For of him, and through him, and to him, *are* all things: to whom *be* glory for ever. Amen" (Ro.11:33-36).**
> **"Because the foolishness of God is wiser than men; and the weakness of God is stronger than men" (1 Co.1:25).**
> **"For who hath known the mind of the Lord, that he may instruct him? But we have the mind of Christ" (1 Co.2:16).**
> **"He revealeth the deep and secret things: he knoweth what *is* in the darkness, and the light dwelleth with him" (Da.2:22).**

c. The LORD is greater than all the nations of the earth in all their power and glory (vv.15-17). In comparison to God, the power and glory of all nations throughout history are nothing more than a drop of water in a bucket or a piece of dust

---

2 Stanley M. Horton. *The Complete Biblical Library, Isaiah.* (Springfield, MO: World Library Press, Inc., 1995), p.311.

on a set of scales (v.15). Of course, the nations of the earth are important to God. What nations do—how they rule and exercise their power and care for their citizens—matters to God. But when the power and glory of nations are matched against the omnipotent glory of God, the nations fade into insignificance. If a person were to search the earth for something valuable enough to offer God, the individual would find nothing. Even the forests and animals of Lebanon would not be enough to make a sacrificial offering worthy of Him. Nothing among the nations could ever be offered to God that would be worthy of His glory. God's greatness—His power and glory—supercedes all the power and glory of all nations for all of time. There is nothing in heaven or earth worthy of His greatness. In comparison to God's significance, the importance of nations is worthless, less than nothing before Him, total vanity.

> "Neither is worshipped with men's hands, as though he needed any thing, seeing he giveth to all life, and breath, and all things; And hath made of one blood all nations of men for to dwell on all the face of the earth, and hath determined the times before appointed, and the bounds of their habitation; That they should seek the Lord, if haply they might feel after him, and find him, though he be not far from every one of us: For in him we live, and move, and have our being; as certain also of your own poets have said, For we are also his offspring. Forasmuch then as we are the offspring of God, we ought not to think that the Godhead is like unto gold, or silver, or stone, graven by art and man's device. And the times of this ignorance God winked at; but now commandeth all men every where to repent: Because he hath appointed a day, in the which he will judge the world in righteousness by *that* man whom he hath ordained; *whereof* he hath given assurance unto all *men,* in that he hath raised him from the dead" (Ac.17:25-31).

> "Both riches and honour *come* of thee, and thou reignest over all; and in thine hand *is* power and might; and in thine hand it *is* to make great, and to give strength unto all" (1 Chr.29:12).

> "He divideth the sea with his power, and by his understanding he smiteth through the proud" (Jb.26:12).

> "I know that thou canst do every *thing,* and *that* no thought can be withholden from thee" (Jb.42:2).

> "For he knoweth our frame; he remembereth that we *are* dust" (Ps.103:14).

d. The LORD is greater than all the images and false gods of this world (vv.18-21). No idol or false god can even be compared to the LORD. Comparisons are ridiculous. Idols and false gods are nothing more than man-made objects, the creation of people's imagination. A skilled craftsman using metal, gold, silver, or wood creates these gods from images he pictures in his mind.

Note the four questions asked in verse 21. Scripture clearly says that a people—an individual, a family, a tribe, a community, a nation—should know the truth, for they have heard the truth from the beginning of human history, ever since creation. Therefore, a person is without excuse if he or she worships a false god rather than the LORD Himself, Who is the Truth. The truth is twofold: there is only one living and true God, the LORD Himself (Jehovah, Yahweh). And God alone is the Creator of the universe. He is *far greater* than all the images and false gods of this world.

> "And saying, Sirs, why do ye these things? We also are men of like passions with you, and preach unto you that ye should turn from these vanities unto the living God, which made heaven, and earth, and the sea, and all things that are therein" (Ac.14:15).

> "Forasmuch then as we are the offspring of God, we ought not to think that the Godhead is like unto gold, or silver, or stone, graven by art and man's device" (Ac.17:29).

> "For the wrath of God is revealed from heaven against all ungodliness and unrighteousness of men, who hold the truth in unrighteousness; Because that which may be known of God is manifest in them; for God hath showed *it* unto them. For the invisible things of him from the creation of the world are clearly seen, being understood by the things that are made, *even* his eternal power and Godhead; so that they are without excuse: Because that, when they knew God, they glorified *him* not as God, neither were thankful; but became vain in their imaginations, and their foolish heart was darkened. Professing themselves to be wise, they became fools, And changed the glory of the uncorruptible God into an image made like to corruptible man, and to birds, and fourfooted beasts, and creeping things. Wherefore God also gave them up to uncleanness through the lusts of their own hearts, to dishonour their own bodies between themselves: Who changed the truth of God into a lie, and worshipped and served the creature more than the Creator, who is blessed for ever. Amen" (Ro.1:18-25).

> "The heavens declare the glory of God; and the firmament showeth his handywork" (Ps.19:1).

> "The heavens declare his righteousness, and all the people see his glory" (Ps.97:6).

e. The LORD is greater than all the people of the earth (vv.22-24). When the LORD sits enthroned above the earth, looking down upon the people, they appear as nothing more than grasshoppers in His sight. The LORD is so great that He can stretch out the heavens that He created and spread them out like a tent in which He lives and demonstrates His presence and glory. In comparison to the rulers and judges of this earth God is *far greater.* He alone judges the great, the powerful of this earth. If their works have been evil, He erases and makes their works useless. They are nothing more than plants that are sown in the ground. As soon as they take root and appear, their lives and positions of power are snuffed out. Blasting them with the fury of His breath, the LORD causes the great and powerful to wither away like a plant or to be swept away like chaff by a whirlwind (vv.23-24).

> "John answered and said, A man can receive nothing, except it be given him from heaven" (Jn.3:27).

"Not that we are sufficient of ourselves to think any thing as of ourselves; but our sufficiency *is* of God" (2 Co.3:5).

"Shall mortal man be more just than God? shall a man be more pure than his maker? Behold, he put no trust in his servants; and his angels he charged with folly: How much less *in* them that dwell in houses of clay, whose foundation *is* in the dust, *which* are crushed before the moth? They are destroyed from morning to evening: they perish for ever without any regarding *it*. Doth not their excellency *which is* in them go away? they die, even without wisdom" (Jb.4:17-21).

"What *is* man, that thou shouldest magnify him? and that thou shouldest set thine heart upon him?" (Jb.7:17).

"When I consider thy heavens, the work of thy fingers, the moon and the stars, which thou hast ordained; What is man, that thou art mindful of him? and the son of man, that thou visitest him?" (Ps.8:3-4).

"Nevertheless man *being* in honour abideth not: he is like the beasts *that* perish" (Ps.49:12).

"But our God *is* in the heavens: he hath done whatsoever he hath pleased" (Ps.115:3).

f. The LORD is greater than any being in the entire universe (vv.25-26). To whom can the LORD be compared? Who is His equal? No one. The LORD alone is the *Holy One*. He alone created all the heavens of the starry sky (v.26). No one else is great enough nor has the power to create such a vast universe. Note that the LORD Himself is speaking. He challenges the reader: "Lift up your eyes and look at the heavens above and ask yourself: 'who created all these?'" Certainly not some little god, a piece of wood or metal created by the imagination of a corrupt human being, the *Holy One*, the LORD Himself who created everything. He is so great that He not only created the stars of the heavens, but He also named them and calls them by their names. It is His power and His power alone that established the laws of the universe that keep the stars functioning according to those laws. Again the LORD is *far greater* than any being in the entire universe. He alone is the *Holy One*, totally set apart and distinct from all other beings. Any person should be able to stand out under the starry sky at night and understand this fact: the universe did not happen by chance. It has been created by the *Holy One*, the Supreme Being who is totally set apart from all other beings in the universe.

"And the scribe said unto him, Well, Master, thou hast said the truth: for there is one God; and there is none other but he" (Mk.12:32).

"And saying, Sirs, why do ye these things? We also are men of like passions with you, and preach unto you that ye should turn from these vanities unto the living God, which made heaven, and earth, and the sea, and all things that are therein: Who in times past suffered all nations to walk in their own ways. Nevertheless he left not himself without witness, in that he did good, and gave us rain from heaven, and fruitful seasons, filling our hearts with food and gladness" (Ac.14:15-17).

"Wherefore thou art great, O LORD God: for *there is* none like thee, neither *is there any* God beside thee" (2 S.7:22).

"And he said, LORD God of Israel, *there is* no God like thee, in heaven above, or on earth beneath, who keepest covenant and mercy with thy servants that walk before thee with all their heart" (1 K.8:23).

"For who in the heaven can be compared unto the LORD? *who* among the sons of the mighty can be likened unto the LORD?" (Ps.89:6).

g. The LORD is greater than any trial or temptation (vv.27-31). Due to the Jews' oppressive enemies as well as their hardships and sufferings, they were complaining and accusing God of forgetting them. They felt as though God were far away, unconcerned about their welfare or else unaware of their hardships. But the LORD knew, and His heart reached out in compassion to His people. Stirring Isaiah to encourage them, the LORD gave four assurances to His people:

⇒ He is the everlasting God, the Creator of the whole earth (v.28). Thus He oversees the earth and knows everything that is happening. Because He is everlasting—no beginning and no end—He is able to oversee and control all events of human history.

⇒ He never faints or becomes weary in overseeing the earth and His people. Again, being everlasting, God is always available to help those who truly trust and obey Him.

⇒ He strengthens both the weary and the weak who trust Him (v.29).

⇒ He will renew the strength of all who wait on the LORD (vv.30-31). No matter their chronological age, the LORD will strengthen them with more energy and vigor than even young men have. Note this fact: the word *wait* does not mean sitting around doing nothing. Rather it means to *hope* in the LORD, praying and trusting the LORD to meet one's need (Is.26:3-4; 30:15). Also, the word *renew* means to exchange, such as exchanging old clothes for new.[3] The believer who truly places his hope in the LORD will renew his strength, exchange his weaknesses for the LORD's strength (2 Co.12:9). The LORD will build up the believer, empower his spirit to soar above the trials and temptations that afflict him, to soar just like an eagle above the earth. A believer who truly hopes in the LORD will be strengthened so that he can run through the problems, hardships, trials, and temptations of life. And he will not grow weary. He will walk victoriously, triumphantly, and not faint (v.31).

"But when ye pray, use not vain repetitions, as the heathen *do:* for they think that they shall be heard for their much speaking. Be not ye therefore like unto them: for your Father knoweth what things ye have need of, before ye ask him" (Mt.6:7-8).

---

3 Warren W. Wiersbe. *Be Comforted.* (Wheaton, IL: Victor Books, 1992), pp.111-112.

"But seek ye first the kingdom of God, and his righteousness; and all these things [housing, food, clothing] shall be added unto you" (Mt.6:33).

"And he said unto me, My grace is sufficient for thee: for my strength is made perfect in weakness. Most gladly therefore will I rather glory in my infirmities, that the power of Christ may rest upon me. Therefore I take pleasure in infirmities, in reproaches, in necessities, in persecutions, in distresses for Christ's sake: for when I am weak, then am I strong" (2 Co.12:9-10).

"Now unto him that is able to do exceeding abundantly above all that we ask or think, according to the power that worketh in us" (Ep.3:20).

"For God hath not given us the spirit of fear; but of power, and of love, and of a sound mind" (2 Ti.1:7).

"Who through faith subdued kingdoms, wrought righteousness, obtained promises, stopped the mouths of lions, Quenched the violence of fire, escaped the edge of the sword, out of weakness were made strong, waxed valiant in fight, turned to flight the armies of the aliens" (He.11:33-34).

"But I *am* poor and needy; *yet* the Lord thinketh upon me: thou *art* my help and my deliverer; make no tarrying, O my God" (Ps.40:17).

"Fear thou not; for I *am* with thee: be not dismayed; for I *am* thy God: I will strengthen thee; yea, I will help thee; yea, I will uphold thee with the right hand of my righteousness" (Is.41:10).

"Fear not: for I have redeemed thee, I have called *thee* by thy name; thou *art* mine. When thou passest through the waters, I *will be* with thee; and through the rivers, they shall not overflow thee: when thou walkest through the fire, thou shalt not be burned; neither shall the flame kindle upon thee" (Is.43:1-2).

CHAPTER 41

1. God's power to execute judgment upon all who defy Him

a. God's summons for the nations to gather for a court trial: A picture of future judgment

b. God's two key questions put forward to the people

1) Who has the power to raise up a ruler to execute judgment on the nations? A prediction of Cyrus, king of Persia (559–530 B.C.), 13:17-18; 44:28; 45:1
   • He would destroy nations
   • He would be unscathed, unstoppable

2) Who has the power to control the affairs of the human race—down through the generations of history?

c. God's answer: He, the LORD—He alone has such power

d. God's twofold purpose for the coming judgment

1) To strike fear in the people: Giving them a chance to repent

2) To expose their wicked hearts, their trust in one another (v.6) & in their false gods (v.7): Giving them a chance to turn back to the LORD

2. God's power to protect & provide for Israel (His people)

a. God's assurance: They were His chosen servants

1) He would, therefore, regather them from the ends of the earth: Set them free from Babylonian captivity, 43:1-7

2) He would not reject them

b. God's promise to protect His people

1) They were not to fear, because He would be with them, help them, & uphold them

   • God would shame & confuse all who opposed them: All enemies

B. Set Free Through God's Power to Control Human History, the Very Deeds of People, 41:1-29

Keep silence before me, O islands; and let the people renew *their* strength: let them come near; then let them speak: let us come near together to judgment.
2 Who raised up the righteous *man* from the east, called him to his foot, gave the nations before him, and made *him* rule over kings? he gave *them* as the dust to his sword, *and* as driven stubble to his bow.
3 He pursued them, *and* passed safely; *even* by the way *that* he had not gone with his feet.
4 Who hath wrought and done *it,* calling the generations from the beginning? I the LORD, the first, and with the last; I *am* he.
5 The isles saw *it,* and feared; the ends of the earth were afraid, drew near, and came.
6 They helped every one his neighbour; and *every one* said to his brother, Be of good courage.
7 So the carpenter encouraged the goldsmith, *and* he that smootheth *with* the hammer him that smote the anvil, saying, It is ready for the sodering: and he fastened it with nails, *that* it should not be moved.
8 But thou, Israel, *art* my servant, Jacob whom I have chosen, the seed of Abraham my friend.
9 *Thou* whom I have taken from the ends of the earth, and called thee from the chief men thereof, and said unto thee, Thou *art* my servant; I have chosen thee, and not cast thee away.
10 Fear thou not; for I *am* with thee: be not dismayed; for I *am* thy God: I will strengthen thee; yea, I will help thee; yea, I will uphold thee with the right hand of my righteousness.
11 Behold, all they that were incensed against thee shall be ashamed and confounded:

they shall be as nothing; and they that strive with thee shall perish.
12 Thou shalt seek them, and shalt not find them, *even* them that contended with thee: they that war against thee shall be as nothing, and as a thing of nought.
13 For I the LORD thy God will hold thy right hand, saying unto thee, Fear not; I will help thee.
14 Fear not, thou worm Jacob, *and* ye men of Israel; I will help thee, saith the LORD, and thy redeemer, the Holy One of Israel.
15 Behold, I will make thee a new sharp threshing instrument having teeth: thou shalt thresh the mountains, and beat *them* small, and shalt make the hills as chaff.
16 Thou shalt fan them, and the wind shall carry them away, and the whirlwind shall scatter them: and thou shalt rejoice in the LORD, *and* shalt glory in the Holy One of Israel.
17 *When* the poor and needy seek water, and *there is* none, *and* their tongue faileth for thirst, I the LORD will hear them, *I* the God of Israel will not forsake them.
18 I will open rivers in high places, and fountains in the midst of the valleys: I will make the wilderness a pool of water, and the dry land springs of water.
19 I will plant in the wilderness the cedar, the shittah tree, and the myrtle, and the oil tree; I will set in the desert the fir tree, *and* the pine, and the box tree together:
20 That they may see, and know, and consider, and understand together, that the hand of the LORD hath done this, and the Holy One of Israel hath created it.
21 Produce your cause, saith the LORD; bring forth your strong *reasons,* saith the King of Jacob.
22 Let them bring *them* forth, and show us what shall happen: let them show the former things, what they *be,* that we may consider them, and know the latter end of them; or declare us things for to come.
23 Show the things that are to come hereafter, that we

would perish

   • God would totally eliminate all the enemies who opposed & waged war against His people

2) They were not to fear, because He would hold their right hands & help them

3) They were not to fear, because He was their Redeemer: He would deliver them from captivity despite the fact that they were mere worms (weak & helpless)

   • God would empower them to defeat their enemies: Make them like a threshing sledge with sharp teeth, threshing their enemies & reducing them to chaff with the wind blowing their enemies away

   • God would give His people a reason to rejoice & to glory in Him

c. God's promise to provide for His people as they suffered in exile or returned from captivity

1) The people would be poor & needy, parched with thirst

2) The LORD would hear their cry & prayer
   • He would provide water

   • He would provide a fruitful land: Would even restore the desert into productive land

3) The LORD's purpose: To demonstrate His power, showing the people that He alone could free His people & meet their needs, 14, 16

3. God's power to prove that He is the only living & true God

a. God's challenge to idolaters: Prove your case

1) Prove that idols or false gods can predict the future & fulfill the events
   • Prove they can explain past events, showing how the events relate to the present & are leading to a specific outcome
   • Prove they can foretell coming events

2) Prove that idols can do mighty works—good or bad—that would fill us with amazement & fear b. God's verdict on idolatry 1) Idols are less than nothing, worthless 2) Idolaters are detestable c. God's proof that He alone is the only living & true God 1) He alone has the power to control history: He would raise up Cyrus of Persia to conquer the earth & free Israel 2) He alone predicted the historical rise of Cyrus: His execution of God's judgment upon the nations	may know that ye *are* gods: yea, do good, or do evil, that we may be dismayed, and behold *it* together. 24 Behold, ye *are* of nothing, and your work of nought: an abomination *is he that* chooseth you. 25 I have raised up *one* from the north, and he shall come: from the rising of the sun shall he call upon my name: and he shall come upon princes as *upon* morter, and as the potter treadeth clay. 26 Who hath declared from the beginning, that we may know? and beforetime, that we may say, *He is* righteous?	yea, *there is* none that showeth, yea, *there is* none that declareth, yea, *there is* none that heareth your words. 27 The first *shall say* to Zion, Behold, behold them: and I will give to Jerusalem one that bringeth good tidings. 28 For I beheld, and *there was* no man; even among them, and *there was* no counsellor, that, when I asked of them, could answer a word. 29 Behold, they *are* all vanity; their works *are* nothing: their molten images *are* wind and confusion.	& the freeing of God's people, 41:1-3; 44:28; 45:1 3) He alone could predict that a messenger would proclaim the good news: His people would be set free d. God's verdict on all idols, all false gods 1) They cannot answer, reveal anything 2) They are false gods, amounting to nothing: As empty as the wind, causing confusion

DIVISION V

THE PROPHECIES OF COMFORT AND FREEDOM: A PICTURE OF BELIEVERS BEING SET FREE FROM THE CAPTIVITY OF SIN AND DEATH, 40:1–48:22

B. Set Free Through God's Power to Control Human History, the Very Deeds of People, 41:1-29

(41:1-29) **Introduction**: freedom is one of the major cravings of the human heart. People want to be free to live, worship, work, and move about as they wish. The human heart rebels against restraint, bondage, and enslavement. Yet when the human heart and the experiences of day-to-day life are objectively and honestly evaluated, one tragic fact jumps to the forefront: we are enslaved to sin and death. No person can keep from committing sin, and no person can keep from dying. From the moment we are born, we are doomed to sin, to act selfishly and commit wicked deeds. And we are doomed to die. Fundamentally, to be human means to be a sinner doomed to die. As much as we may dislike this truth, we are all held in bondage to sin and death.

But there is wonderful news: God can free us from sin and from death. We can live righteously and godly in this present life, and we can inherit eternal life, but only by the power of God. This is the important message of this Scripture: *Set Free Through God's Power to Control Human History, the Very Deeds of People*, 41:1-29.

1. God's power to execute judgment upon all who defy Him (vv.1-7).
2. God's power to protect and provide for Israel (His people) (vv.8-20).
3. God's power to prove that He is the only living and true God (vv.21-29).

1 (41:1-7) **Power, of God, to Execute Judgment—Judgment, Executed by, God's Power—Judgment, Executed by, God's Agent Cyrus—Cyrus, King of Persia, Agent of God, to Execute Judgment—Nations, Judgment of, by God's Agent Cyrus—Judgment, of the Nations, Example of—Judgment, Purpose for, Twofold—Sovereignty of God, Facts Concerning, God Controls Nations—Prophecy, Concerning the Nations, Judgment of**: God has the power to execute judgment on the wicked, and history is rapidly moving toward that climactic day when that point in time arrives, the struggle between light and darkness, good and evil, righteousness and wickedness, faith and unbelief will be over. Only the LORD and those who truly believe and follow Him will survive the final and terrifying day of judgment. But note: God does not always wait to execute judgment on the wicked. Sometimes, His hand of judgment begins to fall even as acts of wickedness (sin, evil, unrighteousness) are being committed. This was the case in Isaiah's day and in succeeding generations. Sadly, people and nations were living in a cesspool of immorality, unrighteousness, lawlessness, and violence. The people were steeped in idolatry and false worship. Despite that, God still loved the world, every individual and every nation. Thus He inspired Isaiah to issue another prophecy, a warning of coming judgment. All the people and nations needed to know this fact: God has the power to execute judgment upon all who defy Him.

OUTLINE	SCRIPTURE	SCRIPTURE	OUTLINE
1. God's power to execute judgment upon all who defy Him a. God's summons for the nations to gather for a court trial: A picture of future judgment b. God's two key questions put forward to the people 1) Who has the power to	Keep silence before me, O islands; and let the people renew *their* strength: let them come near; then let them speak: let us come near together to judgment. 2 Who raised up the righteous *man* from the east, called him to his foot, gave the nations before	him, and made *him* rule over kings? he gave *them* as the dust to his sword, *and* as driven stubble to his bow. 3 He pursued them, *and* passed safely; *even* by the way *that* he had not gone with his feet. 4 Who hath wrought and	raise up a ruler to execute judgment on the nations: A prediction of Cyrus, king of Persia (559–530 B.C.), 13:17-18; 44:28; 45:1 • He would destroy nations • He would be unscathed, unstoppable 2) Who has the power to

OUTLINE	SCRIPTURE	SCRIPTURE	OUTLINE
control the affairs of the human race—down through the generations of history?	done *it,* calling the generations from the beginning? I the LORD, the first, and with the last; I *am* he.	said to his brother, Be of good courage.	chance to repent
c. God's answer: He, the LORD—He alone has such power	5 The isles saw *it,* and feared; the ends of the earth were afraid, drew near, and came.	7 So the carpenter encouraged the goldsmith, *and* he that smootheth *with* the hammer him that smote the anvil, saying, It is ready for the soldering: and he fastened it with nails, *that* it should not be moved.	2) To expose their wicked hearts, their trust in one another (v.6) & in their false gods (v.7): Giving them a chance to turn back to the LORD
d. God's twofold purpose for the coming judgment			
1) To strike fear in the people: Giving them a	6 They helped every one his neighbour; and *every one*		

a. God issued a summons for the nations of the earth to gather for a trial (v.1). Attendance at the trial was compulsory not optional. The summons was issued to *all the islands,* to all people and nations from the most distant corner of the earth. They were instructed to approach the LORD in reverence and silence, for they were being summoned to face the judgment of God because of their terrible, destructive, and wicked behavior.

b. God asked the people and the nations two key questions (vv.2-4). Keep in mind that God was giving Isaiah insight into the future day when judgment would be executed against the Babylonian Empire.

1) God's first question directly addresses the issue of judgment: Who has the power to raise up a ruler to execute judgment on the nations? Note that the ruler to be raised up would come from the *east* (v.2). He would conquer nations, subduing king after king and defeating numerous armies with his sword and bow. This is a clear prediction of Cyrus, king of Persia (559–530 B.C.).

In a compelling demonstration of the prophecy's accuracy, Isaiah revealed that the name of the king would be Cyrus even though it was years before this king appeared on the scene of human history (Is.44:28; 45:1). In an earlier prophecy, Isaiah had revealed that the agent of God's wrath on Babylon would be the Median Empire, which is another prophecy predicting the rise of Cyrus (Is.13:17-18).

The point being stressed here is God's power. It was His power alone that raised up Cyrus to execute judgment on the wicked nations who had defied Him and persecuted His people. Cyrus would destroy these nations, pursuing their kings as well as their citizens, killing some and capturing others, until all the people were subjected and made a part of the great Persian Empire. Cyrus and Persia would be unscathed and unstoppable, all because God was using Cyrus as His agent of judgment.

2) God's second question has to do with the issue of sovereignty: Who has the power to control the affairs of mankind, the behavior of nations and people down through history (v.4)? Today, we can look back through history and see that the prophecy concerning Cyrus actually took place. What God predicted happened. Cyrus conquered Babylon and all the nations within the Babylonian Empire, carrying out God's judgment upon the nations of that day and time. From a historical perspective, it is evident that God controlled the affairs of the human race from Isaiah's day to the day of the Persian Empire, a period of more than 160 years. Yet it was not only during that brief period that God exercised His power and sovereignty over the affairs of the human race. God is sovereign over the entire world at all times. He controls the affairs of all nations through all the generations of history.

c. So far in this passage, the one who executes judgment and controls the affairs of the human race has not been identified. But now the answers to the two questions are given, and they are given by God Himself. He alone, the LORD, has this power (v.4b). He is the First and the Last. By *First* is meant that He preceded all the generations of people and nations on earth and, in fact, brought them into being. By *Last* is meant that He will still be existing and overseeing the last generation of human history. He is the eternal God, the LORD of history (Is.44:6; He.13:8; Re.1:8; 2:8; 21:6; 22:13).

d. In descriptive language, God states the twofold purpose of the coming judgment (vv.5-7). These two purposes reveal the true heart of God. Even when He has to execute judgment against the wicked, God's heart is full of compassion and love, not vengeance.

In executing judgment, God's first purpose is to strike fear in people to arouse them to repent. When people are stricken with fear, they sometimes turn away from their sins and back to the LORD, crying out for His help. Isaiah predicted that when the nations and islands, the very ends of the earth, saw the hand of God's judgment being executed through Cyrus, they would fear and tremble under the weight of the judgment.

God's second purpose for executing judgment is to show that the people trusted in one another and in their false gods (vv.6-7) rather than in the LORD. Isaiah predicted that the nations would run to one another to seek help and to form alliances against the Persians. They would encourage one another to be strong, to turn to their idols and false gods for help. They would even build new and better idols, hoping to secure their favor as they opposed the Persian war machine. Of course, their idols and false gods were of no use when the Persians attacked. Keep in mind that God's purpose was to execute judgment against the people and nations because of their wickedness and their false worship. Once the wicked hearts and idolatry of the people were exposed, there was hope that they would turn back to the LORD in repentance.

Thought 1. God alone can execute judgment against all the wicked people and nations of this earth. He alone has the power to oversee and control all nations in addition to all the leaders and citizens of all generations. God dwells in pure holiness and perfection, possessing all knowledge and all power. In view of that, He knows the truth about every nation, every leader, and every citizen. God knows the heart and behavior of us all, whether good or bad, righteous or wicked. As He warned the generations of Isaiah's time, so He warns all generations, including ours today: the Day of Judgment is coming. We must all give an account for what we have done and are doing. If we live good, righteous lives, we will be rewarded. But if we live sinful, wicked lives, we will face the hand of God's judgment and be doomed to eternal separation from Him. Listen to God's warning to the wicked of the earth:

"For the Son of man shall come in the glory of his Father with his angels; and then he shall reward every man according to his works" (Mt.16:27).

"And then shall appear the sign of the Son of man in heaven: and then shall all the tribes of the earth mourn, and they shall see the Son of man coming in the clouds of heaven with power and great glory" (Mt.24:30).

"When the Son of man shall come in his glory, and all the holy angels with him, then shall he sit upon the throne of his glory: And before him shall be gathered all nations: and he shall separate them one from another, as a shepherd divideth *his* sheep from the goats: And he shall set the sheep on his right hand, but the goats on the left...Then shall he say also unto them on the left hand, Depart from me, ye cursed, into everlasting fire, prepared for the devil and his angels" (Mt.25:31-33, 41).

"The Lord knoweth how to deliver the godly out of temptations, and to reserve the unjust unto the day of judgment to be punished" (2 Pe.2:9).

"But the heavens and the earth, which are now, by the same word are kept in store, reserved unto fire against the day of judgment and perdition of ungodly men" (2 Pe.3:7).

"And Enoch also, the seventh from Adam, prophesied of these, saying, Behold, the Lord cometh with ten thousands of his saints, To execute judgment upon all, and to convince all that are ungodly among them of all their ungodly deeds which they have ungodly committed, and of all their hard *speeches* which ungodly sinners have spoken against him" (Jude 1:14-15).

"Behold, he cometh with clouds; and every eye shall see him, and they *also* which pierced him: and all kindreds of the earth shall wail because of him. Even so, Amen" (Re.1:7).

"And I saw a great white throne, and him that sat on it, from whose face the earth and the heaven fled away; and there was found no place for them. And I saw the dead, small and great, stand before God; and the books were opened: and another book was opened, which is *the book* of life: and the dead were judged out of those things which were written in the books, according to their works. And the sea gave up the dead which were in it; and death and hell delivered up the dead which were in them: and they were judged every man according to their works. And death and hell were cast into the lake of fire. This is the second death. And whosoever was not found written in the book of life was cast into the lake of fire" (Re.20:11-15).

"I the LORD search the heart, *I* try the reins, even to give every man according to his ways, *and* according to the fruit of his doings" (Je.17:10).

Thought 2. The motivation for God's judgment must always be remembered. Judging us from a heart of love and compassion, He seeks to save us from harming ourselves and others. Our sinful behavior is what causes so much of the destruction of life and property and the pollution of the environment in the world. An honest evaluation of the devastation we cause reveals that our hearts are wicked, selfish, and greedy, and it should strike fear in us. Exposing the truth of our sinful hearts and behavior should arouse us to repent. It is for this reason that God disciplines and judges us when we commit evil. Repentance is our only hope to escape God's judgment:

"Repent ye therefore, and be converted, that your sins may be blotted out, when the times of refreshing shall come from the presence of the Lord" (Ac.3:19).

"For godly sorrow worketh repentance to salvation not to be repented of: but the sorrow of the world worketh death" (2 Co.7:10).

"For if I have boasted any thing to him of you, I am not ashamed; but as we spake all things to you in truth, even so our boasting, which *I made* before Titus, is found a truth" (2 Co.7:14).

"But the heavens and the earth, which are now, by the same word are kept in store, reserved unto fire against the day of judgment and perdition of ungodly men. But, beloved, be not ignorant of this one thing, that one day *is* with the Lord as a thousand years, and a thousand years as one day. The Lord is not slack concerning his promise, as some men count slackness; but is longsuffering to us-ward, not willing that any should perish, but that all should come to repentance. But the day of the Lord will come as a thief in the night; in the which the heavens shall pass away with a great noise, and the elements shall melt with fervent heat, the earth also and the works that are therein shall be burned up" (2 Pe.3:7-10).

"Because sentence against an evil work is not executed speedily, therefore the heart of the sons of men is fully set in them to do evil. Though a sinner do evil an hundred times, and his *days* be prolonged, yet surely I know that it shall be well with them that fear God, which fear before him: But it shall not be well with the wicked, neither shall he prolong *his* days, *which are* as a shadow; because he feareth not before God" (Ecc.8:11-13).

"And now, because ye have done all these works, saith the LORD, and I spake unto you, rising up early and speaking, but ye heard not; and I called you, but ye answered not; Therefore will I do unto *this* house, which is called by my name, wherein ye trust, and unto the place which I gave to you and to your fathers, as I have done to Shiloh. And I will cast you out of my sight, as I have cast out all your brethren, *even* the whole seed of Ephraim. Therefore pray not thou for this people, neither lift up cry nor prayer for them, neither make intercession to me: for I will not hear thee" (Je.7:13-16).

"But if the wicked will turn from all his sins that he hath committed, and keep all my statutes, and do that which is lawful and right, he shall surely live, he shall not die" (Eze.18:21).

"Cast away from you all your transgressions, whereby ye have transgressed; and make you a new heart and a new spirit: for why will ye die, O house of Israel?" (Eze.18:31).

2 (41:8-20) **Power, of God, to Protect and Provide—Protection, Promised by God—Provision, of God, Promised—Israel, Promises to, God's Protection and Provision—Strength, Promised, to God's People—Deliverance, Promised, from Enemies—Help, Promised, to God's People—God, Names - Titles, Redeemer; Holy One of Israel—Israel, Promises to, Deliverance from Captivity—Prophecy, Concerning Israel, Deliverance from Captivity—Babylon, Captivity of Israel, Deliverance from—Promises, God's Protection, Given to Israel, (His People)—Promises, God's Provision, Given to Israel—Power, of God, to Deliver from Captivity**: God has the power to protect and provide for Israel (His people). This is a wonderful assurance to all believers who sense that they fail the LORD often and fall so short of His glory. Israel too failed the LORD repeatedly and miserably disappointing God over and over again. Nevertheless, the LORD loved His people and never ceased to reach out to them. For generations the Israelites were oppressed, not only by the Assyrians and Babylonians but also by all the surrounding nations who preceded those two world empires. They suffered continual hardship and domination from a stream of tyrants down through history—all due to their sins. In Isaiah's day, few of the Jews genuinely trusted the LORD or lived righteous lives. Most were living in unbelief, rejecting God and engaging in sinful, unrighteous behavior. Still the LORD loved His people and reached out in compassion to them. In the present Scripture, God stirred Isaiah to give strong encouragement and hope to His people. If they truly believed and followed Him, He would use His power to deliver them from their captivity and would protect and provide for them. Note the assurance and promises given by the LORD:

OUTLINE	SCRIPTURE	SCRIPTURE	OUTLINE

2. God's power to protect & provide for Israel (His people)
a. God's assurance: They were His chosen servants
  1) He would, therefore, regather them from the ends of the earth: Set them free from Babylonian captivity, 43:1-7
  2) He would not reject them
b. God's promise to protect His people
  1) They were not to fear, because He would be with them, help them, & uphold them
 	
    • God would shame & confuse all who opposed them: All enemies would perish
 	
    • God would totally eliminate all the enemies who opposed & waged war against His people
 	
  2) They were not to fear, because He would hold their right hands & help them
  3) They were not to fear, because He was their Redeemer: He would deliver them from captivity despite the fact that they
	8 But thou, Israel, *art* my servant, Jacob whom I have chosen, the seed of Abraham my friend.
	9 *Thou* whom I have taken from the ends of the earth, and called thee from the chief men thereof, and said unto thee, Thou *art* my servant; I have chosen thee, and not cast thee away.
	10 Fear thou not; for I *am* with thee: be not dismayed; for I *am* thy God: I will strengthen thee; yea, I will help thee; yea, I will uphold thee with the right hand of my righteousness.
	11 Behold, all they that were incensed against thee shall be ashamed and confounded: they shall be as nothing; and they that strive with thee shall perish.
	12 Thou shalt seek them, and shalt not find them, *even* them that contended with thee: they that war against thee shall be as nothing, and as a thing of nought.
	13 For I the LORD thy God will hold thy right hand, saying unto thee, Fear not; I will help thee.
	14 Fear not, thou worm Jacob, *and* ye men of Israel; I will help thee, saith the LORD, and thy redeemer, the Holy One of Israel.
		15 Behold, I will make thee a new sharp threshing instrument having teeth: thou shalt thresh the mountains, and beat *them* small, and shalt make the hills as chaff.
		16 Thou shalt fan them, and the wind shall carry them away, and the whirlwind shall scatter them: and thou shalt rejoice in the LORD, *and* shalt glory in the Holy One of Israel.
		17 *When* the poor and needy seek water, and *there is* none, *and* their tongue faileth for thirst, I the LORD will hear them, *I* the God of Israel will not forsake them.
		18 I will open rivers in high places, and fountains in the midst of the valleys: I will make the wilderness a pool of water, and the dry land springs of water.
		19 I will plant in the wilderness the cedar, the shittah tree, and the myrtle, and the oil tree; I will set in the desert the fir tree, *and* the pine, and the box tree together:
		20 That they may see, and know, and consider, and understand together, that the hand of the LORD hath done this, and the Holy One of Israel hath created it.
			were mere worms (weak & helpless)
			  • God would empower them to defeat their enemies: Make them like a threshing sledge with sharp teeth, threshing their enemies & reducing them to chaff with the wind blowing their enemies away
			  • God would give His people a reason to rejoice & to glory in Him
			c. God's promise to provide for His people as they suffered in exile or returned from captivity
			  1) The people would be poor & needy, parched with thirst
			  2) The LORD would hear their cry & prayer
			    • He would provide water
			
			    • He would provide a fruitful land: Would even restore the desert into productive land
			
			  3) The LORD's purpose: To demonstrate His power, showing the people that He alone could free His people & meet their needs, 14, 16

a. God assured His people that they were His *chosen* servants (vv.8-9). Note that God Himself addressed the people as Israel, *my servant* and Jacob, *whom I have chosen*. He then called them the descendants of Abraham, *my friend* (v.8). These are titles of great honor. Consider what a privilege it is to be a servant of God, chosen by Him, and to be a descendant of Abraham, the friend of God Himself. God had always pursued a close relationship with the Israelites, even those of Isaiah's day, and offered them the privilege of knowing Him intimately. In fact, God has usually offered the privilege of knowing Him personally to both Jew and Gentile. But the human race has always chosen to reject His offer. Even though God had chosen the Israelites to be His very special servants, they had often proved unfaithful. Consequently, God was forced to continually discipline and punish them.

Here, it is God's purpose to give His people great assurance. Though God used the Assyrians and Babylonians to punish them, the LORD would one day gather them from the ends of the earth. They were His servants, chosen by Him;

therefore, He would not forget them in their hour of trial. He would not reject them (v.9). He would set them free them from the Babylonian captivity so they could return to the promised land.

b. God assured His people that He would protect them in the here and now, in the present distress they were experiencing (vv.10-16). No doubt God's promise of freeing His people from the coming captivity was very encouraging, especially to the true believers who were to endure the Babylonian captivity. But they needed far more than just a distant, future hope of deliverance. Righteous believers needed to know that God was with them day by day in their present painful circumstances. So God met their need and gave them a most wonderful promise: whether in the present or in the future and in whatever circumstances, God's people were not to fear. Three reasons are given why righteous believers should not be anxious, afraid.

First, God's people were not to fear because He Himself would be with them. He would strengthen and help them and uphold them with His right hand—His righteous, victorious hand. God's promise to be with His people applies to all righteous believers of all generations. Even in the very worst times believers are not to be dismayed or frightened by the oppression of any enemy. Even if the enemy seems much stronger and the believers feel extremely weak, the LORD promises to strengthen His people. Even when believers fall and collapse before the enemy, the LORD will uphold them with His right hand, a hand of righteousness and justice (2 Ti.4:18).

⇒ The LORD will shame and confuse all who oppose His people; their enemies will perish by the LORD's victorious, righteous hand (v.11).

⇒ The LORD will totally eliminate all the enemies who contend with or wage war against His people (v.12).

Second, God's people were not to fear because He would hold their right hands and help them as they faced their enemies (v.13). Note the close relationship being stressed here: the LORD tells righteous believers that He is "your God" and that He will "hold your right hand." He will "help you." Meditating upon this promise should give enormous encouragement to believers who are facing oppression and hardships.

Third, God's people were not to fear because He was their Redeemer (v.14). *Redeemer* here refers to the kinsman redeemer *(goel),* who in ancient history was the family protector. The redeemer was a person who saved or rescued a family member who was suffering or distressed due to financial trouble, the death of a spouse, loss of property, or some other heavy burden (see DEEPER STUDY #1—Ru.2:20 for more discussion). In the present Scripture, the LORD calls Himself the Redeemer, the family protector of His people. As their Redeemer, He promises to help them. The implication for the Israelites was that He would deliver them from their captivity. Note also the other title the LORD claims for Himself: the Holy One of Israel (His people). As the Holy One, He is distinct, completely set apart from all other creatures by His power, knowledge, and understanding. Thus, He is able to completely fulfill His purpose in the lives of His people despite their hardships or difficult circumstances. Note that He refers to His people as *worms,* which simply means that they are weak and helpless. Though they are too weak to help themselves, they are not to fear the enemies who oppress them, for God is their Redeemer. And as their Redeemer, God will do two things for His people:

⇒ The LORD will empower them to defeat their enemies (v.15). He will make them like a threshing sledge with sharp teeth. They will thresh their enemies and reduce them to chaff, and the enemies will be blown away as if by a strong wind (vv.15-16).

⇒ The LORD will give them hearts that rejoice and glory in Him (v.16).

c. God assured His people that He would provide for them (vv.17-20). This specific promise of God refers to God's provision for His people during the Babylonian exile and their return from captivity. However, the promise is applicable to every generation of believers. Whenever God's people are poor and needy or parched with thirst, the LORD will hear their cry for help (vv.17-19). He will provide water and a fruitful land for them. He will even turn the desert into fertile soil so that it will be productive and fruitful. Note the LORD's *purpose* in providing for the needs of His people: it is to demonstrate His power and to show that He alone can free them and meet their needs (v.20). The world needs to witness God's miraculous provision for His people when they are suffering and facing difficult circumstances. When unbelievers see the miraculous power of God in action, some will turn to the LORD and become genuine followers of Him.

Thought 1. Two of the great promises of God are that of His protection and provision. If we are believers who truly follow the LORD, He promises to protect and deliver us when any enemy attacks or oppresses us. Although God does not always deliver us *from* difficult circumstances, He will always deliver us *through* them. No matter what trial, hardship, temptation, or adversary confronts us, the LORD will protect us and give us whatever provision we need to overcome the difficult circumstance.

If we genuinely trust the LORD, obey His commandments, and live righteously, the LORD promises to deliver us through...

- financial difficulties
- unemployment
- broken relationships
- family divisions
- business problems
- emotional difficulties
- sorrow
- disease
- hunger
- thirst

The LORD will even deliver us from ever having to taste or experience death. When the moment of our departure comes, quicker than the eye can blink, the LORD will transfer us from this world into heaven. One moment we will be in this world, and the next we will be in the very presence of God.

(1) The LORD promises to protect us through all the trials of life and from all the enemies who oppress us.

> **"Behold, I give unto you power to tread on serpents and scorpions, and over all the power of the enemy: and nothing shall by any means hurt you" (Lu.10:19).**
> **"But there shall not an hair of your head perish" (Lu.21:18).**

"Who shall separate us from the love of Christ? *shall* tribulation, or distress, or persecution, or famine, or nakedness, or peril, or sword?...Nay, in all these things we are more than conquerors through him that loved us. For I am persuaded, that neither death, nor life, nor angels, nor principalities, nor powers, nor things present, nor things to come, Nor height, nor depth, nor any other creature, shall be able to separate us from the love of God, which is in Christ Jesus our Lord" (Ro.8:35, 37-39).

"There hath no temptation taken you but such as is common to man: but God *is* faithful, who will not suffer you to be tempted above that ye are able; but will with the temptation also make a way to escape, that ye may be able to bear *it*" (1 Co.10:13).

"And the Lord shall deliver me from every evil work, and will preserve *me* unto his heavenly kingdom: to whom *be* glory for ever and ever. Amen" (2 Ti.4:18).

"For whatsoever is born of God overcometh the world: and this is the victory that overcometh the world, *even* our faith. Who is he that overcometh the world, but he that believeth that Jesus is the Son of God?" (1 Jn.5:4-5).

"The LORD shall fight for you, and ye shall hold your peace" (Ex.14:14).

"The eternal God *is* thy refuge, and underneath *are* the everlasting arms: and he shall thrust out the enemy from before thee; and shall say, Destroy *them*" (De.33:27).

"For the eyes of the LORD run to and fro throughout the whole earth, to show himself strong in the behalf of *them* whose heart *is* perfect toward him. Herein thou hast done foolishly: therefore from henceforth thou shalt have wars" (2 Chr.16:9).

"The angel of the LORD encampeth round about them that fear him, and delivereth them" (Ps.34:7).

"Through thee will we push down our enemies: through thy name will we tread them under that rise up against us" (Ps.44:5).

"He shall cover thee with his feathers, and under his wings shalt thou trust: his truth *shall be thy* shield and buckler" (Ps.91:4).

(2) The LORD will provide for us and meet every need we have.

"But seek ye first the kingdom of God, and his righteousness; and all these things [housing, food, clothing] shall be added unto you" (Mt.6:33).

"But my God shall supply all your need according to his riches in glory by Christ Jesus" (Ph.4:19).

"*Let your* conversation [conduct, behavior] *be* without covetousness; *and be* content with such things as ye have: for he hath said, I will never leave thee, nor forsake thee. So that we may boldly say, The Lord *is* my helper, and I will not fear what man shall do unto me" (He.13:5-6).

"But if from thence thou shalt seek the LORD thy God, thou shalt find *him,* if thou seek him with all thy heart and with all thy soul" (De.4:29).

"And thou shalt return and obey the voice of the LORD, and do all his commandments which I command thee this day. And the LORD thy God will make thee plenteous in every work of thine hand, in the fruit of thy body, and in the fruit of thy cattle, and in the fruit of thy land, for good: for the LORD will again rejoice over thee for good, as he rejoiced over thy fathers" (De.30:8-9).

"For the oppression of the poor, for the sighing of the needy, now will I arise, saith the LORD; I will set *him* in safety *from him that* puffeth at him" (Ps.12:5).

"Thou hast also given me the shield of thy salvation: and thy right hand hath holden me up, and thy gentleness hath made me great" (Ps.18:35).

"The LORD *is* my strength and my shield; my heart trusted in him, and I am helped: therefore my heart greatly rejoiceth; and with my song will I praise him" (Ps.28:7).

"*Oh* how great *is* thy goodness, which thou hast laid up for them that fear thee; *which* thou hast wrought for them that trust in thee before the sons of men!" (Ps.31:19).

"But I *am* poor and needy; *yet* the Lord thinketh upon me: thou *art* my help and my deliverer; make no tarrying, O my God" (Ps.40:17).

"Thou visitest the earth, and waterest it: thou greatly enrichest it with the river of God, *which* is full of water: thou preparest them corn, when thou hast so provided for it" (Ps.65:9).

"Blessed *be* the Lord, *who* daily loadeth us *with benefits, even* the God of our salvation. Selah" (Ps.68:19).

"I will abundantly bless her provision: I will satisfy her poor with bread" (Ps.132:15).

"For thou hast been a strength to the poor, a strength to the needy in his distress, a refuge from the storm, a shadow from the heat, when the blast of the terrible ones *is* as a storm *against* the wall" (Is.25:4).

"Fear thou not; for I *am* with thee: be not dismayed; for I *am* thy God: I will strengthen thee; yea, I will help thee; yea, I will uphold thee with the right hand of my righteousness" (Is.41:10).

"Fear not: for I have redeemed thee, I have called *thee* by thy name; thou *art* mine. When thou passest through the waters, I *will be* with thee; and through the rivers, they shall not overflow thee: when thou walkest through the fire, thou shalt not be burned; neither shall the flame kindle upon thee" (Is.43:1-2).

"And *even* to *your* old age I *am* he; and *even* to hoar [gray] hairs will I carry *you:* I have made, and I will bear; even I will carry, and will deliver *you*" (Is.46:4).

3 (41:21-29) **Idolatry, Inadequacy, Discussed—Gods, False, Inadequacy of, Discussed—Idolaters, Court Trial of, Must Prove Their Case—Worship, False, Inadequacy of, Discussed—Idols - Idolatry, Verdict of God, Worthless—Proofs, of God, Contrasted with Idols—God, Proof, Only Living and True God**: God has the power to prove that He is the only living and true God. Every one of the events prophesied by Isaiah would be fulfilled exactly as revealed by God:

⇒ the Persian king, Cyrus, would be raised up by God
⇒ the Jews would be taken captive by the Babylonians
⇒ the Jews would be set free by Cyrus and allowed to return to the promised land

Along with that, God promised to protect righteous believers and to meet their needs day by day as they experienced these three significant events. God's power to fulfill these prophecies and to perform these miraculous works proves that He is the only living and true God. When people objectively and honestly study the prophecies of God's Word and their fulfillment, they immediately understand the most basic truth in the universe: the LORD (Jehovah, Yahweh) is the only living and true God.

In the face of this indisputable evidence, all people who choose to reject the LORD and worship false gods must appear in court to stand before the Judge of the universe to present their case. And when idolaters step forth to present the defense for their idols, their arguments for idolatry must be just as strong as the case for the LORD's power and existence.

OUTLINE	SCRIPTURE	SCRIPTURE	OUTLINE

3. God's power to prove that He is the only living & true God
a. God's challenge to idolaters: Prove your case
  1) Prove that idols or false gods can predict the future & fulfill the events
    • Prove they can explain past events, showing how the events relate to the present & are leading to a specific outcome
    • Prove they can foretell coming events
  2) Prove that idols can do mighty works—good or bad—that would fill us with amazement & fear
b. God's verdict on idolatry
  1) Idols are less than nothing, worthless
  2) Idolaters are detestable
c. God's proof that He alone is the only living & true God
  1) He alone has the power to control history: He would
	21 Produce your cause, saith the LORD; bring forth your strong *reasons,* saith the King of Jacob.
	22 Let them bring *them* forth, and show us what shall happen: let them show the former things, what they *be,* that we may consider them, and know the latter end of them; or declare us things for to come.
	23 Show the things that are to come hereafter, that we may know that ye *are* gods: yea, do good, or do evil, that we may be dismayed, and behold *it* together.
	24 Behold, ye *are* of nothing, and your work of nought: an abomination *is he that* chooseth you.
	25 I have raised up *one* from the north, and he shall come: from the rising of the sun shall he call upon my name:
		and he shall come upon princes as *upon* morter, and as the potter treadeth clay.
		26 Who hath declared from the beginning, that we may know? and beforetime, that we may say, *He is* righteous? yea, *there is* none that showeth, yea, *there is* none that declareth, yea, *there is* none that heareth your words.
		27 The first *shall say* to Zion, Behold, behold them: and I will give to Jerusalem one that bringeth good tidings.
		28 For I beheld, and *there was* no man; even among them, and *there was* no counsellor, that, when I asked of them, could answer a word.
		29 Behold, they *are* all vanity; their works *are* nothing: their molten images *are* wind and confusion.
			raise up Cyrus of Persia to conquer the earth & free Israel
			  2) He alone predicted the historical rise of Cyrus: His execution of God's judgment upon the nations & the freeing of God's people, 41:1-3; 44:28; 45:1
			
			  3) He alone could predict that a messenger would proclaim the good news: His people would be set free
			d. God's verdict on all idols, all false gods
			  1) They cannot answer, reveal anything
			
			  2) They are false gods, amounting to nothing: As empty as the wind, causing confusion

a. God challenges the idolaters of Isaiah's day and of all succeeding generations to present their case for worshipping idols, false gods (vv.21-23). "Prove that your false gods can predict the future and make the predictions come true. Prove that they can explain past events, then show how they relate to the present and are leading to a specific outcome, to a future that has already been destined and determined by *their* power." If false worshippers could foretell coming events and bring those events to pass, they could prove that their so-called gods were true. Not only that, idolaters must prove that their false gods can do mighty works, works (good or bad) so miraculous that they would fill people with amazement and fear. But no so-called god can do these things. Only the one living and true LORD can do them, and only He has proven that He can.

These are exactly the things God has done down through the generations of human history. In addition to working mightily in the lives of righteous believers, the LORD has fulfilled every prophecy of His Holy Word, explaining past events and how they relate to the present and to the predictions of what will take place in the future. Beginning with the woman's seed, who would crush the head of the serpent, stretching through the birth of Israel as a descendant of Abraham, and reaching on down through history to the coming of Christ, the LORD has fulfilled the wonderful predictions concerning the coming seed, the Savior of the world. (See outline and notes—Ge.3:15; 12:2-3; 15:1-21; Is.49:1-50:11; 52:13–53:12; Mt.1:18-25 for more discussion.) In addition to predicting and fulfilling past events, the LORD also gives prophecy after prophecy concerning the future of the world. As the events of past predictions have come true, so the predictions of future events will be fulfilled. Not a single word of His promises will fail (1 K.8:56; Mt.5:18; Lu.21:33).

b. Of course, idolaters can make no case for their false gods. Subsequently, God issues His verdict on all idolaters and their idols. His verdict shatters the hopes and the trust of all idolaters, for when facing the scrutiny of God's holy judgment, idols are exposed as less than nothing, utterly worthless. The verdict God pronounces against idolaters dooms them for eternity. They are abominable, detestable, filthy in the sight of God.

c. The proof that the LORD is the only living and true God is of critical importance (vv.25-27). To emphasize the truth, the LORD stresses three astounding facts:

⇒ He alone had the power to control history, and He would prove His power by raising up Cyrus of Persia to conquer the earth and free Israel (also see vv.2-4).

⇒ He alone could predict the historical rise of Cyrus and that the Persian king would carry out God's judgment upon the nations and free God's people from their Babylonian captivity (13:17-18: 41:1-3; 44:28; 45:1). No one else could ever make a prediction that revealed the name of the coming ruler more than a century before his birth. No one else in heaven or earth could even hint that such an event would take place, much less cause it to occur.

⇒ He alone could predict that a messenger would proclaim the good news, the fact that His people would be set free from their captivity and return to the promised land.

d. As God looks around the courtroom, waiting for a response from the idolaters, not even the slightest evidence can be presented to support false gods. Apparently, God issues His final verdict on all idols and idolaters (vv.28-29). They are false—each and every one—false gods and false worshippers. They are empty, useless, and worthless. And the worship and works of the idolaters amount to nothing in the sight of God. Their images and false gods are as empty as the wind and nothing but confusion.

Thought 1. We all worship something. None of us is free from worshipping while we walk upon the face of the earth. We either worship the LORD Himself, or we worship ourselves, some other person, material possessions, or false gods created by the human imagination. Even an atheist who denies that God exists gives his heart to something. When we worship something, we commit our heart and life to it; and we focus our devotion, energy, and ambition on it. God demands that we focus upon Him, the only living and true God, and that we commit and devote ourselves to Him, giving Him our utmost attention and greatest energy. But many of us do the very opposite.

Only the LORD is to receive our devotion and worship, but many of us are more focused upon living in impressive houses, wearing the latest style of clothing, and securing more wealth and property than we are upon wor-shipping God. Many of us spend more time in front of a mirror than we do in daily prayer. Some put girl-friends, boyfriends, wives, husbands, children, and friends before the LORD. Still others put recreation, relaxation, and comfort before the LORD. Any person or thing that becomes dominant in our lives, any person or thing we put before the LORD, becomes an idol, the focus of our devotion and worship. God forbids such idolatry and false worship:

"For as I passed by, and beheld your devotions, I found an altar with this inscription, TO THE UNKNOWN GOD. Whom therefore ye ignorantly worship, him declare I unto you. God that made the world and all things therein, seeing that he is Lord of heaven and earth, dwelleth not in temples made with hands; Neither is worshipped with men's hands, as though he needed any thing, seeing he giveth to all life, and breath, and all things; And hath made of one blood all nations of men for to dwell on all the face of the earth, and hath determined the times before appointed, and the bounds of their habitation; That they should seek the Lord, if haply they might feel after him, and find him, though he be not far from every one of us: For in him we live, and move, and have our being; as certain also of your own poets have said, For we are also his offspring. Forasmuch then as we are the offspring of God, we ought not to think that the Godhead is like unto gold, or silver, or stone, graven by art and man's device. And the times of this ignorance God winked at; but now commandeth all men every where to repent: Because he hath appointed a day, in the which he will judge the world in righteousness by *that* man whom he hath ordained; *whereof* he hath given assurance unto all *men*, in that he hath raised him from the dead" (Ac.17:23-31).

"For the wrath of God is revealed from heaven against all ungodliness and unrighteousness of men, who hold the truth in unrighteousness; Because that which may be known of God is manifest in them; for God hath showed *it* unto them. For the invisible things of him from the creation of the world are clearly seen, being understood by the things that are made, *even* his eternal power and Godhead; so that they are without excuse: Because that, when they knew God, they glorified *him* not as God, neither were thankful; but became vain in their imaginations, and their foolish heart was darkened. Professing themselves to be wise, they became fools, And changed the glory of the uncorruptible God into an image made like to corruptible man, and to birds, and fourfooted beasts, and creeping things. Wherefore God also gave them up to uncleanness through the lusts of their own hearts, to dishonour their own bodies between themselves: Who changed the truth of God into a lie, and worshipped and served the creature more than the Creator, who is blessed for ever. Amen" (Ro.1:18-25).

"As concerning therefore the eating of those things that are offered in sacrifice unto idols, we know that an idol *is* nothing in the world, and that *there is* none other God but one. For though there be that are called gods, whether in heaven or in earth, (as there be gods many, and lords many,) But to us *there is but* one God, the Father, of whom *are* all things, and we in him; and one Lord Jesus Christ, by whom *are* all things, and we by him" (1 Co.8:4-6).

"Little children, keep yourselves from idols. Amen" (1 Jn.5:21).

"Thou shalt have no other gods before me. Thou shalt not make unto thee any graven image, or any likeness *of any thing* that *is* in heaven above, or that *is* in the earth beneath, or that *is* in the water under the earth: Thou shalt not bow down thyself to them, nor serve them: for I the LORD thy God *am* a jealous God, visiting the iniquity of the fathers upon the children unto the third and fourth *generation* of them that hate me" (Ex.20:3-5).

"Ye shall make you no idols nor graven image, neither rear you up a standing image, neither shall ye set up *any* image of stone in your land, to bow down unto it: for I *am* the LORD your God" (Le.26:1).

"Take heed to yourselves, that your heart be not deceived, and ye turn aside, and serve other gods, and worship them" (De.11:16).

"There shall no strange god be in thee; neither shalt thou worship any strange god" (Ps.81:9).

"I *am* the LORD: that *is* my name: and my glory will I not give to another, neither my praise to graven images" (Is.42:8).

CHAPTER 42

C. Set Free Through God's Perfect Servant, the Messiah, the Lord Jesus Christ (the First of Four *Servant Songs*), 42:1-25

49:1-13; 50:1-11; 52:12–53:12

1. The introduction of the Messiah
  a. He is God's Servant
  b. He is God's Chosen One
  c. He possesses God's Spirit
  d. He is righteous (perfect) & brings justice to the world
  e. He is peaceful, not threatening or lawless

  f. He is compassionate
    1) Helps the bruised (weak)
    2) Helps the smoldering wicks (the hopeless)
    3) Executes true justice
  g. He is steadfast, persevering
    1) In establishing justice
    2) In teaching God's law (Word) & giving hope

2. The mission of the Messiah
  a. The mission guaranteed by God the LORD
    1) By His creative power
      • Created the heavens & earth
      • Gave breath & life to people
    2) By His righteousness
    3) By His presence & care
  b. The mission spelled out by God
    1) To institute God's new covenant, 49:8; 55:3; Je.31:31-34; Eze.34:25
    2) To be God's light for all nations, Jn.8:12; 9:39-41; Co.1:13
      • To open the eyes of the spiritually blind
      • To free the captives who are in darkness

  c. The mission assured by God
    1) His name & glory would not be given to another

    2) His power had fulfilled former predictions
    3) His power would fulfill the predictions concerning the promised Messiah
3. The response to the Messiah
  a. God's challenge to those who accepted the Messiah: Demanded a song of praise
    1) Everyone must sing
      • The sailors & islanders
      • The people who lived in the desert & its towns
      • The few people who

Behold my servant, whom I uphold; mine elect, *in whom* my soul delighteth; I have put my spirit upon him: he shall bring forth judgment to the Gentiles.
2 He shall not cry, nor lift up, nor cause his voice to be heard in the street.
3 A bruised reed shall he not break, and the smoking flax shall he not quench: he shall bring forth judgment unto truth.
4 He shall not fail nor be discouraged, till he have set judgment in the earth: and the isles shall wait for his law.
5 Thus saith God the LORD, he that created the heavens, and stretched them out; he that spread forth the earth, and that which cometh out of it; he that giveth breath unto the people upon it, and spirit to them that walk therein:
6 I the LORD have called thee in righteousness, and will hold thine hand, and will keep thee, and give thee for a covenant of the people, for a light of the Gentiles;
7 To open the blind eyes, to bring out the prisoners from the prison, *and* them that sit in darkness out of the prison house.
8 I *am* the LORD: that *is* my name: and my glory will I not give to another, neither my praise to graven images.
9 Behold, the former things are come to pass, and new things do I declare: before they spring forth I tell you of them.
10 Sing unto the LORD a new song, *and* his praise from the end of the earth, ye that go down to the sea, and all that is therein; the isles, and the inhabitants thereof.
11 Let the wilderness and the cities thereof lift up *their voice,* the villages *that* Kedar

doth inhabit: let the inhabitants of the rock sing, let them shout from the top of the mountains.
12 Let them give glory unto the LORD, and declare his praise in the islands.
13 The LORD shall go forth as a mighty man, he shall stir up jealousy like a man of war: he shall cry, yea, roar; he shall prevail against his enemies.
14 I have long time holden my peace; I have been still, *and* refrained myself: *now* will I cry like a traveiling woman; I will destroy and devour at once.
15 I will make waste mountains and hills, and dry up all their herbs; and I will make the rivers islands, and I will dry up the pools.
16 And I will bring the blind by a way *that* they knew not; I will lead them in paths *that* they have not known: I will make darkness light before them, and crooked things straight. These things will I do unto them, and not forsake them.
17 They shall be turned back, they shall be greatly ashamed, that trust in graven images, that say to the molten images, Ye *are* our gods.
18 Hear, ye deaf; and look, ye blind, that ye may see.
19 Who *is* blind, but my servant? or deaf, as my messenger *that* I sent? who *is* blind as *he that is* perfect, and blind as the LORD'S servant?
20 Seeing many things, but thou observest not; opening the ears, but he heareth not.
21 The LORD is well pleased for his righteousness' sake; he will magnify the law, and make *it* honourable.
22 But this *is* a people robbed and spoiled; *they are* all of them snared in holes, and they are hid in prison houses: they are for a prey, and none delivereth; for a spoil, and none saith, Restore.
23 Who among you will give ear to this? *who* will hearken and hear for the time to come?
24 Who gave Jacob for a spoil, and Israel to the robbers? did not the LORD, he against whom we have

lived in the villages of Kedar (or Arabia)
      • The mass of people in the city of Sela
    2) Everyone must glorify the LORD & praise Him

  b. God's warning to those who rejected the Messiah & stood as God's enemies
    1) God would go forth & triumph over His enemies

      • He had kept silent & been patient a long time
      • The day for judgment had now come—just like the day for a woman to give birth
    2) God would destroy the land owned by His enemies, all those who reject the Messiah

  c. God's promise to the spiritually blind who confessed their need for the Messiah
    1) God would lead & guide them
      • Light their path
      • Remove all obstacles
    2) God would not forsake them

  d. God's indictment against the idolaters
    1) They trusted in false gods
    2) They would be turned away—in shame

4. The summons to believe God's promise
  a. Reason 1: Because they were blind servants & deaf messengers
    1) They failed to serve & bear witness to the LORD
    2) They paid no attention to the works of God nor to His Word
  b. Reason 2: Because God had magnified His law (Word)—to teach people to believe Him & to live righteously
  c. Reason 3: Because God's people (Israel) had disobeyed His law & were suffering His punishment
    1) Were being robbed, entrapped, imprisoned, & enslaved
    2) Had no one to rescue them
  d. Reason 4: Because they refused to learn from past experience
    1) They refused to accept the fact that it was the LORD who had punished them: Due to their refusal to

| follow His ways & obey His commandments | sinned? for they would not walk in his ways, neither were they obedient unto his law. | anger, and the strength of battle: and it hath set him on fire round about, yet he knew | (chastisement) |
| 2) They refused to understand God's discipline | 25 Therefore he hath poured upon him the fury of his | not; and it burned him, yet he laid *it* not to heart. | |

DIVISION V

THE PROPHECIES OF COMFORT AND FREEDOM: A PICTURE OF BELIEVERS BEING SET FREE FROM THE CAPTIVITY OF SIN AND DEATH, 40:1–48:22

C. Set Free Through God's Perfect Servant, the Messiah, the Lord Jesus Christ (the First of Four *Servant Songs*), 42:1-25

(42:1-25) **Introduction**: if there has ever been a day when people needed help, encouragement, rescuing, it is today. People are sinking ever deeper in the sand under the weight of heavy burdens, constant and brazen temptations, unimaginable evil, and a growing insensitivity and indifference to it all. In addition, a host of personal problems are overwhelming people's spirits today, problems such as...

- dissatisfaction, purposelessness, emptiness
- tension, pressure, and anxiety
- insufficient income, financial difficulty, bankruptcy
- unemployment, loss of job, lack of skills
- a sense of discouragement, failure, inadequacy

People's need for help is the reason for the present Scripture. God knows our desperate need, and with deep compassion He has stepped forward to meet it. This He did by sending His Servant, the Messiah, into the world. Through His very own Servant, the Lord Jesus Christ, God gives us the power to endure and conquer the hardships that threaten to crush us. He meets all the needs of the human heart, which He created to love and have fellowship with Him. This passage is the first of four "Servant Songs" in the book of *Isaiah* (49:1-13; 50:1-11; 52:12-53:12). This is, *Set Free Through God's Perfect Servant, the Messiah, the Lord Jesus Christ (the First of Four Servant Songs)*, 42:1-25.

1. The promise to send the Messiah (vv.1-4).
2. The mission of the Messiah (vv.5-9).
3. The response to the Messiah (vv.10-17).
4. The summons to believe God's promise (vv.18-25).

1 (42:1-4) **Messiah, Names – Titles, God's Servant—Messiah, Nature and Character of, Sevenfold—Jesus Christ, Names – Titles, God's Servant—Jesus Christ, Nature – Character of, Sevenfold**: this is a prophecy predicting the coming of the Messiah, a prophecy given some seven hundred years before the Lord Jesus Christ came to earth. The godly nature and character of the Messiah is discussed first, for the eternal fate of people hinges on their understanding of who the Messiah is. God Himself is speaking about the Messiah, which indicates the extreme importance of this passage:

OUTLINE	SCRIPTURE	SCRIPTURE	OUTLINE
1. The introduction of the Messiah	Behold my servant, whom I uphold; mine elect, *in whom* my soul delighteth; I have put my spirit upon him: he shall bring forth judgment to the Gentiles. 2 He shall not cry, nor lift up, nor cause his voice to be heard in the street.	3 A bruised reed shall he not break, and the smoking flax shall he not quench: he shall bring forth judgment unto truth. 4 He shall not fail nor be discouraged, till he have set judgment in the earth: and the isles shall wait for his law.	f. He is compassionate
a. He is God's Servant			1) Helps the bruised (weak)
b. He is God's Chosen One			2) Helps the smoldering
c. He possesses God's Spirit			wicks (the hopeless)
d. He is righteous (perfect) & brings justice to the world			3) Executes true justice
			g. He is steadfast, persevering
e. He is peaceful, not threatening or lawless			1) In establishing justice
			2) In teaching God's law (Word) & giving hope

a. The Messiah will be *God's Servant* (v.1). "Behold! My Servant." *Behold* means to sit up and take notice. "Here is my Servant" (NIV). Pay attention to Him. "Look at my Servant" (NLT). God is presenting His Servant, the Messiah, to the world. So He commands the world to look, to pay attention to Him. Being God's Servant means that the Messiah will be *devoted* to God. His heart will be set on doing exactly what God commands. God is sending the Messiah into the world on a very specific mission, and since He is God's *Servant,* the Messiah's task will be to carry out the mission assigned Him. This is the announcement God is making. "Behold! My Servant." He is coming to accomplish God's will on earth, and God declares that He will uphold Him. No matter what the difficulties or how great the opposition, God Almighty will sustain, strengthen, and protect His Servant. He will make sure the Messiah accomplishes His task. Nothing will defeat Him or keep Him from doing God's will.

b. The Messiah will be God's *Chosen One*. He has been called, appointed by God Himself. He has not been conceived or sent on His mission by an earthly ruler or heavenly being, but rather by God Himself. The coming of the Messiah into the world was not determined by the wisdom of men, but rather by the infinite wisdom of God. God and God alone appointed the Messiah. He is God's Chosen One. And God takes great delight in the Messiah, in all that He is in His nature and character and in all the work that He accomplishes. God expressed His delight in the Lord Jesus Christ on two different occasions—at His baptism and at His transfiguration:

> "And Jesus, when he was baptized, went up straightway out of the water: and, lo, the heavens were opened unto him, and he saw the Spirit of God descending like a dove, and lighting upon him: And lo a voice from heaven, saying, This is my beloved Son, in whom I am well pleased" (Mt.3:16-17).
>
> "And after six days Jesus taketh Peter, James, and John his brother, and bringeth them up into an high mountain apart, And was transfigured before them: and his face did shine as the sun, and his raiment was white as the light. And, behold, there appeared unto them Moses and Elias talking with him. Then answered Peter, and said unto Jesus, Lord, it is good for us to be here: if thou wilt, let us make here three tabernacles; one for thee, and one for Moses, and one for Elias. While he yet spake, behold, a bright cloud overshadowed them: and behold a voice out of the cloud, which said, This is my beloved Son, in whom I am well pleased; hear ye him" (Mt.17:1-5).

c. The Messiah will have God's very own Spirit. This passage stresses that the Messiah will be filled with the fullness of God's Spirit. God's Spirit will rest on Him, fully equipping Him to carry out His task. Down through history, God had given His Spirit to His servants, but they were mere human beings, so the power of the Spirit to work through them was always limited. But that will not be the case with the Messiah, the Savior of the world. The Spirit of the LORD—all the fullness of God Himself—will rest upon Him (11:2; Col.2:8).

d. The Messiah will be righteous and just, possessing within His very nature the perfection of virtue and decency. Thus, He will bring true justice to the nations and the people of the world. Note how important this is to God, for it is mentioned three times in these four verses (v.1, 3, 4). Keep in mind that *true justice* is the result of acting exactly as one should, always doing what is right, and treating others as they should be treated. *True justice* and *salvation* are strong counterparts in that righteous behavior is oftentimes a good indication of a person's salvation, and salvation leads to righteous behavior. The point being emphasized is this: the Messiah's very nature compels Him to save the world by establishing justice among its nations and peoples. Of course, when the Lord Jesus Christ returns to set up God's kingdom on earth, His justice will be all that is needed to save the world and to eliminate all wicked and evil behavior.

e. The Messiah will be peaceful, not boisterous, threatening, or lawless (v.2). He will not be a rabble-rouser or a trouble-maker. He will not take part in riots, uprisings, or revolts. He will not be violent, but rather have a calm, restful spirit. As a man of peace, He will share the message of harmony between people and between God and people.

> "And suddenly there was with the angel a multitude of the heavenly host praising God, and saying, Glory to God in the highest, and on earth peace, good will toward men" (Lu.2:13-14).
>
> "Peace I leave with you, my peace I give unto you: not as the world giveth, give I unto you. Let not your heart be troubled, neither let it be afraid" (Jn.14:27).
>
> "These things I have spoken unto you, that in me ye might have peace. In the world ye shall have tribulation: but be of good cheer; I have overcome the world" (Jn.16:33).
>
> "The word which *God* sent unto the children of Israel, preaching peace by Jesus Christ: (he is Lord of all:)" (Ac.10:36).
>
> "Therefore being justified by faith, we have peace with God through our Lord Jesus Christ" (Ro.5:1).
>
> "For he is our peace, who hath made both one, and hath broken down the middle wall of partition *between us*" (Ep.2:14).
>
> "And, having made peace through the blood of his cross, by him to reconcile all things unto himself; by him, *I say,* whether *they be* things in earth, or things in heaven" (Col.1:20).
>
> "But he *was* wounded for our transgressions, *he was* bruised for our iniquities: the chastisement of our peace *was* upon him; and with his stripes we are healed" (Is.53:5).

f. The Messiah will be compassionate (v.3). His very nature will be one of love, mercy, and understanding. Because of His nature, His entire life will be focused on pastoral care. Note the reference to a bruised reed. Bruised reeds are useless, so people break them and discard them. But because the Messiah's heart is full of compassion, He will not break or throw any-one away as useless. To the contrary, His very purpose for coming to earth will be to help the bruised, those who have been wounded and weakened by the trials and hardships of life. *Smoking flax*, or *smoldering wick* (NIV) is a picture of people whose lives lack purpose and meaning, who have lost almost all faith and hope. Whatever desires or expectations they did have nearly been snuffed out, and a sense of despair grips their hearts. But God promises that the Messiah will have compassion on the smoldering wicks of the earth. He will cup them in His hands and keep the flame—their hope and sense of purpose—from burning out. The Messiah will be faithful to treat them justly, just as they should be treated, and to strengthen and lift them up. By meeting their need, He will prove faithful and bring true justice to earth.

Thought 1. Note the people upon whom Christ had compassion:
(1) Christ had compassion upon the weak, the purposeless, and the aimless—upon all who had lost faith and hope.

> "But when he saw the multitudes, he was moved with compassion on them, because they fainted, and were scattered abroad, as sheep having no shepherd" (Mt.9:36).

(2) Christ had compassion on the sick, those who were diseased.

"**And Jesus went about all the cities and villages, teaching in their synagogues, and preaching the gospel of the kingdom, and healing every sickness and every disease among the people**" (Mt.9:35).
"**And Jesus went forth, and saw a great multitude, and was moved with compassion toward them, and he healed their sick**" (Mt.14:14).

(3) Christ had compassion on the hungry, those who had nothing to eat and were faint from hunger.

"**Then Jesus called his disciples *unto him*, and said, I have compassion on the multitude, because they continue with me now three days, and have nothing to eat: and I will not send them away fasting, lest they faint in the way**" (Mt.15:32).

(4) Christ had compassion on those who could not pay their debts.

"**Then the lord of that servant was moved with compassion, and loosed him, and forgave him the debt**" (Mt.18:27).

(5) Christ had compassion on the blind.

"**So Jesus had compassion *on them*, and touched their eyes: and immediately their eyes received sight, and they followed him**" (Mt.20:34).

(6) Christ had compassion on lepers, those considered most unclean.

"**The blind receive their sight, and the lame walk, the lepers are cleansed, and the deaf hear, the dead are raised up, and the poor have the gospel preached to them**" (Mt.11:5).
"**And there came a leper to him, beseeching him, and kneeling down to him, and saying unto him, If thou wilt, thou canst make me clean. And Jesus, moved with compassion, put forth *his* hand, and touched him, and saith unto him, I will; be thou clean**" (Mk.1:40-41).

(7) Christ had compassion on the bereaved, the grief-stricken who had lost loved ones.

"**Now when he came nigh to the gate of the city, behold, there was a dead man carried out, the only son of his mother, and she was a widow: and much people of the city was with her. And when the Lord saw her, he had compassion on her, and said unto her, Weep not. And he came and touched the bier: and they that bare *him* stood still. And he said, Young man, I say unto thee, Arise**" (Lu.7:12-14).

(8) Christ had compassion on people who repented, who turned away from their sins and returned to God.

"**And he arose, and came to his father. But when he was yet a great way off, his father saw him, and had compassion, and ran, and fell on his neck, and kissed him**" (Lu.15:20).

g. The Messiah will be steadfast and persevering (v.4). He will not falter, fail, or become discouraged. No matter what difficulty, hardship, or opposition confronts Him, He will persist in His task. He will not give up or stop until true justice—truth and righteousness—are established on earth. He will be totally committed to teaching God's law, His Holy Word, and to giving hope to the people of the earth. And He will not rest until He has accomplished His purpose—until all the islands, all the distant lands beyond the sea, place their trust and hope in His law (Holy Word).

Thought 1. What a powerful example for us! We must be steadfast and persevering in the task of reaching the world for Christ. We must not falter or be discouraged by hardship or opposition. We must not allow anything to stop us from taking the glory of God to the farthest ends of the earth. We must press on until the task is fully accomplished.

"**And ye shall be hated of all *men* for my name's sake: but he that endureth to the end shall be saved**" (Mt.10:22).
"**Therefore, my beloved brethren, be ye stedfast, unmovable, always abounding in the work of the Lord, forasmuch as ye know that your labour is not in vain in the Lord**" (1 Co.15:58).
"**And let us not be weary in well doing: for in due season we shall reap, if we faint not**" (Ga.6:9).
"**Only let your conversation [conduct, behavior] be as it becometh the gospel of Christ: that whether I come and see you, or else be absent, I may hear of your affairs, that ye stand fast in one spirit, with one mind striving together for the faith of the gospel**" (Ph.1:27).
"**I charge *thee* therefore before God, and the Lord Jesus Christ, who shall judge the quick and the dead at his appearing and his kingdom; Preach the word; be instant in season, out of season; reprove, rebuke, exhort with all longsuffering and doctrine. For the time will come when they will not endure sound doctrine; but after their own lusts shall they heap to themselves teachers, having itching ears; And they shall turn away *their* ears from the truth, and shall be turned unto fables. But watch thou in all things, endure afflictions, do the work of an evangelist, make full proof of thy ministry. For I am now ready to be offered, and the time of my departure is at hand. I have fought a good fight, I have finished *my* course, I have kept the faith: Henceforth there is laid up for me a crown of righteousness,**

which the Lord, the righteous judge, shall give me at that day: and not to me only, but unto all them also that love his appearing" (2 Ti.4:1-8).

"Wherefore gird up the loins of your mind, be sober, and hope to the end for the grace that is to be brought unto you at the revelation of Jesus Christ" (1 Pe.1:13).

"Be sober, be vigilant; because your adversary the devil, as a roaring lion, walketh about, seeking whom he may devour: Whom resist stedfast in the faith, knowing that the same afflictions are accomplished in your brethren that are in the world" (1 Pe.5:8-9).

"Ye therefore, beloved, seeing ye know *these things* before, beware lest ye also, being led away with the error of the wicked, fall from your own stedfastness. But grow in grace, and *in* the knowledge of our Lord and Saviour Jesus Christ. To him *be* glory both now and for ever. Amen" (2 Pe.3:17-18).

2 (42:5-9) **Purpose, of the Messiah, Described—Mission, of the Messiah, Stated—Messiah, Mission of, Discussed—New Covenant, Instituted, by Christ—Assurance, of Christ's First Coming, Guaranteed by God—Life, of Christ, Guaranteed by God—Christ, Purpose of, Twofold:** having described the character of the Messiah, God now discusses His Servant's mission, which He says will not fail. Of this, people can rest assured. It is almost incomprehensible that God would send His Son into the world as a Servant of the human race. And yet God has always known that many would not believe His Servant (Jesus Christ) and would reject Him. He knew that some would refuse to bow the knee before Him in worship and that others would defy and curse Him. For these very reasons He wants the world to clearly understand three facts.

OUTLINE	SCRIPTURE	SCRIPTURE	OUTLINE
2. The mission of the Messiah a. The mission guaranteed by God the LORD 1) By His creative power • Created the heavens & earth • Gave breath & life to people 2) By His righteousness 3) By His presence & care b. The mission spelled out by God 1) To institute God's new covenant, 49:8; 55:3; Je.31:31-34; Eze.34:25 2) To be God's light for all	5 Thus saith God the LORD, he that created the heavens, and stretched them out; he that spread forth the earth, and that which cometh out of it; he that giveth breath unto the people upon it, and spirit to them that walk therein: 6 I the LORD have called thee in righteousness, and will hold thine hand, and will keep thee, and give thee for a covenant of the people, for a light of the Gentiles;	7 To open the blind eyes, to bring out the prisoners from the prison, *and* them that sit in darkness out of the prison house. 8 I *am* the LORD: that *is* my name: and my glory will I not give to another, neither my praise to graven images. 9 Behold, the former things are come to pass, and new things do I declare: before they spring forth I tell you of them.	nations, Jn.8:12; 9:39-41; Co.1:13 • To open the eyes of the spiritually blind • To free the captives who are in darkness c. The mission assured by God 1) His name & glory would not be given to another 2) His power had fulfilled former predictions 3) His power would fulfill the predictions concerning the promised Messiah

a. *God the LORD* guarantees the success of the Servant's mission (v.5). The guarantee is not being given by a mere human being or by any so-called god people might worship. It is given by *God the LORD* Himself, the only true and living God. Because He is true and living, He has the power to guarantee the coming of the Messiah and the fulfillment of His mission. But this is not the only power of God that guarantees the success of the Servant's mission.

1) God's creative power also guarantees that He will send the Messiah and fulfill His mission on earth. God is the great Creator of the entire universe, of earth and heaven with all the planets and stars throughout space. And He is the One who has given breath and life to every person in the world.

2) God's righteousness also guarantees that the Messiah will come and fulfill His purpose on earth (v.6). God will always do what is *right;* He will always do the *righteous* thing. Because the world so desperately needs salvation, God will send the Messiah to save the world and to bring His righteousness to people. God's Servant will also establish a righteous relationship with people, teaching them to do what is *right* as they live together and walk day by day acknowledging and worshipping God.

3) God's presence and care also guarantee the coming of the Messiah and the fulfillment of His mission on earth (v.6). God actually says that He will hold the hand of the Messiah. He will guide and take care of Him. God says that He will *keep* His Servant, or hold Him up and protect Him, as He goes about fulfilling His mission. Nothing, absolutely nothing, will keep God's Servant from doing exactly what God sends Him into the world to do.

b. The Messiah's mission was to have two very specific and important purposes. Note how these purposes meet the desperate needs of the world, the deepest needs of the human heart.

1) First, God's Servant will institute God's *new covenant,* a new relationship with His people. Note that the Messiah Himself is the new covenant. This fact is of critical importance. God will make the Lord Jesus Christ Himself the basis of the new relationship that He establishes with people. Formerly, God had established a covenant, a relationship, with Abraham through the wonderful promise of the *promised seed.* The promised seed was a reference to the coming Messiah, who would bring God's blessings to all the families of the earth (see outline and note—Ge.12:3 for more discussion). Later, God expanded His relationship with His people by promising David a descendant who would rule as king forever (see outline and note—2 S.7:11-17 for more discussion).

In the present Scripture, God expands the covenant again by promising a new relationship that His Servant will establish (Is.49:8; 55:3; Je.31:31-34; Eze.34:25). The Messiah will fulfill both the Abrahamic covenant of the *promised seed* and the Davidic covenant of the *promised king.* And shockingly the new covenant will be established by the death of God's Servant. Through His death, the Messiah will bring people into a right relationship with God, making it possible for Him to forgive their sins, satisfy their hunger and thirst for God, and fulfill their longing to live eternally.

"For this is my blood of the new testament, which is shed for many for the remission of sins" (Mt.26:28).

"But God commendeth his love toward us, in that, while we were yet sinners, Christ died for us. Much more then, being now justified by his blood, we shall be saved from wrath through him" (Ro.5:8-9).

"But now hath he obtained a more excellent ministry, by how much also he is the mediator of a better covenant, which was established upon better promises. For if that first *covenant* had been faultless, then should no place have been sought for the second. For finding fault with them, he saith, Behold, the days come, saith the Lord, when I will make a new covenant with the house of Israel and with the house of Judah: Not according to the covenant that I made with their fathers in the day when I took them by the hand to lead them out of the land of Egypt; because they continued not in my covenant, and I regarded them not, saith the Lord. For this *is* the covenant that I will make with the house of Israel after those days, saith the Lord; I will put my laws into their mind, and write them in their hearts: and I will be to them a God, and they shall be to me a people: And they shall not teach every man his neighbour, and every man his brother, saying, Know the Lord: for all shall know me, from the least to the greatest. For I will be merciful to their unrighteousness, and their sins and their iniquities will I remember no more. In that he saith, A new *covenant,* he hath made the first old. Now that which decayeth and waxeth old *is* ready to vanish away" (He.8:6-13).

"Neither by the blood of goats and calves, but by his own blood he entered in once into the holy place, having obtained eternal redemption *for us.* For if the blood of bulls and of goats, and the ashes of an heifer sprinkling the unclean, sanctifieth to the purifying of the flesh: How much more shall the blood of Christ, who through the eternal Spirit offered himself without spot to God, purge your conscience from dead works to serve the living God? And for this cause he is the mediator of the new testament, that by means of death, for the redemption of the transgressions *that were* under the first testament, they which are called might receive the promise of eternal inheritance" (He.9:12-15).

"And to Jesus the mediator of the new covenant, and to the blood of sprinkling, that speaketh better things than *that of* Abel" (He.12:24).

"He is despised and rejected of men; a man of sorrows, and acquainted with grief: and we hid as it were *our* faces from him; he was despised, and we esteemed him not. Surely he hath borne our griefs, and carried our sorrows: yet we did esteem him stricken, smitten of God, and afflicted. But he *was* wounded for our transgressions, *he was* bruised for our iniquities: the chastisement of our peace *was* upon him; and with his stripes we are healed. All we like sheep have gone astray; we have turned every one to his own way; and the LORD hath laid on him the iniquity of us all" (Is.53:3-6).

"Behold, the days come, saith the LORD, that I will make a new covenant with the house of Israel, and with the house of Judah: Not according to the covenant that I made with their fathers in the day *that* I took them by the hand to bring them out of the land of Egypt; which my covenant they brake, although I was an husband unto them, saith the LORD: But this *shall be* the covenant that I will make with the house of Israel; After those days, saith the LORD, I will put my law in their inward parts, and write it in their hearts; and will be their God, and they shall be my people. And they shall teach no more every man his neighbour, and every man his brother, saying, Know the LORD: for they shall all know me, from the least of them unto the greatest of them, saith the LORD; for I will forgive their iniquity, and I will remember their sin no more" (Je.31:31-34).

2) Second, God's Servant will be God's light for all nations (v.6). No longer will people have to stumble through life in darkness, wondering which way to go or how to handle the problems and hardships of life. No longer will people have to wonder where they have come from, why they are here, and where they are going. God promises that the Messiah will eliminate darkness from the face of the earth...

- all the darkness of ignorance, purposelessness, emptiness, aimlessness, loneliness
- all the darkness of restlessness, anger, hostility, discrimination, prejudice, and warfare

God's Servant will be sent to earth to bring God's light to the world. He will open the eyes of all who are spiritually blind and set free captives held in the darkness of sin and death. Through the light of God's Servant, the Lord Jesus Christ, people can now be freed from the captivity of sin and death. The light of God's Servant has vanquished even the darkness of death and eternal separation from God. Jesus Christ is the light of the world.

"The people which sat in darkness saw great light; and to them which sat in the region and shadow of death light is sprung up" (Mt.4:16).

"And thou, child, shalt be called the prophet of the Highest: for thou shalt go before the face of the Lord to prepare his ways; To give knowledge of salvation unto his people by the remission of their sins, Through the tender mercy of our God; whereby the dayspring from on high hath visited us, To give light to them that sit in darkness and *in* the shadow of death, to guide our feet into the way of peace" (Lu.1:76-79).

"In him was life; and the life was the light of men" (Jn.1:4).

"Then spake Jesus again unto them, saying, I am the light of the world: he that followeth me shall not walk in darkness, but shall have the light of life" (Jn.8:12).

"Then Jesus said unto them, Yet a little while is the light with you. Walk while ye have the light, lest darkness come upon you: for he that walketh in darkness knoweth not whither he goeth" (Jn.12:35).

"I am come a light into the world, that whosoever believeth on me should not abide in darkness" (Jn.12:46).

"For God, who commanded the light to shine out of darkness, hath shined in our hearts, to *give* the light of the knowledge of the glory of God in the face of Jesus Christ" (2 Co.4:6).

"Wherefore he saith, Awake thou that sleepest, and arise from the dead, and Christ shall give thee light" (Ep.5:14).

"And the city had no need of the sun, neither of the moon, to shine in it: for the glory of God did lighten it, and the Lamb *is* the light thereof" (Re.21:23).

"The people that walked in darkness have seen a great light: they that dwell in the land of the shadow of death, upon them hath the light shined" (Is.9:2).

"I the LORD have called thee in righteousness, and will hold thine hand, and will keep thee, and give thee for a covenant of the people, for a light of the Gentiles" (Is.42:6).

c. The LORD Himself ensures the mission of the Messiah (vv.8-9). Note that God uses His distinctive name, *the LORD*, to guarantee its success. "That is my name!" He declares. He is the true and living God; therefore He will fulfill His promise. God will send His Servant into the world to fulfill His mission on behalf of God's people. He will not give His name or glory to anyone other than His Servant, the Messiah. He will not give His glory to another person, and He will never, ever allow any false god or idol to take credit for sending the Messiah into the world.

God's power, and His power alone, has fulfilled former predictions (v.9). Therefore, His power will fulfill the predictions concerning the coming Messiah. Just as promised, He will send His Servant into the world, and He will make sure the Messiah fulfills His mission.

"Think not that I am come to destroy the law, or the prophets: I am not come to destroy, but to fulfil" (Mt.5:17).

"Even as the Son of man came not to be ministered unto, but to minister, and to give his life a ransom for many" (Mt.20:28).

"For the Son of man is come to seek and to save that which was lost" (Lu.19:10).

"For God so loved the world, that he gave his only begotten Son, that whosoever believeth in him should not perish, but have everlasting life. For God sent not his Son into the world to condemn the world; but that the world through him might be saved" (Jn.3:16-17).

"I can of mine own self do nothing: as I hear, I judge: and my judgment is just; because I seek not mine own will, but the will of the Father which hath sent me" (Jn.5:30).

"And Jesus said, For judgment I am come into this world, that they which see not might see; and that they which see might be made blind" (Jn.9:39).

"The thief cometh not, but for to steal, and to kill, and to destroy: I am come that they might have life, and that they might have *it* more abundantly" (Jn.10:10).

"This *is* a faithful saying, and worthy of all acceptation, that Christ Jesus came into the world to save sinners; of whom I am chief" (1 Ti.1:15).

"Then said I, Lo, I come (in the volume of the book it is written of me,) to do thy will, O God....Then said he, Lo, I come to do thy will, O God. He taketh away the first, that he may establish the second. By the which will we are sanctified through the offering of the body of Jesus Christ once *for all*" (He.10:7, 9-10).

3 (42:10-17) **Messiah, Response to, Demanded by God—Messiah, Response to, a Fourfold Response—Jesus Christ, Response to, Demanded by God—Praise, for the Messiah, Demanded by God**: God foresaw the various responses to the Savior, His Servant. In truth, every human being should praise God for sending the Messiah into the world on such a great mission. No greater gift could have been given to the world. Through the Messiah, all human beings can be saved, become acceptable to God, and have a personal relationship with the LORD. Furthermore, they can have all the darkness of sin, guilt, and death erased from their hearts. For these reasons, all people should respond to God's gift of the Messiah by lifting up their voices in resounding praise to the LORD. Note the responses that God foresaw.

OUTLINE	SCRIPTURE	SCRIPTURE	OUTLINE
3. The response to the Messiah a. God's challenge to those who accepted the Messiah: Demanded a song of praise 1) Everyone must sing • The sailors & islanders • The people who lived in the desert & its towns • The few people who lived in the villages of Kedar (or Arabia) • The mass of people in the city of Sela	10 Sing unto the LORD a new song, *and* his praise from the end of the earth, ye that go down to the sea, and all that is therein; the isles, and the inhabitants thereof. 11 Let the wilderness and the cities thereof lift up *their voice,* the villages *that* Kedar doth inhabit: let the inhabitants of the rock sing, let them shout from the top of the mountains.	12 Let them give glory unto the LORD, and declare his praise in the islands. 13 The LORD shall go forth as a mighty man, he shall stir up jealousy like a man of war: he shall cry, yea, roar; he shall prevail against his enemies. 14 I have long time holden my peace; I have been still, *and* refrained myself: *now* will I cry like a travailing woman; I will destroy and	2) Everyone must glorify the LORD & praise Him b. God's warning to those who rejected the Messiah & stood as God's enemies 1) God would go forth & triumph over His enemies • He had kept silent & been patient a long time • The day for judgment had now come—just like the day for a wom-

OUTLINE	SCRIPTURE	SCRIPTURE	OUTLINE
an to give birth 2) God would destroy the land owned by His enemies, all those who reject the Messiah c. God's promise to the spiritually blind who confessed their need for the Messiah 1) God would lead & guide them	devour at once. 15 I will make waste mountains and hills, and dry up all their herbs; and I will make the rivers islands, and I will dry up the pools. 16 And I will bring the blind by a way *that* they knew not; I will lead them in paths *that* they have not known: I will	make darkness light before them, and crooked things straight. These things will I do unto them, and not forsake them. 17 They shall be turned back, they shall be greatly ashamed, that trust in graven images, that say to the molten images, Ye *are* our gods.	• Light their path • Remove all obstacles 2) God would not forsake them d. God's indictment against the idolaters 1) They trusted in false gods 2) They would be turned away—in shame

a. God saw that some people's response would be positive. They would accept and believe in His Servant. Of these people God demanded praise (vv.10-12). Because of His great gift to the world in the person of the Messiah, God expected everyone to worship Him in song and praise.
⇒ the sailors and islanders
⇒ the people who live in the desert and its towns
⇒ the few people living in the villages of Kedar or the desert wilderness of Arabia
⇒ the many people in the city of Sela, the capital of Edom

All the people were to shout from the mountaintops, singing for joy because God had made the most glorious and sacrificial contribution possible to the world. He sent His only Son, His perfect Son, the Lord Jesus Christ, into the world to save men and to set them free. Thus, everyone should glorify the LORD and praise His name to the farthest islands, the ends of the world.

b. The LORD knew that His enemies would not respond favorably to the Messiah. He knew that they would reject Christ and remain His enemies (vv.13-15). Consequently, the LORD foretold that He would march forth like a mighty conqueror against them and triumph over them. Filled with righteous anger due to the rejection of His Servant, God would shout out the battle cry and take vengeance against them. No longer would He keep silent or be patient as He had been, hoping they would repent and praise Him for sending the Messiah. Due to their continued defiance, the day for judgment would come, just as the day comes for a woman to give birth. Like a woman in labor, God would groan, pant, and gasp as He gave birth to a new era, the period of judgment on earth. All the enemies' land and vegetation would be destroyed. Their rivers and water resources would dry up—all because they rejected the Messiah and refused to praise the LORD for sending His Servant into the world.

c. God also foresaw the response of people who confessed that they were blind (v.16). The blind would have no difficulty confessing their darkness and need for God's Servant. Therefore, God promised to lead and guide them. He promised to turn their darkness into light and to remove all obstacles in their path as they walked through life day by day. God also promised to never forsake those who confessed their spiritual blindness and their desperate need for the Messiah.

"Through the tender mercy of our God; whereby the dayspring from on high hath visited us, To give light to them that sit in darkness and *in* the shadow of death, to guide our feet into the way of peace" (Lu.1:78-79).

"Also I say unto you, Whosoever shall confess me before men, him shall the Son of man also confess before the angels of God: But he that denieth me before men shall be denied before the angels of God" (Lu.12:8-9).

"Howbeit when he, the Spirit of truth, is come, he will guide you into all truth: for he shall not speak of himself; but whatsoever he shall hear, *that* shall he speak: and he will show you things to come" (Jn.16:13).

"To open their eyes, *and* to turn *them* from darkness to light, and *from* the power of Satan unto God, that they may receive forgiveness of sins, and inheritance among them which are sanctified by faith that is in me" (Ac.26:18).

"That if thou shalt confess with thy mouth the Lord Jesus, and shalt believe in thine heart that God hath raised him from the dead, thou shalt be saved" (Ro.10:9).

"For God, who commanded the light to shine out of darkness, hath shined in our hearts, to *give* the light of the knowledge of the glory of God in the face of Jesus Christ" (2 Co.4:6).

"The eyes of your understanding being enlightened; that ye may know what is the hope of his calling, and what the riches of the glory of his inheritance in the saints" (Ep.1:18).

"For ye were sometimes darkness, but now *are ye* light in the Lord: walk as children of light: (For the fruit of the Spirit is in all goodness and righteousness and truth;) Proving what is acceptable unto the Lord. And have no fellowship with the unfruitful works of darkness, but rather reprove *them*" (Ep.5:8-11).

"But ye *are* a chosen generation, a royal priesthood, an holy nation, a peculiar people; that ye should show forth the praises of him who hath called you out of darkness into his marvellous light" (1 Pe.2:9).

"Whosoever shall confess that Jesus is the Son of God, God dwelleth in him, and he in God" (1 Jn.4:15).

"The meek will he guide in judgment: and the meek will he teach his way" (Ps.25:9).

"For this God *is* our God for ever and ever: he will be our guide *even* unto death" (Ps.48:14).

"Thou shalt guide me with thy counsel, and afterward receive me *to* glory" (Ps.73:24).

d. God also foresaw the response of idolaters (v.17). Although many would refuse to worship God's Servant, they would still choose to worship idols and false gods. Despite the fact that God had demonstrated His love by sending His Servant into the world, they would deliberately choose to place their trust in the false gods conceived in their own imaginations. As a result, God declared that He would turn them away from His presence in utter shame. He would reject and condemn them. And they would be utterly embarrassed by their idolatry, ashamed for having worshipped trivial material possessions made by their own hands.

> **"Know ye not that the unrighteous shall not inherit the kingdom of God? Be not deceived: neither fornicators, nor idolaters, nor adulterers, nor effeminate, nor abusers of themselves with mankind, Nor thieves, nor covetous, nor drunkards, nor revilers, nor extortioners, shall inherit the kingdom of God"** (1 Co.6:9-10).
>
> **"But fornication, and all uncleanness, or covetousness, let it not be once named among you, as becometh saints; Neither filthiness, nor foolish talking, nor jesting, which are not convenient: but rather giving of thanks. For this ye know, that no whoremonger, nor unclean person, nor covetous man, who is an idolater, hath any inheritance in the kingdom of Christ and of God. Let no man deceive you with vain words: for because of these things cometh the wrath of God upon the children of disobedience"** (Ep.5:3-6).
>
> **"Little children, keep yourselves from idols. Amen"** (1 Jn.5:21).
>
> **"Thou shalt have no other gods before me. Thou shalt not make unto thee any graven image, or any likeness *of any thing* that *is* in heaven above, or that *is* in the earth beneath, or that *is* in the water under the earth: Thou shalt not bow down thyself to them, nor serve them: for I the LORD thy God *am* a jealous God, visiting the iniquity of the fathers upon the children unto the third and fourth *generation* of them that hate me"** (Ex.20:3-5).
>
> **"Take heed to yourselves, that your heart be not deceived, and ye turn aside, and serve other gods, and worship them"** (De.11:16).
>
> **"There shall no strange god be in thee; neither shalt thou worship any strange god"** (Ps.81:9).
>
> **"I *am* the LORD: that *is* my name: and my glory will I not give to another, neither my praise to graven images"** (Is.42:8).

4 **(42:18-25) Summons, to Believe God, Fourfold Reasons—Belief, Reason for, Fourfold—Israel, Duty, to Believe God—Spiritual Blindness, Caused by, Fourfold Causes—Law of God, Greatness of—Word of God, Greatness of—Punishment, Caused by, Several Causes—Messiah, Duty Toward, to Believe—Jesus Christ, Duty, to Believe, Fourfold Reasons—Servant of God, Duty, to Believe**: God now calls on the Israelites to believe the promise concerning His Servant. When Isaiah gave this prophecy, he was standing before the Israelites of his day. Naturally, the heart of God would have already reached out to them first. But God was also giving this prophecy to all the Jews who, in the future, would suffer during the Babylonian captivity. He spoke as well to all the deaf and blind people of succeeding generations. "Hear, you deaf!" God cried. "Look, you blind, that you may see" (v.18). Four clear reasons are given why God summoned the Israelites to believe the promise regarding the coming of the Messiah:

OUTLINE	SCRIPTURE	SCRIPTURE	OUTLINE
4. The summons to believe God's promise	18 Hear, ye deaf; and look, ye blind, that ye may see.	spoil, and none saith, Restore. 23 Who among you will give ear to this? *who* will hearken and hear for the time to come?	enslaved 2) Had no one to rescue them
a. Reason 1: Because they were blind servants & deaf messengers	19 Who *is* blind, but my servant? or deaf, as my messenger *that* I sent? who *is* blind as he that *is* perfect, and blind as the LORD'S servant?		d. Reason 4: Because they refused to learn from past experience
1) They failed to serve & bear witness to the LORD		24 Who gave Jacob for a spoil, and Israel to the robbers? did not the LORD, he against whom we have sinned? for they would not walk in his ways, neither were they obedient unto his law.	1) They refused to accept the fact that it was the LORD who had punished them: Due to their refusal to follow His ways & obey His commandments
2) They paid no attention to the works of God nor to His Word	20 Seeing many things, but thou observest not; opening the ears, but he heareth not.		
b. Reason 2: Because God had magnified His law (Word)—to teach people to believe Him & to live righteously	21 The LORD is well pleased for his righteousness' sake; he will magnify the law, and make *it* honourable.		
c. Reason 3: Because God's people (Israel) had disobeyed His law & were suffering His punishment	22 But this *is* a people robbed and spoiled; *they are* all of them snared in holes, and they are hid in prison houses: they are for a prey, and none delivereth; for a	25 Therefore he hath poured upon him the fury of his anger, and the strength of battle: and it hath set him on fire round about, yet he knew not; and it burned him, yet he laid *it* not to heart.	2) They refused to understand God's discipline (chastisement)
1) Were being robbed, entrapped, imprisoned, &			

a. The Israelites were blind servants and deaf messengers (vv.19-20). Like so many people through the ages, most of the Israelites had blinded their eyes and shut their ears to God's Word and His marvelous works. Although the LORD had called them to be His servants and the messengers of His promises to the world, nearly all refused to serve God or share His Word with others. In fact, they themselves disobeyed God's Word and refused to keep His commandments. Even when God performed mighty works among them, they paid no attention. They shut their eyes and ears to both the works and the Word of God.

"But if thine eye be evil, thy whole body shall be full of darkness. If therefore the light that is in thee be darkness, how great *is* that darkness!" (Mt.6:23).

"And every one that heareth these sayings of mine, and doeth them not, shall be likened unto a foolish man, which built his house upon the sand: And the rain descended, and the floods came, and the winds blew, and beat upon that house; and it fell: and great was the fall of it" (Mt.7:26-27).

"And he said unto him, If they hear not Moses and the prophets, neither will they be persuaded, though one rose from the dead" (Lu.16:31).

"But their minds were blinded: for until this day remaineth the same veil untaken away in the reading of the old testament; which *veil* is done away in Christ. But even unto this day, when Moses is read, the veil is upon their heart. Nevertheless when it shall turn to the Lord, the veil shall be taken away" (2 Co.3:14-16).

"In whom the god of this world hath blinded the minds of them which believe not, lest the light of the glorious gospel of Christ, who is the image of God, should shine unto them. For we preach not ourselves, but Christ Jesus the Lord; and ourselves your servants for Jesus' sake" (2 Co.4:4-5).

"This I say therefore, and testify in the Lord, that ye henceforth walk not as other Gentiles walk, in the vanity of their mind, Having the understanding darkened, being alienated from the life of God through the ignorance that is in them, because of the blindness of their heart: Who being past feeling have given themselves over unto lasciviousness, to work all uncleanness with greediness" (Ep.4:17-19).

"And they shall turn away *their* ears from the truth, and shall be turned unto fables" (2 Ti.4:4).

"But he that hateth his brother is in darkness, and walketh in darkness, and knoweth not whither he goeth, because that darkness hath blinded his eyes" (1 Jn.2:11).

"To whom shall I speak, and give warning, that they may hear? behold, their ear *is* uncircumcised, and they cannot hearken: behold, the word of the LORD is unto them a reproach; they have no delight in it" (Je.6:10).

"Son of man, thou dwellest in the midst of a rebellious house, which have eyes to see, and see not; they have ears to hear, and hear not: for they *are* a rebellious house" (Eze.12:2).

"But they refused to hearken, and pulled away the shoulder, and stopped their ears, that they should not hear" (Zec.7:11).

b. God had magnified His law, or Word, among the Israelites (v.21). He had given them His Word to teach them to believe Him and to live righteously. No people had ever been blessed as richly as they. God had given them the awesome responsibility of sharing His Word with the world. And His Word included the wonderful promise of the *promised seed*, God's Servant and Messiah, the Lord Jesus Christ Himself. For this reason, the spiritually blind and deaf had to open their eyes and ears. They had to repent, turn back to the LORD, and obey His law.

"Wherefore the law *is* holy, and the commandment holy, and just, and good. Was then that which is good made death unto me? God forbid. But sin, that it might appear sin, working death in me by that which is good; that sin by the commandment might become exceeding sinful" (Ro.7:12-13).

"For we know that the law is spiritual: but I am carnal, sold under sin. For that which I do I allow not: for what I would, that do I not; but what I hate, that do I. If then I do that which I would not, I consent unto the law that *it is* good. Now then it is no more I that do it, but sin that dwelleth in me. For I know that in me (that is, in my flesh,) dwelleth no good thing: for to will is present with me; but *how* to perform that which is good I find not. For the good that I would I do not: but the evil which I would not, that I do. Now if I do that I would not, it is no more I that do it, but sin that dwelleth in me. I find then a law, that, when I would do good, evil is present with me. For I delight in the law of God after the inward man" (Ro.7:14-22).

"But we know that the law *is* good, if a man use it lawfully; Knowing this, that the law is not made for a righteous man, but for the lawless and disobedient, for the ungodly and for sinners, for unholy and profane, for murderers of fathers and murderers of mothers, for manslayers, For whoremongers, for them that defile themselves with mankind, for menstealers, for liars, for perjured persons, and if there be any other thing that is contrary to sound doctrine" (1 Ti.1:8-10).

"The law of the LORD *is* perfect, converting the soul: the testimony of the LORD *is* sure, making wise the simple" (Ps.19:7).

c. The Israelites were suffering God's punishment because they had disobeyed His law (v.22). Down through the generations, Israel and all other nations who disobeyed God's Word had suffered the judgment and discipline of God. Due to their sins, God had allowed them to be imprisoned and enslaved by enemies. In Israel's case, there was no one to rescue them from God's judgment. And there will be no one to rescue any of the wicked who continue to disobey God's Holy Word and commandments.

"But fornication, and all uncleanness, or covetousness, let it not be once named among you, as becometh saints; Neither filthiness, nor foolish talking, nor jesting, which are not convenient: but rather giving of thanks. For this ye know, that no whoremonger, nor unclean person, nor covetous man, who is an idolater, hath any inheritance in the kingdom of Christ and of God. Let no man deceive you with vain words: for because of these things cometh the wrath of God upon the children of disobedience" (Ep.5:3-6).

"And to you who are troubled rest with us, when the Lord Jesus shall be revealed from heaven with his mighty angels, In flaming fire taking vengeance on them that know not God, and that obey not the gospel of our Lord Jesus Christ: Who shall be punished with everlasting destruction from the presence of the Lord, and from the glory of his power" (2 Th.1:7-9).

"For if the word spoken by angels was stedfast, and every transgression and disobedience received a just recompence of reward; How shall we escape, if we neglect so great salvation; which at the first began to be spoken by the Lord, and was confirmed unto us by them that heard *him*" (He.2:2-3).

"And a curse, if ye will not obey the commandments of the LORD your God, but turn aside out of the way which I command you this day, to go after other gods, which ye have not known" (De.11:28).

"But if ye will not obey the voice of the LORD, but rebel against the commandment of the LORD, then shall the hand of the LORD be against you, as *it was* against your fathers" (1 S.12:15).

d. The Israelites needed to believe God's Servant because they had refused to learn from past experience (vv.23-25). Isaiah asked a critical question: "Who will listen and pay close attention to the summons of God to believe His servant, the Messiah?" Few people seem to learn from past experience, and the Israelites were no exception. In the future, God would discipline and punish them through the Babylonian captivity and exile. But like their forefathers, they would refuse to believe that God would actually judge and punish them. The thought that their sin would cause God to judge them so severely would never cross their minds. They would still choose to be blinded by sin and refuse to follow the LORD or obey His Word (vv.24-25). Due to their terrible sin, God would pour out His anger on them in judgment; still they would refuse to understand His discipline. Like so many people down through the years, they would refuse to heed God's warnings. They would harden their hearts toward Him and become insensitive to His warnings.

"For the heart of this people is waxed gross, and their ears are dull of hearing, and their eyes have they closed; lest they should see with *their* eyes, and hear with *their* ears, and understand with *their* heart, and should be converted, and I should heal them" (Ac.28:27).

"But after thy hardness and impenitent heart treasurest up unto thyself wrath against the day of wrath and revelation of the righteous judgment of God; Who will render to every man according to his deeds: To them who by patient continuance in well doing seek for glory and honour and immortality, eternal life: But unto them that are contentious, and do not obey the truth, but obey unrighteousness, indignation and wrath, Tribulation and anguish, upon every soul of man that doeth evil, of the Jew first, and also of the Gentile" (Ro.2:5-9).

"They are all gone out of the way, they are together become unprofitable; there is none that doeth good, no, not one. Their throat *is* an open sepulchre; with their tongues they have used deceit; the poison of asps *is* under their lips" (Ro.3:12-13).

"This I say therefore, and testify in the Lord, that ye henceforth walk not as other Gentiles walk, in the vanity of their mind, Having the understanding darkened, being alienated from the life of God through the ignorance that is in them, because of the blindness of their heart: Who being past feeling have given themselves over unto lasciviousness, to work all uncleanness with greediness" (Ep.4:17-19).

"Now the Spirit speaketh expressly, that in the latter times some shall depart from the faith, giving heed to seducing spirits, and doctrines of devils; Speaking lies in hypocrisy; having their conscience seared with a hot iron" (1 Ti.4:1-2).

"Harden not your heart, as in the provocation, *and as in* the day of temptation in the wilderness: When your fathers tempted me, proved me, and saw my work. Forty years long was I grieved with *this* generation, and said, It *is* a people that do err in their heart, and they have not known my ways: Unto whom I sware in my wrath that they should not enter into my rest" (Ps.95:8-11).

"Happy *is* the man that feareth alway: but he that hardeneth his heart shall fall into mischief" (Pr.28:14).

"He, that being often reproved hardeneth *his* neck, shall suddenly be destroyed, and that without remedy" (Pr.29:1).

CHAPTER 43

D. Set Free Through the Redeemer, the LORD Your God: A Study of Redemption, 43:1-28

1. The source of redemption: The LORD
a. He created & formed you
b. He encourages you: Fear not
1) The LORD has redeemed you
2) The LORD knows you by name
2. The promises of the Redeemer
a. He will be with you
1) Through all the deep waters (trials, hardships) of life
2) Through all the fiery oppressions of life

b. He will rescue you, set you free from all oppressors (Egypt, Cush, & Sheba)
1) Because He is your God, the Holy One, your Savior
2) Because you are precious to Him, you will be honored & loved

c. He will gather you from the ends of the earth, return you to the promised land (a symbol of heaven)
1) The identity of those gathered: Israel (true believers)
• All the children—sons & daughters—of God, Ro.8:16-17; 2 Co.6:17-18; Ga.4:4-6
• All who are believers & created for His glory (see the new creation, 2 Co.5:17; Ep.2:10; 4:24)

2) The summons for unbelieving Jews to see & hear: Believe God
3) The summons for the unbelieving nations to assemble
• To acknowledge that the LORD foretold the restoration of Israel
• To prove their claim that their gods were real, that they could predict future events
d. He will appoint you to be His special witness & servant
1) The reason: That you may know, believe, & understand Him
2) The facts
• He alone is God

But now thus saith the LORD that created thee, O Jacob, and he that formed thee, O Israel, Fear not: for I have redeemed thee, I have called *thee* by thy name; thou *art* mine.
2 When thou passest through the waters, I *will be* with thee; and through the rivers, they shall not overflow thee: when thou walkest through the fire, thou shalt not be burned; neither shall the flame kindle upon thee.
3 For I *am* the LORD thy God, the Holy One of Israel, thy Saviour: I gave Egypt *for* thy ransom, Ethiopia and Seba for thee.
4 Since thou wast precious in my sight, thou hast been honourable, and I have loved thee: therefore will I give men for thee, and people for thy life.
5 Fear not: for I *am* with thee: I will bring thy seed from the east, and gather thee from the west;
6 I will say to the north, Give up; and to the south, Keep not back: bring my sons from far, and my daughters from the ends of the earth;
7 *Even* every one that is called by my name: for I have created him for my glory, I have formed him; yea, I have made him.
8 Bring forth the blind people that have eyes, and the deaf that have ears.
9 Let all the nations be gathered together, and let the people be assembled: who among them can declare this, and show us former things? let them bring forth their witnesses, that they may be justified: or let them hear, and say, *It is* truth.
10 Ye *are* my witnesses, saith the LORD, and my servant whom I have chosen: that ye may know and believe me, and understand that I *am* he: before me there was no God formed, neither shall there be after me.

11 I, *even* I, *am* the LORD; and beside me *there is* no saviour.
12 I have declared, and have saved, and I have showed, when *there was* no strange *god* among you: therefore ye *are* my witnesses, saith the LORD, that I *am* God.
13 Yea, before the day *was* I *am* he; and *there is* none that can deliver out of my hand: I will work, and who shall let it?
14 Thus saith the LORD, your redeemer, the Holy One of Israel; For your sake I have sent to Babylon, and have brought down all their nobles, and the Chaldeans, whose cry *is* in the ships.
15 I *am* the LORD, your Holy One, the creator of Israel, your King.
16 Thus saith the LORD, which maketh a way in the sea, and a path in the mighty waters;
17 Which bringeth forth the chariot and horse, the army and the power; they shall lie down together, they shall not rise: they are extinct, they are quenched as tow.
18 Remember ye not the former things, neither consider the things of old.
19 Behold, I will do a new thing; now it shall spring forth; shall ye not know it? I will even make a way in the wilderness, *and* rivers in the desert.
20 The beast of the field shall honour me, the dragons and the owls: because I give waters in the wilderness, *and* rivers in the desert, to give drink to my people, my chosen.
21 This people have I formed for myself; they shall show forth my praise.
22 But thou hast not called upon me, O Jacob; but thou hast been weary of me, O Israel.
23 Thou hast not brought me the small cattle of thy burnt offerings; neither hast thou honoured me with thy sacrifices. I have not caused thee to serve with an offering, nor wearied thee with incense.
24 Thou hast bought me no sweet cane with money, neither hast thou filled me with the fat of thy sacrifices: but

• He alone is the Savior

3) The witness you are to bear
• He has revealed the truth
• He has saved you
• He alone is God
• He alone possesses eternal power & judgment: No one can stop or reverse His works

e. He will defeat all the enemies who oppress you
1) He guarantees deliverance: Because He is your Redeemer, the Holy One
2) He guarantees the defeat of Babylon
• The reason: He is the LORD, your Holy One, Creator, King
• The surety of judgment: He will utterly destroy the enemy—just as surely as He destroyed the Egyptian army in the Red Sea, Ex.14:26-28

f. He will do great things, even a new thing: Will guide & provide for you as never before
1) His guidance: Will make a way to return to the promised land

2) His provision: Water & all other necessities of life
• The wild animals will drink & be glad
• The returning exiles will have their thirst quenched

3) His purpose: To stir you to proclaim His praise

3. The failure of God's people to live like the redeemed
a. The charge
1) You have not prayed to, worshipped, or approached God as He prescribed
• Not sought Him with a pure, righteous heart
• Not sought to be cleansed by the blood of the sacrifice
2) You have not faithfully brought your special offerings to the LORD
3) You have burdened the

LORD with your sins	thou hast made me to serve with thy sins, thou hast wearied me with thine iniquities.	thou, that thou mayest be justified.	your case, your innocence
b. The appeal of the LORD: He alone blots out your transgressions	25 I, *even* I, *am* he that blotteth out thy transgressions for mine own sake, and will not remember thy sins.	27 Thy first father hath sinned, and thy teachers have transgressed against me.	2) God's charge: Your ancestors—even leaders—have always sinned
c. The trial of hypocrites 1) God's demand: Prove	26 Put me in remembrance: let us plead together: declare	28 Therefore I have profaned the princes of the sanctuary, and have given Jacob to the curse, and Israel to reproaches.	3) God's judgment: The religious leaders will be disgraced & the people destroyed

DIVISION V

THE PROPHECIES OF COMFORT AND FREEDOM: A PICTURE OF BELIEVERS BEING SET FREE FROM THE CAPTIVITY OF SIN AND DEATH, 40:1–48:22

D. Set Free Through the Redeemer, the LORD Your God: A Study of Redemption, 43:1-28

(43:1) **Introduction**: people can be kidnapped to be sold as slaves, for sexual pleasure, for building up a workforce, for revenge, or for a host of other reasons. When a ransom is demanded for the release of the kidnapped person, the cost is usually huge.

The enormous price God paid to ransom His people is the subject of the present Scripture. In the previous chapter, Isaiah said that the people of his day were continuing in their sin and refusing to turn back to the LORD. As a result, God's anger burned against them (42:23-25). Now we would expect God's hand of judgment to immediately fall upon the Israelites. We would expect Him to abandon and destroy them. But the very opposite is true. God is longsuffering and not willing that any person should perish and be doomed to eternal separation from Him. With a broken heart over the people's failure, the LORD reached out to ransom them from both their sins and their enemies. Remember that Isaiah had predicted the destruction of Jerusalem and the exile of the Jewish people. But he had also predicted that the Persians would miraculously free God's people from their Babylonian captivity (41:1-20). Furthermore, the LORD would set them free from all the enslavements and bondages of this life through the coming of God's very special Servant, the Messiah (42:1-25). Now God declares that His people can be set free through the wonderful redemption provided by the LORD. This is, *Set Free Through the Redeemer, the LORD Your God: A Study of Redemption*, 43:1-28.

1. The source of redemption: the LORD (v.1).
2. The promises of the Redeemer (vv.2-21).
3. The failure of God's people to live like the redeemed (vv.22-28).

1 (43:1) **Redemption, Source of, the LORD—Fear, Deliverance from, God's Love and Redemption—Redemption, Result of, Deliverance from Fear—Israel, Creation of, by God—Love, of God, Results, Redemption—Believers, Known by God, Believers, Relationship with God, Are His—Encouragement, Source of, the LORD**: the source of redemption is the LORD Himself. Despite Israel's continued sin and rejection of Him, the LORD still loved His people. He still reached out in mercy and goodness to them. "Where sin abounded, grace did much more abound" (Ro.5:20). Looking ahead to the terrible hardships His people would face, the LORD wanted them to know that He would not forsake them. He would reach out to rescue them. Remember that Isaiah was predicting the Babylonian captivity, which still lay ahead for the Jews. The LORD promises to be with His people, even in the midst of such a terrifying experience as enslavement and exile. This verse is one of the great promises in the Holy Bible:

OUTLINE	SCRIPTURE	SCRIPTURE	OUTLINE
1. The source of redemption: The LORD a. He created & formed you b. He encourages you: Fear not	**B**ut now thus saith the LORD that created thee, O Jacob, and he that formed thee, O Israel, Fear	not: for I have redeemed thee, I have called *thee* by thy name; thou *art* mine.	1) The LORD has redeemed you 2) The LORD knows you by name

a. In the midst of their awful affliction, the people needed to remember a significant fact: the LORD Himself had created and formed them into the nation of Israel. The words *created* and *formed* are the same words used to describe the creation of man and woman (Ge.1:1; 2:7). Thus, Israel is as much a creation of the LORD as the human race is. God has a distinctive purpose for each, a purpose that must be fulfilled, just as His Word states. Although the Israelites would be exiled and scattered throughout the Babylonian Empire, those who trusted the LORD could rest assured that He would not forget them. They were still His chosen people, created by His own hand. True, due to the destruction of Jerusalem and the exile of the people, Israel's future as a nation looked very bleak. Nothing less than extinction was staring Israel in the face. [1]

b. But note how God encouraged His people: He told them two things they needed to remember. First, He had redeemed them. In the very midst of their hardship, they could know that God would redeem them again. Their deliverance from the Babylonian captivity was as good as done. The day would come when they would be set free from their bondage

---

[1] H.C. Leupold. *Exposition of Isaiah,* Vol.1. (Grand Rapids, Michigan: Baker Book House, 1968), p.78.

and sufferings. Centuries earlier, the LORD had delivered His people from Egyptian bondage. Now He was promising to deliver them from their captivity in Babylon. But the LORD wanted His people to know a second fact: He knew every one of them personally and called each by name. They were His people, and He was very concerned about them. They were bound to Him in a unique way, for He had a very special purpose for them. Remember that when Israel or the Jews are being discussed, their relationship to the LORD was based upon God's purpose for them, a threefold purpose that blessed the entire world:

⇒ They were the people through whom God would send His Son, the promised seed, the Lord Jesus Christ into the world.
⇒ They were the people through whom God would send His Word, the Holy Bible, to the world.
⇒ They were the people God chose to be His witnesses to the world that He is the only living and true God.

Thought 1. The source of redemption is the Lord Himself. Only the Lord can save us from the enslavement of sin, death, and hell. Being enslaved to sin means that we cannot keep from sinning. All of us sin because we have inherited a depraved nature from our parents (Ro.5:12). Consequently, we cannot keep from sinning. We cannot live a perfect or righteous life. And since we have inherited a corruptible nature from our parents, we are also enslaved by death. From the day we are born, we are ever progressing to that inevitable day when our bodies will return to dust. But because God loves us, He has provided redemption for us. Jesus Christ paid the ransom for us by giving His life for us. We are redeemed by the shed blood of Christ. This is exactly what God's Holy Word says:

"For all have sinned, and come short of the glory of God; Being justified freely by his grace through the redemption that is in Christ Jesus" (Ro.3:23-24).

"But of him are ye in Christ Jesus, who of God is made unto us wisdom, and righteousness, and sanctification, and redemption" (1 Co.1:30).

"Christ hath redeemed us from the curse of the law, being made a curse for us: for it is written, Cursed *is* every one that hangeth on a tree" (Ga.3:13).

"In whom [Christ] we have redemption through his blood, *even* the forgiveness of sins" (Col.1:14).

"Looking for that blessed hope, and the glorious appearing of the great God and our Saviour Jesus Christ; Who gave himself for us, that he might redeem us from all iniquity, and purify unto himself a peculiar people, zealous of good works" (Tit.2:13-14).

"Neither by the blood of goats and calves, but by his own blood he entered in once into the holy place, having obtained eternal redemption *for us*. For if the blood of bulls and of goats, and the ashes of an heifer sprinkling the unclean, sanctifieth to the purifying of the flesh: How much more shall the blood of Christ, who through the eternal Spirit offered himself without spot to God, purge your conscience from dead works to serve the living God?" (He.9:12-14).

"Forasmuch as ye know that ye were not redeemed with corruptible things, *as* silver and gold, from your vain conversation *received* by tradition from your fathers; But with the precious blood of Christ, as of a lamb without blemish and without spot" (1 Pe.1:18-19).

"And they sung a new song, saying, Thou art worthy to take the book, and to open the seals thereof: for thou wast slain, and hast redeemed us to God by thy blood out of every kindred, and tongue, and people, and nation" (Re.5:9).

---

2 (43:2-21) **Redeemer, Promises of, Sixfold—Presence, of the LORD, Promised—Trials, Deliverance Through, Promised—Ransom, Source, God's Love—Love, of God, for His People—Restoration, of Israel, Promised—Witnessing, Message of, God and Christ—Servant of God, Purpose for, Threefold—Believers, Chosen by God, Threefold Purpose—God, Facts Concerning, Only True God—Victory, Over Enemies, Assured—Israel, Promises, Deliverance from Captivity—God, Names – Titles of, Holy One of Israel; Redeemer—Guidance, Promised—Provision, of God, Promised—Promises, of God, Sixfold**: the Redeemer's promises to Israel are now spelled out. Think how these promises have been fulfilled since the Messiah, the Lord Jesus Christ, has come. Although these promises were fulfilled to some degree in the lives of true believers in ancient Israel, they were completely fulfilled when the Messiah came to earth to pay the redemption price for the salvation of the human race. Note how applicable all of these promises are to believers down through history:

OUTLINE	SCRIPTURE	SCRIPTURE	OUTLINE

2. The promises of the Redeemer
a. He will be with you
  1) Through all the deep waters (trials, hardships) of life
  2) Through all the fiery oppressions of life
 	
b. He will rescue you, set you free from all oppressors (Egypt, Cush, & Sheba)
  1) Because He is your God,
	2 When thou passest through the waters, I *will be* with thee; and through the rivers, they shall not overflow thee: when thou walkest through the fire, thou shalt not be burned; neither shall the flame kindle upon thee.
	3 For I *am* the LORD thy God, the Holy One of Israel, thy Saviour: I gave Egypt *for* thy ransom, Ethiopia and Se-
		ba for thee.
		4 Since thou wast precious in my sight, thou hast been honourable, and I have loved thee: therefore will I give men for thee, and people for thy life.
		5 Fear not: for I *am* with thee: I will bring thy seed from the east, and gather thee from the west;
		6 I will say to the north, Give up; and to the south,
			the Holy One, your Savior
			  2) Because you are precious to Him, you will be honored & loved
			
			c. He will gather you from the ends of the earth, return you to the promised land (a symbol of heaven)
			  1) The identity of those gathered: Israel (true believers)

114

OUTLINE	SCRIPTURE	SCRIPTURE	OUTLINE

• All the children—sons & daughters—of God, Ro.8:16-17; 2 Co.6:17-18; Ga.4:4-6
• All who are believers & created for His glory (see the new creation, 2 Co.5:17; Ep.2:10; 4:24)
2) The summons for unbelieving Jews to see & hear: Believe God
3) The summons for the unbelieving nations to assemble
  • To acknowledge that the LORD foretold the restoration of Israel
  • To prove their claim that their gods were real, that they could predict future events
d. He will appoint you to be His special witness & servant
1) The reason: That you may know, believe, & understand Him
2) The facts
  • He alone is God
  • He alone is the Savior
 	
3) The witness you are to bear
  • He has revealed the truth
  • He has saved you
  • He alone is God
  • He alone possesses eternal power & judgment: No one can stop
	Keep not back: bring my sons from far, and my daughters from the ends of the earth;
	7 *Even* every one that is called by my name: for I have created him for my glory, I have formed him; yea, I have made him.
	8 Bring forth the blind people that have eyes, and the deaf that have ears.
	9 Let all the nations be gathered together, and let the people be assembled: who among them can declare this, and show us former things? let them bring forth their witnesses, that they may be justified: or let them hear, and say, It is truth.
	10 Ye *are* my witnesses, saith the LORD, and my servant whom I have chosen: that ye may know and believe me, and understand that I *am* he: before me there was no God formed, neither shall there be after me.
	11 I, *even* I, *am* the LORD; and beside me *there is* no saviour.
	12 I have declared, and have saved, and I have showed, when *there was* no strange god among you: therefore ye *are* my witnesses, saith the LORD, that I *am* God.
	13 Yea, before the day *was* I *am* he; and *there is* none that can deliver out of my hand: I
		will work, and who shall let it?
		14 Thus saith the LORD, your redeemer, the Holy One of Israel; For your sake I have sent to Babylon, and have brought down all their nobles, and the Chaldeans, whose cry *is* in the ships.
		15 I *am* the LORD, your Holy One, the creator of Israel, your King.
		16 Thus saith the LORD, which maketh a way in the sea, and a path in the mighty waters;
		17 Which bringeth forth the chariot and horse, the army and the power; they shall lie down together, they shall not rise: they are extinct, they are quenched as tow.
		18 Remember ye not the former things, neither consider the things of old.
		19 Behold, I will do a new thing; now it shall spring forth; shall ye not know it? I will even make a way in the wilderness, *and* rivers in the desert.
		20 The beast of the field shall honour me, the dragons and the owls: because I give waters in the wilderness, *and* rivers in the desert, to give drink to my people, my chosen.
		21 This people have I formed for myself; they shall show forth my praise.
			or reverse His works
			e. He will defeat all the enemies who oppress you
			1) He guarantees deliverance: Because He is your Redeemer, the Holy One
			2) He guarantees the defeat of Babylon
			  • The reason: He is the LORD, your Holy One, Creator, King
			  • The surety of judgment: He will utterly destroy the enemy—just as surely as He destroyed the Egyptian army in the Red Sea, Ex.14:26-28
			
			f. He will do great things, even a new thing: Will guide & provide for you as never before
			1) His guidance: Will make a way to return to the promised land
			
			2) His provision: Water & all other necessities of life
			  • The wild animals will drink & be glad
			  • The returning exiles will have their thirst quenched
			3) His purpose: To stir you to proclaim His praise

a. The LORD promises to be with His people as they pass through all the deep waters and fiery trials of life (v.2). When trials and hardships threaten to engulf believers, they will not drown. The LORD will be with them to strengthen and uphold them. When fiery persecutions threaten to overwhelm believers, the flames will not burn them, for the LORD's presence and power will protect them. This promise was literally fulfilled when the LORD protected Shadrach, Meshcach, and Abednego in the fiery furnace (Da.3:25-27). No matter how deep the trial or hardship and no matter how fiery the oppression or persecution, the LORD promises to be with His people.

> **"For where two or three are gathered together in my name, there am I in the midst of them"** (Mt.18:20).
> **"Lo, I am with you alway, *even* unto the end of the world. Amen"** (Mt.28:20).
> **"And, behold, I *am* with thee, and will keep thee in all *places* whither thou goest, and will bring thee again into this land; for I will not leave thee, until I have done *that* which I have spoken to thee of"** (Ge.28:15).
> **"And he said, My presence shall go *with thee,* and I will give thee rest"** (Ex.33:14).
> **"When thou goest out to battle against thine enemies, and seest horses, and chariots, *and* a people more than thou, be not afraid of them: for the LORD thy God *is* with thee, which brought thee up out of the land of Egypt"** (De.20:1).
> **"But thou, O LORD, be merciful unto me, and raise me up, that I may requite them"** (Ps.41:10).

b. The LORD promises to ransom His people and set them free from all their oppressors (vv.3-4). Note that the weight of the LORD'S promise rests solely on His own shoulders. He reinforces His promise by using three different titles for Himself:

⇒ "your God" guarantees this promise
⇒ "the Holy One of Israel" guarantees this promise
⇒ "your Savior" guarantees this promise

God's people can rest assured that He will ransom them. He will set them free from all who oppress them. In fact, all who tyrannize God's people will themselves be the ransom paid to free His people. Three nations in particular are mentioned, but the truth applies to all the nations of earth. When Egypt, Cush (Ethiopia), or Seba oppressed Israel, the LORD sacrificed (doomed) these nations. Instead of allowing them to continue subjecting His people, He destroyed them. God gave up three oppressors rather than give up His people. The point is striking, a clear warning to any person or nation that persecutes God's people. They will not succeed. Either immediately or one day in the future, God will execute judgment against them. He will "give them up" to suffer the very oppression and cruelty they inflicted upon His people. God will always ransom His people from their oppressors. And the ransom price for those who are enemies of God and His people is very high: they will pay with their very own lives. Note why God does such a remarkable thing for His people: they are precious to Him and He loves them.

"Take heed therefore unto yourselves, and to all the flock, over the which the Holy Ghost hath made you overseers, to feed the church of God, which he hath purchased with his own blood" (Ac.20:28).

"For God so loved the world, that he gave his only begotten Son, that whosoever believeth in him should not perish, but have everlasting life. For God sent not his Son into the world to condemn the world; but that the world through him might be saved" (Jn.3:16-17).

"And the Lord shall deliver me from every evil work, and will preserve *me* unto his heavenly kingdom: to whom *be* glory for ever and ever. Amen" (2 Ti.4:18).

"But because the LORD loved you, and because he would keep the oath which he had sworn unto your fathers, hath the LORD brought you out with a mighty hand, and redeemed you out of the house of bondmen, from the hand of Pharaoh king of Egypt" (De.7:8).

"But I *am* poor and needy; *yet* the Lord thinketh upon me: thou *art* my help and my deliverer; make no tarrying, O my God" (Ps.40:17).

"Surely he shall deliver thee from the snare of the fowler, *and* from the noisome pestilence" (Ps.91:3).

"Be not afraid of their faces: for I *am* with thee to deliver thee, saith the LORD" (Je.1:8).

"For thus saith the LORD of hosts; After the glory hath he sent me unto the nations which spoiled you: for he that toucheth you toucheth the apple of his eye" (Zec.2:8).

"And the LORD their God shall save them in that day as the flock of his people: for they *shall be as* the stones of a crown, lifted up as an ensign upon his land" (Zec.9:16).

"And they shall be mine, saith the LORD of hosts, in that day when I make up my jewels; and I will spare them, as a man spareth his own son that serveth him" (Mal.3:17).

c. The LORD promises to gather His people from the ends of the earth and return them to the promised land (vv.5-9). This is a clear reference to the Israelites' being set free from their captivity in Babylon and returning to Jerusalem. But it is also applicable to any of God's people who are living in exile from their true home. And it applies particularly to the restoration of Israel in the latter days of human history (see outline and notes—Ro.11:25-36 for more discussion). Note that the LORD calls Israel His sons and daughters (v.6). Of course, God's children are those who truly believe and follow Him. After the Persians released the Jews from Babylonian captivity, only a few Jews truly believed the promises of God and chose to return to the promised land. The vast majority chose to remain in Babylon with all its pleasures and possessions (see outlines and notes—Ezr.1:1–2:70; 8:1-20 for more discussion). Note that God once again reminds His people that He has created them for His glory.

Longing for each of His chosen people to trust Him as Redeemer, the LORD summons all unbelieving Jews—the spiritually blind and deaf—to see and hear His promises. No greater promises could be given; consequently, the spiritually blind and deaf should believe them (v.8). Clearly, God longs for unbelieving nations to believe also, for He issues a summons for them to assemble before Him (v.9). He challenges them to acknowledge that He has foretold the restoration of Israel. At the same time, if they are unwilling to believe in Him, He challenges them to prove that their so-called gods are true. To do this, they will have to be able to predict future events like the regathering of Israel. Any god should care enough for his people to do what the LORD is doing—preparing His people for the terrifying trials and hardships that are coming upon them in the future.

Thought 1. What is said of the Israelites is applicable to all true believers.
(1) All genuine believers are sons and daughters of God, created for His glory.

"But as many as received him, to them gave he power to become the sons of God, *even* to them that believe on his name" (Jn.1:12).

"The Spirit itself beareth witness with our spirit, that we are the children of God: And if children, then heirs; heirs of God, and joint-heirs with Christ; if so be that we suffer with *him*, that we may be also glorified together" (Ro.8:16-17).

"Wherefore come out from among them, and be ye separate, saith the Lord, and touch not the unclean *thing;* and I will receive you, And will be a Father unto you, and ye shall be my sons and daughters, saith the Lord Almighty" (2 Co.6:17-18).

"But when the fulness of the time was come, God sent forth his Son, made of a woman, made under the law, To redeem them that were under the law, that we might receive the adoption of sons. And because ye are sons, God hath sent forth the Spirit of his Son into your hearts, crying, Abba, Father" (Ga.4:4-6).

"When Israel *was* a child, then I loved him, and called my son out of Egypt" (Ho.11:1).

(2) All genuine believers are re-created by the Spirit of God, made into new people.

"Therefore we are buried with him by baptism into death: that like as Christ was raised up from the dead by the glory of the Father, even so we also should walk in newness of life" (Ro.6:4).

"But now we are delivered from the law, that being dead wherein we were held; that we should serve in newness of spirit, and not *in* the oldness of the letter" (Ro.7:6).

"Therefore if any man *be* in Christ, *he is* a new creature: old things are passed away; behold, all things are become new" (2 Co.5:17).

"For in Christ Jesus neither circumcision availeth any thing, nor uncircumcision, but a new creature" (Ga.6:15).

"For we are his workmanship, created in Christ Jesus unto good works, which God hath before ordained that we should walk in them" (Ep.2:10).

"Having abolished in his flesh the enmity, *even* the law of commandments *contained* in ordinances; for to make in himself of twain one new man, *so* making peace" (Ep.2:15).

"And that ye put on the new man, which after God is created in righteousness and true holiness" (Ep.4:24).

"And have put on the new *man,* which is renewed in knowledge after the image of him that created him" (Col.3:10).

d. The LORD has appointed His people to be His special witnesses and servants (vv.10-13). Verse 10 is one of the most significant verses in all of Scripture. It spells out exactly why God chooses and saves His people day by day. Three purposes are listed:

⇒ that His people might *know Him*—know Him personally and intimately as they walk through life
⇒ that His people might *believe Him*—entrust all to Him, believe every word that proceeds out of His mouth, and stand upon the promises of God
⇒ that His people might *understand Him*—grasp, comprehend, appreciate, esteem, and value Him for all He is within His majestic glory and person

As His witnesses and servants, believers are to know that the LORD is the only living and true God and that He alone is the Savior of the world. Apart from Him, there is no Savior. No person can be saved without trusting and following Him and Him alone (v.11). Saving His people from the Babylonian captivity, the LORD proves that He is the only living and true God and the Savior of the human race. He, not some false god, is the One who will save His people from their captivity. Since He alone is God and there is no other Savior, His people are to bear strong testimony to four facts:

⇒ that He has revealed the truth about Himself both to Israel and to the other nations of the world
⇒ that He is the Savior of the human race who alone has saved and redeemed those who truly believe and follow Him
⇒ that He alone is the living and true God
⇒ that He alone possesses eternal power and that judgment rests with Him

"And he said unto them, Go ye into all the world, and preach the gospel to every creature" (Mk.16:15).

"Then said Jesus to them again, Peace *be* unto you: as *my* Father hath sent me, even so send I you" (Jn.20:21).

"And they were all filled with the Holy Ghost, and began to speak with other tongues, as the Spirit gave them utterance" (Ac.2:4).

"For we cannot but speak the things which we have seen and heard" (Ac.4:20).

"Go, stand and speak in the temple to the people all the words of this life. And when they heard *that,* they entered into the temple early in the morning, and taught. But the high priest came, and they that were with him, and called the council together, and all the senate of the children of Israel and sent to the prison to have them brought" (Ac.5:20-21).

"And we are his witnesses of these things; and *so is* also the Holy Ghost, whom God hath given to them that obey him" (Ac.5:32).

"And he said, The God of our fathers hath chosen thee [Paul], that thou shouldest know his will, and see that Just One, and shouldest hear the voice of his mouth. For thou shalt be his witness unto all men of what thou hast seen and heard" (Ac.22:14-15).

"But when the Jews spake against *it,* I was constrained to appeal unto Caesar; not that I had ought to accuse my nation of. For this cause therefore have I called for you, to see *you,* and to speak with *you:* because that for the hope of Israel I am bound with this chain" (Ac.28:19-20).

"We having the same spirit of faith, according as it is written, I believed, and therefore have I spoken; we also believe, and therefore speak" (2 Co.4:13).

"These things speak, and exhort, and rebuke with all authority. Let no man despise thee" (Tit.2:15).

"Come *and* hear, all ye that fear God, and I will declare what he hath done for my soul" (Ps.66:16).

"I will mention the lovingkindnesses of the LORD, *and* the praises of the LORD, according to all that the LORD hath bestowed on us, and the great goodness toward the house of Israel, which he hath bestowed on them according to his mercies, and according to the multitude of his lovingkindnesses" (Is.63:7).

"Then I said, I will not make mention of him, nor speak any more in his name. But *his word* was in mine heart as a burning fire shut up in my bones, and I was weary with forbearing, and I could not *stay*" (Je.20:9).

"Then they that feared the LORD spake often one to another: and the LORD hearkened, and heard *it*, and a book of remembrance was written before him for them that feared the LORD, and that thought upon his name" (Mal.3:16).

e.   No one can stop or reverse the works God does among His people on earth. The LORD will ultimately defeat all enemies who oppress His people (vv.14-17). He guarantees the deliverance of His people because He is their Redeemer, the Holy One. By declaring Himself the *Holy One*, God indicates that redeeming His people from their enemies is the righteous and ethical thing to do. And since He is the Redeemer, He must guarantee that His people will be delivered. His holy perfection demands that He do what is right. Thus, His people can rest assured that He will take action on their behalf. They will be delivered from Babylon, and their oppressors will be defeated. Again note why: because He is the LORD, the Holy One, Israel's Creator, their king (v.15). His judgment of Babylon is sure. He will utterly destroy them as surely as He destroyed the Egyptian army in the Red Sea (Ex.14:26-28).

Thought 1. In dealing with His people, the LORD always does the righteous thing. When His people are oppressed, the ethical action is always to deliver them from their persecutors. In righteousness, He condemns their oppressors, dooming them to utter defeat and judgment. Through His awesome power, God promises His people victory over all their enemies.

"Who shall separate us from the love of Christ? *shall* tribulation, or distress, or persecution, or famine, or nakedness, or peril, or sword?...Nay, in all these things we are more than conquerors through him that loved us. For I am persuaded, that neither death, nor life, nor angels, nor principalities, nor powers, nor things present, nor things to come, Nor height, nor depth, nor any other creature, shall be able to separate us from the love of God, which is in Christ Jesus our Lord" (Ro.8:35, 37-39).

"Now thanks *be* unto God, which always causeth us to triumph in Christ, and maketh manifest the savour of his knowledge by us in every place" (2 Co.2:14).

"For though we walk in the flesh, we do not war after the flesh: (For the weapons of our warfare *are* not carnal, but mighty through God to the pulling down of strong holds;) Casting down imaginations, and every high thing that exalteth itself against the knowledge of God, and bringing into captivity every thought to the obedience of Christ" (2 Co.10:3-5).

"Finally, my brethren, be strong in the Lord, and in the power of his might. Put on the whole armour of God, that ye may be able to stand against the wiles of the devil. For we wrestle not against flesh and blood, but against principalities, against powers, against the rulers of the darkness of this world, against spiritual wickedness in high *places*. Wherefore take unto you the whole armour of God, that ye may be able to withstand in the evil day, and having done all, to stand" (Ep.6:10-13).

"This charge I commit unto thee, son Timothy, according to the prophecies which went before on thee, that thou by them mightest war a good warfare; Holding faith, and a good conscience; which some having put away concerning faith have made shipwreck" (1 Ti.1:18-19).

"But thou, O man of God, flee these things; and follow after righteousness, godliness, faith, love, patience, meekness. Fight the good fight of faith, lay hold on eternal life, whereunto thou art also called, and hast professed a good profession before many witnesses" (1 Ti.6:11-12).

"Thou therefore endure hardness, as a good soldier of Jesus Christ. No man that warreth entangleth himself with the affairs of *this* life; that he may please him who hath chosen him to be a soldier" (2 Ti.2:3-4).

"And the Lord shall deliver me from every evil work, and will preserve *me* unto his heavenly kingdom: to whom *be* glory for ever and ever. Amen" (2 Ti.4:18).

"Be sober, be vigilant; because your adversary the devil, as a roaring lion, walketh about, seeking whom he may devour: Whom resist stedfast in the faith, knowing that the same afflictions are accomplished in your brethren that are in the world. But the God of all grace, who hath called us unto his eternal glory by Christ Jesus, after that ye have suffered a while, make you perfect, stablish, strengthen, settle *you*" (1 Pe.5:8-10).

"For whatsoever is born of God overcometh the world: and this is the victory that overcometh the world, *even* our faith. Who is he that overcometh the world, but he that believeth that Jesus is the Son of God?" (1 Jn.5:4-5).

"Through thee will we push down our enemies: through thy name will we tread them under that rise up against us" (Ps.44:5).

f.   The LORD will do greater things than ever before for His people; He will perform a *new thing* on their behalf (vv.18-21). What is this *new thing*? He will guide and provide for them as never before. Although the cruel Babylonians will hold them in captivity, God will work through the nations of the world to restore His people to the promised land (a symbol of heaven) (vv.5-6). Nations from the four corners of the earth will help Israel return to the land God promised them. And when they return, God will take care of them and provide for all their necessities (v.20). Of course, water is the most essential need in a desert region. As scarce as water is, God promises to provide so much water that even the wild animals will have enough to drink. Note why God promises to guide and provide for His people: so they would bear strong witness to Him and praise His name before the entire world (v.21).

Thought 1. The LORD promises to guide us day by day as we walk through life. No matter how difficult the path, if we believe and follow Him, He promises to guide us. Listen to His wonderful promises:

"Through the tender mercy of our God; whereby the dayspring from on high hath visited us, To give light to them that sit in darkness and *in* the shadow of death, to guide our feet into the way of peace" (Lu.1:78-79).

"Howbeit when he, the Spirit of truth, is come, he will guide you into all truth: for he shall not speak of himself; but whatsoever he shall hear, *that* shall he speak: and he will show you things to come" (Jn.16:13).

"As an eagle stirreth up her nest, fluttereth over her young, spreadeth abroad her wings, taketh them, beareth them on her wings: *So* the LORD alone did lead him, and *there was* no strange god with him" (De.32:11-12).

"The LORD *is* my shepherd; I shall not want. He maketh me to lie down in green pastures: he leadeth me beside the still waters. He restoreth my soul: he leadeth me in the paths of righteousness for his name's sake. Yea, though I walk through the valley of the shadow of death, I will fear no evil: for thou *art* with me; thy rod and thy staff they comfort me. Thou preparest a table before me in the presence of mine enemies: thou anointest my head with oil; my cup runneth over. Surely goodness and mercy shall follow me all the days of my life: and I will dwell in the house of the LORD for ever" (Ps.23:1-6).

"The meek will he guide in judgment: and the meek will he teach his way" (Ps.25:9).

"Teach me thy way, O LORD, and lead me in a plain path, because of mine enemies" (Ps.27:11).

"For this God *is* our God for ever and ever: he will be our guide *even* unto death" (Ps.48:14).

"Thou shalt guide me with thy counsel, and afterward receive me *to* glory" (Ps.73:24).

"*If* I take the wings of the morning, *and* dwell in the uttermost parts of the sea; Even there shall thy hand lead me, and thy right hand shall hold me" (Ps.139:9-10).

"And thine ears shall hear a word behind thee, saying, This *is* the way, walk ye in it, when ye turn to the right hand, and when ye turn to the left" (Is.30:21).

"And I will bring the blind by a way *that* they knew not; I will lead them in paths *that* they have not known: I will make darkness light before them, and crooked things straight. These things will I do unto them, and not forsake them" (Is.42:16).

Thought 2. Another great promise of the LORD is that He will provide for our needs. He will look after and take care of true believers who follow Him. All believers will have the necessities to sustain life until the day the LORD is ready to take them to heaven.

"But seek ye first the kingdom of God, and his righteousness; and all these things shall be added unto you" (Mt.6:33).

"Give, and it shall be given unto you; good measure, pressed down, and shaken together, and running over, shall men give into your bosom. For with the same measure that ye mete withal it shall be measured to you again" (Lu.6:38).

"But my God shall supply all your need according to his riches in glory by Christ Jesus" (Ph.4:19).

"And ye shall serve the LORD your God, and he shall bless thy bread, and thy water; and I will take sickness away from the midst of thee" (Ex.23:25).

"And thou shalt return and obey the voice of the LORD, and do all his commandments which I command thee this day. And the LORD thy God will make thee plenteous in every work of thine hand, in the fruit of thy body, and in the fruit of thy cattle, and in the fruit of thy land, for good: for the LORD will again rejoice over thee for good, as he rejoiced over thy fathers" (De.30:8-9).

"Blessed *be* the Lord, *who* daily loadeth us *with benefits, even* the God of our salvation. Selah" (Ps.68:19).

"I will abundantly bless her provision: I will satisfy her poor with bread" (Ps.132:15).

"Bring ye all the tithes into the storehouse, that there may be meat in mine house, and prove me now herewith, saith the LORD of hosts, if I will not open you the windows of heaven, and pour you out a blessing, that *there shall* not *be room* enough *to receive it*" (Mal.3:10).

3 (43:22-28) **Israel, Sins of, Failure to Pray and Worship—Prayerlessness, Sin of, Example—Worship, Failure to, Example—Israel, Sins of, Failure to Pray and Worship—Forgiveness, Source of, the LORD**: the failure of God's people to live like *the redeemed* is now discussed. Although God promises to save His people, they in no way deserve to be saved. God's salvation will be totally by His grace. He will rescue His people from Babylonian captivity because He loves them.

Isaiah levels a very serious charge against God's people: they are offering up empty prayer and worship. Apparently many of the Jews were praying and worshipping, but they were not approaching God as He had prescribed (vv.22-24). They were not seeking Him with pure, righteous hearts. When they prayed and worshipped, they approached God with the stain of sin upon their lives, and they did not seek to be cleansed by the blood of the sacrifice. They did not even offer the occasional special offerings such as fragrant cane or incense or the fat from sacrifices to the LORD (v.24). Approaching God for the forgiveness of sins was the furthest thing from their minds. They were not obeying God's commandments but, rather, living immoral and unrighteous lives. They were focused upon the world, and their hearts were full of covetousness and the selfish pursuit of pleasure. As Isaiah charged earlier, they were worshipping the LORD hypocritically (1:11-12). Obviously, the people had no *sense* of sin, no awareness of having committed wickedness. Their hearts and consciences were hardened against God. Note the strong charge God levels against them: they are burdening Him with their sins and wearying Him with their iniquities. They are breaking His holy commandments (v.24).

As a result of Israel's terrible offenses against the LORD, we would expect the hand of God's judgment to fall upon the people. But instead, His heart reaches out in an appeal to them. He longs to blot out their transgressions and remember their sins no more. Clearly, this is a call for them to repent and seek His forgiveness.

There is no forgiveness apart from repentance. To stress the utter necessity for seeking His forgiveness, the LORD again summons the people to appear at a legal trial (vv.26-28). He calls upon them to review what they have done and to state the case for their innocence. But before they can speak, the LORD charges them with being just like their father who sinned. This is a reference either to Adam, the father of the human race, or to Abraham, the father of the Jews. Both Adam and Abraham rebelled against the LORD (see outline and notes—Ge.3:1-13; 12:17-20; 20:8-10 for more discussion).

Due to their continued sin, God's hand of judgment was certain to fall upon the Jews. Because of their false worship and hypocrisy, their religious leaders would be disgraced, the people shamed, and their nation destroyed. Keep in mind that God's Word was fulfilled when the Babylonians destroyed Jerusalem, including the temple, and scattered the survivors throughout the Babylonian Empire.

OUTLINE	SCRIPTURE	SCRIPTURE	OUTLINE

3. **The failure of God's people to live like the redeemed**
a. The charge
  1) You have not prayed to, worshipped, or approached God as He prescribed
    • Not sought Him with a pure, righteous heart
    • Not sought to be cleansed by the blood of the sacrifice
  2) You have not faithfully brought your special offerings to the LORD
  3) You have burdened the LORD with your sins
	22 But thou hast not called upon me, O Jacob; but thou hast been weary of me, O Israel.
	23 Thou hast not brought me the small cattle of thy burnt offerings; neither hast thou honoured me with thy sacrifices. I have not caused thee to serve with an offering, nor wearied thee with incense.
	24 Thou hast bought me no sweet cane with money, neither hast thou filled me with the fat of thy sacrifices: but thou hast made me to serve with thy sins, thou hast wea-
		ried me with thine iniquities.
		25 I, *even* I, *am* he that blotteth out thy transgressions for mine own sake, and will not remember thy sins.
		26 Put me in remembrance: let us plead together: declare thou, that thou mayest be justified.
		27 Thy first father hath sinned, and thy teachers have transgressed against me.
		28 Therefore I have profaned the princes of the sanctuary, and have given Jacob to the curse, and Israel to reproaches.
			b. The appeal of the LORD: He alone blots out your transgressions
			
			c. The trial of hypocrites
			  1) God's demand: Prove your case, your innocence
			
			  2) God's charge: Your ancestors—even leaders—have always sinned
			
			  3) God's judgment: The religious leaders will be disgraced & the people destroyed

Thought 1. Prayer and worship are synonymous, the very same act. When people pray to the LORD, they are worshipping Him; and when people worship, they are praying through their praise, thanksgiving, and requests. Their prayers are also a proclamation of the gospel, of God's working in the hearts of believers. Through prayer, every act of worship is being performed, and through worship, every act of prayer is being demonstrated. Moreover, worship and prayer are both communication and fellowship with God. When people pray or worship, they commune with the LORD through the various acts of praise, thanksgiving, and presenting their requests.

But the Israelites were not sincere in their approach to the LORD, neither in their prayers nor in their worship. Like most people, the majority of the Jews were not praying or seeking the LORD. And those who were worshipping were uttering empty prayers. Prayerlessness and empty worship were two of the major characteristics of their lives. (1) Listen to what God's Holy Word says about prayerlessness.

"From whence *come* wars and fightings among you? *come they* not hence, *even* of your lusts that war in your members? Ye lust, and have not: ye kill, and desire to have, and cannot obtain: ye fight and war, yet ye have not, because ye ask not. Ye ask, and receive not, because ye ask amiss, that ye may consume *it* upon your lusts. Ye adulterers and adulteresses, know ye not that the friendship of the world is enmity with God? whosoever therefore will be a friend of the world is the enemy of God" (Js.4:1-4, esp. v.2).

"Not forsaking the assembling of ourselves together, as the manner of some *is;* but exhorting *one another:* and so much the more, as ye see the day approaching" (He.10:25).

"Have the workers of iniquity no knowledge? who eat up my people *as* they eat bread: they have not called upon God" (Ps.53:4).

"And *there is* none that calleth upon thy name, that stirreth up himself to take hold of thee: for thou hast hid thy face from us, and hast consumed us, because of our iniquities" (Is.64:7).

"For the pastors are become brutish, and have not sought the LORD: therefore they shall not prosper, and all their flocks shall be scattered" (Je.10:21).

"As *it is* written in the law of Moses, all this evil is come upon us: yet made we not our prayer before the LORD our God, that we might turn from our iniquities, and understand thy truth" (Da.9:13).

"They are all hot as an oven, and have devoured their judges; all their kings are fallen: *there is* none among them that calleth unto me" (Ho.7:7).

"I will also stretch out mine hand upon Judah, and upon all the inhabitants of Jerusalem; and I will cut off the remnant of Baal from this place, *and* the name of the Chemarims with the priests; And them that worship the host of heaven upon the housetops; and them that worship *and* that swear by the

LORD, and that swear by Malcham; And them that are turned back from the LORD; and *those* that have not sought the LORD, nor enquired for him" (Zep.1:4-6, esp.v.6).

(2) Listen to what God's Holy Word says about empty, formal worship.

"Woe unto you, scribes and Pharisees, hypocrites! for ye pay tithe of mint and anise and cummin, and have omitted the weightier *matters* of the law, judgment, mercy, and faith: these ought ye to have done, and not to leave the other undone" (Mt.23:23).

"Ye observe days, and months, and times, and years. I am afraid of you, lest I have bestowed upon you labour in vain." (Ga.4:10-11).

"Wherefore if ye be dead with Christ from the rudiments of the world, why, as though living in the world, are ye subject to ordinances" (Col.2:20).

"Having a form of godliness, but denying the power thereof: from such turn away" (2 Ti.3:5).

"And another angel came out of the temple which is in heaven, he also having a sharp sickle" (Re.14:17).

"And Samuel said, Hath the LORD *as great* delight in burnt offerings and sacrifices, as in obeying the voice of the LORD? Behold, to obey *is* better than sacrifice, *and* to hearken than the fat of rams" (1 S.15:22).

"For thou desirest not sacrifice; else would I give *it:* thou delightest not in burnt offering. The sacrifices of God *are* a broken spirit: a broken and a contrite heart, O God, thou wilt not despise" (Ps.51:16-17).

"Keep thy foot when thou goest to the house of God, and be more ready to hear, than to give the sacrifice of fools: for they consider not that they do evil" (Ecc.5:1).

"Bring no more vain oblations; incense is an abomination unto me; the new moons and sabbaths, the calling of assemblies, I cannot away with; *it is* iniquity, even the solemn meeting" (Is.1:13).

"Wherefore the Lord said, Forasmuch as this people draw near *me* with their mouth, and with their lips do honour me, but have removed their heart far from me, and their fear toward me is taught by the precept of men" (Is.29:13).

"For I desired mercy, and not sacrifice; and the knowledge of God more than burnt offerings" (Ho.6:6).

CHAPTER 44

E. Set Free by the LORD, the Only Living & True God, 44:1-28

1. God's people are set free by His promise: He will *help* Israel (redeemed believers)

a. God helps by assuring the redeemed: They belong to Him
   1) Because He created them
   2) Because He chose them to be His servants
   3) Because He helps them: Delivers from fear, v.2, 8

b. God helps by pouring His blessings on the land & His Spirit on true believers, Is.32:15; 59:21; Ac.2:14-36; see also Nu.11:29; Eze.36:24-28; 37:14; 39:29; Joel 2:25-29; Zec.12:10
   1) The redeemed & their descendants will prosper
   2) The unbeliever who is redeemed will unashamedly identify with the LORD & His people

c. God helps by declaring His preeminence—who He is
   1) He is their King & Redeemer
   2) He is the LORD Almighty
   3) He is the First & the Last
   4) He alone is God

d. God helps by proving no one is like Him
   1) He alone appointed Israel long ago to be His people
   2) He alone knows the future: He is omniscient, knowing all things

e. God helps by delivering the redeemed from fear & captivity
   1) He had foretold the events
   2) The redeemed bear witness to God's deliverance

f. God helps by giving assurance: He is the Rock, the only foundation to life

2. God's people are set free by knowing the folly of idolatry

a. The stupidity of idolatry
   1) Idols are worthless
   2) Idol worshippers are blind & ignorant

   3) Idolatry is foolish & profits nothing

b. The judgment of idolatry & idolaters: Will face God's wrath
   1) Will be put to shame
   2) Will stand before God in

Yet now hear, O Jacob my servant; and Israel, whom I have chosen:

2 Thus saith the LORD that made thee, and formed thee from the womb, *which* will help thee; Fear not, O Jacob, my servant; and thou, Jesurun, whom I have chosen.

3 For I will pour water upon him that is thirsty, and floods upon the dry ground: I will pour my spirit upon thy seed, and my blessing upon thine offspring:

4 And they shall spring up as among the grass, as willows by the water courses.

5 One shall say, I *am* the LORD'S; and another shall call *himself* by the name of Jacob; and another shall subscribe *with* his hand unto the LORD, and surname *himself* by the name of Israel.

6 Thus saith the LORD the King of Israel, and his redeemer the LORD of hosts; I *am* the first, and I *am* the last; and beside me *there is* no God.

7 And who, as I, shall call, and shall declare it, and set it in order for me, since I appointed the ancient people? and the things that are coming, and shall come, let them show unto them.

8 Fear ye not, neither be afraid: have not I told thee from that time, and have declared *it?* ye *are* even my witnesses. Is there a God beside me? yea, *there is* no God; I know not *any.*

9 They that make a graven image *are* all of them vanity; and their delectable things shall not profit; and they *are* their own witnesses; they see not, nor know; that they may be ashamed.

10 Who hath formed a god, or molten a graven image *that* is profitable for nothing?

11 Behold, all his fellows shall be ashamed: and the workmen, they *are* of men: let them all be gathered together, let them stand up; *yet*

they shall fear, *and* they shall be ashamed together.

12 The smith with the tongs both worketh in the coals, and fashioneth it with hammers, and worketh it with the strength of his arms: yea, he is hungry, and his strength faileth: he drinketh no water, and is faint.

13 The carpenter stretcheth out *his* rule; he marketh it out with a line; he fitteth it with planes, and he marketh it out with the compass, and maketh it after the figure of a man, according to the beauty of a man; that it may remain in the house.

14 He heweth him down cedars, and taketh the cypress and the oak, which he strengtheneth for himself among the trees of the forest: he planteth an ash, and the rain doth nourish *it.*

15 Then shall it be for a man to burn: for he will take thereof, and warm himself; yea, he kindleth *it,* and baketh bread; yea, he maketh a god, and worshippeth *it;* he maketh it a graven image, and falleth down thereto.

16 He burneth part thereof in the fire; with part thereof he eateth flesh; he roasteth roast, and is satisfied: yea, he warmeth *himself,* and saith, Aha, I am warm, I have seen the fire:

17 And the residue thereof he maketh a god, *even* his graven image: he falleth down unto it, and worshippeth *it,* and prayeth unto it, and saith, Deliver me; for thou *art* my god.

18 They have not known nor understood: for he hath shut their eyes, that they cannot see; *and* their hearts, that they cannot understand.

19 And none considereth in his heart, neither *is there* knowledge nor understanding to say, I have burned part of it in the fire; yea, also I have baked bread upon the coals thereof; I have roasted flesh, and eaten *it:* and shall I make the residue thereof an abomination? shall I fall down to the stock of a tree?

20 He feedeth on ashes: a deceived heart hath turned him aside, that he cannot deliver his soul, nor say, *Is*

terror & shame

c. The physical nature of idols & idolaters
   1) The blacksmith is a mere man & his tools are only physical, material objects
      • He himself makes the tools & the idols
      • He himself is only flesh: He hungers & tires
   2) The carpenter is a mere man & his tools are only material objects
      • He makes an outline of an image: Has an idea of what the god should look like

      • He chisels & shapes the god in man's image
      • He makes the idol from a tree he had cut down in a forest or else had planted

d. The utter stupidity of idolatry restated & illustrated
   1) An idol is made from a physical substance: Wood that is used for heating & cooking
      • An idol is not spirit, not from the spiritual, eternal world
      • A person uses half the wood for heating & cooking

      • A person uses the other half to make an idol
   2) The person actually worships & prays to his man-made idol: "Save me"

e. The cause of idolatry
   1) A person is spiritually blind: His or her eyes & mind are closed

   2) A person is non-thinking: Does not have the knowledge, understanding, or honesty to face the truth, that the idol is only a material substance (not from the spiritual, eternal world)

   3) A person is deceived
      • He feeds his soul on ashes
      • He trusts something that

cannot save him	*there* not a lie in my right hand?	ens alone; that spreadeth abroad the earth by myself;	2) Guaranteed by God's power to expose the errors of false teachers: The false prophets, diviners, & wise of the world
3. God's people are set free by returning to the LORD & by renewing their great hope in the promised land	21 Remember these, O Jacob and Israel; for thou *art* my servant: I have formed thee; thou *art* my servant: O Israel, thou shalt not be forgotten of me.	25 That frustrateth the tokens of the liars, and maketh diviners mad; that turneth wise *men* backward, and maketh their knowledge foolish;	
a. The charge to God's people		26 That confirmeth the word of his servant, and performeth the counsel of his messengers; that saith to Jerusalem, Thou shalt be inhabited; and to the cities of Judah, Ye shall be built, and I will raise up the decayed places thereof:	3) Guaranteed by God's power to fulfill His Word & the predictions of His messengers
1) Must remember that they are God's servants & that they have been forgiven their sins	22 I have blotted out, as a thick cloud, thy transgressions, and, as a cloud, thy sins: return unto me; for I have redeemed thee.		• That His people would return to the promised land
2) Must repent: Because the LORD has redeemed them	23 Sing, O ye heavens; for the LORD hath done *it:* shout, ye lower parts of the earth: break forth into singing, ye mountains, O forest, and every tree therein: for the LORD hath redeemed Jacob, and glorified himself in Israel.		• That Jerusalem & the other cities would be rebuilt, 58:12; 61:4; Je.32:15
3) Must join all creation in praising God		27 That saith to the deep, Be dry, and I will dry up thy rivers:	4) Guaranteed by God's power to work miracles such as crossing the Red Sea
• Because the LORD has redeemed them			5) Guaranteed by God's power to use King Cyrus of Persia to set the Jewish exiles free: They would rebuild Jerusalem & the temple (2 Chr.36:22-23; Ezr.1:1-11; 6:1-22
• Because the LORD displays His glory in them	24 Thus saith the LORD, thy redeemer, and he that formed thee from the womb, I *am* the LORD that maketh all *things;* that stretcheth forth the heav-	28 That saith of Cyrus, *He is* my shepherd, and shall perform all my pleasure: even saying to Jerusalem, Thou shalt be built; and to the temple, Thy foundation shall be laid.	
b. The wonderful promise of God: The redeemed will return to the promised land			
1) Guaranteed by God's power to create the universe			

DIVISION V

THE PROPHECIES OF COMFORT AND FREEDOM: A PICTURE OF BELIEVERS BEING SET FREE FROM THE CAPTIVITY OF SIN AND DEATH, 40:1–48:22

E. Set Free by the LORD, the Only Living and True God, 44:1-28

(44:1-28) **Introduction**: freedom is one of the most prized possessions of the human race. People who live in a free nation are usually able to move around without restraints, exercise their initiatives, pursue their ambitions, choose their work, marry the person of their choice, and worship freely. But people who are not free are severely restricted, sometimes even persecuted or enslaved. In a restrictive, oppressive society, people often have to deal with prejudice, discrimination, and favoritism. They are seldom allowed to travel freely, worship, or choose the work they want to do. Personal ambition, goals, and initiative are usually repressed, and people have to work at jobs determined by government officials, which includes forced labor.

Freedom is the subject of the present Scripture. The LORD clearly shows that He has a vital interest in people being set free from the bondages and enslavements of this life. Remember that Isaiah is predicting the Babylonian captivity of the Jews. But he also predicts that God will use human events in order to set His people free from their captivity. By His own power God will liberate and restore His people to the promised land. But more important, true liberty—an inner peace and freedom—can come only through the LORD, the only living and true God. He and He alone has the power to set people free from the enslavements of this life, including the terrifying bondages of sin and death. This is the subject of the present Scripture: *Set Free by the LORD, the Only Living and True God,* 44:1-28.

1. God's people are set free by His promise: He will *help* Israel (redeemed believers) (vv.1-8).
2. God's people are set free by knowing the folly of idolatry (vv.9-20).
3. God's people are set free by returning to the LORD and by renewing their great hope in the promised land (vv.21-28).

1 (44:1-8) **Liberty, Source of, God's Promise—Set Free, Source of, God's Promise—Help – Helping, Source, God, Sixfold Help—Holy Spirit, Prophecy Concerning, Spirit Outpouring—God, Names – Titles of—God, Proofs of, Prophecy—Israel, Prophecies Concerning, Deliverance from Captivity**: God's people are set free by His wonderful promise to *help* them as they walk through life. Note verse 2, where the LORD claims to be the only true God, the only One who can truly help people and deliver them from fear (v.2; also see v.8). The striking opening words, "now hear" (or "now listen"), set this Scripture off sharply from what has just been said. At the close of chapter 43, the LORD pronounced judgment upon the Israelites (vv.26-28). But now the LORD gives an astounding promise: the destruction and shame of His people will not be total. He will not allow them to be completely destroyed, for they are His *servant,* whom He has chosen to be His righteous people. They are His witnesses to unbelievers who rebel against Him.

Note in God's address to the people that the names "Jacob" and "Israel" are both used to refer to the entire nation. In God's mind, there is no Northern or Southern Kingdom. His people are one nation, one people before Him. Hereafter, the division of the nation will be a thing of the past. His people are not to be divided but rather united in serving Him.

But as seen in the previous chapter, as well as throughout the book of Isaiah, the vast majority of the Israelites failed to serve God. Consequently, the hand of God's judgment fell upon them. Even in the present Scripture, Isaiah predicts the future destruction of the nation and the exile of the survivors, as well as their return from captivity (vv.8, 24-28). And yet again God makes a remarkable the most wonderful promise: in the midst of this terrifying trial, He will *assist* His people by helping them in six specific ways:

OUTLINE	SCRIPTURE	SCRIPTURE	OUTLINE

1. God's people are set free by His promise: He will *help* Israel (redeemed believers)
a. God helps by assuring the redeemed: They belong to Him
  1) Because He created them
  2) Because He chose them to be His servants
  3) Because He helps them: Delivers from fear, v.2 8
b. God helps by pouring His blessings on the land & His Spirit on true believers, Is. 32:15; 59:21; Ac.2:14-36; see also Nu.11:29; Eze. 36:24-28; 37:14; 39:29; Joel 2:25-29; Zec.12:10
  1) The redeemed & their descendants will prosper
  2) The unbeliever who is redeemed will unashamedly identify with the LORD & His people
	Yet now hear, O Jacob my servant; and Israel, whom I have chosen: 2 Thus saith the LORD that made thee, and formed thee from the womb, *which* will help thee; Fear not, O Jacob, my servant; and thou, Jesurun, whom I have chosen. 3 For I will pour water upon him that is thirsty, and floods upon the dry ground: I will pour my spirit upon thy seed, and my blessing upon thine offspring: 4 And they shall spring up as among the grass, as willows by the water courses. 5 One shall say, I *am* the LORD'S; and another shall call *himself* by the name of Jacob; and another shall sub-	scribe *with* his hand unto the LORD, and surname *himself* by the name of Israel. 6 Thus saith the LORD the King of Israel, and his redeemer the LORD of hosts; I *am* the first, and I *am* the last; and beside me *there is* no God. 7 And who, as I, shall call, and shall declare it, and set it in order for me, since I appointed the ancient people? and the things that are coming, and shall come, let them show unto them. 8 Fear ye not, neither be afraid: have not I told thee from that time, and have declared *it?* ye *are* even my witnesses. Is there a God beside me? yea, *there is* no God; I know not *any.*	c. God helps by declaring His preeminence—who He is
			  1) He is their King & Redeemer
			  2) He is the LORD Almighty
			  3) He is the First & the Last
			  4) He alone is God
			d. God helps by proving no one is like Him
			  1) He alone appointed Israel long ago to be His people
			  2) He alone knows the future: He is omniscient, knowing all things
			e. God helps by delivering the redeemed from fear & captivity
			  1) He had foretold the events
			  2) The redeemed bear witness to God's deliverance
			f. God helps by giving assurance: He is the Rock, the only foundation to life

a. God will help His people by assuring them that they belong to Him (v.2). They are His people, His possession. This is a wonderful truth that should give every believer great reassurance. When believers know that they belong to God, they know that the LORD loves and cares for them and will provide whatever security, protection, and provision they need. Note that God gives believers three assurances to prove that they belong to Him:

⇒ God created them, formed them from the womb. This has a twofold application with Israel. Not only was each Israelite created by God, but also the nation as a whole. As a nation Israel was created when God delivered the people from Egyptian bondage and based their society upon His laws at Mount Sinai. As individuals and as a nation, they were the LORD's, and they belonged to Him because He was their Creator.

⇒ God chose the Israelites to be His servants, His very special witnesses to the world. Therefore, they could expect to have a very distinctive relationship with the LORD, a relationship that assured them of His presence and care.

⇒ God helps His people as they walk through life day by day. Hence, they need not fear when they face enemies and the hardships of life (vv.2, 8).

> "Blessed *be* the God and Father of our Lord Jesus Christ, who hath blessed us with all spiritual blessings in heavenly *places* in Christ: According as he hath chosen us in him before the foundation of the world, that we should be holy and without blame before him in love: Having predestinated us unto the adoption of children by Jesus Christ to himself, according to the good pleasure of his will" (Ep.1:3-5).
>
> "But ye *are* a chosen generation, a royal priesthood, an holy nation, a peculiar people; that ye should show forth the praises of him who hath called you out of darkness into his marvellous light: Which in time past *were* not a people, but *are* now the people of God: which had not obtained mercy, but now have obtained mercy" (1 Pe.2:9-10).
>
> "For thou *art* an holy people unto the LORD thy God: the LORD thy God hath chosen thee to be a special people unto himself, above all people that *are* upon the face of the earth" (De.7:6).
>
> "But know that the LORD hath set apart him that is godly for himself: the LORD will hear when I call unto him" (Ps.4:3).

b. God will help His people by blessing them both physically and spiritually (vv.3-5). Physically they will prosper because the LORD will send rain to water their fields and produce rich crops. Spiritually they will prosper because the LORD will pour out His Spirit on believers and their descendants. The same power that created physical life will create spiritual life. And by the power of God's Spirit, the believer becomes a *new creation*, a *new person* (2 Co.5:17; Ga.6:15; Ep.2:15; Ep.4:22-24; Col.3:10). Centuries earlier, the LORD had predicted the coming of His Spirit through Moses and the prophets (Nu.11:29; Is.32:15; 59:21; Eze.36:24-28; 37:14; 39:29; Joel 2:25-29; Zec.12:10). This prophecy was fulfilled by the coming of Christ to save and empower His people (Ac.1:1-8; 2:1-4, 14-36). He empowers them through the gifts of the Holy Spirit. It is God's Spirit that causes believers to spring up and multiply in number as rapidly as grass and trees near streams of water (v.4). Through the power of God's Spirit, unbelievers will turn to the LORD and unashamedly identify with Him and His people (v.5). True believers will profess that they belong to the LORD, and they will call themselves true Israelites (true Christians). With boldness they will honor the LORD by confessing His Name.

Thought 1. The work of the Holy Spirit in the lives of believers cannot be overemphasized. His work is stressed time and again throughout Scripture. Here are several of the Spirit's major functions:

(1) The Holy Spirit comforts believers, just as Christ comforted His followers when He was on earth.

"And I will pray the Father, and he shall give you another Comforter, that he may abide with you for ever" (Jn.14:16).
"The Spirit itself beareth witness with our spirit, that we are the children of God: And if children, then heirs; heirs of God, and joint-heirs with Christ; if so be that we suffer with *him*, that we may be also glorified together" (Ro.8:16-17).
"And because ye are sons, God hath sent forth the Spirit of his Son into your hearts, crying, Abba, Father" (Ga.4:6).
"Hereby know we that we dwell in him, and he in us, because he hath given us of his Spirit" (1 Jn.4:13).

(2) The Holy Spirit teaches believers.

"But the Comforter, *which is* the Holy Ghost, whom the Father will send in my name, he shall teach you all things, and bring all things to your remembrance, whatsoever I have said unto you" (Jn.14:26).
"Howbeit when he, the Spirit of truth, is come, he will guide you into all truth: for he shall not speak of himself; but whatsoever he shall hear, *that* shall he speak: and he will show you things to come" (Jn.16:13).
"Which things also we speak, not in the words which man's wisdom teacheth, but which the Holy Ghost teacheth; comparing spiritual things with spiritual" (1 Co.2:13).
"But the anointing which ye have received of him abideth in you, and ye need not that any man teach you: but as the same anointing teacheth you of all things, and is truth, and is no lie, and even as it hath taught you, ye shall abide in him" (1 Jn.2:27).

(3) The Holy Spirit bears strong witness to the work of Christ and salvation.

"But when the Comforter is come, whom I will send unto you from the Father, *even* the Spirit of truth, which proceedeth from the Father, he shall testify of me" (Jn.15:26).
"He [the Holy Spirit] shall glorify me: for he shall receive of mine, and shall show *it* unto you. All things that the Father hath are mine: therefore said I, that he shall take of mine, and shall show *it* unto you" (Jn.16:14-15).
"This is he that came by water and blood, *even* Jesus Christ; not by water only, but by water and blood. And it is the Spirit that beareth witness, because the Spirit is truth" (1 Jn.5:6).

(4) The Holy Spirit convicts believers of their sin, their lack of righteousness, and the coming judgment.

"Nevertheless I tell you the truth; It is expedient for you that I go away: for if I go not away, the Comforter will not come unto you; but if I depart, I will send him unto you. And when he is come, he will reprove the world of sin, and of righteousness, and of judgment: Of sin, because they believe not on me; Of righteousness, because I go to my Father, and ye see me no more; Of judgment, because the prince of this world is judged" (Jn.16:7-11).

(5) The Holy Spirit leads and guides believers.

"Howbeit when he, the Spirit of truth, is come, he will guide you into all truth: for he shall not speak of himself; but whatsoever he shall hear, *that* shall he speak: and he will show you things to come" (Jn.16:13).
"For as many as are led by the Spirit of God, they are the sons of God" (Ro.8:14).

(6) The Holy Spirit quickens, or gives life to, believers.

"It is the spirit that quickeneth; the flesh profiteth nothing: the words that I speak unto you, *they* are spirit, and *they* are life" (Jn.6:63).
"But if the Spirit of him that raised up Jesus from the dead dwell in you, he that raised up Christ from the dead shall also quicken your mortal bodies by his Spirit that dwelleth in you" (Ro.8:11).
"For Christ also hath once suffered for sins, the just for the unjust, that he might bring us to God, being put to death in the flesh, but quickened by the Spirit" (1 Pe.3:18).

(7) The Holy Spirit dwells within believers, making them the very temples of God Himself.

"*Even* the Spirit of truth; whom the world cannot receive, because it seeth him not, neither knoweth him: but ye know him; for he dwelleth with you, and shall be in you" (Jn.14:17).
"But ye are not in the flesh, but in the Spirit, if so be that the Spirit of God dwell in you. Now if any man have not the Spirit of Christ, he is none of his" (Ro.8:9).
"Know ye not that ye are the temple of God, and *that* the Spirit of God dwelleth in you?" (1 Co.3:16).

"What? know ye not that your body is the temple of the Holy Ghost *which is* in you, which ye have of God, and ye are not your own? For ye are bought with a price: therefore glorify God in your body, and in your spirit, which are God's" (1 Co.6:19-20).

"That good thing which was committed unto thee keep by the Holy Ghost which dwelleth in us" (2 Ti.1:14).

"But the anointing which ye have received of him abideth in you, and ye need not that any man teach you: but as the same anointing teacheth you of all things, and is truth, and is no lie, and even as it hath taught you, ye shall abide in him" (1 Jn.2:27).

"And he that keepeth his commandments dwelleth in him, and he in him. And hereby we know that he abideth in us, by the Spirit which he hath given us" (1 Jn.3:24).

c. God will help His people by declaring who He is, the majestic nature of his being (v.6). The four titles claimed by God should give great assurance to believers.

1) The LORD is the *King* and *Redeemer* of His people. As their King, He rules over them, governing and taking care of them, making sure their most basic needs are met. As Redeemer, He saves His people from all the bondages and enslavements of this life.

2) The LORD is *the LORD of hosts*, or *the LORD Almighty*. The LORD possesses supreme power in the universe and controls all the hosts of beings, both in heaven and on earth. Thus the believer can rest assured of God's help when needs arise. No matter the severity of hardship or trial, the LORD Almighty will help His people. He is able to help them because He has the power to control all the beings in the universe.

3) The LORD is the *First* and *Last*, the *Eternal Being*, who exists above the universe and oversees its entire operation. He was first, existing before the universe was created; and He will be last, existing when the history of the present universe ends. The LORD has always been on the scene, and He will be on the scene when it disappears in flames with a loud roar (2 Pe.3:10-13). The LORD is the *First* and *Last*, the *Beginning* and *Ending*.

4) The LORD alone is God. Apart from Him, there is no *God*. All other gods claimed by people are false. Therefore, believers who truly follow the LORD can rest assured that they have the LORD's help. As the only living and true God, the LORD obviously loves His creation and possesses the power to help all who truly believe and follow Him.

d. God will help His people by proving that no one—no person and no so-called god—is like Him (v.7). If any people think that they or their gods are equal to the LORD, let them stand up and defend their claim. Here, Isaiah is painting a picture of a legal trial. God puts these people and their gods on *trial*. They must appear before God and show that the prophecies they have proclaimed have actually come true. As far as the LORD is concerned, He can prove His case. By calling Abraham, He chose and established Israel to be His people (Ge.12:1-3; 15:1-21). Then He not only foretold the building of a nation from this one man, but He also predicted event after event throughout the nation's history. And now He is predicting their future captivity by Babylon and their release by the Persians (vv.8, 21-28). No one is like the LORD, for He alone is omniscient. He alone knows all things and as such He alone is able to foretell the future. Believers can be assured of God's help and care in the future, for *nothing takes Him by surprise*.

"And the scribe said unto him, Well, Master, thou hast said the truth: for there is one God; and there is none other but he" (Mk.12:32).

"Who *is* like unto thee, O LORD, among the gods? who *is* like thee, glorious in holiness, fearful *in* praises, doing wonders?" (Ex.15:11).

"Wherefore thou art great, O LORD God: for *there is* none like thee, neither *is there any* God beside thee, according to all that we have heard with our ears" (2 S.7:22).

"And he said, LORD God of Israel, *there is* no God like thee, in heaven above, or on earth beneath, who keepest covenant and mercy with thy servants that walk before thee with all their heart" (1 K.8:23).

"For who in the heaven can be compared unto the LORD? *who* among the sons of the mighty can be likened unto the LORD?" (Ps.89:6).

"To whom then will ye liken God? or what likeness will ye compare unto him?" (Is.40:18).

e. God will help His people by delivering them—the redeemed—from fear and captivity (v.8). This promise of help will be a great encouragement to God's people, especially to those who will be taken captive by Babylon. Note that Isaiah is foretelling the Babylonian captivity years before it will take place. If God foresees the captivity and it actually takes place, the people can rest in His promise of their release and return to the promised land. Restoration is a certainty. Note why: because they are God's witnesses, a people very special to Him. They are His people, His servants. There is no chance He will forget His people or forsake His servants.

"But the very hairs of your head are all numbered. Fear ye not therefore, ye are of more value than many sparrows" (Mt.10:30-31).

"Forasmuch then as the children are partakers of flesh and blood, he also himself likewise took part of the same; that through death he might destroy him that had the power of death, that is, the devil; And deliver them who through fear of death were all their lifetime subject to bondage" (He.2:14-15).

"Fear thou not; for I *am* with thee: be not dismayed; for I *am* thy God: I will strengthen thee; yea, I will help thee; yea, I will uphold thee with the right hand of my righteousness" (Is.41:10).

"But now thus saith the LORD that created thee, O Jacob, and he that formed thee, O Israel, Fear not: for I have redeemed thee, I have called *thee* by thy name; thou *art* mine. When thou passest through the waters, I *will be* with thee; and through the rivers, they shall not overflow thee: when thou walkest through the fire, thou shalt not be burned; neither shall the flame kindle upon thee" (Is.43:1-2).

f. God will help His people by assuring them that He is the Rock, the very foundation of life. No other person or so-called god can claim to be the Rock of life. No one can build a foundation solid enough for people to build their lives and faith upon, not eternally. Only the LORD is the Rock, the foundation that can provide eternal stability and security for people. As the Rock, the LORD is the believer's foundation, strength, refuge, and security, both in this life and the next.

> "Therefore whosoever heareth these sayings of mine, and doeth them, I will liken him unto a wise man, which built his house upon a rock: And the rain descended, and the floods came, and the winds blew, and beat upon that house; and it fell not: for it was founded upon a rock. And every one that heareth these sayings of mine, and doeth them not, shall be likened unto a foolish man, which built his house upon the sand: And the rain descended, and the floods came, and the winds blew, and beat upon that house; and it fell: and great was the fall of it." (Mt.7:24-27).
>
> "Wherefore also it is contained in the scripture, Behold, I lay in Sion a chief corner stone, elect, precious: and he that believeth on him shall not be confounded." (1 Pe.2:6).
>
> "*He is* the Rock, his work *is* perfect: for all his ways *are* judgment: a God of truth and without iniquity, just and right *is* he" (De.32:4).
>
> "For their rock *is* not as our Rock, even our enemies themselves *being* judges" (De.32:31).
>
> "*There is* none holy as the LORD: for *there is* none beside thee: neither *is there* any rock like our God" (1 S.2:2).
>
> "The LORD *is* my rock, and my fortress, and my deliverer; my God, my strength, in whom I will trust; my buckler, and the horn of my salvation, *and* my high tower" (Ps.18:2).
>
> "For who *is* God save the LORD? or who *is* a rock save our God?" (Ps.18:31).
>
> "Unto thee will I cry, O LORD my rock; be not silent to me: lest, *if* thou be silent to me, I become like them that go down into the pit" (Ps.28:1).
>
> "Truly my soul waiteth upon God: from him *cometh* my salvation. He only *is* my rock and my salvation; *he is* my defence; I shall not be greatly moved" (Ps.62:1-2).
>
> "But the LORD is my defence; and my God *is* the rock of my refuge" (Ps.94:22).

---

2 (44:9-20) **Idolatry, Discussed—Idolatry, Stupidity of; Judgment of—Worship, False, Caused by—Gods, False, Discussed—Worship, False, Discussed—Liberty, from Idolatry—Set Free, from False Worship and False Gods**: God's people are set free by knowing the absurdity and folly of idolatry and false worship. It took great courage for Isaiah to preach about idols and false worship. He lived in a society in which almost every person practiced idolatry. In fact, the people and nations who seemed to be the most successful and powerful were those who honored false gods. True believers of the LORD were ridiculed and oppressed by the society of Isaiah's day. Thus it required enormous courage to bear witness to the LORD and to oppose the people's idolatrous practices. In these verses, Isaiah launches a sharp attack against the idols and false gods of his day:

OUTLINE	SCRIPTURE	SCRIPTURE	OUTLINE
2. God's people are set free by knowing the folly of idolatry	9 They that make a graven image *are* all of them vanity; and their delectable things shall not profit; and they *are* their own witnesses; they see not, nor know; that they may be ashamed.	faileth: he drinketh no water, and is faint.	flesh: He hungers & tires
a. The stupidity of idolatry		13 The carpenter stretcheth out *his* rule; he marketh it out with a line; he fitteth it with planes, and he marketh it out with the compass, and maketh it after the figure of a man, according to the beauty of a man; that it may remain in the house.	2) The carpenter is a mere man & his tools are only material objects
1) Idols are worthless			
2) Idol worshippers are blind & ignorant			• He makes an outline of an image: Has an idea of what the god should look like
3) Idolatry is foolish & profits nothing	10 Who hath formed a god, or molten a graven image *that* is profitable for nothing?		
b. The judgment of idolatry & idolaters: Will face God's wrath	11 Behold, all his fellows shall be ashamed: and the workmen, they *are* of men: let them all be gathered together, let them stand up; *yet* they shall fear, *and* they shall be ashamed together.	14 He heweth him down cedars, and taketh the cypress and the oak, which he strengtheneth for himself among the trees of the forest: he planteth an ash, and the rain doth nourish *it*.	• He chisels & shapes the god in man's image • He makes the idol from a tree he had cut down in a forest or else had planted
1) Will be put to shame			
2) Will stand before God in terror & shame			
c. The physical nature of idols & idolaters			
1) The blacksmith is a mere man & his tools are only physical, material objects	12 The smith with the tongs both worketh in the coals, and fashioneth it with hammers, and worketh it with the strength of his arms: yea, he is hungry, and his strength	15 Then shall it be for a man to burn: for he will take thereof, and warm himself; yea, he kindleth *it,* and baketh bread; yea, he maketh a god, and worshippeth *it;* he	d. The utter stupidity of idolatry restated & illustrated 1) An idol is made from a physical substance: Wood that is used for heating & cooking
• He himself makes the tools & the idols			
• He himself is only			

OUTLINE	SCRIPTURE	SCRIPTURE	OUTLINE
• An idol is not spirit, not from the spiritual, eternal world	maketh it a graven image, and falleth down thereto.	see; *and* their hearts, that they cannot understand.	mind are closed
• A person uses half the wood for heating & cooking	16 He burneth part thereof in the fire; with part thereof he eateth flesh; he roasteth roast, and is satisfied: yea, he warmeth *himself,* and saith, Aha, I am warm, I have seen the fire:	19 And none considereth in his heart, neither *is there* knowledge nor understanding to say, I have burned part of it in the fire; yea, also I have baked bread upon the coals thereof; I have roasted flesh, and eaten *it:* and shall I make the residue thereof an abomination? shall I fall down to the stock of a tree?	2) A person is non-thinking: Does not have the knowledge, understanding, or honesty to face the truth, that the idol is only a material substance (not from the spiritual, eternal world)
• A person uses the other half to make an idol	17 And the residue thereof he maketh a god, *even* his graven image: he falleth down unto it, and worshippeth *it,* and prayeth unto it, and saith, Deliver me; for thou *art* my god.		
2) The person actually worships & prays to his man-made idol: "Save me"			
e. The cause of idolatry	18 They have not known nor understood: for he hath shut their eyes, that they cannot	20 He feedeth on ashes: a deceived heart hath turned him aside, that he cannot deliver his soul, nor say, *Is there* not a lie in my right hand?	3) A person is deceived • He feeds his soul on ashes • He trusts something that cannot save him
1) A person is spiritually blind: His or her eyes &			

a. True believers know the stupidity of idolatry (vv.9-10). In God's eyes, idols are utterly worthless, amounting to nothing. Idol worshippers are blind and ignorant, failing to see or know the truth. They are like the blind who stumble and stagger about as they try to find their way in a world of darkness. To their discredit, they are ignorant of the truth and will ultimately be ashamed.

b. True believers know that idolaters will be judged (v.11). The day is coming when idolaters and the craftsmen who make the idols will face the wrath of God. They are mere men, appointed to stand before the God of the universe to give an account of their deeds, whether good or bad. If they have had anything whatsoever to do with idols, they will stand before God terrified. And they will be ashamed because they rejected the only living and true God and chose instead to worship idols and false gods.

c. True believers know the physical, material nature of idolatry (vv.12-14). They know that idol makers—both the blacksmith and carpenter—are only human beings and that the works of their hands are only material objects. The blacksmith who makes an idol is only flesh like every other person, a being who hungers and tires. So it is with the carpenter. Being a mere human, he creates his so-called god out of his own imagination (vv.13-14). Based upon his idea, he chisels and shapes the god into a form resembling man's image. Furthermore, he carves the idol from a tree he cuts down, either one he finds in the forest or has planted. Everything and everyone involved in idolatry—the idol maker, the idol, and the idolater—are just physical matter. All have a material nature.

d. True believers know the importance of re-emphasizing the utter foolishness of idolatry (vv.15-17). Courageously, Isaiah stressed that an idol is nothing but physical, material substance. In this example, Isaiah spells out that the idol is made of wood, which is used for heating and cooking (v.15). The implication is that it is not from the spiritual or eternal world. Half of the wood is used for heat and cooking, and the other half is used to make an idol. And incredibly, the unbeliever actually worships and prays to the idol. In times of desperation and hardship, he cries out: "Save me; you are my god" (v.17).

e. True believers know the cause of idolatry (vv.18-20). Three causes are mentioned:

1) People worship idols because they are spiritually blind. Their eyes and mind are closed, shut tight and hardened against the LORD. As a consequence they do not know the LORD, nor can they understand the truths He reveals.
2) People worship idols because they lack a sense of judgment or reasoning and are unthinking (v.19). Idol worshippers do not have enough knowledge or understanding to accept the truth. It takes an honest heart to confess that one's so-called god is a mere creation of man's hands, only an idea in one's mind about who God is.
3) People who worship idols or false gods are deceived (v.20). Thinking they have the approval and blessing of their so-called god, they try to feed their souls on something that is no better than ashes. They are trusting something that can neither save nor help them. They are totally deceived.

Thought 1. Idolatry is worshipping anything other than the LORD Himself. We commit idolatry when we put ourselves, our families, and our loved ones before the LORD. It is even possible to put work, recreation, food, pleasure, and comfort before the LORD. If our major focus is on anything other than God, we are placing God second. And God will not take second place. He demands first place in our lives. Our thoughts and energy and activities should all be dedicated to the LORD. At the beginning of every day, our hearts and lives should be so devoted to Him that He is the focus of our very being. Anything less than this is idolatry. Listen to what God's Holy Word says about idolatry:

> "For as I passed by, and beheld your devotions, I found an altar with this inscription, TO THE UNKNOWN GOD. Whom therefore ye ignorantly worship, him declare I unto you. God that made the world and all things therein, seeing that he is Lord of heaven and earth, dwelleth not in temples made with hands; Neither is worshipped with men's hands, as though he needed any thing, seeing he giveth to all life, and breath, and all things; And hath made of one blood all nations of men for to dwell on all the face of the earth, and hath determined the times before appointed, and the bounds of their habitation; That they should seek the Lord, if haply they might feel after him, and find him, though he be not far from every one of us: For in him we live, and move, and have our being; as certain also of your

own poets have said, For we are also his offspring. Forasmuch then as we are the offspring of God, we ought not to think that the Godhead is like unto gold, or silver, or stone, graven by art and man's device. And the times of this ignorance God winked at; but now commandeth all men every where to repent: Because he hath appointed a day, in the which he will judge the world in righteousness by *that* man whom he hath ordained; *whereof* he hath given assurance unto all *men,* in that he hath raised him from the dead" (Ac.17:23-31).

"For the wrath of God is revealed from heaven against all ungodliness and unrighteousness of men, who hold the truth in unrighteousness; Because that which may be known of God is manifest in them; for God hath showed *it* unto them. For the invisible things of him from the creation of the world are clearly seen, being understood by the things that are made, *even* his eternal power and Godhead; so that they are without excuse: Because that, when they knew God, they glorified *him* not as God, neither were thankful; but became vain in their imaginations, and their foolish heart was darkened. Professing themselves to be wise, they became fools....And even as they did not like to retain God in *their* knowledge, God gave them over to a reprobate mind, to do those things which are not convenient; Being filled with all unrighteousness, fornication, wickedness, covetousness, maliciousness; full of envy, murder, debate, deceit, malignity; whisperers, Backbiters, haters of God, despiteful, proud, boasters, inventors of evil things, disobedient to parents, Without understanding, covenantbreakers, without natural affection, implacable, unmerciful: Who knowing the judgment of God, that they which commit such things are worthy of death, not only do the same, but have pleasure in them that do them" (Ro.1:18-22, 28-32).

"Know ye not that the unrighteous shall not inherit the kingdom of God? Be not deceived: neither fornicators, nor idolaters, nor adulterers, nor effeminate, nor abusers of themselves with mankind, Nor thieves, nor covetous, nor drunkards, nor revilers, nor extortioners, shall inherit the kingdom of God. And such were some of you: but ye are washed, but ye are sanctified, but ye are justified in the name of the Lord Jesus, and by the Spirit of our God" (1 Co.6:9-11).

"Now the works of the flesh are manifest, which are *these;* Adultery, fornication, uncleanness, lasciviousness, Idolatry, witchcraft, hatred, variance, emulations, wrath, strife, seditions, heresies, Envyings, murders, drunkenness, revellings, and such like: of the which I tell you before, as I have also told *you* in time past, that they which do such things shall not inherit the kingdom of God" (Ga.5:19-21).

"And walk in love, as Christ also hath loved us, and hath given himself for us an offering and a sacrifice to God for a sweetsmelling savour. But fornication, and all uncleanness, or covetousness, let it not be once named among you, as becometh saints; Neither filthiness, nor foolish talking, nor jesting, which are not convenient: but rather giving of thanks. For this ye know, that no whoremonger, nor unclean person, nor covetous man, who is an idolater, hath any inheritance in the kingdom of Christ and of God. Let no man deceive you with vain words: for because of these things cometh the wrath of God upon the children of disobedience" (Ep.5:2-6).

"Little children, keep yourselves from idols. Amen" (1 Jn.5:21).

"But the fearful, and unbelieving, and the abominable, and murderers, and whoremongers, and sorcerers, and idolaters, and all liars, shall have their part in the lake which burneth with fire and brimstone: which is the second death" (Re.21:8).

"Thou shalt have no other gods before me. Thou shalt not make unto thee any graven image, or any likeness *of any thing* that *is* in heaven above, or that *is* in the earth beneath, or that *is* in the water under the earth: Thou shalt not bow down thyself to them, nor serve them: for I the LORD thy God *am* a jealous God, visiting the iniquity of the fathers upon the children unto the third and fourth *generation* of them that hate me" (Ex.20:3-5).

"Ye shall make you no idols nor graven image, neither rear you up a standing image, neither shall ye set up *any* image of stone in your land, to bow down unto it: for I *am* the LORD your God" (Le.26:1).

"Take heed to yourselves, that your heart be not deceived, and ye turn aside, and serve other gods, and worship them" (De.11:16).

"Not unto us, O LORD, not unto us, but unto thy name give glory, for thy mercy, *and* for thy truth's sake. Wherefore should the heathen say, Where *is* now their God? But our God *is* in the heavens: he hath done whatsoever he hath pleased. Their idols *are* silver and gold, the work of men's hands. They have mouths, but they speak not: eyes have they, but they see not: They have ears, but they hear not: noses have they, but they smell not: They have hands, but they handle not: feet have they, but they walk not: neither speak they through their throat. They that make them are like unto them; *so is* every one that trusteth in them" (Ps.115:1-8).

"I *am* the LORD: that *is* my name: and my glory will I not give to another, neither my praise to graven images" (Is.42:8).

3 (44:21-28) **Hope, for Restoration, Promise by God—Hope, for the Promised Land, Given by God—Heaven, Hope for, Given by God—Repentance, Stirred by, Forgiveness of Sins—Spiritual Forgiveness, Secured by, Repentance—Liberty, Secured by, Repentance—Freedom, Secured by, Repentance—Israel, Restoration of, Prophecy of—Jerusalem, Restoration of, Prophecy of—Cyrus, Prophecy Concerning, Setting Jewish Exiles Free—Babylon, Deliverance from, Prophecy Concerning**: God's people are set free by returning to the LORD and renewing their hope in the promised land. Isaiah now draws a sharp contrast between idolaters and God's people. Remember that the prophet is looking ahead to the time when the Israelites will be a conquered people, deported and scattered all over the Babylonian

Empire. The Babylonians were an unbelieving, idolatrous people, as many of the Israelites themselves were. Only a few of the Jews were true believers in Isaiah's day, and the same would be true during the Babylonian captivity. But God still loves His people, so He reaches out to them in compassion. Through His prophet Isaiah He issues a strong charge to His people and gives them a wonderful promise. Note the Scripture and outline:

OUTLINE	SCRIPTURE	SCRIPTURE	OUTLINE
3. God's people are set free by returning to the LORD & by renewing their great hope in the promised land a. The charge to God's people 1) Must remember that they are God's servants & that they have been forgiven their sins 2) Must repent: Because the LORD has redeemed them 3) Must join all creation in praising God • Because the LORD has redeemed them • Because the LORD displays His glory in them b. The wonderful promise of God: The redeemed will return to the promised land 1) Guaranteed by God's power to create the universe	21 Remember these, O Jacob and Israel; for thou *art* my servant: I have formed thee; thou *art* my servant: O Israel, thou shalt not be forgotten of me. 22 I have blotted out, as a thick cloud, thy transgressions, and, as a cloud, thy sins: return unto me; for I have redeemed thee. 23 Sing, O ye heavens; for the LORD hath done *it:* shout, ye lower parts of the earth: break forth into singing, ye mountains, O forest, and every tree therein: for the LORD hath redeemed Jacob, and glorified himself in Israel. 24 Thus saith the LORD, thy redeemer, and he that formed thee from the womb, I *am* the LORD that maketh all *things;* that stretcheth forth the heavens alone; that	spreadeth abroad the earth by myself; 25 That frustrateth the tokens of the liars, and maketh diviners mad; that turneth wise *men* backward, and maketh their knowledge foolish; 26 That confirmeth the word of his servant, and performeth the counsel of his messengers; that saith to Jerusalem, Thou shalt be inhabited; and to the cities of Judah, Ye shall be built, and I will raise up the decayed places thereof: 27 That saith to the deep, Be dry, and I will dry up thy rivers: 28 That saith of Cyrus, *He is* my shepherd, and shall perform all my pleasure: even saying to Jerusalem, Thou shalt be built; and to the temple, Thy foundation shall be laid.	2) Guaranteed by God's power to expose the errors of false teachers: The false prophets, diviners, & wise of the world 3) Guaranteed by God's power to fulfill His Word & the predictions of His messengers • That His people would return to the promised land • That Jerusalem & the other cities would be rebuilt, 58:12; 61:4; Je.32:15 4) Guaranteed by God's power to work miracles such as crossing the Red Sea 5) Guaranteed by God's power to use King Cyrus of Persia to set the Jewish exiles free: They would rebuild Jerusalem & the temple (2 Chr.36:22-23; Ezr.1:1-11; 6:1-22

a. God's strong charge to His people is threefold. First, they are to remember that they are God's servants; therefore, He will not forget them (vv.21-22). Even when they are in captivity, suffering horribly, they will still be His servants, the people He has chosen to be His witnesses on earth. Although they will forget and forsake Him, He will not forget or forsake them. His offer of forgiveness will still stand. Their sins can still be blotted out, as though washed away by the rain of a cloud or the moisture from a morning mist.

Second, to be forgiven their sins, they must repent. They must turn away from their sins and turn back to the LORD. Once they have repented, the LORD will forgive and redeem them. Redemption looks ahead to the coming of the Messiah, the Lord Jesus Christ. He alone has paid the ransom to set people free from the bondages of sin and death.

Third, His people must join all creation in praising Him (v.23). Redemption and forgiveness of sins are the greatest of gifts, gifts that should arouse people everywhere to praise God's name. But even if every human being praised the LORD, their praise would not be enough. So all nature is summoned to burst into song and sing for joy. The heavens above and the earth beneath—including all its mountains, forests, and trees—are to praise the LORD for His redemption.

b. God's wonderful promise to His people is that those who are truly redeemed will return to the promised land (vv.24-28). Israel will be restored to its homeland; Jerusalem and other towns of Judah will be rebuilt. The Redeemer Himself will liberate the Jewish exiles from Babylon and return them to their homeland. And it is the Redeemer's power that will set them free. God will use His power in five ways to guarantee the restoration of Israel:

1) Israel's restoration is guaranteed by God's power to create both the human race and the universe (v.24). He formed each individual Israelite in the womb, as well as the nation of Israel. The same LORD who created them also created all things, both in the heavens and the earth. God's enormous creative power ensures the restoration of Israel. He who possesses such power can certainly free His people from any bondage or enslavement.

2) Israel's restoration is guaranteed by God's power to expose the errors of false teachers. These include false prophets, diviners, and the wise of the world (v.25). When occult practices deceive and enslave people, the LORD has the power to set them free. Whereas false prophets teach lies and diviners use deception and double-talk to secure followers, the LORD speaks only the truth. Through revealing the truth about people's sinful nature, the LORD is able to arouse them to repent. And through revealing the truth of redemption, He gives them a way to be forgiven of their sins and set free from the penalty of sin, which is death. In dealing with those who are considered wise in this world, the LORD has the power to refute their so-called wisdom and expose its foolishness. He is able to exercise the same power to free His people from all the bondages of this world.

3) Israel's restoration is guaranteed by God's power to fulfill His Word and the predictions of His messengers (v.26). A sharp contrast is being drawn between this verse and the previous one, between false teachers of the occult and the messengers of God. False teachers of the occult are involved in pseudoscience, whereas the messengers of God make predictions based upon God's Word. Consequently, the predictions of God's messengers come true. Two predictions in particular are mentioned:
⇒ the prediction that Israel will return to the promised land

⇒ the prediction that Jerusalem and the other cities of the nation will be rebuilt (58:12; 61:4; Je.32:15). But note this fact: it is God's power that fulfills the predictions of His messengers. Because of God's power, the wonderful restoration of His people and the rebuilding of the nation will take place in the future.

d. Israel's restoration is guaranteed by God's power to work. Down through history, the LORD had performed miracle after miracle, spectacular events such as crossing the Red Sea and the Jordan River (see outline and notes— Ex.14:1-21; Jos.3:1-17 for more discussion). If the LORD is strong enough to perform such great miracles as those, He is bound to be strong enough to deliver the Israelites from the bondage of any earthly power or nation.

e. Israel's restoration is guaranteed by God's power to raise up King Cyrus of Persia to set the Jewish exiles free (v.28). He has the power to guarantee that they would rebuild Jerusalem and the temple (see outline and notes— 2 Chr.36:22-23; Ezr.1:1-11; 6:1-22 for more discussion). As history shows, King Cyrus liberated Israel, and this prediction was fulfilled exactly as God foretold.

Thought 1. God gives the same strong charges and wonderful promises to believers today that He gave to believers in Isaiah's day. But remember, the LORD commands us to repent of our sins and acknowledge that redemption can be secured only through Him. He alone has paid the ransom to set us free from sin and death. The ransom price for our sins was the death of His Son. If we trust Christ to save us from the bondages of sin and death, God redeems us. He allows the death of His Son to count as the payment for our sin. Thus, through Christ and Christ alone we are set free from sin, counted righteous before God, and made acceptable to Him.

Once we have trusted Christ and been redeemed, God promises to give us the promised land of heaven. When we have spent our last moment on earth, more quickly than the eye can blink, God will transfer us into His presence. We will immediately move from this natural world into the spiritual world. There we will live eternally with the LORD.

(1) When we trust Christ, God forgives our sins and redeems us. Redemption is through the Messiah, the Lord Jesus Christ.

> **"For all have sinned, and come short of the glory of God; Being justified freely by his grace through the redemption that is in Christ Jesus" (Ro.3:23-24).**
>
> **"Christ hath redeemed us from the curse of the law, being made a curse for us: for it is written, Cursed *is* every one that hangeth on a tree" (Ga.3:13).**
>
> **"In whom we have redemption through his blood, the forgiveness of sins, according to the riches of his grace" (Ep.1:7).**
>
> **"In whom we have redemption through his blood, *even* the forgiveness of sins" (Col.1:14).**
>
> **"Looking for that blessed hope, and the glorious appearing of the great God and our Saviour Jesus Christ; Who gave himself for us, that he might redeem us from all iniquity, and purify unto himself a peculiar people, zealous of good works" (Tit.2:13-14).**
>
> **"Neither by the blood of goats and calves, but by his own blood he entered in once into the holy place, having obtained eternal redemption *for us*. For if the blood of bulls and of goats, and the ashes of an heifer sprinkling the unclean, sanctifieth to the purifying of the flesh: How much more shall the blood of Christ, who through the eternal Spirit offered himself without spot to God, purge your conscience from dead works to serve the living God?" (He.9:12-14).**
>
> **"Forasmuch as ye know that ye were not redeemed with corruptible things, *as* silver and gold, from your vain conversation *received* by tradition from your fathers; But with the precious blood of Christ, as of a lamb without blemish and without spot" (1 Pe.1:18-19).**
>
> **"And they sung a new song, saying, Thou art worthy to take the book, and to open the seals thereof: for thou wast slain, and hast redeemed us to God by thy blood out of every kindred, and tongue, and people, and nation" (Re.5:9).**

(2) Once we have accepted Jesus Christ as our Savior, we are redeemed and forgiven of our sins. And God gives us the most wonderful assurance: we will inherit the promised land of heaven.

> **"Let not your heart be troubled: ye believe in God, believe also in me. In my Father's house are many mansions: if *it were* not so, I would have told you. I go to prepare a place for you. And if I go and prepare a place for you, I will come again, and receive you unto myself; that where I am, *there* ye may be also" (Jn.14:1-3).**
>
> **"For we know that if our earthly house of *this* tabernacle were dissolved, we have a building of God, an house not made with hands, eternal in the heavens" (2 Co.5:1).**
>
> **"For our conversation [citizenship] is in heaven; from whence also we look for the Saviour, the Lord Jesus Christ: Who shall change our vile body, that it may be fashioned like unto his glorious body, according to the working whereby he is able even to subdue all things unto himself" (Ph.3:20-21).**
>
> **"We give thanks to God and the Father of our Lord Jesus Christ, praying always for you, Since we heard of your faith in Christ Jesus, and of the love *which ye have* to all the saints, For the hope which is laid up for you in heaven, whereof ye heard before in the word of the truth of the gospel" (Col.1:3-5).**
>
> **"By faith Abraham, when he was called to go out into a place which he should after receive for an inheritance, obeyed; and he went out, not knowing whither he went. By faith he sojourned in the land of promise, as *in* a strange country, dwelling in tabernacles with Isaac and Jacob, the heirs with him of**

the same promise: For he looked for a city which hath foundations, whose builder and maker *is* God" (He.11:8-10).

"These all died in faith, not having received the promises, but having seen them afar off, and were persuaded of *them,* and embraced *them,* and confessed that they were strangers and pilgrims on the earth. For they that say such things declare plainly that they seek a country. And truly, if they had been mindful of that *country* from whence they came out, they might have had opportunity to have returned. But now they desire a better *country,* that is, an heavenly: wherefore God is not ashamed to be called their God: for he hath prepared for them a city" (He.11:13-16).

"Blessed *be* the God and Father of our Lord Jesus Christ, which according to his abundant mercy hath begotten us again unto a lively hope by the resurrection of Jesus Christ from the dead, To an inheritance incorruptible, and undefiled, and that fadeth not away, reserved in heaven for you" (1 Pe.1:3-4).

"And the city [holy city, the capital of heaven] had no need of the sun, neither of the moon, to shine in it: for the glory of God did lighten it, and the Lamb *is* the light thereof. And the nations of them which are saved shall walk in the light of it: and the kings of the earth do bring their glory and honour into it. And the gates of it shall not be shut at all by day: for there shall be no night there. And they shall bring the glory and honour of the nations into it. And there shall in no wise enter into it any thing that defileth, neither *whatsoever* worketh abomination, or *maketh* a lie: but they which are written in the Lamb's book of life" (Re.21:23-27).

CHAPTER 45

F. Set Free by God's Power to Work Through People & Nations: A Look at the Extent of God's Extra-ordinary Power, 45:1-25

Thus saith the LORD to his anointed, to Cyrus, whose right hand I have holden, to subdue nations before him; and I will loose the loins of kings, to open before him the two leaved gates; and the gates shall not be shut;

2 I will go before thee, and make the crooked places straight: I will break in pieces the gates of brass, and cut in sunder the bars of iron:

3 And I will give thee the treasures of darkness, and hidden riches of secret places, that thou mayest know that I, the LORD, which call *thee* by thy name, *am* the God of Israel.

4 For Jacob my servant's sake, and Israel mine elect, I have even called thee by thy name: I have surnamed thee, though thou hast not known me.

5 I *am* the LORD, and *there is* none else, *there is* no God beside me: I girded thee, though thou hast not known me:

6 That they may know from the rising of the sun, and from the west, that *there is* none beside me. I *am* the LORD, and *there is* none else.

7 I form the light, and create darkness: I make peace, and create evil: I the LORD do all these *things.*

8 Drop down, ye heavens, from above, and let the skies pour down righteousness: let the earth open, and let them bring forth salvation, and let righteousness spring up together; I the LORD have created it.

9 Woe unto him that striveth with his Maker! *Let* the potsherd *strive* with the potsherds of the earth. Shall the clay say to him that fashioneth it, What makest thou? or thy work, He hath no hands?

10 Woe unto him that saith unto *his* father, What begettest thou? or to the woman,

What hast thou brought forth?

11 Thus saith the LORD, the Holy One of Israel, and his Maker, Ask me of things to come concerning my sons, and concerning the work of my hands command ye me.

12 I have made the earth, and created man upon it: I, *even* my hands, have stretched out the heavens, and all their host have I commanded.

13 I have raised him up in righteousness, and I will direct all his ways: he shall build my city, and he shall let go my captives, not for price nor reward, saith the LORD of hosts.

14 Thus saith the LORD, The labour of Egypt, and merchandise of Ethiopia and of the Sabeans, men of stature, shall come over unto thee, and they shall be thine: they shall come after thee; in chains they shall come over, and they shall fall down unto thee, they shall make supplication unto thee, *saying,* Surely God *is* in thee; and *there is* none else, *there is* no God.

15 Verily thou *art* a God that hidest thyself, O God of Israel, the Saviour.

16 They shall be ashamed, and also confounded, all of them: they shall go to confusion together *that are* makers of idols.

17 *But* Israel shall be saved in the LORD with an everlasting salvation: ye shall not be ashamed nor confounded world without end.

18 For thus saith the LORD that created the heavens; God himself that formed the earth and made it; he hath established it, he created it not in vain, he formed it to be inhabited: I *am* the LORD; and *there is* none else.

19 I have not spoken in secret, in a dark place of the earth: I said not unto the seed of Jacob, Seek ye me in vain: I the LORD speak righteousness, I declare things that are right.

20 Assemble yourselves and come; draw near together, ye *that are* escaped of the nations: they have no knowledge that set up the wood of their graven image, and pray

1. God's power to use Cyrus to free Israel from captivity: A picture of Christ setting people free from sin & death
a. God's anointing & working through Cyrus to be His agent
b. God's fivefold purpose
  1) To execute His justice against wicked, oppressive nations
    • He would empower Cyrus to conquer great cities, fortresses, & nations
    • He would give Cyrus great wealth: The hidden wealth of nations
  2) To stir Cyrus to know He is the LORD

  3) To stir Cyrus to free Israel from captivity
    • Because God named & honored him in prophecy: Called him God's *shepherd* (40:11; 44:28) & *anointed* (45:1)
    • Because God proved He alone is the LORD: By foretelling & working through Cyrus
  4) To prove to the world that He alone is God
    • He alone is the Creator

    • He alone is sovereign, controlling both good & evil, peace & calamity

  5) To bring the righteousness & salvation of heaven to the world

c. God's warning to those who questioned His ways & works
  1) The questions…
    • Opposed God's choice of Israel as His people
    • Opposed God's anointing & use of a pagan king
  2) The doom pronounced
    • On those who argued with their Creator
    • On those who argued with the way He worked

d. God's answer to those who questioned their Creator & the way He worked

  1) He is the Creator of the heavens & earth & of mankind: Has the right to do as He wills

  2) He would raise up Cyrus (a type of Christ) to fulfill His righteous purpose: To rebuild Jerusalem & to set the captives free

2. God's power to stir the nations to submit & bow before Him: A picture of the Messiah's kingdom, 2:2-4; 18:7; 23:15-18
a. The picture of the submission
  1) Nations would willingly come to Israel to surrender their worship & wealth to the LORD
  2) Nations would confess the Name of Israel's God
    • That He alone is the LORD
    • That He alone is the Savior: A fact that had been a mystery to all unbelievers
b. The results of the nations' submission
  1) All idolaters would be ashamed & disgraced

  2) All the redeemed of Israel would be saved eternally: Never ashamed or disgraced

3. God's power to save everyone within the nations who turn to Him
a. God's surety of salvation
  1) His enormous power: Created the universe
  2) His purpose: Made the universe to be inhabited
  3) His Word: He speaks only the truth
    • He does not speak in secret but openly
    • He does not encourage people to seek Him in vain
b. God's appeal to the people of all nations: To escape the coming judgment
  1) To turn from their idols: They were only material objects & could not save them

2) To acknowledge that He alone is God • He alone foretold the judgment (of Babylon) & the setting free of His people from captivity • He alone is God: A just God & a Savior 3) To look to Him & be saved: He alone is God & He alone can save	unto a god *that* cannot save. 21 Tell ye, and bring *them* near; yea, let them take counsel together: who hath declared this from ancient time? *who* hath told it from that time? *have* not I the LORD? and *there is* no God else beside me; a just God and a Saviour; *there is* none beside me. 22 Look unto me, and be ye saved, all the ends of the earth: for I *am* God, and *there is* none else.	23 I have sworn by myself, the word is gone out of my mouth *in* righteousness, and shall not return, That unto me every knee shall bow, every tongue shall swear. 24 Surely, shall *one* say, in the LORD have I righteousness and strength: *even* to him shall *men* come; and all that are incensed against him shall be ashamed. 25 In the LORD shall all the seed of Israel be justified, and shall glory.	c. God's warning to the people of all nations: A solemn threefold oath 1) Every knee will bow & confess to Him: Applies to Christ, Ro.14:11-12; Ph.2:9-11 2) Every person who opposes Him & lives an unrighteous life will face judgment: Be put to shame 3) Every descendant of Israel (all true believers) will be declared righteous & enter glory with Him

DIVISION V

THE PROPHECIES OF COMFORT AND FREEDOM: A PICTURE OF BELIEVERS BEING SET FREE FROM THE CAPTIVITY OF SIN AND DEATH, 40:1–48:22

F. Set Free by God's Power to Work Through People and Nations: A Look at the Extent of God's Extraordinary Power, 45:1-25

(45:1-25) **Introduction**: the lust for power is a strong craving within the human heart. Holding power is not wrong or evil. In fact, there must be leaders in positions of authority for society to function properly. But craving power for the purpose of dominating or enslaving others arises from an evil heart. Tragically, many rulers of the world down through history have sought power for the purpose of controlling the citizens of a nation and then reveling in the wealth and luxury of their top government positions.

But for most of us, the craving for power is far more limited. Most of us simply want the power to command people's attention, to and convince them of the worth of our opinions or our way of doing things. Having enough power to influence people to do what we desire or think seems to satisfy most people. But even this limited longing for power arises from hearts that are self-centered. No matter what position of authority we hold, we must always keep our motives pure. We must use whatever power or influence we have for the welfare of our neighbors, our community, and for society as a whole.

God's enormous power is the subject of this Scripture. God uses His power for good at all times. He never uses it for evil. Down through history, He has always used His power to work all things out for good, both for the human race in general and for His people. This fact is clearly seen in the present Scripture. This is, *Set Free by God's Power to Work Through People and Nations: A Look at the Extent of God's Extraordinary Power*, 45:1-25.

1. God's power to use Cyrus to free Israel from captivity: a picture of Christ setting people free from sin and death (vv.1-13).
2. God's power to arouse the nations to submit and bow before Him: a picture of the Messiah's kingdom, 2:2-4; 18:7; 23:15-18 (vv.14-17).
3. God's power to save everyone within the nations who turn to Him (vv.18-25).

[1] (45:1-13) **Sovereignty, of God, Example—Power, of God, to Work Through Nations—Deliverance, of Israel, from Captivity—Cyrus, Appointed by God, to Free Israel—Captivity, of Israel, Liberated by Cyrus—Israel, Chosen by God, Questioned—Sovereignty, of God, Questioned—Power, of God, to Free His People**: Isaiah predicts that God's power will work through Cyrus, the pagan king of Persia. God's power will arouse King Cyrus to free Israel from the Babylonian captivity. Remember, this prophecy is being given more than 150 years before the event. Isaiah not only pinpoints the nation that will free the Jews, but he gives the name of the ruler—and Cyrus has not even been born yet. His birth and rule still lie several generations in the future. Only because of God's eternal knowledge (omniscience) and infinite power (omnipotence) could He have known these facts and revealed them to Isaiah. God is *omniscient*, knowing all things past, present, and future. And God is *omnipotent*, possessing supreme, unlimited, and unrestricted power. God rules and reigns over the entire universe. He oversees all affairs worldwide, working through both people and nations to accomplish His purpose of redemption. At the same time God gave *free will* to the human race. Sadly, the great majority of people down through the ages have chosen to defy or reject Him. Nevertheless, the LORD has determined to provide the way of salvation for all who will trust Him and repent their sins. The LORD works all things out for good, orchestrating human events in order to save those who truly trust and follow Him. That is why God used His power to raise up Cyrus to free the true believers in Israel from their captivity. This event is a clear picture of Christ setting people free from sin and death. Note the Scripture and outline:

OUTLINE	SCRIPTURE	SCRIPTURE	OUTLINE
1. God's power to use Cyrus to free Israel from captivity: A picture of Christ setting people free from sin & death a. God's anointing & working through Cyrus to be His agent b. God's fivefold purpose 　1) To execute His justice against wicked, oppressive nations 　　• He would empower Cyrus to conquer great cities, fortresses, & nations 　　• He would give Cyrus great wealth: The hidden wealth of nations 　2) To stir Cyrus to know He is the LORD 　3) To stir Cyrus to free Israel from captivity 　　• Because God named & honored him in prophecy: Called him God's *shepherd* (40:11; 44:28) & *anointed* (45:1) 　　• Because God proved He alone is the LORD: By foretelling & working through Cyrus 　4) To prove to the world that He alone is God 　　• He alone is the Creator 　　• He alone is sovereign, controlling both good & evil, peace & calamity	Thus saith the LORD to his anointed, to Cyrus, whose right hand I have holden, to subdue nations before him; and I will loose the loins of kings, to open before him the two leaved gates; and the gates shall not be shut; 2 I will go before thee, and make the crooked places straight: I will break in pieces the gates of brass, and cut in sunder the bars of iron: 3 And I will give thee the treasures of darkness, and hidden riches of secret places, that thou mayest know that I, the LORD, which call *thee* by thy name, *am* the God of Israel. 4 For Jacob my servant's sake, and Israel mine elect, I have even called thee by thy name: I have surnamed thee, though thou hast not known me. 5 I *am* the LORD, and *there is* none else, *there is* no God beside me: I girded thee, though thou hast not known me: 6 That they may know from the rising of the sun, and from the west, that *there is* none beside me. I *am* the LORD, and *there is* none else. 7 I form the light, and create darkness: I make peace, and create evil: I the LORD do all these *things*.	8 Drop down, ye heavens, from above, and let the skies pour down righteousness: let the earth open, and let them bring forth salvation, and let righteousness spring up together; I the LORD have created it. 9 Woe unto him that striveth with his Maker! *Let* the potsherd *strive* with the potsherds of the earth. Shall the clay say to him that fashioneth it, What makest thou? or thy work, He hath no hands? 10 Woe unto him that saith unto *his* father, What begettest thou? or to the woman, What hast thou brought forth? 11 Thus saith the LORD, the Holy One of Israel, and his Maker, Ask me of things to come concerning my sons, and concerning the work of my hands command ye me. 12 I have made the earth, and created man upon it: I, *even* my hands, have stretched out the heavens, and all their host have I commanded. 13 I have raised him up in righteousness, and I will direct all his ways: he shall build my city, and he shall let go my captives, not for price nor reward, saith the LORD of hosts.	5) To bring the righteousness & salvation of heaven to the world c. God's warning to those who questioned His ways & works 　1) The questions… 　　• Opposed God's choice of Israel as His people 　　• Opposed God's anointing & use of a pagan king 　2) The doom pronounced 　　• On those who argued with their Creator 　　• On those who argued with the way He worked d. God's answer to those who questioned their Creator & the way He worked 　1) He is the Creator of the heavens & earth & of mankind: Has the right to do as He wills 　2) He would raise up Cyrus (a type of Christ) to fulfill His righteous purpose: To rebuild Jerusalem & to set the captives free

a. God would anoint Cyrus to be His special agent (vv.1-3). Surprisingly, the LORD called the pagan king *his anointed*. The term *anointed* was a term of honor usually reserved for righteous kings, prophets, priests, patriarchs, and for the people of God themselves (1 S.12:3; Ps.2:2; 105:15; Da.9:25; Hab.3:13). Even Christ Himself is called the *Anointed One* (Da.9:25-26). In light of the traditional use of the term, the people must have been utterly shocked when Isaiah referred to Cyrus as *God's anointed*. But unknown to them, God was planning a marvelous thing for His people, those who truly believed and followed Him. He was going to rescue them from the Babylonian captivity. To perform this unusual feat, it was necessary to raise up a ruler through whom He could work and accomplish His purposes.

b. God had a fivefold purpose for raising up Cyrus to be His agent. These purposes clearly show how God works through both people and nations to fulfill His will and accomplish His wonderful plan of salvation.

1) First, God was going to use Cyrus to execute His justice upon the wicked nations of the earth. He would empower Cyrus to be a world conqueror and subdue nations with the Persian war machine. In some cases, Cyrus would defeat and strip kings of their armor and military power. In other cases, kings would tremble in so much fear that they would swing open their gates and surrender without a fight (v.1). All over the known world of that time, the mountains would be leveled, the great cities and fortresses of the world would be conquered (v.2). Through these conquests, the LORD would give Cyrus great wealth, the hidden treasures of nations (v.3a).

2) Second, God was going to stir up Cyrus to know that He is the LORD (Jehovah, Yahweh), the only true and living God (v.3b). How could Cyrus know that God had appointed him to conquer the world and free the Israelites from captivity? How could he know that the LORD had called him by name generations before he was born? Most likely through the prophet Daniel, who would be an elderly prime minister in Cyrus's court. Daniel would undoubtedly have told the king about some of the great prophecies of Isaiah (Da.6:28; 10:1). Josephus, the first-century Jewish historian, actually said that it was Isaiah's prophecy that aroused Cyrus to free the Jews. He states:

When Cyrus read this [Isaiah's prophecy], and admired the divine power, an earnest desire and ambition seized upon him to fulfill what was so written. So he called for the most imminent Jews that were in Babylon and said to them, that he gave them leave to go back to their own country, and to rebuild their city Jerusalem, and the temple of God, for that he would be their assistant, and that he would write to the rulers and governors that were in their neighborhood of their country of Judea, that they should contribute to them gold and silver for the building of the temple, and, besides that, beast for their sacrifices.[1]

The source from which Josephus got his information is not known. But since Daniel was Cyrus's prime minister, it is likely that he showed Isaiah's prophecy to the king. And as a strong witness for the LORD, Daniel almost certainly did all he could to lead the king to acknowledge the only true and living God. Although we cannot know if Cyrus ever truly turned to the LORD, Scripture does say that the LORD Himself raised up Cyrus so that he might know that the LORD is the God of Israel, the only living and true God.

3) Third, God was going to raise up Cyrus to free the Israelites from captivity and allow them to return to the promised land of Judah (vv.4-5). Although the LORD honored Cyrus by appointing him to be His agent, God's purpose was not focused upon the king. His purpose was to fulfill His promises to Israel, to set the exiles free from captivity and return them to their homeland. When God called King Cyrus His *shepherd* (40:11; 44:28) and His *anointed* (45:1), He bestowed a great honor on the Persian king. However Cyrus was not honored because of any personal merit or righteousness. Scripture clearly says that Cyrus did not acknowledge or know the LORD during the days when God was preparing him to help Israel. God *chose* to use Cyrus to free His people from captivity.

4) Fourth, God was going to raise up Cyrus to prove to the world and His people that He alone is God (vv.6-7). From the rising to the setting of the sun, from one end of the earth to the other, all people were to know that there is no God but the LORD Himself (Jehovah, Yahweh). He alone is the Creator, for He alone has created both light and darkness. And He alone is sovereign, controlling both good and evil, peace and calamity.

God's prediction and use of Cyrus—and even naming the as yet unborn king—would arouse the attention of all who were truly objective and honest. It would also prove beyond any reasonable doubt that the LORD alone is God.

5) Fifth, God was going to raise up Cyrus to bring heaven's righteousness and salvation to the world (v.8). By releasing His people from captivity, God would prove His righteousness, prove that He always does the right thing by fulfilling His Word and promises. And He would prove His salvation by delivering His people from their captivity. God would pour the righteousness and salvation of heaven, of God Himself, upon His people.

c. God now issues a strong warning to those who question His will and the way He works with people (vv.9-13). Naturally, some people in Isaiah's day opposed God's will. A number of unbelievers opposed God's choice of Israel as His people. Others opposed His use of a pagan king to free His people. They believed that a pagan such as King Cyrus was not worthy to be used for God's great purposes. In their minds, Cyrus was far too evil, immoral, and corrupt for God to anoint him for any service, much less to free His people from captivity.

But note God's response to those who second-guess or criticize the way He chooses to work. He pronounces the certain doom of all who argue with their Creator (v.9). People who challenge the LORD expose their true hearts. They show that their hearts are hard and stubborn against God. Consider a potter and his clay. A clay pot does not argue with its maker. It does not question what the potter is making or the way he is doing it. Think about newborn babies. While they are being born, babies do not ask why their parents are bringing them into the world or question the way they are being delivered into it.

d. God's answer to those who question their Creator is very straightforward (vv.11-13). They must think about what they are really doing. In questioning the LORD about His children and about the way He works, they are actually issuing orders to the LORD, telling Him what they think should be done and the way it should be done. Simply stated, they are seeking to *play God*. Those who question and argue with God must remember two facts:

⇒ The LORD is the Creator of the heavens and earth and of all mankind. For this reason He has the right to do as He chooses (v.12).

⇒ The LORD will raise up Cyrus to fulfill His righteous purpose. His purpose is to rebuild the holy city of Jerusalem and to set Israel free from its captivity.

Thought 1. Cyrus is a clear picture of Christ in that the king was the anointed of God, appointed to set God's people free from their captivity so they could return to the promised land. Jesus Christ was also anointed by God, appointed to set the human race free from the bondages of sin and death. Through Christ, all believers can live eternally with God. Unfortunately, when Cyrus issued the great proclamation of freedom to the Jews, only a few chose to return to the promised land. So it is today with the great proclamation of the gospel: only a few choose to follow the LORD and place their hope in the promised land of heaven. Jesus Christ has provided the way for us to be set free from sin and death. But we must believe Him. To lay claim to the freedom Christ offers, listen to what God's Holy Word says about Him:

> **"For all have sinned, and come short of the glory of God; Being justified freely by his grace through the redemption that is in Christ Jesus: Whom God hath set forth *to be* a propitiation through faith in his blood, to declare his righteousness for the remission of sins that are past, through the forbearance of God" (Ro.3:23-25).**

> **"In whom we have redemption through his blood, the forgiveness of sins, according to the riches of his grace" (Ep.1:7).**

> **"But is now made manifest by the appearing of our Saviour Jesus Christ, who hath abolished death, and hath brought life and immortality to light through the gospel" (2 Ti.1:10).**

> **"Forasmuch then as the children are partakers of flesh and blood, he also himself likewise took part of the same; that through death he might destroy him that had the power of death, that is, the devil; And deliver them who through fear of death were all their lifetime subject to bondage" (He.2:14-15).**

---

[1] Josephus. *Complete Works. Antiquities of the Jews.* Book 11, Ch.1, Para.2, p.228.

2 (45:14-17) **Messiah, Kingdom of—Power, of God, to Subdue Nations—Nations, in the Millennium, Described—Submission, of Nations, in Messiah's Kingdom**: God has the power to arouse nations to submit and bow before Him, the God of Israel. This is a clear picture of what will happen in the future kingdom of the Messiah. The Lord Jesus Christ will return to establish God's kingdom on earth (2:2-4; 18:7; 23:15-18; 60:5-14). This period of history is known as the Millennium, an era that includes the return of Christ and His reign on earth. In that day, nations will willingly come to Israel to surrender their worship and wealth to the LORD (v.14). Coming *in chains* simply means they come willingly, voluntarily as prisoners of the LORD. The nations will also bow before Israel's God and make two confessions:

⇒ That the LORD is the only true and living God.
⇒ That the God of Israel is the true Savior, a God who works in mysterious ways.

This means that the only citizens of the Messiah's kingdom will be those who believe in the Savior of Israel, who is the LORD Himself. Only the Jews and Gentiles who truly trust the Lord Jesus Christ as their personal Savior will be left on earth.

When the nations submit themselves to the LORD, all idol makers will be put out of business. And they will be shamed and disgraced because of their horrible profession. This is a clear reference to God's coming judgment on all idolaters who reject Him and turn to false gods. Their fate will be sealed—they are doomed to shame and disgrace under the hand of God's judgment. However, all the redeemed of Israel will be eternally saved by the LORD (v.17). They will never be ashamed or disgraced.

OUTLINE	SCRIPTURE	SCRIPTURE	OUTLINE

2. **God's power to stir the nations to submit & bow before Him: A picture of the Messiah's kingdom, 2:2-4; 18:7; 23:15-18**
 a. The picture of the submission
   1) Nations would willingly come to Israel to surrender their worship & wealth to the LORD
   2) Nations would confess the Name of Israel's God
     • That He alone is the LORD
	14 Thus saith the LORD, The labour of Egypt, and merchandise of Ethiopia and of the Sabeans, men of stature, shall come over unto thee, and they shall be thine: they shall come after thee; in chains they shall come over, and they shall fall down unto thee, they shall make supplication unto thee, *saying,* Surely God *is* in thee; and *there is* none else, *there is* no God.	15 Verily thou *art* a God that hidest thyself, O God of Israel, the Saviour.
		 16 They shall be ashamed, and also confounded, all of them: they shall go to confusion together *that are* makers of idols.
		 17 *But* Israel shall be saved in the LORD with an everlasting salvation: ye shall not be ashamed nor confounded world without end.
			• That He alone is the Savior: A fact that had been a mystery to all unbelievers
			 b. The results of the nations' submission
			   1) All idolaters would be ashamed & disgraced
			
			   2) All the redeemed of Israel would be saved eternally: Never ashamed or disgraced

Thought 1. In the Messiah's kingdom, every knee will bow and every tongue confess that Jesus Christ is the true LORD of the universe. Therefore, it is far better to bow before Christ now, while we live on earth, than to be forced to bow and confess Christ in the future and face the terrifying judgment of God. If we humble ourselves and acknowledge Christ as Savior, we will be saved. God will rescue us from sin, death, and the condemnation to come. Therefore God strongly appeals to us today, encouraging us to surrender to Christ. Listen to what God's Holy Word says about confessing and denying Christ:

"Whosoever therefore shall confess me before men, him will I confess also before my Father which is in heaven. But whosoever shall deny me before men, him will I also deny before my Father which is in heaven" (Mt.10:32-33).

"Whosoever therefore shall be ashamed of me and of my words in this adulterous and sinful generation; of him also shall the Son of man be ashamed, when he cometh in the glory of his Father with the holy angels" (Mk.8:38).

"That if thou shalt confess with thy mouth the Lord Jesus, and shalt believe in thine heart that God hath raised him from the dead, thou shalt be saved. For with the heart man believeth unto righteousness; and with the mouth confession is made unto salvation" (Ro.10:9-10).

"Who [Jesus Christ], being in the form of God, thought it not robbery to be equal with God: But made himself of no reputation, and took upon him the form of a servant, and was made in the likeness of men: And being found in fashion as a man, he humbled himself, and became obedient unto death, even the death of the cross. Wherefore God also hath highly exalted him, and given him a name which is above every name: That at the name of Jesus every knee should bow, of *things* in heaven, and *things* in earth, and *things* under the earth; And *that* every tongue should confess that Jesus Christ *is* Lord, to the glory of God the Father" (Ph.2:6-11).

"If we suffer, we shall also reign with *him:* if we deny *him,* he also will deny us" (2 Ti.2:12).

"They profess that they know God; but in works they deny *him,* being abominable, and disobedient, and unto every good work reprobate" (Tit.1:16).

"But there were false prophets also among the people, even as there shall be false teachers among you, who privily shall bring in damnable heresies, even denying the Lord that bought them, and bring upon themselves swift destruction" (2 Pe.2:1).

"Who is a liar but he that denieth that Jesus is the Christ? He is antichrist, that denieth the Father and the Son. Whosoever denieth the Son, the same hath not the Father: *(but) he that acknowledgeth the Son hath the Father also*" (1 Jn.2:22-23).

"Whosoever shall confess that Jesus is the Son of God, God dwelleth in him, and he in God" (1 Jn.4:15).

3 (45:18-25) **Salvation, Source of, God's Power—Power, of God, Work of, Salvation—Salvation, Surety of, Threefold Assurance—Warning, to Unbelievers, Will Bow Before God—Unbelievers, Appeal to, Threefold**: God has the power to save all people, no matter where they are from. There is only one requirement: they must turn to the LORD. In discussing His power to save people, the LORD first declares that salvation is sure. He then makes an appeal to the people of all nations. Finally, He issues a strong warning to everyone. Note the Scripture and outline:

OUTLINE	SCRIPTURE	SCRIPTURE	OUTLINE

3. God's power to save everyone within the nations who turn to Him
a. God's surety of salvation
  1) His enormous power: Created the universe
  2) His purpose: Made the universe to be inhabited
  3) His Word: He speaks only the truth
    • He does not speak in secret but openly
    • He does not encourage people to seek Him in vain
b. God's appeal to the people of all nations: To escape the coming judgment
  1) To turn from their idols: They were only material objects & could not save them
 	
  2) To acknowledge that He alone is God
	18 For thus saith the LORD that created the heavens; God himself that formed the earth and made it; he hath established it, he created it not in vain, he formed it to be inhabited: I am the LORD; and there is none else.
	19 I have not spoken in secret, in a dark place of the earth: I said not unto the seed of Jacob, Seek ye me in vain: I the LORD speak righteousness, I declare things that are right.
	20 Assemble yourselves and come; draw near together, ye that are escaped of the nations: they have no knowledge that set up the wood of their graven image, and pray unto a god that cannot save.
	21 Tell ye, and bring them near; yea, let them take counsel together: who hath de-
		clared this from ancient time? who hath told it from that time? have not I the LORD? and there is no God else beside me; a just God and a Saviour; there is none beside me.
		22 Look unto me, and be ye saved, all the ends of the earth: for I am God, and there is none else.
		23 I have sworn by myself, the word is gone out of my mouth in righteousness, and shall not return, That unto me every knee shall bow, every tongue shall swear.
		24 Surely, shall one say, in the LORD have I righteousness and strength: even to him shall men come; and all that are incensed against him shall be ashamed.
		25 In the LORD shall all the seed of Israel be justified, and shall glory.
			• He alone foretold the judgment (of Babylon) & the setting free of His people from captivity
			• He alone is God: A just God & a Savior
			
			  3) To look to Him & be saved: He alone is God & He alone can save
			
			c. God's warning to the people of all nations: A solemn threefold oath
			  1) Every knee will bow & confess to Him: Applies to Christ, Ro.14:11-12; Ph.2:9-11
			  2) Every person who opposes Him & lives an unrighteous life will face judgment: Be put to shame
			  3) Every descendant of Israel (all true believers) will be declared righteous & enter glory with Him

a. God wants everyone to know and be confident in His power to save all people. No matter who they are—Gentile or Jew, idolater or true worshipper—the LORD can save all those who genuinely trust Him. God gives three assurances to prove He has the power to save even the most stubborn and defiant of the earth:

1) God's enormous power to create the universe proves that He has unlimited power. Any power strong enough to create the universe can save anyone.

2) God created the earth for a very specific purpose—so that it might be fruitful and inhabited by the human race. The earth is not supposed to be empty or desolate. Given that, God will not destroy all the people of earth. He will save those who turn to the Savior for redemption (v.15).

3) God's Word gives the assurance of salvation, for God speaks only the truth. Longing for people to be saved, the LORD does not speak in a whisper or in a dark corner where people can barely hear. He does not encourage people to seek Him in vain; nor does He deceive people and leave them empty because they cannot understand what He is saying. Rather, the LORD *speaks* the truth and encourages people to *seek* the truth.

b. God longs for people to be saved and to escape the coming judgment (vv.20-22). Therefore, He makes a threefold appeal to the people of all nations.

1) God appeals to people to turn from their idols, because they are only material objects that cannot save them. Worshipping idols only exposes people's ignorance. Idols have no life, so of course they are powerless to help those who pray to them and cry out for their help.

2) God appeals to people to acknowledge that He alone is God (v.21). He has proven His claim by foretelling the judgment of Babylon and the release of His people from captivity (v.21). Predicting these two phenomenal events and fulfilling them in every detail are unquestionable proof that He alone is God, the righteous LORD and Savior of the world. There is no other God.

3) God appealed to the people to look to Him in order to be saved (v.22). He alone is God, There is no other person or so-called god who can save people from all the ends of the earth people are to look to Him for salvation.

c. In closing His discussion of salvation, God issues a strong warning to the people of all nations (vv.23-25). The warning must be heeded, especially because it is issued under a threefold oath. The LORD swears that three events will take place:

1) Every knee will bow and every tongue confess to Him. This means that the entire world will bow before Christ:

> "For it is written, *As* I live, saith the Lord, every knee shall bow to me, and every tongue shall confess to God. So then every one of us shall give account of himself to God" (Ro.14:11-12).
>
> "Wherefore God also hath highly exalted him, and given him a name which is above every name: That at the name of Jesus every knee should bow, of *things* in heaven, and *things* in earth, and *things* under the earth; And *that* every tongue should confess that Jesus Christ *is* Lord, to the glory of God the Father" (Ph.2:9-11).

2) Every individual who opposes the LORD and lives an unrighteous life will face God's judgment (v.24).
3) Every descendant of Israel (all true believers) will be declared righteous by the LORD and will enter glory with Him (v.25).

Thought 1. God has the power to save not just everyone but *anyone*. No matter how sinful, wicked, or corrupt a person may be, the LORD can save that person. Christ did not came to save the righteous, Those who already know and love the LORD but the unrighteous. The person who lives in a cesspool of immorality can be saved. The person who has worshipped idols and false gods can be saved. The person who has stolen, lied, deceived, burned with hostility or hatred, abused or assaulted others, maimed or murdered, or committed any other sinful behavior can be saved. No matter what wrong we have done, we can be saved.

But salvation is conditional. We must believe in the Lord Jesus Christ and repent of our sins. To repent means to turn away from sin and follow Christ, to live obediently and righteously by obeying God's holy commandments. All who heed God's warning—who sincerely turn away from their sins, repent, and follow Christ—will be saved. Salvation is open to all, regardless of social class, wealth, ethnicity, or past behavior. Listen to God's Holy Word:

"For the Son of man is come to seek and to save that which was lost" (Lu.19:10).

"For God so loved the world, that he gave his only begotten Son, that whosoever believeth in him should not perish, but have everlasting life. For God sent not his Son into the world to condemn the wold; but that the world through him might be saved" (Jn.3:16-17).

"And it shall come to pass, *that* whosoever shall call on the name of the Lord shall be saved" (Ac.2:21).

"Him hath God exalted with his right hand *to be* a Prince and a Saviour, for to give repentance to Israel, and forgiveness of sins" (Ac.5:31).

"That if thou shalt confess with thy mouth the Lord Jesus, and shalt believe in thine heart that God hath raised him from the dead, thou shalt be saved. For with the heart man believeth unto righteousness; and with the mouth confession is made unto salvation...For whosoever shall call upon the name of the Lord shall be saved" (Ro.10:9-10, 13).

"This *is* a faithful saying, and worthy of all acceptation, that Christ Jesus came into the world to save sinners; of whom I am chief" (1 Ti.1:15).

"For the grace of God that bringeth salvation hath appeared to all men, Teaching us that, denying ungodliness and worldly lusts, we should live soberly, righteously, and godly, in this present world" (Tit.2:11-12).

"Wherefore he is able also to save them to the uttermost that come unto God by him, seeing he ever liveth to make intercession for them" (He.7:25).

"The Lord is not slack concerning his promise, as some men count slackness; but is longsuffering to us-ward, not willing that any should perish, but that all should come to repentance" (2 Pe.3:9).

"Come now, and let us reason together, saith the LORD: though your sins be as scarlet, they shall be as white as snow; though they be red like crimson, they shall be as wool" (Is.1:18).

"Ho, every one that thirsteth, come ye to the waters, and he that hath no money; come ye, buy, and eat; yea, come, buy wine and milk without money and without price" (Is.55:1).

CHAPTER 46

G. Set Free by Turning Away from Idolatry: A Study of Idolatry, 46:1-13

1. The fate of idolaters & their idols
  a. They will be bowed down: Conquered by enemies
  b. They will be led into captivity: Unsaved by the false gods they worshipped

2. The contrasting fate of genuine believers
  a. The LORD created them & will carry them from the womb to the grave
  b. The LORD will always sustain & carry them through all the trials & temptations of life

3. The powerlessness of false gods to save their worshippers
  a. They are not like the LORD nor equal to the LORD
  b. They are only the creation of man's mind, thoughts, ideas
  c. They are only tangible, physical objects: They are made by mere man

Bel boweth down, Nebo stoopeth, their idols were upon the beasts, and upon the cattle: your carriages *were* heavy loaden; *they are* a burden to the weary *beast.*
2 They stoop, they bow down together; they could not deliver the burden, but themselves are gone into captivity.
3 Hearken unto me, O house of Jacob, and all the remnant of the house of Israel, which are borne *by me* from the belly, which are carried from the womb:
4 And *even* to *your* old age I *am* he; and *even* to hoar hairs will I carry *you:* I have made, and I will bear; even I will carry, and will deliver *you.*
5 To whom will ye liken me, and make *me* equal, and compare me, that we may be like?
6 They lavish gold out of the bag, and weigh silver in the balance, *and* hire a goldsmith; and he maketh it a god: they fall down, yea,

they worship.
7 They bear him upon the shoulder, they carry him, and set him in his place, and he standeth; from his place shall he not remove: yea, *one* shall cry unto him, yet can he not answer, nor save him out of his trouble.
8 Remember this, and show yourselves men: bring it again to mind, O ye transgressors.
9 Remember the former things of old: for I *am* God, and *there is* none else; *I am* God, and *there is* none like me,
10 Declaring the end from the beginning, and from ancient times *the things* that are not *yet* done, saying, My counsel shall stand, and I will do all my pleasure:
11 Calling a ravenous bird from the east, the man that executeth my counsel from a far country: yea, I have spoken it, I will also bring it to pass; I have purposed it, I will also do it.
12 Hearken unto me, ye stouthearted, that *are* far from righteousness:
13 I bring near my righteousness; it shall not be far off, and my salvation shall not tarry: and I will place salvation in Zion for Israel my glory.

  d. They are unable to help or sustain people in life: They have to be carried
  e. They cannot move (to guide, protect, or provide for people)
  f. They cannot answer or save when called upon

4. The strong appeal of God to idolaters (all false worshippers)
  a. Remember the powerlessness of your idols
  b. Remember God's works down through history: He has proven He is God

  1) He has revealed the truth to man, foretold important future events even of the end time: His purpose & plan will come to pass
  2) He will raise up a *bird of prey*—a world leader (Cyrus)—to fulfill His purpose: He will execute judgment upon idolaters & free His people (a picture of Christ's work)
  c. Listen to the LORD
  1) Because you are stubborn, & unrighteous
  2) Because God is bringing His righteousness near: It is right at hand
  3) Because God is ready to save Zion & to give His glory to Israel (all genuine believers)

DIVISION V

THE PROPHECIES OF COMFORT AND FREEDOM: A PICTURE OF BELIEVERS BEING SET FREE FROM THE CAPTIVITY OF SIN AND DEATH, 40:1–48:22

G.   Set Free by Turning Away from Idolatry: A Study of Idolatry, 46:1-13

(46:1-13) **Introduction**: idolatry, worshipping something other than the LORD, is a horrifying evil. It is bound to be repugnant in the sight of the LORD, the only living and true God, the Creator of the universe with its hundreds of billions of stars and galaxies. Think about it. There are over 200 billion stars in our galaxy alone, and there are also over 200 hundred billions galaxies? The numbers are staggering, beyond our comprehension or imagination? The vastness of our universe just explodes the human mind! The LORD Himself dwells in a glory that mere men cannot possibly fathom. In light of His radiant glory and magnificence, the LORD must be totally repelled when anyone worships something or someone other than Him, the only living and true God. Considering God's creation and the wonderful salvation He has provided for the human race, it is inconceivable how anyone could deny God.

Idolatry is the subject of the present Scripture. Isaiah had already predicted that Babylon would be the agent of the judgment God had pronounced upon Israel. In the present Scripture, Isaiah predicts that the LORD would also eventually judge Babylon because of its cruelty and wickedness. And the false gods and idols worshipped by the citizens of Babylon would be powerless to stop God's judgment. Despite the people's crying out to their gods for deliverance, the great empire would fall. The idols in which the people trusted would be helpless, unable to save them. This is the subject of the present Scripture: *Set Free by Turning Away from Idolatry: A Study of Idolatry,* 46:1-13.

  1. The fate of idolaters and their idols (vv.1-2).
  2. The contrasting fate of genuine believers (vv.3-4).
  3. The powerlessness of false gods to save their worshippers (vv.5-7).
  4. The strong appeal of God to idolaters (all false worshippers) (vv.8-13).

1 (46:1-2) **Idolaters, Fate of—Idols, Fate of—Babylon, Fate of—Babylon, Idols of, Fate—Gods, False, Fate of—Worship, False, Fate of**: the fate of idolaters and their idols is described in a sad, tragic picture of war. Babylon was to be defeated in war, with all the bloody carnage of slain and wounded soldiers, the cruel slaughter and rape of citizens, and the destruction of property. As a result of Babylon's defeat, the truth about the people's gods would be exposed: they were false and powerless to help their worshippers. They were supposed to bring deliverance and give victory over Babylon's enemies. But instead they were just like the citizens of Babylon, stooping in utter defeat and bowing down before the conquering enemy (v.1).

OUTLINE	SCRIPTURE	SCRIPTURE	OUTLINE
1. The fate of idolaters & their idols a. They will be bowed down: Conquered by enemies b. They will be led into captivity: Unsaved by the false	**B**el boweth down, Nebo stoopeth, their idols were upon the beasts, and upon the cattle: your carriages *were* heavy loaden; *they are* a burden to the weary	*beast.* 2 They stoop, they bow down together; they could not deliver the burden, but themselves are gone into captivity.	gods they worshipped

Bel, meaning *lord*, was another name for Marduk, the chief god of Babylon. Bel was the same false god the Canaanites worshipped as *Baal*. The other chief god of Babylon, *Nebo*, was thought to be Bel's son. He was worshipped as the god of fate, wisdom, writing, learning, and astronomy.

The Babylonians were a very religious people and totally devoted to their so-called gods. This is clearly seen in the frequency with which the Babylonians combined the names of their gods with the names of the children. For example, Nebo (or Nebu) is part of the names Nebuchadnezzar, Nebopolassar, and Nebonidus, while Bel is part of the name Belshazzar. Naming their children after their gods shows just how much the people placed their trust in them.

Obviously, when the Babylonians faced the hardships and misfortunes of life, they turned to their so-called gods in prayer and worship, seeking their help. In particular, at times of desperation such as war or personal assault, the people would cry out to their gods to save them. But the Babylonians were to learn a much-needed lesson: their gods were false and therefore could not help them, could not meet their needs. These false gods could not carry the people through their fiery trial. Instead, the idols themselves would be carried away by their victorious enemy. Rather than rescuing the Babylonians from their burden, their so-called gods would suffer a humiliating defeat and become a burden to the weary animals that would carry them away as plunder of war (v.2).

The graphic picture being painted of both idols and idolaters is that of utter defeat, of being either destroyed or led into captivity. False gods are not able to help or save those who worship them. Worshippers of a false god are doomed to defeat and death without the help of the LORD, the only living and true God. And when their lives are over, worshippers of false gods will feel the hand of God's judgment. They will not inherit the kingdom of God. This is the undeniable pronouncement of God's Holy Word:

> "Know ye not that the unrighteous shall not inherit the kingdom of God? Be not deceived: neither fornicators, nor idolaters, nor adulterers, nor effeminate, nor abusers of themselves with mankind, Nor thieves, nor covetous, nor drunkards, nor revilers, nor extortioners, shall inherit the kingdom of God" (1 Co.6:9-10).

> "Now the works of the flesh are manifest, which are *these;* Adultery, fornication, uncleanness, lasciviousness, Idolatry, witchcraft, hatred, variance, emulations, wrath, strife, seditions, heresies, Envyings, murders, drunkenness, revellings, and such like: of the which I tell you before, as I have also told *you* in time past, that they which do such things shall not inherit the kingdom of God" (Ga.5:19-21).

> "But fornication, and all uncleanness, or covetousness, let it not be once named among you, as becometh saints; Neither filthiness, nor foolish talking, nor jesting, which are not convenient: but rather giving of thanks. For this ye know, that no whoremonger, nor unclean person, nor covetous man, who is an idolater, hath any inheritance in the kingdom of Christ and of God. Let no man deceive you with vain words: for because of these things cometh the wrath of God upon the children of disobedience" (Ep.5:3-6).

> "But the fearful, and unbelieving, and the abominable, and murderers, and whoremongers, and sorcerers, and idolaters, and all liars, shall have their part in the lake which burneth with fire and brimstone: which is the second death" (Re.21:8).

2 (46:3-4) **Believers, Fate of—Assurance, of God's Support—Deliverance, Source, God—Deliverance, Through Trials and Temptations—Support, God's, Promise—Promises, of God, to Support—Believers, Contrasted with Idolaters—Israel, Promises to, God's Support**: the fate of true believers is the exact opposite of the fate of idolaters. Down through the centuries, the Israelites had suffered terrifying trials and enormous loss of life due to oppression and warfare. Now as Isaiah foresaw the future Babylonian conquest and captivity, he saw that few Israelites would survive the slaughter of the war and the harsh deportation of the survivors. Those who were taken captive and dispersed throughout the Babylonian Empire would suffer greatly. But note God's admonition to listen to Him, for He had a wonderful promise for Israel, in particular for those who truly believed and followed Him.

The Israelites were God's creation, both as individuals and as a nation. From their very conception, the LORD had taken care of them. From the day of their birth, He had carried them, nurturing and nourishing them (v.3). Remember that Israel's birth as a nation took place when the people were delivered from Egyptian slavery and given God's law at Mount Sinai. Down through the centuries, the LORD had always looked after and protected His people. When they suffered defeat and destruction at the hands of enemies, it was always due to their own wicked behavior and the need for

God to discipline them. But even in times of disaster and chastisement, the LORD was looking after His people. He was using the discipline to correct them lest they bring further harm to themselves or to others. Although the discipline sometimes seemed oppressive, and even destructive, the LORD had always brought His people through the harsh ordeals.

Now the Israelites were about to face more grave challenges, and the LORD wanted them to know a very significant fact: He would always be with His people, even to their old age (v.4). He is the LORD (Jehovah, Yahweh), the only living and true God, who is the same yesterday, today, and forever (He.13:8). Therefore, He would continue to carry His people through all of their hardships. He would sustain them, hold them up, and give them the strength to walk through all the trials and temptations of the future. Just as He has done for the believers of the past, so He will do for the believers of the present and the future. The LORD will protect, guide, and provide whatever we need throughout all of life, even to our old age.

OUTLINE	SCRIPTURE	SCRIPTURE	OUTLINE
2. The contrasting fate of genuine believers a. The LORD created them & will carry them from the womb to the grave	3 Hearken unto me, O house of Jacob, and all the remnant of the house of Israel, which are borne *by me* from the belly, which are carried from the womb:	4 And *even* to *your* old age I *am* he; and *even* to hoar hairs will I carry *you:* I have made, and I will bear; even I will carry, and will deliver *you.*	b. The LORD will always sustain & carry them through all the trials & temptations of life

"*Let your* conversation [conduct, behavior] *be* without covetousness; *and be* content with such things as ye have: for he hath said, I will never leave thee, nor forsake thee. So that we may boldly say, The Lord *is* my helper, and I will not fear what man shall do unto me" (He.13:5-6).

"Ye have seen what I did unto the Egyptians, and *how* I bare you on eagles' wings, and brought you unto myself" (Ex.19:4).

"The eternal God *is thy* refuge, and underneath *are* the everlasting arms: and he shall thrust out the enemy from before thee; and shall say, Destroy *them*" (De.33:27).

"Thou hast also given me the shield of thy salvation: and thy right hand hath holden me up, and thy gentleness hath made me great" (Ps.18:35).

"The LORD *is* my strength and my shield; my heart trusted in him, and I am helped: therefore my heart greatly rejoiceth; and with my song will I praise him" (Ps.28:7).

"But I *am* poor and needy; *yet* the Lord thinketh upon me: thou *art* my help and my deliverer; make no tarrying, O my God" (Ps.40:17).

"For he shall give his angels charge over thee, to keep thee in all thy ways. They shall bear thee up in *their* hands, lest thou dash thy foot against a stone" (Ps.91:11-12).

"Fear thou not; for I *am* with thee: be not dismayed; for I *am* thy God: I will strengthen thee; yea, I will help thee; yea, I will uphold thee with the right hand of my righteousness" (Is.41:10).

"Fear not: for I have redeemed thee, I have called *thee* by thy name; thou *art* mine. When thou passest through the waters, I *will be* with thee; and through the rivers, they shall not overflow thee: when thou walkest through the fire, thou shalt not be burned; neither shall the flame kindle upon thee" (Is.43:1-2).

"And *even* to *your* old age I *am* he; and *even* to hoar hairs will I carry *you:* I have made, and I will bear; even I will carry, and will deliver *you*" (Is.46:4).

"Behold, the Lord GOD will help me; who *is* he *that* shall condemn me? lo, they all shall wax old as a garment; the moth shall eat them up" (Is.50:9).

3 (46:5-7) **Powerlessness, of False Gods, Sixfold Proof—Idols, Powerlessness of, Sixfold Truth—Idolaters, Errors of—Idolatry, Results of**: false gods are worthless, for they are unable to help their followers and powerless to save their worshippers. Six facts prove their powerlessness:

a. Idols *are not* like the LORD nor equal with the LORD (v.5). As the living and true God, the LORD is able to help His people by strengthening them through all the difficult situations and worldly enticements of life. Idols cannot do this, for they are neither true nor living.

b. Idols *are only* the creation of a person's mind (v.6a). An honest, realistic evaluation of idols reveals that every idol has its beginning in people's thoughts. When people conceive an idea of who God is and what He does, a god is born in their minds. Sadly, most people worship the gods of their own imaginations rather than the LORD. The LORD alone has revealed Himself in His Holy Word, the Bible, and has came to earth to reveal Himself in the Person of Jesus Christ.

c. Idols *are only* material objects or ideas that are made or conceived by mere man (v.7). In some cases, craftsmen manufacture an idol out of gold or silver, and people bow down to worship it. But today, most people worship the idols of their own thoughts such as...

- athletes
- movie stars
- models
- sports
- television
- recreation
- sex
- wealth
- possessions
- comfort, a life of ease
- religion
- family or other loved one

A person's idol is whatever receives the primary devotion and commitment of that person's heart, whatever consumes that person's life. The LORD, the true and living God, demands our highest devotion and commitment, our best time, and the greatest energy of our bodies. If we give our greatest devotion, commitment, time, and energy to something else, we place that thing ahead of God. If a person or thing, not the LORD, becomes first in our lives, it is an idol, an object of our own creation that we worship.

d. Idols *are unable* to carry people through life; instead, they have to be carried. Consider any of the idols already mentioned or any other idol in the minds or possessions of people. In all cases, idols have to be carried by their creators or worshippers, whether in their minds or in their hands. Idols are lifeless, totally incapable of helping or carrying anyone through the severe hardships or wicked snares of this world.

e. Idols *cannot move.* They have no ability to move for they exist only in the mind of the worshipper or else at the spot where they sit. Lifeless and immobile, idols are not able to help, guide, protect, or provide for people.

f. Idols *cannot answer* people who cry out to them for help. Nor can idols save those people when they face great problems. No matter how much people pray or how loudly they cry when in distress, idols cannot answer them. Idols cannot deliver or rescue them. Idols can do nothing. They have no life; consequently, they are worthless, utterly useless to their worshippers. Idols are absolutely nothing like the LORD, who is the true and living God. Because He lives, He can give believers supernatural strength to walk through any circumstances, no matter how difficult or frightening. And when believers face the final trial of life, which is death, God gives them the wonderful promise of being immediately transferred into His presence (2 Ti.4:18).

OUTLINE	SCRIPTURE	SCRIPTURE	OUTLINE
3. The powerlessness of false gods to save their worshippers a. They are not like the LORD nor equal to the LORD b. They are only the creation of man's mind, thoughts, ideas c. They are only tangible, physical objects: They are made by	5 To whom will ye liken me, and make *me* equal, and compare me, that we may be like? 6 They lavish gold out of the bag, and weigh silver in the balance, *and* hire a goldsmith; and he maketh it a god: they fall down, yea,	they worship. 7 They bear him upon the shoulder, they carry him, and set him in his place, and he standeth; from his place shall he not remove: yea, *one* shall cry unto him, yet can he not answer, nor save him out of his trouble.	mere man d. They are unable to help or sustain people in life: They have to be carried e. They cannot move (to guide, protect, or provide for people) f. They cannot answer or save when called upon

"For as I passed by, and beheld your devotions, I found an altar with this inscription, TO THE UNKNOWN GOD. Whom therefore ye ignorantly worship, him declare I unto you. God that made the world and all things therein, seeing that he is Lord of heaven and earth, dwelleth not in temples made with hands; Neither is worshipped with men's hands, as though he needed any thing, seeing he giveth to all life, and breath, and all things; And hath made of one blood all nations of men for to dwell on all the face of the earth, and hath determined the times before appointed, and the bounds of their habitation; That they should seek the Lord, if haply they might feel after him, and find him, though he be not far from every one of us: For in him we live, and move, and have our being; as certain also of your own poets have said, For we are also his offspring. Forasmuch then as we are the offspring of God, we ought not to think that the Godhead is like unto gold, or silver, or stone, graven by art and man's device. And the times of this ignorance God winked at; but now commandeth all men every where to repent: Because he hath appointed a day, in the which he will judge the world in righteousness by *that* man whom he hath ordained; *whereof* he hath given assurance unto all *men,* in that he hath raised him from the dead" (Ac.17:23-31).

"For the invisible things of him from the creation of the world are clearly seen, being understood by the things that are made, *even* his eternal power and Godhead; so that they are without excuse: Because that, when they knew God, they glorified *him* not as God, neither were thankful; but became vain in their imaginations, and their foolish heart was darkened. Professing themselves to be wise, they became fools, And changed the glory of the uncorruptible God into an image made like to corruptible man, and to birds, and fourfooted beasts, and creeping things. Wherefore God also gave them up to uncleanness through the lusts of their own hearts, to dishonour their own bodies between themselves: Who changed the truth of God into a lie, and worshipped and served the creature more than the Creator, who is blessed for ever. Amen" (Ro.1:20-25).

"As concerning therefore the eating of those things that are offered in sacrifice unto idols, we know that an idol *is* nothing in the world, and that *there is* none other God but one. For though there be that are called gods, whether in heaven or in earth, (as there be gods many, and lords many,) But to us *there is but* one God, the Father, of whom *are* all things, and we in him; and one Lord Jesus Christ, by whom *are* all things, and we by him" (1 Co.8:4-6).

"Now concerning spiritual *gifts,* brethren, I would not have you ignorant. Ye know that ye were Gentiles, carried away unto these dumb idols, even as ye were led. Wherefore I give you to understand, that no man speaking by the Spirit of God calleth Jesus accursed: and *that* no man can say that Jesus is the Lord, but by the Holy Ghost" (1 Co.12:1-3).

"Assemble yourselves and come; draw near together, ye *that are* escaped of the nations: they have no knowledge that set up the wood of their graven image, and pray unto a god *that* cannot save. Tell ye, and bring *them* near; yea, let them take counsel together: who hath declared this from ancient time? *who* hath told it from that time? *have* not I the LORD? and *there is* no God else beside me; a just God and a Saviour; *there is* none beside me. Look unto me, and be ye saved, all the ends of the earth: for I *am* God, and *there is* none else" (Is.45:20-22).

"They *are* upright as the palm tree, but speak not: they must needs be borne, because they cannot go. Be not afraid of them; for they cannot do evil, neither also *is it* in them to do good. Forasmuch as *there is* none like unto thee, O LORD; thou *art* great, and thy name is great in might" (Je.10:5-6).

4 (46:8-13) **Appeal, of God, to Idolaters—Idolaters, Warning to, Judgment—Invitation, to Idolaters, Remember the LORD—Worshipers, False, Appeal to, Remember the LORD—Rebels, Appeal to, Remember the LORD—Hard–Hearted, Appeal to—Stubborn, Warning to—Cyrus, Prophecy Concerning—Israel, Prophecy Concerning, Restoration**: God issued both a strong appeal and a strong warning to all idolaters. They must immediately take three steps to become acceptable to Him and to escape His coming judgment. These three steps are clearly marked by Scripture:

OUTLINE	SCRIPTURE	SCRIPTURE	OUTLINE
4. The strong appeal of God to idolaters (all false worshippers) a. Remember the powerlessness of your idols b. Remember God's works down through history: He has proven He is God 1) He has revealed the truth to man, foretold important future events even of the end time: His purpose & plan will come to pass 2) He will raise up a *bird of*	8 Remember this, and show yourselves men: bring it again to mind, O ye transgressors. 9 Remember the former things of old: for I *am* God, and *there is* none else; *I am* God, and *there is* none like me, 10 Declaring the end from the beginning, and from ancient times *the things* that are not *yet* done, saying, My counsel shall stand, and I will do all my pleasure: 11 Calling a ravenous bird	from the east, the man that executeth my counsel from a far country: yea, I have spoken *it,* I will also bring it to pass; I have purposed *it,* I will also do it. 12 Hearken unto me, ye stouthearted, that *are* far from righteousness: 13 I bring near my righteousness; it shall not be far off, and my salvation shall not tarry: and I will place salvation in Zion for Israel my glory.	*prey*—a world leader (Cyrus)—to fulfill His purpose: He will execute judgment upon idolaters & free His people (a picture of Christ's work) c. Listen to the LORD 1) Because you are stubborn, & unrighteous 2) Because God is bringing His righteousness near: It is right at hand 3) Because God is ready to save Zion & to give His glory to Israel (all genuine believers)

a. Idolaters must remember that they are sinners, transgressors, rebels before God. Note that God Himself is still speaking. It is God who calls idolaters "rebels"—a most serious charge. During Isaiah's day, most of the people in the world were worshipping idols, including most of the Israelites. Practically every Israelite professed to believe in the LORD. To their own minds they were worshipping the LORD, but what they were really worshipping was their *own idea* of who God is. They rejected God's righteousness and His holy commandments, choosing instead to live immoral and wicked lives.

The false worship practiced by their neighbors appealed to the Israelites. These religions allowed people to live as they wanted, fulfilling their fleshly desires for more and more…
* possessions and wealth
* pleasure and recreation
* power and honor

Most of the Jews followed a religion that mixed the worship of God with the worship of idols. They accepted only part of God's revelation of Himself, rejecting His righteousness and His demand for them to live righteously. As a result, their religion became eclectic, a mixture of the truth and error. Although they considered themselves to be followers of the LORD, they had become idolaters. Rejecting God's full revelation of Himself, they became *rebels*.

Again, it was the LORD Himself making this harsh but accurate charge against those who professed to worship Him. Idolaters must remember this and prove themselves mature men and women by turning away from idolatry. They must not act like children, who are too young to know the truth. They must take responsibility for their behavior. They are transgressors who are rebelling against the only living and true God.

b. Idolaters must remember God's works down through history, for His former works prove that He is the LORD, the only living and true God (vv.9-11). Time and again, the LORD has demonstrated that He alone is God. He has demonstrated His existence and power throughout history, beginning with Creation. He demonstrated His power in the great flood of Noah's day, in the deliverance of Israel from Egyptian slavery, in the giving of the law on Mount Sinai, and in the choosing of Abraham to be the father of several great nations, but especially in the *promised seed*, which was fulfilled in Christ and in those who believe and follow Him. These are just a few of the marvelous works of God that idolaters must remember, for God's mighty works prove His existence and power.

From the beginning of human history, God has revealed the truth to man and foretold important future events, even those that will take place at the end of the world. Many of the events have already taken place, giving further evidence that God alone is the LORD, the only living and true God. His purpose and plan for His people, those who truly believe and follow Him, will come to pass. As Isaiah stood there proclaiming this prophecy to his audience, God gave him insight into the future. Isaiah predicted that the LORD would raise up a "bird of prey"—a world leader—from the east to fulfill His purpose (v.11). This was a direct reference to King Cyrus of Persia (41:2-3, 25). God would raise up Cyrus for two very specific purposes: to execute the LORD's judgment on idolaters and to free His people from the Babylonian captivity (13:17–14:2). To give full assurance, God gave a double guarantee that these two events would take place:
⇒ "I have spoken…I will also bring it to pass."
⇒ "I have purposed it, I will also do it."

c. Idolaters must listen to the LORD (vv.12-13). Three compelling reasons are given why they must listen:
1) Idolaters are stubborn, and they are far from righteousness. Although they profess to know the LORD, they are actually worshipping idols, the creation of their thoughts and the figment of their imaginations. They are not living lives of righteousness by obeying the commandments of God. Instead of treating people justly, they are lying, stealing, cheating and falsely accusing. Instead of living moral and pure lives, they are forsaking the natural use of sex and committing all kinds of illicit behavior, including fornication, adultery, and homosexuality. God warns idolators, and they must listen, for they have become stubborn, hard-hearted, and far from righteousness.

> **"For the wrath of God is revealed from heaven against all ungodliness and unrighteousness of men, who hold the truth in unrighteousness; Because that which may be known of God is manifest in them; for God hath showed *it* unto them. For the invisible things of him from the creation of the world are clearly seen, being understood by the things that are made, *even* his eternal power and Godhead; so that they are without excuse: Because that, when they knew God, they glorified *him* not as God, neither were thankful; but became vain in their imaginations, and their foolish heart was darkened. Professing themselves to be wise, they became fools, And changed the glory of the uncorruptible God into an image made like to corruptible man, and to birds, and fourfooted beasts, and creeping things. Wherefore God also gave them up to uncleanness through the lusts of their own hearts, to dishonour their own bodies between themselves: Who changed the truth of God into a lie, and worshipped and served the creature more than the Creator, who is blessed for ever. Amen. For this cause God gave them up unto vile affections: for even their women did change the natural use into that which is against nature: And likewise also the men, leaving the natural use of the woman, burned in their lust one toward another; men with men working that which is unseemly, and receiving in themselves that recompence of their error which was meet. And even as they did not like to retain God in *their* knowledge, God gave them over to a reprobate mind, to do those things which are not convenient; Being filled with all unrighteousness, fornication, wickedness, covetousness, maliciousness; full of envy, murder, debate, deceit, malignity; whisperers, Backbiters, haters of God, despiteful, proud, boasters, inventors of evil things, disobedient to parents, Without understanding, covenantbreakers, without natural affection, implacable, unmerciful: Who knowing the judgment of God, that they which commit such things are worthy of death, not only do the same, but have pleasure in them that do them"** (Ro.1:18-32).

> **"But glory, honour, and peace, to every man that worketh good, to the Jew first, and also to the Gentile: For there is no respect of persons with God. For as many as have sinned without law shall also perish without law: and as many as have sinned in the law shall be judged by the law; (For not the hearers of the law *are* just before God, but the doers of the law shall be justified. For when the Gentiles, which have not the law, do by nature the things contained in the law, these, having not the law, are a law unto themselves: Which show the work of the law written in their hearts, their conscience also bearing witness, and *their* thoughts the mean while accusing or else excusing one another;) In the day when God shall judge the secrets of men by Jesus Christ according to my gospel. Behold, thou art called a Jew, and restest in the law, and makest thy boast of God, And knowest *his* will, and approvest the things that are more excellent, being instructed out of the law"** (Ro.2:10-18).

> **"And then shall that Wicked [the antichrist] be revealed, whom the Lord shall consume with the spirit of his mouth, and shall destroy with the brightness of his coming: *Even him,* whose coming is after the working of Satan with all power and signs and lying wonders, And with all deceivableness of unrighteousness in them that perish; because they received not the love of the truth, that they might be saved. And for this cause God shall send them strong delusion, that they should believe a lie: That they all might be damned who believed not the truth, but had pleasure in unrighteousness"** (2 Th.2:8-12).

> **"But exhort one another daily, while it is called To day; lest any of you be hardened through the deceitfulness of sin"** (He.3:13).

> **"And [they] shall receive the reward of unrighteousness, *as* they that count it pleasure to riot in the daytime. Spots *they are* and blemishes, sporting themselves with their own deceivings while they feast with you; Having eyes full of adultery, and that cannot cease from sin; beguiling unstable souls: an heart they have exercised with covetous practices; cursed children"** (2 Pe.2:13-14).

> **"Whosoever committeth sin transgresseth also the law: for sin is the transgression of the law"** (1 Jn.3:4).

> **"And GOD saw that the wickedness of man *was* great in the earth, and *that* every imagination of the thoughts of his heart *was* only evil continually"** (Ge.6:5).

> **"The wicked, through the pride of his countenance, will not seek *after God:* God *is* not in all his thoughts"** (Ps.10:4).

> **"Every one of them is gone back: they are altogether become filthy; *there is* none that doeth good, no, not one"** (Ps.53:3).

> **"But we are all as an unclean *thing,* and all our righteousnesses *are* as filthy rags; and we all do fade as a leaf; and our iniquities, like the wind, have taken us away"** (Is.64:6).

2) Idolaters must listen because God is bringing His righteousness near, right next to them, right at their hand. Because righteousness will be so close, the idolater will be without excuse if he continues to reject God. This was a clear prediction of God's power to set the Jews free from their captivity in Babylon. But it was also a prediction that pointed forward to God's gift of the Messiah, the Savior of the world. The Messiah, the Lord Jesus Christ, would embody the very righteousness of God Himself. Christ would demonstrate God's righteousness before the entire world. And the world would be without excuse if they rejected Christ, the very image of God's righteousness.

"But now the righteousness of God without the law is manifested, being witnessed by the law and the prophets; Even the righteousness of God *which is* by faith of Jesus Christ unto all and upon all them that believe: for there is no difference: For all have sinned, and come short of the glory of God; Being justified freely by his grace through the redemption that is in Christ Jesus: Whom God hath set forth *to be* a propitiation through faith in his blood, to declare his righteousness for the remission of sins that are past, through the forbearance of God; To declare, *I say,* at this time his righteousness: that he might be just, and the justifier of him which believeth in Jesus" (Ro.3:21-26).

"For he hath made him *to be* sin for us, who knew no sin; that we might be made the righteousness of God in him" (2 Co.5:21).

"For we have not an high priest which cannot be touched with the feeling of our infirmities; but was in all points tempted like as *we are, yet* without sin" (He.4:15).

"Wherefore he is able also to save them to the uttermost that come unto God by him, seeing he ever liveth to make intercession for them. For such an high priest became us, *who is* holy, harmless, undefiled, separate from sinners, and made higher than the heavens" (He.7:25-26).

"Yea doubtless, and I count all things *but* loss for the excellency of the knowledge of Christ Jesus my Lord: for whom I have suffered the loss of all things, and do count them *but* dung, that I may win Christ, And be found in him, not having mine own righteousness, which is of the law, but that which is through the faith of Christ, the righteousness which is of God by faith: That I may know him, and the power of his resurrection, and the fellowship of his sufferings, being made conformable unto his death" (Ph.3:8-10).

"Forasmuch as ye know that ye were not redeemed with corruptible things, *as* silver and gold, from your vain conversation *received* by tradition from your fathers; But with the precious blood of Christ, as of a lamb without blemish and without spot" (1 Pe.1:18-19).

"Who did no sin, neither was guile found in his mouth: Who, when he was reviled, reviled not again; when he suffered, he threatened not; but committed *himself* to him that judgeth righteously: Who his own self bare our sins in his own body on the tree, that we, being dead to sins, should live unto righteousness: by whose stripes ye were healed" (1 Pe.2:22-24).

"Thou lovest righteousness, and hatest wickedness: therefore God, thy God, hath anointed thee with the oil of gladness above thy fellows" (Ps.45:7).

"Behold, the days come, saith the LORD, that I will raise unto David a righteous Branch, and a King shall reign and prosper, and shall execute judgment and justice in the earth" (Je.23:5).

3) The idolater must listen because God is ready to save Zion and give His glory to Israel. This is a clear prediction of God's coming salvation. All who truly believed the LORD would be rescued, set free from the coming Babylonian captivity. When the event actually happened, not many truly believed the LORD or still placed their hope in the promised land. Most—the vast majority—stayed behind in Babylon. They had become comfortable, prosperous, and wrapped up in the world of unbelievers. And as this prophecy indicates, many had become devoted to the idolatrous worship of the world.

But God warned the idolaters: the LORD's salvation was at hand. He was ready to bring the oppression and captivity of His people to an end. The great day of salvation and the glorification of His people was approaching. Thus the idolaters stood forewarned: they will miss out on God's wonderful salvation and the coming glory promised to true believers and worshippers of the LORD. This is a strong warning to all idolaters and unbelievers of every generation. God's Holy Word declares that the climactic day of God's salvation, the deliverance of His people from the bondages of this earth, is coming. Soon the Messiah, the Lord Jesus Christ, will return to earth to close the pages of human history. In that day, a most wonderful event will take place: all righteous believers will be glorified.

"Then shall the righteous shine forth as the sun in the kingdom of their Father. Who hath ears to hear, let him hear" (Mt.13:43).

"The Spirit itself beareth witness with our spirit, that we are the children of God: And if children, then heirs; heirs of God, and joint-heirs with Christ; if so be that we suffer with *him,* that we may be also glorified togetherd" (Ro.8:16-17).

"For our conversation is in heaven; from whence also we look for the Saviour, the Lord Jesus Christ: Who shall change our vile body, that it may be fashioned like unto his glorious body, according to the working whereby he is able even to subdue all things unto himself" (Ph.3:20-21).

"When Christ, *who is* our life, shall appear, then shall ye also appear with him in glory" (Col.3:4).

"The elders which are among you I exhort, who am also an elder, and a witness of the sufferings of Christ, and also a partaker of the glory that shall be revealed" (1 Pe.5:1).

"After this I beheld, and, lo, a great multitude, which no man could number, of all nations, and kindreds, and people, and tongues, stood before the throne, and before the Lamb, clothed with white robes, and palms in their hands; And cried with a loud voice, saying, Salvation to our God which sitteth upon the throne, and unto the Lamb" (Re.7:9-10).

"And there shall be no night there; and they need no candle, neither light of the sun; for the Lord God giveth them light: and they shall reign for ever and ever" (Re.22:5).

"Because he hath set his love upon me, therefore will I deliver him: I will set him on high, because he hath known my name" (Ps.91:14).

"And they that be wise shall shine as the brightness of the firmament; and they that turn many to righteousness as the stars for ever and ever" (Da.12:3).

CHAPTER 47

H. Set Free by God's Judgment of the Oppressor, Babylon: A Warning to All Who Oppress Others, 47:1-15

1. The defeat of the oppressor: A picture of God's vengeance
  a. The oppressor—Babylon, the unconquered virgin—would be humiliated
    1) Would be dethroned, lose all authority & honor
    2) Would be enslaved
    3) Would face severe hardship

    4) Would be exposed & shamed
  b. The defeat would be *certain*
    1) The LORD's Word: Would execute vengeance

    2) The LORD's purpose
      • To redeem, rescue His people: By His Name
      • To cast the oppressor into darkness: To remove the oppressor forever

2. The sins of the oppressor: Wicked acts that provoked God
  a. Cruelty to God's people
    1) God had used Babylon to discipline His people
    2) The oppressor had shown no mercy, even to the aged
  b. Boasting & misplacing their security: Failing to think about God & the consequences of sin
  c. Fleshly, carnal pleasure: Living carelessly, immorally
  d. Pride, self-sufficiency, & self-exaltation (humanism): Exalting self (man) as supreme—self-deification

Come down, and sit in the dust, O virgin daughter of Babylon, sit on the ground: *there is* no throne, O daughter of the Chaldeans: for thou shalt no more be called tender and delicate.
2 Take the millstones, and grind meal: uncover thy locks, make bare the leg, uncover the thigh, pass over the rivers.
3 Thy nakedness shall be uncovered, yea, thy shame shall be seen: I will take vengeance, and I will not meet *thee as* a man.
4 *As for* our redeemer, the LORD of hosts *is* his name, the Holy One of Israel.
5 Sit thou silent, and get thee into darkness, O daughter of the Chaldeans: for thou shalt no more be called, The lady of kingdoms.
6 I was wroth with my people, I have polluted mine inheritance, and given them into thine hand: thou didst show them no mercy; upon the ancient hast thou very heavily laid thy yoke.
7 And thou saidst, I shall be a lady for ever: *so that* thou didst not lay these *things* to thy heart, neither didst remember the latter end of it.
8 Therefore hear now this, *thou that art* given to pleasures, that dwellest carelessly, that sayest in thine heart, I *am,* and none else beside me; I shall not sit *as* a widow, neither shall I know the loss of children:

9 But these two *things* shall come to thee in a moment in one day, the loss of children, and widowhood: they shall come upon thee in their perfection for the multitude of thy sorceries, *and* for the great abundance of thine enchantments.
10 For thou hast trusted in thy wickedness: thou hast said, None seeth me. Thy wisdom and thy knowledge, it hath perverted thee; and thou hast said in thine heart, I *am,* and none else beside me.
11 Therefore shall evil come upon thee; thou shalt not know from whence it riseth: and mischief shall fall upon thee; thou shalt not be able to put if off: and desolation shall come upon thee suddenly, *which* thou shalt not know.
12 Stand now with thine enchantments, and with the multitude of thy sorceries, wherein thou hast laboured from thy youth; if so be thou shalt be able to profit, if so be thou mayest prevail.
13 Thou art wearied in the multitude of thy counsels. Let now the astrologers, the stargazers, the monthly prognosticators, stand up, and save thee from *these things* that shall come upon thee.
14 Behold, they shall be as stubble; the fire shall burn them; they shall not deliver themselves from the power of the flame: *there shall* not *be* a coal to warm at, *nor* fire to sit before it.
15 Thus shall they be unto thee with whom thou hast laboured, *even* thy merchants, from thy youth: they shall wander every one to his quarter; none shall save thee.

3. The sudden, catastrophic end of the oppressor
  a. The oppressor's false security would be lost—suddenly
    1) Would lose family & all hope for the future
    2) Would lose all despite their trust in sorcery

  b. The oppressor's wickedness, wisdom, & knowledge would mislead & deceive him

  c. The oppressor's end would be disastrous: An unforeseen calamity or catastrophe would suddenly fall upon him

4. The powerlessness of false religion—the world of the occult—to deliver the oppressor
  a. The occult rituals can never save you: Even if you keep seeking

  b. The occult concepts & notions only wear you out: Leave you hopeless & exhausted
  c. The occult leaders cannot save you from the future, from what is to come upon you

  d. The occult leaders will be burned up like dried grass: Cannot save themselves, much less you

  e. The occult leaders can only give you empty counsel for money
  f. The occult leaders will continue on in their error: Not one can save you

DIVISION V

THE PROPHECIES OF COMFORT AND FREEDOM: A PICTURE OF BELIEVERS BEING SET FREE FROM THE CAPTIVITY OF SIN AND DEATH, 40:1–48:22

H. Set Free by God's Judgment of the Oppressor, Babylon: A Warning to All Who Oppress Others, 47:1-15

(47:1-15) **Introduction**: throughout the world people are being oppressed. Oppressive behavior is a common problem, one that exists within many families as well as in businesses, organizations, religions, and governments of this world. Oppression can exist even between two people, when one person is overbearing or too demanding. Husbands and wives can be oppressive when they dominate each other. Children can be oppressive when they are too demanding of their parents or abusive toward other children. Governments can be oppressive by passing preferential laws that discriminate among various classes or races of citizens. Leaders can be oppressive by abusing dictatorial powers. Much of the suffering throughout the world is due to the oppressive and greedy behavior of governments and leaders against their own people, of one race against another, one social class against another, and one religion against another.

In the ancient world, the Babylonians were one of the most oppressive people ever to come on the scene of world history. They were an ambitious people who set their sights on building a worldwide empire. An attempt was made to make Babylon the mightiest and most glorious capital of the world. But in pursuing this ambition for world power, the Babylonians became a vicious and ruthless people, tyrannizing and conquering one nation after another. After defeating a people, the Babylonians enslaved and then deported the entire population into other nations. Their purpose in this was to break the population's allegiance to their own nation by forcing them to become citizens of other nations. But loyalty to any nation other than Babylon was not tolerated. The world was to become a Babylonian world. Every nation was to be subjected under the rule and law of Babylon. To achieve its ends, all forms of cruelty and savagery were used against the people of other nations. Individuals either subjected themselves under the thumb of Babylon or else faced harsh punishment or even death.

Because of Babylon's vicious tyranny, in particular their mistreatment of God's people, God pronounced judgment upon the cruel oppressor. However, this prophecy was pronounced more than 150 years before the hand of God's judgment would fall. God was determined to set His people free. Through the destruction of Babylon, they would be set free to return to the promised land. This is, *Set Free by God's Judgment of the Oppressor, Babylon: A Warning to All Who Oppress Others*, 47:1-15.

1. The defeat of the oppressor: a picture of God's vengeance (vv.1-5).
2. The sins of the oppressor: wicked acts that provoked God (vv.6-8).
3. The sudden, catastrophic end of the oppressor (vv.9-11).
4. The powerlessness of false religion—the world of the occult—to deliver the oppressor (vv.12-15).

1 (47:1-5) **Vengeance, of God, Prophecy Concerning—Babylon, Prophecy Concerning, Conquered—Oppressors, Judgment of, Example—Word of God, Prophecies of, Surety of Fulfillment—Judgment, of God, Prophecy Concerning**: any oppressor of God's people will ultimately be defeated. For that reason Babylon, the cruel persecutors of God's people in Biblical times, was doomed to fall. Remember that Babylon was the capital of a worldwide empire, probably the greatest empire to rule over the nations of ancient history. But Babylon had been a ruthless, bloodthirsty master as she conquered and ruled over the nations of the earth. Thus Isaiah predicted that Babylon would face the hand of God's judgment. Babylon would be humiliated and conquered (vv.1-3a). Although the conqueror is not named here, Isaiah did identify Persia elsewhere as the conqueror (44:28; 45:1-13). And history has proven the fulfillment of the prophecy, for Persia conquered Babylon in 539 B.C. Note that Babylon is referred to as a *virgin daughter*, a tender, delicate nation, which simply means that she was a young nation; she had never been sexually conquered, never raped by other nations up until that time. However, Isaiah was predicting that God would work through Persia to conquer or rape the nation of Babylon. In the vast world empire, the brutal persecutors of God's people would sit in dust. The acclaimed nation of Babylon would be dethroned, lose all her authority and honor throughout the world. The once legendary capital would be conquered and utterly humiliated. No longer would the Babylonian citizens be pampered, living lives of luxury and pleasure and possessing most of the wealth of the world. The oppressors themselves would now be enslaved and led into captivity. They would face the severe hardships of slaves, being forced to do the most menial and difficult tasks within society. Instead of using animals to turn the heavy millstones for grinding flour, the conquering nation would force the Babylonian people to do the work of the animals. Furthermore, the enslaved women would no longer be able to show concern for beautiful clothes or modesty. Rather, they would be treated as slaves, forced to lift up their skirts and bare their legs. They would be forced to expose themselves and be at the disposal of the conquerors. In other words, the Babylonian women would reap the same mistreatment that their own husbands and fathers had forced upon female citizens of other nations. They would be abused, raped, and shamed.

Note that the fall of Babylon was guaranteed by the LORD Himself (vv.3b-5). He would personally take vengeance and execute his justice against Babylon. And all citizens of the cruel, oppressive nation would feel the weight of His hand against them. No citizen would be spared. Judgment is non-negotiable. It is a surety for two reasons: first, the LORD has determined to rescue His people. He is the *Redeemer*; therefore He is bound to deliver all who trust and follow Him. Moreover, He is the LORD *of hosts*, the LORD Almighty. He has the power to rule and control all beings and events throughout the universe. He is also the *Holy One of Israel*, the God who has a covenant relationship with His people, caring for and looking after them, demanding that they live holy and righteous lives. Due to this relationship, God is bound to rescue His people from their adversaries. His very Name—*Our Redeemer, the LORD of hosts, the Holy One of Israel*—shows that He will deliver His people from their oppressors.

Second, God's purpose is to execute justice against any who repress or tyrannize His people. The oppressor will be cast into darkness and removed forever. Hence, no longer would Babylon be the leader, the queen of nations and kingdoms.

OUTLINE	SCRIPTURE	SCRIPTURE	OUTLINE
1. The defeat of the oppressor: A picture of God's vengeance	Come down, and sit in the dust, O virgin daughter of Babylon, sit on the ground: *there is* no throne, O daughter of the Chaldeans: for thou shalt no more be called tender and delicate.	2 Take the millstones, and grind meal: uncover thy locks, make bare the leg, uncover the thigh, pass over the rivers.	2) Would be enslaved
a. The oppressor—Babylon, the unconquered virgin would be humiliated			3) Would face severe hardship
1) Would be dethroned, lose all authority & honor		3 Thy nakedness shall be uncovered, yea, thy shame	4) Would be exposed & shamed
			b. The defeat would be *certain*

OUTLINE	SCRIPTURE	SCRIPTURE	OUTLINE
1) The LORD's Word: Would execute vengeance 2) The LORD's purpose • To redeem, rescue His people: By His Name	shall be seen: I will take vengeance, and I will not meet *thee as* a man. 4 *As for* our redeemer, the LORD of hosts *is* his name, the Holy One of Israel.	5 Sit thou silent, and get thee into darkness, O daughter of the Chaldeans: for thou shalt no more be called, The lady of kingdoms.	• To cast the oppressor into darkness: To remove the oppressor forever

Thought 1. One of the most despised behaviors in the eyes of God is that of mistreating or oppressing other people. Why? Because God loves and cares for every human being. He hates and despises our sins, but He loves us; and He expects us to love our neighbors. For this reason He will not tolerate the mistreatment or oppression of others. All forms of oppression and mistreatment are despised by God:

⇒ degrading or ignoring people
⇒ crushing or beating them down
⇒ disheartening or causing distress for them
⇒ harassing or hounding them
⇒ persecuting them sexually, emotionally, mentally, or spiritually
⇒ tormenting or torturing them
⇒ enslaving or trampling them under foot

No matter how we mistreat people, God despises it and He will hold us accountable. His hand of judgment will fall upon us, and He will repay with vengeance accordingly. Listen to God's Holy Word:

"Woe unto you, scribes and Pharisees, hypocrites! for ye make clean the outside of the cup and of the platter, but within they are full of extortion and excess" (Mt.23:25).

"But unto them that are contentious, and do not obey the truth, but obey unrighteousness, indignation and wrath, Tribulation and anguish, upon every soul of man that doeth evil, of the Jew first, and also of the Gentile" (Ro.2:8-9).

"Dearly beloved, avenge not yourselves, but *rather* give place unto wrath: for it is written, Vengeance *is* mine; I will repay, saith the Lord" (Ro.12:19).

"Know ye not that the unrighteous shall not inherit the kingdom of God? Be not deceived: neither fornicators, nor idolaters, nor adulterers, nor effeminate, nor abusers of themselves with mankind, Nor thieves, nor covetous, nor drunkards, nor revilers, nor extortioners, shall inherit the kingdom of God" (1 Co.6:9-10).

"Now the works of the flesh are manifest, which are *these*; Adultery, fornication, uncleanness, lasciviousness, Idolatry, witchcraft, hatred, variance, emulations, wrath, strife, seditions, heresies, Envyings, murders, drunkenness, revellings, and such like: of the which I tell you before, as I have also told *you* in time past, that they which do such things shall not inherit the kingdom of God" (Ga.5:19-21).

"Let no man deceive you with vain words: for because of these things cometh the wrath of God upon the children of disobedience" (Ep.5:6).

"And to you who are troubled rest with us, when the Lord Jesus shall be revealed from heaven with his mighty angels, In flaming fire taking vengeance on them that know not God, and that obey not the gospel of our Lord Jesus Christ: Who shall be punished with everlasting destruction from the presence of the Lord, and from the glory of his power" (2 Th.1:7-9).

"To me *belongeth* vengeance, and recompence; their foot shall slide in *due* time: for the day of their calamity *is* at hand, and the things that shall come upon them make haste" (De.32:35).

"O LORD God, to whom vengeance belongeth; O God, to whom vengeance belongeth, show thyself" (Ps.94:1).

"He that oppresseth the poor reproacheth his Maker: but he that honoureth him hath mercy on the poor" (Pr.14:31).

"If thou seest the oppression of the poor, and violent perverting of judgment and justice in a province, marvel not at the matter: for *he that is* higher than the highest regardeth; and *there be* higher than they" (Ecc.5:8).

"And I will execute great vengeance upon them with furious rebukes; and they shall know that I *am* the LORD, when I shall lay my vengeance upon them" (Eze.25:17).

"And I will execute vengeance in anger and fury upon the heathen, such as they have not heard" (Mi.5:15).

"God *is* jealous, and the LORD revengeth; the LORD revengeth, and *is* furious; the LORD will take vengeance on his adversaries, and he reserveth *wrath* for his enemies" (Na.1:2).

2 (47:6-8) **Oppression, Sins of—Sins, Listed, of the Oppressor—Evil, Results of, Provoked God—Evil, Listed, of the Oppressor**: the oppressors of God's people were to be judged because of their terrible sins, in particular their cruelty toward God's people. Historically, Babylon, as the capital of a worldwide empire, was the center of the world, the focus of the world's attention. But it was the small nation of Israel and her people that were the focus of God's eye. Within Israel there were a small number of people who truly trusted and loved the LORD, who obeyed His commandments and lived righteously. Thus God was working behind the scenes through world events to save His people from the persecutions and bondages of this world. But in this present point, God spelled out even more sins of the oppressor, sins that explain exactly why Babylon was to be destroyed.

OUTLINE	SCRIPTURE	SCRIPTURE	OUTLINE

2. The sins of the oppressor: Wicked acts that provoked God
a. Cruelty to God's people
  1) God had used Babylon to discipline His people
  2) The oppressor had shown no mercy, even to the aged
b. Boasting & misplacing their security: Failed to think about God & the conse-
	6 I was wroth with my people, I have polluted mine inheritance, and given them into thine hand: thou didst show them no mercy; upon the ancient hast thou very heavily laid thy yoke.
	7 And thou saidst, I shall be a lady for ever: *so* that thou didst not lay these *things* to
		thy heart, neither didst remember the latter end of it.
		8 Therefore hear now this, *thou that art* given to pleasures, that dwellest carelessly, that sayest in thine heart, I *am,* and none else beside me; I shall not sit *as* a widow, neither shall I know the loss of children:
			quences of sin
			
			c. Fleshly, carnal pleasure: Living carelessly, immorally
			d. Pride, self-sufficiency, & self-exaltation (humanism): Exalting self (man) as supreme, self-deification

a. The first sin of the oppressor was the mistreatment of God's people, the cruel abuse inflicted upon them (v.6). Some generations before, the LORD had actually raised up and worked through Babylon to execute judgment against the savage Assyrians and other wicked nations of the earth. Then, due to Israel's terrible sins, God had used Babylon as His agent to execute judgment against His own people. Israel's sins had aroused His anger; therefore, the LORD had used Babylon as the rod of His discipline. Through disciplining His people, the LORD sought to stir them to return to Him (Is.42:23-25; 43:22-28; La.2:2; also see Is.9:8–10:34 to compare how God uses nations to discipline His people). But Babylon failed to respect the *basic human rights* of other people. They showed no mercy to Israel, God's very own *inheritance* whom He had chosen to be His people. Even the elderly were forced to do slave labor, grueling work. These actions exposed in the most vile traits of human nature were exposed in the Babylonians vicious, merciless spirits and coldhearted cruelty. This was the first sin for which the oppressor was to be condemned.

> "Their feet *are* swift to shed blood: Destruction and misery *are* in their ways: And the way of peace have they not known: There is no fear of God before their eyes" (Ro.3:15-18).
> "For their feet run to evil, and make haste to shed blood" (Pr.1:16).
> "For they sleep not, except they have done mischief; and their sleep is taken away, unless they cause *some* to fall" (Pr.4:16).
> "An heart that deviseth wicked imaginations, feet that be swift in running to mischief" (Pr.6:18).
> "Their feet run to evil, and they make haste to shed innocent blood: their thoughts *are* thoughts of iniquity; wasting and destruction *are* in their paths" (Is.59:7).
> "Woe to them that devise iniquity, and work evil upon their beds! when the morning is light, they practise it, because it is in the power of their hand" (Mi.2:1).

b. Boasting in their prosperity and power and placing their security in the things of the world was the second sin of the Babylonian oppressor. The leaders and people of the great empire thought they would continue forever, that their nation would always be the *queen,* the superpower of the world. No thought was ever given to another nation's rising and becoming more powerful than Babylon. No thought was ever given to the only living and true God nor to the consequences of their own immoral, unrighteous and malicious treatment of others. For this reason, the hand of God's judgment was to fall upon Babylon. Note that this sin of boasting and misplacing security will be a trait in the New Babylon. It will arise in the last days of human history and will be one of the reasons why the New Babylon will be destroyed by God (Re.18:7; see outline and notes—Re.18:1-24 for more discussion).

> "And I will say to my soul, Soul, thou hast much goods laid up for many years; take thine ease, eat, drink, *and* be merry. But God said unto him, *Thou* fool, this night thy soul shall be required of thee: then whose shall those things be, which thou hast provided?" (Lu.12:19-20).
> "Wherefore let him that thinketh he standeth take heed lest he fall" (1 Co.10:12).
> "Charge them that are rich in this world, that they be not highminded, nor trust in uncertain riches, but in the living God, who giveth us richly all things to enjoy" (1 Ti.6:17).
> "But he giveth more grace. Wherefore he saith, God resisteth the proud, but giveth grace unto the humble" (Js.4:6).
> "For the wicked boasteth of his heart's desire, and blesseth the covetous, *whom* the LORD abhorreth" (Ps.10:3).
> "They that trust in their wealth, and boast themselves in the multitude of their riches; None *of them* can by any means redeem his brother, nor give to God a ransom for him" (Ps.49:6-7).
> "Boast not thyself of to morrow; for thou knowest not what a day may bring forth" (Pr.27:1).
> "He that trusteth in his own heart is a fool: but whoso walketh wisely, he shall be delivered" (Pr.28:26).
> "They have belied the LORD, and said, *It is* not he; neither shall evil come upon us; neither shall we see sword nor famine" (Je.5:12).
> "Behold, I *am* against thee, O inhabitant of the valley, *and* rock of the plain, saith the LORD; which say, Who shall come down against us? or who shall enter into our habitations?" (Je.21:13).
> "Ye have plowed wickedness, ye have reaped iniquity; ye have eaten the fruit of lies: because thou didst trust in thy way, in the multitude of thy mighty men" (Ho.10:13).

c. The oppressor's third sin was living a fleshly, carnal life (v.8ª). The Babylonians were a people given over to self-gratification, living carefree and careless lives. They were a pleasure-loving people filled with a spirit of selfishness, indulgence, license, partying, and immorality. Little or no thought was given to the fact that they were becoming a reckless and undisciplined society. Satisfying their fleshly cravings and carnal appetites was the full focus of their lives. The Babylonians rarely thought about a future life with the only living and true God. Centuries of worshipping false gods that "allowed" them to indulge in their most lustful desires had hardened their hearts against the LORD. Consequently, the hand of God's judgment was to fall upon this oppressor of His people, Babylon.

"And that [seed] hich fell among thorns are they, which, when they have heard, go forth, and are choked with cares and riches and pleasures of *this* life, and bring no fruit to perfection" (Lu.8:14).

"And I will say to my soul, Soul, thou hast much goods laid up for many years; take thine ease, eat, drink, *and* be merry. But God said unto him, *Thou* fool, this night thy soul shall be required of thee: then whose shall those things be, which thou hast provided? So *is* he that layeth up treasure for himself, and is not rich toward God" (Lu.12:19-21).

"(For many walk, of whom I have told you often, and now tell you even weeping, *that they are* the enemies of the cross of Christ: Whose end *is* destruction, whose God *is their* belly, and *whose* glory *is* in their shame, who mind earthly things.)" (Ph.3:18-19).

"But she that liveth in pleasure is dead while she liveth" (1 Ti.5:6).

"And [they] shall receive the reward of unrighteousness, *as* they that count it pleasure to riot in the daytime. Spots *they are* and blemishes, sporting themselves with their own deceivings while they feast with you; Having eyes full of adultery, and that cannot cease from sin; beguiling unstable souls: an heart they have exercised with covetous practices; cursed children" (2 Pe.2:13-14).

"He that loveth pleasure *shall be* a poor man: he that loveth wine and oil shall not be rich" (Pr.21:17).

"For the drunkard and the glutton shall come to poverty: and drowsiness shall clothe *a man* with rags" (Pr.23:21).

"Come ye, *say they,* I will fetch wine, and we will fill ourselves with strong drink; and to morrow shall be as this day, *and* much more abundant" (Is.56:12).

d. An attitude of pride, self-sufficiency, self-exaltation, and self-deification was the fourth sin of the oppressor. The Babylonians had a firm belief in *humanism* or self-deification, that "I am, and there is none beside me" (v.8). They felt that no one was superior to them, not even God. They even exalted themselves as the supreme society among the human race. And they rested secure in this fact, boasting among the nations that they were the *greatest* among the people and empires of the world. Not surprisingly, they felt that their armies were undefeatable, that their nation would never suffer like the widow nor ever lose so many children (soldiers) that another nation could conquer them. Feeling that they controlled their own lives and destiny, they *deified* themselves. They regarded themselves as the supreme or greatest race on earth. This *humanistic spirit*—puffed up pride, self-sufficiency, self-exaltation, and self-deification—was the fifth sin that was to doom the oppressor.

"And whosoever shall exalt himself shall be abased; and he that shall humble himself shall be exalted" (Mt.23:12).

"But he giveth more grace. Wherefore he saith, God resisteth the proud, but giveth grace unto the humble" (Js.4:6).

"Love not the world, neither the things *that are* in the world. If any man love the world, the love of the Father is not in him. For all that *is* in the world, the lust of the flesh, and the lust of the eyes, and the pride of life, is not of the Father, but is of the world" (1 Jn.2:15-16).

"The wicked in *his* pride doth persecute the poor: let them be taken in the devices that they have imagined" (Ps.10:2).

"Therefore pride compasseth them about as a chain; violence covereth them *as* a garment" (Ps.73:6).

"These six *things* doth the LORD hate: yea, seven *are* an abomination unto him: A proud look, a lying tongue, and hands that shed innocent blood, An heart that deviseth wicked imaginations, feet that be swift in running to mischief, A false witness *that* speaketh lies, and he that soweth discord among brethren" (Pr.6:16-19).

"*When* pride cometh, then cometh shame" (Pr.11:2).

"Pride *goeth* before destruction, and an haughty spirit before a fall" (Pr.16:18).

"An high look, and a proud heart, *and* the plowing of the wicked, *is* sin" (Pr.21:4).

"He that is of a proud heart stirreth up strife" (Pr.28:25).

"A man's pride shall bring him low: but honour shall uphold the humble in spirit" (Pr.29:23).

"For thou hast said in thine heart, I will ascend into heaven, I will exalt my throne above the stars of God: I will sit also upon the mount of the congregation, in the sides of the north: I will ascend above the heights of the clouds; I will be like the most High. Yet thou shalt be brought down to hell, to the sides of the pit" (Is.14:13-15).

"Son of man, say unto the prince of Tyrus, Thus saith the Lord GOD; Because thine heart *is* lifted up, and thou hast said, I *am* a God, I sit *in* the seat of God, in the midst of the seas; yet thou *art* a man, and not God, though thou set thine heart as the heart of God: Behold, thou *art* wiser than Daniel; there is no secret that they can hide from thee: With thy wisdom and with thine understanding thou hast gotten thee riches, and hast gotten gold and silver into thy treasures: By thy great wisdom *and* by thy traffic hast thou increased thy riches, and thine heart is lifted up because of thy riches: Therefore thus saith the Lord GOD; Because thou hast set thine heart as the heart of God; Behold, therefore I will bring strangers upon thee, the terrible of the nations: and they shall draw their swords against the beauty of thy wisdom, and they shall defile thy brightness. They shall bring thee down to the pit, and thou shalt die the deaths of *them that are* slain in the midst of the seas" (Eze.28:2-8).

"Though thou exalt *thyself* as the eagle, and though thou set thy nest among the stars, thence will I bring thee down, saith the LORD" (Ob.1:4).

3 (47:9-11) **Oppression, Example of—Judgment, What Is to Be Judged, the Oppressor—Babylon, Judgment of, Predicted**: the end of the oppressor would be sudden, catastrophic. In one night's time the city of Babylon would be conquered by Darius, the king of the Medo-Persian Empire (Da.5:1-31, esp.30-31). Furthermore, the conquest would happen without a battle. The Babylonian's misplaced security would collapse and be lost in one day. What the people had formerly thought impossible would take place, both the loss of children and women becoming widows. Within a single night the citizens of Babylon would lose their families and all hope for the future. Note where they had placed their trust: in the world of the occult, that is, in sorcery, enchantments, witchcraft, psychics, divinations, and astrology. But in the hour of need the world of the occult would fail the Babylonians, for the occult is merely another counterfeit religion. It is a phony science that is utterly useless in facing the terrifying enemies and hardships of life. Thus, the oppressor's trust in the world of the occult would collapse in their desperate hour of need.

In addition, the oppressor's trust in keeping his wickedness hidden and his sins out of sight would be shattered. No longer could he take comfort in the deception of hiding his evil in the dark, out of sight. He would now know that his sins were exposed and always had been. The oppressor's knowledge had misled or deceived him. Knowledge had given him a false sense of self-importance, causing him to exalt himself above others, even above God Himself. Often the oppressor felt there was no true God in the universe. No supreme being who saw and knew all and would judge all behavior. In his earthly wisdom and knowledge, he believed that the universe was eternal and self-sustaining or else that it began to appear out of nothing. Considering himself wise and knowledgeable, he was misled. However, true believers must keep in mind that a person usually denies the LORD in order to continue on with his life of wickedness, doing as he wishes and desires. By rejecting God and His Word, he is able to live as he wishes without any restraint. Sadly, this same pattern of behavior that was characteristic of the Babylonians has been a trait of many people and societies down through the centuries.

Nevertheless, despite the self-deception of the oppressors, their end would be disaster (v.11). Isaiah predicted that an unforeseen calamity would suddenly fall upon Babylon. And the mighty metropolis would not be able to stop the catastrophic events. The disaster would be totally unexpected and take place suddenly. As pointed out above, the Median king, Darius, launched a surprise attack and conquered the capital in one night. Yet God's prophecy of total destruction would not take place until the second century B.C. Secular history tells us that this mightiest capital of the ancient world was utterly destroyed when the Parthians conquered the metropolis.

OUTLINE	SCRIPTURE	SCRIPTURE	OUTLINE

3. The sudden, catastrophic end of the oppressor
a. The oppressor's false security would be lost—suddenly
  1) Would lose family & all hope for the future
  2) Would lose all despite their trust in sorcery
b. The oppressor's wickedness, wisdom, & knowledge would mislead & deceive him
	9 But these two *things* shall come to thee in a moment in one day, the loss of children, and widowhood: they shall come upon thee in their perfection for the multitude of thy sorceries, *and* for the great abundance of thine enchantments.
	10 For thou hast trusted in thy wickedness: thou hast said, None seeth me. Thy wisdom and thy knowledge,
		it hath perverted thee; and thou hast said in thine heart, I *am,* and none else beside me.
		11 Therefore shall evil come upon thee; thou shalt not know from whence it riseth: and mischief shall fall upon thee; thou shalt not be able to put if off: and desolation shall come upon thee suddenly, *which* thou shalt not know.
			c. The oppressor's end would be disastrous: An unforeseen calamity or catastrophe would suddenly fall upon him

Thought 1. The sudden and unexpected destruction that fell upon Babylon is a picture of what will fall upon all the wicked of the earth in the last days. All who have denied and turned away from the signs, the warnings, the Christian witnesses, and the promptings of the LORD will meet with a sudden and tragic end.

"For then [in the last days] shall be great tribulation, such as was not since the beginning of the world to this time, no, nor ever shall be. And except those days should be shortened, there should no flesh be saved: but for the elect's sake those days shall be shortened. Then if any man shall say unto you, Lo, here *is* Christ, or there; believe *it* not. For there shall arise false Christs, and false prophets, and shall show great signs and wonders; insomuch that, if *it were* possible, they shall deceive the very elect. Behold, I have told you before. Wherefore if they shall say unto you, Behold, *he is* in the desert; go not forth: behold, he is in the secret chambers; believe *it* not. For as the lightning cometh out of the east, and shineth even unto the west; so shall also the coming of the Son of man be" (Mt.24:21-27).

"But of that day and hour knoweth no *man*, no, not the angels of heaven, but my Father only. But as the days of Noe *were,* so shall also the coming of the Son of man be. For as in the days that were before the flood they were eating and drinking, marrying and giving in marriage, until the day that Noe entered into the ark, And knew not until the flood came, and took them all away; so shall also the coming of the Son of man be" (Mt.24:36-39).

"Let your loins be girded about, and *your* lights burning; And ye yourselves like unto men that wait for their lord, when he will return from the wedding; that when he cometh and knocketh, they may open unto him immediately. Blessed *are* those servants, whom the lord when he cometh shall find watching: verily I say unto you, that he shall gird himself, and make them to sit down to meat, and will come forth and serve them. And if he shall come in the second watch, or come in the third watch, and find *them* so, blessed are those servants. And this know, that if the goodman of the house had known what hour the thief would come, he would have watched, and not have suffered his house to be broken through. Be ye therefore ready also: for the Son of man cometh at an hour when ye think not" (Lu.12:35-40).

"But of the times and the seasons, brethren, ye have no need that I write unto you. For yourselves know perfectly that the day of the Lord so cometh as a thief in the night. For when they shall say, Peace and safety; then sudden destruction cometh upon them, as travail upon a woman with child; and they shall not escape" (1 Th.5:1-3).

"Behold, I come as a thief. Blessed *is* he that watcheth, and keepeth his garments, lest he walk naked, and they see his shame" (Re.16:15).

4 (47:12-15) **Powerlessness, of False Religion; of the World of the Occult—Religion, False, Powerlessness of— Occult, Powerlessness of—Sorcery, Powerlessness of—Oppression, Judgment of, Assured**: the occult world of the oppressors—their false religion—would be powerless to save them. In the ancient world, Babylon was known as the major center for astrology and for every conceivable practice of the occult world. It was the center of all the *occult powers* for which people's depraved hearts craved. But they were not true *powers*. They were only deceptive gods or imaginations created in people's minds, evil demonic forces that were misleading people. Because God's people were to be exiled to Babylon, it was necessary to prepare them for the deceptions and lies of the occult world. Thus God offered a challenge to those who searched for help from the occult: "Keep on practicing your enchantments and sorceries that you have worshipped all these years. Perhaps eventually the so-called *powers* will be able to meet your needs and help you." Of course, the LORD was using sarcasm to get across the fact that the entire realm of the occult was powerless, totally unable to help the seeker. In these challenging remarks the LORD outlined six facts that His people had to grasp to withstand the appeal and the pull of the occult world. These facts are just as relevant today as they were in ancient history.

OUTLINE	SCRIPTURE	SCRIPTURE	OUTLINE
4. The powerlessness of false religion—the world of the occult—to deliver the oppressor a. The occult rituals can never save you: Even if you keep seeking	12 Stand now with thine enchantments, and with the multitude of thy sorceries, wherein thou hast laboured from thy youth; if so be thou shalt be able to profit, if so be thou mayest prevail.	14 Behold, they shall be as stubble; the fire shall burn them; they shall not deliver themselves from the power of the flame: *there shall* not *be* a coal to warm at, *nor* fire to sit before it.	d. The occult leaders will be burned up like dried grass: Cannot save themselves, much less you
b. The occult concepts & notions only wear you out: Leave you hopeless & exhausted c. The occult leaders cannot save you from the future, from what is to come upon you	13 Thou art wearied in the multitude of thy counsels. Let now the astrologers, the stargazers, the monthly prognosticators, stand up, and save thee from *these things* that shall come upon thee.	15 Thus shall they be unto thee with whom thou hast laboured, *even* thy merchants, from thy youth: they shall wander every one to his quarter; none shall save thee.	e. The occult leaders can only give you empty counsel for money f. The occult leaders will continue on in their error: Not one can save you

a. Occult rituals can never save a person (v.12). Even if the mind of the participant continually seeks help, the occult *power* can never respond, for it is only a fantasy in the mind of the participant. It is non-existent.

b. Occult concepts and notions only wear a person out, leaving the individual helpless and exhausted (v.13a). No matter how many hours of study a person devotes to an occult practice, no matter how much advice or instruction is received, there will be no help forthcoming. The person is only draining himself physically and mentally and wasting his time.

c. The occult leaders who study the stars and planets and forecast their influence over human affairs cannot save one person from future trouble, from what is coming upon him or her (v.13). In basic terms, a person's true destiny cannot be foretold nor changed by astrology or by stargazing. In particular when dealing with the judgment of God, no person who has rejected the LORD will escape His coming wrath. The Babylonians did not escape, yet they had reached the summit in seeking the forces of the occult world. Just as the hand of God's judgment fell upon them, so it will fall upon all who reject Him and seek their destiny in the imaginary *powers* of the occult.

d. The occult leaders themselves will face the hand of God's judgment (v.14a). God's ruling against them is very straightforward: they and their occult beliefs have no substance. They are nothing more than stubble. Consequently, they will be burned up like dried grass. And they will not be able to save themselves from the power of God's flaming judgment. Moreover, the fire that consumes them will not be for the purpose of providing warmth or light to those who are sitting in darkness. Rather, it will be for the purpose of executing justice and judgment against the deceptive, perverse leaders of the occult world.

e. The occult leaders can only give empty counsel for money (v.15). No matter how much they attempt to look into the future to foresee people's destiny, they themselves are only physical human beings like the seekers. Both the occult leader and the seeker are limited by the physical, material world. Neither can see into the spiritual world, neither can see the future destiny of other people. Only God Himself is omniscient (all-knowing), omnipresent (present everywhere), and omnipotent (all-powerful). Only He knows the future destiny of people and of the world, and only He has the power to execute events in the future. Doing business with a member of the occult is a waste of money, a foolish waste. Such seeking leads to empty, worthless counsel.

f. The occult leaders will continue on in their error (v.15b). As long as people and nations are willing to pay for the advice of occult leaders, they will continue to collect the money and give their erroneous counsel. But not a single occult leader can save a person from his or her future destiny, especially from the coming judgment of God.

Thought 1. God warns us time and again against the world of the occult. Note the references to the occult practices mentioned in these warnings:

"Now the works of the flesh are manifest, which are *these;* Adultery, fornication, uncleanness, lasciviousness, Idolatry, witchcraft, hatred, variance, emulations, wrath, strife, seditions, heresies, Envyings, murders, drunkenness, revellings, and such like: of the which I tell you before, as I have also told *you* in time past, that they which do such things shall not inherit the kingdom of God" (Ga.5:19-21).

"But the fearful, and unbelieving, and the abominable, and murderers, and whoremongers, and sorcerers, and idolaters, and all liars, shall have their part in the lake which burneth with fire and brimstone: which is the second death" (Re.21:8).

"Regard not them that have familiar spirits, neither seek after wizards, to be defiled by them: I *am* the LORD your God" (Le.19:31).

"And the soul that turneth after such as have familiar spirits, and after wizards, to go a whoring after them, I will even set my face against that soul, and will cut him off from among his people" (Le.20:6).

"When thou art come into the land which the LORD thy God giveth thee, thou shalt not learn to do after the abominations of those nations. There shall not be found among you *any one* that maketh his son or his daughter to pass through the fire, or that useth divination, *or* an observer of times, or an enchanter, or a witch, Or a charmer, or a consulter with familiar spirits, or a wizard, or a necromancer. For all that do these things *are* an abomination unto the LORD: and because of these abominations the LORD thy God doth drive them out from before thee. Thou shalt be perfect with the LORD thy God" (De.18:9-13).

"So Saul died for his transgression which he committed against the LORD, *even* against the word of the LORD, which he kept not, and also for asking *counsel* of *one that had* a familiar spirit, to enquire *of it*" (1 Chr.10:13).

"And when they shall say unto you, Seek unto them that have familiar spirits, and unto wizards that peep, and that mutter: should not a people seek unto their God? for the living to the dead? To the law and to the testimony: if they speak not according to this word, *it is* because *there is* no light in them" (Is.8:19-20).

"And I will cut off witchcrafts out of thine hand; and thou shalt have no *more* soothsayers" (Mi.5:12).

CHAPTER 48

I.   Set Free by God's Plan of Redemption: The Hope of Being Delivered from God's Judgment & Wrath, 48:1-22

Hear ye this, O house of Jacob, which are called by the name of Israel, and are come forth out of the waters of Judah, which swear by the name of the LORD, and make mention of the God of Israel, *but* not in truth, nor in righteousness.

2   For they call themselves of the holy city, and stay themselves upon the God of Israel; The LORD of hosts *is* his name.

3   I have declared the former things from the beginning; and they went forth out of my mouth, and I showed them; I did *them* suddenly, and they came to pass.

4   Because I knew that thou *art* obstinate, and thy neck *is* an iron sinew, and thy brow brass;

5   I have even from the beginning declared *it* to thee; before it came to pass I showed *it* thee: lest thou shouldest say, Mine idol hath done them, and my graven image, and my molten image, hath commanded them.

6   Thou hast heard, see all this; and will not ye declare *it?* I have showed thee new things from this time, even hidden things, and thou didst not know them.

7   They are created now, and not from the beginning; even before the day when thou heardest them not; lest thou shouldest say, Behold, I knew them.

8   Yea, thou heardest not; yea, thou knewest not; yea, from that time *that* thine ear was not opened: for I knew that thou wouldest deal very treacherously, and wast called a transgressor from the womb.

9   For my name's sake will I defer mine anger, and for my praise will I refrain for thee, that I cut thee not off.

10 Behold, I have refined thee, but not with silver; I have chosen thee in the furnace of affliction.

11 For mine own sake, *even* for mine own sake, will I do *it:* for how should *my name* be polluted? and I will not give my glory unto another.

12 Hearken unto me, O Jacob and Israel, my called; I *am* he; I *am* the first, I also *am* the last.

13 Mine hand also hath laid the foundation of the earth, and my right hand hath spanned the heavens: *when* I call unto them, they stand up together.

14 All ye, assemble yourselves, and hear; which among them hath declared these *things?* The LORD hath loved him: he will do his pleasure on Babylon, and his arm *shall be on* the Chaldeans.

15 I, *even* I, have spoken; yea, I have called him: I have brought him, and he shall make his way prosperous.

16 Come ye near unto me, hear ye this; I have not spoken in secret from the beginning; from the time that it was, there *am* I: and now the Lord GOD, and his Spirit, hath sent me.

17 Thus saith the LORD, thy Redeemer, the Holy One of Israel; I *am* the LORD thy God which teacheth thee to profit, which leadeth thee by the way *that* thou shouldest go.

18 O that thou hadst hearkened to my commandments! then had thy peace been as a river, and thy righteousness as the waves of the sea:

19 Thy seed also had been as the sand, and the offspring of thy bowels like the gravel thereof; his name should not have been cut off nor destroyed from before me.

20 Go ye forth of Babylon, flee ye from the Chaldeans, with a voice of singing declare ye, tell this, utter it *even* to the end of the earth; say ye, The LORD hath redeemed his servant Jacob.

21 And they thirsted not *when* he led them through the deserts: he caused the waters to flow out of the rock for them: he clave the rock also, and the waters gushed out.

22 *There is* no peace, saith the LORD, unto the wicked.

---

1. God's indictment: His people were hypocritical & stubborn
a. Their hypocrisy
  1) They made four claims
  • Were of Israel & Judah: The right race & tribe
  • Took oaths in the LORD's Name & used His Name to back their own words
  • Esteemed the Holy City
  • Relied on God
  2) They were untruthful: Did not live righteously, v.1

b. Their stubbornness
  1) God had foretold certain events in their history & brought them about because they were an obstinate, stiff-necked people

  • His purpose: To keep them from claiming that their idols or false gods had delivered or helped them

  • His charge: To hear, see, & confess Him as the only true God, the One who had always predicted the future & fulfilled the events
  2) God revealed new things: To keep them from claiming that it was their own efforts that delivered them

  • Because they had never heard nor understood His prophecies
  • Because they were rebels, transgressors from birth

2. God's patience: He delayed His wrath to deliver His people
a. To stir praise for His name: Due to His mercy, not cutting His people off
b. To refine His people in the furnace of affliction
c. To honor His name & keep it from being defamed

d. To protect His glory

3. God's plan: He worked & controlled all events in order to redeem His people
a. The surety of redemption
  1) His person: "I am...," v.12
  2) His power: Created the universe

b. The promise of redemption, deliverance from captivity
  1) His knowledge, not an idol, foretold this
  2) His power would raise up an agent (Cyrus) to destroy Babylon

  3) His Word guaranteed the prophecy: Cyrus would succeed against Babylon

  4) His promise should be heeded: The LORD Himself had clearly predicted the destruction of Babylon & the redemption (deliverance) of His people from captivity
c. The reassurance of their redemption, deliverance
  1) He was their Redeemer, the Holy One
  2) He was the LORD their God who taught & led them in the right way
d. The blessings of redemption God desired for His people
  1) Peace like a river
  2) Righteousness that rolls on like the waves of the sea
  3) Population growth

  4) A name never cut off nor removed from God's presence

e. The great imperative shout of redemption: Flee Babylon (the influence of the world & its unbelievers)
  1) Proclaim redemption to the whole earth
  • The LORD has redeemed His people
  • The LORD will guide His people to the promised land & meet their needs—just as He did in the wilderness journey, Ex.17:1-7; Nu.20:11
  2) Issue a warning: There is no peace for the wicked

DIVISION V

THE PROPHECIES OF COMFORT AND FREEDOM: A PICTURE OF BELIEVERS BEING SET FREE FROM THE CAPTIVITY OF SIN AND DEATH, 40:1–48:22

I. Set Free by God's Plan of Redemption: The Hope of Being Delivered from God's Judgment and Wrath, 48:1-22

(48:1-22) **Introduction**: one of the blackest marks against human society is that of slavery. Forcing people to work under duress or without freedom is a terrible evil. Holding people in captivity, bondage, and chains is inhumane and deserves the severest punishment of the law. People are held in slavery for the purpose of cheap labor, prostitution, warfare, and for the pleasure and will of the powerful and the rich.

But there is wonderful news for the enslaved of this earth. God has a plan to redeem all who are held in bondage, if they will just trust and follow Him. This is the wonderful message of the present Scripture: *Set Free by God's Plan of Redemption: The Hope of Being Delivered from God's Judgment and Wrath*, 48:1-22.

1. God's indictment: His people are hypocritical and stubborn (vv.1-8).
2. God's patience: He delays His wrath and will deliver His people (vv.9-11).
3. God's plan: He works and controls all events so He can redeem His people (vv.12-22).

1 (48:1-8) **Hypocrisy, Example of, Israelites—Hypocrisy, Claims of, Four Claims—Israel, Sins of, Hypocrisy; Stubbornness—Stubbornness, Example of, the Jews—Idolatry, Discredited – Refuted, by Prophetic Fulfillment**: God issued a serious indictment against His people: they were hypocritical and stubborn. Note the word *hear* or *listen*. The people had closed their ears to God's Word and warnings, refusing to turn from their sins and idolatry back to the Lord. Although they professed to know the Lord, they were not living righteous lives, not obeying God's holy commandments. Instead they were living deceitfully, becoming more and more hard-hearted in their resistance to God. Note the Scripture and outline:

OUTLINE	SCRIPTURE	SCRIPTURE	OUTLINE

1. God's indictment: His people were hypocritical & stubborn
a. Their hypocrisy
  1) They made four claims
    • Were of Israel & Judah: The right race & tribe
    • Took oaths in the LORD's Name & used His Name to back their own words
    • Esteemed the Holy City
    • Relied on God
  2) They were untruthful: Did not live righteously, v.1
b. Their stubbornness
  1) God had foretold certain events in their history & brought them about because they were an obstinate, stiff-necked people
 	
    • His purpose: To keep them from claiming
	Hear ye this, O house of Jacob, which are called by the name of Israel, and are come forth out of the waters of Judah, which swear by the name of the LORD, and make mention of the God of Israel, *but* not in truth, nor in righteousness.
	2 For they call themselves of the holy city, and stay themselves upon the God of Israel; The LORD of hosts *is* his name.
	3 I have declared the former things from the beginning; and they went forth out of my mouth, and I showed them; I did *them* suddenly, and they came to pass.
	4 Because I knew that thou art obstinate, and thy neck *is* an iron sinew, and thy brow brass;
	5 I have even from the beginning declared *it* to thee;
		before it came to pass I showed *it* thee: lest thou shouldest say, Mine idol hath done them, and my graven image, and my molten image, hath commanded them.
		6 Thou hast heard, see all this; and will not ye declare *it?* I have showed thee new things from this time, even hidden things, and thou didst not know them.
		7 They are created now, and not from the beginning; even before the day when thou heardest them not; lest thou shouldest say, Behold, I knew them.
		8 Yea, thou heardest not; yea, thou knewest not; yea, from that time *that* thine ear was not opened: for I knew that thou wouldest deal very treacherously, and wast called a transgressor from the womb.
			that their idols or false gods had delivered or helped them
			
			    • His charge: To hear, see, & confess Him as the only true God, the One who had always predicted the future & fulfilled the events
			  2) God then revealed new things: To keep them from claiming that it was their own efforts that delivered them
			
			    • Because they had never heard nor understood His prophecies
			    • Because they were rebels, transgressors from birth

a. The Israelites were sharply rebuked for their hypocrisy (vv.1-2). Isaiah addressed them as the house of Jacob. Remember, Jacob was the ancient ancestor and father of the twelve tribes of Israel. Every Jew considered Jacob and his sons to be the ancient people of God and considered himself to be a descendant of one of the tribes. As a descendant of Jacob and his sons, every Jew was thought to be a member of God's people, a person who had been especially chosen by God. The Jews made four special claims about themselves. Note how these claims are applicable to so many who profess the LORD and who claim to belong to the "right" religion.

First, a Jew claimed that he was "of Israel and Judah." By Israel is meant the right race, the people chosen by God to be His true witnesses on earth and to be especially blessed by Him. By *Judah* is meant the royal tribe of Israel and the tribe through which the Messiah was to come. Apparently a Jew born in the tribe of Judah considered himself especially blessed by God. Applying this to society through the ages, think how many consider themselves to be of a superior class of people, both socially and racially. Think of the problems within societies all over the world due to social and racial prejudice.

Second, a Jew took oaths in the LORD's Name. In other words, he may have sworn that he would take a particular action based on his belief in the LORD. Or perhaps he took an oath or made a promise declaring that God would verify the truthfulness of his word or promise. By using or referring to the Name of the LORD in making promises, the Jew was implying that he believed in the LORD and that he worshipped the LORD.

Third, a Jew claimed to highly esteem the city of Jerusalem. It was the capital of the nation and the location of the temple; thus Jerusalem was the Holy City in the minds of all Israelites. Furthermore, all Israelites identified with the Holy City and claimed to be citizens of Jerusalem.

Fourth, a Jew claimed to trust and rely upon God as he walked through life day by day. Professing to believe in the LORD, a Jew readily claimed to lean and depend on God to guide him and to meet his needs.

Although Jews made these claims, they were hypocritical, untruthful. Most Jews were not living righteously. They were not obeying the LORD, not keeping His holy commandments. Thus their disobedience and hypocrisy proved their disbelief, that they did not accept God as the LORD of the universe. If they had truly believed Him, that He was the Savior and LORD, they would have obeyed Him. But their disobedience discredited their profession. Within the depths of their hearts the Jews did not sincerely believe or accept God as LORD and Savior. Their rejection of His commandments was irrefutable proof of their insincerity.

This indictment of hypocrisy was leveled against the Jews of Isaiah's day and those of succeeding generations, including the Jews who would be taken captive by Babylon in the future. Isaiah foresaw that the Jews in captivity would become comfortable and complacent in their captive state, that most of them would not return to the promised land when given the opportunity. Over the 70 years of their exile, the Jews would become settled, building houses and developing farms and businesses. In addition, when they had the opportunity to return to Jerusalem, the vast majority of Jews would choose not to go. Why? Because most would have been born and reared in Babylon. Consequently, few would have the faith or willingness to give up their homes, comfortable lifestyles, and the pleasures they had come to know in Babylon.

God's indictment against these worldly Jews was sharp. Their professions were false, hypocritical. They were not living righteous lives, obeying God's commandments, nor following Him. Stated simply, their words, actions, and behavior did not back up their claims.

> **"Ye hypocrites, well did Esaias prophesy of you, saying, This people draweth nigh unto me with their mouth, and honoureth me with *their* lips; but their heart is far from me. But in vain they do worship me, teaching *for* doctrines the commandments of men"** (Mt.15:7-9).
>
> **"But woe unto you, scribes and Pharisees, hypocrites! for ye shut up the kingdom of heaven against men: for ye neither go in *yourselves,* neither suffer ye them that are entering to go in"** (Mt.23:13; see vv.14-33).
>
> **"Even so ye also outwardly appear righteous unto men, but within ye are full of hypocrisy and iniquity"** (Mt.23:28).
>
> **"But and if that evil servant shall say in his heart, My lord delayeth his coming; And shall begin to smite *his* fellowservants, and to eat and drink with the drunken; The lord of that servant shall come in a day when he looketh not for *him,* and in an hour that he is not aware of, And shall cut him asunder, and appoint *him* his portion with the hypocrites: there shall be weeping and gnashing of teeth"** (Mt.24:48-51).
>
> **"Either how canst thou say to thy brother, Brother, let me pull out the mote that is in thine eye, when thou thyself beholdest not the beam that is in thine own eye? Thou hypocrite, cast out first the beam out of thine own eye, and then shalt thou see clearly to pull out the mote that is in thy brother's eye"** (Lu.6:42).
>
> **"Beware ye of the leaven of the Pharisees, which is hypocrisy"** (Lu.12:1).
>
> **"Ye hypocrites, ye can discern the face of the sky and of the earth; but how is it that ye do not discern this time? Yea, and why even of yourselves judge ye not what is right?"** (Lu.12:56-57).
>
> **"Now I beseech you, brethren, mark them which cause divisions and offences contrary to the doctrine which ye have learned; and avoid them. For they that are such serve not our Lord Jesus Christ, but their own belly; and by good words and fair speeches deceive the hearts of the simple"** (Ro.16:17-18).
>
> **"Now the Spirit speaketh expressly, that in the latter times some shall depart from the faith, giving heed to seducing spirits, and doctrines of devils; Speaking lies in hypocrisy; having their conscience seared with a hot iron"** (1 Ti.4:1-2).
>
> **"Unto the pure all things *are* pure: but unto them that are defiled and unbelieving *is* nothing pure; but even their mind and conscience is defiled. They profess that they know God; but in works they deny *him,* being abominable, and disobedient, and unto every good work reprobate"** (Tit.1:15-16).

b. The LORD sharply rebuked the Israelites for their stubbornness (vv.3-8). Despite all He had done for them down through the centuries, the Jews had continued to be an obstinate people and a stiff-necked people. In times past the LORD had foretold a number of phenomenal events pertaining to the Jews that lay out in the future. And He had acted to fulfill these events, bringing blessing after blessing upon them. Some of the significant events that God had foretold and brought about were...

- Abraham's call and the promises given him
- the wonderful deliverance of the Jews' forefathers from Egyptian bondage
- the establishment of Israel as a nation when the law was given at Mount Sinai
- the conquest of Canaan, the promised land
- the wonderful deliverance of Israel from Assyrian oppression

Note God's purpose for predicting these events and working to bring them about: so His people could not claim that their idols had delivered or helped them (v.5). Note also God's charge to the Jews: they must hear, see, and confess the LORD as the only true God (v.6). In every case it was He alone who had predicted the future and then redeemed His people. Therefore they had to listen to the prophecies, and when the events occurred, they had to recognize the prophecy and confess the LORD as the only true God. However, the Israelites shut their eyes to the prophecies given and to their fulfillment, exposing their stubborn hearts. Yet the LORD declared that He would now reveal new things to Isaiah's generation, events that had formerly been hidden from them (vv.6-8). These events had been deliberately hidden to prevent the people from claiming they knew about them beforehand. These new prophecies predicted by Isaiah included such future matters as...

* the raising up of Cyrus (v.14)
* the fall of Babylon and Israel's restoration (vv.20-21)
* the coming suffering and atoning death of the Messiah (Is.52:13–53:12)
* the New Age of Salvation (65:1-16)
* the Messianic Age and the creation of new heavens and earth, an eternal universe (65:17-25)

The LORD revealed these events to the Jews and to all succeeding generations of people for one purpose and one purpose only: to prove that He alone is the LORD of the universe, the only living and true God. He alone is to be worshipped and not the idols or false gods worshipped by the majority of the human race. Sadly, as the Jews in the past closed their ears to the prophecies of God, so most people down through the ages have hardened their hearts toward the LORD and His prophetic Word. When God's prophecies are so clearly spelled out in Holy Scripture, why do so many people continue to shut their ears to the LORD and His Word? God answers this question Himself, and His answer exposes a tragic fact. People who refuse to see the fulfillment of God's prophecies are blind, deliberately blind. Moreover they doom themselves, whether Jews or Gentiles. People reject God and His prophetic Word because they are traitors, rebels from birth. They deliberately choose to be stubborn, hard-hearted, and stiff-necked toward the LORD. They reject the LORD despite the fact that His prophetic Word demands belief and righteousness.

"Ye stiffnecked and uncircumcised in heart and ears, ye do always resist the Holy Ghost: as your fathers *did,* **so** *do* **ye" (Ac.7:51).**

"For the heart of this people is waxed gross, and their ears are dull of hearing, and their eyes have they closed; lest they should see with *their* **eyes, and hear with** *their* **ears, and understand with** *their* **heart, and should be converted, and I should heal them" (Ac.28:27).**

"But after thy hardness and impenitent heart treasurest up unto thyself wrath against the day of wrath and revelation of the righteous judgment of God; Who will render to every man according to his deeds: To them who by patient continuance in well doing seek for glory and honour and immortality, eternal life: But unto them that are contentious, and do not obey the truth, but obey unrighteousness, indignation and wrath, Tribulation and anguish, upon every soul of man that doeth evil, of the Jew first, and also of the Gentile" (Ro.2:5-9).

"This I say therefore, and testify in the Lord, that ye henceforth walk not as other Gentiles walk, in the vanity of their mind, Having the understanding darkened, being alienated from the life of God through the ignorance that is in them, because of the blindness of their heart: Who being past feeling have given themselves over unto lasciviousness, to work all uncleanness with greediness" (Ep.4:17-19).

"Now the Spirit speaketh expressly, that in the latter times some shall depart from the faith, giving heed to seducing spirits, and doctrines of devils; Speaking lies in hypocrisy; having their conscience seared with a hot iron" (1 Ti.4:1-2).

"For the time will come when they will not endure sound doctrine; but after their own lusts shall they heap to themselves teachers, having itching ears; And they shall turn away *their* **ears from the truth, and shall be turned unto fables" (2 Ti.4:3-4).**

"Take heed, brethren, lest there be in any of you an evil heart of unbelief, in departing from the living God. But exhort one another daily, while it is called To day; lest any of you be hardened through the deceitfulness of sin" (He.3:12-13).

"Yet he sent prophets to them, to bring them again unto the LORD; and they testified against them: but they would not give ear" (2 Chr.24:19).

"Be ye not as the horse, *or* **as the mule,** *which* **have no understanding: whose mouth must be held in with bit and bridle, lest they come near unto thee. Many sorrows** *shall be* **to the wicked: but he that trusteth in the LORD, mercy shall compass him about" (Ps.32:9-10).**

"Harden not your heart, as in the provocation, *and as in* **the day of temptation in the wilderness: When your fathers tempted me, proved me, and saw my work. Forty years long was I grieved with** *this* **generation, and said, It** *is* **a people that do err in their heart, and they have not known my ways: Unto whom I sware in my wrath that they should not enter into my rest" (Ps.95:8-11).**

"Who rejoice to do evil, *and* **delight in the frowardness of the wicked" (Pr.2:14).**

"He, that being often reproved hardeneth *his* **neck, shall suddenly be destroyed, and that without remedy" (Pr.29:1).**

"Hearken unto me, ye stouthearted, that *are* **far from righteousness" (Is.46:12).**

"Because I knew that thou *art* **obstinate, and thy neck** *is* **an iron sinew, and thy brow brass...***There is* **no peace, saith the LORD, unto the wicked" (Is.48:4, 22).**

"To whom shall I speak, and give warning, that they may hear? behold, their ear *is* **uncircumcised, and they cannot hearken: behold, the word of the LORD is unto them a reproach; they have no delight in it" (Je.6:10).**

"And they have turned unto me the back, and not the face: though I taught them, rising up early and teaching *them,* **yet they have not hearkened to receive instruction" (Je.32:33).**

"*As for* the word that thou hast spoken unto us in the name of the LORD, we will not hearken unto thee" (Je.44:16).

"Son of man, thou dwellest in the midst of a rebellious house, which have eyes to see, and see not; they have ears to hear, and hear not: for they *are* a rebellious house" (Eze.12:2).

"But they refused to hearken, and pulled away the shoulder, and stopped their ears, that they should not hear" (Zec.7:11).

"If ye will not hear, and if ye will not lay *it* to heart, to give glory unto my name, saith the LORD of hosts, I will even send a curse upon you, and I will curse your blessings: yea, I have cursed them already, because ye do not lay *it* to heart" (Mal.2:2).

2 (48:9-11) **Patience, of God, Purpose for, Fivefold—Longsuffering, of God, Purposes—Wrath, of God, Delayed, Five Reasons**: God revealed a wonderful fact to His people: despite their hypocrisy and stubbornness, He was patient and not willing that any of them should perish. With a heart full of love for His people, He suffered a long time with their insincere, obstinate behavior. He delayed His wrath, longing for them to repent and turn back to Him. All who repented would be delivered from the bondage and oppression of their enemies. Although the people deserved to be condemned due to their despicable behavior, the LORD would have mercy on them. He would not cut His people off, not immediately. Four reasons are given explaining why God delayed His wrath:

a. God is patient, showing mercy so that people will praise His Name (v.9). When a person honestly looks at how much sin has infected the world and considers how merciful God has been by delaying His wrath, the person is stirred to praise God for His mercy. However, death is the just reward for sin and rebellion against God. But out of a heart of mercy, the LORD has delayed His wrath. It will not be delayed forever, for the day of final judgment is coming when every person will give an account for His or her behavior. But for now God's mercy provides a way of eternal salvation for all who will believe. Because of His mercy, His Name is to be praised.

b. God is patient, showing mercy in order to refine His people in the furnace of affliction (v.10). Just as silver is refined—made more pure, and more valuable—in a furnace of fire, so God's people are refined through the hardships and suffering they endure. It is through these trials that the LORD makes His people stronger, both in character and in faith. When a true believer suffers, he draws closer to the LORD through prayer and worship. Suffering arouses a person to call upon the LORD for provision, help, guidance, protection, or deliverance. And when the LORD answers the true believer's prayer, the believer draws even closer to the LORD through more prayer, worship, and thanksgiving. Hence, the LORD's patience and mercy are continuously refining His people, making them stronger believers than ever before.

c. The LORD is patient, showing mercy in order to honor His Name and keep His Name from being defamed (v.11a). The words "for my sake" are emphasized, being mentioned twice in this brief verse. God is absolutely determined to protect the integrity of His Name and His Word. This thought should be reassuring to believers, for if God had executed His wrath upon the human race in Isaiah's day, His promise of redemption—that some would be saved—would not have been fulfilled. Neither would many of the prophecies that were given long ago. Therefore God delayed His wrath in order to honor His Word, to fulfill all the predictions and promises He had given to His people. By keeping and fulfilling His Word, He honors His Name. Hence, no person can legitimately defame God's Name by accusing Him of lying to people. The earth is still standing so that God can honor His Name by keeping the promises He has given to the world, in particular to true believers.

d. God is patient, showing mercy to protect His glory (v.11b). As the LORD God of the universe, the Creator of heaven and earth, the LORD is by His very nature the most magnificent being who has ever existed or ever will exist. The very essence of His being is light, a light so brilliant and magnificent that it shines forth with the blazing holiness of God's righteousness. God's glory is so radiant and powerful, so full of splendor, that in the New Jerusalem there will be no need for sunlight. The magnificence of God's glory and being shines so intensely that it will provide the light needed in the capital city of the new heavens and earth. God's majesty and righteousness are so potent that they would consume any sinner or imperfect being who stood in His presence. Because of God's glory and majesty, He is to be praised and honored by true believers. When God is patient and merciful to His people, they are to exalt and worship His Holy Name. It is this glory—the glory of praise and honor—that the LORD will never share with another person or being.

OUTLINE	SCRIPTURE	SCRIPTURE	OUTLINE
2. God's patience: He delayed His wrath to deliver His people a. To stir praise for His name: Due to His mercy, not cutting His people off b. To refine His people in the furnace of affliction	9 For my name's sake will I defer mine anger, and for my praise will I refrain for thee, that I cut thee not off. 10 Behold, I have refined thee, but not with silver;	I have chosen thee in the furnace of affliction. 11 For mine own sake, *even* for mine own sake, will I do *it:* for how should *my name* be polluted? and I will not give my glory unto another.	c. To honor His name & keep it from being defamed d. To protect His glory

Thought 1. God is patient with the human race, delaying the day of His coming wrath against the ungodly and unrighteous of the earth. Although death is the just reward for sin, God has not yet executed His justice and judgment upon the world. The LORD is longsuffering, yearning for individuals and nations to repent, to turn back to Him and away from their sinful behavior. In addition, He is merciful, willing to forgive any who will truly repent. Listen to God's Holy Word:

"And his mercy *is* on them that fear him from generation to generation" (Lu.1:50).

"*What* if God, willing to show *his* wrath, and to make his power known, endured with much longsuffering the vessels of wrath fitted to destruction" (Ro.9:22).

"But God, who is rich in mercy, for his great love wherewith he loved us, Even when we were dead in sins, hath quickened us together with Christ, (by grace ye are saved;) And hath raised *us* up together, and made *us* sit together in heavenly *places* in Christ Jesus: That in the ages to come he might show the exceeding riches of his grace in *his* kindness toward us through Christ Jesus. For by grace are ye saved through faith; and that not of yourselves: *it is* the gift of God" (Ep.2:4-8).

"Not by works of righteousness which we have done, but according to his mercy he saved us, by the washing of regeneration, and renewing of the Holy Ghost; Which he shed on us abundantly through Jesus Christ our Saviour; That being justified by his grace, we should be made heirs according to the hope of eternal life" (Tit.3:5-7).

"Which sometime were disobedient, when once the longsuffering of God waited in the days of Noah, while the ark was a preparing, wherein few, that is, eight souls were saved by water" (1 Pe.3:20).

"The Lord is not slack concerning his promise, as some men count slackness; but is longsuffering to us-ward, not willing that any should perish, but that all should come to repentance" (2 Pe.3:9).

"But the mercy of the LORD *is* from everlasting to everlasting upon them that fear him, and his righteousness unto children's children" (Ps.103:17).

"For my name's sake will I defer mine anger, and for my praise will I refrain for thee, that I cut thee not off" (Is.48:9).

"*It is of* the LORD'S mercies that we are not consumed, because his compassions fail not. *They are* new every morning" (La.3:22-23).

"Nevertheless mine eye spared them from destroying them, neither did I make an end of them in the wilderness" (Eze.20:17).

"And rend your heart, and not your garments, and turn unto the LORD your God: for he *is* gracious and merciful, slow to anger, and of great kindness, and repenteth him of the evil" (Joel 2:13).

"Who *is* a God like unto thee, that pardoneth iniquity, and passeth by the transgression of the remnant of his heritage? he retaineth not his anger for ever, because he delighteth in mercy" (Mic.7:18).

3 **(48:12-22) Plans, of God, Redemption—Redemption, Illustrated, Israel's Deliverance—Israel, Deliverance from, Babylonian Captivity—Captivity, Deliverance from, Promise—Sovereignty, of God, Seen in Israel's Restoration**: God revealed His plan to redeem His people. He declared that He would work through human events, controlling them in order to save and free His people. As seen throughout these verses, the LORD Himself is the Redeemer (v.17), the LORD God of the universe who liberated His people from captivity and rescued them from their enemies. He is the Redeemer who led His people back to the promised land from the land of their captivity. What follows is an excellent study on redemption, showing exactly how God saves and rescues His people:

OUTLINE	SCRIPTURE	SCRIPTURE	OUTLINE

3. God's plan: He worked & controlled all events in order to redeem His people
a. The surety of redemption
  1) His person: "I am...," v.12
  2) His power: Created the universe
 	
b. The promise of redemption, deliverance from captivity
  1) His knowledge, not an idol, foretold this
  2) His power would raise up an agent (Cyrus) to destroy Babylon
  3) His Word guaranteed the prophecy: Cyrus would succeed against Babylon
 	
  4) His promise should be heeded: The LORD Himself had clearly predicted the destruction of Babylon & the redemption (deliverance) of His people from captivity
c. The reassurance of their redemption, deliverance
  1) He was their Redeemer,
	12 Hearken unto me, O Jacob and Israel, my called; I *am* he; I *am* the first, I also *am* the last.
	13 Mine hand also hath laid the foundation of the earth, and my right hand hath spanned the heavens: *when I* call unto them, they stand up together.
	14 All ye, assemble yourselves, and hear; which among them hath declared these *things?* The LORD hath loved him: he will do his pleasure on Babylon, and his arm *shall be on* the Chaldeans.
	15 I, *even* I, have spoken; yea, I have called him: I have brought him, and he shall make his way prosperous.
	16 Come ye near unto me, hear ye this; I have not spoken in secret from the beginning; from the time that it was, there *am* I: and now the Lord GOD, and his Spirit, hath sent me.
	17 Thus saith the LORD, thy Redeemer, the Holy One of
		Israel; I *am* the LORD thy God which teacheth thee to profit, which leadeth thee by the way *that* thou shouldest go.
		18 O that thou hadst hearkened to my commandments! then had thy peace been as a river, and thy righteousness as the waves of the sea:
		19 Thy seed also had been as the sand, and the offspring of thy bowels like the gravel thereof; his name should not have been cut off nor destroyed from before me.
		20 Go ye forth of Babylon, flee ye from the Chaldeans, with a voice of singing declare ye, tell this, utter it *even* to the end of the earth; say ye, The LORD hath redeemed his servant Jacob.
		21 And they thirsted not *when* he led them through the deserts: he caused the waters to flow out of the rock for them: he clave the rock also, and the waters gushed out.
		22 *There is* no peace, saith the LORD, unto the wicked.
			the Holy One
			  2) He was the LORD their God who taught & led them in the right way
			d. The blessings of redemption God desired for His people
			  1) Peace like a river
			  2) Righteousness that rolls on like the waves of the sea
			  3) Population growth
			
			  4) A name never cut off nor removed from God's presence
			e. The great imperative shout of redemption: Flee Babylon (the influence of the world & its unbelievers)
			  1) Proclaim redemption to the whole earth
			  • The LORD has redeemed His people
			  • The LORD will guide His people to the promised land & meet their needs—just as He did in the wilderness journey, Ex.17:1-7; Nu.20:11
			  2) Issue a warning: There is no peace for the wicked

a. God Himself is the surety of redemption, the assurance that His people will be rescued from their captivity (vv.12-13). Two facts about the LORD guarantee redemption. First, the LORD's person—who He is—assures the believer that God will redeem him, deliver him from all the bondages and enslaving powers of this earth. "I am He" means that the LORD alone is God. He is the "First and the Last," signifying that God is sovereign and eternal, spanning all of time. In the beginning of the universe He was there; and when this present universe ends, He will still exist as the eternal, sovereign LORD over all. Because He is the living and true God, His people can be confident about their redemption. The LORD will save them from the enslavements of this life and from the enemies who hold them captive, such as the Babylonians.

Second, God's power that created the universe assures redemption for the genuine believer (v.13). It was God's hand that laid the foundation of the earth on which people live. And it was His right hand that stretched out the heavens, filling the vast expanse with billions of stars and planets. When God spoke the Word to call all things into being, they appeared (40:21-22; 42:5; 44:24; 45:12, 18; 51:13; Ps.102:25). Since God has this infinite and matchless power, His people can rest assured that He has the power to redeem them. The LORD will deliver His people from their captivity and will walk with them through whatever hardships they endure.

b. God's plan was the promise of redemption, the promise that He would deliver His people from their captivity (vv.14-16). Note that the LORD summoned everyone to assemble together to hear what He had to say, for the message of redemption was of critical importance. If a person failed to hear and respond to the message, he would remain in captivity. He would never be set free and would be doomed to remain in Babylon (a symbol of the world with all its immorality, lawlessness, corruption, and idolatry). In giving the promise of redemption, the LORD made four statements that must be understood by the listener or reader:

⇒ It was His knowledge—not an idol—that had foretold the coming redemption of God's people (v.14).
⇒ God's power alone would raise up an agent (Cyrus) to execute justice and judgment against Babylon (v.14ᵇ). And it would be the LORD who stirred Cyrus, the king of Persia, to release God's people, allowing them to return to the promised land of Judah.
⇒ God's Word guaranteed this prophecy (v.15). He had spoken, and once He had spoken the event would come about. Cyrus would succeed in destroying Babylon because the LORD Himself would bless the mission of the Persian king.
⇒ God's promise must be heeded by all the hearers and readers of this prophecy (v.16). The LORD had never spoken in secret but, rather, openly and clearly. He was the One who had predicted the destruction of Babylon and the liberation of His people from captivity. Note the claim of Isaiah: it was the Sovereign LORD who had sent him to proclaim this prophecy. Moreover, the prophecy was being conveyed through him by the LORD's Spirit.

c. God gave yet another assurance that His people would be delivered from Babylonian captivity. Note that He attested to the believers' redemption because of who He, the LORD, was. First, He was their *Redeemer, the Holy One of Israel* (v.17). To be *holy* means to be set apart, distinct, different. In light of the LORD's perfection in being, purity, and righteousness, He would always do the right thing. He would fulfill all His promises and deliver His people from their Babylonian captivity.

Second, He is the LORD their God (v.17). And because He is their God, He would teach and lead them, showing them the road of righteousness, the road they should follow throughout life. They could rest assured of His presence and guidance.

d. God's plan of redemption included the most wonderful blessings in life (vv.18-19). Note the appeal of the LORD, the longing of His heart for His people to obey His commandments. If they obeyed Him, they would receive the blessings. But the opposite is also clearly implied: if they disobeyed, they would not receive the blessings of redemption. Four blessings in particular are mentioned:

1) Being redeemed and obeying God bring peace to the human soul (v.18). Notice the comforting comparison of peace to a deep river that flows steadily, strongly, consistently. God's peace is not shallow but, instead, reaches to the depth of the human soul, giving perfect assurance of God's presence and guidance. Neither is God's peace like a flash flood that only occurs every so often. God's peace is a continuous flow of assurance, fulfillment, satisfaction, and well-being.

2) Being redeemed and obeying God will bring righteousness to a person (v.18ᵇ). Note that the righteousness will faithfully roll on and on like waves of the sea. A person who obeys God becomes more and more conformed to the image of the LORD. He bears more of the fruit of the LORD: love, joy, peace, patience, gentleness, goodness, faithfulness, meekness, control (Ga.5:22-23). The obedient believer becomes more moral and just in his dealings with others, treating others as he himself wants to be treated (Lu.6:31). He becomes more compassionate and merciful, more caring and benevolent, reaching out to help those who are in need. Simply stated, the genuine, obedient believer becomes an ambassador for the Redeemer. He seeks to rescue people from the bondages of this world. Righteousness that is consistent and true is one of the great blessings of redemption.

3) Being redeemed and obeying God would bring population growth to Israel (v.19). Numerous children were promised to the Israelites if they would follow the LORD, obeying and keeping His holy commandments (10:22; Ge.13:16; 22:17; 32:12; Je.33:22). Likewise, when believers of any generation are truly obedient to the LORD, they will lead more and more people to the LORD, ever increasing the population of God's kingdom.

4) Being redeemed and obeying God assure the believer of an eternal name, a name that will never be cut off nor removed from God's presence (v.19ᵇ). As Christ said, "He that endureth to the end shall be saved" (Mt.10:22). The genuine believer will receive the wonderful gift of eternal life.

e. God proclaimed the great imperative of redemption, an imperative that is still in effect even today. He clearly said that the message of redemption was to be carried to the "end of the earth" (v.20). What was the imperative of redemption? Go forth from Babylon! Flee the Chaldeans, the Babylonians! Remember that Babylon and its people symbolize the world of unbelievers who live corrupt, wicked lives, who place their trust in false religion and the world of the occult. Because of their unrighteous lifestyles and their rebellion against God, the Babylonians were doomed to face the hand of God's eternal judgment. Thus the message of redemption was to be shouted out, proclaimed to the whole world. The LORD had redeemed His servant Jacob, the nation Israel, and rescued it from Babylonian captivity. Furthermore, the LORD would meet His people's every need while guiding them to the promised land. He would meet their needs just as He had in the wilderness wanderings when He led Israel from Egyptian bondage (Ex.17:1-7; Nu.20:11). Just as the LORD did not fail His people then, so He would not fail them now. He would fulfill His promise and deliver them. And He will fulfill the promise of redemption in the life of any person who truly trusts Him.

On the other hand, the LORD issued a strong warning: there is no peace for the wicked (v.22). There is a shout of joy from those who are redeemed. But there will be only restlessness, distress, and anguish of soul for the wicked of the earth. They will never have *peace with God* but will, rather, be alienated from Him. And they will never have the *peace of God* that fills the human heart with a sense of well-being, purpose, and fulfillment. The *peace of God* gives the believer perfect assurance...

- that his past sins and failures have been taken care of by Christ
- that his present welfare is being looked after by God Himself
- that his future will be taken care of by the presence and guidance of the LORD

The believer knows that he has eternal life, never again to be alienated or separated from the LORD. He knows that his salvation is due to the redemption found in Christ Jesus, our Lord and Savior.

"Blessed *be* the Lord God of Israel; for he hath visited and redeemed his people" (Lu.1:68).

"For all have sinned, and come short of the glory of God; Being justified freely by his grace through the redemption that is in Christ Jesus" (Ro.3:23-24).

"Christ hath redeemed us from the curse of the law, being made a curse for us: for it is written, Cursed *is* every one that hangeth on a tree" (Ga.3:13).

"In whom we have redemption through his blood, the forgiveness of sins, according to the riches of his grace" (Ep.1:7).

"And grieve not the holy Spirit of God, whereby ye are sealed unto the day of redemption" (Ep.4:30).

"In whom we have redemption through his blood, *even* the forgiveness of sins" (Col.1:14).

"Looking for that blessed hope, and the glorious appearing of the great God and our Saviour Jesus Christ; Who gave himself for us, that he might redeem us from all iniquity, and purify unto himself a peculiar people, zealous of good works" (Tit.2:13-14).

"Neither by the blood of goats and calves, but by his own blood he entered in once into the holy place, having obtained eternal redemption *for us*. For if the blood of bulls and of goats, and the ashes of an heifer sprinkling the unclean, sanctifieth to the purifying of the flesh: How much more shall the blood of Christ, who through the eternal Spirit offered himself without spot to God, purge your conscience from dead works to serve the living God?" (He.9:12-14).

"Forasmuch as ye know that ye were not redeemed with corruptible things, *as* silver and gold, from your vain conversation *received* by tradition from your fathers; But with the precious blood of Christ, as of a lamb without blemish and without spot" (1 Pe.1:18-19).

"And they sung a new song, saying, Thou art worthy to take the book, and to open the seals thereof: for thou wast slain, and hast redeemed us to God by thy blood out of every kindred, and tongue, and people, and nation" (Re.5:9).

"I have redeemed thee, I have called *thee* by thy name; thou *art* mine. When thou passest through the waters, I *will be* with thee; and through the rivers, they shall not overflow thee: when thou walkest through the fire, thou shalt not be burned; neither shall the flame kindle upon thee" (Is.43:1-2).

DIVISION VI

THE PROPHECIES OF THE GREAT DELIVERER:
THE SUFFERING SERVANT OF GOD, THE SAVIOR
OF THE WORLD, 49:1–59:21

(49:1–57:21) **DIVISION OVERVIEW**: Isaiah now turns to some of the most significant prophecies in the Old Testament, prophecies of incomparable magnitude. No doubt, they are among the most quoted. The subject is the Savior, the coming Messiah, who would come to earth as the humble Servant of God and give His life for the sins of the world.

The Savior's mission is to save; His call to every person in the world is to be saved. No matter how wicked or wretched a person is, Isaiah proclaims the hope of deliverance and of a glorious future to all who will repent and turn back to God. The great invitation of the Savior is not only to the Jew, but to every person on the face of the earth. All may come and drink freely of the living water offered by Him, for the price of their redemption has already been paid.

No greater messages have ever been preached than those of Isaiah's prophecies—the good news of the Suffering Servant of God dying for the sins of the world. The Messiah can save, and He will save. He will save all who truly trust in Him, repent of their sins, and follow in His steps of righteousness. This is the glorious message preached by Isaiah, the prophecies of the great Deliverer, the Suffering Servant of God, the Savior of the world.

THE PROPHECIES OF THE GREAT DELIVERER:
THE SUFFERING SERVANT OF GOD, THE SAVIOR
OF THE WORLD, 49:1–59:21

A. The Savior's Mission to the World: Being Eternally Called to Reach the Earth for God, 49:1–50:11

B. The Savior's Cry of Salvation: Listen! Wake Up! Depart! 51:1–52:12

C. The Savior's Suffering, His Atoning Death, 52:13–53:12

D. The Savior's Great Promises to Israel—Restoration: Repentant Backsliders Will Return to Him, 54:1-17

E. The Savior's Great Invitation to the World, 55:1–56:8

F. The Savior's Message to Leaders and Idolaters and to the Prideful and Greedy, 56:9–57:21

G. The Savior's Message to the Hypocrites: Guilty of Deceptive, Phony Behavior, 58:1-14

H. The Savior's Message to the Wicked: Guilty of Sin and Separated from God, 59:1-21

1. The Savior's ninefold mission to the unbelievers of the world: Reaching everyone for God

a. He was called to be God's Servant (v.4), His very special messenger to the world

b. He was called to proclaim the Word of God: To send it forth like an arrow, wounding (convicting) people for their own good

c. He was called to be God's Servant, the new Israel: To do the work Israel should have done

d. He was called to live a life of total trust in God
   1) He had meager results, Jn.1:11
   2) He cast himself & the results totally upon God

e. He was called to redeem & return Israel back to God
   1) God strengthened him for the task
   2) God greatly honored him by enlarging his mission

f. He was called to be a *light* to the Gentiles
   1) To be the Savior
   2) To bring salvation to all the earth

g. He was called to suffer, to be despised & rejected by people, 53:3-7; Mk.15:1-41; Jn.1:9-11

h. He was called to be exalted & honored by the rulers & citizens of the world: To be exalted as LORD by God Himself, 45:24; 52:15; Ph.2:10-11

i. He was called to be God's covenant for the people: To be God's pledge that God would fulfill His promises

CHAPTER 49

VI. THE PROPHECIES OF THE GREAT DELIVERER: THE SUFFERING SERVANT OF GOD, THE SAVIOR OF THE WORLD, 49:1–59:21

A. The Savior's Mission to the World: Being Eternally Called to Reach the World for God, 49:1–50:11

Listen, O isles, unto me; and hearken, ye people, from far; The LORD hath called me from the womb; from the bowels of my mother hath he made mention of my name.
2 And he hath made my mouth like a sharp sword; in the shadow of his hand hath he hid me, and made me a polished shaft; in his quiver hath he hid me;
3 And said unto me, Thou *art* my servant, O Israel, in whom I will be glorified.
4 Then I said, I have laboured in vain, I have spent my strength for nought, and in vain: *yet* surely my judgment *is* with the LORD, and my work with my God.
5 And now, saith the LORD that formed me from the womb *to be* his servant, to bring Jacob again to him, Though Israel be not gathered, yet shall I be glorious in the eyes of the LORD, and my God shall be my strength.
6 And he said, It is a light thing that thou shouldest be my servant to raise up the tribes of Jacob, and to restore the preserved of Israel: I will also give thee for a light to the Gentiles, that thou mayest be my salvation unto the end of the earth.
7 Thus saith the LORD, the Redeemer of Israel, *and* his Holy One, to him whom man despiseth, to him whom the nation abhorreth, to a servant of rulers, Kings shall see and arise, princes also shall worship, because of the LORD that is faithful, *and* the Holy One of Israel, and he shall choose thee.
8 Thus saith the LORD, In an acceptable time have I heard thee, and in a day of salvation have I helped thee: and I will preserve thee, and

give thee for a covenant of the people, to establish the earth, to cause to inherit the desolate heritages;
9 That thou mayest say to the prisoners, Go forth; to them that *are* in darkness, Show yourselves. They shall feed in the ways, and their pastures *shall be* in all high places.
10 They shall not hunger nor thirst; neither shall the heat nor sun smite them: for he that hath mercy on them shall lead them, even by the springs of water shall he guide them.
11 And I will make all my mountains a way, and my highways shall be exalted.
12 Behold, these shall come from far: and, lo, these from the north and from the west; and these from the land of Sinim.
13 Sing, O heavens; and be joyful, O earth; and break forth into singing, O mountains: for the LORD hath comforted his people, and will have mercy upon his afflicted.
14 But Zion said, The LORD hath forsaken me, and my Lord hath forgotten me.
15 Can a woman forget her sucking child, that she should not have compassion on the son of her womb? yea, they may forget, yet will I not forget thee.
16 Behold, I have graven thee upon the palms of *my* hands; thy walls *are* continually before me.
17 Thy children shall make haste; thy destroyers and they that made thee waste shall go forth of thee.
18 Lift up thine eyes round about, and behold: all these gather themselves together, *and* come to thee. As I live, saith the LORD, thou shalt surely clothe thee with them all, as with an ornament, and bind them *on thee,* as a bride *doeth.*
19 For thy waste and thy desolate places, and the land of thy destruction, shall even now be too narrow by reason of the inhabitants, and they that swallowed thee up shall be far away.
20 The children which thou shalt have, after thou hast lost the other, shall say again in

1) The promise to restore the land (earth) & to assign God's inheritance to His people
2) The promise to set the people free from captivity & darkness
3) The promise to guide & protect His people, Mt.6:33

4) The promise to remove all obstacles & to guide His people back to the promised land: Gather them from the north, west, & south, all the way from the region of Sinim (Aswan or Egypt)
5) The promise to comfort His people & to have mercy on them in their afflictions

2. The Savior's threefold mission to the discouraged: Reaching all who feel forsaken, forgotten

a. His mission of revealing God's love: Compared to a loving mother
   1) God would not forget His people
      • They were engraved on His hands
      • They & Jerusalem's walls were ever before Him
   2) God would cause His people's descendants to return & their enemies to flee
      • The return to the promised land was guaranteed by the LORD's oath
      • The returning people would be a spectacular sight: Each person would be like a bridal ornament adding sparkle to the nation
      • The returning people would overflow the land: The land would be too small for the influx of returnees, & more space would be needed for them to live in

- The number of returnees would be surprising, totally unexpected: Because so many had been lost due to their captivity & exile

3) God would arouse the nations to release & return His people to the promised land
  - The nations would even help transport the returning captives, 14:2; 43:6; 60:9
  - The leaders would subject themselves to Zion
4) God would prove two great truths
  - That He alone is the LORD
  - That those who hope in Him will not be ashamed
b. His mission of revealing God's power to deliver His people: Compared to the strength of a mighty warrior
1) He would free, save His people from their captors

2) He would cause the oppressors to turn against one another
3) He would prove the most basic truths in all the universe: That He is…
  - The LORD
  - Your Savior & Redeemer
  - The Mighty One of Jacob (Israel)

c. His mission of redeeming His people by paying the ransom: Compared to the love of a forgiving husband
1) He had not divorced or sold them to creditors
  - They had left him & been sold because of their sin

thine ears, The place *is* too strait for me: give place to me that I may dwell.
21 Then shalt thou say in thine heart, Who hath begotten me these, seeing I have lost my children, and am desolate, a captive, and removing to and fro? and who hath brought up these? Behold, I was left alone; these, where *had* they *been?*
22 Thus saith the Lord GOD, Behold, I will lift up mine hand to the Gentiles, and set up my standard to the people: and they shall bring thy sons in *their* arms, and thy daughters shall be carried upon *their* shoulders.
23 And kings shall be thy nursing fathers, and their queens thy nursing mothers: they shall bow down to thee with *their* face toward the earth, and lick up the dust of thy feet; and thou shalt know that I *am* the LORD: for they shall not be ashamed that wait for me.
24 Shall the prey be taken from the mighty, or the lawful captive delivered?
25 But thus saith the LORD, Even the captives of the mighty shall be taken away, and the prey of the terrible shall be delivered: for I will contend with him that contendeth with thee, and I will save thy children.
26 And I will feed them that oppress thee with their own flesh; and they shall be drunken with their own blood, as with sweet wine: and all flesh shall know that I the LORD *am* thy Saviour and thy Redeemer, the mighty One of Jacob.

CHAPTER 50

Thus saith the LORD, Where *is* the bill of your mother's divorcement, whom I have put away? or which of my creditors *is it* to whom I have sold you? Behold, for your iniquities have ye sold yourselves, and for your transgressions is your mother put away.

2 Wherefore, when I came, *was there* no man? when I called, *was there* none to answer? Is my hand shortened at all, that it cannot redeem? or have I no power to deliver? behold, at my rebuke I dry up the sea, I make the rivers a wilderness: their fish stinketh, because *there is* no water, and dieth for thirst.
3 I clothe the heavens with blackness, and I make sackcloth their covering.
4 The Lord GOD hath given me the tongue of the learned, that I should know how to speak a word in season to *him that is* weary: he wakeneth morning by morning, he wakeneth mine ear to hear as the learned.
5 The Lord GOD hath opened mine ear, and I was not rebellious, neither turned away back.
6 I gave my back to the smiters, and my cheeks to them that plucked off the hair: I hid not my face from shame and spitting.
7 For the Lord GOD will help me; therefore shall I not be confounded: therefore have I set my face like a flint, and I know that I shall not be ashamed.
8 *He is* near that justifieth me; who will contend with me? let us stand together: who *is* mine adversary? let him come near to me.
9 Behold, the Lord GOD will help me; who *is* he *that* shall condemn me? lo, they all shall wax old as a garment; the moth shall eat them up.
10 Who *is* among you that feareth the LORD, that obeyeth the voice of his servant, that walketh *in* darkness, and hath no light? let him trust in the name of the LORD, and stay upon his God.
11 Behold, all ye that kindle a fire, that compass *yourselves* about with sparks: walk in the light of your fire, and in the sparks *that* ye have kindled. This shall ye have of mine hand; ye shall lie down in sorrow.

- They had not responded when he continually came & appealed to them to return to Him
2) He always had the power to redeem (deliver) them
  - Just as He dried up the Red Sea (Ex.14:1-31) & the Jordan River (Js.3:14-17)

  - Just as He darkened the sky in the plagues of Egypt (Ex.20:21)

3. **The Savior's twofold mission to the weary: Reaching out to all who are in bondage to sin & death**
a. His mission to preach to the weary
1) He was taught by God

2) He was not rebellious, turning His ear away from God's instructions

b. His mission to suffer for the weary
1) His sufferings
  - Was beaten, scourged
  - Was mocked & spat upon
2) His obedience & steadfastness: Set His face like a stone to suffer death
  - Was helped by God
  - Was not shamed

3) His vindication by God: No one dared to charge or accuse Him
  - Because God justified Him: Knew that He was just, righteous, sinless
  - Because God helped Him
  - Because all accusers would be like garments that fell apart due to age or being eaten by moths

4. **The Savior's specific mission to the whole human race: To warn each person to fear the LORD & obey the Savior**
a. The person who walks in darkness: Must trust the LORD & persevere in Him

b. The person who is self-sufficient & self-reliant (who walks by his own light): Will lie down in awful torment

DIVISION VI

THE PROPHECIES OF THE GREAT DELIVERER: THE SUFFERING SERVANT OF GOD, THE SAVIOR OF THE WORLD, 49:1–59:21

A. The Savior's Mission to the World: Being Eternally Called to Reach the World for God, 49:1–50:11

(49:1–50:11) **Introduction**: God loves the world. He loves every single person in the world, including murderers, abusers, oppressors, liars, thieves, wife-beaters, naggers, complainers, agnostics, and atheists. Even when people curse, reject, and defy Him, God loves them. No matter how people treat God, He still loves them. He wants to save all people from the terrifying judgment that is coming against all their ungodliness and unrighteousness. Because of His love for the world, God sent His Son, the Lord Jesus Christ, to deliver the human race from the coming judgment.

This present Scripture proclaims the Savior's mission to the world. God sent Christ into the world to save and help people: the unbelievers; the discouraged who feel deserted, alienated, forsaken, forgotten; and the weary and heavily burdened; and the whole human race. This is, *The Savior's Mission to the World: Being Eternally Called to Reach the World for God*, 49:1–50:11.

1. The Savior's ninefold mission to the unbelievers of the world: reaching everyone for God (49:1-13).
2. The Savior's threefold mission to the discouraged: reaching all who feel forsaken, forgotten (49:14–50:3).
3. The Savior's twofold mission to the weary: reaching out to all who are in bondage to sin and death (50:4-9).
4. The Savior's specific mission to the whole human race: to warn each person to fear the LORD and obey the Savior (50:10-11).

1 (49:1-13) **Mission, of Christ, Ninefold—Christ, Mission of, Ninefold—Servant of God, Prophecy Concerning, His Mission—Christ, Prophecies Concerning, Despised and Rejected; Exaltation of—Gentiles, Prophecies Concerning, Salvation—Israel, Prophecies Concerning, Salvation—Christ, Mission of, Meager Results—Christ, Names – Titles, New *Israel*—New Covenant, Established, Christ—Israel, the New, Established by—Word of God, Proclamation of, Mission of Christ**: the Savior was given a very special, ninefold mission when He came into the world. Note that the Savior Himself is speaking, inviting all the people from the islands and distant nations to give close attention. What He has to say is of utmost importance. He has a very special message, good tidings of great joy for the world.

OUTLINE	SCRIPTURE	SCRIPTURE	OUTLINE

1. The Savior's ninefold mission to the unbelievers of the world: Reaching everyone for God
a. He was called to be God's Servant (v.4), His very special messenger to the world
b. He was called to proclaim the Word of God: To send it forth like an arrow, wounding (convicting) people for their own good
 	
c. He was called to be God's Servant, the new Israel: To do the work Israel should have done
d. He was called to live a life of total trust in God
  1) He had meager results, Jn.1:11
  2) He cast himself & the results totally upon God
e. He was called to redeem & return Israel back to God
  1) God strengthened him for the task
  2) God greatly honored him by enlarging his mission
 	
f. He was called to be a *light* to the Gentiles
	Listen, O isles, unto me; and hearken, ye people, from far; The LORD hath called me from the womb; from the bowels of my mother hath he made mention of my name.
	2 And he hath made my mouth like a sharp sword; in the shadow of his hand hath he hid me, and made me a polished shaft; in his quiver hath he hid me;
	3 And said unto me, Thou *art* my servant, O Israel, in whom I will be glorified.
	4 Then I said, I have laboured in vain, I have spent my strength for nought, and in vain: *yet* surely my judgment *is* with the LORD, and my work with my God.
	5 And now, saith the LORD that formed me from the womb *to be* his servant, to bring Jacob again to him, Though Israel be not gathered, yet shall I be glorious in the eyes of the LORD, and my God shall be my strength.
	6 And he said, It is a light thing that thou shouldest be
		my servant to raise up the tribes of Jacob, and to restore the preserved of Israel: I will also give thee for a light to the Gentiles, that thou mayest be my salvation unto the end of the earth.
		7 Thus saith the LORD, the Redeemer of Israel, *and* his Holy One, to him whom man despiseth, to him whom the nation abhorreth, to a servant of rulers, Kings shall see and arise, princes also shall worship, because of the LORD that is faithful, *and* the Holy One of Israel, and he shall choose thee.
		8 Thus saith the LORD, In an acceptable time have I heard thee, and in a day of salvation have I helped thee: and I will preserve thee, and give thee for a covenant of the people, to establish the earth, to cause to inherit the desolate heritages;
		9 That thou mayest say to the prisoners, Go forth; to them that *are* in darkness, Show yourselves. They shall feed in the ways, and their
			1) To be the Savior
			2) To bring salvation to all the earth
			
			g. He was called to suffer, to be despised & rejected by people, 53:3-7; Mk.15:1-41; Jn.1:9-11
			h. He was called to be exalted & honored by the rulers & citizens of the world: To be exalted as LORD by God Himself, 45:24; 52:15; Ph.2:10-11
			
			i. He was called to be God's covenant for the people: To be God's pledge that God would fulfill His promises
			  1) The promise to restore the land (earth) & to assign God's inheritance to His people
			  2) The promise to set the people free from captivity & darkness
			  3) The promise to guide & protect His people, Mt.6:33

OUTLINE	SCRIPTURE	SCRIPTURE	OUTLINE
4) The promise to remove all obstacles & to guide His people back to the	pastures *shall be* in all high places. 10 They shall not hunger nor thirst; neither shall the heat nor sun smite them: for he that hath mercy on them shall lead them, even by the springs of water shall he guide them. 11 And I will make all my mountains a way, and my highways shall be exalted.	12 Behold, these shall come from far: and, lo, these from the north and from the west; and these from the land of Sinim. 13 Sing, O heavens; and be joyful, O earth; and break forth into singing, O mountains: for the LORD hath comforted his people, and will have mercy upon his afflicted.	promised land: Gather them from the north, west, & south, all the way from the region of Sinim (Aswan or Egypt) 5) The promise to comfort His people & to have mercy on them in their afflictions

a. The Savior was called to do God's will. In fact, God appointed Him for His mission before He was born. He even called Him by Name before His birth. These two facts suggest that the Savior has existed eternally and that a very personal relationship existed between Him and God before His birth. From the beginning, before Creation itself, the Savior was called to be God's very special messenger to the world. Before He was born, an angel appeared and announced that He was to be called Jesus, "for He shall save His people from their sins" (Mt.1:21). Later as an adult, Jesus Christ proclaimed: "Lo, I come...to do thy will, O God" (He.10:7).

"I am come that they might have life, and that they might have *it* more abundantly" (Jn.10:10).

b. The Savior was called to proclaim the Word of God (v.2). His mouth was to be like a sharp sword that would divide a person's soul or fleshly desires from his spirit and righteous behavior (He.4:12). While He walked upon the earth, the Savior was to use "the Sword of the Spirit, which is the Word of God" (Ep.6:17). His Word would go forth like an arrow, wounding consciences and convicting people of sin, righteousness, and judgment (Jn.16:8-11). The Savior's Word would be like a fire that melts people's hearts before God and like a hammer that breaks their rock-hard hearts, crushing them into soft powder before God. Note this significant fact: while the Savior proclaimed the Word of God, God protected Him in the shadow of His hand.

> **"And all bare him witness, and wondered at the gracious words which proceeded out of his mouth. And they said, Is not this Joseph's son?" (Lu.4:22).**
> **"And they were astonished at his doctrine: for his word was with power" (Lu.4:32).**
> **"It is the spirit that quickeneth; the flesh profiteth nothing: the words that I speak unto you, *they* are spirit, and *they* are life" (Jn.6:63).**
> **"Then Simon Peter answered him, Lord, to whom shall we go? thou hast the words of eternal life" (Jn.6:68).**
> **"The officers answered, Never man spake like this man" (Jn.7:46).**
> **"He that rejecteth me, and receiveth not my words, hath one that judgeth him: the word that I have spoken, the same shall judge him in the last day" (Jn.12:48).**
> **"He that loveth me not keepeth not my sayings: and the word which ye hear is not mine, but the Father's which sent me" (Jn.14:24).**

c. The Savior was called to be God's Servant, the new *Israel* on earth. The work that Israel as a nation had failed to do, the Savior would do. Remember that God had chosen the Israelites for three primary purposes:
⇒ To be the people who would bear strong testimony that He alone is the LORD (Jehovah, Yahweh), the only living and true God.
⇒ To be the people through whom He would send His Word, the Holy Word of God, to the world.
⇒ To be the people through whom He would send the Messiah, the Savior, to the world.

But the Israelites failed in their God-given task. They failed to be God's witnesses to the unbelievers of the world. They failed to keep God's holy commandments. They chose to live immoral and unrighteous lives, striving to acquire the power, riches, and pleasures of this world. And most tragic, when God sent Christ into the world, they rejected Him (Jn.1:11). Despite Israel's failure, God still loved the world and was determined to save the world (Jn.3:16). Therefore, He appointed His Son to be the new Israel, to be His very special witness of God's love and salvation. God also appointed Christ to be the Savior of the world and to proclaim His Holy Word to the ends of the earth. The Savior, the Lord Jesus Christ, fulfilled every purpose for which God had appointed the old Israel. Christ Himself became God's servant, the new Israel.

Thought 1. Believers often seek the power, riches, and pleasures of this world; consequently, they fail to carry out the mission for which God has called them. Christ came to be God's Servant, and He was faithful in His calling. As the Servant of God, He ministered to the people of the world, fulfilling His mission. God has given us the mission of being His witnesses to a lost and dying world, a world that reels in desperate need. Yet far too many of us became wrapped up in the pleasures and possessions of this world instead of committing ourselves to the task of reaching the lost and meeting the needs of the world. We must follow the example of Christ.

"Even as the Son of man came not to be ministered unto, but to minister, and to give his life a ransom for many" (Mt.20:28).

"For whether *is* greater, he that sitteth at meat, or he that serveth? *is* not he that sitteth at meat? but I am among you as he that serveth" (Lu.22:27).

"He riseth from supper, and laid aside his garments; and took a towel, and girded himself. After that he poureth water into a bason, and began to wash the disciples' feet, and to wipe *them* with the towel wherewith he was girded" (Jn.13:4-5).

"Who, being in the form of God, thought it not robbery to be equal with God: But made himself of no reputation, and took upon him the form of a servant, and was made in the likeness of men: And being found in fashion as a man, he humbled himself, and became obedient unto death, even the death of the cross" (Ph.2:6-8).

d. The Savior was called to live a life of total trust in God (v.4). From a human perspective, the Savior had meager, disappointing results on earth (Jn.1:11). Christ had few followers who really trusted in Him. From all appearances, His mission seemed a failure, especially when He was crucified upon the cross and His apostles scattered for their lives. But note what the Savior said centuries before He came to earth: He would cast Himself and the results totally upon God. The results were in God's hand, and the Savior left them and the reward due Him entirely up to God. Although He had labored faithfully to the point of utter exhaustion and the giving of His life, He trusted that God would make His mission a success.

"And when the tempter came to him, he said, If thou be the Son of God, command that these stones be made bread. But he answered and said, It is written, Man shall not live by bread alone, but by every word that proceedeth out of the mouth of God" (Mt.4:3-4).

"Then saith Jesus unto him, Get thee hence, Satan: for it is written, Thou shalt worship the Lord thy God, and him only shalt thou serve. Then the devil leaveth him, and, behold, angels came and ministered unto him" (Mt.4:10-11).

"Jesus answered and said unto him, If a man love me, he will keep my words: and my Father will love him, and we will come unto him, and make our abode with him" (Jn.14:23).

"If ye keep my commandments, ye shall abide in my love; even as I have kept my Father's commandments, and abide in his love" (Jn.15:10).

"For as by one man's disobedience many were made sinners, so by the obedience of one shall many be made righteous" (Ro.5:19).

"Then said he, Lo, I come to do thy will, O God. He taketh away the first, that he may establish the second" (He.10:9).

e. The Savior was called to redeem and return Israel to God (v.5). He was sent "to the lost sheep of the house of Israel" (Mt.15:24). He was sent to lead them to God so they could be delivered from the bondages of sin and death, live righteous lives, and be assured of living eternally with God (Jn.3:16-17). Although the Jews rejected the Lord Jesus, God honored and strengthened Him for His task of bringing Israel back to God, and the Savior was successful. Remember that the very first followers of Christ were Jewish believers and that the first church was also made up of Jewish believers. Moreover, when the LORD returns to earth, a large number of Jews will know that Jesus Christ is the Savior. They will trust Him and become acceptable to God. God will receive them into His eternal kingdom.

But note what the LORD, the Father of the Savior, says: reaching Israel alone is too small a task for Christ, for He is God's Servant. God's Servant deserves a far greater task. Therefore, God enlarged His mission on earth, that of reaching the Gentiles (point 6).

f. The Savior was called to be a *light* to the Gentiles. In other words, Christ was to be the Savior of the entire world and to bring salvation to every human being. Note that two points are being stressed:

⇒ The Person sent by God is Himself the Savior. If people wish to be saved, they must approach God through the person of Jesus Christ. He is the Mediator, the High Priest, who brings people to God. As He said, "I am the way, the truth, and the life: no man comes to the Father but by Me" (Jn.14:6).

⇒ The Person sent by God was given the awesome task of taking God's salvation to the ends of the earth. Because of its overwhelming importance, God's message of salvation must be taken to every human being. And the task of proclaiming the message must not fail.

"As it is written in the book of the words of Esaias the prophet, saying, The voice of one crying in the wilderness, Prepare ye the way of the Lord, make his paths straight. Every valley shall be filled, and every mountain and hill shall be brought low; and the crooked shall be made straight, and the rough ways *shall be* made smooth; And all flesh shall see the salvation of God" (Lu.3:4-6).

"Then spake Jesus again unto them, saying, I am the light of the world: he that followeth me shall not walk in darkness, but shall have the light of life" (Jn.8:12).

"And Jesus said, For judgment I am come into this world, that they which see not might see; and that they which see might be made blind. And *some* of the Pharisees which were with him heard these words, and said unto him, Are we blind also? Jesus said unto them, If ye were blind, ye should have no sin: but now ye say, We see; therefore your sin remaineth" (Jn.9:39-41).

"And it shall come to pass, *that* whosoever shall call on the name of the Lord shall be saved" (Ac.2:21).

"That if thou shalt confess with thy mouth the Lord Jesus, and shalt believe in thine heart that God hath raised him from the dead, thou shalt be saved. For with the heart man believeth unto righteousness; and with the mouth confession is made unto salvation. For the scripture saith,

Whosoever believeth on him shall not be ashamed. For there is no difference between the Jew and the Greek: for the same Lord over all is rich unto all that call upon him. For whosoever shall call upon the name of the Lord shall be saved" (Ro.10:9-13).

"Who hath delivered us from the power of darkness, and hath translated *us* into the kingdom of his dear Son" (Col.1:13).

"Who will have all men to be saved, and to come unto the knowledge of the truth" (1 Ti.2:4).

"For the grace of God that bringeth salvation hath appeared to all men, Teaching us that, denying ungodliness and worldly lusts, we should live soberly, righteously, and godly, in this present world" (Tit.2:11-12).

g. The Savior was called to suffer, to be despised and rejected by people (53:3-7; Mk.15:1-41; Jn.1:10-11). The Savior would become the *suffering Servant* of God. He would be subjected to humiliation at the hands of people, be ridiculed and mocked, assaulted and abused, despised and rejected, scourged and crucified.

Notice who is revealing that the Savior will be the suffering Servant of God. It is God Himself, the Redeemer, the Holy One of Israel who reveals this fact. The Savior's sufferings have a purpose—to redeem or pay the ransom to set people free from sin, death, and the coming judgment. As the Holy One of Israel, the LORD always acts on the basis of His holiness, always does what is righteous and just. And the right thing to do is to fulfill His promises, in particular the promise to send the Savior into the world to provide redemption. Through the suffering of the Savior, the LORD does the righteous thing for the human race: He provides redemption for all who trust, obey, and follow the Lord Jesus Christ.

"And they that passed by railed on him, wagging their heads, and saying, Ah, thou that destroyest the temple, and buildest *it* in three days, Save thyself, and come down from the cross" (Mk.15:29-30).

"And the Pharisees also, who were covetous, heard all these things: and they derided him" (Lu.16:14).

"And many of them said, He hath a devil, and is mad; why hear ye him?" (Jn.10:20).

"And being found in fashion as a man, he humbled himself, and [He] became obedient unto death, even the death of the cross" (Ph.2:8).

"He is despised and rejected of men; a man of sorrows, and acquainted with grief: and we hid as it were *our* faces from him; he was despised, and we esteemed him not. Surely he hath borne our griefs, and carried our sorrows: yet we did esteem him stricken, smitten of God, and afflicted. But he *was* wounded for our transgressions, *he was* bruised for our iniquities: the chastisement of our peace *was* upon him; and with his stripes we are healed. All we like sheep have gone astray; we have turned every one to his own way; and the LORD hath laid on him the iniquity of us all. He was oppressed, and he was afflicted, yet he opened not his mouth: he is brought as a lamb to the slaughter, and as a sheep before her shearers is dumb, so he openeth not his mouth" (Is.53:3-7).

h. The Savior was called to be honored by the rulers and citizens of the world (v.7). While on earth, the Savior was abused and crucified. However, after His sufferings, He was raised from the dead and exalted as Lord by the power of God Himself. When the Savior returns to set up God's kingdom on earth, all the citizens of the world will honor Him. All kings, princes, and rulers will rise up from their thrones in utter shock and amazement that Jesus Christ is truly Lord. Prostrating themselves before Him, they will willingly surrender the authority of all the nations of the earth, and they will honor Christ as Lord of the universe (45:24; 52:15; Ph.2:10-11).

"So then after the Lord had spoken unto them, he was received up into heaven, and sat on the right hand of God" (Mk.16:19).

"Hereafter shall the Son of man sit on the right hand of the power of God" (Lu.22:69).

"This Jesus hath God raised up, whereof we all are witnesses. Therefore being by the right hand of God exalted, and having received of the Father the promise of the Holy Ghost, he hath shed forth this, which ye now see and hear. For David is not ascended into the heavens: but he saith himself, The LORD said unto my Lord, Sit thou on my right hand, Until I make thy foes thy footstool. Therefore let all the house of Israel know assuredly, that God hath made that same Jesus, whom ye have crucified, both Lord and Christ" (Ac.2:32-36).

"The God of our fathers raised up Jesus, whom ye slew and hanged on a tree. Him hath God exalted with his right hand *to be* a Prince and a Saviour, for to give repentance to Israel, and forgiveness of sins" (Ac.5:30-31).

"Which he wrought in Christ, when he raised him from the dead, and set *him* at his own right hand in the heavenly *places*" (Ep.1:20).

"Wherefore God also hath highly exalted him, and given him a name which is above every name: That at the name of Jesus every knee should bow, of *things* in heaven, and *things* in earth, and *things* under the earth; And *that* every tongue should confess that Jesus Christ *is* Lord, to the glory of God the Father" (Ph.2:9-11).

"And I beheld, and I heard the voice of many angels round about the throne and the beasts and the elders: and the number of them was ten thousand times ten thousand, and thousands of thousands; Saying with a loud voice, Worthy is the Lamb that was slain to receive power, and riches, and wisdom, and strength, and honour, and glory, and blessing" (Re.5:11-12).

i. The Savior was called to be God's covenant for the people (vv.8-13). Note that it is the person of Christ Himself that is the covenant. Through Him, God pledges to fulfill all His promises. The Savior is to be the *Mediator* through whom God brings to the world the promise of salvation and all the other promises He has made down through the ages. The promises given to Israel, as well as to the Gentiles, are to be fulfilled through the Savior. Note that God promised to answer the prayers of his suffering Servant and to help Him in the day of salvation. Throughout His life on earth, the Savior suffered agonizing pain due to the continual hostility of people, in particular the religionists. Bearing the weight of so much opposition broke His heart, causing Him to go before the LORD with loud cries and tears, begging for help and strength to complete His mission. This is exactly what Scripture says:

> **"Who in the days of his flesh, when he had offered up prayers and supplications with strong crying and tears unto him that was able to save him from death, and was heard in that he feared; Though he were a Son, yet learned he obedience by the things which he suffered; And being made perfect, he became the author of eternal salvation unto all them that obey him" (He.5:7-9).**

God heard the strong cries and saw the tears of His suffering Servant. Filled with a heart of love for His Son (Jn.3:16), God answered the Savior's prayers. He met His need, whatever the need of the hour was. God protected the Savior in order to guarantee that He would become the *covenant* for the people, the *pledge* that God would fulfill His promises to His people. Five promises in particular are mentioned:

1) Through the Savior, God promises to restore the land and to assign the inheritance promised to the people (v.8ᵇ). This is a reference to the inheritance God gave each tribe when the land was divided under the leadership of Joshua (see outline and notes—Jos.14:1-15 for more discussion). When Christ returns to earth to set up God's kingdom, the true believers among the Israelites will receive their promised inheritances. But so will all Gentile believers. In that day, God will reward every believer with the inheritance promised in His Holy Word.

> **"And now, brethren, I commend you to God, and to the word of his grace, which is able to build you up, and to give you an inheritance among all them which are sanctified" (Ac.20:32).**
> **"Giving thanks unto the Father, which hath made us meet to be partakers of the inheritance of the saints in light" (Col.1:12).**
> **"Blessed *be* the God and Father of our Lord Jesus Christ, which according to his abundant mercy hath begotten us again unto a lively hope by the resurrection of Jesus Christ from the dead, To an inheritance incorruptible, and undefiled, and that fadeth not away, reserved in heaven for you, Who are kept by the power of God through faith unto salvation ready to be revealed in the last time" (1 Pe.1:3-5).**

2) Through the Savior, God promises to set the people free from captivity and darkness (v.9ᵃ). Israel's deliverance from the captivity in Babylon is a clear picture of the Savior delivering God's people from the bondages of sin, death, and the coming judgment. The Savior *redeems* and *sets free* all those who put their trust in Him.

> **"For all have sinned, and come short of the glory of God; Being justified freely by his grace through the redemption that is in Christ Jesus" (Ro.3:23-24).**
> **"Looking for that blessed hope, and the glorious appearing of the great God and our Saviour Jesus Christ; Who gave himself for us, that he might redeem us from all iniquity, and purify unto himself a peculiar people, zealous of good works" (Tit.2:13-14).**
> **"Neither by the blood of goats and calves, but by his own blood he entered in once into the holy place, having obtained eternal redemption *for us*. For if the blood of bulls and of goats, and the ashes of an heifer sprinkling the unclean, sanctifieth to the purifying of the flesh: How much more shall the blood of Christ, who through the eternal Spirit offered himself without spot to God, purge your conscience from dead works to serve the living God?" (He.9:12-14).**
> **"Forasmuch as ye know that ye were not redeemed with corruptible things, *as* silver and gold, from your vain conversation *received* by tradition from your fathers; But with the precious blood of Christ, as of a lamb without blemish and without spot" (1 Pe.1:18-19).**

3) Through the Savior, God promises to guide His people and to provide for and protect them (vv.9ᵇ-10). God has always given this wonderful promise to His people, to all who truly believe and follow Him. Note that no matter where people go, the LORD promises to meet their needs along the way. Even the barren hills will provide food for true believers. In compassion, the LORD promises to guide and lead His people, meeting whatever needs they have. Whether Jews or Gentiles, if people truly trust the LORD, their needs will be met.

> **"But seek ye first the kingdom of God, and his righteousness; and all these things shall be added unto you" (Mt.6:33).**
> **"The LORD *is* my strength and my shield; my heart trusted in him, and I am helped: therefore my heart greatly rejoiceth; and with my song will I praise him" (Ps.28:7).**
> **"*Oh* how great *is* thy goodness, which thou hast laid up for them that fear thee; *which* thou hast wrought for them that trust in thee before the sons of men!" (Ps.31:19).**
> **"For thou hast been a strength to the poor, a strength to the needy in his distress, a refuge from the storm, a shadow from the heat, when the blast of the terrible ones *is* as a storm *against* the wall" (Is.25:4).**
> **"And thine ears shall hear a word behind thee, saying, This *is* the way, walk ye in it, when ye turn to the right hand, and when ye turn to the left" (Is.30:21).**
> **"Fear thou not; for I *am* with thee: be not dismayed; for I *am* thy God: I will strengthen thee; yea, I will help thee; yea, I will uphold thee with the right hand of my righteousness" (Is.41:10).**

"Fear not: for I have redeemed thee, I have called *thee* by thy name; thou *art* mine. When thou passest through the waters, I *will be* with thee; and through the rivers, they shall not overflow thee: when thou walkest through the fire, thou shalt not be burned; neither shall the flame kindle upon thee" (Is.43:1-2).

4) Through the Savior, God removes all obstacles and guides His people back to the promised land (vv.11-12). This is a wonderful picture of people coming to the Savior from all parts of the earth. No barrier can keep God from bringing believers to the Savior. In the last days of human history, a remnant of the Jews will return to the promised land to worship the Savior, the Lord Jesus Christ, who will establish the seat of His government in Jerusalem.

"And when the Gentiles heard this, they were glad, and glorified the word of the Lord: and as many as were ordained to eternal life believed" (Ac.13:48).

"And when there had been much disputing, Peter rose up, and said unto them, Men *and* brethren, ye know how that a good while ago God made choice among us, that the Gentiles by my mouth should hear the word of the gospel, and believe" (Ac.15:7).

"Be it known therefore unto you, that the salvation of God is sent unto the Gentiles, and *that* they will hear it" (Ac.28:28).

"For the kingdom *is* the LORD'S: and he *is* the governor among the nations" (Ps.22:28).

"Look unto me, and be ye saved, all the ends of the earth: for I *am* God, and *there is* none else" (Is.45:22).

5) Through the Savior, God promises to comfort His people and to have mercy on them in their affliction (v.13).

"Blessed *be* God, even the Father of our Lord Jesus Christ, the Father of mercies, and the God of all comfort; Who comforteth us in all our tribulation, that we may be able to comfort them which are in any trouble, by the comfort wherewith we ourselves are comforted of God" (2 Co.1:3-4).

"And in that day thou shalt say, O LORD, I will praise thee: though thou wast angry with me, thine anger is turned away, and thou comfortedst me" (Is.12:1).

"For the LORD shall comfort Zion: he will comfort all her waste places; and he will make her wilderness like Eden, and her desert like the garden of the LORD; joy and gladness shall be found therein, thanksgiving, and the voice of melody" (Is.51:3).

"But the mercy of the LORD *is* from everlasting to everlasting upon them that fear him, and his righteousness unto children's children" (Ps.103:17).

"Who *is* a God like unto thee, that pardoneth iniquity, and passeth by the transgression of the remnant of his heritage? he retaineth not his anger for ever, because he delighteth *in* mercy" (Mic.7:18).

2 (49:14-26) **Christ, Mission of, to the Discouraged—Discouraged, Answer - Solution to, Christ—Weariness, Answer - Solution to, Christ—Forsaken, Answer - Solution to, Christ—Forgotten, Answer - Solution to, Christ—Alienation, Answer - Solution to, Christ—Israel, Failure - Errors of, Discouragement—Israel, Love for, by God—Restoration, of Israel, Promised—Assurance, of God's Love, Illustrated—Discouraged, Duty to, Help and Assure:** the Savior was given a specific threefold mission to help the discouraged. In these verses, the prophet Isaiah is picturing a conversation between the LORD and Zion. Zion represents the Jews who were suffering through the Babylonian captivity and those who had been left behind in the devastated land of Judah. Due to the hardship of the captivity and the devastation of their land, the people had become extremely discouraged. They knew an important fact from history: once a nation was conquered and its people deported, they never returned to their homeland. After decades of captivity, the Jews began to feel abandoned by God. They felt as though God had forgotten and forsaken them. Even when they prayed, God seemed far, far away, unconcerned with their suffering. It was as if the LORD did not know about their hardships, for their prayers seemed to go unanswered. God appeared totally out of reach.

But this was the furthest thing from the truth, and God spoke up to share the truth of the situation. What He had to say is one of the strongest declarations of His love ever given to His people or, for that matter, to the human race. Assuring His people of His love and His power, the LORD compared Himself to a loving mother (vv.15-23), a mighty warrior (vv.24-26), and a forgiving husband (50:1-3). In comparing Himself to these three people, the LORD was describing His mission to the discouraged. When His people feel forsaken, forgotten, abandoned, and all alone, He reaches out to them in love, seeking to encourage and reassure them.

OUTLINE	SCRIPTURE	SCRIPTURE	OUTLINE
2. The Savior's threefold mission to the discouraged: Reaching all who feel forsaken, forgotten a. His mission of revealing God's love: Compared to a loving mother 1) God would not forget His people • They were engraved on	14 But Zion said, The LORD hath forsaken me, and my Lord hath forgotten me. 15 Can a woman forget her sucking child, that she should not have compassion on the son of her womb? yea, they may forget, yet will I not forget thee. 16 Behold, I have graven	thee upon the palms of *my* hands; thy walls *are* continually before me. 17 Thy children shall make haste; thy destroyers and they that made thee waste shall go forth of thee. 18 Lift up thine eyes round about, and behold: all these gather themselves together,	His hands • They & Jerusalem's walls were ever before Him 2) God would cause His people's descendants to return & their enemies to flee • The return to the promised land was guaranteed by the LORD's oath

OUTLINE	SCRIPTURE	SCRIPTURE	OUTLINE
• The returning people would be a spectacular sight: Each person would be like a bridal ornament adding sparkle to the nation • The returning people would overflow the land: The land would be too small for the influx of returnees, & more space would be needed for them to live in	*and* come to thee. *As* I live, saith the LORD, thou shalt surely clothe thee with them all, as with an ornament, and bind them *on thee,* as a bride *doeth.* 19 For thy waste and thy desolate places, and the land of thy destruction, shall even now be too narrow by reason of the inhabitants, and they that swallowed thee up shall be far away.	from the mighty, or the lawful captive delivered? 25 But thus saith the LORD, Even the captives of the mighty shall be taken away, and the prey of the terrible shall be delivered: for I will contend with him that contendeth with thee, and I will save thy children.	God's power to deliver His people: Compared to the strength of a mighty warrior 1) He would free, save His people from their captors
• The number of returnees would be surprising, totally unexpected: Because so many had been lost due to their captivity & exile	20 The children which thou shalt have, after thou hast lost the other, shall say again in thine ears, The place *is* too strait for me: give place to me that I may dwell. 21 Then shalt thou say in thine heart, Who hath begotten me these, seeing I have lost my children, and am desolate, a captive, and removing to and fro? and who hath brought up these? Behold, I was left alone; these, where *had* they *been?*	26 And I will feed them that oppress thee with their own flesh; and they shall be drunken with their own blood, as with sweet wine: and all flesh shall know that I the LORD *am* thy Saviour and thy Redeemer, the mighty One of Jacob.	2) He would cause the oppressors to turn against one another 3) He would prove the most basic truths in all the universe: That He is… • The LORD • Your Savior & Redeemer • The Mighty One of Jacob (Israel)
3) God would arouse the nations to release & return His people to the promised land • The nations would even help transport the returning captives, 14:2; 43:6; 60:9 • The leaders would subject themselves to Zion 4) God would prove two great truths • That He alone is the LORD • That those who hope in Him will not be ashamed b. His mission of revealing	22 Thus saith the Lord GOD, Behold, I will lift up mine hand to the Gentiles, and set up my standard to the people: and they shall bring thy sons in *their* arms, and thy daughters shall be carried upon *their* shoulders. 23 And kings shall be thy nursing fathers, and their queens thy nursing mothers: they shall bow down to thee with *their* face toward the earth, and lick up the dust of thy feet; and thou shalt know that I *am* the LORD: for they shall not be ashamed that wait for me. 24 Shall the prey be taken	**CHAPTER 50** **T**hus saith the LORD, Where *is* the bill of your mother's divorcement, whom I have put away? or which of my creditors *is* it to whom I have sold you? Behold, for your iniquities have ye sold yourselves, and for your transgressions is your mother put away. 2 Wherefore, when I came, *was there* no man? when I called, *was there* none to answer? Is my hand shortened at all, that it cannot redeem? or have I no power to deliver? behold, at my rebuke I dry up the sea, I make the rivers a wilderness: their fish stinketh, because *there is* no water, and dieth for thirst. 3 I clothe the heavens with blackness, and I make sackcloth their covering.	c. His mission of redeeming His people by paying the ransom: Compared to the love of a forgiving husband 1) He had not divorced or sold them to creditors • They had left him & been sold because of their sin • They had not responded when he continually came & appealed to them to return to Him 2) He always had the power to redeem (deliver) them • Just as He dried up the Red Sea (Ex.14:1-31) & the Jordan River (Js.3:14-17) • Just as He darkened the sky in the plagues of Egypt (Ex.20:21)

a. The LORD's mission is to reveal His love to the discouraged (vv.15-23). His love can be compared to the love of a mother for her nursing child. Could a mother forget to feed and nourish her baby? Could she abandon and have no love for the child? Not likely! But even if she did, God will not forget His people (v.15), for they are engraved, actually carved and chiseled, on the palms of His hands. This means that God's people are permanently in His hands, under His care, protection, and provision. But this is not all: those protected inside Jerusalem's walls are ever before Him. They are always in His sight, and they will stand forever before Him as a memorial. He will always be with His people, looking after them and the Holy City.

For this reason, God will cause the Israelites' descendants to return to the promised land and cause their enemies to flee (vv.17-21). The descendant's return is guaranteed by the LORD's oath (v.18). He swears that as surely as He lives they will return. And the returning people will be a spectacular sight (v.18b), for each returnee will be like a piece of bridal ornament to add sparkle to the nation. Although the land of Judah had been ruined and its population decimated, the influx of returnees will be so great that the land will be too small for them (v.19). They will actually need more space to live in (v.20). The number of returnees will be surprising and totally unexpected because so many had died during their captivity and exile (v.21). Remember that only a few exiles returned to Judah from Babylon when they were released by King Cyrus of Persia. Therefore, this prophecy was not fulfilled in those days. It clearly refers to the coming Messianic Kingdom, the day when Christ will return to establish His kingdom on earth.

When Christ returns to establish God's kingdom on earth, He will arouse the nations to release and return His people to the promised land (vv.22-23). The nations will even help transport the returning captives (14:2; 43:6; 60:9). Moreover, all the rulers of the nations will subject themselves to Jerusalem because the LORD will make it the capital of His government. When Zion becomes the seat of worldwide government, the rulers of the earth will look after and care for the Holy City just as a foster father or a nursing mother would. They will even bow down with their faces to the ground to honor and worship Christ.

In that day, God will prove two great truths: that He alone is the LORD and that those who hope in Him will never be disappointed or ashamed. By keeping their eyes on the future, God's people could conquer their discouragement. Holding fast to God's promises, they could know that they were neither forsaken nor forgotten. They were etched on God's hands, ever before His face. They were under His continued care, protection, and provision.

b. The LORD's mission is to reveal His power to deliver His people (vv.24-26). Note that His power is compared to the strength of a mighty warrior. Who can take plunder or rescue captives from a *mighty warrior*? No one! No one except the LORD, that is. The discouraged can rest assured of three wonderful promises:

⇒ The LORD will save His people from their enemies and free them from their captors (v.25). No matter who opposes or attacks them, God Himself will take up the fight. As surely as He is God, He will rescue His people from their adversaries and their oppression.

⇒ The LORD will cause the oppressors of His people to turn against one another (v.26). The statement that they will eat or feed on their own flesh is a picture of internal strife, conflict, and civil war.

⇒ The LORD will prove the most basic truth in all the universe (v.26)—that He is the LORD, the Savior and Redeemer, the Mighty One of Jacob (Israel).

c. The LORD's mission is to pay the ransom price necessary to redeem His people. He will liberate them from their captivity (ch.50:1-3). Note that God's redemption is compared to the love of a forgiving husband. Although the Israelites were guilty of serious sin, the LORD had not divorced or sold them to creditors, as so many men did their wives in that day. When men divorced or sold their wives, they gave them a certificate of divorce, but Israel had no evidence to prove that God had divorced her. There was no certificate, nothing in the history of Israel to suggest that God had ever severed connections with His people. They were sent away from their homeland and sold into captivity because of their sins, not because God had divorced them. To the contrary, the LORD had continually reached out to be reconciled with His people. But when He appealed to them to return to Him, few responded in repentance. Most of the people continued in their sinful, adulterous ways, refusing to repent and turn back to the LORD.

Nevertheless, the LORD always had the power to redeem His people, the power to rescue and deliver them from their captors (vv.2-3). His power had been proven in the past when He dried up the Red Sea (Ex.14:1-31) and the Jordan River (Js.3:14-17). And it was proven when He darkened the sky in the plagues of Egypt (Ex.20:21). The Israelites' discouragement was due to their own sin, not to the LORD's forsaking or forgetting them. They were in captivity and feeling abandoned because they had chosen to walk in the wicked ways of the world. Nevertheless, the LORD's mission was to reach the discouraged.

Today the LORD still reaches out to those who are disheartened. He reaches out in love to be reconciled with all who feel forsaken or forgotten, deserted or alienated, lonely or friendless, isolated or homeless, outcast or rejected, destitute or unloved.

> "And, behold, they brought to him a man sick of the palsy, lying on a bed: and Jesus seeing their faith said unto the sick of the palsy; Son, be of good cheer; thy sins be forgiven thee" (Mt.9:2).
>
> "And fear not them which kill the body, but are not able to kill the soul: but rather fear him which is able to destroy both soul and body in hell. Are not two sparrows sold for a farthing? and one of them shall not fall on the ground without your Father. But the very hairs of your head are all numbered. Fear ye not therefore, ye are of more value than many sparrows. Whosoever therefore shall confess me before men, him will I confess also before my Father which is in heaven. But whosoever shall deny me before men, him will I also deny before my Father which is in heaven" (Mt.10:28-33).
>
> "Even as the Son of man came not to be ministered unto, but to minister, and to give his life a ransom for many" (Mt.20:28).
>
> "The Spirit of the Lord is upon me, because he hath anointed me to preach the gospel to the poor; he hath sent me to heal the brokenhearted, to preach deliverance to the captives, and recovering of sight to the blind, to set at liberty them that are bruised" (Lu.4:18).
>
> "But as for me, my feet were almost gone; my steps had well nigh slipped. For I was envious at the foolish, *when* I saw the prosperity of the wicked....Until I went into the sanctuary of God; *then* understood I their end" (Ps.73:2-3, 17).
>
> "Thus my heart was grieved, and I was pricked in my reins. So foolish *was* I, and ignorant: I was *as* a beast before thee. Nevertheless I *am* continually with thee: thou hast holden *me* by my right hand. Thou shalt guide me with thy counsel, and afterward receive me *to* glory. Whom have I in heaven *but thee?* and *there is* none upon earth *that* I desire beside thee. My flesh and my heart faileth: *but* God *is* the strength of my heart, and my portion for ever....But *it is* good for me to draw near to God: I have put my trust in the Lord GOD, that I may declare all thy works" (Ps.73:21-26, 28).
>
> "Fear thou not; for I *am* with thee: be not dismayed; for I *am* thy God: I will strengthen thee; yea, I will help thee; yea, I will uphold thee with the right hand of my righteousness....For I the LORD thy God will hold thy right hand, saying unto thee, Fear not; I will help thee" (Is.41:10, 13).
>
> Fear not: for I have redeemed thee, I have called *thee* by thy name; thou *art* mine. When thou passest through the waters, I *will be* with thee; and through the rivers, they shall not overflow thee: when thou walkest through the fire, thou shalt not be burned; neither shall the flame kindle upon thee" (Is.43:1-2).

3 (50:4-9) **Weary, the Answer - Solution to, Christ—Christ, Mission of, to the Weary—Burden, Answer - Solution to, Christ—Tired, Answer - Solution to, Christ—Exhausted, Answer - Solution to, Christ—Disgusted, Answer - Solution to, Christ—Discontent, Answer - Solution to, Christ—Impatience, Answer - Solution to, Christ—Weak - Weakness, Answer to, Christ:** the Savior was given a very special mission to the weary. This is the third of four *Servant songs* that predict the coming Servant or Savior of the world (chs.42:1-7; 49:1-7; 50:4-9; 52:12–53:12). Four times in this passage the Servant refers to the LORD God, or Sovereign LORD, who sent Him on His mission. In each reference the Servant tells how the LORD God met His every need as He carried out His assigned duties (v.4, 5, 7, 9). As the Scripture and outline show, His mission was twofold: to preach to the weary and to suffer for the weary:

OUTLINE	SCRIPTURE	SCRIPTURE	OUTLINE

3. **The Savior's twofold mission to the weary: Reaching out to all who are in bondage to sin & death**
 a. His mission to preach to the weary
   1) He was taught by God
 	
   2) He was not rebellious, turning His ear away from God's instructions
 	
 b. His mission to suffer for the weary
   1) His sufferings
    • Was beaten, scourged
    • Was mocked & spat upon
	4 The Lord GOD hath given me the tongue of the learned, that I should know how to speak a word in season to *him that is* weary: he wakeneth morning by morning, he wakeneth mine ear to hear as the learned.
	 5 The Lord GOD hath opened mine ear, and I was not rebellious, neither turned away back.
	 6 I gave my back to the smiters, and my cheeks to them that plucked off the hair: I hid not my face from shame and spitting.
		7 For the Lord GOD will help me; therefore shall I not be confounded: therefore have I set my face like a flint, and I know that I shall not be ashamed.
		 8 *He is* near that justifieth me; who will contend with me? let us stand together: who *is* mine adversary? let him come near to me.
		 9 Behold, the Lord GOD will help me; who *is* he *that* shall condemn me? lo, they all shall wax old as a garment; the moth shall eat them up.
			2) His obedience & steadfastness: Set His face like a stone to suffer death
			   • Was helped by God
			   • Was not shamed
			
			 3) His vindication by God: No one dared to charge or accuse Him
			   • Because God justified Him: Knew that He was just, righteous, sinless
			   • Because God helped Him
			   • Because all accusers would be like garments that fell apart due to age or else being eaten by moths

a. First, the Messiah's mission was to share God's Word with the weary (v.4). Who are the weary? They are those who are...

- tired
- exhausted
- downtrodden
- unable to go on
- traumatized
- unhappy
- discontented
- disgusted
- overworked
- oppressed
- being seduced
- feeling tempted
- suffering hardship
- experiencing misfortune
- seeking to become acceptable through works, idolatry, or false worship

Anyone who is suffering under the weight of heavy pressure, stress, or burdens is a person who is weary. But there is wonderful news: the Savior was sent into the world to meet the needs of the broken and oppressed. The LORD God of the universe, the Father of the Lord Jesus Christ, gave Christ the very words to share with them. God taught His Servant the words to preach and teach so that He could help sustain them. Note the claim of the Savior, God's Servant: every morning of His life, the LORD awakened Him and quickened His ear to hear the Word of God. The Savior then taught the Word of God. The Savior did not rebel against the LORD God or turn His ear away from God's instructions. Everything God taught the Savior to say and do, Jesus Christ said and did for the sake of the weary.

> "Then answered Jesus and said unto them, Verily, verily, I say unto you, The Son can do nothing of himself, but what he seeth the Father do: for what things soever he doeth, these also doeth the Son likewise" (Jn.5:19).
> "I can of mine own self do nothing: as I hear, I judge: and my judgment is just; because I seek not mine own will, but the will of the Father which hath sent me" (Jn.5:30).
> "For I came down from heaven, not to do mine own will, but the will of him that sent me" (Jn.6:38).
> "Then said Jesus unto them, When ye have lifted up the Son of man, then shall ye know that I am *he,* and *that* I do nothing of myself; but as my Father hath taught me, I speak these things" (Jn.8:28).
> "But that the world may know that I love the Father; and as the Father gave me commandment, even so I do. Arise, let us go hence" (Jn.14:31).
> "Then said he [Christ], Lo, I come to do thy will, O God. He taketh away the first, that he may establish the second. By the which will we are sanctified through the offering of the body of Jesus Christ once *for all*" (He.10:9-10).

b. The Savior's mission was to suffer for the weary (vv.6-9). When Christ died on the cross, He willingly gave Himself up to die as the ransom for the people's sins. He suffered as their *substitute*: in their place, in their stead, in their behalf. Willingly, He offered His back to be scourged, beaten until there was very little flesh left. He offered His cheek to the sinners of the world, and they pulled out His beard. Voluntarily, He offered His face to be spat upon by all who rejected Him as God's Servant, the Savior of the world (see Mt.26:67; 27:26, 30; Mk.14:6; 15:16-20; Lu.18:32; Jn.18:22; 19:1).

Yet through all the suffering, the Savior remained obedient and steadfast to the mission given Him by God. He set His face like a stone to suffer death so that the weary of the earth could be saved. Because Christ remained faithful, obedient to the Father's will, God helped Him by making sure He would never be shamed or disgraced by failing in His mission! Christ would be triumphant in accomplishing His purpose. Down through the centuries, the weary of this earth turned to the Savior by the millions to be delivered from the heavy weight of sin and the stressful burdens of this earth.

In His trial on earth, the Savior and Servant of God was falsely accused. But the Savior knew this important fact: God would vindicate or prove Him right (vv.8-9). The LORD would justify Him because He was sinless. He had always lived a righteous and just life as He shared God's Word with the people. Therefore, God would make His mission triumphant. The weary of the earth who placed their trust in Him would be saved, but the Savior's accusers would be like a garment that falls apart due to age or from being eaten by moths. They would not last but, rather, would face the judgment of the LORD God.

"That it might be fulfilled which was spoken by Esaias the prophet, saying, Himself took our infirmities, and bare *our* **sicknesses" (Mt.8:17).**

"Come unto me, all *ye* **that labour and are heavy laden, and I will give you rest. Take my yoke upon you, and learn of me; for I am meek and lowly in heart: and ye shall find rest unto your souls. For my yoke** *is* **easy, and my burden is light" (Mt.11:28-30).**

"The Spirit of the Lord is upon me, because he hath anointed me to preach the gospel to the poor; he hath sent me to heal the brokenhearted, to preach deliverance to the captives, and recovering of sight to the blind, to set at liberty them that are bruised" (Lu.4:18).

"And ye shall know the truth, and the truth shall make you free" (Jn.8:32).

"And he bearing his cross went forth into a place called *the place* **of a skull, which is called in the Hebrew Golgotha: Where they crucified him, and two others with him, on either side one, and Jesus in the midst" (Jn.19:17-18).**

"Know ye not, that to whom ye yield yourselves servants to obey, his servants ye are to whom ye obey; whether of sin unto death, or of obedience unto righteousness? But God be thanked, that ye were the servants of sin, but ye have obeyed from the heart that form of doctrine which was delivered you. Being then made free from sin, ye became the servants of righteousness" (Ro.6:16-18).

"But now being made free from sin, and become servants to God, ye have your fruit unto holiness, and the end everlasting life. For the wages of sin *is* **death; but the gift of God** *is* **eternal life through Jesus Christ our Lord" (Ro.6:22-23).**

"*There is*** **therefore now no condemnation to them which are in Christ Jesus, who walk not after the flesh, but after the Spirit. For the law of the Spirit of life in Christ Jesus hath made me free from the law of sin and death" (Ro.8:1-2).**

"Surely he hath borne our griefs, and carried our sorrows: yet we did esteem him stricken, smitten of God, and afflicted" (Is.53:4).

4 (50:10-11) **Decision, Duty – Essential, to Obey—Mission, of Christ, Results—Self-Sufficient, Judgment of, Torment—Self-Reliant, End of, Torment—Darkness, Walking in, Duty**: the Savior's mission demands a decision from every person. Being the very Servant of God and the Savior of the world means that Jesus Christ is a Person of unparalleled importance. Since He has come to the world as the Savior, people cannot avoid making a decision concerning Him. People either accept or reject the salvation offered by the Savior. In fact, a person's avoidance is his decision to reject Christ. By sending the Savior into the world, the LORD God has shown that He longs for every person in the world to be saved from the bondages of this life, from discouragement, and from weariness. Because of so great a salvation, God demands that people fear and obey the Word of Christ. As the Scripture points out, God gives two words of warning:

OUTLINE	SCRIPTURE	SCRIPTURE	OUTLINE
4. **The Savior's specific mission to the whole human race: To warn each person to fear the LORD & obey the Savior** a. The person who walks in darkness: Must trust the LORD & persevere in Him	10 Who *is* among you that feareth the LORD, that obeyeth the voice of his servant, that walketh *in* darkness, and hath no light? let him trust in the name of the LORD, and stay upon his God.	11 Behold, all ye that kindle a fire, that compass *yourselves* about with sparks: walk in the light of your fire, and in the sparks *that* ye have kindled. This shall ye have of mine hand; ye shall lie down in sorrow.	b. The person who is self-sufficient & self-reliant (who walks by his own light): Will lie down in awful torment

a. The person who walks in darkness must trust the LORD and persevere in Him.

"And ye shall be hated of all *men* **for my name's sake: but he that endureth to the end shall be saved" (Mt.10:22).**

"For God so loved the world, that he gave his only begotten Son, that whosoever believeth in him should not perish, but have everlasting life" (Jn.3:16).

"Then said they unto him, What shall we do, that we might work the works of God? Jesus answered and said unto them, This is the work of God, that ye believe on him whom he hath sent" (Jn.6:28-29).

"As the Father hath loved me, so have I loved you: continue ye in my love" (Jn.15:9).

"Therefore being justified by faith, we have peace with God through our Lord Jesus Christ" (Ro.5:1).

"Wherefore seeing we also are compassed about with so great a cloud of witnesses, let us lay aside every weight, and the sin which doth so easily beset us, and let us run with patience the race that is set before us, Looking unto Jesus the author and finisher of *our* faith; who for the joy that was set before him endured the cross, despising the shame, and is set down at the right hand of the throne of God. For consider him that endured such contradiction of sinners against himself, lest ye be wearied and faint in your minds. Ye have not yet resisted unto blood, striving against sin" (He.12:1-4).

"Blessed *is* the man that endureth temptation: for when he is tried, he shall receive the crown of life, which the Lord hath promised to them that love him" (Js.1:12).

"Wherefore gird up the loins of your mind, be sober, and hope to the end for the grace that is to be brought unto you at the revelation of Jesus Christ; As obedient children, not fashioning yourselves according to the former lusts in your ignorance" (1 Pe.1:13-14).

"And this is his commandment, That we should believe on the name of his Son Jesus Christ, and love one another, as he gave us commandment" (1 Jn.3:23).

"Behold, I come quickly: hold that fast which thou hast, that no man take thy crown" (Re.3:11).

b. The person who is self-sufficient and self-reliant will face God's judgment. All who reject the light of the Savior and walk by their own light will lie down in *torment,* a picture of eternal punishment due to their unbelief and rejection of the Savior.

"Not every one that saith unto me, Lord, Lord, shall enter into the kingdom of heaven; but he that doeth the will of my Father which is in heaven. Many will say to me in that day, Lord, Lord, have we not prophesied in thy name? and in thy name have cast out devils? and in thy name done many wonderful works? And then will I profess unto them, I never knew you: depart from me, ye that work iniquity" (Mt.7:21-23).

"When Jesus heard *it,* he marvelled, and said to them that followed, Verily I say unto you, I have not found so great faith, no, not in Israel. And I say unto you, That many shall come from the east and west, and shall sit down with Abraham, and Isaac, and Jacob, in the kingdom of heaven. But the children of the kingdom shall be cast out into outer darkness: there shall be weeping and gnashing of teeth" (Mt.8:10-12).

"Then said the king to the servants, Bind him hand and foot, and take him away, and cast *him* into outer darkness; there shall be weeping and gnashing of teeth" (Mt.22:13).

"And these shall go away into everlasting punishment: but the righteous into life eternal" (Mt.25:46).

"He that believeth on the Son hath everlasting life: and he that believeth not the Son shall not see life; but the wrath of God abideth on him" (Jn.3:36).

"Marvel not at this: for the hour is coming, in the which all that are in the graves shall hear his voice, And shall come forth; they that have done good, unto the resurrection of life; and they that have done evil, unto the resurrection of damnation" (Jn.5:28-29).

"How shall we escape, if we neglect so great salvation; which at the first began to be spoken by the Lord, and was confirmed unto us by them that heard *him*" (He.2:3).

"Of how much sorer punishment, suppose ye, shall he be thought worthy, who hath trodden under foot the Son of God, and hath counted the blood of the covenant, wherewith he was sanctified, an unholy thing, and hath done despite unto the Spirit of grace?" (He.10:29).

"For if God spared not the angels that sinned, but cast *them* down to hell, and delivered *them* into chains of darkness, to be reserved unto judgment; And spared not the old world, but saved Noah the eighth *person,* a preacher of righteousness, bringing in the flood upon the world of the ungodly...The Lord knoweth how to deliver the godly out of temptations, and to reserve the unjust unto the day of judgment to be punished" (2 Pe.2:4-5, 9).

"But the fearful, and unbelieving, and the abominable, and murderers, and whoremongers, and sorcerers, and idolaters, and all liars, shall have their part in the lake which burneth with fire and brimstone: which is the second death" (Re.21:8).

CHAPTER 51

B. The Savior's Cry of Salvation: Listen! Wake Up! Depart! 51:1–52:12

1. Listen to the LORD! Take note, you who seek the LORD & His righteousness

a. Look back—remember the rock from which you were cut, born: Israel came from Abraham & Sarah
1) God called Abraham (one person) & promised him a great nation of descendants
2) God will now comfort Zion: Do the same for the returnees being freed from Babylon (a picture of believers being set free from sin & death)
   • Make them a great nation
   • Restore their land

b. Look ahead—in the future the LORD's law & justice will rule the world: A picture of the Messiah's kingdom

1) The glorious truth: *My* righteousness, *My* salvation, *My* arms, will bring justice to all nations
2) The longing & hope of the world: Is found in Him
3) The wonderful promise
   • The corrupt universe with all its wicked people will perish: Wear out & be done away with

   • The salvation & righteousness of God will last forever: To bring life to the redeemed
c. Look inward—you who know what is righteous & have God's Word in your heart: Trust Him
1) Do not fear people's scorn & mockery
2) The reasons
   • They will perish like a moth-eaten garment
   • God's righteousness & salvation will last forever: Impart eternal life to the redeemed
2. Wake up, wake up, O LORD! Help your people
a. The cry for another Exodus
1) The LORD had delivered His redeemed from the mythical sea monster Rahab (Egypt)

Hearken to me, ye that follow after righteousness, ye that seek the LORD: look unto the rock *whence* ye are hewn, and to the hole of the pit *whence* ye are digged.
2 Look unto Abraham your father, and unto Sarah *that* bare you: for I called him alone, and blessed him, and increased him.
3 For the LORD shall comfort Zion: he will comfort all her waste places; and he will make her wilderness like Eden, and her desert like the garden of the LORD; joy and gladness shall be found therein, thanksgiving, and the voice of melody.
4 Hearken unto me, my people; and give ear unto me, O my nation: for a law shall proceed from me, and I will make my judgment to rest for a light of the people.
5 My righteousness *is* near; my salvation is gone forth, and mine arms shall judge the people; the isles shall wait upon me, and on mine arm shall they trust.
6 Lift up your eyes to the heavens, and look upon the earth beneath: for the heavens shall vanish away like smoke, and the earth shall wax old like a garment, and they that dwell therein shall die in like manner: but my salvation shall be for ever, and my righteousness shall not be abolished.
7 Hearken unto me, ye that know righteousness, the people in whose heart *is* my law; fear ye not the reproach of men, neither be ye afraid of their revilings.
8 For the moth shall eat them up like a garment, and the worm shall eat them like wool: but my righteousness shall be for ever, and my salvation from generation to generation.
9 Awake, awake, put on strength, O arm of the LORD; awake, as in the ancient days, in the generations of old. *Art* thou not it that hath cut Rahab, *and* wounded the

dragon?
10 *Art* thou not it which hath dried the sea, the waters of the great deep; that hath made the depths of the sea a way for the ransomed to pass over?
11 Therefore the redeemed of the LORD shall return, and come with singing unto Zion; and everlasting joy *shall be* upon their head: they shall obtain gladness and joy; *and* sorrow and mourning shall flee away.
12 I, *even* I, *am* he that comforteth you: who *art* thou, that thou shouldest be afraid of a man *that* shall die, and of the son of man *which* shall be made as grass;
13 And forgettest the LORD thy maker, that hath stretched forth the heavens, and laid the foundations of the earth; and hast feared continually every day because of the fury of the oppressor, as if he were ready to destroy? and where *is* the fury of the oppressor?
14 The captive exile hasteneth that he may be loosed, and that he should not die in the pit, nor that his bread should fail.
15 But I *am* the LORD thy God, that divided the sea, whose waves roared: The LORD of hosts *is* his name.
16 And I have put my words in thy mouth, and I have covered thee in the shadow of mine hand, that I may plant the heavens, and lay the foundations of the earth, and say unto Zion, Thou *art* my people.
17 Awake, awake, stand up, O Jerusalem, which hast drunk at the hand of the LORD the cup of his fury; thou hast drunken the dregs of the cup of trembling, *and* wrung *them* out.
18 *There is* none to guide her among all the sons *whom* she hath brought forth; neither *is there any* that taketh her by the hand of all the sons *that* she hath brought up.
19 These two *things* are come unto thee; who shall be sorry for thee? desolation, and destruction, and the famine, and the sword: by whom shall I comfort thee?
20 Thy sons have fainted, they lie at the head of all the

2) The Lord had also dried up the Red Sea so they could safely cross
b. The LORD's wonderful promise to the ransomed
1) They would return to Zion (Jerusalem)
2) They would be filled with everlasting joy: Freed form all sorrow & mourning
c. The LORD's assurance: He is the One who comforts them
1) The questions asked by God
   • Why fear mortal man?

   • Why forget the LORD who created you & the universe?

   • Why live in constant terror because of the oppressors?
   • Where is the fury of the oppressor when confronted by God?
2) The assurance of God: The captives would be set free

   • Because the LORD has the power: The LORD who divided & stirs up the waves of the sea
   • Because the LORD has placed His Word into the care & trust of His people
   • Because the LORD protects His people
   • Because the LORD is the Creator & they are His people
3. Wake up, wake up, O Jerusalem! You (the redeemed) will be set free from captivity: A picture of the believer being freed from sin & death
a. The city of Jerusalem must wake up & rise from its suffering of God's judgment
1) The city had no leaders to guide the people

2) The city had suffered a double calamity
   • Desolation & destruction
   • Famine & bloodshed

3) The city's young men had been killed & piled up in

the streets

4) The afflicted city was challenged to heed God's promise
- He defends His people (the redeemed), 12
- He would remove the cup of judgment—His discipline, chastisement—from His people

- He would transfer the cup of judgment over to the persecutors & oppressors
- He would make the redeemed victorious over all enemies

b. The city of Jerusalem must wake up & be clothed with splendor & strength
1) Because it is holy: The impure & godless would no longer enter

2) Because it is to arise from the dust: Be enthroned & freed from captivity

3) Because it is to be redeemed without money—freely, by grace

4) Because God's people had suffered so much
- Had been enslaved by Egypt & oppressed by Assyria

streets, as a wild bull in a net: they are full of the fury of the LORD, the rebuke of thy God. 21 Therefore hear now this, thou afflicted, and drunken, but not with wine: 22 Thus saith thy Lord the LORD, and thy God *that* pleadeth the cause of his people, Behold, I have taken out of thine hand the cup of trembling, *even* the dregs of the cup of my fury; thou shalt no more drink it again: 23 But I will put it into the hand of them that afflict thee; which have said to thy soul, Bow down, that we may go over: and thou hast laid thy body as the ground, and as the street, to them that went over.

CHAPTER 52

Awake, awake; put on thy strength, O Zion; put on thy beautiful garments, O Jerusalem, the holy city: for henceforth there shall no more come into thee the uncircumcised and the unclean. 2 Shake thyself from the dust; arise, *and* sit down, O Jerusalem: loose thyself from the bands of thy neck, O captive daughter of Zion. 3 For thus saith the LORD, Ye have sold yourselves for nought; and ye shall be redeemed without money. 4 For thus saith the Lord GOD, My people went down aforetime into Egypt to sojourn there; and the Assyrian oppressed them without cause.

5 Now therefore, what have I here, saith the LORD, that my people is taken away for nought? they that rule over them make them to howl, saith the LORD; and my name continually every day is blasphemed. 6 Therefore my people shall know my name: therefore *they shall know* in that day that I *am* he that doth speak: behold, *it is* I. 7 How beautiful upon the mountains are the feet of him that bringeth good tidings, that publisheth peace; that bringeth good tidings of good, that publisheth salvation; that saith unto Zion, Thy God reigneth! 8 Thy watchmen shall lift up the voice; with the voice together shall they sing: for they shall see eye to eye, when the LORD shall bring again Zion. 9 Break forth into joy, sing together, ye waste places of Jerusalem: for the LORD hath comforted his people, he hath redeemed Jerusalem. 10 The LORD hath made bare his holy arm in the eyes of all the nations; and all the ends of the earth shall see the salvation of our God. 11 Depart ye, depart ye, go ye out from thence, touch no unclean *thing;* go ye out of the midst of her; be ye clean, that bear the vessels of the LORD. 12 For ye shall not go out with haste, nor go by flight: for the LORD will go before you; and the God of Israel *will be* your rereward.

- Were now in bondage & exiled to Babylon: Being persecuted & mocked & having to hear God's name blasphemed all day long

5) Because God's people would know the LORD's name—know Him personally: Because He would fulfill His promise of redemption, 3
c. The city of Jerusalem must wake up & listen to the watchmen's proclamation of good news
1) The good news of peace & salvation, of God's reign on earth

2) The good news of the LORD's return to Zion (Jerusalem)

3) The good news of the LORD's comfort & redemption

4) The good news that God will destroy the enemies of His people, both in Isaiah's day & when Christ returns to earth

4. **Depart, depart! Flee the captivity of Babylon: A picture of spiritual separation**
a. The charge: Not to touch any unclean thing, to be pure

b. The promise: Would not be threatened, forced to flee
1) God would lead the way
2) God would also be their rear guard, protect their back

DIVISION VI

THE PROPHECIES OF THE GREAT DELIVERER: THE SUFFERING SERVANT OF GOD, THE SAVIOR OF THE WORLD, 49:1–59:21

B. The Savior's Cry of Salvation: Listen! Wake Up! Depart! 51:1–52:12

(51:1–52:12) **Introduction**: Listen! Wake up! Depart! These are three admonitions most of us hear often in our lives. Parents, supervisors, teachers, politicians, preachers, or even just friends are always encouraging or warning us to listen, to wake up, to leave, to move on.

These three imperatives are the subject of the present Scripture. Remember that Isaiah is looking into the future, predicting the coming Babylonian Captivity and the liberation of the Jews by the Persian king, Cyrus. Earlier, God's prophet had addressed the unfaithful in Israel (48:1-22). Now he addresses the faithful, those who seek the LORD and His righteousness. During their captivity, the Jews would endure terrible hardship and almost break under the weight of their suffering. But the LORD had a wonderful message for them, telling them exactly what to do to prepare for the future He had planned for them. This chapter is that message, a message for all the faithful who truly believe and follow the LORD. This is, *The Savior's Cry of Salvation: Listen! Wake Up! Depart! 51:1–52:12.*

1. Listen to the LORD! Take note, you who seek the LORD and His righteousness (51:1-8).
2. Wake up, wake up, O LORD! Help your people (51:9-16).
3. Wake up, wake up, O Jerusalem! You (the redeemed) will be set free from captivity: a picture of the believer being freed from sin and death (51:17–52:10).
4. Depart, depart! Flee the captivity of Babylon: a picture of spiritual separation (52:11-12).

1 (51:1-8) **Listen – Listening, Duty, to the LORD—Attention, Duty—Look – Looking, Duty, to Look Back, Ahead, Inward—Righteousness, Duty, to Seek—Seek – Seeking, the LORD—Believers, Duty—Promises, Comfort; Deliverance; Messiah's Kingdom—Prophecy, Concerning Israel, Deliverance from Captivity—Messiah's Kingdom, Prophecy Concerning—Encouragement, to the Righteous—Admonition, to Believers, Threefold—Counsel, to Believers—Faithful – Faithfulness, Admonition to, Threefold**: Hearken! Listen to the LORD! You who seek the LORD and His righteousness—listen to Me! This is the cry of the LORD, who is challenging and encouraging His people to pay attention because what He has to say is of paramount importance. Note the three strong imperatives: Listen and look back (v.1), listen and look ahead (v.4), listen and look inward (v.7).

Who are the people who seek the LORD and His righteousness? Glance quickly at the Scripture and outline. Verse seven below tells us: they are people who know righteousness and keep God's law and Word in their hearts. This righteousness is *imputed*. In other words, God credits or applies this righteousness to people when they believe in Him. When people place their faith in the LORD, the LORD counts their faith as righteousness, and they become *justified* before Him and acceptable to Him. That is what is meant by *imputed* righteousness. But knowing righteousness also means knowing right from wrong and doing what is right. It means righteous behavior. After people have placed their faith in the LORD, they live righteous lives by keeping the commandments of God's Holy Word. These are the people who truly seek the LORD and His righteousness, and all the promises and admonitions of this Scripture are addressed to them.

OUTLINE	SCRIPTURE	SCRIPTURE	OUTLINE
1. Listen to the LORD! Take note, you who seek the LORD & His righteousness a. Look back—remember the rock from which you were cut, born: Israel came from Abraham & Sarah 1) God called Abraham (one person) & promised him a great nation of descendants 2) God will now comfort Zion: Do the same for the returnees being freed from Babylon (a picture of believers being set free from sin & death) • Make them a great nation • Restore their land b. Look ahead—in the future the LORD's law & justice will rule the world: A picture of the Messiah's kingdom 1) The glorious truth: *My* righteousness, *My* salva-	Hearken to me, ye that follow after righteousness, ye that seek the LORD: look unto the rock *whence* ye are hewn, and to the hole of the pit *whence* ye are digged. 2 Look unto Abraham your father, and unto Sarah *that* bare you: for I called him alone, and blessed him, and increased him. 3 For the LORD shall comfort Zion: he will comfort all her waste places; and he will make her wilderness like Eden, and her desert like the garden of the LORD; joy and gladness shall be found therein, thanksgiving, and the voice of melody. 4 Hearken unto me, my people; and give ear unto me, O my nation: for a law shall proceed from me, and I will make my judgment to rest for a light of the people. 5 My righteousness *is* near; my salvation is gone forth,	and mine arms shall judge the people; the isles shall wait upon me, and on mine arm shall they trust. 6 Lift up your eyes to the heavens, and look upon the earth beneath: for the heavens shall vanish away like smoke, and the earth shall wax old like a garment, and they that dwell therein shall die in like manner: but my salvation shall be for ever, and my righteousness shall not be abolished. 7 Hearken unto me, ye that know righteousness, the people in whose heart *is* my law; fear ye not the reproach of men, neither be ye afraid of their revilings. 8 For the moth shall eat them up like a garment, and the worm shall eat them like wool: but my righteousness shall be for ever, and my salvation from generation to generation.	tion, *My* arms, will bring justice to all nations 2) The longing & hope of the world: Is found in Him 3) The wonderful promise • The corrupt universe with all its wicked people will perish: Wear out & be done away with • The salvation & righteousness of God will last forever: To bring life to the redeemed c. Look inward—you who know what is righteous & have God's Word in your heart: Trust Him 1) Do not fear people's scorn & mockery 2) The reasons • They will perish like a moth-eaten garment • God's righteousness & salvation will last forever: Impart eternal life to the redeemed

a. The righteous must look back. They must remember the rock from which they were hewn, or cut, and the quarry from which they were dug (vv.1-3). The rock is identified as Abraham and the quarry as Sarah (v.2). God is saying that the righteous of Israel must look back to their ancestors, Abraham and Sarah, from whom they descended. When God called Abraham, he was but one person, a single individual, but God gave him the wonderful promise of a great nation of descendants. From a human perspective, there was no possibility that Abraham would have many descendants and develop into a great nation, for Sarah was unable to have children. But with God all things are possible, and He fulfilled His promise by giving Abraham and Sarah a child when Abraham was about 100 years old and Sarah 90 (Ro.4:19).

If the LORD performed such a marvelous miracle for Abraham, think what He would do for His people who were held in captivity by Babylon (v.3). Although they were a broken people, weak and small in number due to their severe hardships, the LORD would comfort them. He would have compassion on His people and on Zion, their capital (Jerusalem), which lay in ruins.

Picture the few surviving Israelites as exiles in Babylon, a subjected and broken people, trying for seventy long years to survive the harsh circumstances and the brutal oppression of the Babylonians. To help His people get through those trying days, the LORD gave them this prophecy many decades before the Babylonian captivity. He wanted the righteous to be comforted and to rest assured that He had not forgotten His promises. Despite their captivity and terrible sufferings, He would still make them a great nation and restore their land. In fact, their land would become so fruitful that its deserts and wastelands would become like the Garden of Eden, the very garden of the LORD Himself. In that day, joy and gladness, thanksgiving and song would fill the land. Obviously, this prophecy has a double reference, referring to the rebuilding of the nation by the exiles who returned from Babylonian captivity and also to the establishment of the Messiah's kingdom when Christ returns to earth.

Thought 1. We who are true believers must look back and remember the Rock from which we were cut. That Rock is Jesus Christ, our Savior. He is the Rock, the foundation of our lives. It is He who gave us the *new birth*, causing us to be *born again*. In Christ we have a new life in that we are made acceptable to God and given the wonderful inheritance of the promised land of heaven.

> "But as many as received him, to them gave he power to become the sons of God, *even* to them that believe on his name: Which were born, not of blood, nor of the will of the flesh, nor of the will of man, but of God" (Jn.1:12-13).

> "Jesus answered and said unto him, Verily, verily, I say unto thee, Except a man be born again, he cannot see the kingdom of God. Nicodemus saith unto him, How can a man be born when he is old? can he enter the second time into his mother's womb, and be born? Jesus answered, Verily, verily, I say unto thee, Except a man be born of water and *of* the Spirit, he cannot enter into the kingdom of God. That which is born of the flesh is flesh; and that which is born of the Spirit is spirit. Marvel not that I said unto thee, Ye must be born again. The wind bloweth where it listeth, and thou hearest the sound thereof, but canst not tell whence it cometh, and whither it goeth: so is every one that is born of the Spirit" (Jn.3:3-8).

> "Therefore if any man *be* in Christ, *he is* a new creature: old things are passed away; behold, all things are become new" (2 Co.5:17).

> "That ye put off concerning the former conversation [behavior, conduct] the old man, which is corrupt according to the deceitful lusts; And be renewed in the spirit of your mind; And that ye put on the new man, which after God is created in righteousness and true holiness" (Ep.4:22-24).

> "For our conversation [citizenship] is in heaven; from whence also we look for the Saviour, the Lord Jesus Christ: Who shall change our vile body, that it may be fashioned like unto his glorious body, according to the working whereby he is able even to subdue all things unto himself" (Ph.3:20-21).

> "Not by works of righteousness which we have done, but according to his mercy he saved us, by the washing of regeneration, and renewing of the Holy Ghost; Which he shed on us abundantly through Jesus Christ our Saviour; That being justified by his grace, we should be made heirs according to the hope of eternal life" (Tit.3:5-7).

> "Blessed *be* the God and Father of our Lord Jesus Christ, which according to his abundant mercy hath begotten us again unto a lively hope by the resurrection of Jesus Christ from the dead, To an inheritance incorruptible, and undefiled, and that fadeth not away, reserved in heaven for you" (1 Pe.1:3-4).

> "Being born again, not of corruptible seed, but of incorruptible, by the word of God, which liveth and abideth for ever" (1 Pe.1:23).

> "Whosoever believeth that Jesus is the Christ is born of God: and every one that loveth him that begat loveth him also that is begotten of him" (1 Jn.5:1).

> "And the city had no need of the sun, neither of the moon, to shine in it: for the glory of God did lighten it, and the Lamb *is* the light thereof. And the nations of them which are saved shall walk in the light of it: and the kings of the earth do bring their glory and honour into it. And the gates of it shall not be shut at all by day: for there shall be no night there. And they shall bring the glory and honour of the nations into it. And there shall in no wise enter into it any thing that defileth, neither *whatsoever* worketh abomination, or *maketh* a lie: but they which are written in the Lamb's book of life" (Re.21:23-27).

b. The righteous must look ahead—into the future to the glorious day when God's law and justice will rule the world (vv.4-6). "Listen to Me," God says to His people. The day is coming when the Messiah, the Savior (the Lord Jesus Christ) will return to earth to establish God's kingdom. In that day, God's law will govern people's lives. Every human being will respect the dignity of life, protect the property and rights of others, and promote the well-being of all nations. God's justice will become a light to the nations, showing them how to establish a strong society of righteousness, equality, and justice for all. Everyone will treat his neighbor as he wishes to be treated (Mt.7:12; Lu.6:31).

As God's people look ahead to the future, they will know that God is going to bring His justice to earth. How? He told them (v.5a):

⇒ By establishing His righteousness—His law and Word—as the light, the guide to be followed by everyone on earth.

⇒ By bringing salvation to earth and setting His people free from their captivity and the suffering of this world.

⇒ By raising His arm, His power, to execute judgment and to subject all nations to His rule.

The longing and hope of the world is found only in the LORD and in the strength of His arm. Note the reference to the *islands*, which refers to the most distant parts of the earth (v.5b). Only God's power can bring true righteousness and justice to mankind. Thus the only hope for peace in the world is found in the LORD and in His promise that He will establish His kingdom of righteousness and justice on earth.

Still another wonderful promise is given to us. When the day of the Messiah's kingdom comes, both this corrupted universe and all the wicked people in it will perish (v.6). Although it might seem that the heavens above and the earth below will last forever, they will not. The starry heavens will disintegrate in smoke, and the earth will wear out like a piece of old clothing. Then all the wicked of the earth will be eternally separated from God and perish under the hand of His judgment. But all who put their trust in God's salvation and righteousness will live forever.

Thought 1. Believers of all generations must look ahead to the future, to the wonderful hope the LORD gives us of living forever in His kingdom.

> "**But lay up for yourselves treasures in heaven, where neither moth nor rust doth corrupt, and where thieves do not break through nor steal**" (Mt.6:20).
> "**Notwithstanding in this rejoice not, that the spirits are subject unto you; but rather rejoice, because your names are written in heaven**" (Lu.10:20).
> "**In my Father's house are many mansions: if *it were* not so, I would have told you. I go to prepare a place for you. And if I go and prepare a place for you, I will come again, and receive you unto myself; that where I am, *there* ye may be also**" (Jn.14:2-3).
> "**For we know that if our earthly house of *this* tabernacle were dissolved, we have a building of God, an house not made with hands, eternal in the heavens**" (2 Co.5:1).
> "**We give thanks to God and the Father of our Lord Jesus Christ, praying always for you, Since we heard of your faith in Christ Jesus, and of the love *which ye have* to all the saints, For the hope which is laid up for you in heaven, whereof ye heard before in the word of the truth of the gospel**" (Col.1:3-5).
> "**By faith Abraham, when he was called to go out into a place which he should after receive for an inheritance, obeyed; and he went out, not knowing whither he went. By faith he sojourned in the land of promise, as *in* a strange country, dwelling in tabernacles with Isaac and Jacob, the heirs with him of the same promise: For he looked for a city which hath foundations, whose builder and maker *is* God**" (He.11:8-10).
> "**These all died in faith, not having received the promises, but having seen them afar off, and were persuaded of *them*, and embraced *them*, and confessed that they were strangers and pilgrims on the earth. For they that say such things declare plainly that they seek a country. And truly, if they had been mindful of that *country* from whence they came out, they might have had opportunity to have returned. But now they desire a better *country*, that is, an heavenly: wherefore God is not ashamed to be called their God: for he hath prepared for them a city**" (He.11:13-16).
> "**Blessed *are* they that do his commandments, that they may have right to the tree of life, and may enter in through the gates into the city**" (Re.22:14).

c. The righteous must look inward and trust God during their hardships and suffering (vv.7-8). They must continue to live righteously and keep God's Word in their hearts. Only by remaining faithful can God's people keep from collapsing under the weight of their afflictions. The Israelites were bitterly persecuted by the Babylonians—mocked, cursed, reviled, and abused. But note God's encouragement: they must not fear the abuse, for their enemies would perish just like a moth-eaten garment (v.8). God's righteousness and salvation, however, would last forever, imparting eternal life to the true believers of this earth.

Thought 1. Believers today face the same problems, difficulties, and trials of life that everyone else experiences. But in addition to the regular hardships, believers oftentimes face persecution, just as they did under Babylonian captivity. Unbelievers taunt, mock, and sometimes assault, imprison, and even murder believers. During such times of trial and suffering, the LORD has a special message for us: trust Him. He cares for us, and He will take care of us through all the trials of life. Listen to the wonderful promises God gives to those who trust Him:

> "**The LORD *is* my light and my salvation; whom shall I fear? the LORD *is* the strength of my life; of whom shall I be afraid?**" (Ps.27:1).
> "***Oh* how great *is* thy goodness, which thou hast laid up for them that fear thee; *which* thou hast wrought for them that trust in thee before the sons of men! Thou shalt hide them in the secret of thy presence from the pride of man: thou shalt keep them secretly in a pavilion from the strife of tongues**" (Ps.31:19-20).
> "**Many sorrows *shall be* to the wicked: but he that trusteth in the LORD, mercy shall compass him about**" (Ps.32:10).
> "**The LORD redeemeth the soul of his servants: and none of them that trust in him shall be desolate**" (Ps.34:22).
> "**Trust in the LORD, and do good; *so* shalt thou dwell in the land, and verily thou shalt be fed**" (Ps.37:3).
> "**Commit thy way unto the LORD; trust also in him; and he shall bring *it* to pass**" (Ps.37:5).
> "**But the salvation of the righteous *is* of the LORD: *he is* their strength in the time of trouble**" (Ps.37:39).
> "**They that trust in the LORD *shall be* as mount Zion, *which* cannot be removed, *but* abideth for ever**" (Ps.125:1).
> "**Trust in the LORD with all thine heart; and lean not unto thine own understanding. In all thy ways acknowledge him, and he shall direct thy paths**" (Pr.3:5-6).
> "**The fear of man bringeth a snare: but whoso putteth his trust in the LORD shall be safe**" (Pr.29:25).

"Thou wilt keep *him* in perfect peace, *whose* mind *is* stayed *on thee:* because he trusteth in thee. Trust ye in the LORD for ever: for in the LORD JEHOVAH *is* everlasting strength" (Is.26:3-4).

"Who *is* among you that feareth the LORD, that obeyeth the voice of his servant, that walketh *in* darkness, and hath no light? let him trust in the name of the LORD, and stay upon his God" (Is.50:10).

"Behold, God *is* my salvation; I will trust, and not be afraid: for the LORD JEHOVAH *is* my strength and *my* song; he also is become my salvation" (Is.12:2).

"And it shall be said in that day, Lo, this *is* our God; we have waited for him, and he will save us: this *is* the LORD; we have waited for him, we will be glad and rejoice in his salvation" (Is.25:9).

"The LORD thy God in the midst of thee *is* mighty; he will save, he will rejoice over thee with joy; he will rest in his love, he will joy over thee with singing" (Zep.3:17).

2 (51:9-16) **Deliverance, Source, the LORD—Promises, of Deliverance, from Captivity—Prophecy, Concerning Israel, Freed from Captivity—Assurance, of Deliverance—Deliverance, from Fear, by God**: Wake up, wake up, O Lord! Awake to help your people! Note that while the cry above was addressed to true believers (vv.1-8), the cry here is addressed to the LORD. In his vision of the future, Isaiah foresaw that the people would suffer unimaginable, agonizing pain, and the sight of their suffering clearly weighed heavily upon his heart. Although the events lay decades out in the future, the prophet cried out for God to awaken and arise in behalf of His people who would face the coming trials.

OUTLINE	SCRIPTURE	SCRIPTURE	OUTLINE
2. Wake up, wake up, O LORD! Help your people a. The cry for another Exodus 1) The LORD had delivered His redeemed from the mythical sea monster Rahab (Egypt) 2) The Lord had also dried up the Red Sea so they could safely cross b. The Lord's wonderful promise to the ransomed 1) They would return to Zion (Jerusalem) 2) They would be filled with everlasting joy: Freed form all sorrow & mourning c. The LORD's assurance: He is the One who comforts them 1) The questions asked by God • Why fear mortal man?	9 Awake, awake, put on strength, O arm of the LORD; awake, as in the ancient days, in the generations of old. *Art* thou not it that hath cut Rahab, *and* wounded the dragon? 10 *Art* thou not it which hath dried the sea, the waters of the great deep; that hath made the depths of the sea a way for the ransomed to pass over? 11 Therefore the redeemed of the LORD shall return, and come with singing unto Zion; and everlasting joy *shall be* upon their head: they shall obtain gladness and joy; *and* sorrow and mourning shall flee away. 12 I, *even* I, *am* he that comforteth you: who *art* thou, that thou shouldest be afraid of a man *that* shall die, and of the son of man *which* shall be made as grass;	13 And forgettest the LORD thy maker, that hath stretched forth the heavens, and laid the foundations of the earth; and hast feared continually every day because of the fury of the oppressor, as if he were ready to destroy? and where *is* the fury of the oppressor? 14 The captive exile hasteneth that he may be loosed, and that he should not die in the pit, nor that his bread should fail. 15 But I *am* the LORD thy God, that divided the sea, whose waves roared: The LORD of hosts *is* his name. 16 And I have put my words in thy mouth, and I have covered thee in the shadow of mine hand, that I may plant the heavens, and lay the foundations of the earth, and say unto Zion, Thou *art* my people.	• Why forget the LORD who created you & the universe? • Why live in constant terror because of the oppressors? • Where is the fury of the oppressor when confronted by God? 2) The assurance of God: The captives would be set free • Because the LORD has the power: The LORD who divided & stirs up the waves of the sea • Because the LORD has placed His Word into the care & trust of His people • Because the LORD protects His people • Because the LORD is the Creator & they are His people

a. Isaiah called upon the LORD to lift His arm and power to deliver His people from Babylon, just as He delivered their forefathers from Egypt (called Rahab, the mythical sea monster, Jb.26:12; Ps.87:4; 89:10; Is.30:7). When the LORD delivered Israel from Egyptian bondage, He miraculously dried up the Red Sea so the *redeemed* could safely cross (vv.9-10). Once again, God's people would need Him to miraculously deliver them. More than 150 years before the event, God in His sovereignty and mercy revealed to His prophet the terrible sufferings that were coming upon God's people. Therefore, Isaiah prayed for God to help His dear people and to miraculously deliver them when the sufferings fell upon His people.

b. As soon as Isaiah prayed, the LORD gave a most wonderful promise: the ransomed of the LORD would return to Zion (Jerusalem). All true believers in Israel would be set free from the intense sorrow and mourning experienced during their captivity. Furthermore, they would be filled with everlasting joy. Gladness and gratification would flood their souls.

c. Note that the LORD gave more than a promise; He gave assurance that He would give them comfort (vv.12-16). God is the God of all comfort. He and He alone could bring solace and security to their souls. He alone had the power to deliver them from captivity and fill them with joy. In light of this fact, God had several questions to ask:

⇒ Why would His people fear mortal man, who withers like the grass and disappears? Even if they were held in captivity, true believers had the promise that the God of comfort would care for them (2 Co.1:3-4; 1 Pe.5:7; 5:10).

⇒ Why would God's people forget the LORD who created them and the universe? He who has this kind of power has the power to comfort them through all the sufferings of life and to fill them with joy (v.13).

⇒ Why would God's people live in constant terror of oppressors (v.13)? Many people in the world defied God and persecuted His people, but the God who had the power to create could deliver His people from the terror and threat of oppressors.

⇒ Where was the fury of the oppressor when confronted by God (v.13c)? In comparison to the LORD, the strength of the oppressor was as nothing, ridiculously small.

No matter what circumstances the true believers found themselves in, there was no room for fear. It was absurd to fear when their God possessed omnipotent power, the power to do anything. In light of this, God's people could rest assured that they would be set free (vv.14-16). They would not die in prison, and they would never lack the basic necessities of life. Note that four facts guaranteed that God would deliver believers from captivity and provide for them:

⇒ The LORD has the power to deliver them (v.15). The same power that stirred up the waves of the sea was available to believers (v.15).
⇒ The LORD had given His Word to His people with many promises and assurances of His love and care for them (v.16).
⇒ The LORD protected His people, covering them with the shadow of His hand (v.16).
⇒ The LORD was their Creator, and they were His people. Therefore, He would neither forget nor forsake them. He would fulfill His purposes for creating them (v.16).

Thought 1. God has awakened, risen up, to meet our need. We are held in bondage to sin and death. We cannot keep from sinning and falling short of God's glory. Nor can we keep from dying. Death is inevitable; every human being will die. Sin and death have taken us captive, enslaved us, and put us in bondage. But God has given us a wonderful promise: we can be delivered from sin and death. Jesus Christ has paid the ransom to set us free from captivity. No one has to continue walking in sin, and no one has to die and be separated from God. Through Jesus Christ, we can be saved both from sin and death. Victory over sin and eternal life are priceless gifts bestowed on believers through the redemption that is in Christ Jesus.

"**For God so loved the world, that he gave his only begotten Son, that whosoever believeth in him should not perish, but have everlasting life. For God sent not his Son into the world to condemn the world; but that the world through him might be saved**" (Jn.3:16-17).

"**For all have sinned, and come short of the glory of God; Being justified freely by his grace through the redemption that is in Christ Jesus**" (Ro.3:23-24).

"**Christ hath redeemed us from the curse of the law, being made a curse for us: for it is written, Cursed** *is* **every one that hangeth on a tree**" (Ga.3:13).

"**In whom we have redemption through his blood,** *even* **the forgiveness of sins**" (Col.1:14).

"**Looking for that blessed hope, and the glorious appearing of the great God and our Saviour Jesus Christ; Who gave himself for us, that he might redeem us from all iniquity, and purify unto himself a peculiar people, zealous of good works**" (Tit.2:13-14).

"**Neither by the blood of goats and calves, but by his own blood he entered in once into the holy place, having obtained eternal redemption** *for us.* **For if the blood of bulls and of goats, and the ashes of an heifer sprinkling the unclean, sanctifieth to the purifying of the flesh: How much more shall the blood of Christ, who through the eternal Spirit offered himself without spot to God, purge your conscience from dead works to serve the living God?**" (He.9:12-14).

"**Forasmuch as ye know that ye were not redeemed with corruptible things,** *as* **silver and gold, from your vain conversation** *received* **by tradition from your fathers; But with the precious blood of Christ, as of a lamb without blemish and without spot**" (1 Pe.1:18-19).

"**And they sung a new song, saying, Thou art worthy to take the book, and to open the seals thereof: for thou wast slain, and hast redeemed us to God by thy blood out of every kindred, and tongue, and people, and nation**" (Re.5:9).

---

3 (51:17–52:10) **Deliverance, from Captivity, Promise of—Jerusalem, Challenge to, to Awaken—Jerusalem, Prophecy Concerning, Destruction—Israel, Prophecy Concerning, Destruction; Restoration—Restoration, of Israel, Prophecy Concerning—Awake – Awaken, to Heed God's Promise; to Heed Prophecy**: Wake up, wake up, O Jerusalem! You—the redeemed of Jerusalem—will be set free from captivity. In these verses, the great city of Jerusalem is pictured as a mother whose children have been killed in war or else taken captive. As a result, there is no one left to help her. She has drained the cup of God's wrath, and now she staggers in a drunken stupor. But the LORD gives her great hope, the hope that her children would be freed from captivity and return home to give her a new beginning.[1] For that reason the mother should awaken and prepare for her returning children. The LORD Himself challenged the city to awaken, giving Jerusalem and its citizens three wake-up calls. (51:17-23; 52:1-10). Note the Scripture and outline:

OUTLINE	SCRIPTURE	SCRIPTURE	OUTLINE
3. **Wake up, wake up, O Jerusalem! You (the redeemed) will be set free from captivity: A picture of the believer being freed from sin & death** a. The city of Jerusalem must wake up & rise from its suffering of God's judgment 1) The city had no leaders to	17 Awake, awake, stand up, O Jerusalem, which hast drunk at the hand of the LORD the cup of his fury; thou hast drunken the dregs of the cup of trembling, *and* wrung *them* out. 18 *There is* none to guide her among all the sons *whom*	she hath brought forth; neither *is there any* that taketh her by the hand of all the sons *that* she hath brought up. 19 These two *things* are come unto thee; who shall be sorry for thee? desolation, and destruction, and the famine, and the sword: by whom	guide the people 2) The city had suffered a double calamity • Desolation & destruction • Famine & bloodshed

---

1 Warren W. Wiersbe. *Be Comforted*, p.129.

OUTLINE	SCRIPTURE	SCRIPTURE	OUTLINE
3) The city's young men had been killed & piled up in the streets 4) The afflicted city was challenged to heed God's promise • He defends His people (the redeemed), 12 • He would remove the cup of judgment—His	shall I comfort thee? 20 Thy sons have fainted, they lie at the head of all the streets, as a wild bull in a net: they are full of the fury of the LORD, the rebuke of thy God. 21 Therefore hear now this, thou afflicted, and drunken, but not with wine: 22 Thus saith thy Lord the LORD, and thy God *that* pleadeth the cause of his people, Behold, I have taken	out of thine hand the cup of trembling, *even* the dregs of the cup of my fury; thou shalt no more drink it again: 23 But I will put it into the hand of them that afflict thee; which have said to thy soul, Bow down, that we may go over: and thou hast laid thy body as the ground, and as the street, to them that went over.	discipline, chastisement—from His people • He would transfer the cup of judgment over to the persecutors & oppressors • He would make the redeemed victorious over all enemies

a. Jerusalem must wake up from the stupor caused by suffering God's judgment (vv.17-23). Because of the people's wickedness and idolatry, the cup of God's righteous wrath had been given to the city, and the citizens had drunk the LORD's fury to the last drop. They had no choice, for they were guilty of the most heinous sins against the LORD. Sadly, the city had no capable sons or leaders to guide the people (v.18), and most of the people were living selfish, wicked lives, disobeying the commandments of God. There were not enough righteous leaders to keep God's judgment from fall-ing upon the nation, and there was no one to stand in the gap as a mediator between the people and God.

As a result, the cup of God's judgment was poured out upon the city (v.19). Jerusalem suffered a double calamity—desolation and destruction, famine and sword. Isaiah predicted that the Babylonian war machine would march across the land of Judah and leave the nation utterly devastated. The young men of Jerusalem would fall in the street, dying either at the enemy's hands or from hunger (v.20). And Jerusalem would be like an antelope caught in a net, unable to escape its coming death.

But judgment was not the last word from the LORD. He offered wonderful hope to the city of Jerusalem and invited the citizens to hear His marvelous promises (vv.21-23). Note who was making these promises: "your Lord," "the LORD," and "your God." What was being stressed is the sovereignty of God, His power and control over all things, including the affairs of people and nations. His sovereign power and the fact that He was their God guaranteed that He would fulfill these promises to the city of Jerusalem and its citizens. He gave four specific promises:

⇒ The LORD would defend His people (the redeemed, vv.11-16). Since He was their God and possessed sovereign power, He was bound to defend them.

⇒ The LORD would remove the cup of judgment—His discipline and chastisement—from the people (v.22). His discipline would not last forever. He disciplined His people only to correct them, to stir them up to forsake their sins and return to Him in repentance.

⇒ The LORD would transfer the cup of judgment to the persecutors and oppressors of His people, and they would reap the torment and terror they had sown (v.23).

⇒ The LORD would cause the redeemed to be victorious over all their enemies (v.23). They would be more than conquerors.

Thought 1. A victorious life is one of the great promises God makes to believers. No matter what we face, a simple trial or a terrible hardship, persecution or even enslavement, the LORD promises to be with us and to meet our every need. Conquering, overcoming, triumphing over all the trials and temptations of life is possible through the LORD's presence and strength. Listen to the wonderful promises of God's Word:

"**But there shall not an hair of your head perish**" (Lu.21:18).

"**Who shall separate us from the love of Christ?** *shall* **tribulation, or distress, or persecution, or famine, or nakedness, or peril, or sword?...Nay, in all these things we are more than conquerors through him that loved us. For I am persuaded, that neither death, nor life, nor angels, nor principalities, nor powers, nor things present, nor things to come, Nor height, nor depth, nor any other creature, shall be able to separate us from the love of God, which is in Christ Jesus our Lord**" (Ro.8:35, 37-39).

"**Now thanks** *be* **unto God, which always causeth us to triumph in Christ, and maketh manifest the savour of his knowledge by us in every place**" (2 Co.2:14).

"**For though we walk in the flesh, we do not war after the flesh: (For the weapons of our warfare** *are* **not carnal, but mighty through God to the pulling down of strong holds;) Casting down imaginations, and every high thing that exalteth itself against the knowledge of God, and bringing into captivity every thought to the obedience of Christ**" (2 Co.10:3-5).

"**For the which cause I also suffer these things: nevertheless I am not ashamed: for I know whom I have believed, and am persuaded that he is able to keep that which I have committed unto him against that day**" (2 Ti.1:12).

"**And the Lord shall deliver me from every evil work, and will preserve** *me* **unto his heavenly kingdom: to whom** *be* **glory for ever and ever. Amen**" (2 Ti.4:18).

"*Let your* **conversation [conduct, conversation]** *be* **without covetousness;** *and be* **content with such things as ye have: for he hath said, I will never leave thee, nor forsake thee. So that we may boldly say, The Lord** *is* **my helper, and I will not fear what man shall do unto me**" (He.13:5-6).

"**Casting all your care upon him; for he careth for you**" (1 Pe.5:7).

"For whatsoever is born of God overcometh the world: and this is the victory that overcometh the world, *even* our faith. Who is he that overcometh the world, but he that believeth that Jesus is the Son of God?" (1 Jn.5:4-5).

"And, behold, I *am* with thee, and will keep thee in all *places* whither thou goest, and will bring thee again into this land; for I will not leave thee, until I have done *that* which I have spoken to thee of" (Ge.28:15).

"For the eyes of the LORD run to and fro throughout the whole earth, to show himself strong in the behalf of *them* whose heart *is* perfect toward him. Herein thou hast done foolishly: therefore from henceforth thou shalt have wars" (2 Chr.16:9).

"The angel of the LORD encampeth round about them that fear him, and delivereth them" (Ps.34:7).

"Through thee will we push down our enemies: through thy name will we tread them under that rise up against us" (Ps.44:5).

"He shall cover thee with his feathers, and under his wings shalt thou trust: his truth *shall be thy* shield and buckler" (Ps.91:4).

"Thou shalt not be afraid for the terror by night; *nor* for the arrow *that* flieth by day" (Ps.91:5).

"He shall not be afraid of evil tidings: his heart is fixed, trusting in the LORD" (Ps.112:7).

"When thou liest down, thou shalt not be afraid: yea, thou shalt lie down, and thy sleep shall be sweet" (Pr.3:24).

"For thou hast been a strength to the poor, a strength to the needy in his distress, a refuge from the storm, a shadow from the heat, when the blast of the terrible ones *is* as a storm *against* the wall" (Is.25:4).

b. The city of Jerusalem must wake up and be clothed with splendor and strength (52:1-6). It was not enough for Jerusalem to put off the stupor caused by drinking God's wrath. It must also put on the beautiful garment of splendor and strength, the only garment suitable for the *Holy City* of God. Five reasons are given why Jerusalem must reclothe itself:

1) Jerusalem must put on new garments because it is the Holy City (v.1). To be *holy* means to be set apart to God, to be distinct and different in morality and righteousness. Note that the *uncircumcised*, which refers to unbelievers, and the unclean will no longer be allowed to enter Jerusalem. This is a clear indication that this prophecy refers to the Messiah's kingdom. When Jesus Christ returns to set up God's kingdom on earth, Jerusalem will be the seat of God's worldwide government.

2) Jerusalem must put on new garments because it is to arise from the dust (v.2). Not only during the Babylonian captivity but also down through the centuries, Jerusalem has suffered bondage, oppression, and destruction time and again. But in the Messiah's kingdom, the city will sit enthroned as the capital of the world, never again to be held captive by a foreign nation or people. In that day, Jerusalem will definitely be the *Holy City*, the very seat of God's government and kingdom on earth.

3) Jerusalem must put on new garments because it will be redeemed without money, set free totally by God's grace (v.3). Nation after nation had conquered Jerusalem throughout history, yet none had paid the Jews for the right to rule over them. But the day was coming when God Himself would provide redemption for the city. Clearly, this is a reference to the redemption provided through the Messiah, the Lord Jesus Christ.

4) Jerusalem must put on new garments because suffering had tainted God's people (vv.4-5). Centuries earlier, the Israelites had been enslaved by Egypt. More recently, they had been oppressed by Assyria, and now they were about to be exiled to Babylon. Through all these terrible enslavements, God's people were persecuted, mocked, and forced to hear God's name blasphemed and cursed all day long. Living in the midst of such foul behavior and language contaminated the people, even true believers. Thus, Jerusalem and its people must awaken and put on new clothing, the clothing of God's righteousness.

5) Jerusalem must put on new garments because God's people will know the LORD's name, know Him personally (v.6). The new clothing is the redemption provided by the Lord Jesus Christ. To be accepted in the Messiah's kingdom, people must *put on* the Lord Jesus Christ Himself and the redemption He provides.

OUTLINE	SCRIPTURE	SCRIPTURE	OUTLINE
	CHAPTER 52	Ye have sold yourselves for nought; and ye shall be redeemed without money.	deemed without money— freely, by grace
b. The city of Jerusalem must wake up & be clothed with splendor & strength	Awake, awake; put on thy strength, O Zion; put on thy beautiful garments, O Jerusalem, the holy city: for	4 For thus saith the Lord GOD, My people went down aforetime into Egypt to sojourn there; and the Assyrian	4) Because God's people had suffered so much
1) Because it is holy: The impure & godless would no longer enter	henceforth there shall no more come into thee the uncircumcised and the unclean.	oppressed them without cause.	• Had been enslaved by Egypt & oppressed by Assyria
2) Because it is to arise from the dust: Be enthroned & freed from captivity	2 Shake thyself from the dust; arise, *and* sit down, O Jerusalem: loose thyself from the bands of thy neck, O captive daughter of Zion.	5 Now therefore, what have I here, saith the LORD, that my people is taken away for nought? they that rule over them make them to howl, saith the LORD; and my name continually every day is blas-	• Were now in bondage & exiled to Babylon: Being persecuted & mocked & having to hear God's name blasphemed all day long
3) Because it is to be re-	3 For thus saith the LORD,		

OUTLINE	SCRIPTURE	SCRIPTURE	OUTLINE
5) Because God's people would know the LORD's name—	phemed. 6　Therefore my people shall know　my　name:　therefore	*they shall know* in that day that I *am* he that doth speak: behold, *it is* I.	know Him personally: Because He would fulfill His promise of redemption, 3

"But put ye on the Lord Jesus Christ, and make not provision for the flesh, to *fulfil* the lusts *thereof*" (Ro.13:14).

"Therefore if any man *be* in Christ, *he is* a new creature: old things are passed away; behold, all things are become new" (2 Co.5:17).

"That ye put off concerning the former conversation [conduct, conversation] the old man, which is corrupt according to the deceitful lusts; And be renewed in the spirit of your mind; And that ye put on the new man, which after God is created in righteousness and true holiness. Wherefore putting away lying, speak every man truth with his neighbour: for we are members one of another. Be ye angry, and sin not: let not the sun go down upon your wrath: Neither give place to the devil. Let him that stole steal no more: but rather let him labour, working with *his* hands the thing which is good, that he may have to give to him that needeth. Let no corrupt communication proceed out of your mouth, but that which is good to the use of edifying, that it may minister grace unto the hearers. And grieve not the holy Spirit of God, whereby ye are sealed unto the day of redemption. Let all bitterness, and wrath, and anger, and clamour, and evil speaking, be put away from you, with all malice: And be ye kind one to another, tenderhearted, forgiving one another, even as God for Christ's sake hath forgiven you" (Ep.4:22-32).

"But now ye also put off all these; anger, wrath, malice, blasphemy, filthy communication out of your mouth. Lie not one to another, seeing that ye have put off the old man with his deeds; And have put on the new *man*, which is renewed in knowledge after the image of him that created him" (Col.3:8-10).

c.　The city of Jerusalem must wake up and listen to the watchmen's proclamation of the good news (vv.7-10). The runner who brought good news was the messenger who raced from a battlefield with the latest news of victory or defeat. The watchmen were people within the city appointed to stand watch, looking for the arrival of the messengers bringing their news. In the present case, the news was coming from the LORD Himself. He had *good news* to be proclaimed to His people. Keep in mind that the Israelites had been taken captive and scattered all over the Babylonian Empire. All the cities of Judah had been destroyed and the land devastated. Jerusalem itself lay in shambles, utterly ruined. Thus, when God challenged the city to listen to the watchmen's proclamation, the Jews scattered throughout the Babylonian Empire experienced a great anticipation rising in their hearts. The runner brought the glorious news that King Cyrus of Persia had defeated Babylon and was now freeing the Jews to return to their homeland. Thus, the feet of the messenger bringing such wonderful news were beautiful. The message sent by God had four aspects:

⇒　The message was the good news of peace and salvation (v.7). The LORD reigns over the earth, and He had proven His sovereign power by saving His people. They were free to return to the promised land.

⇒　The message was the good news of the LORD's return to Zion, or Jerusalem (v.8). When Christ returns to earth, Jerusalem will be the seat of both government and religion. Every eye on earth will see Christ and witness the glory of His person and kingdom.

⇒　The message is the good news of the LORD's comfort and redemption (v.9). No greater comfort can come to the human soul than that of salvation. Being saved from the bondages of this world brings comfort to the human soul.

⇒　The message was the good news that the ends of the earth would see God's salvation (v.10). Isaiah prophesied that God's arm of power would rise against Babylon, destroy the enemy of His people, and set His people free. Note the reference to the *ends of the earth*. This points to the Messiah's kingdom, the time when Christ will return to set up God's kingdom on earth. When He returns, He will exercise His absolute power against all the brutal, wicked nations of earth in the battle that is commonly called Armageddon (see outline and notes—Re.19:17-21 for more discussion).

OUTLINE	SCRIPTURE	SCRIPTURE	OUTLINE
c.　The city of Jerusalem must wake up & listen to the watchmen's proclamation of good news 1) The good news of peace & salvation, of God's reign on earth 2) The good news of the LORD's return to Zion (Jerusalem)	7　How beautiful upon the mountains are the feet of him that　bringeth　good　tidings, that　publisheth　peace;　that bringeth　good　tidings　of good, that publisheth salvation; that saith unto Zion, Thy God reigneth! 8　Thy　watchmen　shall lift up the voice; with the voice together shall they sing: for they　shall　see　eye　to　eye,	when the LORD shall bring again Zion. 9　Break forth into joy, sing together, ye waste places of Jerusalem: for the LORD hath comforted his people, he hath redeemed Jerusalem. 10 The LORD hath made bare his holy arm in the eyes of all the nations; and all the ends of the earth shall see the salvation of our God.	3) The good news of the LORD's comfort & redemption 4) The good news that God will destroy the enemies of His people, both in Isaiah's day & when Christ returns to earth

Thought 1. The *good news* of salvation is to be proclaimed around the world. God loves the world and everyone in it. Therefore He longs to save us all. This was the very purpose for which He sent His Son into the world. Christ was not sent to condemn us but to save us. This is the wonderful message of salvation through Christ:

"For God so loved the world, that he gave his only begotten Son, that whosoever believeth in him should not perish, but have everlasting life. For God sent not his Son into the world to condemn the world; but that the world through him might be saved. He that believeth on him is not condemned: but he that believeth not is condemned already, because he hath not believed in the name of the only begotten Son of God" (Jn.3:16-18).

"I am the door: by me if any man enter in, he shall be saved, and shall go in and out, and find pasture. The thief cometh not, but for to steal, and to kill, and to destroy: I am come that they might have life, and that they might have *it* more abundantly" (Jn.10:9-10).

"Neither is there salvation in any other: for there is none other name under heaven given among men, whereby we must be saved" (Ac.4:12).

"But God commendeth his love toward us, in that, while we were yet sinners, Christ died for us. Much more then, being now justified by his blood, we shall be saved from wrath through him" (Ro.5:8-9).

"For by grace are ye saved through faith; and that not of yourselves: *it is* the gift of God: Not of works, lest any man should boast" (Ep.2:8-9).

"For God hath not appointed us to wrath, but to obtain salvation by our Lord Jesus Christ" (1 Th.5:9).

"Though he were a Son, yet learned he obedience by the things which he suffered; And being made perfect, he became the author of eternal salvation unto all them that obey him" (He.5:8-9).

"So Christ was once offered to bear the sins of many; and unto them that look for him shall he appear the second time without sin unto salvation" (He.9:28).

4 (52:11-12) **Spiritual Separation, Duty—Separation, Spiritual, Duty—Purity, Duty—Morality, Duty—Righteousness, Duty—Israel, Duty—Believers, Duty:** Depart, depart! Flee the captivity of Babylon. When liberty was proclaimed, God's people were to immediately leave the land of their bondage. They were to get out and never return because Babylon was the epitome of wickedness and idolatry. Babylonian society was steeped in the pollutions of this world:

⇒ sexual immorality	⇒ discord	⇒ greed
⇒ impurity	⇒ prejudice	⇒ covetousness
⇒ debauchery	⇒ jealousy	⇒ injustice
⇒ idolatry	⇒ rage	⇒ envy
⇒ witchcraft	⇒ hostility	⇒ drunkenness
⇒ hatred	⇒ selfish ambition	⇒ orgies

Babylon was no place for God's people. Believers were to turn away from the sinful nation and its people and return to the promised land. They were not to touch any unclean thing nor were they to take any unclean thing—whether behavior or object—with them. They were to make a complete break from the world of their captivity. They were not to continue or even be reminded of the wicked world that had held them in bondage.

Note that priests in particular were to keep themselves pure, for they would be carrying the holy vessels (utensils) and furnishings that belonged in Jerusalem's temple. Cyrus would return the holy vessels that Nebuchadnezzar had taken as plunder from the temple (Ezr.1:7). Handling the holy vessels of the LORD was a very special privilege that God had given the priests. Therefore, the priests were to prepare themselves for the task through ritual cleansings (see outlines and notes—Nu.3:5-13; 2 Chr.5:2-10 for more discussion).

God gave His people a wonderful promise: they would not be threatened or forced to flee as they left Babylon. Centuries before when the Israelites were set free by the Egyptians, they had to flee for their lives (Ex.12:33-39; see outline and note—Ex.14:5-12 for more discussion). Although they did not have to flee from this captivity, God's people were not to linger. The LORD instructed them to depart *immediately,* to make haste to get out of Babylon (the world). If they would leave the world of wickedness and false worship without delay, God would personally go before them and guide them, and He would grant His presence as a rear guard to protect them. With His guidance and protection, they would reach the promised land.

OUTLINE	SCRIPTURE	SCRIPTURE	OUTLINE
4. Depart, depart! Flee the captivity of Babylon: A picture of spiritual separation a. The charge: Not to touch any unclean thing, to be pure	11 Depart ye, depart ye, go ye out from thence, touch no unclean *thing;* go ye out of the midst of her; be ye clean, that bear the vessels of the LORD.	12 For ye shall not go out with haste, nor go by flight: for the LORD will go before you; and the God of Israel *will be* your reward.	b. The promise: Would not be threatened, forced to flee 1) God would lead the way 2) God would also be their rear guard, protect their back

Thought 1. Note this important fact: the events described above had not yet taken place when God's prophet Isaiah was predicting them. Think about this fact for a moment. It would be more than 150 years before King Cyrus defeated Babylon and set God's people free. This is an astounding prophecy and clear proof of the accuracy of God's Holy Word. What God is saying in this passage is of paramount importance, and it is applicable to believers of all generations. When we as believers hear the message that sets us free, we are to immediately leave the world of wickedness and false worship. We are to spiritually separate ourselves from the pollutions of this world. We are to touch no unclean thing. "Depart, Depart, go out from there!" This is God's strong charge to us. After we have been

set free from sin and death by Christ, we must have nothing else to do with the evil and the idols of this world. We are to renounce all sin and idol worship, put them behind us, and be totally separated to God.

"And with many other words did he testify and exhort, saying, Save yourselves from this untoward generation" (Ac.2:40).

"I wrote unto you in an epistle not to company with fornicators: Yet not altogether with the fornicators of this world, or with the covetous, or extortioners, or with idolaters; for then must ye needs go out of the world. But now I have written unto you not to keep company, if any man that is called a brother be a fornicator, or covetous, or an idolater, or a railer, or a drunkard, or an extortioner; with such an one no not to eat" (1 Co.5:9-11).

"Be ye not unequally yoked together with unbelievers: for what fellowship hath righteousness with unrighteousness? and what communion hath light with darkness? And what concord hath Christ with Belial? or what part hath he that believeth with an infidel? And what agreement hath the temple of God with idols? for ye are the temple of the living God; as God hath said, I will dwell in them, and walk in *them;* and I will be their God, and they shall be my people" (2 Co.6:14-16).

"Wherefore come out from among them, and be ye separate, saith the Lord, and touch not the unclean *thing;* and I will receive you, And will be a Father unto you, and ye shall be my sons and daughters, saith the Lord Almighty" (2 Co.6:17-18).

"And have no fellowship with the unfruitful works of darkness, but rather reprove *them.* For it is a shame even to speak of those things which are done of them in secret" (Ep.5:11-12).

"Now we command you, brethren, in the name of our Lord Jesus Christ, that ye withdraw yourselves from every brother that walketh disorderly, and not after the tradition which he received of us" (2 Th.3:6).

"Thou shalt not follow a multitude to *do* evil; neither shalt thou speak in a cause to decline after many to wrest *judgment*" (Ex.23:2).

"Take heed to thyself, lest thou make a covenant with the inhabitants of the land whither thou goest, lest it be for a snare in the midst of thee" (Ex.34:12).

"Blessed *is* the man that walketh not in the counsel of the ungodly, nor standeth in the way of sinners, nor sitteth in the seat of the scornful" (Ps.1:1).

"My son, if sinners entice thee, consent thou not....My son, walk not thou in the way with them; refrain thy foot from their path" (Pr.1:10, 15).

"Enter not into the path of the wicked, and go not in the way of evil *men*" (Pr.4:14).

"Be not thou envious against evil men, neither desire to be with them" (Pr.24:1).

"Make no friendship with an angry man; and with a furious man thou shalt not go: Lest thou learn his ways, and get a snare to thy soul" (Pr.22:24-25).

"Eat thou not the bread of *him that hath* an evil eye, neither desire thou his dainty meats: For as he thinketh in his heart, so *is* he: Eat and drink, saith he to thee; but his heart *is* not with thee" (Pr.23:6-7).

CHAPTER 52

C. The Savior's Suffering, His Atoning Death,[DS1] 52:13–53:12

1. The Savior came for four very specific purposes
   a. To live wisely: Obey God
   b. To be highly exalted, Ph.2:7-11
   c. To be crucified
      1) His appearance marred: Beaten & bloodied
      2) His body disfigured: Unrecognizable—no longer looked like a man
   d. To sprinkle (cleanse) & redeem people from many nations
      1) Kings (& people) would be speechless before Him
      2) People would understand the gospel, Ro.15:20-21

2. The Savior suffered rejection
   a. His coming had been predicted but rejected: God's arm, His power, was denied
   b. His coming as a child was unexpected & rejected
      1) He grew up in God's care but on dry ground: Poverty
      2) He had nothing attractive or majestic about His appearance
   c. His coming as a man of sorrows who had to suffer for the human race was rejected
      1) He was despised & scorned by people
      2) He was turned away from, not esteemed

3. The Savior bore the penalty for man's sin
   a. The sad fact: He suffered for us, yet many felt He was justly executed as a criminal
   b. The truth: He died for us
      1) Our griefs & sorrows, 4
      2) Our transgressions & iniquities

13 Behold, my servant shall deal prudently, he shall be exalted and extolled, and be very high.
14 As many were astonied at thee; his visage was so marred more than any man, and his form more than the sons of men:
15 So shall he sprinkle many nations; the kings shall shut their mouths at him: for *that* which had not been told them shall they see; and *that* which they had not heard shall they consider.

CHAPTER 53

Who hath believed our report? and to whom is the arm of the LORD revealed?
2 For he shall grow up before him as a tender plant, and as a root out of a dry ground: he hath no form nor comeliness; and when we shall see him, *there is* no beauty that we should desire him.
3 He is despised and rejected of men; a man of sorrows, and acquainted with grief: and we hid as it were *our* faces from him; he was despised, and we esteemed him not.
4 Surely he hath borne our griefs, and carried our sorrows: yet we did esteem him stricken, smitten of God, and afflicted.
5 But he *was* wounded for our transgressions, *he was* bruised for our iniquities: the chastisement of our peace

was upon him; and with his stripes we are healed.
6 All we like sheep have gone astray; we have turned every one to his own way; and the LORD hath laid on him the iniquity of us all.
7 He was oppressed, and he was afflicted, yet he opened not his mouth: he is brought as a lamb to the slaughter, and as a sheep before her shearers is dumb, so he openeth not his mouth.
8 He was taken from prison and from judgment: and who shall declare his generation? for he was cut off out of the land of the living: for the transgression of my people was he stricken.
9 And he made his grave with the wicked, and with the rich in his death; because he had done no violence, neither *was any* deceit in his mouth.
10 Yet it pleased the LORD to bruise him; he hath put *him* to grief: when thou shalt make his soul an offering for sin, he shall see *his* seed, he shall prolong *his* days, and the pleasure of the LORD shall prosper in his hand.
11 He shall see of the travail of his soul, *and* shall be satisfied: by his knowledge shall my righteous servant justify many; for he shall bear their iniquities.
12 Therefore will I divide him *a portion* with the great, and he shall divide the spoil with the strong; because he hath poured out his soul unto death: and he was numbered with the transgressors; and he bare the sin of many, and made intercession for the transgressors.

   c. The purpose of His death
      1) To give us peace & healing
      2) To save us from the sin of going astray & its penalty: Death, Eze.18:4; Ro.6:23
   d. The way He saved us: By bearing sin for us

4. The Savior suffered willingly but unjustly: Was the sinless Son of God
   a. He willingly & silently suffered harsh treatment: Just like a lamb led to the slaughter
   b. He willingly suffered an illegal arrest, trial, & execution
      1) He was cut off—put to death—for the transgression of God's people
      2) He was stricken for the sins of God's people
   c. He willingly suffered a burial with the wicked, even though He was the sinless Son of God

5. The results of the Savior's suffering
   a. He became the *substitute sacrifice* for sin
   b. He produces many offspring, righteous believers
   c. He prolonged His days: Arose to carry on & advance God's work
   d. He conquered death & brought satisfaction to everyone involved
   e. He justified many: By bearing their iniquities
   f. He is honored as the great Victor: He will divide the wealth of His conquests with the strong (believers)
      1) Because He died as a transgressor
      2) Because He bore the sin of many
      3) Because He made intercession for sinners

DIVISION VI

THE PROPHECIES OF THE GREAT DELIVERER: THE SUFFERING SERVANT OF GOD, THE SAVIOR OF THE WORLD, 49:1–59:21

C. The Savior's Suffering, His Atoning Death, 52:13–53:12

(52:13–53:12) **Introduction**: *Isaiah 53* is the summit, the Mount Everest of biblical prophecy.[1] In this chapter, the Savior of the world is seen suffering for the sins of the human race, and the scene and meaning of His death are described in surprising detail. For true believers, Isaiah 53 is one of the most heartbreaking yet cherished passages of Scripture, for it describes the brutal treatment and horrible sufferings Christ endured *on our behalf*.

---

1 Warren Wiersbe. *Be Comforted*, p.132. Wiersbe gleaned the quote from the Biblical Scholar, Dr. Kyle M. Yates.

A marked feature of *Isaiah 53* is the vicarious, substitutionary death of God's "suffering Servant," the promised Messiah. Emphasizing this theme time and again, Isaiah predicts that the Savior will die "for our sins." He will die "in our place," "on our behalf," "in our stead," "for us," "as our *substitute*." Paying the penalty of sin *for us*, the Savior will set us free from the bondage of sin, death, and hell. Through His death, we have received from God the most amazing healing and salvation. We have been saved from the bondages of sin and death, and from the coming terrifying judgment of God against all unrepentant sinners.

Meditating on the sufferings of Christ will break a person's heart, for they overwhelm human imagination. Christ bore all the sadistic, brutal treatment due us—every one of us. Grasping this truth is bound to drive us to the ground on our faces before Him.

Interestingly, this prophecy about the Messiah's sufferings was written more than seven hundred years before the coming of Jesus Christ. How then do we know that this Scripture is a prophecy about Christ and not someone else? There are several facts that show beyond any doubt that Jesus Christ is the suffering Servant of God, the Savior of the world.

First, Isaiah predicts time and again that God's Servant will definitely be the Messiah (42:1f; 49:1f; 50:1f; 52:12f; also see 9:6-7). And passages throughout the New Testament repeatedly identify Jesus Christ as the Messiah promised by God (Mt.8:16-17; 11:2-6; 16:16; 26:63-64; Mk.15:25-28; Lu.2:10-11; 2:25-32; 4:41; 24:45-48; Jn.1:41; 1:49; 4:25-26; 6:14, 68-69; 8:28; 11:25-27; Ac.8:26-40; 9:22; 17:2-4; 1 Pe.2:21-24; 1 Jn.5:1).

Second, Philip the evangelist identified the suffering Servant of Isaiah 53 with Christ. An Ethiopian eunuch was once reading from the fifty-third chapter of Isaiah, and he asked Philip who the suffering Servant was. Without hesitation or equivocation, Philip replied that it was Jesus. Then he explained how Jesus fulfilled the prophecy of the suffering Savior (Ac.8:26-40).

Third, Paul says that this chapter refers to the preaching of the gospel and to a person's confession of Christ as the Savior of the world (Ro.10:9-10, 13, 16; compared with 53:1).

Fourth, the apostle John says that Isaiah 53 applies to Christ (Jn.12:37-38; compared with 53:1).

Fifth, as Warren W. Wiersbe points out, up until the twelfth century, Jewish scholars interpreted Isaiah 53 as Messianic and identified God's Servant as the Messiah. After the twelfth century, however, scholars began interpreting the passage as a reference to the sufferings of the nation Israel. But how could Israel die for the sins of Israel (v.8)? Also, how could anyone declare that Israel was innocent of sin and had suffered unjustly (v.9)? Isaiah 53 presents a suffering Servant who is sinless, completely innocent and unworthy of death. The prophecy does not concern a nation of innocent people, but rather an individual who suffers for the sins of the entire world, for people such as the Ethiopian eunuch (52:15; Ac.8:26-40).[2]

Isaiah 53 is a graphic description of the suffering Servant of God, who is identified in the New Testament as Jesus Christ. Because God loved the world so much, He sent His Son to save the human race from the bondages of sin, death, and the terrifying judgment to come. Jesus Christ is the Savior of the world, who forgives the sins of all who truly believe and love Him, obeying His holy commandments. This is, *The Savior's Suffering, His Atoning Death*, 52:13–53:12.

1. The Savior came for four very specific purposes (52:13-15).
2. The Savior suffered rejection (53:1-3).
3. The Savior suffered for the penalty of sin (53:4-6).
4. The Savior suffered willingly but unjustly: Was the sinless Son of God (53:7-9).
5. The results of the Savior's suffering (53:10-12).

DEEPER STUDY # 1

(52:13–53:12) **Scripture, Fulfilled—Prophecy, Fulfilled**: Because of the length of this Deeper Study, it is being placed at the end of this commentary, p.204.

---

1 (52:13-15) **Servant of God, Prophecy Concerning, His Death—Christ, Death of, Purposes—Suffering, of Christ, Purposes—Savior, Sufferings of, Purposes—Christ, Wisdom of, to Do God's Will—Wisdom, of Christ, Did God's Will—Christ, Obedience of, Did God's Will—Christ, Exaltation, Prophecy Concerning—Prophecies, Concerning Christ, Exaltation—Crucifixion, of Christ, Prophecy Concerning—Christ, Crucifixion of, Severity Predicted—Redemption, of Christ, Prophecy Concerning**: God Himself is speaking here, and He says that He will send His Servant, the Savior, for four very specific purposes. Through Isaiah, God reveals exactly why He will send the Messiah into the world.

OUTLINE	SCRIPTURE	SCRIPTURE	OUTLINE

1. The Savior came for four very specific purposes
a. To live wisely: Obey God
b. To be highly exalted, Ph.2:7-11
c. To be crucified
  1) His appearance marred: Beaten & bloodied
  2) His body disfigured:
	13 Behold, my servant shall deal prudently, he shall be exalted and extolled, and be very high.
	14 As many were astonied at thee; his visage was so marred more than any man, and his form more than the
		sons of men:
		15 So shall he sprinkle many nations; the kings shall shut their mouths at him: for *that* which had not been told them shall they see; and *that* which they had not heard shall they consider.
			Unrecognizable—no longer looked like a man
			d. To sprinkle (cleanse) & redeem people from many nations
			  1) Kings (& people) would be speechless before Him
			  2) People would understand the gospel, Ro.15:20-21

a. God's Servant, the Savior, came to live *wisely*, which means that He came to carry out God's will on earth. God has a very specific purpose for the world, and His Servant came to make sure that purpose is carried out. The word *prudently*

---

2 Warren W. Wiersbe. *Be Comforted*, p.132.

or *wisely*, means to be circumspect, intelligent, or to act with wisdom. But it can also mean *to prosper* or *have good success*. It is not surprising then that some translations of the Bible say that the Servant will act *prudently* or *wisely*, while others say that He will *prosper*, which means that He will succeed in carrying out God's will on earth. Combining both thoughts stresses a significant truth: the Savior would act wisely in that He would do exactly what God sent Him to do, and He would accomplish His task. He would obey God perfectly, coming up short in nothing. As Isaiah predicted earlier, "the Spirit of the LORD shall rest upon Him, the Spirit of wisdom and understanding, the Spirit of counsel and might, the Spirit and of the fear of the LORD" (11:2).

Christ lived wisely. He obeyed God, did exactly what God wanted done, and accomplished God's will on earth. Of course, God's will is for all people to obey Him, to know and worship Him, living righteously as they walk through life. By never failing to obey God, Christ became the *Ideal Righteousness*—the very embodiment, the representative, the pattern of righteousness. Just like the pattern of any product, many copies are made from the pattern, each being exactly like the original. Because Christ is the *Ideal Righteousness*, His righteousness can stand for or cover all people who put their trust in Him. In other words, when people place their faith in Christ, God no longer sees them as sinners, but as *righteous*, covered by the righteousness of Christ.

"Think not that I am come to destroy the law, or the prophets: I am not come to destroy, but to fulfil" (Mt.5:17).

"He went away again the second time, and prayed, saying, O my Father, if this cup may not pass away from me, except I drink it, thy will be done" (Mt.26:42).

"Jesus saith unto them, My meat [food] is to do the will of him that sent me, and to finish his work" (Jn.4:34).

"I can of mine own self do nothing: as I hear, I judge: and my judgment is just; because I seek not mine own will, but the will of the Father which hath sent me" (Jn.5:30).

"If ye keep my commandments, ye shall abide in my love; even as I have kept my Father's commandments, and abide in his love" (Jn.15:10).

"I have glorified thee on the earth: I have finished the work which thou gavest me to do" (Jn.17:4).

"For as by one man's disobedience many were made sinners, so by the obedience of one shall many be made righteous" (Ro.5:19).

"For he hath made him *to be* sin for us, who knew no sin; that we might be made the righteousness of God in him" (2 Co.5:21).

"For as many as are of the works of the law are under the curse: for it is written, Cursed *is* every one that continueth not in all things which are written in the book of the law to do them. But that no man is justified by the law in the sight of God, *it is* evident: for, The just shall live by faith. And the law is not of faith: but, The man that doeth them shall live in them. Christ hath redeemed us from the curse of the law, being made a curse for us: for it is written, Cursed *is* every one that hangeth on a tree" (Ga.3:10-13).

"But the scripture hath concluded all under sin, that the promise by faith of Jesus Christ might be given to them that believe. But before faith came, we were kept under the law, shut up unto the faith which should afterwards be revealed. Wherefore the law was our schoolmaster *to bring us* unto Christ, that we might be justified by faith. But after that faith is come, we are no longer under a schoolmaster. For ye are all the children of God by faith in Christ Jesus" (Ga.3:22-26).

"For it became him, for whom *are* all things, and by whom *are* all things, in bringing many sons unto glory, to make the captain of their salvation perfect through sufferings" (He.2:10).

"For we have not an high priest which cannot be touched with the feeling of our infirmities; but was in all points tempted like as *we are, yet* without sin. Let us therefore come boldly unto the throne of grace, that we may obtain mercy, and find grace to help in time of need" (He.4:15-16).

"Though he were a Son, yet learned he obedience by the things which he suffered; And being made perfect, he became the author of eternal salvation unto all them that obey him" (He.5:8-9).

"Wherefore he is able also to save them to the uttermost that come unto God by him, seeing he ever liveth to make intercession for them. For such an high priest became us, *who is* holy, harmless, undefiled, separate from sinners, and made higher than the heavens" (He.7:25-26).

"Then said he, Lo, I come to do thy will, O God. He taketh away the first, that he may establish the second" (He.10:9, see v.13).

"Forasmuch as ye know that ye were not redeemed with corruptible things, *as* silver and gold, from your vain conversation [conduct, behavior] *received* by tradition from your fathers; But with the precious blood of Christ, as of a lamb without blemish and without spot" (1 Pe.1:18-19).

b. God's Servant, the Savior, came to be highly exalted (v.13). As is seen throughout this Scripture, the Savior suffered and died, but He did not remain dead. He rose from the dead, ascended into heaven, and sat down at the right hand of God. Because Christ lived wisely, obeying His Father in all things, He finished His ministry on earth both *completely* and *perfectly*. He achieved the greatest degree of success possible in that He wholly fulfilled and satisfied God's purpose for Him on earth. He was then raised from the dead, lifted up, and highly exalted by God Himself, both "now and forever" (Jude 25; Re.5:12).

⇒　The Savior, the Lord Jesus Christ, has been exalted to sit at the right hand of God.

"So then after the Lord had spoken unto them, he was received up into heaven, and sat on the right hand of God" (Mk.16:19).

"Hereafter shall the Son of man sit on the right hand of the power of God" (Lu.22:69).

"This Jesus hath God raised up, whereof we all are witnesses. Therefore being by the right hand of God exalted, and having received of the Father the promise of the Holy Ghost, he hath shed forth this, which ye now see and hear. For David is not ascended into the heavens: but he saith himself, The LORD said unto my Lord, Sit thou on my right hand, Until I make thy foes thy footstool. Therefore let all the house of Israel know assuredly, that God hath made that same Jesus, whom ye have crucified, both Lord and Christ" (Ac.2:32-36).

"The God of Abraham, and of Isaac, and of Jacob, the God of our fathers, hath glorified his Son Jesus; whom ye delivered up, and denied him in the presence of Pilate, when he was determined to let *him* go" (Ac.3:13).

"The God of our fathers raised up Jesus, whom ye slew and hanged on a tree. Him hath God exalted with his right hand *to be* a Prince and a Saviour, for to give repentance to Israel, and forgiveness of sins" (Ac.5:30-31).

⇒ All power and authority have been given to the Savior, the Lord Jesus Christ.

"And Jesus came and spake unto them, saying, All power is given unto me in heaven and in earth" (Mt.28:18).

⇒ All beings and all things have been put under the Savior's feet, and He is head over all.

"Which he wrought in Christ, when he raised him from the dead, and set *him* at his own right hand in the heavenly *places*, Far above all principality, and power, and might, and dominion, and every name that is named, not only in this world, but also in that which is to come: And hath put all *things* under his feet, and gave him *to be* the head over all *things*" (Ep.1:20-22).

⇒ All beings and all things will bow before the Savior and confess that Jesus Christ is Lord, to the glory of God the Father.

"[Christ] Who, being in the form of God, thought it not robbery to be equal with God: But made himself of no reputation, and took upon him the form of a servant, and was made in the likeness of men: And being found in fashion as a man, he humbled himself, and became obedient unto death, even the death of the cross. Wherefore God also hath highly exalted him, and given him a name which is above every name: That at the name of Jesus every knee should bow, of *things* in heaven, and *things* in earth, and *things* under the earth; And *that* every tongue should confess that Jesus Christ *is* Lord, to the glory of God the Father" (Ph.2:6-11).

c. God's Servant, the Savior was sent to suffer and die for our transgressions and iniquities (v.14; also see 53:5). The human mind staggers at the extreme severity of the sufferings inflicted upon and endured by Him. He was so beaten and bloody, so badly mutilated that His appearance was marred or ruined. And His body was disfigured, unrecognizable. He no longer looked like a man, no longer like a human being. Note that Scripture actually says this: that His form or body was so disfigured it was beyond recognition. People who saw Him were utterly horrified, shocked at His disfigurement. Most likely Scripture does not give a full account of the beatings and abuse inflicted upon the Savior. But what is shared causes the believer to cringe and feel sick at heart. The believer knows that the Lord Jesus Christ bore all these sufferings for his sins, as well as for the sins of the entire human race.

⇒ First, when Christ stood trial before the High Priest Caiaphas, the Jews spat in His face and beat Him with their fists and the palms of their hands.

"Then did they spit in his face, and buffeted him; and others smote *him* with the palms of their hands, Saying, Prophesy unto us, thou Christ, Who is he that smote thee?" (Mt.26:67-68).

"And some began to spit on him, and to cover his face, and to buffet him, and to say unto him, Prophesy: and the servants did strike him with the palms of their hands" (Mk.14:65).

"And the men that held Jesus mocked him, and smote *him*. And when they had blindfolded him, they struck him on the face, and asked him, saying, Prophesy, who is it that smote thee? And many other things blasphemously spake they against him" (Lu.22:63-65).

⇒ Second, Pilate had Christ scourged. By law, the Jews limited scourging to no more than 40 lashes, but the Romans had no such limitation. The extreme mockery and abuse painted by Scripture seems to indicate that Pilate had Him lashed many more times in order to please the Jews.

"Then released he Barabbas unto them: and when he had scourged Jesus, he delivered *him* to be crucified" (Mt.27:26).

"And *so* Pilate, willing to content the people, released Barabbas unto them, and delivered Jesus, when he had scourged *him*, to be crucified" (Mk.15:15).

"Then Pilate therefore took Jesus, and scourged *him*" (Jn.19:1).

⇒ Third, when Christ was turned over to the Roman soldiers, they not only scourged Him but they also twisted together a crown of thorns and clamped it down on His head. The soldiers then beat Him with their fists, probably until He collapsed.

> **"And the soldiers platted a crown of thorns, and put *it* on his head, and they put on him a purple robe, And said, Hail, King of the Jews! and they smote him with their hands" (Jn.19:2-3).**

⇒ Fourth, shockingly, the Roman soldiers even plucked off some, if not all, of His beard.

> **"I gave my back to the smiters, and my cheeks to them that plucked off the hair: I hid not my face from shame and spitting" (Is.50:6).**

⇒ Fifth, in His sufferings Christ was bearing sin for the human race. As Christ hung on the cross, He actually became "sin for us" (2 Co.5:21). And in becoming sin and dying, Christ was experiencing all that was contrary to the nature of God, which is *life and holiness*. Thus, Christ had to face the very judgment of God against Him as He bore the sins of the world. The spiritual suffering that took place far exceeded the physical suffering. God Himself was forsaking His own Son, executing His holy judgment against the sins that Christ was bearing on behalf of the human race. (See outline and note—Mt.27:46-49 for more discussion.) Christ undoubtedly sensed very deeply the *curse of separation* from God that sin causes. We should always remember that sin is the only thing that causes God to separate Himself from anyone. And if He separated Himself from Christ due to the sins He bore for mankind, He will certainly separate Himself from any sinner.

> **"And about the ninth hour Jesus cried with a loud voice, saying, Eli, Eli, lama sabachthani? that is to say, My God, my God, why hast thou forsaken me?" (Mt.27:46).**
> **"And at the ninth hour Jesus cried with a loud voice, saying, Eloi, Eloi, lama sabachthani? which is, being interpreted, My God, my God, why hast thou forsaken me?" (Mk.15:34).**
> **"But your iniquities have separated between you and your God, and your sins have hid *his* face from you, that he will not hear" (Is.59:2).**

d. God's Servant, the Savior, came to sprinkle (cleanse) and redeem many people in many nations (v.15). Sprinkling refers to the sacrificial blood of animals that had to be shed and sprinkled on the altar for forgiveness of sins (see outline and notes—Le.1:1-17; esp.vv.5, 11, 15 for more discussion; also see Le.3:2, 8, 13; 4:6, 16-17, 25, 30, 34; 5:9). Before Christ came, the blood of the sacrificial animals brought atonement and reconciliation between the worshippers and God. But now, since the coming of Christ, atonement for sin is secured through the shedding of His blood. And through His blood, many people in many nations are being redeemed, cleansed from their sins.

Although Christ would be rejected and crucified by the people of His day, once His mission and the gospel were understood, kings and citizens alike would stand speechless before Him. While He walked upon earth, most people would consider the Savior insignificant and unimportant. But after His death and resurrection, many would stand in stark amazement, stunned at how wrong the world had been to reject Him. In fact, their mouths would be shut, dumbfounded because Christ's coming had been misinterpreted so badly. As a result, many would hear the gospel, understand it, and accept Jesus Christ as their Savior. The apostle Paul clearly said that this prophecy refers to the preaching of Christ to the people of the world. Warren W. Wiersbe makes an excellent statement that is well worth quoting:

> *Many people have been tortured and killed in an inhumane way, but knowing about their suffering does not touch our conscience, though it might arouse our sympathy. Our Lord's sufferings and death were different, because they involved everybody in the world. The Gospel message is not "Christ died," for that is only a fact in history, like "Napoleon died." The Gospel message is that "Christ died for our sins (1 Cor.15:1-4). You and I are as guilty of Christ's death as Annas, Caiaphas, Herod Antipas, and Pilate.*[3]

> **"For this is my blood of the new testament, which is shed for many for the remission of sins" (Mt.26:28).**
> **"But God commendeth his love toward us, in that, while we were yet sinners, Christ died for us. Much more then, being now justified by his blood, we shall be saved from wrath through him" (Ro.5:8-9).**
> **"That I should be the minister of Jesus Christ to the Gentiles, ministering the gospel of God, that the offering up of the Gentiles might be acceptable, being sanctified by the Holy Ghost. I have therefore whereof I may glory through Jesus Christ in those things which pertain to God. For I will not dare to speak of any of those things which Christ hath not wrought by me, to make the Gentiles obedient, by word and deed. Through mighty signs and wonders, by the power of the Spirit of God; so that from Jerusalem, and round about unto Illyricum, I have fully preached the gospel of Christ. Yea, so have I strived to preach the gospel, not where Christ was named, lest I should build upon another man's foundation: But as it is written [in Isaiah], To whom he was not spoken of, they shall see: and they that have not heard shall understand" (Ro.15:16-21).**
> **"How much more shall the blood of Christ, who through the eternal Spirit offered himself without spot to God, purge your conscience from dead works to serve the living God?" (He.9:14).**

---

3 Warren W. Wiersbe. *Be Comforted*, p.135.

"Forasmuch as ye know that ye were not redeemed with corruptible things, *as* silver and gold, from your vain conversation *received* by tradition from your fathers; But with the precious blood of Christ, as of a lamb without blemish and without spot" (1 Pe.1:18-19).

"But if we walk in the light, as he is in the light, we have fellowship one with another, and the blood of Jesus Christ his Son cleanseth us from all sin. If we say that we have no sin, we deceive ourselves, and the truth is not in us. If we confess our sins, he is faithful and just to forgive us *our* sins, and to cleanse us from all unrighteousness" (1 Jn.1:7-9).

"And from Jesus Christ, *who is* the faithful witness, *and* the first begotten of the dead, and the prince of the kings of the earth. Unto him that loved us, and washed us from our sins in his own blood" (Re.1:5).

2 (53:1-3) **Rejection, of Christ, Prophecy Concerning—Unbelief, in Christ, Prophecy Concerning—Savior, Unbelief in, Prophecy Concerning—Prophecy, Concerning, Rejection of Christ**: a new speaker now comes to the forefront. While the speaker is not identified, the picture is that of believers discussing the Savior's death and the world's rejection of Him. While Christ walked on earth, He suffered rejection because He seemed to be of no consequence and was totally misunderstood. Down through the centuries, the vast majority of people have continued to reject God's Servant, the Savior of the world, the Lord Jesus Christ. Note the Scripture and outline:

OUTLINE	SCRIPTURE	SCRIPTURE	OUTLINE

2. The Savior suffered rejection
a. His coming had been predicted but rejected: God's arm, His power, was denied
b. His coming as a child was unexpected & rejected
  1) He grew up in God's care but on dry ground: Poverty
  2) He had nothing attractive
	Who hath believed our report? and to whom is the arm of the LORD revealed? 2 For he shall grow up before him as a tender plant, and as a root out of a dry ground: he hath no form nor comeliness; and when we shall see him, *there is* no	beauty that we should desire him. 3 He is despised and rejected of men; a man of sorrows, and acquainted with grief: and we hid as it were *our* faces from him; he was despised, and we esteemed him not.	or majestic about His appearance
			c. His coming as a man of sorrows who had to suffer for the human race was rejected
			  1) He was despised & scorned by people
			  2) He was turned away from, not esteemed

a. The Savior's coming had been predicted, but the prophecy had been rejected (v.1). Time and again, God had foretold that He would send the Messiah into the world. But very few believed the prophecies. They denied that God could or would use His power (arms), to do such a thing as send a savior to the world. Or else they denied the need for a savior, believing that people were capable and wise enough to meet their own needs. Thus, the prophecies concerning a coming Savior were rejected. In light of the coming of Jesus Christ and His clear fulfillment of so many Old Testament prophecies, one would think that the prophecies would be universally accepted and believed. But, tragically, few have believed, and believers down through the ages have cried out: "Who has believed our report (our message)? To whom has the arm of the LORD (His saving power) been revealed?"

b. The Savior's coming as a baby was totally unexpected and therefore it too was rejected (v.2). The people expected the son of David, a descendant of the great king, who would free the Jewish state from all its oppressors and make it one of the greatest nations the world has ever known (see DEEPER STUDY #2—Mt.1:18 for more discussion). The Jews expected the Messiah to come in great power and majesty, anticipating that He would immediately set them free from their captivity and oppression. But when the Messiah came into the world, He did not come as a conqueror, deliverer, or mighty prince. Instead the Messiah entered the world as a baby in totally unexpected and undesirable circumstances.

Jesus grew up in God's care, like a tender shoot of a plant that is barely noticed. Although He was a descendant of the royal, illustrious line of David, the family of David had sunk into insignificance and poverty. And Jesus' supposed father Joseph was only a poor carpenter. Even Nazareth, the place of Jesus' upbringing, was not a respected city (Jn.1:43-46). Thus Jesus grew and developed unnoticed, out of "dry ground," that is, in a humble and little known family. There was nothing to appeal or draw attention to His family, His environment, or even His country of birth. In fact, the nation Israel was a barren country of little importance to the rest of the world. At the time Christ was born, Israel had been conquered and was being ruled by the Romans.

Most people also expected the Messiah to be an attractive, charismatic person, someone who would stir hope in the hearts of all who saw Him. But as Scripture says (v.26), He was not physically attractive. He did not have a charismatic personality that naturally drew people to Him. Nothing about His appearance was striking or majestic. Nothing about it made Him any different from any other person. In outward appearance, Jesus was an average, ordinary person who would fit into any crowd, never attracting attention.

c. The Savior's coming as a man of sorrows was rejected. The very thought of His suffering for the human race was unacceptable to people (v.3). People dismiss the idea that they are...
- so sinful that they need a Savior to make them acceptable to God
- so sinful that God had to send His Son to die for their sins

To a variety of people, the cross and all it represents—the blood, the gore, the suffering—are repulsive, making Christianity a *bloody religion*. In their minds, individuals become acceptable to God by *good works*, doing the best they can throughout life. They believe that they do enough good works to be acceptable to God and that, in the final analysis, God would never reject them. As a result, they reject the idea of a Savior having to die for the sins of the human race.

Tragically, Christ was despised and rejected by men throughout His life. Many actually avoided Him because they detested Him so. As a result, Christ suffered not just when He died upon the cross but also during his day-to-day experiences throughout His life. Not only was He reared in poverty, but...

- He was born to a virgin mother (Mt.1:18-19).
- He was born in a stable under shocking conditions (Lu.2:7).
- He was born to poor parents (Lu.2:24).
- He had His life threatened as a baby (Mt.2:13f).
- He was the object of Herod's ambitious wrath, which led to the slaughter of all the male children two years and under (in Bethlehem and surrounding areas (Mt.2:16f).
- He had to be moved about for protection when He was a baby (Mt.2:13f).
- He was reared in a despicable place, Nazareth (Lu.2:39).
- He apparently lost His earthly father (Joseph) during His youth, for His father's name is not mentioned in the list of His family (Mt.13:55-56).
- He had no home as an adult, not even a place to lay His head (Mt.8:20; Lu.9:58).
- He had to depend upon others for financial support (Mt.8:2-3).
- He faced relentless temptation (Mt.4:1; He.2:18; 4:15).
- He was hated and opposed by religionists and had to face their continual hostility (Mk.14:1-2; He.12:3).
- He had the charge of insanity leveled against Him (Mk.3:21).
- He was charged with being demon possessed (Mk.3:22).
- He was opposed by His own family (Mk.3:31-32).
- He was rejected, hated and opposed by His audiences (Mt.13:53-58; Lu.4:28-29).
- He was betrayed by a close friend, Judas, one of the apostles (Mk.14:10-11, 18).
- He was left all alone at the end of His life, rejected and forsaken by all His friends (Mk.14:50).
- He was tried before the high court of the land on the charge of treason (Jn.18:33).
- He was put to death by crucifixion, the worst possible manner of death (Jn.19:16f).

The rejection, hostility, and sufferings of Christ during His life undoubtedly took their toll upon His body. Apparently He appeared so worn and aged that he was thought to be nearly 50 years old (Jn.8:57).[4] The depth of Christ's sufferings can be seen in three facts:

⇒ In coming to earth, Christ set aside all the glory, worship, and service given Him by the hosts of heaven itself, all of which He had always had.

"**Who, being in the form of God, thought it not robbery to be equal with God: But made himself of no reputation, and took upon him the form of a servant, and was made in the likeness of men**" (**Ph.2:6-7**).

"**Forasmuch then as the children are partakers of flesh and blood, he also himself likewise took part of the same; that through death he might destroy him that had the power of death, that is, the devil; And deliver them who through fear of death were all their lifetime subject to bondage. For verily he took not on** *him the nature of* **angels; but he took on** *him* **the seed of Abraham. Wherefore in all things it behoved him to be made like unto** *his* **brethren, that he might be a merciful and faithful high priest in things** *pertaining* **to God, to make reconciliation for the sins of the people. For in that he himself hath suffered being tempted, he is able to succour them that are tempted**" (**He.2:14-18**).

"**For we have not an high priest which cannot be touched with the feeling of our infirmities; but was in all points tempted like as** *we are, yet* **without sin**" (**He.4:15**).

⇒ In coming to earth, Christ bore all the temptations and trials of the human flesh as well as the mockery, hostility, and rejection of sinful people.

"**And when he was come into his own country, he taught them in their synagogue, insomuch that they were astonished, and said, Whence hath this** *man* **this wisdom, and** *these* **mighty works? Is not this the carpenter's son? is not his mother called Mary? and his brethren, James, and Joses, and Simon, and Judas? And his sisters, are they not all with us? Whence then hath this** *man* **all these things? And they were offended in him. But Jesus said unto them, A prophet is not without honour, save in his own country, and in his own house**" (**Mt.13:54-57**).

"**And the Pharisees also, who were covetous, heard all these things: and they derided him**" (**Lu.16:14**).

"**He was in the world, and the world was made by him, and the world knew him not. He came unto his own, and his own received him not**" (**Jn.1:10-11**).

"**And many of them said, He hath a devil, and is mad; why hear ye him?**" (**Jn.10:20**).

⇒ In coming to earth, Christ took the sins of the entire human race upon Himself and died for those sins, suffering the rejection of God and God's judgment upon them.

"**The next day John seeth Jesus coming unto him, and saith, Behold the Lamb of God, which taketh away the sin of the world**" (**Jn.1:29**).

"**Who gave himself for our sins, that he might deliver us from this present evil world, according to the will of God and our Father**" (**Ga.1:4**).

"**Forasmuch as ye know that ye were not redeemed with corruptible things,** *as* **silver and gold, from your vain conversation** *received* **by tradition from your fathers; But with the precious blood of Christ, as of a lamb without blemish and without spot**" (**1 Pe.1:18-19**).

---

4 *Matthew Henry's Commentary*, Vol. 4, p.302.

"Who his own self bare our sins in his own body on the tree, that we, being dead to sins, should live unto righteousness: by whose stripes ye were healed" (1 Pe.2:24).

"For Christ also hath once suffered for sins, the just for the unjust, that he might bring us to God, being put to death in the flesh, but quickened by the Spirit" (1 Pe.3:18).

3 (53:4-6) **Christ, Death of, Purposes—Sufferings, of Christ, Purposes for—Sin, Penalty of, Paid by Christ—Man, Sins of, Penalty Paid—Christ, Death, Opinions Concerning—Grief, Answer - Solution to, Christ—Sorrow, Answer - Solution to, Christ—Christ, Ministry, to Bear People's Sorrows—Christ, Death, Substitutionary—Peace, Source, Christ's Death—Healing, Source, Christ's Death:** God's Servant, the Savior, bore the penalty for the sins of the human race. Note the word *surely* in verse 4. A sharp contrast is being drawn between Christ bearing our sins and the unbelief, hostility, and rejection of the Messiah mentioned in verse 3. The thought here is, "Surely He bore the grief and sorrow due our flesh, the penalty for our sins." No matter what people may think or believe, the fact is that Christ suffered and paid the ultimate penalty for our sins.

Remember that this prophecy was given more than seven hundred years before Christ came to earth. Yet note the guarantee God gives concerning the coming of the Messiah. Although He was speaking about a future event, He spoke in the past tense, as though the event had already taken place. Being omniscient and eternal, God naturally saw into the future. Therefore He could speak in the past tense, guaranteeing that His prophecy would be fulfilled. His Servant, the Savior, would definitely come and He would pay the ultimate penalty for sin. Note the Scripture and outline:

OUTLINE	SCRIPTURE	SCRIPTURE	OUTLINE

3. The Savior bore the penalty for man's sin
a. The sad fact: He suffered for us, yet many felt He was justly executed as a criminal
b. The truth: He died for us
  1) Our griefs & sorrows, 4
  2) Our transgressions &
	4 Surely he hath borne our griefs, and carried our sorrows: yet we did esteem him stricken, smitten of God, and afflicted.
	5 But he *was* wounded for our transgressions, *he was* bruised for our iniquities: the
		chastisement of our peace *was* upon him; and with his stripes we are healed.
		6 All we like sheep have gone astray; we have turned every one to his own way; and the LORD hath laid on him the iniquity of us all.
			iniquities
			c. The purpose of His death
			  1) To give us peace & healing
			  2) To save us from the sin of going astray & its penalty: Death, Eze.18:4; Ro.6:23
			d. The way He saved us: By bearing sin for us

a. How sad it is that so many in Christ's day reacted against Him, rejecting, mocking, and even crucifying the Savior. A number felt that He was justly executed as a criminal (v.4). During His trial and crucifixion, they thought He was being executed for His own sins, for having broken the law of both God and man. Various religionists believed that His sufferings in life and on the cross were due to His sins and were proof that the hand of God's judgment was upon Him. In their minds, Christ was being "stricken, smitten by God, and afflicted." He was indeed "smitten by God, and afflicted," but not for His own sins. God put His Son to death for the sins of the world, including the sins of His enemies, the very ones who were rejecting and crucifying Him.

It was for our sins that God sent His Son, Jesus Christ, into the world. When Christ came to earth, He bore all of our grief and sorrow, our infirmities and weaknesses—not only on the cross, but also throughout His entire life. Daily, Christ bore the penalty for our sin, suffering on our behalf, identifying with us, and experiencing all the trials and temptations of life that continually confront us. The apostle Matthew even says that Christ's bearing our infirmities and sorrows applies to His healing ministry (Mt.8:14-17, esp.17).

In another verse, Matthew says that "the Son of man [Christ] came not to be ministered to, but to minister, and to give His life a ransom for many" (Mt.20:28). In this one statement, Matthew summed up the entire ministry of Christ. First, Christ came to minister to us, identifying with our grief and sorrow, our infirmities and weaknesses. Throughout His life, He experienced the suffering, the trials, and the temptations that we face. Second, He came to give His life as a ransom for us. He gave Himself up to pay for our sin so that we might be set free from sin and death and be given the wonderful privilege of worshipping and living with God eternally.

All our sufferings on earth are due to our flesh and the corruptible world in which we live. They are the result of sin, the penalty for sin, the consequences of Adam's sin (Ro.3:23). That is not to say that every person who is suffering physical pain is being punished, but as Scripture says, when Adam sinned, death with all its corruption entered into the world. When Adam and Eve bore children, those children inherited their parents' sinful nature. And so the sin nature with all that it entails was passed on down to the entire human race (Ro.5:12). Because we all sin and come short of the glory of God, we bear the consequences of grief and sorrow, weaknesses and infirmities (Ro.6:23).

"For all have sinned, and come short of the glory of God" (Ro.3:23).

"Wherefore, as by one man sin entered into the world, and death by sin; and so death passed upon all men, for that all have sinned" (Ro.5:12).

"For the wages of sin *is* death; but the gift of God *is* eternal life through Jesus Christ our Lord" (Ro.6:23).

b. The truth is that Christ died for us all (v.5). We deserve to pay the penalty for sin, for we are the ones who have broken the law, both of man and of God. At the very least, every one of us has mistreated other people or had evil thoughts. And we have broken the Ten Commandments. Thus, we stand accused before God. He has pronounced the verdict—guilty—and the sentence is spiritual death, eternal separation from Him. But there is wonderful news: God has not executed judgment upon us. He executed His judgment upon Christ. It was Christ who died to pay the penalty for our sins.

Note the emphasis throughout these verses: God's Servant, the Savior Jesus Christ, died for our *transgressions* and *iniquities*. *Transgressions (pesha)* are acts that cross over a line drawn by God. To transgress means to revolt, rebel, rise up against, reject God. It means Picture violating or ignoring a posting of *No Trespassing* on a piece of property. A transgressor deliberately disregards the warning, *chooses to sin*. Iniquity *(adown, or awon)* means the perverse, crooked, moral evil that lies within the human heart and nature, which means that we are sinners *by nature*.[5] As Warren W. Wiersbe says, we are sinners both *by choice* and *by nature*.[6] Simply stated, Christ died for all our transgressions, for our *sinful nature* as well as for the sins we choose to commit day by day.

Note the word *wounded*, or *pierced*. Christ was wounded for us on the cross when His hands and feet were pierced by nails (Ps.22:16; Lu.24:39-40) and when a spear was thrust into His side (Jn.19:31-37; Re.1:7; Zec.12:10). Also note the word *bruised*, or *crushed*. It was the heavy weight of our sins that crushed the very life out of Christ.

c. The purpose of Christ's death was twofold (v.5b-6). First, He died to provide peace and healing for us (v.5b). Sin contaminates God's presence and separates us from God. Because God is holy and perfect, He can have nothing to do with sin. Consequently, a great barrier or gulf separates sinful people from God. And no one can climb the barrier or bridge the gulf, for a sinner is unacceptable to God. God loves the sinner, but He hates the sin. He hates sin…

⇒   because it is sin that has brought so much brutality, wickedness, and death into the world
⇒   because it is sin that alienates man from God, putting hostility between them and making them enemies. It is this *alienation* that causes some people to curse God and His Son Jesus Christ and others to deny or defy God.

It was for this very reason that God sent His Son, the Lord Jesus Christ, into the world. Christ came to make peace between God and man. By giving His Son to die for the sins of the world, God demonstrated His great love for people. By dying on the cross, Christ provided the way for people to be reconciled with God. Peace with God is possible. If people will turn from their sins and approach God through Christ, believing that Christ died for their sins, God will accept them. No longer does God have to seem far away, unconcerned, and out of touch. No longer does the barrier, the separation, have to exist between God and us. Through Christ we can be reconciled to God and have peace. Christ forgives our sin and saves us from the coming judgment that will fall upon all the enemies and rejecters of God. Oh, the wonder of it all! "By His stripes we are healed"—spiritually healed.

> **"The word which *God* sent unto the children of Israel, preaching peace by Jesus Christ: (he is Lord of all:)" (Ac.10:36).**
> **"Therefore being justified by faith, we have peace with God through our Lord Jesus Christ" (Ro.5:1).**
> **"Therefore if any man *be* in Christ, *he is* a new creature: old things are passed away; behold, all things are become new. And all things *are* of God, who hath reconciled us to himself by Jesus Christ, and hath given to us the ministry of reconciliation; To wit, that God was in Christ, reconciling the world unto himself, not imputing their trespasses unto them; and hath committed unto us the word of reconciliation. Now then we are ambassadors for Christ, as though God did beseech *you* by us: we pray *you* in Christ's stead, be ye reconciled to God. For he hath made him *to be* sin for us, who knew no sin; that we might be made the righteousness of God in him" (2 Co.5:17-21).**
> **"But now in Christ Jesus ye who sometimes were far off are made nigh by the blood of Christ. For he is our peace, who hath made both one, and hath broken down the middle wall of partition *between us;* Having abolished in his flesh the enmity, *even* the law of commandments *contained* in ordinances; for to make in himself of twain one new man, *so* making peace; And that he might reconcile both unto God in one body by the cross, having slain the enmity thereby" (Ep.2:13-16).**
> **"And, having made peace through the blood of his cross, by him to reconcile all things unto himself; by him, *I say,* whether *they be* things in earth, or things in heaven. And you, that were sometime alienated and enemies in *your* mind by wicked works, yet now hath he reconciled: In the body of his flesh through death, to present you holy and unblameable and unreproveable in his sight" (Col.1:20-22).**
> **"Wherefore in all things it behoved him to be made like unto *his* brethren, that he might be a merciful and faithful high priest in things *pertaining* to God, to make reconciliation for the sins of the people. For in that he himself hath suffered being tempted, he is able to succour them that are tempted" (He.2:17-18).**

Second, Christ died to deliver us from the penalty for going astray, which is death (v.6; Ro.6:23). Note that God compares people to sheep, for sheep have a tendency to go astray. It is also within the very nature of people to wander, to reject God and break His commandments. Three aspects of our human nature cause us to drift away:

⇒   By its very nature, our flesh lusts after the things of this world (1 Jn.2:15-16). Desiring and coveting more and more is a constant battle faced by the human soul. The flesh constantly lusts for more and more: a second helping of cake, a larger house, more wealth or power, more recognition or honor. The flesh lusts for sex, even if it involves adultery, fornication (extramarital sex), or some form of abnormal, illicit sex. Such sinful behavior is what Scripture calls the *lust of the flesh.*

⇒   In looking around, we see things that are attractive, desirable, enticing, or valuable. And we want what we see, even if it is wrong and sinful. This is what the Scripture calls the *lust of the eyes.*

⇒   The *pride of life* also causes us to go astray. Our selfish desire for recognition, honor, position, power, and fame is sinful, because it exalts us above others for selfish purposes. Position, power, and fame are to be used to serve and help others, not to exalt ourselves over them or to accumulate and hoard wealth.

---

5   James Strong. *The New Strong's Exhaustive Concordance of the Bible.* (Nashville, TN: Thomas Nelson Publishers, 1990), # 6588, 5771.
6   Warren W. Wiersbe. *Be Comforted*, p.138.

When sheep go astray, they are in danger of getting lost, being attacked, or dooming themselves. Within our very nature there is a tendency for us to go astray, following the lusts of our flesh and eyes and pursuing the pride of life. When we do this, we run the risk of getting lost and forgetting the way back to God. Furthermore, when we turn away from the LORD, one enemy after another will attack us through mockery, ridicule, or charges of hypocrisy. And, of course, getting lost can doom us to eternal separation from God.

But there is wonderful news: Christ died to deliver us from the sin of going astray and from its penalty, which is death. This He did by bearing sin for us. It was for this very reason that Christ died. Note exactly what Scripture says: God "laid on Him" the iniquity of us all. Our sins were actually lifted off of us and *placed upon* Christ. He *bore* the weight and the penalty of sin for us. This is what is known as the *substitutionary*, *vicarious* death of Christ. He died as our Substitute, in our place and on our behalf. Because He died *for* us, we are delivered from the experience of death. When we are ready to leave this earth, quicker than the eye can blink, God will transfer us right into His presence. One moment we are in this world, and the next moment we are in heaven standing in the very presence of God.

"I am the good shepherd: the good shepherd giveth his life for the sheep" (Jn.10:11).

"For when we were yet without strength, in due time Christ died for the ungodly. For scarcely for a righteous man will one die: yet peradventure for a good man some would even dare to die. But God commendeth his love toward us, in that, while we were yet sinners, Christ died for us" (Ro.5:6-8).

"For the wages of sin *is* death; but the gift of God *is* eternal life through Jesus Christ our Lord" (Ro.6:23).

"For I delivered unto you first of all that which I also received, how that Christ died for our sins according to the scriptures; And that he was buried, and that he rose again the third day according to the scriptures" (1 Co.15:3-4).

"And as it is appointed unto men once to die, but after this the judgment: So Christ was once offered to bear the sins of many; and unto them that look for him shall he appear the second time without sin unto salvation" (He.9:27-28).

"Who his own self bare our sins in his own body on the tree, that we, being dead to sins, should live unto righteousness: by whose stripes ye were healed" (1 Pe.2:24).

"For Christ also hath once suffered for sins, the just for the unjust, that he might bring us to God, being put to death in the flesh, but quickened by the Spirit" (1 Pe.3:18).

"And ye know that he was manifested to take away our sins; and in him is no sin" (1 Jn.3:5).

4 (53:7-9) **Servant, of God, Sufferings of—Savior, Sufferings of, Willingly Died—Christ, Death of, Voluntary—Christ, Sinlessness of, Prophecy Concerning—Sinlessness, of Christ, Prophecy Concerning**: God's Servant, the Savior, suffered unjustly, but willingly. As the sinless Son of God, Christ did not have to suffer. He had the foreknowledge (omniscience) and the power (omnipotence) to avoid the cross and all that led up to it. Yet He undertook the mission of His own free will, not only out of obedience to God the Father but also out of love for the human race. He died for the sins of the world, to save mankind from the penalty of sin, which is death, eternal separation from God. Christ's *selflessness* and humility are now emphasized by stressing three facts: although He was the sinless Son of God...

- He willingly suffered harsh treatment (v.7)
- He willingly endured an illegal arrest, trial, and execution (v.8)
- He willingly subjected to being buried with the wicked (v.9)

OUTLINE	SCRIPTURE	SCRIPTURE	OUTLINE
4. The Savior suffered willingly but unjustly: Was the sinless Son of God a. He silently, willingly suffered harsh treatment: Just like a lamb led to the slaughter b. He willingly suffered an illegal arrest, trial, & execution	7 He was oppressed, and he was afflicted, yet he opened not his mouth: he is brought as a lamb to the slaughter, and as a sheep before her shearers is dumb, so he openeth not his mouth. 8 He was taken from prison and from judgment: and who shall declare his generation?	for he was cut off out of the land of the living: for the transgression of my people was he stricken. 9 And he made his grave with the wicked, and with the rich in his death; because he had done no violence, neither *was any* deceit in his mouth.	1) He was cut off—put to death—for the transgression of God's people 2) He was stricken for the sins of God's people c. He willingly suffered a burial with the wicked, even though He was the sinless Son of God

a. Christ silently endured brutal treatment (v.7). Throughout His life, Christ was oppressed, afflicted, and treated cruelly by unbelievers. But He never opened His mouth to take vengeance or to react violently toward His oppressors. Even when they led Him like a lamb to the slaughter as sacrifices for the people's sins, He willingly went to the cross to die for the sins of the human race. Just as a sheep before her shearers is silent, so Christ never opened His mouth to object or retaliate against those who were mistreating Him. Note this fact: just as in the Old Testament unblemished lambs were led to slaughter, so Christ is the spotless Lamb of God who takes away the sins of the world (Jn.1:29, 36; 1 Co.5:7; Re.5:6, 12; 13:8). Remember that a lamb was sacrificed for each Jewish household at Passover (Ex.12:1-13). Christ is the Passover Lamb who died for the sins of the whole world (Jn.1:29). Again, as a sheep is silent before her shearers, Christ was silent as He endured the cruel punishment of His enemies. He was silent...

- before Caiaphas (Mt.26:62-63)
- before the chief priest and elders (Mt.27:12)
- before Pilate (Mt.27:14; Jn.19:9)

- before Herod Antipas (Lu.23:9)
- before the soldiers who mocked, beat, and crucified Him (1 Pe.2:21-23).

b. Christ willingly suffered an illegal arrest, trial, and execution (v.8). After being unjustly seized in the Garden of Gethsemane, Christ was illegally tried before all the officials mentioned above. False witnesses even testified against Him (Mt.26:60-61). He was then unjustly executed. But note: Christ's death was misunderstood just as His life and ministry had been. When the enemies cut Him off from the land of the living and put Him to death, they thought they were through with Him and His claim to be the Savior, the Son of the living God. But they completely misunderstood His death. Christ was being put to death for the transgressions of the entire human race. He was being stricken by *God Himself* for those sins. It was for that purpose that He knowingly and voluntarily surrendered Himself to God.

Note also the statements that Christ "was cut off" and "for...my people He was stricken." The verbs are in the *passive voice*, which indicates actions that were taken by God Himself. It was God who cut Christ off, God who put Him to death for the sins of the people. As the New Testament says, "God made Him...to be sin for us" (2 Co.5:21).[7]

c. Christ willingly suffered a burial with the wicked, even though He was the sinless Son of God (v.9). No act of violence was ever committed by Christ, and no word of deceit ever flowed from His mouth. He was, as Scripture declares time and again, without sin. Nevertheless, He suffered the horrific penalty for sin, which is death. Consequently, He was buried with the wicked, right along with mere men, sinners of the earth just like you and me.

The actual burial of Jesus Christ is important, for it proves that He did indeed die (1 Co.15:1-5). Remember that the Roman authorities released Christ's body to Joseph and Nicodemus. They never would have released His body to them unless Christ was truly dead (Jn.19:38-42; Mk.15:42-47).

Thought 1. Christ's death was voluntary. He willingly died for the sins of people that they might become acceptable to God.

"Greater love hath no man than this, that a man lay down his life for his friends" (Jn.15:13).

"Who gave himself for our sins, that he might deliver us from this present evil world, according to the will of God and our Father" (Ga.1:4).

"And walk in love, as Christ also hath loved us, and hath given himself for us an offering and a sacrifice to God for a sweetsmelling savour" (Ep.5:2).

"Who gave himself for us, that he might redeem us from all iniquity, and purify unto himself a peculiar people, zealous of good works" (Tit.2:14).

"Hereby perceive we the love *of God*, because he laid down his life for us: and we ought to lay down *our* lives for the brethren" (1 Jn.3:16).

"And from Jesus Christ, *who is* the faithful witness, *and* the first begotten of the dead, and the prince of the kings of the earth. Unto him that loved us, and washed us from our sins in his own blood" (Re.1:5).

Thought 2. Jesus Christ is the sinless Son of God.

"And one of the malefactors which were hanged railed on him, saying, If thou be Christ, save thyself and us. But the other answering rebuked him, saying, Dost not thou fear God, seeing thou art in the same condemnation? And we indeed justly; for we receive the due reward of our deeds: but this man hath done nothing amiss. And he said unto Jesus, Lord, remember me when thou comest into thy kingdom. And Jesus said unto him, Verily I say unto thee, To day shalt thou be with me in paradise" (Lu.23:39-43).

"Which of you convinceth me of sin? And if I say the truth, why do ye not believe me?" (Jn.8:46).

"For he hath made him *to be* sin for us, who knew no sin; that we might be made the righteousness of God in him" (2 Co.5:21).

"But unto the Son *he saith*, Thy throne, O God, *is* for ever and ever: a sceptre of righteousness *is* the sceptre of thy kingdom. Thou hast loved righteousness, and hated iniquity; therefore God, *even* thy God, hath anointed thee with the oil of gladness above thy fellows" (He.1:8-9).

"For we have not an high priest which cannot be touched with the feeling of our infirmities; but was in all points tempted like as *we are, yet* without sin" (He.4:15).

"Wherefore he is able also to save them to the uttermost that come unto God by him, seeing he ever liveth to make intercession for them. For such an high priest became us, *who is* holy, harmless, undefiled, separate from sinners, and made higher than the heavens" (He.7:25-26).

"Forasmuch as ye know that ye were not redeemed with corruptible things, *as* silver and gold, from your vain conversation *received* by tradition from your fathers; But with the precious blood of Christ, as of a lamb without blemish and without spot" (1 Pe.1:18-19).

"Who did no sin, neither was guile found in his mouth: Who, when he was reviled, reviled not again; when he suffered, he threatened not; but committed *himself* to him that judgeth righteously: Who his own self bare our sins in his own body on the tree, that we, being dead to sins, should live unto righteousness: by whose stripes ye were healed" (1 Pe.2:22-24).

5 (53:10-12) **Savior, Sufferings of, Results—Christ, Death of, Results—Prophecy, Concerning Christ, Results of, Death—Sacrifice, of Christ, Prophecy Concerning—Sacrifice, Christ, Death, Substitute Sacrifice—Sacrifice, Animal, Type of, Christ**: the closing verses of this great prophecy about Christ's death describe the results of the

---

7 John F. Walvoord and Roy B. Zuck, Editors. *The Bible Knowledge Commentary, Old Testament,* p.1108.

Savior's sufferings. Up to this point, the bitter hatred and hostility of the Savior's enemies, the cruel and brutal mistreatment of the Savior, and the horrible sufferings endured by the Savior have been the focus. But now the great victory of the cross is discussed. Six wonderful results have taken place since the death of God's Servant, the Messiah and Savior of the world, the Lord Jesus Christ:

OUTLINE	SCRIPTURE	SCRIPTURE	OUTLINE
5. **The results of the Savior's suffering** a. He became the *substitute sacrifice* for sin b. He produces many offspring, righteous believers c. He prolonged His days: Arose to carry on & advance God's work d. He conquered death & brought satisfaction to everyone involved e. He justified many: By	10 Yet it pleased the LORD to bruise him; he hath put *him* to grief: when thou shalt make his soul an offering for sin, he shall see *his* seed, he shall prolong *his* days, and the pleasure of the LORD shall prosper in his hand. 11 He shall see of the travail of his soul, *and* shall be satisfied: by his knowledge shall my righteous servant justify	many; for he shall bear their iniquities. 12 Therefore will I divide him *a portion* with the great, and he shall divide the spoil with the strong; because he hath poured out his soul unto death: and he was numbered with the transgressors; and he bare the sin of many, and made intercession for the transgressors.	bearing their iniquities f. He is honored as the great Victor: He will divide the wealth of His conquests with the strong (believers) 1) Because He died as a transgressor 2) Because He bore the sin of many 3) Because He made intercession for sinners

a. The Savior became the substitute sacrifice for sin (v.10). His *substitutionary death* is the major theme of this great chapter of Isaiah. Jesus Christ did not die as a martyr, as someone put to death for his beliefs. Nor did He die as an example, as someone showing us how to face death with a positive attitude. He died neither by accident nor because fate decided it was time for Him to die. Jesus Christ died deliberately, purposefully, and at the hands of God the Father. God Himself had determined that His Son would die for the sins of the world. His death was predetermined, planned by God before human history even began:

> "Ye men of Israel, hear these words; Jesus of Nazareth, a man approved of God among you by miracles and wonders and signs, which God did by him in the midst of you, as ye yourselves also know: Him, being delivered by the determinate counsel and foreknowledge of God, ye have taken, and by wicked hands have crucified and slain" (Ac.2:22-23).
>
> "[God] Who hath saved us, and called *us* with an holy calling, not according to our works, but according to his own purpose and grace, which was given us in Christ Jesus before the world began, But is now made manifest by the appearing of our Saviour Jesus Christ, who hath abolished death, and hath brought life and immortality to light through the gospel" (2 Ti.1:9-10).

From the beginning, knowing that man would sin and need to be saved, it was God's plan to bruise (crush) Christ on the cross. God filled Christ with the grief or suffering for the sins of the world. Christ Himself was to be offered up as the *perfect sacrifice* for the sins of every human being who ever lived. Never again would animal sacrifices be needed, for with Christ's death, the perfect sacrifice to which they pointed had been offered. Jesus Christ, God's very own Son, had died as the perfect offering, the *substitute sacrifice* for the sins of the entire world. Note how this fact is emphasized throughout the entire chapter:

⇒ He bore our griefs and sorrows (v.4).
⇒ He was wounded for our transgression and bruised for our iniquities (v.5).
⇒ The LORD laid on Him the iniquity of us all (v.6).
⇒ He was brought as a lamb to the slaughter to be offered to God as a *substitute sacrifice* (v.7).
⇒ He was stricken for the transgression of God's people (v.8).
⇒ God made His soul an offering for sin (v.10).
⇒ He bore their iniquities (v.11).
⇒ He bore the sins of many (v.12).

> "The next day John seeth Jesus coming unto him, and saith, Behold the Lamb of God, which taketh away the sin of the world" (Jn.1:29).
>
> "For when we were yet without strength, in due time Christ died for the ungodly" (Ro.5:6).
>
> "Purge out therefore the old leaven, that ye may be a new lump, as ye are unleavened. For even Christ our passover is sacrificed for us" (1 Co.5:7).
>
> "For I delivered unto you first of all that which I also received, how that Christ died for our sins according to the scriptures" (1 Co.15:3).
>
> "And *that* he died for all, that they which live should not henceforth live unto themselves, but unto him which died for them, and rose again" (2 Co.5:15).
>
> "And walk in love, as Christ also hath loved us, and hath given himself for us an offering and a sacrifice to God for a sweetsmelling savour" (Ep.5:2).
>
> "Who gave himself for us, that he might redeem us from all iniquity, and purify unto himself a peculiar people, zealous of good works" (Tit.2:14).
>
> "Hereby perceive we the love *of God*, because he laid down his life for us: and we ought to lay down *our* lives for the brethren" (1 Jn.3:16).

b. Through death, the Savior has produced many offspring, a multitude of people who truly believe in Him and follow His righteous commandments. Looking down through the centuries, Christ saw the true believers of every generation, those who would repent of their sins and turn back to God. He foresaw a victorious people who would conquer the temptations and trials of life, who would bear strong testimony to the gospel through His atoning sacrifice. A great, spiritual family of true believers has been born because the Savior died on the cross for their sins.

"But as many as received him, to them gave he power to become the sons of God, *even* to them that believe on his name" (Jn.1:12).

"For God so loved the world, that he gave his only begotten Son, that whosoever believeth in him should not perish, but have everlasting life" (Jn.3:16).

"For I am not ashamed of the gospel of Christ: for it is the power of God unto salvation to every one that believeth; to the Jew first, and also to the Greek" (Ro.1:16).

"That if thou shalt confess with thy mouth the Lord Jesus, and shalt believe in thine heart that God hath raised him from the dead, thou shalt be saved. For with the heart man believeth unto righteousness; and with the mouth confession is made unto salvation" (Ro.10:9-10).

"And you *hath he quickened,* who were dead in trespasses and sins; Wherein in time past ye walked according to the course of this world, according to the prince of the power of the air, the spirit that now worketh in the children of disobedience: Among whom also we all had our conversation in times past in the lusts of our flesh, fulfilling the desires of the flesh and of the mind; and were by nature the children of wrath, even as others. But God, who is rich in mercy, for his great love wherewith he loved us, Even when we were dead in sins, hath quickened us together with Christ, (by grace ye are saved;) And hath raised *us* up together, and made *us* sit together in heavenly *places* in Christ Jesus: That in the ages to come he might show the exceeding riches of his grace in *his* kindness toward us through Christ Jesus. For by grace are ye saved through faith; and that not of yourselves: *it is* the gift of God: Not of works, lest any man should boast" (Ep.2:1-9).

c. The Savior prolonged His days. He rose from the dead and now advances God's work throughout the world (v.10). Jesus Christ is not dead. He did not remain in the grave. He arose and ascended into heaven, where He is seated at the right hand of God the Father. For the remainder of human history, Christ will be busy *working all things out for good* on behalf of true believers, those who genuinely love and obey Him. Working through His true followers, He is continuing to carry the gospel of salvation to the world. The deep longing of the Savior's heart is for many more to be delivered from sin and death, for many to live eternally with Him.

1) Jesus Christ arose from the dead.

"But ye denied the Holy One and the Just, and desired a murderer to be granted unto you; And killed the Prince of life, whom God hath raised from the dead; whereof we are witnesses" (Ac.3:14-15).

"And with great power gave the apostles witness of the resurrection of the Lord Jesus: and great grace was upon them all" (Ac.4:33).

"And we are witnesses of all things which he did both in the land of the Jews, and in Jerusalem; whom they slew and hanged on a tree: Him God raised up the third day, and showed him openly; Not to all the people, but unto witnesses chosen before of God, *even* to us, who did eat and drink with him after he rose from the dead" (Ac.10:39-41).

"And Paul, as his manner was, went in unto them, and three sabbath days reasoned with them out of the scriptures, Opening and alleging, that Christ must needs have suffered, and risen again from the dead; and that this Jesus, whom I preach unto you, is Christ" (Ac.17:2-3).

"Concerning his [God's] Son Jesus Christ our Lord, which was made of the seed of David according to the flesh; And declared *to be* the Son of God with power, according to the spirit of holiness, by the resurrection from the dead" (Ro.1:3-4).

"That if thou shalt confess with thy mouth the Lord Jesus, and shalt believe in thine heart that God hath raised him from the dead, thou shalt be saved. For with the heart man believeth unto righteousness; and with the mouth confession is made unto salvation" (Ro.10:9-10).

"Moreover, brethren, I declare unto you the gospel which I preached unto you, which also ye have received, and wherein ye stand; By which also ye are saved, if ye keep in memory what I preached unto you, unless ye have believed in vain. For I delivered unto you first of all that which I also received, how that Christ died for our sins according to the scriptures; And that he was buried, and that he rose again the third day according to the scriptures" (1 Co.15:1-4).

"Blessed *be* the God and Father of our Lord Jesus Christ, which according to his abundant mercy hath begotten us again unto a lively hope by the resurrection of Jesus Christ from the dead, To an inheritance incorruptible, and undefiled, and that fadeth not away, reserved in heaven for you" (1 Pe.1:3-4).

2) Jesus Christ is actively working to carry out and advance God's work on earth. Through the presence of the Holy Spirit in the lives of believers, Christ helps them as they bear testimony to the message of salvation.

a) Christ comforts believers through the Person of the Holy Spirit.

"But the Comforter, *which is* the Holy Ghost, whom the Father will send in my name, he shall teach you all things, and bring all things to your remembrance, whatsoever I have said unto you" (Jn.14:26).

b) Christ bears strong testimony to the salvation He provides through the Person of the Holy Spirit.

"But when the Comforter is come, whom I will send unto you from the Father, *even* the Spirit of truth, which proceedeth from the Father, he shall testify of me" (Jn.15:26).

c) Christ pierces and convicts the heart of people through the Person of the Holy Spirit.

"Nevertheless I tell you the truth; It is expedient for you that I go away: for if I go not away, the Comforter will not come unto you; but if I depart, I will send him unto you. And when he is come, he will reprove the world of sin, and of righteousness, and of judgment: Of sin, because they believe not on me; Of righteousness, because I go to my Father, and ye see me no more; Of judgment, because the prince of this world is judged" (Jn.16:7-11).

d) Christ sets people free from the law of sin and death through the law of His Spirit.

"*There is* therefore now no condemnation to them which are in Christ Jesus, who walk not after the flesh, but after the Spirit. For the law of the Spirit of life in Christ Jesus hath made me free from the law of sin and death" (Ro.8:1-2).

e) Christ guarantees the security of those who truly believe and obey His Holy commandments.

"Who *is* he that condemneth? *It is* Christ that died, yea rather, that is risen again, who is even at the right hand of God, who also maketh intercession for us. Who shall separate us from the love of Christ? *shall* tribulation, or distress, or persecution, or famine, or nakedness, or peril, or sword? As it is written, For thy sake we are killed all the day long; we are accounted as sheep for the slaughter. Nay, in all these things we are more than conquerors through him that loved us. For I am persuaded, that neither death, nor life, nor angels, nor principalities, nor powers, nor things present, nor things to come, Nor height, nor depth, nor any other creature, shall be able to separate us from the love of God, which is in Christ Jesus our Lord" (Ro.8:34-39).

f) Christ encourages and helps believers when they are tempted or confronted with any severe trial or hardship.

"Wherefore in all things it behoved him to be made like unto *his* brethren, that he might be a merciful and faithful high priest in things *pertaining* to God, to make reconciliation for the sins of the people. For in that he himself hath suffered being tempted, he is able to succour them that are tempted" (He.2:17-18).
"For we have not an high priest which cannot be touched with the feeling of our infirmities; but was in all points tempted like as *we are, yet* without sin. Let us therefore come boldly unto the throne of grace, that we may obtain mercy, and find grace to help in time of need" (He.4:15-16).

g) Christ continually intercedes for believers. His ministry of intercession means that He represents, upholds, and prays for true believers throughout their entire lives. Through His death on the cross, Christ guaranteed eternal salvation for every true believer.

"Wherefore he is able also to save them to the uttermost that come unto God by him, seeing he ever liveth to make intercession for them. For such an high priest became us, *who is* holy, harmless, undefiled, separate from sinners, and made higher than the heavens; Who needeth not daily, as those high priests, to offer up sacrifice, first for his own sins, and then for the people's: for this he did once, when he offered up himself" (He.7:25-27).

h) Christ works all things out for good for His people as they carry on the work of God.

"And we know that all things work together for good to them that love God, to them who are the called according to *his* purpose" (Ro.8:28).
"Then said they unto him, What shall we do, that we might work the works of God? Jesus answered and said unto them, This is the work of God, that ye believe on him whom he hath sent" (Jn.6:28-29).

d. The Savior conquered death and brought *satisfaction* to everyone involved (v.11). When Christ looked back at all He had achieved, He felt a deep sense of fulfillment, for He had carried out God's will *perfectly*. He had fully achieved that which He had set out to do, making it possible for all people to be forgiven their sins and to become acceptable to God. On the cross, Christ uttered these astounding words: "It is finished" (Jn.19:30). The work of redemption was finished, and now any person who wishes can be reconciled with God.

"When Jesus therefore had received the vinegar, he said, It is finished: and he bowed his head, and gave up the ghost" (Jn.19:30).

God the Father was also satisfied, very pleased with the work of His Son. At both the baptism and the resurrection of Jesus Christ, God announced, "This is my beloved Son, in whom I am well pleased" (Mt.3:17; 17:5; Mk.1:11; 9:7;

Lu.3:22; 9:35; 2 Pe.1:17). God put His stamp of approval upon His Son throughout His entire life, for Christ always did those things that pleased the Father, in particular dying upon the cross.

> **"And he that sent me is with me: the Father hath not left me alone; for I do always those things that please him"** (Jn.8:29).
> **"Ye men of Israel, hear these words; Jesus of Nazareth, a man approved of God among you by miracles and wonders and signs, which God did by him in the midst of you, as ye yourselves also know: Him, being delivered by the determinate counsel and foreknowledge of God, ye have taken, and by wicked hands have crucified and slain: Whom God hath raised up, having loosed the pains of death: because it was not possible that he should be holden of it"** (Ac.2:22-24).

Naturally, believers find deep satisfaction and fulfillment in the cross. When believers turn to the LORD by faith, they are set free from their sin, death, and the judgment to come. Furthermore, they are given the wonderful inheritance of living eternally with God in the promised land of heaven.

> **"The word which *God* sent unto the children of Israel, preaching peace by Jesus Christ: (he is Lord of all:)"** (Ac.10:36).
> **"And, having made peace through the blood of his cross, by him to reconcile all things unto himself; by him, *I say*, whether *they be* things in earth, or things in heaven"** (Col.1:20).
> **"Let us therefore fear, lest, a promise being left *us* of entering into his rest, any of you should seem to come short of it. For unto us was the gospel preached, as well as unto them: but the word preached did not profit them, not being mixed with faith in them that heard *it*. For we which have believed do enter into rest, as he said, As I have sworn in my wrath, if they shall enter into my rest: although the works were finished from the foundation of the world"** (He.4:1-3).
> **"There remaineth therefore a rest to the people of God. For he that is entered into his rest, he also hath ceased from his own works, as God *did* from his. Let us labour therefore to enter into that rest, lest any man fall after the same example of unbelief"** (He.4:9-11).
> **"As for me, I will behold thy face in righteousness: I shall be satisfied, when I awake, with thy likeness"** (Ps.17:15).
> **"For he satisfieth the longing soul, and filleth the hungry soul with goodness"** (Ps.107:9).

e. The Savior made justification possible through His death on the cross (v.11). To *justify* means to declare a person righteous. Justice always demands that the lawbreaker be condemned and the righteous be set free. Since all of us have broken God's law, we all stand condemned to bear the penalty, which is death. But Christ has already died for us, bearing the penalty of death on our behalf. Therefore, if we trust Christ as our Savior, allowing Him to cover us with His righteousness, God justifies us. He declares us righteous. He credits righteousness to our account. This is the meaning of justification. We are not righteous, but God declares us righteous when we give our lives to His Son, the Lord Jesus Christ. Justification is one of the greatest gifts we receive as a result of Christ's death on the cross.

> **"Repent ye therefore, and be converted, that your sins may be blotted out, when the times of refreshing shall come from the presence of the Lord"** (Ac.3:19).
> **"For all have sinned, and come short of the glory of God; Being justified freely by his grace through the redemption that is in Christ Jesus: Whom God hath set forth *to be* a propitiation through faith in his blood, to declare his righteousness for the remission of sins that are past, through the forbearance of God"** (Ro.3:23-25).
> **"Therefore as by the offence of one [Adam] *judgment came* upon all men to condemnation; even so by the righteousness of one *the free gift came* upon all men unto justification of life. For as by one man's disobedience many were made sinners, so by the obedience of one shall many be made righteous"** (Ro.5:18-19).
> **"Therefore being justified by faith, we have peace with God through our Lord Jesus Christ"** (Ro.5:1).
> **"Know ye not that the unrighteous shall not inherit the kingdom of God? Be not deceived: neither fornicators, nor idolaters, nor adulterers, nor effeminate, nor abusers of themselves with mankind, Nor thieves, nor covetous, nor drunkards, nor revilers, nor extortioners, shall inherit the kingdom of God. And such were some of you: but ye are washed, but ye are sanctified, but ye are justified in the name of the Lord Jesus, and by the Spirit of our God"** (1 Co.6:9-11, esp. v.11).
> **"Even as Abraham believed God, and it was accounted to him for righteousness"** (Ga.3:6).
> **"But the scripture hath concluded all under sin, that the promise by faith of Jesus Christ might be given to them that believe. But before faith came, we were kept under the law, shut up unto the faith which should afterwards be revealed. Wherefore the law was our schoolmaster *to bring us* unto Christ, that we might be justified by faith"** (Ga.3:22-24).

f. The Savior is now honored by believers as the great conqueror and victor, the LORD and Sovereign Majesty of the universe (v.12). Believers look to Christ as the great conqueror of sin, death, and hell. But not everyone believes that Jesus Christ is the Savior, the promised Messiah. Some do not even believe in God, much less in Jesus Christ. Nevertheless, the day is coming when God the Father will send Jesus Christ back to earth. In the last days of human history, Christ will return to set up God's kingdom on earth. In that day, every knee will bow and every tongue confess that Jesus Christ is indeed who He claimed to be: the promised Messiah, the Savior of the world. In that day, even the unbelievers—those who rejected the Savior, the great and the small, the rulers and the citizens—will bow the knee before Him.

When that day arrives, believers will receive their reward. Christ will divide the wealth of His conquests with the strong, those who have placed their trust in Christ. Believers will appropriately exalt His name to the highest...

- because He died as a transgressor for them
- because He bore their sins
- because He made intercession for all sinners

For these reasons and so many more, Jesus Christ will be exalted on high. He will be given all the praise from all creatures of all time, both in this and any other universe that might exist. He will be given all the glory, majesty, dominion, and power, forever and ever. And in that day, believers will stand in stark amazement because Christ will share His inheritance with all who truly believe and love Him.

"In my Father's house are many mansions: if *it were* not so, I would have told you. I go to prepare a place for you. And if I go and prepare a place for you, I will come again, and receive you unto myself; that where I am, *there* ye may be also" (Jn.14:2-3).

"The Spirit itself beareth witness with our spirit, that we are the children of God: And if children, then heirs; heirs of God, and joint-heirs with Christ; if so be that we suffer with *him*, that we may be also glorified together. For I reckon that the sufferings of this present time *are* not worthy *to be compared* with the glory which shall be revealed in us" (Ro.8:16-18).

"For it is written, *As* I live, saith the Lord, every knee shall bow to me, and every tongue shall confess to God" (Ro.14:11).

"Who, being in the form of God, thought it not robbery to be equal with God: But made himself of no reputation, and took upon him the form of a servant, and was made in the likeness of men: And being found in fashion as a man, he humbled himself, and became obedient unto death, even the death of the cross. Wherefore God also hath highly exalted him, and given him a name which is above every name: That at the name of Jesus every knee should bow, of *things* in heaven, and *things* in earth, and *things* under the earth; And *that* every tongue should confess that Jesus Christ *is* Lord, to the glory of God the Father. Wherefore, my beloved, as ye have always obeyed, not as in my presence only, but now much more in my absence, work out your own salvation with fear and trembling" (Ph.2:6-12).

"For our conversation [conversation] is in heaven; from whence also we look for the Saviour, the Lord Jesus Christ: Who shall change our vile body, that it may be fashioned like unto his glorious body, according to the working whereby he is able even to subdue all things unto himself" (Ph.3:20-21).

"When Christ, *who is* our life, shall appear, then shall ye also appear with him in glory" (Col.3:4).

"Therefore I endure all things for the elect's sakes, that they may also obtain the salvation which is in Christ Jesus with eternal glory" (2 Ti.2:10).

"For the Lord himself shall descend from heaven with a shout, with the voice of the archangel, and with the trump of God: and the dead in Christ shall rise first: Then we which are alive *and* remain shall be caught up together with them in the clouds, to meet the Lord in the air: and so shall we ever be with the Lord. Wherefore comfort one another with these words" (1 Th.4:16-18).

"The elders which are among you I exhort, who am also an elder, and a witness of the sufferings of Christ, and also a partaker of the glory that shall be revealed" (1 Pe.5:1).

"Who shall not fear thee, O Lord, and glorify thy name? for *thou* only *art* holy: for all nations shall come and worship before thee; for thy judgments are made manifest" (Re.15:4).

"And there shall be no night there; and they need no candle, neither light of the sun; for the Lord God giveth them light: and they shall reign for ever and ever" (Re.22:5).

"Look unto me, and be ye saved, all the ends of the earth: for I *am* God, and *there is* none else. I have sworn by myself, the word is gone out of my mouth *in* righteousness, and shall not return, That unto me every knee shall bow, every tongue shall swear" (Is.45:22-23).

"And it shall come to pass, *that* from one new moon to another, and from one sabbath to another, shall all flesh come to worship before me, saith the LORD" (Is.66:23).

DEEPER STUDY # 1
(52:13–53:12) **Scripture, Fulfilled—Prophecy, Fulfilled:**

OLD TESTAMENT PROPHECIES ABOUT JESUS AND THEIR FULFILLMENT IN THE NEW TESTAMENT

SCRIPTURE REFERENCE	PROPHECY	FULFILLMENT
Ge.3:15	The Promised Seed of a Woman	Lu.2:7; Ga.4:4; Re.12:5
Ge.12:3; 18:18; 22:18	The Promised Seed of Abraham	Ac.3:25; Ga.3:8 (Mt.1:1; Lu.3:34)
Ge.17:19; 21:12; 22:16-17 26:2	The Promised Seed of Isaac	Mt.1:2; Lu.1:55, 72-74
Ge.28:14 (Nu.24:17)	The Promised Seed of Jacob	Lu.3:34 (Mt.1:2)
Ge.49:10[a]	Will Spring from the Royal Tribe of Judah	Lu.3:33; He.7:14
De.18:15, 18	Will Be a Prophet	Jn.6:14; Ac.3:22-23

Scripture Reference	Prophecy	Fulfillment
(continued)	*(continued)*	*(continued)*
2 S.7:13[b] (Is.9:1, 7; 11:1-5)	Will Be the Eternal Heir to David's Throne	Mt.1:1 (Mt.1:6; Lu.1:32-33)
2 S.7:14[a]	Will Be God's Son	Mk.1:1
Jb.17:3	Will Ransom Men	Ep.1:7 (1 Jn.2:1-2)
Ps.2:1-2	Will Be Rejected by the Nations	Lu.23:36[a], 38
Ps.2:7	The Son of God	Ac.13:33; He.1:5; 5:5
Ps.8:2	Is to Be Praised	Mt.21:16
Ps.16:8-11	Will Be Resurrected	Ac.2:25-28, 31; 13:34-35 (Mt.28:1-2; Mk.16:6, 12, 14; Lu.24:1-53)
Ps.22:1	Will Be Forsaken by God	Mt.27:46; Mk.15:34
Ps.22:6-8	People Will Mock, Wag Their Heads at the Cross	Mt.27:39
Ps.22:16	Hands and Feet Will Be Pierced	Mt.27:35
Ps.22:18	Clothes Gambled for	Mt.27:35; Mk.15:24; Lu.23:34; Jn.19:24
Ps.22:22	To Secure Many Brothers	He.2:12
Ps.27:12	Accused by False Witnesses	Mk.14:56
Ps.31:5	Commends His Spirit to God	Lu.23:46
Ps.34:20	No Bones Broken	Jn.19:32-36
Ps.40:6-8	Fulfills God's Will	He.10:5-7
Ps.41:9	Is Betrayed by Judas	Jn.13:18; Ac.1:16
Ps.45:6, 7	Is Eternal and Preeminent	He.1:8, 9
Ps.68:18	Will Lead Captivity Captive and Return to Heaven	Ep.4:8-10
Ps.69:4	Hated Without a Cause	Mt.27:22-23
Ps.69:21	Offered Drugs on the Cross	Mt.27:48; Mk.15:36; Lu.23:36; Jn.19:28, 29
Ps.69:25; 109:8	Judas' Fate	Ac.1:20
Ps.78:1-2; Is.6:9-10	Will Speak in Parables	Mt.13:13; Mk.4:11-13
Ps.89:26-27	Exaltation	Ph.2:9 (Re.11:15)
Ps.95:7-11	Hearts Hardened Against	He.3:7-11; 4:3, 5-7
Ps.102:25-27	Is Creator and Is Eternal	He.1:10-12
Ps.110:1	To Be Exalted	Mt.22:44; Mk.12:36; Lu.20:42; Ac.2:34, 35; He.1:13
Ps.110:4	The High Priest	He.5:6
Ps.118:22, 23	The Stone	Mt.21:42; Mk.12:10; Lu.20:17; Ac.4:11
Ps.118:25, 26	The Triumphal Entry	Mt.21:9; Mk.11:9; Jn.12:13
Ps.132:11, 17	The Son of David	Lu.1:69; Ac.2:30
Is.7:14	The Virgin Birth	Mt.1:23
Is.9:1, 2	A Light to Those in Darkness	Mt.4:15, 16
Is.11:1	Will Be from Nazareth	Mt.2:23
Is.11:2	The Spirit Rests Upon in a Special Way	Lu.4:18-21 (Mt.12:18; Jn.3:34)
Is.11:10	To Save the Gentiles	Ro.15:12
Is.25:8	To Conquer Death	1 Co.15:54
Is.28:16	The Stone	Ro.9:33; 1 Pe.2:6
Is.35:5-6	Do Miracles	Mt.11:4-6; 15:30; 21:14; Jn.6:1-2; 20:30-31
Is.35:6; 61:1-2 (Ps.72:2; 146:8; Zec.11:11)	Will Meet the Desperate Needs of Men	Mt.11:4-6
Is.42:1-4	To Minister to the Gentiles	Mt.12:17-21
Is.49:6-7; 52:15	A Light to the Gentiles	Lu.2:32; Ac.13:47, 48; 26:23
Is.50;4-9	Obedient to the Father	Lu.22:42; Ph.2:8
Is.50:6	Smitten and Spat Upon	Mt.26:67; 27:30
Is.50:6; Mi.5:1	Hit in the Face	Mt.26:67; 27:30
Is.52:13	Exalted	Ac.1:9; 2:33-35; Ph.2:9-10
Is.52:14; 53:2	Disfigured	Mk.15:15-19
Is.53:1-3	Would Not Be Believed	Jn.12:38; Ro.10:16
Is.53:3-6; Ps.16:10	To Die and Arise	Ac.26:22, 23; 2:27
Is.53:4-6, 11	To Die for Man's Sins	1 Pe.2:24, 25
Is.53:4	To Heal and Bear Man's Sickness	Mt.8:17
Is.53:7	Silent When Accused	Mk.14:61
Is.53:9	To Be Sinless and Buried with the Rich	1 Pe.2:22

SCRIPTURE REFERENCE	PROPHECY	FULFILLMENT
(continued)	*(continued)*	*(continued)*
Is.53:12	To Be Counted a Sinner	Mk.15:28; Lu.22:37
Is.54:13	To Teach As God	Jn.6:45
Is.55:3	To Be Raised	Ac.13:34
Is.59:20, 21	To Save Israel	Ro.11:26, 27
Is.61:1-2	Proclaim the Year of the Lord	Lu.4:18-19
Je.31:15	Herod Tries to Kill Christ	Mt.2:16-18
Je.31:31-34	To Make a New Covenant with Man	He.8:8-12; 10:16, 17
Je.32:6-9	Betrayal Money Used to Buy Field	Mt.27:9-10
Da.9:25	Would Be Rejected 483 Years After Cyrus' Declaration to Rebuild the Temple	Mt.21:42
Hos.1:10-11	To Bring About the Restoration of Israel	Ro.9:26; 11:1-36
Hos.2:23	The Conversion of the Gentiles	Ro.9:25; 1 Pe.2:10
Hos.11:1	Will Flee to Egypt	Mt.2:13
Joel 2:28-32	The Promise of the Spirit	Ac.2:16-21
Amos 9:11, 12	The LORD's Return and David's Kingdom Reestablished	Ac.15:16, 17
Mic.5:2	The Birthplace of Messiah	Mt.2:5, 6; Jn.7:42
Hab.1:5	The Jews' Unbelief	Ac.13:40, 41
Hag.2:6	The Return of Christ	He.12:26
Zec.9:9	The Triumphal Entry	Mt.21:4, 5; Jn.12:14, 15
Zec.11:12-13	Judas' Betrayal	Mt.27:9, 10
Zec.12:10	The Spear Pierced in Side	Jn.19:37
Zec.13:7	The Scattering of the Disciples at the Cross	Mt.26:31, 56; Mk.14:27, 50
Mal.3:1	The Forerunner, John the Baptist	Mt.11:10; Mk.1:2; Lu.7:27
Mal.4:5, 6	The Forerunner, John the Baptist	Mt.11:13, 14; 17:10-13; Mk.9:11-13; Lu.1:16, 17

CHAPTER 54

D. The Savior's Great Promise to Israel—Restoration: Repentant Backsliders Would Return to Him, 54:1-17

1. The repentant backsliders would be set free & filled with joy

a. Because they would no longer be barren children due to their forsaking God (their husband)

b. Because they would grow in numbers: Be fruitful & reproduce, Ga.4:26-27

  1) They would need to enlarge their tents: Make more room for the growing population (of believers)

  2) They would spread out over the entire earth: Settle in the foreign nations & cities of the earth

2. The repentant backsliders would be delivered from fear, shame, & disgrace

a. The fear of oppression

b. The shame of youthful sins

c. The humiliation of captivity or any other bondage

3. The repentant backsliders would be reconciled to God

a. A reconciliation aroused by their Maker, God Himself

  1) He was like a loving husband

  2) He had called them back: As if they were deserted, rejected wives

  3) He would no longer judge (chastise, discipline) them: No longer hide His face from them

  4) He would have compassion & shower them with kindness & mercy

Sing, O barren, thou *that* didst not bear; break forth into singing, and cry aloud, thou *that* didst not travail with child: for more *are* the children of the desolate than the children of the married wife, saith the LORD.

2 Enlarge the place of thy tent, and let them stretch forth the curtains of thine habitations: spare not, lengthen thy cords, and strengthen thy stakes;

3 For thou shalt break forth on the right hand and on the left; and thy seed shall inherit the Gentiles, and make the desolate cities to be inhabited.

4 Fear not; for thou shalt not be ashamed: neither be thou confounded; for thou shalt not be put to shame: for thou shalt forget the shame of thy youth, and shalt not remember the reproach of thy widowhood any more.

5 For thy Maker *is* thine husband; the LORD of hosts *is* his name; and thy Redeemer the Holy One of Israel; The God of the whole earth shall he be called.

6 For the LORD hath called thee as a woman forsaken and grieved in spirit, and a wife of youth, when thou wast refused, saith thy God.

7 For a small moment have I forsaken thee; but with great mercies will I gather thee.

8 In a little wrath I hid my face from thee for a moment; but with everlasting kindness will I have mercy on thee,

saith the LORD thy Redeemer.

9 For this *is as* the waters of Noah unto me: for *as* I have sworn that the waters of Noah should no more go over the earth; so have I sworn that I would not be wroth with thee, nor rebuke thee.

10 For the mountains shall depart, and the hills be removed; but my kindness shall not depart from thee, neither shall the covenant of my peace be removed, saith the LORD that hath mercy on thee.

11 O thou afflicted, tossed with tempest, *and* not comforted, behold, I will lay thy stones with fair colors, and lay thy foundations with sapphires.

12 And I will make thy windows of agates, and thy gates of carbuncles, and all thy borders of pleasant stones.

13 And all thy children *shall be* taught of the LORD; and great *shall be* the peace of thy children.

14 In righteousness shalt thou be established: thou shalt be far from oppression; for thou shalt not fear: and from terror; for it shall not come near thee.

15 Behold, they shall surely gather together, *but* not by me: whosoever shall gather together against thee shall fall for thy sake.

16 Behold, I have created the smith that bloweth the coals in the fire, and that bringeth forth an instrument for his work; and I have created the waster to destroy.

17 No weapon that is formed against thee shall prosper; and every tongue *that* shall rise against thee in judgment thou shalt condemn. This *is* the heritage of the servants of the LORD, and their righteousness *is* of me, saith the LORD.

b. A reconciliation guaranteed by God's sworn oath

  1) This oath was more sure than the oath given to Noah: God would never again rebuke or be angry with them

  2) This oath was more sure than the mountains & hills that were shaken & removed: God's unfailing love & peace would never be taken from them

4. The repentant backsliders would be given a glorious future: A picture of the Savior's kingdom

a. The new Jerusalem will be a city of unparalleled beauty & value, Re.21:9-23

  1) God Himself will build the city

  2) God will use only the most valued & best quality materials

b. The citizens will be taught by the LORD Himself & be filled with peace of heart, mind, & soul

c. The citizens will live in righteousness: Under a fair & just government

  1) Will be no oppression, no social evil or lawlessness

  2) Will be no fear or terror

d. The citizens will be protected

  1) God will defeat the enemies of His people, Lu.20:18

  2) God created & used the nations' weapons as His agents: To execute justice & judgment within the world

  3) God will not allow an attack against His people in the day of His kingdom: Not even a verbal attack

e. The glorious future is guaranteed by God's promise, His Word

DIVISION VI

THE PROPHECIES OF THE GREAT DELIVERER: THE SUFFERING SERVANT OF GOD, THE SAVIOR OF THE WORLD, 49:1–59:21

D. The Savior's Great Promise to Israel—Restoration: Repentant Backsliders Will Return to Him, 54:1-17

(54:1-17) **Introduction**: to *backslide* means to revert to a worse condition, to lapse morally, or to back away from one's practice of religion. When believers backslide, they turn away from the LORD and His holy commandments, which demand righteous living. A backsliding believer returns to the selfishness and sins of the world. A backsliding believer ignores or neglects worship, the reading of God's Word, prayer, witnessing, and reaching out to meet the desperate needs of the world. A backsliding believer sometimes slips into immoral, lawless, or even violent behavior. Backsliding shames Christ by giving the world a chance to ridicule and mock His name. How? By presenting a terrible testimony or impression of the Christian life.

Backsliding is the practical subject of the present Scripture. The Israelites were a backsliding people, a people who continually turned away from the LORD to follow the wicked ways and the false gods of the world. Nevertheless, God loved His chosen people, both the believers and the unbelievers. As seen in Isaiah 53, God sent the Savior into the world to die for the sins of the entire human race. To the world, the Messiah's salvation means the offer of a great invitation (55:1–56:8). To the hypocrites and the wicked of this earth, the Messiah's salvation means a strong warning (58:1–59:21). To Israel, the Messiah's salvation means *restoration* (54:1-17). [1] This is, *The Savior's Great Promise to Israel—Restoration: Repentant Backsliders Will Return to Him*, 54:1-17.

1. The repentant backsliders would be set free and filled with joy (vv.1-3).
2. The repentant backsliders would be delivered from fear, shame, and disgrace (v.4).
3. The repentant backsliders would be reconciled to God (vv.5-10).
4. The repentant backsliders would be given a glorious future: a picture of the Savior's kingdom (vv.11-17).

[1] (54:1-3) **Backsliders, Repentance of, Results—Restoration, of Israel, Results—Prophecy, Concerning Israel, Restoration of—Population, of Israel, Growth Promised—Church, Growth in Numbers, Prophecy Concerning—Believers, Growth in Numbers, Promised—Joy, Promised, to Repentant Backsliders**: the repentant backsliders would experience joy, and the nation would grow. Israel is the backsliding nation described throughout this passage. Isaiah called Israel a *barren* woman; she was unfruitful and unproductive because she had been an unfaithful wife. Israel had turned away from her husband, God Himself (50:1-3; 62:4; Je.3:8; Ho.2:1f; Eze.16:1f; 23:1f). She had broken her vow to be faithful to the LORD, to belong to Him and Him alone. The people had turned away from the LORD to live as they wanted and to do their own thing, which meant embracing false gods and committing acts of wickedness. So far as godliness and righteousness were concerned, the nation had been drained. The people had become utterly *barren*. For that reason, the LORD had to abandon the Israelites. Because of her sin, the nation was destroyed and the citizens taken captive by Babylon.

However, the day was coming when backsliding Israel would return to the LORD, experiencing joy and great growth within the nation. As a result of the war and the hardship of their exile, the Israelite population was greatly diminished. But when the Israelites were set free from Babylonian captivity and allowed to return to the promised land, they would grow in numbers. They would be fruitful and reproduce their population. Although the immediate occasion for this prophecy was Israel's restoration to the promised land after their captivity in Babylon, the prophecy will not be totally fulfilled until the Messiah returns to set up God's kingdom on earth. No expansion in the history of Israel has ever come close to the population explosion described in these verses. Yet, when the Lord Jesus Christ returns to set up God's kingdom on earth, Israel will need to enlarge her tents even more to make room for the growing population.

But just who is the population? Does this verse refer only to the true believers of Israel, or is it a reference to all believers of all nations? Clearly, the Scripture carries a double application. It refers both to the Jews who were returning from Babylonian captivity and to all the citizens who will live in the kingdom of Christ when He returns to earth. In fact, this is exactly what other Scriptures say. The apostle Paul applies this passage to all believers of all nations when he says that the heavenly Jerusalem is the mother of all believers (Ga.4:26-27; also see He.12:22). What is being described is the enormous number of Gentile believers birthed through the witness of the early church, which consisted of the apostles and the earliest Jewish believers. Down through the centuries, the number of believers has grown significantly. And when Christ returns to earth, believers will do exactly what verse three says: they will spread out over the entire earth, settling in all the nations and cities of the world. Keep in mind that only believers will be allowed to live on earth when Christ returns to set up God's kingdom.

OUTLINE	SCRIPTURE	SCRIPTURE	OUTLINE
1. **The returning backsliders would be set free & be filled with joy** a. Because they would no longer be barren children due to their forsaking God (their husband) b. Because they would grow in numbers: Be fruitful & reproduce, Ga.4:26-27 1) They would need to en-	Sing, O barren, thou *that* didst not bear; break forth into singing, and cry aloud, thou *that* didst not travail with child: for more *are* the children of the desolate than the children of the married wife, saith the LORD. 2 Enlarge the place of thy tent, and let them stretch forth	the curtains of thine habitations: spare not, lengthen thy cords, and strengthen thy stakes; 3 For thou shalt break forth on the right hand and on the left; and thy seed shall inherit the Gentiles, and make the desolate cities to be inhabited.	large their tents: Make more room for the growing population (of believers) 2) They would spread out over the entire earth: Settle in the foreign nations & cities of the earth

Thought 1. God warns us against backsliding, against turning away from Him. Far too many of us have turned to this world and its wicked ways instead of remaining true to the LORD. Think how many of us have forsaken the Lord for the pleasures, power, fame, possessions, and wealth of this world. Think how many of us have worshipped so-called gods—the sun, moon, and stars; celebrities, heroes, and other public figures; television, movies, music, and so on—rather than the Father of the Lord Jesus Christ, the only living and true God. God has given us His Holy

---

[1] Warren W. Wiersbe. *Be Comforted*, p.142. The wording of these last three statements was gleaned from Warren W. Wiersbe.

Word in the Bible, and His Word is sufficient to meet every need we have. Still, far too many of us have backslidden by abandoning God, committing adultery with this world and its false gods.

(1) Listen to God's warning against backsliding.

"And because iniquity shall abound, the love of many shall wax cold" (Mt.24:12).

"And Jesus said unto him, No man, having put his hand to the plough, and looking back, is fit for the kingdom of God" (Lu.9:62).

"For the wrath of God is revealed from heaven against all ungodliness and unrighteousness of men, who hold the truth in unrighteousness" (Ro.1:18).

"And even as they did not like to retain God in *their* knowledge, God gave them over to a reprobate mind, to do those things which are not convenient; Being filled with all unrighteousness, fornication, wickedness, covetousness, maliciousness; full of envy, murder, debate, deceit, malignity; whisperers, Backbiters, haters of God, despiteful, proud, boasters, inventors of evil things, disobedient to parents, Without understanding, covenantbreakers, without natural affection, implacable, unmerciful: Who knowing the judgment of God, that they which commit such things are worthy of death, not only do the same, but have pleasure in them that do them" (Ro.1:28-32).

"But now, after that ye have known God, or rather are known of God, how turn ye again to the weak and beggarly elements, whereunto ye desire again to be in bondage?" (Ga.4:9).

"Now the just shall live by faith: but if *any man* draw back, my soul shall have no pleasure in him" (He.10:38).

"They went out from us, but they were not of us; for if they had been of us, they would *no doubt* have continued with us: but *they went out*, that they might be made manifest that they were not all of us" (1 Jn.2:19).

"Nevertheless I have *somewhat* against thee, because thou hast left thy first love" (Re.2:4).

"The backslider in heart shall be filled with his own ways" (Pr.14:14).

(2) Listen to the wonderful promises God makes to backsliders who repent and return to Him.

"Blessed *are* they that mourn: for they shall be comforted" (Mt.5:4).

"I say unto you, that likewise joy shall be in heaven over one sinner that repenteth, more than over ninety and nine just persons, which need no repentance" (Lu.15:7).

"Hitherto have ye asked nothing in my name: ask, and ye shall receive, that your joy may be full" (Jn.16:24).

"Then Peter said unto them, Repent, and be baptized every one of you in the name of Jesus Christ for the remission of sins, and ye shall receive the gift of the Holy Ghost" (Ac.2:38).

"Repent ye therefore, and be converted, that your sins may be blotted out, when the times of refreshing shall come from the presence of the Lord" (Ac.3:19).

"For the kingdom of God is not meat and drink; but righteousness, and peace, and joy in the Holy Ghost" (Ro.14:17).

"For godly sorrow worketh repentance to salvation not to be repented of: but the sorrow of the world worketh death" (2 Co.7:10).

"If my people, which are called by my name, shall humble themselves, and pray, and seek my face, and turn from their wicked ways; then will I hear from heaven, and will forgive their sin, and will heal their land" (2 Chr.7:14).

"Thou wilt show me the path of life: in thy presence *is* fulness of joy; at thy right hand *there are* pleasures for evermore" (Ps.16:11).

"The LORD *is* nigh unto them that are of a broken heart; and saveth such as be of a contrite spirit" (Ps.34:18).

"They that sow in tears shall reap in joy" (Ps.126:5).

"Therefore with joy shall ye draw water out of the wells of salvation" (Is.12:3).

"And the ransomed of the LORD shall return, and come to Zion with songs and everlasting joy upon their heads: they shall obtain joy and gladness, and sorrow and sighing shall flee away" (Is.35:10).

"Let the wicked forsake his way, and the unrighteous man his thoughts: and let him return unto the LORD, and he will have mercy upon him; and to our God, for he will abundantly pardon" (Is.55:7).

"For all those *things* hath mine hand made, and all those *things* have been, saith the LORD: but to this *man* will I look, *even* to *him that is* poor and of a contrite spirit, and trembleth at my word" (Is.66:2).

"Return, ye backsliding children, *and* I will heal your backslidings. Behold, we come unto thee; for thou *art* the LORD our God" (Je.3:22).

"But if the wicked will turn from all his sins that he hath committed, and keep all my statutes, and do that which is lawful and right, he shall surely live, he shall not die" (Eze.18:21).

"Cast away from you all your transgressions, whereby ye have transgressed; and make you a new heart and a new spirit: for why will ye die, O house of Israel?" (Eze.18:31).

---

2 (54:4) **Backsliders, Repentant, Promises to—Deliverance, from What, Three Things—Fear, Deliverance from, Promised—Shame, Deliverance from, Promised—Disgrace, Deliverance from, Promised**: the repentant backsliders would be delivered from fear, shame, and humiliation. This promise and the great promises given above seem far-fetched and hard to believe. At the time of this prophecy the Israelites were in bondage, held captive by Babylon. From all appearances, they would continue to live in the fear of daily oppression, hardship, and deprivation. And as slaves to Babylon, they would continue to bear the shame and disgrace of their bondage. Remember that their enslavement was due to their continual rejection of God and their wicked behavior down through the centuries from the time they were a young nation. Nevertheless the wonderful promise of God to backsliding Israel was *deliverance*. Some day in the future they would repent and return to the LORD.

a. In that day, they would no longer fear the oppression of enemies or of any other trial or seductive temptation. Fear would be erased from their hearts and replaced with a spirit of peace and complete confidence in the LORD'S care.

b. In that day, the shame of sin would no longer be remembered, neither the transgressions of youth, nor the sins committed as an adult. Israel's youth probably refers to the entire history of the nation from its birth at Mount Sinai until the time of the Babylonian captivity, the time of this present Scripture.

⇒ The nation's childhood would have been its birth beginning with Abraham up until the time the people were formed into a nation under Moses.

⇒ The adult life of the nation would most likely stand for the time between Christ's coming and the end of human history.

Whatever the case, the shame of Israel's sins as a young nation plagued the people up through the Babylonian captivity. But a wonderful promise was being given to them in this Scripture: the day was coming when the shame of their youthful sins would no longer be remembered. Their transgressions and all the disgrace and oppression that occurred because of them would be erased from their minds. Of course, this will take place when the Messiah, the Lord Jesus Christ, returns to earth to establish the kingdom of God.

c. In that day, the humiliation of enslavement, of being held in bondage, would also be erased. The word *widowhood* refers to the time Israel abandoned the LORD (her husband) and committed spiritual adultery against Him by turning to other gods and to the wickedness of this world. Forsaking God is just as disgraceful as a woman forsaking her husband to commit adultery with another man. But when Christ returns, the disgrace of forsaking the Lord will be removed and remembered no more.

OUTLINE	SCRIPTURE	SCRIPTURE	OUTLINE
2. The returning backsliders would be delivered from fear, shame, & disgrace a. The fear of oppression	4 Fear not; for thou shalt not be ashamed: neither be thou confounded; for thou shalt not be put to shame: for	thou shalt forget the shame of thy youth, and shalt not remember the reproach of thy widowhood any more.	b. The shame of youthful sins c. The humiliation of captivity or any other bondage

Thought 1. These same three promises are applicable to us. God will accept all backsliders who truly return to Him in repentance. He will deliver them from fear, shame, and humiliation.

(1) Backsliders who truly repent will be delivered from fear—the fear of oppression from enemies, trials, and seductive temptations. God's presence and power will fill believers, strengthening them to conquer their fear. However, believers must trust the Lord, truly follow Him, and draw close to Him in times of trial and temptation. Listen to what God's Holy Word says about fear:

"But the very hairs of your head are all numbered. Fear ye not therefore, ye are of more value than many sparrows" (Mt.10:30-31).

"For God hath not given us the spirit of fear; but of power, and of love, and of a sound mind" (2 Ti.1:7).

"And when I saw him, I fell at his feet as dead. And he laid his right hand upon me, saying unto me, Fear not; I am the first and the last: I *am* he that liveth, and was dead; and, behold, I am alive for evermore, Amen; and have the keys of hell and of death [the keys to eternal life]" (Re.1:17-18).

"I laid me down and slept; I awaked; for the LORD sustained me. I will not be afraid of ten thousands of people, that have set *themselves* against me round about" (Ps.3:5-6).

"The LORD *is* my light and my salvation; whom shall I fear? the LORD *is* the strength of my life; of whom shall I be afraid? When the wicked, *even* mine enemies and my foes, came upon me to eat up my flesh, they stumbled and fell. Though an host should encamp against me, my heart shall not fear: though war should rise against me, in this *will* I *be* confident" (Ps.27:1-3).

"I will say of the LORD, *He is* my refuge and my fortress: my God; in him will I trust. Surely he shall deliver thee from the snare of the fowler, *and* from the noisome pestilence. He shall cover thee with his feathers, and under his wings shalt thou trust: his truth *shall be thy* shield and buckler. Thou shalt not be afraid for the terror by night; *nor* for the arrow *that* flieth by day; *Nor* for the pestilence *that* walketh in darkness; *nor* for the destruction *that* wasteth at noonday" (Ps.91:2-6).

"The LORD *is* on my side; I will not fear: what can man do unto me?" (Ps.118:6).

"When thou liest down, thou shalt not be afraid: yea, thou shalt lie down, and thy sleep shall be sweet" (Pr.3:24).

"Behold, God *is* my salvation; I will trust, and not be afraid: for the LORD JEHOVAH *is* my strength and *my* song; he also is become my salvation" (Is.12:2).

"Fear thou not; for I *am* with thee: be not dismayed; for I *am* thy God: I will strengthen thee; yea, I will help thee; yea, I will uphold thee with the right hand of my righteousness" (Is.41:10).

"Fear not: for I have redeemed thee, I have called *thee* by thy name; thou *art* mine. When thou passest through the waters, I *will be* with thee; and through the rivers, they shall not overflow thee:

when thou walkest through the fire, thou shalt not be burned; neither shall the flame kindle upon thee. For I *am* the LORD thy God, the Holy One of Israel, thy Saviour: I gave Egypt *for* thy ransom, Ethiopia and Seba for thee" (Is.43:1-3).

(2) Backsliders who truly repent will be delivered from the shame of sin. When professing believers live worldly lives of sinful pleasure, immorality, greed, and covetousness and engage in lying, stealing, and cheating, they are hypocrites. Professing one thing, they do something else. By their false profession they are attempting to deceive others, but they are only deceiving themselves and smearing God's name and holy character. Sadly, sin does not always cause a person to sense shame, and many people do not even consider sin shameful. Nonetheless, all sins are degrading acts of treachery to God. In His eyes, every wrongdoing committed is a shameful, humiliating, contemptible act and each act places a stigma of shame upon the world, magnifying the spirit of wickedness, lawlessness, violence, and immorality that is sweeping across the earth.

In spite of everything, though, God will forgive our sins. This verse gives us His wonderful promise. God will erase the shame of sin from our lives. Our task is to repent of our backsliding. Listen to the LORD's wonderful promise concerning the forgiveness of sins:

"And said unto them, Thus it is written, and thus it behoved Christ to suffer, and to rise from the dead the third day: And that repentance and remission of sins should be preached in his name among all nations, beginning at Jerusalem" (Lu.24:46-47).

"Then Peter said unto them, Repent, and be baptized every one of you in the name of Jesus Christ for the remission of sins, and ye shall receive the gift of the Holy Ghost" (Ac.2:38).

"The God of our fathers raised up Jesus, whom ye slew and hanged on a tree. Him hath God exalted with his right hand *to be* a Prince and a Saviour, for to give repentance to Israel, and forgiveness of sins. And we are his witnesses of these things; and *so is* also the Holy Ghost, whom God hath given to them that obey him" (Ac.5:30-32).

"In whom we have redemption through his blood, the forgiveness of sins, according to the riches of his grace" (Ep.1:7).

"If we confess our sins, he is faithful and just to forgive us *our* sins, and to cleanse us from all unrighteousness" (1 Jn.1:9).

"I, *even* I, *am* he that blotteth out thy transgressions for mine own sake, and will not remember thy sins" (Is.43:25).

"Let the wicked forsake his way, and the unrighteous man his thoughts: and let him return unto the LORD, and he will have mercy upon him; and to our God, for he will abundantly pardon" (Is.55:7).

"Return, ye backsliding children, *and* I will heal your backslidings. Behold, we come unto thee; for thou *art* the LORD our God" (Je.3:22).

(3) Backsliders who truly repent will be delivered from the humiliation of bondage. The entire world is held in bondage to sin. No person can keep from sinning nor can any person live a sinless life. "All have sinned and come short of the glory of God" (Ro.3:23). Tragically, many of us are held in bondage to sinful habits: alcohol, drugs, smoking, sexual immorality, stealing, lying, gluttony, cursing, and a host of other enslaving sins.

To be enslaved to any wicked behavior is an utter disgrace, for it shows lack of discipline and self-control. To be controlled or manipulated by any sinful or harmful behavior exposes a weak mind or a heart hardened toward God. But again God makes a wonderful promise to us: He will deliver us from the humiliation of bondage. However, His promise is conditional. As long as we live out in the world and continue to forsake the Lord, He cannot help us. But if we return to Him, He will help us. Through Christ, He will remove the dishonor and humiliation of our bondage to sin. Listen to the promises of God's Holy Word:

"Who gave himself for our sins, that he might deliver us from this present evil world, according to the will of God and our Father" (Ga.1:4).

"And the Lord shall deliver me from every evil work, and will preserve *me* unto his heavenly kingdom: to whom *be* glory for ever and ever. Amen" (2 Ti.4:18).

"Who his own self bare our sins in his own body on the tree, that we, being dead to sins, should live unto righteousness: by whose stripes ye were healed. For ye were as sheep going astray; but are now returned unto the Shepherd and Bishop of your souls" (1 Pe.2:24-25).

"The Lord knoweth how to deliver the godly out of temptations, and to reserve the unjust unto the day of judgment to be punished" (2 Pe.2:9).

"My little children, these things write I unto you, that ye sin not. And if any man sin, we have an advocate with the Father, Jesus Christ the righteous: And he is the propitiation for our sins: and not for ours only, but also for *the sins of* the whole world" (1 Jn.2:1-2).

3 (54:5-10) **Reconciliation, Source, God—Repentance, Results, Reconciliation—Israel, Prophecies Concerning, Reconciliation with God—Prophecies, Concerning Israel, Reconciliation—Reconciliation, Promises of, to Backsliders**: the repentant backsliders would be reconciled to God. Note that reconciliation is initiated by God Himself, "your Maker" and "your husband." This is a startling statement, for it claims that the bond between God and His people is just like the loving bond between a husband and his wife. As their *Maker* who truly loves them, God could never abandon His people to their enemies or to the enslaving power of their sin. He was bound to be reaching out to His wayward people, longing for them to return to Him. God has the power to reconcile backsliders to Him because He is the LORD *of hosts*, the LORD *Almighty* who controls all beings in both heaven and earth. God is also the *Holy One* of Israel, which means that He is flawless and righteous. He will always do the right thing, always show His love by accepting backsliders who return to Him. Moreover, God is the *Redeemer*, which means that His very nature is to save His people from their enemies and from the sins of the world. Note who the Redeemer is: He is *God of all the earth*. It is He who seeks to be reconciled to His people who have gone astray. They, or anyone else for that matter, can be reconciled and have a relationship with the *God of all the earth*. What a staggering thought! But that is the promise of this passage.

Like a loving husband, the LORD calls His people to return to His arms. Despite the fact that His people had abandoned Him for the gods and wickedness of this world, He still desired to be reconciled to them. Note the stress upon God's love for His people. His love is like the love of a young married man who is ardently attracted to and single-minded in the pursuit of his wife. God is passionately in love with His people and longs for close fellowship and communion with them. Even when God's people drift away, He seeks after them with the hope that they will return to Him.

Even as the love of God is stressed, His justice must be acknowledged as well. Sin can arouse His anger and force Him to act (vv.7-8). God will chastise any of His people who turn away from Him. When believers are unfaithful and commit spiritual adultery by turning to false gods or to the sins of this world, God will discipline them. God will abandon and hide His face from carnal, worldly sinners, but only for a short time.

God is merciful and compassionate (vv.7-8). For that reason He assures His backsliding people that He will show mercy to them. Although they may seem far away by living in unbelief and sin, the day is coming when God will take His people back. He will receive all who repent and turn back to Him. No longer will He hide His face in anger against them; instead, He will have compassion and redeem them (v.8).

The LORD'S sworn oath guarantees this reconciliation (vv.9-10). The day is coming when the LORD will never again rebuke or be angry with His people. This oath is more sure than the oath God swore to Noah when He promised to never again judge the earth with a worldwide flood. And it is more sure than the presence of the mountains and hills, which are sometimes shaken and removed. In summary, God will never take His unfailing peace and love from His people (v.10).

OUTLINE	SCRIPTURE	SCRIPTURE	OUTLINE

3. The returning backsliders would be reconciled to God
a. A reconciliation aroused by their Maker, God Himself
  1) He was like a loving husband
  2) He had called them back: As if they were deserted, rejected wives
 	
  3) He would no longer judge (chastise, discipline) them: No longer hide His face from them
  4) He would have compassion & shower them with
	5 For thy Maker *is* thine husband; the LORD of hosts *is* his name; and thy Redeemer the Holy One of Israel; The God of the whole earth shall he be called.
	6 For the LORD hath called thee as a woman forsaken and grieved in spirit, and a wife of youth, when thou wast refused, saith thy God.
	7 For a small moment have I forsaken thee; but with great mercies will I gather thee.
	8 In a little wrath I hid my face from thee for a moment; but with everlasting kindness
		will I have mercy on thee, saith the LORD thy Redeemer.
		9 For this *is as* the waters of Noah unto me: for *as* I have sworn that the waters of Noah should no more go over the earth; so have I sworn that I would not be wroth with thee, nor rebuke thee.
		10 For the mountains shall depart, and the hills be removed; but my kindness shall not depart from thee, neither shall the covenant of my peace be removed, saith the LORD that hath mercy on thee.
			kindness & mercy
			
			b. A reconciliation guaranteed by God's sworn oath
			  1) This oath was more sure than the oath given to Noah: God would never again rebuke or be angry with them
			  2) This oath was more sure than the mountains & hills that were shaken & removed: God's unfailing love & peace would never be taken from them

Thought 1. God loves His people and longs to be reconciled to every individual who has strayed from Him. Backsliders are those who have deserted God, turned away from Him to form adulterous relationships with the sinful world and the gods of false religion. When backsliders abandon God, they wound His heart and cause Him excruciating pain, all because God loves His people and longs for a close relationship with them. He wants His people to continually speak to Him through prayer and listen to Him by meditating on His Holy Word. And He wants His people to obey Him, for His commandments tell a person how to live a victorious, productive, and meaningful life. When we drift away, the Lord reaches out to us in love. He wants us to forsake our adulterous, sinful ways and return to Him. If we will return from our backsliding, the Lord will have mercy upon us. He is perfectly willing to be reconciled to any backslider. But we must know this one fact: reconciliation comes only through Jesus Christ. In other words, if we desire to be reconciled to God, we must approach Him through Christ. Christ alone has brought peace between God and the human race. Christ alone can forgive our sins, for He alone died for the sins of the world. Reconciliation with God is possible only if we approach the Father through His Son, the Lord Jesus Christ.

> **"For God so loved the world, that he gave his only begotten Son, that whosoever believeth in him should not perish, but have everlasting life" (Jn.3:16).**
> **"But God commendeth his love toward us, in that, while we were yet sinners, Christ died for us. Much more then, being now justified by his blood, we shall be saved from wrath through him. For if, when we were enemies, we were reconciled to God by the death of his Son, much more, being reconciled, we shall be saved by his life" (Ro.5:8-10).**
> **"Therefore if any man *be* in Christ, *he is* a new creature: old things are passed away; behold, all things are become new. And all things *are* of God, who hath reconciled us to himself by Jesus Christ, and hath given to us the ministry of reconciliation; To wit, that God was in Christ, reconciling the world unto himself, not imputing their trespasses unto them; and hath committed unto us the word of**

reconciliation. Now then we are ambassadors for Christ, as though God did beseech *you* by us: we pray *you* in Christ's stead, be ye reconciled to God. For he hath made him *to be* sin for us, who knew no sin; that we might be made the righteousness of God in him" (2 Co.5:17-21).

"But God, who is rich in mercy, for his great love wherewith he loved us, Even when we were dead in sins, hath quickened us together with Christ, (by grace ye are saved;)" (Ep.2:4-5).

"But now in Christ Jesus ye who sometimes were far off are made nigh by the blood of Christ. For he is our peace, who hath made both one, and hath broken down the middle wall of partition *between us;* Having abolished in his flesh the enmity, *even* the law of commandments *contained* in ordinances; for to make in himself of twain one new man, *so* making peace; And that he might reconcile both unto God in one body by the cross, having slain the enmity thereby" (Ep.2:13-16).

"In whom we have redemption through his blood, *even* the forgiveness of sins" (Col.1:14).

"And, having made peace through the blood of his cross, by him to reconcile all things unto himself; by him, *I say,* whether *they be* things in earth, or things in heaven. And you, that were sometime alienated and enemies in *your* mind by wicked works, yet now hath he reconciled: In the body of his flesh through death, to present you holy and unblameable and unreproveable in his sight" (Col.1:20-22).

"Wherefore in all things it behoved him to be made like unto *his* brethren, that he might be a merciful and faithful high priest in things *pertaining* to God, to make reconciliation for the sins of the people. For in that he himself hath suffered being tempted, he is able to succour them that are tempted" (He.2:17-18).

4 (54:11-17) **Backsliders, Repentant, Promises to—Prophecy, Concerning Israel, Restoration—Restoration, of Israel, Prophecy Concerning—Messiah, Kingdom of, Prophecy Concerning—Christ, Future Kingdom, Prophecy Concerning—Kingdom, of Christ, Prophecy Concerning—End Times, Prophecy Concerning, Christ's Kingdom—Inheritance, of Believers, Christ's Kingdom—Promises, to Believers, Christ's Kingdom**: the repentant backsliders would be given a glorious future. This Scripture is clearly describing a society far beyond any ever known on earth. God is giving an unmistakable picture of the kingdom that will be established in the future when Christ returns to earth. Note that the prophecy is addressed to Jerusalem, the afflicted city that has been battered by army after army, hardly ever knowing a moment of peace or comfort. God has wonderful news for this downtrodden city: it has been destined for a glorious future. This fact may stun and dumbfound many in the world; nevertheless, Jerusalem is to become the capital of the Messiah's kingdom when He returns to earth. Note exactly what is said in these verses:

OUTLINE	SCRIPTURE	SCRIPTURE	OUTLINE
4. **The returning backsliders would be given a glorious future: A picture of the Savior's kingdom**	11 O thou afflicted, tossed with tempest, *and* not comforted, behold, I will lay thy stones with fair colors, and lay thy foundations with sapphires.	come near thee. 15 Behold, they shall surely gather together, *but* not by me: whosoever shall gather together against thee shall fall for thy sake.	2) Will be no fear or terror
a. The new Jerusalem will be a city of unparalleled beauty & value, Re.21:9-23			d. The citizens will be protected
1) God Himself will build the city	12 And I will make thy windows of agates, and thy gates of carbuncles, and all thy borders of pleasant stones.	16 Behold, I have created the smith that bloweth the coals in the fire, and that bringeth forth an instrument for his work; and I have created the waster to destroy.	1) God will defeat the enemies of His people, Lu.20:18
2) God will use only the most valued & best quality materials			2) God created & used the nations' weapons as His agents: To execute justice & judgment within the world
b. The citizens will be taught by the LORD Himself & be filled with peace of heart, mind, & soul	13 And all thy children *shall be* taught of the LORD; and great *shall be* the peace of thy children.	17 No weapon that is formed against thee shall prosper; and every tongue *that* shall rise against thee in judgment thou shalt condemn. This *is* the heritage of the servants of the LORD, and their righteousness *is* of me, saith the LORD.	3) God will not allow an attack against His people in the day of His kingdom: Not even a verbal attack
c. The citizens will live in righteousness: Under a fair & just government	14 In righteousness shalt thou be established: thou shalt be far from oppression; for thou shalt not fear: and from terror; for it shall not		e. The glorious future is guaranteed by God's promise, His Word
1) Will be no oppression, no social evil or lawlessness			

a. The citizens of the New Jerusalem will live in a city of unparalleled beauty and value. God Himself will build the city using only the finest and most valuable materials. The city will be so glorious that it will be indescribable. Thus, Isaiah uses the most precious stones on earth to picture what the New Jerusalem will look like. All buildings in the city will be constructed from precious jewels, and the foundations will be laid with sapphires. All the towers and pentacles will be made of sparkling rubies, while the gates and walls will be made of other precious jewels and crystal. Remember that all stones and rocks in the universe deteriorate and eventually waste away. But the sparkling jewels used to construct the Holy City will be incorruptible. Therefore, the chemical makeup of God's incorruptible throne is unknown to man. A study of *Revelation*, both the Scripture and commentary, is helpful in understanding the New Jerusalem (see outline and notes—Re.21:9-23 for more discussion).

b. The citizens of the New Jerusalem will be taught by the LORD Himself. As a result, their hearts will be flooded with the peace of God. God's *peace* suggests a victorious life free from the oppression of enemies, trials, and temptations. Also suggested are well-being, good health, and prosperity in all things. The peace of God means to be free from all restlessness, disturbance, instability, anxiety, distress, discouragement, depression, weakness, and any other feeling or emotion that creates problems for people. God's peace means inward strength, purpose, meaning, significance, and a deep sense of fulfillment and satisfaction. It means living a victorious, conquering, and triumphant life that is full of meaning and purpose. Listen to what other Scriptures say about God's peace:

> "Peace I leave with you, my peace I give unto you: not as the world giveth, give I unto you. Let not your heart be troubled, neither let it be afraid" (Jn.14:27).
>
> "These things I have spoken unto you, that in me ye might have peace. In the world ye shall have tribulation: but be of good cheer; I have overcome the world" (Jn.16:33).
>
> "Therefore being justified by faith, we have peace with God through our Lord Jesus Christ" (Ro.5:1).
>
> "But now in Christ Jesus ye who sometimes were far off are made nigh by the blood of Christ. For he is our peace, who hath made both one, and hath broken down the middle wall of partition *between us*" (Ep.2:13-14).
>
> "Be careful for nothing; but in every thing by prayer and supplication with thanksgiving let your requests be made known unto God. And the peace of God, which passeth all understanding, shall keep your hearts and minds through Christ Jesus" (Ph.4:6-7).
>
> "And, having made peace through the blood of his cross, by him to reconcile all things unto himself; by him, *I say,* whether *they be* things in earth, or things in heaven" (Col.1:20).
>
> "The LORD will give strength unto his people; the LORD will bless his people with peace" (Ps.29:11).
>
> "Great peace have they which love thy law: and nothing shall offend them" (Ps.119:165).
>
> "Thou wilt keep *him* in perfect peace, *whose* mind *is* stayed *on thee:* because he trusteth in thee" (Is.26:3).
>
> "O that thou hadst hearkened to my commandments! then had thy peace been as a river, and thy righteousness as the waves of the sea" (Is.48:18).

c. The citizens of the New Jerusalem will live in a righteous society, for the LORD Himself will establish a fair and just government that shows no partiality or favoritism. There will be no prejudice or discrimination in the New Jerusalem. There will be no evil or lawlessness running rampant throughout society. Tyranny and violence will be gone forever. Within society there will be nothing whatsoever to fear. The righteous, fair, and just society of Christ's kingdom is exactly the kind of society that God admonishes us to be building today.

d. The citizens of the New Jerusalem will be protected (vv.15-17a). No nation will be allowed to defeat God's people when Christ establishes God's kingdom on earth. In fact, no nation will be allowed to assemble for the purpose of waging war. In the past, God raised up and used the nations as His agents to execute justice in the world. But in the Messiah's kingdom, God will not allow an attack against His people. No weapon will be forged to be used in war. Not even a verbal attack will be allowed against God's people. Peace will rule within the hearts and minds of people and within their social relationships. God will personally protect His people.

Even today, God promises security to His people. He promises to protect those who truly believe and follow Him. In all trials and sufferings God is present with His people. He carries them or walks with them through every possible hardship *if* they call upon him. Even when they face death, He promises to be with them and to transfer them into His presence. Quicker than the eye can blink, true believers are taken from this earth into the presence of God Himself.

> "These things I have spoken unto you, that in me ye might have peace. In the world ye shall have tribulation: but be of good cheer; I have overcome the world" (Jn.16:33).
>
> "Who shall separate us from the love of Christ? *shall* tribulation, or distress, or persecution, or famine, or nakedness, or peril, or sword?...Nay, in all these things we are more than conquerors through him that loved us. For I am persuaded, that neither death, nor life, nor angels, nor principalities, nor powers, nor things present, nor things to come, Nor height, nor depth, nor any other creature, shall be able to separate us from the love of God, which is in Christ Jesus our Lord" (Ro.8:35, 37-39).
>
> "For the which cause I also suffer these things: nevertheless I am not ashamed: for I know whom I have believed, and am persuaded that he is able to keep that which I have committed unto him against that day" (2 Ti.1:12).
>
> "And the Lord shall deliver me from every evil work, and will preserve *me* unto his heavenly kingdom: to whom *be* glory for ever and ever. Amen" (2 Ti.4:18).
>
> "*Let your* conversation [conduct, behavior] *be* without covetousness; *and be* content with such things as ye have: for he hath said, I will never leave thee, nor forsake thee. So that we may boldly say, The Lord *is* my helper, and I will not fear what man shall do unto me" (He.13:5-6).
>
> "For whatsoever is born of God overcometh the world: and this is the victory that overcometh the world, *even* our faith. Who is he that overcometh the world, but he that believeth that Jesus is the Son of God?" (1 Jn.5:4-5).
>
> "And, behold, I *am* with thee, and will keep thee in all *places* whither thou goest, and will bring thee again into this land; for I will not leave thee, until I have done *that* which I have spoken to thee of" (Ge.28:15).
>
> "For the eyes of the LORD run to and fro throughout the whole earth, to show himself strong in the behalf of *them* whose heart *is* perfect toward him. Herein thou hast done foolishly: therefore from henceforth thou shalt have wars" (2 Chr.16:9).

"The angel of the LORD encampeth round about them that fear him, and delivereth them" (Ps.34:7).

"He shall cover thee with his feathers, and under his wings shalt thou trust: his truth *shall be thy shield and buckler*" (Ps.91:4).

"Thou shalt not be afraid for the terror by night; *nor* for the arrow *that* flieth by day" (Ps.91:5).

"He shall not be afraid of evil tidings: his heart is fixed, trusting in the LORD" (Ps.112:7).

"As the mountains *are* round about Jerusalem, so the LORD *is* round about his people from henceforth even for ever" (Ps.125:2).

"When thou liest down, thou shalt not be afraid: yea, thou shalt lie down, and thy sleep shall be sweet" (Pr.3:24).

"Fear thou not; for I *am* with thee: be not dismayed; for I *am* thy God: I will strengthen thee; yea, I will help thee; yea, I will uphold thee with the right hand of my righteousness" (Is.41:10).

"And *even* to *your* old age I *am* he; and *even* to hoar [gray] hairs will I carry *you:* I have made, and I will bear; even I will carry, and will deliver *you*" (Is.46:4).

e. The citizens of Jerusalem as well as all other believers will have a glorious future in Jerusalem. This promise is guaranteed by God's Holy Word (v.17b). All these blessings are to be the heritage of those who serve the LORD. All true servants of God—genuine believers—will inherit the New Jerusalem, be taught by the LORD, and be flooded with His peace. And they will live in a righteous society under a fair and just government. Moreover, God Himself will protect them. These promises, this heritage, is guaranteed by God's very own Word.

"And now, brethren, I commend you to God, and to the word of his grace, which is able to build you up, and to give you an inheritance among all them which are sanctified" (Ac.20:32).

"Giving thanks unto the Father, which hath made us meet to be partakers of the inheritance of the saints in light" (Col.1:12).

"And whatsoever ye do, do *it* heartily, as to the Lord, and not unto men; Knowing that of the Lord ye shall receive the reward of the inheritance: for ye serve the Lord Christ" (Col.3:23-24).

"Blessed *be* the God and Father of our Lord Jesus Christ, which according to his abundant mercy hath begotten us again unto a lively hope by the resurrection of Jesus Christ from the dead, To an inheritance incorruptible, and undefiled, and that fadeth not away, reserved in heaven for you" (1 Pe.1:3-4).

CHAPTER 55

E. The Savior's Great Invitation to the World, 55:1–56:8

1. The invitation to come to the LORD
a. The people invited: The thirsty & poor
b. The offer: Salvation
   1) Water: Spiritual fullness
   2) Wine & milk: All needs met
c. The price: Free
d. The urgent plea
   1) Do not waste money & labor on things that do not satisfy
   2) Listen to the LORD: Be filled with His nourishment

e. The promise: If you come to the LORD...
   1) You will live
   2) You will receive all the mercies & love promised to David, 2 S.7:11-17
f. The agent of salvation: The Savior
   1) He is God's Witness, Leader, & Commander
   2) He is God's Witness who issues the call for the people (Gentile nations) to come
      • They will rush to Him
      • They will see Him glorified by God

2. The invitation to seek the LORD
a. The danger: Waiting too late
b. The person invited: The wicked, evil person
   1) He must repent
      • Forsake his evil way
      • Turn to the LORD
   2) He will receive mercy & forgiveness—freely
c. The urgent need to seek
   1) God's thoughts & ways are perfect, far beyond our understanding
   2) God's thoughts & ways are righteous, far higher than ours: Ours are imperfect & wicked

d. The way God calls the wicked: By His Word, Mt.13:1-9, 18-33
   1) His Word is as powerful as rain & snow that water the earth & cause the grain to grow

   2) His Word will not return empty: It will bear fruit, accomplish God's purpose

---

Ho, every one that thirsteth, come ye to the waters, and he that hath no money; come ye, buy, and eat; yea, come, buy wine and milk without money and without price.
2 Wherefore do ye spend money for *that which is* not bread? and your labour for *that which* satisfieth not? hearken diligently unto me, and eat ye *that which is* good, and let your soul delight itself in fatness.
3 Incline your ear, and come unto me: hear, and your soul shall live; and I will make an everlasting covenant with you, *even* the sure mercies of David.
4 Behold, I have given him *for* a witness to the people, a leader and commander to the people.
5 Behold, thou shalt call a nation *that* thou knowest not, and nations *that* knew not thee shall run unto thee because of the LORD thy God, and for the Holy One of Israel; for he hath glorified thee.
6 Seek ye the LORD while he may be found, call ye upon him while he is near:
7 Let the wicked forsake his way, and the unrighteous man his thoughts: and let him return unto the LORD, and he will have mercy upon him; and to our God, for he will abundantly pardon.
8 For my thoughts *are* not your thoughts, neither *are* your ways my ways, saith the LORD.
9 For *as* the heavens are higher than the earth, so are my ways higher than your ways, and my thoughts than your thoughts.
10 For as the rain cometh down, and the snow from heaven, and returneth not thither, but watereth the earth, and maketh it bring forth and bud, that it may give seed to the sower, and bread to the eater:
11 So shall my word be that goeth forth out of my mouth: it shall not return unto me

void, but it shall accomplish that which I please, and it shall prosper *in the thing* whereto I sent it.
12 For ye shall go out with joy, and be led forth with peace: the mountains and the hills shall break forth before you into singing, and all the trees of the field shall clap *their* hands.
13 Instead of the thorn shall come up the fir tree, and instead of the brier shall come up the myrtle tree: and it shall be to the LORD for a name, for an everlasting sign *that* shall not be cut off.

CHAPTER 56

Thus saith the LORD, Keep ye judgment, and do justice: for my salvation *is* near to come, and my righteousness to be revealed.
2 Blessed *is* the man *that* doeth this, and the son of man *that* layeth hold on it; that keepeth the sabbath from polluting it, and keepeth his hand from doing any evil.
3 Neither let the son of the stranger, that hath joined himself to the LORD, speak, saying, The LORD hath utterly separated me from his people: neither let the eunuch say, Behold, I *am* a dry tree.
4 For thus saith the LORD unto the eunuchs that keep my sabbaths, and choose *the things* that please me, and take hold of my covenant;
5 Even unto them will I give in mine house and within my walls a place and a name better than of sons and of daughters: I will give them an everlasting name, that shall not be cut off.
6 Also the sons of the stranger, that join themselves to the LORD, to serve him, and to love the name of the LORD, to be his servants, every one that keepeth the sabbath from polluting it, and taketh hold of my covenant;
7 Even them will I bring to my holy mountain, and make them joyful in my house of prayer: their burnt offerings and their sacrifices *shall be* accepted upon mine altar; for mine house shall be called an house of prayer for all people.

---

e. The results of seeking the LORD
   1) The repentant sinner will live in joy & peace
   2) The earth will be transformed
      • All nature will rejoice

      • All thorns will be removed & all vegetation will become fruitful
   3) The transformation will be for the purpose of honoring the LORD: Be a sign of His love & power

3. The invitation to live righteously & to worship the LORD
a. The urgent plea of the LORD
   1) Be just & righteous: God's salvation & righteousness are both near
   2) Keep the Sabbath: Do not defile God's day by working or neglecting worship

b. The persons invited—the foreigners & the eunuchs: All who feel excluded, shut out, separated, & cut off from God's salvation & promises
c. The assurance to eunuchs (the single & chaste by force or by choice): They will not be excluded, cut off
   1) The conditions: Must keep the Sabbath & live righteously
   2) The promises
      • Will be given a place before God & a name better than children
      • Will be given an everlasting name

d. The promises to foreigners (Gentiles): All unbelievers
   1) The condition
      • Must be committed to the LORD, love & serve Him
      • Must worship the LORD & keep the Sabbath

   2) The promises
      • Will be accepted in God's holy mountain (temple)
      • Will be given joy in worship
      • Will have their worship accepted

• Will be accepted by God just as the Jews are accepted: A sworn oath	8 The Lord GOD which gathereth the outcasts of Israel saith, Yet will I	gather *others* to him, beside those that are gathered unto him.	by God

DIVISION VI

THE PROPHECIES OF THE GREAT DELIVERER: THE SUFFERING SERVANT OF GOD, THE SAVIOR OF THE WORLD, 49:1–59:21

E.   The Savior's Great Invitation to the World, 55:1–56:8

(55:1–56:8) **Introduction**: the human race has the most unique opportunity imaginable, that of having worldwide peace, economic prosperity, and justice. Peace among all people is possible. A society in which need has been eliminated is possible. A society in which citizens live in comfort and joy, treat others fairly, and always do what is right is possible. Incomprehensible! Unimaginable! Yet this is the very offer that God extends to the world—the salvation of society. His great invitation to every society and group of people of the world is to receive His gift of peace, prosperity, joy, justice, and righteousness. This is the great message of the present Scripture. As seen earlier, God's very special Servant, His Son Jesus Christ, died for the sins of the entire world (Is.52:13–53:12). He died to offer salvation to the world. This is, *The Savior's Great Invitation to the World*, 55:1–56:8.

1. The invitation to come to the LORD (55:1-5).
2. The invitation to seek the LORD (55:6-13).
3. The invitation to live righteously and to worship the LORD (56:1-8).

1 (55:1-5) **Invitation, Offered to, the Thirsty and Poor—Invitation, Extended by, the LORD—Thirsty, Invitation Offered, to Come—Poor, Invitation to, to Come—Promises, Given to, the Poor; the Thirsty—Salvation, Offered to, Thirsty and Poor—David, Promises to, Offered to Believers—Jesus Christ, Names-Titles—Gentiles, Prophecies Concerning, Salvation**: the first invitation is a cry from the depth of God's heart: Come! Everyone come. The invitation is not extended only to the Jews. God does not call only the religious and righteous to come. He calls everyone, including the ungodly and unrighteous. Note the Scripture and outline:

OUTLINE	SCRIPTURE	SCRIPTURE	OUTLINE

1. **The invitation to come to the LORD**
   a. The people invited: The thirsty & poor
   b. The offer: Salvation
     1) Water: Spiritual fullness
     2) Wine & milk: All needs met
   c. The price: Free
   d. The urgent plea
     1) Do not waste money & labor on things that do not satisfy
     2) Listen to the LORD: Be filled with His nourishment
   e. The promise: If you come to the LORD…
	Ho, every one that thirsteth, come ye to the waters, and he that hath no money; come ye, buy, and eat; yea, come, buy wine and milk without money and without price.
	 2 Wherefore do ye spend money for *that which is* not bread? and your labour for *that which* satisfieth not? Hearken diligently unto me, and eat ye that which is good, and let your soul delight itself in fatness.
	 3 Incline your ear, and come unto me: hear, and your
		soul shall live; and I will make an everlasting covenant with you, *even* the sure mercies of David.
		 4 Behold, I have given him *for* a witness to the people, a leader and commander to the people.
		 5 Behold, thou shalt call a nation *that* thou knowest not, and nations *that* knew not thee shall run unto thee because of the LORD thy God, and for the Holy One of Israel; for he hath glorified thee.
			1) You will live
			 2) You will receive all the mercies & love promised to David, 2 S.7:11-17
			 f. The agent of salvation: The Savior
			   1) He is God's Witness, Leader, & Commander
			   2) He is God's Witness who issues the call for the people (Gentile nations) to come
			    • They will rush to Him
			    • They will see Him glorified by God

a. The people invited to come are those who have thirsty souls and poverty-stricken hearts. To thirst means to desire, crave, long after, yearn for, eagerly seek. To those whose souls are like a desert—dry and barren, eagerly seeking and yearning to have their thirst quenched—God says, "Come to me!"

To be poverty-stricken means to be poor, impoverished, distressed, and in desperate need. To those whose souls are poverty-stricken—utterly famished, destitute, unable to find anything that will satisfy their emptiness—the LORD cries out, "Come to me!" Let all who are thirsty and poor come to the LORD.

b. The offer of the LORD is salvation (v.1). The thirsty, hungry soul can be saved and delivered from its thirst and hunger. The LORD offers streams of *living waters* to satisfy the dry, thirsty soul, and He offers wine and milk to satisfy the hungry heart. Keep in mind that water and food are the most valuable commodities in a dry, barren country. When traveling through desert areas, people will perish unless they have prepared themselves by securing water and food. So it is with the human soul. As people walk through life, they must secure the water and food that the LORD provides or else they will perish. What is the water and food that God provides?

⇒   Jesus Christ is the living water of God.

> **"Jesus answered and said unto her, If thou knewest the gift of God, and who it is that saith to thee, Give me to drink; thou wouldest have asked of him, and he would have given thee living water"** (Jn.4:10).
> **"In the last day, that great _day_ of the feast, Jesus stood and cried, saying, If any man thirst, let him come unto me, and drink. He that believeth on me, as the scripture hath said, out of his belly shall flow rivers of living water"** (Jn.7:37-38; also see Re.7:17; 22:1-2; 22:17).

⇒   Jesus Christ is the bread of life.

> **"And Jesus said unto them, I am the bread of life: he that cometh to me shall never hunger; and he that believeth on me shall never thirst"** (Jn.6:35).
> **"I am that bread of life. Your fathers did eat manna in the wilderness, and are dead. This is the bread which cometh down from heaven, that a man may eat thereof, and not die. I am the living bread which came down from heaven: if any man eat of this bread, he shall live for ever: and the bread that I will give is my flesh, which I will give for the life of the world. The Jews therefore strove among themselves, saying, How can this man give us _his_ flesh to eat?"** (Jn.6:48-52).

c. What is the cost for God's water and food? Astoundingly, they are free, absolutely free. This fact suggests several points:

First, God's salvation is a _free gift_. It cannot be secured by money or by giving religious offerings or by working for it. If salvation were by works, the good deeds of people would put God in debt to them. God would _owe_ them. If that were the case, God would be _subjected_ to them, owing them salvation to pay His debt. But God cannot be subjected to any man. God is the LORD of the universe, ruling and reigning over all. All creatures are in debt to Him; He is in debt to no creature. Whatever He gives is from _grace,_ freely given. He restates the point: God's salvation—the water and food that satisfy the human soul—is _freely_ given. It is a gift.

> **"And by him all that believe are justified from all things, from which ye could not be justified by the law of Moses"** (Ac.13:39).
> **"For all have sinned, and come short of the glory of God; Being justified freely by his grace through the redemption that is in Christ Jesus"** (Ro.3:23-24).
> **"For what saith the scripture? Abraham believed God, and it was counted unto him for righteousness. Now to him that worketh is the reward not reckoned of grace, but of debt. But to him that worketh not, but believeth on him that justifieth the ungodly, his faith is counted for righteousness. Even as David also describeth the blessedness of the man, unto whom God imputeth righteousness without works, _Saying,_ Blessed _are_ they whose iniquities are forgiven, and whose sins are covered"** (Ro.4:3-7).
> **"But not as the offence, so also _is_ the free gift. For if through the offence of one many be dead, much more the grace of God, and the gift by grace, _which is_ by one man, Jesus Christ, hath abounded unto many"** (Ro.5:15).
> **"Therefore as by the offence of one [Adam] _judgment came_ upon all men to condemnation; even so by the righteousness of one _the free gift came_ upon all men unto justification of life. For as by one man's disobedience many were made sinners, so by the obedience of one shall many be made righteous"** (Ro.5:18-19).
> **"For the wages of sin _is_ death; but the gift of God _is_ eternal life through Jesus Christ our Lord"** (Ro.6:23).
> **"For as many as are of the works of the law are under the curse: for it is written, Cursed _is_ every one that continueth not in all things which are written in the book of the law to do them. But that no man is justified by the law in the sight of God, _it is_ evident: for, The just shall live by faith. And the law is not of faith: but, The man that doeth them shall live in them. Christ hath redeemed us from the curse of the law, being made a curse for us: for it is written, Cursed _is_ every one that hangeth on a tree: That the blessing of Abraham might come on the Gentiles through Jesus Christ; that we might receive the promise of the Spirit through faith"** (Gal.3:10-14).
> **"For by grace are ye saved through faith; and that not of yourselves: _it is_ the gift of God: Not of works, lest any man should boast"** (Ep.2:8-9).

Second, the LORD cares deeply for us. He longs to meet the hunger and thirst of our hearts by freely giving us the living water and the bread of life. When a gift is given without any expectation of payment, the gift reveals a caring heart. God is interested in our welfare. He is concerned about us, cherishes us, and holds us in the highest esteem. And He has proven His love by _freely_ offering us the gift of salvation.

Third, the price of salvation was extremely costly to God. Salvation cost God the death of His very own Son. Christ paid the ransom for our sin. Through His death we are redeemed, set free from the bondages of sin and death, and given eternal life. Although we receive salvation freely, God paid an enormous price for our redemption.

> **"The next day John seeth Jesus coming unto him, and saith, Behold the Lamb of God, which taketh away the sin of the world"** (Jn.1:29).
> **"For God so loved the world, that he gave his only begotten Son, that whosoever believeth in him should not perish, but have everlasting life"** (Jn.3:16).

"Him, being delivered by the determinate counsel and foreknowledge of God, ye have taken, and by wicked hands have crucified and slain" (Ac.2:23).

"But God commendeth his love toward us, in that, while we were yet sinners, Christ died for us" (Ro.5:8).

"For as by one man's disobedience many were made sinners, so by the obedience of one shall many be made righteous" (Ro.5:19).

"Hereby perceive we the love *of God*, because he laid down his life for us: and we ought to lay down *our* lives for the brethren" (1 Jn.3:16).

d. The plea of God for people to come is urgent and compelling (v.2). *Come* is an imperative that demands immediate attention. The life or death of the human soul is at stake, for the soul is as thirsty as a barren desert, and as empty as a starving man. Thus the appeal by God is pressing, requiring our utmost and immediate consideration. God makes a two-fold plea:

1) Do not waste money or labor on things that do not satisfy. Note that God puts this plea in the form of a question, focusing on the fact that many people do just that. They spend their money on things that do not satisfy the human soul, things such as...

- worldly pleasures and activities
- immoral and illicit sexual behavior
- material possessions
- fleeting and worthless adventures
- acquiring or buying position, authority, power, or fame

Carnal pleasures and worldly possessions cannot satisfy the human soul. Stimulating the flesh and securing the possessions or fame of this world will leave a person empty inside. This world with its bright lights, cheap thrills, and get-rich-quick schemes will only make an individual more destitute. The person's soul will be like a *wasteland*, hungry and starving for something that will give it a sense of fulfillment and satisfaction.

Think of all the people whose primary objective in life is to get more—more money, more cars, more houses, more property, and so on. They work as hard as they can, laboring day and night to make more money to buy even more things. Once people have enough to meet the necessities of life, they accumulate more money for one of at least three purposes:

⇒ to hoard it to satisfy the emptiness within their souls
⇒ to become recognized as persons of wealth, authority, and power
⇒ to use it to meet the needs of the world and to carry the gospel of Christ to every living soul. (This is the only purpose that is truly justified in the eyes of God.)

2) God's second plea is "Listen, listen carefully to me! Eat what is good! Be filled with my nourishment!" In most cases, excess money is used for worldly, carnal, and selfish purposes. For this reason, God pleads with all of us to ask ourselves this question: Why do we spend money on things that do not nourish us and feed us spiritually? And why do we labor to purchase material things that do not satisfy? God provides the Water and Bread of life, the Lord Jesus Christ Himself. Everyone who truly comes to God receives the fullness of Christ. Christ floods the thirsty, hungry soul with the fullness of His Spirit:

⇒ love	⇒ goodness	⇒ fulfillment
⇒ joy	⇒ faithfulness	⇒ satisfaction
⇒ peace	⇒ meekness	⇒ assurance
⇒ patience	⇒ self control or discipline	⇒ confidence
⇒ gentleness or kindness	⇒ purpose	⇒ value

When Jesus Christ fills a person's soul, the individual walks victoriously in life, conquering and triumphing through all the trials and temptations that arise. Day by day the person is filled with assurance and confidence in the LORD's presence and guidance. This is the nourishment that Christ brings. He alone is the Water and Bread of life. He alone can meet every need to fill the human soul. He alone can keep man from dying of thirst and hunger.

e. God makes a wonderful promise to those who come to the LORD (v.3). However, before the promise is stated, God again stresses how critical it is for people to come to Him. Two times in this one verse the LORD urges people to *hear*, to open their ears, because the issue involved is the life or death of the human soul. If people will listen and then heed what God says, that is, come to the LORD, God promises them two things:

1) Their souls will live. They will be given *real life*, the Water and Bread of God Himself. They will receive all the fullness of Christ described above (v.2).

"The thief cometh not, but for to steal, and to kill, and to destroy: I am come that they might have life, and that they might have *it* more abundantly" (Jn.10:10).

"But [God's purpose] is now made manifest by the appearing of our Saviour Jesus Christ, who hath abolished death, and hath brought life and immortality to light through the gospel" (2 Ti.1:10).

"And this is the record, that God hath given to us eternal life, and this life is in his Son. He that hath the Son hath life; *and* he that hath not the Son of God hath not life. These things have I written unto you that believe on the name of the Son of God; that ye may know that ye have eternal life, and that ye may believe on the name of the Son of God" (1 Jn.5:11-13).

2) They will receive all the mercies and love God promised to David (see outline and notes—2 S.7:11-17 for more discussion). God will make the same covenant with those who truly come to Him that He made with David. His covenant with David included the great promise of an eternal descendant, a throne, and a kingdom, all of which are fulfilled in Jesus Christ (Lu.1:30-33). Jesus Christ is the covenant, the fulfillment of the promises that God gives to man. Any agreement between God and man is based solely upon Christ. If people wish to approach God, they must approach Him through Christ and Christ alone (Jn.14:6).

"And the angel said unto her, Fear not, Mary: for thou hast found favour with God. And, behold, thou shalt conceive in thy womb, and bring forth a son, and shalt call his name Jesus. He shall be great, and shall be called the Son of the Highest: and the Lord God shall give unto him the throne of his father David: And he shall reign over the house of Jacob for ever; and of his kingdom there shall be no end" (Lu.1:30-33).

"Jesus saith unto him, I am the way, the truth, and the life: no man cometh unto the Father, but by me" (Jn.14:6).

"And we declare unto you glad tidings, how that the promise which was made unto the fathers, God hath fulfilled the same unto us their children, in that he hath raised up Jesus again; as it is also written in the second psalm, Thou art my Son, this day have I begotten thee. And as concerning that he raised him up from the dead, *now* no more to return to corruption, he said on this wise, I will give you the sure mercies of David. Wherefore he saith also in another *psalm*, Thou shalt not suffer thine Holy One to see corruption. For David, after he had served his own generation by the will of God, fell on sleep, and was laid unto his fathers, and saw corruption: But he, whom God raised again, saw no corruption. Be it known unto you therefore, men *and* brethren, that through this man is preached unto you the forgiveness of sins: And by him all that believe are justified from all things, from which ye could not be justified by the law of Moses" (Ac.13:32-39).

f. The agent of salvation is the Savior Himself, the Lord Jesus Christ (vv.4-5). It is the Messiah who fulfills God's promises to David, the Messiah who secures salvation for every living soul of every generation. Note that God has sent the Messiah to be His Witness to the people as well as their Leader and Commander. As their Leader and Commander, Christ has been given all authority throughout the universe: "All power is given unto me in heaven and in earth" (Mt.28:18; also see Nu.24:17-19; Is.9:6-7; Re.12:5; 19:15-16). As God's witness, the Messiah will issue the call for all the Gentile nations of the earth to come to the LORD (v.5).

While Christ was on earth, He ministered only in Palestine. No other nation felt the *direct impact* of His ministry during His lifetime. In addition, there were many nations that did not even exist while Christ was on earth. Yet Isaiah predicts that the day will come when nations will rush to Christ and see Him glorified. Since His death on the cross, Christ has been bearing strong witness to the nations of the earth. As a result, multitudes of people have rushed to Him for the salvation He purchased through His death on the cross of Calvary. This prophecy is being carried out day by day as people from all nations hear God's invitation to come to Him for salvation. But the ultimate fulfillment will take place when Christ returns to set up God's kingdom on earth. In that day, every human being will either come to the LORD or else face His terrifying judgment. For all men will worship Him as He sits on the throne of God's glory in the Holy City, Jerusalem (54:11-17). However until that day, the invitation of the LORD is extended to every human being:

"Ho, every one that thirsteth, come ye to the waters, and he that hath no money; come ye, buy, and eat; yea, come, buy wine and milk without money and without price. Wherefore do ye spend money for *that which is* not bread? and your labour for *that which* satisfieth not? hearken diligently unto me, and eat ye *that which is* good, and let your soul delight itself in fatness" (Is.55:1-2).

"Come unto me, all *ye* that labour and are heavy laden, and I will give you rest. Take my yoke upon you, and learn of me; for I am meek and lowly in heart: and ye shall find rest unto your souls. For my yoke *is* easy, and my burden is light" (Mt.11:28-30).

"The kingdom of heaven is like unto a certain king, which made a marriage for his son, And sent forth his servants to call them that were bidden to the wedding: and they would not come....Then saith he to his servants, The wedding is ready, but they which were bidden were not worthy. Go ye therefore into the highways, and as many as ye shall find, bid to the marriage. So those servants went out into the highways, and gathered together all as many as they found, both bad and good: and the wedding was furnished with guests" (Mt.22:2-3, 8-10).

"For there is no difference between the Jew and the Greek: for the same Lord over all is rich unto all that call upon him. For whosoever shall call upon the name of the Lord shall be saved" (Ro.10:12-13).

"For this *is* good and acceptable in the sight of God our Saviour; Who will have all men to be saved, and to come unto the knowledge of the truth. For *there is* one God, and one mediator between God and men, the man Christ Jesus" (1 Ti.2:3-5).

"And the Spirit and the bride say, Come. And let him that heareth say, Come. And let him that is athirst come. And whosoever will, let him take the water of life freely" (Re.22:17).

"Come now, and let us reason together, saith the LORD: though your sins be as scarlet, they shall be as white as snow; though they be red like crimson, they shall be as wool" (Is.1:18).

"Look unto me, and be ye saved, all the ends of the earth: for I *am* God, and *there is* none else" (Is.45:22).

2 (55:6-13) **Invitation, Duty, to Seek God—Seeking, Duty—Seeking, Danger of Delay—Seeking, Results of—Call, Source, God's Word—Word of God, Power of—Wicked, Invitation to—God, Thoughts of, Superior—Ways, of God, Superior**: the second invitation is a strong imperative to seek the LORD. *To seek* means to look for and search for, inquire about, investigate, pursue, strive after. It also means to plead and cry for something to the point of struggling. Only a person who senses a deep need will seek the LORD with such urgency. And this is exactly the objective of God's invitation. There is an urgent need for every human being to seek the LORD. Note the Scripture and outline.

OUTLINE	SCRIPTURE	SCRIPTURE	OUTLINE

2. The invitation to seek the LORD
a. The danger: Waiting too late
b. The person invited: The wicked, evil person
  1) He must repent
  • Forsake his evil way
  • Turn to the LORD
  2) He will receive mercy & forgiveness—freely
c. The urgent need to seek
  1) God's thoughts & ways are perfect, far beyond our understanding
  2) God's thoughts & ways are righteous, far higher than ours: Ours are imperfect & wicked
 	
d. The way God calls the wicked: By His Word, Mt.13:1-9, 18-33
  1) His Word is as powerful as rain & snow that water
	6 Seek ye the LORD while he may be found, call ye upon him while he is near:
	7 Let the wicked forsake his way, and the unrighteous man his thoughts: and let him return unto the LORD, and he will have mercy upon him; and to our God, for he will abundantly pardon.
	8 For my thoughts *are* not your thoughts, neither *are* your ways my ways, saith the LORD.
	9 For *as* the heavens are higher than the earth, so are my ways higher than your ways, and my thoughts than your thoughts.
	10 For as the rain cometh down, and the snow from heaven, and returneth not thither, but watereth the earth, and maketh it bring
		forth and bud, that it may give seed to the sower, and bread to the eater:
		11 So shall my word be that goeth forth out of my mouth: it shall not return unto me void, but it shall accomplish that which I please, and it shall prosper *in the thing* whereto I sent it.
		12 For ye shall go out with joy, and be led forth with peace: the mountains and the hills shall break forth before you into singing, and all the trees of the field shall clap *their* hands.
		13 Instead of the thorn shall come up the fir tree, and instead of the brier shall come up the myrtle tree: and it shall be to the LORD for a name, for an everlasting sign *that* shall not be cut off.
			the earth & cause the grain to grow
			
			2) His Word will not return empty: It will bear fruit, accomplish God's purpose
			
			e. The results of seeking the LORD
			  1) The repentant sinner will live in joy & peace
			  2) The earth will be transformed
			  • All nature will rejoice
			
			  • All thorns will be removed & all vegetation will become fruitful
			  3) The transformation will be for the purpose of honoring the LORD: Be a sign of His love & power

a. This second invitation includes a warning: people can wait too long. They fail to seek the LORD while He is near and still can be found. *Opportunities* are not always available to seek the LORD. Throughout the day, people's minds have to be focused on their work and other duties. A far greater opportunity to seek the LORD is found in the quietness of one's home or in the setting of the church. It is far easier to sense the LORD's presence in a quiet atmosphere than in the hustle and bustle of noisy surroundings. It is also not always easy for people to find God. People can harden their hearts to such a degree that they feel God is far off, completely out of reach. Add the fact that people are creatures of conditioning, which means the more they misbehave, the more acceptable their sinful behavior appears. For example, if people repeatedly commit immoral acts, their consciences can become dead, insensitive to sin. In that frame of mind they will naturally not seek the LORD as readily as they would if their hearts were not hardened but instead were open and sensitive to God. More important, God will have nothing to do with sinful behavior. He is holy and cannot look upon sin; therefore, if people continue in their sinful ways, the LORD is forced to withdraw His presence. Thus, God gives this strong exhortation: "Seek the LORD while He may be found; call on Him while He is near." Do not wait too long. Do not wait until your heart becomes hard and insensitive to the convictions of God's Spirit. God's warning is clear and it is directed to the entire human race: Do not wait until it is too late.

> "And the LORD said, my spirit shall not always strive with man" (Ge.6:3).
> "But after thy hardness and impenitent heart treasurest up unto thyself wrath against the day of wrath and revelation of the righteous judgment of God; Who will render to every man according to his deeds: To them who by patient continuance in well doing seek for glory and honour and immortality, eternal life: But unto them that are contentious, and do not obey the truth, but obey unrighteousness, indignation and wrath, Tribulation and anguish, upon every soul of man that doeth evil, of the Jew first, and also of the Gentile" (Ro.2:5-9).
> "Take heed, brethren, lest there be in any of you an evil heart of unbelief, in departing from the living God. But exhort one another daily, while it is called To day; lest any of you be hardened through the deceitfulness of sin" (He.3:12-13).
> "He, that being often reproved hardeneth *his* neck, shall suddenly be destroyed, and that without remedy" (Pr.29:1).
> "Happy *is* the man that feareth alway: but he that hardeneth his heart shall fall into mischief" (Pr.28:14).

b. Those invited to seek the LORD are the wicked of the earth (v.7). No matter how much wickedness people commit, the LORD still reaches out to them, encouraging them to seek Him. What is involved in seeking? Repentance. Simply and plainly, repentance means to forsake an evil way of life to turn to the LORD. People who truly repent turn away from their wicked behavior, banish evil thoughts from their minds, and turn to the LORD. They believe Him and obey His commandments. When people truly repent, the LORD has mercy upon them and forgives their sins. They are freely, abundantly pardoned.

"That the God of our Lord Jesus Christ, the Father of glory, may give unto you the spirit of wisdom and revelation in the knowledge of him" (Ep.1:17).

"But after that the kindness and love of God our Saviour toward man appeared, Not by works of righteousness which we have done, but according to his mercy he saved us, by the washing of regeneration, and renewing of the Holy Ghost; Which he shed on us abundantly through Jesus Christ our Saviour; That being justified by his grace, we should be made heirs according to the hope of eternal life" (Tit.3:4-7).

"If we confess our sins, he is faithful and just to forgive us *our* sins, and to cleanse us from all unrighteousness" (1 Jn.1:9).

c. The need to seek the LORD is urgent, for God's thoughts and ways are far beyond our comprehension (vv.8-9). God is holy and dwells in perfection, and no one could ever come close to understanding His ways. Why would God create the world and then allow sin to cause so much devastation and the death of every human being? The answers to this question and so many more are partially revealed in Scripture, but only partially. God's thoughts and ways are perfect and righteous, far beyond our understanding. On the other hand our thoughts and ways are blemished, imperfect, wicked, and simplistic. Therefore, we must never try to "second-guess" God.[1] Although many people try to diminish God's image into nothing more than a super-man, a person whose thoughts and ways are only a *little above* man's, nothing could be further from the truth. God's thoughts and ways are as high above ours as the heavens are above the earth. Imagine the incomprehensible distance between the highest star in existence and the earth. God's thoughts and ways exceed man's by a far greater distance than even that because He created the highest star. God clearly does not think or act like we do. Although Scripture does not give us complete answers to all questions, it does give us enough information to enable us to trust God and to know right from wrong. Through the truths revealed in Scripture, we can know much about God, and we can have assurance that Jesus Christ is the Savior of the world. Therefore, when God extends to people the invitation to seek Him, people must seek Him. The LORD knows that the issue involves life and death, eternity in heaven or eternity in hell. But it is up to every individual to accept or reject HIm.

"For God hath concluded them all in unbelief, that he might have mercy upon all. O the depth of the riches both of the wisdom and knowledge of God! how unsearchable *are* his judgments, and his ways past finding out! For who hath known the mind of the Lord? or who hath been his counsellor? Or who hath first given to him, and it shall be recompensed unto him again? For of him, and through him, and to him, *are* all things: to whom *be* glory for ever. Amen" (Ro.11:32-36).

"And they sing the song of Moses the servant of God, and the song of the Lamb, saying, Great and marvellous *are* thy works, Lord God Almighty; just and true *are* thy ways, thou King of saints" (Re.15:3).

d. What will stir the wicked to repent of their sins and return to the LORD for salvation? God's Word (vv.10-11). God's Holy Word is the point of contact between Him and the people of earth. Without the Word of God, people would have no way to know the LORD. If the Holy Bible did not exist, the LORD would have to personally appear or verbally speak out in order to communicate with people. But by giving us the Holy Bible, the LORD has given us continued access to what He wishes to teach us. It is the Word of God that convicts the wicked of their sins and stirs them to repent. It is the Word of God that tells people to cleanse their minds of evil thoughts and correct their wicked behavior. Note what Scripture says: God's Word is as powerful as the rain and snow that water the earth and causes the seed to grow (v.10). God's Word will not return to Him empty. His Word will bear fruit, will accomplish His purpose. It will convict sinners, lead them to Christ, and instruct them in the way of righteousness.

"Heaven and earth shall pass away, but my words shall not pass away" (Mt.24:35).

"Let the word of Christ dwell in you richly in all wisdom; teaching and admonishing one another in psalms and hymns and spiritual songs, singing with grace in your hearts to the Lord" (Col.3:16).

"Study to show thyself approved unto God, a workman that needeth not to be ashamed, rightly dividing the word of truth" (2 Ti.2:15).

"All scripture *is* given by inspiration of God, and *is* profitable for doctrine, for reproof, for correction, for instruction in righteousness" (2 Ti.3:16).

"For the word of God *is* quick, and powerful, and sharper than any twoedged sword, piercing even to the dividing asunder of soul and spirit, and of the joints and marrow, and *is* a discerner of the thoughts and intents of the heart" (He.4:12).

"But the word of the Lord endureth for ever. And this is the word which by the gospel is preached unto you" (1 Pe.1:25).

"As newborn babes, desire the sincere milk of the word, that ye may grow thereby: If so be ye have tasted that the Lord *is* gracious" (1 Pe.2:2-3).

"We have also a more sure word of prophecy; whereunto ye do well that ye take heed, as unto a light that shineth in a dark place, until the day dawn, and the day star arise in your hearts: Knowing this first, that no prophecy of the scripture is of any private interpretation. For the prophecy came not

---

[1] Warren W. Wiersbe. *Be Comforted*, p.147.

in old time by the will of man: but holy men of God spake *as they were* moved by the Holy Ghost" (2 Pe.1:19-21).

"Wherewithal shall a young man cleanse his way? by taking heed *thereto* according to thy word....Thy word have I hid in mine heart, that I might not sin against thee" (Ps.119:9, 11).

"Thy word *is* a lamp unto my feet, and a light unto my path" (Ps.119:105).

"The entrance of thy words giveth light; it giveth understanding unto the simple" (Ps.119:130).

e. The results of seeking the LORD show what great things God does for His people. When God set His people free from the Babylonian captivity, He made three wonderful promises to them, promises that are applicable to believers of all generations (vv.12-13).

1) The people who were set free—repentant sinners—would live in joy and peace (v.12). Their new life would begin as soon as they were released from their captivity, and it would continue on throughout their lives. A sense of fullness—inner joy and inner peace—would continually flood the hearts of faithful, obedient believers.

"Peace I leave with you, my peace I give unto you: not as the world giveth, give I unto you. Let not your heart be troubled, neither let it be afraid" (Jn.14:27).

"These things have I spoken unto you, that my joy might remain in you, and *that* your joy might be full" (Jn.15:11).

"Hitherto have ye asked nothing in my name: ask, and ye shall receive, that your joy may be full" (Jn.16:24).

"These things I have spoken unto you, that in me ye might have peace. In the world ye shall have tribulation: but be of good cheer; I have overcome the world" (Jn.16:33).

"And this is life eternal, that they might know thee the only true God, and Jesus Christ, whom thou hast sent" (Jn.17:3).

"For the kingdom of God is not meat and drink; but righteousness, and peace, and joy in the Holy Ghost" (Ro.14:17).

"Be careful for nothing; but in every thing by prayer and supplication with thanksgiving let your requests be made known unto God. And the peace of God, which passeth all understanding, shall keep your hearts and minds through Christ Jesus" (Ph.4:6-7).

"Wherein ye greatly rejoice, though now for a season, if need be, ye are in heaviness through manifold temptations: That the trial of your faith, being much more precious than of gold that perisheth, though it be tried with fire, might be found unto praise and honour and glory at the appearing of Jesus Christ: Whom having not seen, ye love; in whom, though now ye see *him* not, yet believing, ye rejoice with joy unspeakable and full of glory: Receiving the end of your faith, *even* the salvation of *your* souls" (1 Pe.1:6-9).

"The LORD will give strength unto his people; the LORD will bless his people with peace" (Ps.29:11).

"Great peace have they which love thy law: and nothing shall offend them" (Ps.119:165).

"Therefore with joy shall ye draw water out of the wells of salvation" (Is.12:3).

"Thou wilt keep *him* in perfect peace, *whose* mind *is* stayed *on thee:* because he trusteth in thee" (Is.26:3).

"O that thou hadst hearkened to my commandments! then had thy peace been as a river, and thy righteousness as the waves of the sea" (Is.48:18).

2) The repentant sinners were also given the wonderful promise of a great future, a time when the earth would be transformed, made perfect (vv.12-13a). This is a clear prophecy of the Messianic kingdom, the kingdom that Christ will establish on earth when He returns. In that day all nature will rejoice, for the creation will be delivered from its corruption, its struggle, and its suffering (see outline and notes—Ro.8:18-27 for more discussion). All thorns will be removed from the earth and all vegetation will become fruitful, producing its maximum capacity. There will be a new earth, as well as a new heaven.

"But chiefly them that walk after the flesh in the lust of uncleanness, and despise government. Presumptuous *are they,* selfwilled, they are not afraid to speak evil of dignities. Whereas angels, which are greater in power and might, bring not railing accusation against them before the Lord. But these, as natural brute beasts, made to be taken and destroyed, speak evil of the things that they understand not; and shall utterly perish in their own corruption; And shall receive the reward of unrighteousness, *as* they that count it pleasure to riot in the daytime. Spots *they are* and blemishes, sporting themselves with their own deceivings while they feast with you" (2 Pe.2:10-13).

"And I saw a new heaven and a new earth: for the first heaven and the first earth were passed away; and there was no more sea" (Re.21:1).

"And there shall be no more curse: but the throne of God and of the Lamb shall be in it; and his servants shall serve him: And they shall see his face; and his name *shall be* in their foreheads. And there shall be no night there; and they need no candle, neither light of the sun; for the Lord God giveth them light: and they shall reign for ever and ever" (Re.22:3-5).

"For, behold, I create new heavens and a new earth: and the former shall not be remembered, nor come into mind" (Is.65:17).

"For as the new heavens and the new earth, which I will make, shall remain before me, saith the LORD, so shall your seed and your name remain" (Is.66:22).

3) The transformation of the universe will be for the purpose of honoring the LORD (v.13). It will be a sign of God's wonderful love for His people and of His great power that works for the good of His people.

> "Now the God of patience and consolation grant you to be likeminded one toward another according to Christ Jesus: That ye may with one mind *and* one mouth glorify God, even the Father of our Lord Jesus Christ" (Ro.15:5-6).
>
> "Let us be glad and rejoice, and give honour to him: for the marriage of the Lamb is come, and his wife hath made herself ready" (Re.19:7).
>
> "Give unto the LORD the glory due unto his name; worship the LORD in the beauty of holiness" (Ps.29:2).
>
> "O magnify the LORD with me, and let us exalt his name together" (Ps.34:3).
>
> "Be thou exalted, O God, above the heavens; *let* thy glory *be* above all the earth" (Ps.57:5).
>
> "Let them exalt him also in the congregation of the people, and praise him in the assembly of the elders" (Ps.107:32).
>
> "O LORD, thou *art* my God; I will exalt thee, I will praise thy name; for thou hast done wonderful *things; thy* counsels of old *are* faithfulness *and* truth" (Is.25:1).

3 (56:1-8) **Invitation, Extended to, Foreigners and Eunuchs; the Excluded—Righteousness, Duty, Essential—Worship, Duty, Essential—Sabbath, Duty, to Keep—Eunuch, Promises to; Duty of—Gentiles, Duty; Promises to—Invitation, Extended to, the Rejected, Excluded—Unbelievers, Invitation to, Extended by God—Handicapped, God's Invitation to—Single, the, Invitation to, Extended by God—Lost, Invitation to—Unsaved, Invitation to:** the third invitation is also a demand, a twofold plea. God's people are invited to live righteously and to worship Him. No greater privilege could be given a person than that of worshiping the LORD and being conformed to His righteous image. To be holy as God is holy and to live righteously as God is righteous is beyond comprehension; yet this is precisely the privilege offered to God's people. God's people are also invited to worship the LORD. To know the LORD personally is the summit of human experience. Imagine fellowshipping and communing with, praying and listening to God speak through His Holy Word, being assured and led by His Spirit, praising Him, and offering up thanks to Him—all this and so much more is the high privilege of every true believer. But note that the invitation is also a demand. An option is not given. God's people have no choice. They *must* live righteously and faithfully worship the LORD.

OUTLINE	SCRIPTURE	SCRIPTURE	OUTLINE

3. The invitation to live righteously & to worship the LORD
a. The urgent plea of the LORD
  1) Be just & righteous: God's salvation & righteousness are both near
  2) Keep the Sabbath: Do not defile God's day by working or neglecting worship
 	
b. The persons invited—the foreigners & the eunuchs: All who feel excluded, shut out, separated, & cut off from God's salvation & promises
c. The assurance to eunuchs (the single & chaste by force or by choice): They will not be excluded, cut off
  1) The conditions: Must keep the Sabbath & live righteously
  2) The promises
   • Will be given a place before God & a name
	Thus saith the LORD, Keep ye judgment, and do justice: for my salvation *is* near to come, and my righteousness to be revealed. 2 Blessed *is* the man *that* doeth this, and the son of man *that* layeth hold on it; that keepeth the sabbath from polluting it, and keepeth his hand from doing any evil. 3 Neither let the son of the stranger, that hath joined himself to the LORD, speak, saying, The LORD hath utterly separated me from his people: neither let the eunuch say, Behold, I *am* a dry tree. 4 For thus saith the LORD unto the eunuchs that keep my sabbaths, and choose *the* things that please me, and take hold of my covenant; 5 Even unto them will I give in mine house and within my walls a place and a	name better than of sons and of daughters: I will give them an everlasting name, that shall not be cut off. 6 Also the sons of the stranger, that join themselves to the LORD, to serve him, and to love the name of the LORD, to be his servants, every one that keepeth the sabbath from polluting it, and taketh hold of my covenant; 7 Even them will I bring to my holy mountain, and make them joyful in my house of prayer: their burnt offerings and their sacrifices *shall be* accepted upon mine altar; for mine house shall be called an house of prayer for all people. 8 The Lord GOD which gathereth the outcasts of Israel saith, Yet will I gather *others* to him, beside those that are gathered unto him.	better than children
			  • Will be given an everlasting name
			
			d. The promises to foreigners (Gentiles): All unbelievers
			  1) The condition
			   • Must be committed to the LORD, love & serve Him
			   • Must worship the LORD & keep the Sabbath
			  2) The promises
			   • Will be accepted in God's holy mountain (temple)
			   • Will be given joy in worship
			   • Will have their worship accepted
			
			   • Will be accepted by God just as the Jews are accepted: A sworn oath by God

a. The first plea is solemn and forceful, an urgent plea coming from God Himself. "Thus says the LORD" (vv.1-2).
   1) First, God pleaded with the people to live just and righteous lives. Observe God's law. Keep His commandments. Obey Him. Treat people justly and always do what is right. Why was God so forceful in demanding that the people live righteously? Because God's salvation was at hand. Isaiah foresaw that Israel would be set free from the Babylonian captivity. They would be given the opportunity to return to the promised land. Thus, the people would need to prepare themselves by turning back to the LORD and obeying His commandments. However, when the day of liberty came, only a few Israelites were prepared. Only a few accepted God's offer of salvation and

returned to Jerusalem. Most stayed behind. Why? Through the years, God's people had become settled in worldly Babylon. A spirit of unbelief gripped their hearts, and they were simply not willing to give up the jobs, homes, investments, and businesses they had secured nor the carnal pleasures, comforts, and recreation they enjoyed among the worldly Babylonians. Many had even begun to worship their idols, the false gods of the world.

For these reasons, God's people desperately needed to turn their lives around. Repentance and righteousness were demanded. The people needed to forsake their sins and turn back to God. They needed to respond to the invitation, the plea of God to live righteously. They needed to obey God and keep His holy commandments.

But note: God's plea was not given only to the exiles in Babylon. God's demand for all generations is for people to live righteous lives. Even the Jews who returned to the promised land soon slipped back into their worldly, wicked ways. Reading the prophets who preached during the period of restoration—Ezra, Nehemiah, Haggai, and Malachi—clearly shows this. Thus God's plea and demand for righteousness is extended to all people of all times. Everyone must turn away from the carnal comforts and fleshly pleasures of this world. They must turn away from and forsake wickedness, evil, and sin. In the words of Scripture, God demands that we "live self-controlled, righteous and godly lives in this present world, while we look for that blessed hope—the glorious appearing of the great God and our Savior Jesus Christ" (Tit.2:12-13).

> "For I say unto you, That except your righteousness shall exceed *the righteousness* of the scribes and Pharisees [hypocrites, false religionists], ye shall in no case enter into the kingdom of heaven" (Mt.5:20).
>
> "Awake to righteousness, and sin not; for some have not the knowledge of God: I speak *this* to your shame" (1 Co.15:34).
>
> "Wherefore take unto you the whole armour of God, that ye may be able to withstand in the evil day, and having done all, to stand. Stand therefore, having your loins girt about with truth, and having on the breastplate of righteousness" (Ep.6:13-14).
>
> "And this I pray, that your love may abound yet more and more in knowledge and *in* all judgment; That ye may approve things that are excellent; that ye may be sincere and without offence till the day of Christ; Being filled with the fruits of righteousness, which are by Jesus Christ, unto the glory and praise of God" (Ph.1:9-11).
>
> "But refuse profane and old wives' fables, and exercise thyself *rather* unto godliness" (1 Ti.4:7).
>
> "But thou, O man of God, flee these things; and follow after righteousness, godliness, faith, love, patience, meekness. Fight the good fight of faith, lay hold on eternal life, whereunto thou art also called, and hast professed a good profession before many witnesses" (1 Ti.6:11-12).
>
> "Teaching us that, denying ungodliness and worldly lusts, we should live soberly, righteously, and godly, in this present world; Looking for that blessed hope, and the glorious appearing of the great God and our Saviour Jesus Christ" (Tit.2:12-13).
>
> "But the day of the Lord will come as a thief in the night; in the which the heavens shall pass away with a great noise, and the elements shall melt with fervent heat, the earth also and the works that are therein shall be burned up. *Seeing* then *that* all these things shall be dissolved, what manner *of persons* ought ye to be in *all* holy conversation and godliness, Looking for and hasting unto the coming of the day of God, wherein the heavens being on fire shall be dissolved, and the elements shall melt with fervent heat? Nevertheless we, according to his promise, look for new heavens and a new earth, wherein dwelleth righteousness. Wherefore, beloved, seeing that ye look for such things, be diligent that ye may be found of him in peace, without spot, and blameless" (2 Pe.3:10-14).

Note another fact as well. God forcefully demanded righteousness because the *day of righteousness*, the day of final judgment, would soon be revealed (v.1). Judgment day was at hand. This is the meaning of the statement: "My righteousness will soon be revealed" (v.1, NIV).[2] Isaiah was predicting that a righteous *intervention* was about to take place on earth. God will soon execute a final judgment on all the unrighteous and ungodly of the earth. For this reason, people must turn away from sin and turn to God and His righteousness.

> "For the Son of man shall come in the glory of his Father with his angels; and then he shall reward every man according to his works" (Mt.16:27).
>
> "When the Son of man shall come in his glory, and all the holy angels with him, then shall he sit upon the throne of his glory: And before him shall be gathered all nations: and he shall separate them one from another, as a shepherd divideth *his* sheep from the goats: And he shall set the sheep on his right hand, but the goats on the left....Then shall he say also unto them on the left hand, Depart from me, ye cursed, into everlasting fire, prepared for the devil and his angels" (Mt.25:31-33, 41).
>
> "Marvel not at this: for the hour is coming, in the which all that are in the graves shall hear his voice, And shall come forth; they that have done good, unto the resurrection of life; and they that have done evil, unto the resurrection of damnation" (Jn.5:28-29).
>
> "And Enoch also, the seventh from Adam, prophesied of these, saying, Behold, the Lord cometh with ten thousands of his saints, To execute judgment upon all, and to convince all that are

---

2 H. C. Leupold. *Exposition of Isaiah*, Vol.1, p.263.

ungodly among them of all their ungodly deeds which they have ungodly committed, and of all their hard *speeches* which ungodly sinners have spoken against him" (Jude 1:14-15).

"And I saw a great white throne, and him that sat on it, from whose face the earth and the heaven fled away; and there was found no place for them. And I saw the dead, small and great, stand before God; and the books were opened: and another book was opened, which is *the book* of life: and the dead were judged out of those things which were written in the books, according to their works. And the sea gave up the dead which were in it; and death and hell delivered up the dead which were in them: and they were judged every man according to their works. And death and hell were cast into the lake of fire. This is the second death. And whosoever was not found written in the book of life was cast into the lake of fire" (Re.20:11-15).

2) The second plea of God is to observe the Sabbath or weekly day of worship (v.2). Keep in mind that observing the Sabbath was a *special sign* that God's people worshipped the true and living God (Jehovah, Yahweh). God established the Sabbath as a day of rest and worship so that people could rest their bodies and replenish their spirits. He even made the observance of the Sabbath one of His Ten Commandments: "Remember the seventh day to keep it holy" (Ex.20:8). Do not defile God's day of rest by working and neglecting worship. God established the day of rest and worship for every generation of people. The Jews set aside the seventh day as a day of rest because God had rested on the seventh day after creating the world. After Christ's resurrection, the early believers switched the day of rest and worship to the first day of the week because the Lord had risen on the first day. The first day of the week became known as "the Lord's day."

"Now when *Jesus* was risen early the first *day* of the week, he appeared first to Mary Magdalene, out of whom he had cast seven devils" (Mk.16:9).

"And upon the first *day* of the week, when the disciples came together to break bread, Paul preached unto them, ready to depart on the morrow; and continued his speech until midnight" (Ac.20:7).

"Upon the first *day* of the week let every one of you lay by him in store, as *God* hath prospered him, that there be no gatherings when I come" (1 Co.16:2).

"I was in the Spirit on the Lord's day, and heard behind me a great voice, as of a trumpet, Saying, I am Alpha and Omega, the first and the last: and, What thou seest, write in a book, and send *it* unto the seven churches" (Re.1:10-11).

"Remember the sabbath day, to keep it holy. Six days shalt thou labour, and do all thy work: But the seventh day *is* the sabbath of the LORD thy God: *in it* thou shalt not do any work, thou, nor thy son, nor thy daughter, thy manservant, nor thy maidservant, nor thy cattle, nor thy stranger that *is* within thy gates" (Ex.20:8-10).

b. The LORD invites the foreigner and the eunuch to be part of His people (v.3). Throughout the ancient world, there were Gentiles who became heartsick over the immoral and unjust cesspool society had become. As a result, the moral and just laws of Israel attracted them; and some turned to the LORD to become followers (proselytes), of the Jewish religion. The LORD had always had His arms open for people of all races to come to Him (Nu.10:29; Ex.12:48-49; Ru.1:16). But when foreigners turned to the LORD, they feared they would not be as acceptable to Him as the Jews were. This was a natural fear, for God had appointed the Israelites to be His special witnesses to the world, the people through whom He would send His Word and the promised Messiah. Thus, the Israelites were set apart as a distinct, different people. Sometimes foreigners felt excluded, shut out, separated, and cut off from God's promises and people. This was usually due to the fact that the Jews became prideful and exclusive in their religion, prejudiced and discriminatory toward others. Thus, some foreigners—even when they wanted to turn to the Jewish religion because of its high moral demands—felt unqualified, detached from God's people and unacceptable to God.

Eunuchs had a special handicap. Whether castrated, crushed, or born disfigured, they could not bear children. Bearing children was extremely important to the Jewish race, for God had given Abraham the special promise of a large nation of descendants. Bearing children was so important that God had forbidden any Israelite to ever become a eunuch (De.23:1). But as with some other Scriptures, the Jews apparently misinterpreted this to mean that no eunuch could become a true follower of the LORD. However, this was never the meaning of the law. God's arms and invitation were always open to save eunuchs and to receive their worship (Ac.8:27-38).

c. God gives strong assurance to all foreigners and eunuchs. No person is excluded, shut out, separated, or cut off from God's salvation or promises. His salvation is open to all eunuchs (all who have no spouse or are handicapped or disabled). However, note that God's promise to eunuchs is conditional (vv.4-5). They must keep the Sabbath and live righteous lives, pleasing the LORD and holding fast to His covenant of commitment. If they are faithful to the LORD, they will be given a place before God in the temple and a name that is better than children. Their names will never be cut off but will live forever.

d. God's acceptance of foreigners is also conditional (vv.6-8). For any unbelievers of any race to be accepted by the LORD, they must commit themselves to Him. They must love, obey, and serve the LORD, and they must keep the day of worship holy. All unbelievers who make this commitment to the LORD are given four wonderful promises:
⇒ They will be accepted in God's Holy mountain, His temple, His presence (v.7).
⇒ They will be filled with joy as they pray and worship the LORD.
⇒ They will have their worship and offerings accepted by the LORD. This suggests that prior to their commitment, their worship was false, empty, and unacceptable to God.
⇒ They will be accepted by God just as the Jews are accepted. Note that this is an oath sworn by God Himself.

226

No matter who people are—foreigners or eunuchs, unbelievers or backsliders, able or disabled, Jews or Gentiles, if they accept the salvation of the Savior and commit their lives to the LORD, they will never be excluded. They will never be shut out, separated, or cut off from God's salvation and promises.

"Go ye therefore, and teach all nations, baptizing them in the name of the Father, and of the Son, and of the Holy Ghost: Teaching them to observe all things whatsoever I have commanded you: and, lo, I am with you alway, *even* unto the end of the world. Amen" (Mt.28:19-20).

"And the gospel must first be published among all nations" (Mk.13:10).

"And he said unto them, Go ye into all the world, and preach the gospel to every creature" (Mk.16:15).

"Also I say unto you, Whosoever shall confess me before men, him shall the Son of man also confess before the angels of God" (Lu.12:8).

"But we believe that through the grace of the Lord Jesus Christ we shall be saved, even as they" (Ac.15:11).

"For whosoever shall call upon the name of the Lord shall be saved" (Ro.10:13).

"For by grace are ye saved through faith; and that not of yourselves: *it is* the gift of God: Not of works, lest any man should boast" (Ep.2:8-9).

"For the grace of God that bringeth salvation hath appeared to all men, Teaching us that, denying ungodliness and worldly lusts, we should live soberly, righteously, and godly, in this present world; Looking for that blessed hope, and the glorious appearing of the great God and our Saviour Jesus Christ; Who gave himself for us, that he might redeem us from all iniquity, and purify unto himself a peculiar people, zealous of good works" (Tit.2:11-14).

"Whosoever believeth that Jesus is the Christ is born of God: and every one that loveth him that begat loveth him also that is begotten of him" (1 Jn.5:1).

"And the Spirit and the bride say, Come. And let him that heareth say, Come. And let him that is athirst come. And whosoever will, let him take the water of life freely" (Re.22:17).

1. The message to the leaders: The nation will be judged, devoured by beasts (invaders)

a. The reasons
  1) The leaders are blind watchmen who lack knowledge
  2) The leaders are sleeping dogs who fail to warn people
  3) The leaders are greedy dogs who are self-centered
  4) The leaders are shepherds who lack discernment
    • They ignore the people's welfare & seek their own gain
    • They are materialistic, indulgent drunkards: They give no thought to God or their own frailty

b. The love & care of God for the righteous
  1) They died before the judgment fell: Were taken away & protected by God from the terrible suffering
  2) They entered into their heavenly, eternal rest & peace

2. The message to idolaters & those addicted to the occult: You are adulterers & prostitutes

a. Their terrible evil
  1) They mocked the righteous
  2) They rebelled against God
  3) They were children of liars, idolatrous leaders

b. Their false worship
  1) They worshipped fertility gods (sexual pleasure)
  2) They worshipped cruel gods: Allowed violence & human sacrifice (children)
  3) They worshipped so-called gods of nature: Made these particular gods their prized, most valuable possessions
    • Idols of the valley & streams
    • Idols of the hills & mountains: Set up beds for sex, fertility worship
  4) They had family gods or idols in their homes: They

F. The Savior's Message to Leaders & Idolaters, the Prideful & Greedy, 56:9–57:21

9 All ye beasts of the field, come to devour, *yea,* all ye beasts in the forest.
10 His watchmen *are* blind: they are all ignorant, they *are* all dumb dogs, they cannot bark; sleeping, lying down, loving to slumber.
11 Yea, *they are* greedy dogs *which* can never have enough, and they *are* shepherds *that* cannot understand: they all look to their own way, every one for his gain, from his quarter.
12 Come ye, *say they,* I will fetch wine, and we will fill ourselves with strong drink; and to morrow shall be as this day, *and* much more abundant.

CHAPTER 57

The righteous perisheth, and no man layeth *it* to heart: and merciful men *are* taken away, none considering that the righteous is taken away from the evil *to come.*
2 He shall enter into peace: they shall rest in their beds, *each one* walking *in* his uprightness.
3 But draw near hither, ye sons of the sorceress, the seed of the adulterer and the whore.
4 Against whom do ye sport yourselves? against whom make ye a wide mouth, *and* draw out the tongue? *are* ye not children of transgression, a seed of falsehood,
5 Enflaming yourselves with idols under every green tree, slaying the children in the valleys under the clifts of the rocks?
6 Among the smooth *stones* of the stream *is* thy portion; they, they *are* thy lot: even to them hast thou poured a drink offering, thou hast offered a meat offering. Should I receive comfort in these?
7 Upon a lofty and high mountain hast thou set thy bed: even thither wentest thou up to offer sacrifice.
8 Behind the doors also and the posts hast thou set up

thy remembrance: for thou hast discovered *thyself to another* than me, and art gone up; thou hast enlarged thy bed, and made thee *a covenant* with them; thou lovedst their bed where thou sawest *it.*
9 And thou wentest to the king with ointment, and didst increase thy perfumes, and didst send thy messengers far off, and didst debase *thyself even* unto hell.
10 Thou art wearied in the greatness of thy way; *yet* saidst thou not, There is no hope: thou hast found the life of thine hand; therefore thou wast not grieved.
11 And of whom hast thou been afraid or feared, that thou hast lied, and hast not remembered me, nor laid *it* to thy heart? have not I held my peace even of old, and thou fearest me not?
12 I will declare thy righteousness, and thy works; for they shall not profit thee.
13 When thou criest, let thy companies deliver thee; but the wind shall carry them all away; vanity shall take *them:* but he that putteth his trust in me shall possess the land, and shall inherit my holy mountain;
14 And shall say, Cast ye up, cast ye up, prepare the way, take up the stumblingblock out of the way of my people.
15 For thus saith the high and lofty One that inhabiteth eternity, whose name *is* Holy; I dwell in the high and holy *place,* with him also *that is* of a contrite and humble spirit, to revive the spirit of the humble, and to revive the heart of the contrite ones.
16 For I will not contend for ever, neither will I be always wroth: for the spirit should fail before me, and the souls *which* I have made.
17 For the iniquity of his covetousness was I wroth, and smote him: I hid me, and was wroth, and he went on frowardly in the way of his heart.
18 I have seen his ways, and will heal him: I will lead him also, and restore comforts unto him and to his mourners.
19 I create the fruit of the

secretly engaged in false worship behind closed doors
    • Loved the sexual fertility worship
    • Took delight in nakedness, indecent exposure

  5) They trusted worldly kings instead of God
    • Sent envoys to seek their help
    • Descended to hell seeking help from evil men

c. Their sad tragedy, judgment
  1) Their souls will become weary, empty, burdened down, hopeless

  2) Their hearts will suffer deception: Will forget the LORD, that He does judge sin
    • Because they do not fear the LORD
    • Because they place their trust in idols
    • Because God is patient
  3) They will suffer exposure of their false righteousness & works: Will not save them
  4) They will be desperate, helpless: Will be at the mercy of their lifeless, powerless false gods

d. Their only hope
  1) They must trust God to inherit the promised land

  2) They must travel the road, the way of salvation: It has been prepared with all obstacles removed

3. The message to the prideful & greedy: The LORD alone is the high & lofty One

a. The warning to the prideful: God alone lives in the high & lofty place (heaven)
  1) God lives only with the humble & repentant, not the prideful
  2) God will not always convict (contend, fight with) a person who goes astray: He will not always be angry lest He cause man to perish

b. The warning to the greedy & covetous
  1) God punished them (Israel)
  2) God hid His face, withdrew His presence

c. The only hope for the prideful & greedy: God's promise of healing (salvation) & guidance

  1) God will comfort & fill

them with praise 2) God will give peace to all who come to Him for healing d. The fate of the prideful &	lips; Peace, peace to *him that is* far off, and to *him that is* near, saith the LORD; and I will heal him. 20 But the wicked *are* like	the troubled sea, when it cannot rest, whose waters cast up mire and dirt. 21 *There is* no peace, saith my God, to the wicked.	greedy—the wicked 1) They will be restless like the sea 2) They will have no peace

DIVISION VI

THE PROPHECIES OF THE GREAT DELIVERER: THE SUFFERING SERVANT OF GOD, THE SAVIOR OF THE WORLD, 49:1–59:21

F.   The Savior's Message to Leaders and Idolaters, to the Prideful and Greedy, 56:9–57:21

(56:9–57:21) **Introduction**: corruption in leadership, idolatry, pride, greed, and covetousness—these were major problems within the society of Isaiah's day. And sadly, they became major problems within every generation including today. We often read or hear about leaders who have become corrupt, who have sought personal gain instead of the welfare of the people they were supposed to serve. Countless people in the world are idolaters. They worship man-made ideas or objects or other mere beings instead of the Father of the Lord Jesus Christ and the Creator of all things. We all know people who are prideful, who exalt themselves and demean others because they consider themselves more worthy of recognition, honor, or attention. Others we know covet more and more, hoarding what they have while so many desperate needs exist throughout the world. God has a very special message for all who have failed in any one of these areas. And the message is just as relevant today as it was in Isaiah's day. This is, *The Savior's Message to Leaders and Idolaters, to the Prideful and Greedy*, 56:9–57:21.

1. The message to the leaders: the nation (Judah) will be judged, devoured by beasts (invaders) (56:9–57:2).
2. The message to idolaters and those addicted to the occult: you are adulterers and prostitutes (57:3-14).
3. The message to the prideful and greedy: the LORD alone is the high and lofty One (57:15-21).

[1] (56:9–57:2) **Leaders, Failure of, Fourfold—Leaders, Described as, Watchmen; Dogs; Shepherds—Judah, Leaders of, Failure of—Leaders, Warning to, Judgment—Prophecy, Concerning Judah, Destruction of—Believers, Deliverance from, Judgment—Protection, God's, of Believers, from Judgment—Righteous, Protected by God, from Judgment**: the LORD spoke forcefully and directly to the leaders of Judah: their nation would be judged by being devoured by *beasts*. Apparently, this is a reference to the conquest of Judah by the soldiers of Babylon. Corrupt, degenerate leadership was the primary reason Judah fell. If the leaders had led the people to repent and turn back to the LORD, God would have delivered them. But the leaders had become totally self-centered, deceitful, and negligent in their official duties. In a spirit of defiance and rebellion against God, they were living unrighteous, wicked lives. Their behavior stood diametrically opposed to the will and commandments of God. Note the Scripture and outline:

OUTLINE	SCRIPTURE	SCRIPTURE	OUTLINE

1. The message to the leaders: The nation will be judged, devoured by beasts (invaders)
a. The reasons
  1) The leaders are blind watchmen who lack knowledge
  2) The leaders are sleeping dogs who fail to warn people
  3) The leaders are greedy dogs who are self-centered
  4) The leaders are shepherds who lack discernment
   • They ignore the people's welfare & seek their own gain
   • They are materialistic,
	9 All ye beasts of the field, come to devour, *yea,* all ye beasts in the forest.
	10 His watchmen *are* blind: they are all ignorant, they *are* all dumb dogs, they cannot bark; sleeping, lying down, loving to slumber.
	11 Yea, *they are* greedy dogs *which* can never have enough, and they *are* shepherds *that* cannot understand: they all look to their own way, every one for his gain, from his quarter.
	12 Come ye, *say they,* I will
		fetch wine, and we will fill ourselves with strong drink; and to morrow shall be as this day, *and* much more abundant.
		
		CHAPTER 57
		
		The righteous perisheth, and no man layeth *it* to heart: and merciful men *are* taken away, none considering that the righteous is taken away from the evil *to come.*
		2 He shall enter into peace: they shall rest in their beds, *each one* walking *in* his uprightness.
			indulgent drunkards: They give no thought to God or their own frailty
			
			b. The love & care of God for the righteous
			1) They died before the judgment fell: Were taken away & protected by God from the terrible suffering
			2) They entered into their heavenly, eternal rest & peace

a. God's message to the leaders is a message of condemnation. As leaders, they were far more responsible for the welfare of the nation than the average citizen. Consequently, God held them far more accountable. Four reasons are given for God's strong condemnation:

1) The leaders were the watchmen of the nation, but who were the leaders? They were the rulers, government officials, priests, and prophets, and sadly they had proven to be blind. As watchmen, they were to stay alert to any approaching danger. Once a danger was spotted, they were to warn the people. However, a serious indictment was being pronounced against the leaders of Judah: they were *blind*, unable to see the coming threats to the nation. They were totally ignorant and lacked the understanding they needed to perceive the impending danger. As watchmen, they should have been guarding God's people by warning them to obey the LORD, keep His commandments, and live righteous lives. But because they were blind, they could not see how people's behavior and

decisions were related to God and His righteousness. Nor could they see the importance of living righteously day by day. They simply could not recognize the dangers of disobeying God and His commandments. Thus, they failed to warn the people.

> "But if thine eye be evil, thy whole body shall be full of darkness. If therefore the light that is in thee be darkness, how great *is* that darkness!" (Mt.6:23).
> "Let them alone: they be blind leaders of the blind. And if the blind lead the blind, both shall fall into the ditch" (Mt.15:14).
> "For the heart of this people is waxed gross, and their ears are dull of hearing, and their eyes have they closed; lest they should see with *their* eyes, and hear with *their* ears, and understand with *their* heart, and should be converted, and I should heal them" (Ac.28:27).
> "This I say therefore, and testify in the Lord, that ye henceforth walk not as other Gentiles walk, in the vanity of their mind, Having the understanding darkened, being alienated from the life of God through the ignorance that is in them, because of the blindness of their heart: Who being past feeling have given themselves over unto lasciviousness, to work all uncleanness with greediness" (Ep.4:17-19).
> "We grope for the wall like the blind, and we grope as if *we had* no eyes: we stumble at noonday as in the night; *we are* in desolate places as dead *men*" (Is.59:10).
> "Son of man, I have made thee a watchman unto the house of Israel: therefore hear the word at my mouth, and give them warning from me" (Eze.3:17).

2) The leaders were sleeping dogs that failed to bark and warn the people (v.10). When a thief enters a house, a watchdog should be alert, bark, and warn the homeowner. But the leaders were *asleep*, which means they were complacent, at ease, and unconcerned. Their primary focus was their own comfort and self-interest, not their duty to the nation or the people.

> "Watch ye therefore: for ye know not when the master of the house cometh, at even, or at midnight, or at the cockcrowing, or in the morning" (Mk.13:35).
> "And that, knowing the time, that now *it is* high time to awake out of sleep: for now *is* our salvation nearer than when we believed. The night is far spent, the day is at hand: let us therefore cast off the works of darkness, and let us put on the armour of light" (Ro.13:11-12).
> "Therefore let us not sleep, as *do* others; but let us watch and be sober" (1 Th.5:6).

3) The leaders were greedy dogs, totally self-centered (v.11a). A spirit of covetousness gripped their souls, and they craved more and more authority, power, and wealth. Misusing their authority, they took advantage of their official positions in the government to build up their personal estates and to gain more influence and control.

> "And he said unto them, Take heed, and beware of covetousness: for a man's life consisteth not in the abundance of the things which he possesseth. And he spake a parable unto them, saying, The ground of a certain rich man brought forth plentifully: And he thought within himself, saying, What shall I do, because I have no room where to bestow my fruits? And he said, This will I do: I will pull down my barns, and build greater; and there will I bestow all my fruits and my goods. And I will say to my soul, Soul, thou hast much goods laid up for many years; take thine ease, eat, drink, *and* be merry. But God said unto him, *Thou* fool, this night thy soul shall be required of thee: then whose shall those things be, which thou hast provided? So *is* he that layeth up treasure for himself, and is not rich toward God" (Lu.12:15-21).
> "Mortify therefore your members which are upon the earth; fornication, uncleanness, inordinate affection, evil concupiscence, and covetousness, which is idolatry: For which things' sake the wrath of God cometh on the children of disobedience" (Col.3:5-6).
> "For the love of money is the root of all evil: which while some coveted after, they have erred from the faith, and pierced themselves through with many sorrows" (1 Ti.6:10).
> "The desire of the slothful killeth him; for his hands refuse to labour. He coveteth greedily all the day long: but the righteous giveth and spareth not" (Pr.21:25-26).
> "He that is greedy of gain troubleth his own house; but he that hateth gifts shall live" (Pr.15:27).
> "Thou shalt not covet thy neighbour's house, thou shalt not covet thy neighbour's wife, nor his manservant, nor his maidservant, nor his ox, nor his ass, nor any thing that *is* thy neighbour's" (Ex.20:17).
> "And they covet fields, and take *them* by violence; and houses, and take *them* away: so they oppress a man and his house, even a man and his heritage" (Mi.2:2).

4) The leaders were shepherds who lacked discernment (v.11b-12). Ignoring the people's welfare, they sought their own gain. Instead of taking care of the flock, they fleeced it. They were materialistic, indulgent, and drunken (v.12). They felt confident in their prosperity and secure in their comfortable lifestyle. They believed that when tomorrow came, it would be just like today, leaving them undisturbed to enjoy and revel in carnal pleasures. They gave no thought whatsoever to the frailty of human life, and they neither feared God nor dreaded His judgment. The uncertainty of this life with all its pleasures and prosperity never crossed their minds. They lacked

discernment, so they continued to be unworthy, corrupt leaders diametrically opposed to God and His righteousness.

"And take heed to yourselves, lest at any time your hearts be overcharged with surfeiting, and drunkenness, and cares of this life, and so that day come upon you unawares" (Lu.21:34).

"But he that is an hireling, and not the shepherd, whose own the sheep are not, seeth the wolf coming, and leaveth the sheep, and fleeth: and the wolf catcheth them, and scattereth the sheep" (Jn.10:12).

"Let us walk honestly, as in the day; not in rioting and drunkenness, not in chambering and wantonness, not in strife and envying. But put ye on the Lord Jesus Christ, and make not provision for the flesh, to *fulfil* the lusts *thereof*" (Ro.13:13-14).

"Now the works of the flesh are manifest, which are *these;* Adultery, fornication, uncleanness, lasciviousness, Idolatry, witchcraft, hatred, variance, emulations, wrath, strife, seditions, heresies, Envyings, murders, drunkenness, revellings, and such like: of the which I tell you before, as I have also told *you* in time past, that they which do such things shall not inherit the kingdom of God" (Ga.5:19-21).

"Wine *is* a mocker, strong drink *is* raging: and whosoever is deceived thereby is not wise" (Pr.20:1).

"Who hath woe? who hath sorrow? who hath contentions? who hath babbling? who hath wounds without cause? who hath redness of eyes? They that tarry long at the wine; they that go to seek mixed wine. Look not thou upon the wine when it is red, when it giveth his colour in the cup, *when* it moveth itself aright" (Pr.23:29-31).

"Woe to the crown of pride, to the drunkards of Ephraim, whose glorious beauty is a fading flower, which *are* on the head of the fat valleys of them that are overcome with wine!" (Is.28:1).

"Therefore thus saith the LORD God of Israel against the pastors [shepherds] that feed my people; Ye have scattered my flock, and driven them away, and have not visited them: behold, I will visit upon you the evil of your doings, saith the LORD" (Je.23:2).

"My people hath been lost sheep: their shepherds have caused them to go astray, they have turned them away *on* the mountains: they have gone from mountain to hill, they have forgotten their restingplace" (Je.50:6).

"Son of man, prophesy against the shepherds of Israel, prophesy, and say unto them, Thus saith the Lord GOD unto the shepherds; Woe *be* to the shepherds of Israel that do feed themselves! should not the shepherds feed the flocks? Ye eat the fat, and ye clothe you with the wool, ye kill them that are fed: *but* ye feed not the flock" (Eze.34:2-3).

"Woe unto him that giveth his neighbour drink, that puttest thy bottle to *him,* and makest *him* drunken also, that thou mayest look on their nakedness!" (Hab.2:15).

b. Although God would judge the *unrighteous* leaders and citizens, He took very special care of the *righteous* (57:1-2). Before the judgment fell upon Judah, God took them to heaven to be with Him. In His love, He made sure they died an early death in order to escape the impending disaster. Fulfilling the promise He gives to all believers, God protected the righteous of that day by taking them away through an unexpected death, thus sparing them the terrifying judgment and horrible suffering that would soon come upon the wicked.

Note that unbelievers did not understand what was happening. The thought that God was saving the righteous from the coming judgment never crossed their minds. To the wicked there is no hope in death, but to the righteous there is the greatest of hope. The righteous enter into peace and find rest even as they lie on their deathbeds. When they pass from this world into the next, more quickly than the eye can blink, they enter into eternal rest and peace to live with God forever. Even as true believers face death, God gives them perfect assurance of being immediately transferred into His presence.

H.C. Leupold, the excellent Lutheran commentator says this:

Good men have been dying off in surprising numbers (cf.Ps.12:1; Mic.7:2). By this fact God is trying to say something to his people [Israel], but they have failed to take notice. So the prophet is telling them what it all means. Good people, the "salt of the earth," have been taken away, very likely by an unexpected death. Why does God allow that? That is the way things usually go before great calamities break in: "The righteous are always taken away from the evil to come." This phenomenon has been observed so often that it may be laid down as a general rule. Thus the righteous man is spared, being off the scene before the calamity breaks....generally speaking, men are so dull-willed that they usually fail to see what God has in mind, and how he is sparing his saints much grief.[1]

"And it came to pass, that the beggar died, and was carried by the angels into Abraham's bosom: the rich man also died, and was buried" (Lu.16:22).

"We are confident, *I say,* and willing rather to be absent from the body, and to be present with the Lord" (2 Co.5:8).

"For to me to live *is* Christ, and to die *is* gain. But if I live in the flesh, this *is* the fruit of my labour: yet what I shall choose I wot not. For I am in a strait betwixt two, having a desire to depart, and to be with Christ; which is far better" (Ph.1:21-23).

---

[1] H.C. Leupold. *Exposition of Isaiah,* Vol.2, p.272

"For I know whom I have believed, and am persuaded that he is able to keep that which I have committed unto him against that day" (2 Ti.1:12).

"And the Lord shall deliver me from every evil work, and will preserve [transfer, transport] *me* unto his heavenly kingdom: to whom *be* glory for ever and ever. Amen" (2 Ti.4:18).

"There remaineth therefore a rest to the people of God. For he that is entered into his rest, he also hath ceased from his own works, as God *did* from his. Let us labour therefore to enter into that rest, lest any man fall after the same example of unbelief" (He.4:9-11).

"These all died in faith, not having received the promises, but having seen them afar off, and were persuaded of *them,* and embraced *them,* and confessed that they were strangers and pilgrims on the earth. For they that say such things declare plainly that they seek a country….But now they desire a better *country,* that is, an heavenly: wherefore God is not ashamed to be called their God: for he hath prepared for them a city" (He.11:13-14, 16).

"Yea, though I walk through the valley of the shadow of death, I will fear no evil: for thou *art* with me; thy rod and thy staff they comfort me" (Ps.23:4).

"Precious in the sight of the LORD *is* the death of his saints" (Ps.116:15).

"The wicked is driven away in his wickedness: but the righteous hath hope in his death" (Pr.14:32).

---

2 (57:3-14) **Adulterers, Discussed—Sorcery, Discussed—Occult, World of, Discussed—Spirits, of Occult World, Discussed—Adultery, Spiritual, Discussed—Spiritual Adultery, Discussed—Prostitution, Spiritual, Discussed—Worship, False, Discussed—Judah, Adultery of, Discussed—Persecution, Caused by, Adultery**: the LORD spoke forcefully and directly to idolaters and those who practiced sorcery, black magic, and other forms of witchcraft. Down through the centuries, most Israelites had been deeply influenced by their unbelieving neighbors, and eventually the nation became steeped in sorcery and the world of the occult (see outline and note—2 K.21:1-18 for more discussion). As a result, idolatry and every kind of occult practice flourished throughout the nation of Judah, including within Jerusalem itself. Thus God charged the people with being addicted to idolatry and sorcery—a very serious indictment. Having turned away from the LORD to idols, they were committing spiritual adultery and prostitution (Je.3:8-11; Eze.23:37). Note that God issued a summons for the idolaters and sorcerers to approach Him. He had a very special message for them:

OUTLINE	SCRIPTURE	SCRIPTURE	OUTLINE

2. The message to idolaters & those addicted to the occult: You are adulterers & prostitutes
a. Their terrible evil
  1) They mocked the righteous
  2) They rebelled against God
  3) They were children of liars, idolatrous leaders
b. Their false worship
  1) They worshipped fertility gods (sexual pleasure)
  2) They worshipped cruel gods: Allowed violence & human sacrifice (children)
  3) They worshipped so-called gods of nature: Made these particular gods their prized, most valuable possessions
   • Idols of the valley & streams
   • Idols of the hills & mountains: Set up beds for sex, fertility worship
  4) They had family gods or idols in their homes: They secretly engaged in false worship behind closed doors
   • Loved the sexual fertility worship
   • Took delight in nakedness, indecent exposure
	3 But draw near hither, ye sons of the sorceress, the seed of the adulterer and the whore.
	4 Against whom do ye sport yourselves? against whom make ye a wide mouth, *and* draw out the tongue? *are* ye not children of transgression, a seed of falsehood,
	5 Enflaming yourselves with idols under every green tree, slaying the children in the valleys under the clifts of the rocks?
	6 Among the smooth *stones* of the stream *is* thy portion; they, they *are* thy lot: even to them hast thou poured a drink offering, thou hast offered a meat offering. Should I receive comfort in these?
	7 Upon a lofty and high mountain hast thou set thy bed: even thither wentest thou up to offer sacrifice.
	8 Behind the doors also and the posts hast thou set up thy remembrance: for thou hast discovered *thyself to another* than me, and art gone up; thou hast enlarged thy bed, and made thee *a covenant* with them; thou lovedst their bed where thou sawest *it.*
		9 And thou wentest to the king with ointment, and didst increase thy perfumes, and didst send thy messengers far off, and didst debase *thyself even* unto hell.
		10 Thou art wearied in the greatness of thy way; *yet* saidst thou not, There is no hope: thou hast found the life of thine hand; therefore thou wast not grieved.
		11 And of whom hast thou been afraid or feared, that thou hast lied, and hast not remembered me, nor laid *it* to thy heart? have not I held my peace even of old, and thou fearest me not?
		12 I will declare thy righteousness, and thy works; for they shall not profit thee.
		13 When thou criest, let thy companies deliver thee; but the wind shall carry them all away; vanity shall take *them:* but he that putteth his trust in me shall possess the land, and shall inherit my holy mountain;
		14 And shall say, Cast ye up, cast ye up, prepare the way, take up the stumblingblock out of the way of my people.
			5) They trusted worldly kings instead of God
			   • Sent envoys to seek their help
			   • Descended to hell seeking help from evil men
			c. Their sad tragedy, judgment
			  1) Their souls will become weary, empty, burdened down, hopeless
			
			  2) Their hearts will suffer deception: Will forget the LORD, that He does judge sin
			   • Because they do not fear the LORD
			   • Because they place their trust in idols
			   • Because God is patient
			  3) They will suffer exposure of their false righteousness & works: Will not save them
			  4) They will be desperate, helpless: Will be at the mercy of their lifeless, powerless false gods
			d. Their only hope
			  1) They must trust God to inherit the promised land
			
			  2) They must travel the road, the way of salvation: It has been prepared with all obstacles removed

a. People addicted to idolatry and sorcery are guilty of a most terrible evil, that of mocking and ridiculing the righteous (v.4). Being the majority, they feel spiritually superior, looking down on, insulting, and persecuting true believers. But in reality they are rebelling against the LORD, for He alone is the true and living God. By worshipping idols and engaging in occult practices, they make themselves liars and hypocrites, for while they profess to know the LORD, they are following false gods.

b. People addicted to idolatry and sorcery are guilty of gross false worship (vv.5-11). In Isaiah's day, altars and worship centers had been built everywhere in Judah. Considering that people traveled by foot, a multitude of worship sites was necessary for the convenience of the people. They could be found on practically every street corner in the cities and on every available site in the countryside (De.12:2-3; 2 K.17:9-12; Eze.6:13-14). Note how Scripture stresses the corruption and depravity of the people's false worship at these altars:

1) The people worshipped fertility gods, claiming that they blessed the earth with growth, fruitfulness, and production (v.5ᵃ). This included the fruitfulness of the plant world as well as the reproduction of people and animals. The basic belief of the fertility religion was that the sexual experience pleased the gods of fertility. Because of the emphasis on fertility and the fact that sex is the means of human and animal reproduction, sexual pleasure became a way to seek he favor of these gods. Through the sexual experience the priests and priestesses "helped" people secure the favor of their so-called gods so they would give them whatever fruitfulness they were requesting.

In fact, the priests and priestesses were nothing more than socially accepted prostitutes. As this verse says, the people became "inflamed with lust" in worshipping their idols. And because there was an altar on practically every corner and every beautiful spot in the countryside, people were engaging in sexual pleasure as often as they liked. Illicit passion was running wild throughout the nation. The people completely ignored God's commandment against adultery and fornication (sex outside of marriage).

> **"Ye have heard that it was said by them of old time, Thou shalt not commit adultery: But I say unto you, That whosoever looketh on a woman to lust after her hath committed adultery with her already in his heart. And if thy right eye offend thee, pluck it out, and cast *it* from thee: for it is profitable for thee that one of thy members should perish, and not *that* thy whole body should be cast into hell. And if thy right hand offend thee, cut if off, and cast it from thee: for it is profitable for thee that one of thy members should perish, and not *that* thy whole body should be cast into hell"** (Mt.5:27-30).
>
> **"Thou shalt not commit adultery"** (Ex.20:14).
>
> **"Know ye not that the unrighteous shall not inherit the kingdom of God? Be not deceived: neither fornicators, nor idolaters, nor adulterers, nor effeminate, nor abusers of themselves with mankind, Nor thieves, nor covetous, nor drunkards, nor revilers, nor extortioners, shall inherit the kingdom of God....Flee fornication. Every sin that a man doeth is without the body; but he that committeth fornication sinneth against his own body"** (1 Co.6:9-10, 18).
>
> **"But fornication, and all uncleanness, or covetousness, let it not be once named among you, as becometh saints"** (Ep.5:3).
>
> **"For this is the will of God, *even* your sanctification, that ye should abstain from fornication: That every one of you should know how to possess his vessel in sanctification and honour; Not in the lust of concupiscence, even as the Gentiles which know not God: That no *man* go beyond and defraud his brother in *any* matter: because that the Lord *is* the avenger of all such, as we also have forewarned you and testified"** (1 Th.4:3-6).

2) The people also followed religions that worshipped cruel gods and promoted violence (v.5ᵇ). Shockingly, some people practiced human sacrifice. They even sacrificed children as they sought to please their false gods. This was a common practice in the worship of demons and of the false god Molech (2 K.23:10; Je.7:31; 19:5; 32:35; Eze.20:31; 23:39).

3) The people worshipped so-called gods of nature, making them their most valuable possession (vv.6-7). Idols and altars were built in the valleys (v.6) and on the hills and mountains (v.7). By worshipping these gods and giving them their offerings, loyalty, and devotion, the people were misplacing their trust. They were dooming themselves, for in time of need their false gods were utterly powerless to help them. No matter how highly prized an idol may be, it represents a false god that is nothing more than an idea in the idolater's mind or an object made by man himself.

Again note the reference to the immorality of the people. Setting up beds at the worship sites, they engaged in sexual immorality to gain the favor of the fertility gods (v.7). In light of this behavior, God asked if He should relent, or change His mind about judging their sinful behavior. No response was given, but the answer is obvious. The hand of God's judgment will fall on all people who are addicted to adultery and sorcery and against all who commit wickedness and break His holy commandments.

4) The people worshipped family gods or idols that they kept in their homes (v.8). Apparently this is a reference to those people who professed to worship the LORD but instead worshipped idols behind the closed doors of their homes. Hypocrisy was the major characteristic of their lives. They professed the LORD, but they secretly worshipped idols or engaged in sorcery. For a third time the people's sexual immorality is emphasized. Behind the closed doors of their homes, they sought the so-called gods of fertility by "uncovering their beds" and engaging in sexual pleasure. Taking delight in their nakedness—their indecent exposure—they hoped to be blessed with a good harvest, an increase of livestock, a child, or some other gift.

5) The people trusted worldly, idolatrous kings instead of God (v.9). This is a reference to seeking political alliances for protection instead of turning to the LORD for deliverances. Sending envoys to seek the help of idolatrous kings was the same as seeking the help of their idols or false gods. Why? Because idolatrous kings were trusting in and depending upon their false gods. Therefore, trusting an unbelieving king and his army was the same as

233

trusting the false gods they worshipped (30:1-7; 31:1-3).[2] Seeking the help of unbelieving kings and their gods instead of the LORD was the same as seeking the help of hell (Sheol) itself.

c. People addicted to idolatry and sorcery will face God's judgment. Sadly, they will suffer four consequences when God's hand of justice strikes them.

1) They will become weary, and their souls will be burdened with a sense of emptiness and hopelessness. Rushing here and there seeking help from others will prove fruitless, for no one will have the wisdom or power to help them in their time of crisis. Seeking help from someone other than the LORD will prove utterly futile, pointless, useless. Remember that Isaiah was predicting what would happen to the Jews who had become addicted to idolatry and sorcery. But his message is applicable to every human being down through the centuries. Only the LORD can meet people's needs when they face the crises of life. If they worship anything other than the LORD Himself and live wicked lives, their souls will become weary and weighed down with a sense of emptiness and hopelessness. As Scripture suggests in this verse, people may find a *temporary* renewal of their strength by seeking the help of others, even their false gods. But the renewal of strength is momentary. It will not last. It will crumble, and those who so desperately need help in facing the crisis or hardship will suffer grief.

> "Come unto me, all *ye* that labour and are heavy laden, and I will give you rest. Take my yoke upon you, and learn of me; for I am meek and lowly in heart: and ye shall find rest unto your souls. For my yoke *is* easy, and my burden is light" (Mt.11:28-30).
>
> "Wherefore is light given to him that is in misery, and life unto the bitter *in* soul; Which long for death, but it *cometh* not; and dig for it more than for hid treasures; Which rejoice exceedingly, *and* are glad, when they can find the grave?" (Jb.3:20-22).
>
> "My days are swifter than a weaver's shuttle, and are spent without hope" (Jb.7:6).
>
> "So that my soul chooseth strangling, *and* death rather than my life" (Jb.7:15).
>
> "When I say, My bed shall comfort me, my couch shall ease my complaint; Then thou scarest me with dreams, and terrifiest me through visions: So that my soul chooseth strangling, *and* death rather than my life. I loathe *it;* I would not live alway: let me alone; for my days *are* vanity" (Jb.7:13-16).
>
> "My soul is weary of my life; I will leave my complaint upon myself; I will speak in the bitterness of my soul" (Jb.10:1).
>
> "And where *is* now my hope? as for my hope, who shall see it?" (Jb.17:15).
>
> "O my God, my soul is cast down within me" (Ps.42:6).
>
> "But as for me, my feet were almost gone; my steps had well nigh slipped. For I was envious at the foolish, *when* I saw the prosperity of the wicked" (Ps.73:2-3).
>
> "Then I saw that wisdom excelleth folly, as far as light excelleth darkness. The wise man's eyes *are* in his head; but the fool walketh in darkness: and I myself perceived also that one event happeneth to them all. Then said I in my heart, As it happeneth to the fool, so it happeneth even to me; and why was I then more wise? Then I said in my heart, that this also *is* vanity. For *there is* no remembrance of the wise more than of the fool for ever; seeing that which now *is* in the days to come shall all be forgotten. And how dieth the wise *man?* as the fool. Therefore I hated life; because the work that is wrought under the sun is grievous unto me: for all *is* vanity and vexation of spirit" (Ecc.2:13-17).
>
> "So I returned, and considered all the oppressions that are done under the sun: and behold the tears of *such as were* oppressed, and they had no comforter; and on the side of their oppressors *there was* power; but they had no comforter. Wherefore I praised the dead which are already dead more than the living which are yet alive" (Ecc.4:1-2).
>
> "But Zion said, The LORD hath forsaken me, and my Lord hath forgotten me" (Is.49:14).
>
> "Surely he hath borne our griefs, and carried our sorrows: yet we did esteem him stricken, smitten of God, and afflicted" (Is.53:4).
>
> "They have heard that I sigh: *there is* none to comfort me: all mine enemies have heard of my trouble; they are glad that thou hast done *it:* thou wilt bring the day *that* thou hast called, and they shall be like unto me" (La.1:21).
>
> "And I said, My strength and my hope is perished from the LORD" (La.3:18).

2) They will suffer deception. When people worship idols or engage in some form of sorcery, they soon forget the LORD and the fact that He does judge sin (v.11). By placing their trust in idols, they reveal that they do not *fear the LORD*. And it never crosses their minds that God's judgment has not yet fallen because He is longsuffering and not willing that any should perish. They are deceived, misled by their false worship.

> "For such *are* false apostles, deceitful workers, transforming themselves into the apostles of Christ" (2 Co.11:13).
>
> "But evil men and seducers shall wax worse and worse, deceiving, and being deceived" (2 Ti.3:13).
>
> "For there are many unruly and vain talkers and deceivers, specially they of the circumcision: Whose mouths must be stopped, who subvert whole houses, teaching things which they ought not, for filthy lucre's sake" (Tit.1:10-11).
>
> "For many deceivers are entered into the world, who confess not that Jesus Christ is come in the flesh. This is a deceiver and an antichrist" (2 Jn.1:7).

---

2 Warren W. Wiersbe. *Be Comforted,* pp. 150-151.

3) They will suffer exposure of their false righteousness and works (v.12). People may feel confident because they are faithful in their false worship. Through keeping the rules, ceremonies, and rituals of their religion, they feel they have attained the *righteousness* demanded. A sense of securing the favor of their so-called god gives them confidence. So they continue in their false worship, seeking to accumulate more and more righteousness and to become more and more acceptable to the god they picture in their minds. But the LORD is strikingly clear: He will expose their *false righteousness and works*. As Scripture says elsewhere, the righteousness and works in which they have clothed themselves will prove to be nothing more than "filthy rags" (64:6).[3]

> "But we are all as an unclean *thing,* and all our righteousnesses *are* as filthy rags; and we all do fade as a leaf; and our iniquities, like the wind, have taken us away" (Is.64:6).
> "Therefore by the deeds of the law there shall no flesh be justified in his sight: for by the law *is* the knowledge of sin" (Ro.3:20; also see vv.20-27).
> "Therefore we conclude that a man is justified by faith without the deeds of the law" (Ro.3:28).
> "Knowing that a man is not justified by the works of the law, but by the faith of Jesus Christ, even we have believed in Jesus Christ, that we might be justified by the faith of Christ, and not by the works of the law: for by the works of the law shall no flesh be justified" (Ga.2:16).
> "For as many as are of the works of the law are under the curse: for it is written, Cursed *is* every one that continueth not in all things which are written in the book of the law to do them. But that no man is justified by the law in the sight of God, *it is* evident: for, The just shall live by faith" (Ga.3:10-11).
> "For by grace are ye saved through faith; and that not of yourselves: *it is* the gift of God: Not of works, lest any man should boast" (Ep.2:8-9).
> "If I justify myself, mine own mouth shall condemn me: *if I say, I am* perfect, it shall also prove me perverse" (Jb.9:20).
> "*There is* a generation *that are* pure in their own eyes, and *yet* is not washed from their filthiness" (Pr.30:12).

4) They will not be helped when they face a crisis or hardship (v.13a). Their idols are helpless, lifeless, and possess no ability or power to think or move or do anything else. Idols and false gods are nothing more than an *idea* in a person's mind or an inanimate object made from wood, metal, stone, plastic, or some other substance. Being lifeless, an idol is totally unable to help in times of desperation or need. Note what God says: the day is coming when His hand of judgment will fall, and the idols will be blown away by the breath of His mighty power.

> "For the wrath of God is revealed from heaven against all ungodliness and unrighteousness of men, who hold the truth in unrighteousness; Because that which may be known of God is manifest in them; for God hath showed *it* unto them. For the invisible things of him from the creation of the world are clearly seen, being understood by the things that are made, *even* his eternal power and Godhead; so that they are without excuse: Because that, when they knew God, they glorified *him* not as God, neither were thankful; but became vain in their imaginations, and their foolish heart was darkened. Professing themselves to be wise, they became fools, And changed the glory of the uncorruptible God into an image made like to corruptible man, and to birds, and fourfooted beasts, and creeping things....And even as they did not like to retain God in *their* knowledge, God gave them over to a reprobate mind, to do those things which are not convenient; Being filled with all unrighteousness, fornication, wickedness, covetousness, maliciousness; full of envy, murder, debate, deceit, malignity; whisperers, Backbiters, haters of God, despiteful, proud, boasters, inventors of evil things, disobedient to parents, Without understanding, covenantbreakers, without natural affection, implacable, unmerciful: Who knowing the judgment of God, that they which commit such things are worthy of death, not only do the same, but have pleasure in them that do them" (Ro.1:18-23, 28-32).
> "As concerning therefore the eating of those things that are offered in sacrifice unto idols, we know that an idol *is* nothing in the world, and that *there is* none other God but one. For though there be that are called gods, whether in heaven or in earth, (as there be gods many, and lords many,) But to us *there is but* one God, the Father, of whom *are* all things, and we in him; and one Lord Jesus Christ, by whom *are* all things, and we by him" (1 Co.8:4-6).
> "And there ye shall serve gods, the work of men's hands, wood and stone, which neither see, nor hear, nor eat, nor smell" (De.4:28).
> "Their idols *are* silver and gold, the work of men's hands. They have mouths, but they speak not: eyes have they, but they see not: They have ears, but they hear not: noses have they, but they smell not: They have hands, but they handle not: feet have they, but they walk not: neither speak they through their throat. They that make them are like unto them; *so is* every one that trusteth in them" (Ps.115:4-8).
> "Assemble yourselves and come; draw near together, ye *that are* escaped of the nations: they have no knowledge that set up the wood of their graven image, and pray unto a god *that* cannot save" (Is.45:20).
> "They *are* upright as the palm tree, but speak not: they must needs be borne, because they cannot go. Be not afraid of them; for they cannot do evil, neither also *is it* in them to do good" (Je.10:5).

---

3 H.C. Leupold. *Exposition of Isaiah,* Vol. 1, p.278.

d. Despite the terrible evil being committed by people who are addicted to idolatry and sorcery, there is still great hope for them. God is very patient and longsuffering, and He wants every human being to be saved from the terrifying judgment that is coming. Therefore, there is still hope for idolaters and those who participate in sorcery. Those who will put their trust in God and *seek refuge* in Him will inherit the promised land (a symbol of heaven). But there is no other way for people to be saved and to receive the inheritance of heaven. As this verse says, the LORD has prepared the way of salvation and removed all the obstacles. (v.14). The only hope for idolaters and those who engage in sorcery is to trust the LORD and travel the road of salvation He has prepared (11:16; 35:8-10; 40:3-5; 62:10-12).

"**Even as Abraham believed God, and it was accounted to him for righteousness. Know ye therefore that they which are of faith, the same are the children of Abraham. And the scripture, foreseeing that God would justify the heathen through faith, preached before the gospel unto Abraham, *saying*, In thee shall all nations be blessed. So then they which be of faith are blessed with faithful Abraham. For as many as are of the works of the law are under the curse: for it is written, Cursed *is* every one that continueth not in all things which are written in the book of the law to do them. But that no man is justified by the law in the sight of God, *it is* evident: for, The just shall live by faith. And the law is not of faith: but, The man that doeth them shall live in them. Christ hath redeemed us from the curse of the law, being made a curse for us: for it is written, Cursed *is* every one that hangeth on a tree: That the blessing of Abraham might come on the Gentiles through Jesus Christ; that we might receive the promise of the Spirit through faith**" (Ga.3:6-14).

"**Trust in the LORD, and do good; *so* shalt thou dwell in the land, and verily thou shalt be fed**" (Ps.37:3).

"**Commit thy way unto the LORD; trust also in him; and he shall bring *it* to pass**" (Ps.37:5).

"*It is* **better to trust in the LORD than to put confidence in man**" (Ps.118:8).

"**Trust in the LORD with all thine heart; and lean not unto thine own understanding. In all thy ways acknowledge him, and he shall direct thy paths**" (Pr.3:5-6).

"**Thou wilt keep *him* in perfect peace, *whose* mind *is* stayed *on* thee: because he trusteth in thee. Trust ye in the LORD for ever: for in the LORD JEHOVAH *is* everlasting strength**" (Is.26:3-4).

"**And an highway shall be there, and a way, and it shall be called The way of holiness; the unclean shall not pass over it; but it *shall be* for those: the wayfaring men, though fools, shall not err *therein***" (Is.35:8).

"**Go through, go through the gates; prepare ye the way of the people; cast up, cast up the highways; gather out the stones; lift up a standard for the people. Behold, the LORD hath proclaimed unto the end of the world, Say ye to the daughter of Zion, Behold, thy salvation cometh; behold, his reward *is* with him, and his work before him. And they shall call them, The holy people, The redeemed of the LORD**" (Is.62:10-12).

---

3 (57:15-21) **Prideful, Warning to, Judgment—Prideful, Fate of—Hope for, Salvation and Peace—Greed – Greedy, Warning, Judgment—Greed – Greedy, Fate of—Greedy, Hope for, Salvation and Peace**: the LORD spoke forcefully and directly to the prideful and greedy: He alone is the high and lofty One. He alone whose very name is Holy inhabits eternity. This means that the LORD, His very nature, is the perfection of holiness, is the only living and true God. For that reason He demands that people acknowledge Him as such, that they obey Him and live righteous lives. In these few verses the LORD issues a strong warning to the prideful and greedy.

OUTLINE	SCRIPTURE	SCRIPTURE	OUTLINE
3. The message to the prideful & greedy: The LORD alone is the high & lofty One	15 For thus saith the high and lofty One that inhabiteth eternity, whose name *is* Holy;	frowardly in the way of his heart.	2) God hid His face, withdrew His presence
a. The warning to the prideful: God alone lives in the high & lofty place (heaven)	I dwell in the high and holy *place,* with him also *that is* of a contrite and humble spirit,	18 I have seen his ways, and will heal him: I will lead him also, and restore comforts unto him and to his	c. The only hope for the prideful & greedy: God's promise of healing (salvation) & guidance
1) God lives only with the humble & repentant, not the prideful	to revive the spirit of the humble, and to revive the heart of the contrite ones.	mourners. 19 I create the fruit of the	1) God will comfort & fill them with praise
2) God will not always convict (contend, fight with) a person who goes astray: He will not always be angry lest He cause man to perish	16 For I will not contend for ever, neither will I be always wroth: for the spirit should fail before me, and the souls *which* I have made.	lips; Peace, peace to *him that is* far off, and to *him that is* near, saith the LORD; and I will heal him. 20 But the wicked *are* like	2) God will give peace to all who come to Him for healing
b. The warning to the greedy & covetous	17 For the iniquity of his covetousness was I wroth, and smote him: I hid me, and	the troubled sea, when it cannot rest, whose waters cast up mire and dirt.	d. The fate of the prideful & greedy—the wicked
1) God punished them (Israel)	was wroth, and he went on	21 *There is* no peace, saith my God, to the wicked.	1) They will be restless like the sea
			2) They will have no peace

First, the LORD issues a very straightforward warning to the prideful (vv.15-16). The prideful must remember that God is *omnipresent* and that He alone lives in the high and lofty place, a place that spans all created worlds, the dimension of heaven itself. Being the high and lofty One, God lives only with those who humble themselves before Him and repent for having disobeyed His Word. The implication is that He does not live with the prideful, those who exalt themselves above

Him. Pride separates people from God by causing Him to withdraw His presence from them. Note God's warning: His patience and longsuffering will come to an end. By His Spirit, He convicts the hearts of the prideful, making them aware of their wicked behavior and of the fact that He is actually the true and living God. But if the prideful ignore or deny the conviction, God's patience will run out, and the prideful will face His judgment.

Still, God's anger will not last forever. If He remained angry forever, no one would be saved, much less the prideful. The inference is that God's anger will be set aside when the prideful repent. If people will humble themselves before the LORD, His anger will cease and He will accept them into His presence. The prideful who repent will live with the LORD, and the LORD will live with them.

> **"And whosoever shall exalt himself shall be abased; and he that shall humble himself shall be exalted"** (Mt.23:12).
>
> **"For the wrath of God is revealed from heaven against all ungodliness and unrighteousness of men, who hold the truth in unrighteousness....Being filled with all unrighteousness, fornication, wickedness, covetousness, maliciousness; full of envy, murder, debate, deceit, malignity; whisperers, Backbiters, haters of God, despiteful, proud, boasters, inventors of evil things, disobedient to parents, Without understanding, covenantbreakers, without natural affection, implacable, unmerciful: Who knowing the judgment of God, that they which commit such things are worthy of death, not only do the same, but have pleasure in them that do them"** (Ro.1:18, 29-32).
>
> **"Love not the world, neither the things** *that are* **in the world. If any man love the world, the love of the Father is not in him. For all that** *is* **in the world, the lust of the flesh, and the lust of the eyes, and the pride of life, is not of the Father, but is of the world"** (1 Jn.2:15-16).
>
> **"Pride** *goeth* **before destruction, and an haughty spirit before a fall"** (Pr.16:18).
>
> **"He loveth transgression that loveth strife:** *and* **he that exalteth his gate seeketh destruction"** (Pr.17:19).
>
> **"An high look, and a proud heart,** *and* **the plowing of the wicked,** *is* **sin"** (Pr.21:4).
>
> **"Seest thou a man wise in his own conceit?** *there is* **more hope of a fool than of him"** (Pr.26:12).
>
> **"Though thou exalt** *thyself* **as the eagle, and though thou set thy nest among the stars, thence will I bring thee down, saith the LORD"** (Ob.4).

Second, the LORD issues a strong warning to the greedy and covetous (v.17). Covetousness is a disease that has plagued the human race throughout history. The human heart is filled with a spirit of selfishness and greed. Down through the centuries, many of the Israelites coveted the wealth, possessions, power, and pleasures of their neighbors. As Scripture says, many coveted their neighbor's houses, wives, servants, livestock, and anything else a neighbor owned (Ex.20:17). As a result, they committed the heinous sins that the greedy always commit: lying, stealing, cheating, and oppressing people—particularly the poor, disabled, and defenseless—in order to get what they want. They would often bribe judges and use the courts to secure the desires of their hearts. Because of their sin, the LORD punished the Israelites by hiding His face from them and withdrawing His presence. He did this as a judgment, hoping to arouse them to repent of their covetousness and turn back to Him.

> **"And he said unto them, Take heed, and beware of covetousness: for a man's life consisteth not in the abundance of the things which he possesseth"** (Lu.12:15).
>
> **"Mortify therefore your members which are upon the earth; fornication, uncleanness, inordinate affection, evil concupiscence, and covetousness, which is idolatry: For which things' sake the wrath of God cometh on the children of disobedience"** (Col.3:5-6).
>
> **"Thou shalt not covet thy neighbour's house, thou shalt not covet thy neighbour's wife, nor his manservant, nor his maidservant, nor his ox, nor his ass, nor any thing that** *is* **thy neighbour's"** (Ex.20:17).
>
> **"And they come unto thee as the people cometh, and they sit before thee as my people, and they hear thy words, but they will not do them: for with their mouth they shew much love,** *but* **their heart goeth after their covetousness"** (Eze.33:31).
>
> **"For from the least of them even unto the greatest of them every one** *is* **given to covetousness; and from the prophet even unto the priest every one dealeth falsely"** (Je.6:13).
>
> **"Woe to him that coveteth an evil covetousness to his house, that he may set his nest on high, that he may be delivered from the power of evil!"** (Hab.2:9).

Third, the LORD offers great hope to the prideful and greedy, despite their terrible sins. He offers them the healing of salvation and His own personal guidance (vv.18-19). But note that only *mourners* (v.19) will be saved and guided by the LORD. All within Israel or anywhere else who fell on their faces before the LORD, *mourning* and crying out to Him in repentance, would receive God's peace and the healing of His salvation. In fact, so much peace would flood the souls of repentant sinners that they would cry, "Peace, peace to all who are far and near."

> **"Peace I leave with you, my peace I give unto you: not as the world giveth, give I unto you. Let not your heart be troubled, neither let it be afraid"** (Jn.14:27).
>
> **"These things I have spoken unto you, that in me ye might have peace. In the world ye shall have tribulation: but be of good cheer; I have overcome the world"** (Jn.16:33).
>
> **"Therefore being justified by faith, we have peace with God through our Lord Jesus Christ"** (Ro.5:1).

"But now in Christ Jesus ye who sometimes were far off are made nigh by the blood of Christ. For he is our peace, who hath made both one, and hath broken down the middle wall of partition *between us*" (Ep.2:13-14).

"Be careful for nothing; but in every thing by prayer and supplication with thanksgiving let your requests be made known unto God. And the peace of God, which passeth all understanding, shall keep your hearts and minds through Christ Jesus" (Ph.4:6-7).

"And, having made peace through the blood of his cross, by him to reconcile all things unto himself; by him, *I say*, whether *they be* things in earth, or things in heaven" (Col.1:20).

"The LORD will give strength unto his people; the LORD will bless his people with peace" (Ps.29:11).

"Great peace have they which love thy law: and nothing shall offend them" (Ps.119:165).

"Thou wilt keep *him* in perfect peace, *whose* mind *is* stayed *on thee:* because he trusteth in thee" (Is.26:3).

"But he *was* wounded for our transgressions, *he was* bruised for our iniquities: the chastisement of our peace *was* upon him; and with his stripes we are healed" (Is.53:5).

Fourth, the LORD says that the fate of the prideful and greedy will be entirely different from the fate of those who repent (vv.20-21). The wicked and unrepentant will be restless, like a turbulent sea whose waves never rest due to their being tossed about. In addition, their lives will always be filled with the filth and smut of sin, just like the slimy sand and mud that is stirred up by the tossing waves of the sea. "There is no peace...to the wicked" (v.21).

"For the kingdom of God is not meat and drink; but righteousness, and peace, and joy in the Holy Ghost" (Ro.14:17).

"And in those times *there was* no peace to him that went out, nor to him that came in, but great vexations *were* upon all the inhabitants of the countries" (2 Chr.15:5).

"In the morning thou shalt say, Would God it were even! and at even thou shalt say, Would God it were morning! for the fear of thine heart wherewith thou shalt fear, and for the sight of thine eyes which thou shalt see" (De.28:67).

"For all his days *are* sorrows, and his travail grief; yea, his heart taketh not rest in the night. This is also vanity" (Ecc.2:23).

"The way of peace they know not; and *there is* no judgment in their goings: they have made them crooked paths: whosoever goeth therein shall not know peace" (Is.59:8).

"Destruction cometh; and they shall seek peace, and *there shall be* none" (Eze.7:25).

"Our necks *are* under persecution: we labour, *and* have no rest" (La.5:5).

CHAPTER 58

G. The Savior's Message to the Hypocrites: Guilty of Deceptive, Phony Behavior

1. The phony, deceptive behavior of religious hypocrites

a. The phony behavior they flaunt
   1) They seek God daily: Are pious
   2) They seem eager to learn God's ways, His Word
   3) They pray for guidance, for right decisions
   4) They worship, seek God
b. The actual day-to-day behavior they conceal
   1) They complain to God that He has not noticed their fasting or prayer: Has not met their needs or blessed them
   2) They live selfishly
   3) They exploit people
   4) They are divisive, arguing & fighting: Right after fasting or leaving worship
   5) They expect God to bless them despite their wicked behavior
   6) They wrongly think the LORD will accept their religious behavior

2. The specific behavior demanded by God

a. To be humble before God
b. To bow one's head: Pray
c. To obey the LORD: Make every day acceptable to God
d. To be just & fair to all
   1) Bring an end to the stream of injustice
   2) Set the oppressed free
e. To minister to the needy, Ga.6:10
   1) Must provide food, shelter, & clothing
   2) Must not turn away from a family member who genuinely needs help

Cry aloud, spare not, lift up thy voice like a trumpet, and show my people their transgression, and the house of Jacob their sins.
2 Yet they seek me daily, and delight to know my ways, as a nation that did righteousness, and forsook not the ordinance of their God: they ask of me the ordinances of justice; they take delight in approaching to God.
3 Wherefore have we fasted, *say they,* and thou seest not? *wherefore* have we afflicted our soul, and thou takest no knowledge? Behold, in the day of your fast ye find pleasure, and exact all your labours.
4 Behold, ye fast for strife and debate, and to smite with the fist of wickedness: ye shall not fast as *ye do this* day, to make your voice to be heard on high.
5 Is it such a fast that I have chosen? a day for a man to afflict his soul? *is it* to bow down his head as a bulrush, and to spread sackcloth and ashes *under him?* wilt thou call this a fast, and an acceptable day to the LORD?
6 *Is* not this the fast that I have chosen? to loose the bands of wickedness, to undo the heavy burdens, and to let the oppressed go free, and that ye break every yoke?
7 *Is it* not to deal thy bread to the hungry, and that thou bring the poor that are cast out to thy house? when thou seest the naked, that thou cover him; and that thou hide

not thyself from thine own flesh?
8 Then shall thy light break forth as the morning, and thine health shall spring forth speedily: and thy righteousness shall go before thee; the glory of the LORD shall be thy rereward.
9 Then shalt thou call, and the LORD shall answer; thou shalt cry, and he shall say, Here I *am.* If thou take away from the midst of thee the yoke, the putting forth of the finger, and speaking vanity;
10 And *if* thou draw out thy soul to the hungry, and satisfy the afflicted soul; then shall thy light rise in obscurity, and thy darkness *be* as the noonday:
11 And the LORD shall guide thee continually, and satisfy thy soul in drought, and make fat thy bones: and thou shalt be like a watered garden, and like a spring of water, whose waters fail not.
12 And *they that shall be* of thee shall build the old waste places: thou shalt raise up the foundations of many generations; and thou shalt be called, The repairer of the breach, The restorer of paths to dwell in.
13 If thou turn away thy foot from the sabbath, *from* doing thy pleasure on my holy day; and call the sabbath a delight, the holy of the LORD, honourable; and shalt honour him, not doing thine own ways, nor finding thine own pleasure, nor speaking *thine own* words:
14 Then shalt thou delight thyself in the LORD; and I will cause thee to ride upon the high places of the earth, and feed thee with the heritage of Jacob thy father: for the mouth of the LORD hath spoken *it.*

3. The results of righteous behavior: God's promises

a. Light & healing: Salvation
b. Righteousness & protection: Assured by God's glory

c. Answered prayer: After doing away with oppression, pointing the finger, & malicious talk

d. Light: Will be a strong witness & beacon in the dark to those in need

e. God's guidance
f. Abundant provision & strength to meet every need

g. An honorable name
   1) Will rebuild ancient ruins: Both ruined lives & property
   2) Will be called *The Repairer of the Breach (Broken Walls)*

4. The importance of keeping the Sabbath day holy

a. God's commandment
   1) Must not break the Sabbath, doing as you please
   2) Must make the day a delight
   3) Must not engage in idle, useless talk
b. God's promises
   1) Joy in the LORD
   2) Great honor: Will ride or be victorious over the high places or enemies of the earth
   3) A full share of the inheritance promised to Jacob (the promised land)

DIVISION VI

THE PROPHECIES OF THE GREAT DELIVERER: THE SUFFERING SERVANT OF GOD, THE SAVIOR OF THE WORLD, 49:1–59:21

G. The Savior's Message to the Hypocrites: Guilty of Deceptive, Phony Behavior, 58:1-14

(58:1–59:21) **Introduction**: a hypocrite is a person who pretends, puts on a show, acts out something he or she is not. Many people are hypocrites:
   ⇒ They act as though they believe and love God, yet they do not truly trust or obey God's holy commandments.
   ⇒ They pretend to be seeking God, but their hearts are in reality seeking recognition, esteem, position, power, fame, or wealth.

⇒ They act humble and helpful; nevertheless, they are full of pride, envy, selfishness, and covetousness.
⇒ They show a concern for the things of God at the same time their hearts are set on the things of the world.
⇒ They profess to know and believe God's Word, but they add to or take away from His Word at their own discretion and live as they wish instead of obeying God's Word.

In the present Scripture, God spoke directly to the hypocrites of Isaiah's day. What He said is applicable to every generation. This is, *The Savior's Message to the Hypocrites: Guilty of Deceptive, Phony Behavior*, 58:1-14.
1. The deceptive behavior of religious hypocrites (vv.1-5ᵃ).
2. The specific behavior demanded by God (vv.5ᵇ-7).
3. The results of righteous behavior: God's promises (vv.8-12).
4. The importance of keeping the Sabbath day holy (vv.13-14).

1 (58:1-5ᵃ) **Hypocrite, Behavior of; Traits—Believers, Duty—Hypocrite, Message to—Behavior, Hypocritical**: hypocrites must be told their behavior is phony, hypocritical. They are guilty of dangerous transgression and sin. God instructed Isaiah to address this message to the *house of Jacob*, which is Israel. But God also said that the message was addressed to *my people*. This makes the message applicable to every generation of believers. This message is very important. It is so significant that the prophet was to shout it aloud, raising his voice like a trumpet: "Spare not. Do not hold back from proclaiming the truth," God says. Make sure everyone hears the message and that they hear the truth. They are guilty of dangerous transgression and sin. By *transgression* is meant rebellion. God's people are deliberately rebelling against Him, turning away from His holy commandments. Although they professed to know the LORD and to be following Him, they lived hypocritical lives. They were living dangerous lives that could doom them to the judgment of God:

OUTLINE	SCRIPTURE	SCRIPTURE	OUTLINE
1. The phony, deceptive behavior of religious hypocrites	Cry aloud, spare not, lift up thy voice like a trumpet, and show my people their transgression, and the house of Jacob their sins.	takest no knowledge? Behold, in the day of your fast ye find pleasure, and exact all your labours.	ing or prayer: Has not met their needs or blessed them
			2) They live selfishly
a. The phony behavior they flaunt	2 Yet they seek me daily, and delight to know my	4 Behold, ye fast for strife and debate, and to smite with	3) They exploit people
1) They seek God daily: Are pious	ways, as a nation that did righteousness, and forsook	the fist of wickedness: ye shall not fast as *ye do this*	4) They are divisive, arguing & fighting: Right after fasting or leaving worship
2) They seem eager to learn God's ways, His Word	not the ordinance of their God: they ask of me the ordi-	day, to make your voice to be heard on high.	5) They expect God to bless them despite their wicked behavior
3) They pray for guidance, for right decisions	nances of justice; they take delight in approaching to	5 Is it such a fast that I have chosen? a day for a man	
4) They worship, seek God	God.	to afflict his soul? *is it* to bow down his head as a bulrush,	6) They wrongly think the LORD will accept their religious behavior
b. The actual day-to-day behavior they conceal	3 Wherefore have we fasted, *say they,* and thou seest	and to spread sackcloth and ashes *under him?* wilt thou	
1) They complain to God that He has not noticed their fast-	not? *wherefore* have we afflicted our soul, and thou	call this a fast, and an acceptable day to the LORD?	

a. The devious behavior of hypocrites is sad, for in most cases they do not see their own sins. They have actually deceived themselves. Despite being guilty of terrible sin, they continue their regular religious activities in the belief that God accepts them. They believe they are good enough and do enough good works that, in the final analysis, God will never reject them. No matter how deeply sin is rooted in their lives, they still believe they are acceptable to God. They are convinced that they are *eternally secure*. Many religious hypocrites can make some strong pious claims because they are consistently faithful to their religious beliefs despite their sinful behavior. God says that some hypocrites can even make the following four claims:

⇒ They seek God daily; that is, they have a daily devotional or worship time, either in their home or worship center (v.2).
⇒ They are eager to learn God's ways, to study His Word so they will know how to live righteous lives and please the LORD.
⇒ They pray for guidance, seeking to make right and just decisions in their behavior toward others.
⇒ They worship and seek the LORD on a regular basis throughout the day, drawing near to Him in fellowship and communion.

b. But note what Scripture says: these are deceptive claims, for the hypocrites have forsaken the commandments of God and are not living righteously. Their hearts and day-to-day behavior are a far cry from what God requires (vv.3ᵇ-5). God demands a *personal relationship* with and *obedience* from His true followers. Hypocrites, however, confuse the issue. They substitute religion or church membership for a personal relationship with the LORD; and they equate *good works* with obedience to His commands. For the most part, hypocrites believe that good deeds are what make them acceptable to God. Therefore, they feel they can do what they wish just as long as they do enough good deeds.

Seeking God daily, being eager to learn His Word, praying, and drawing near to the LORD throughout the day are all necessary to maintain a strong spiritual life and relationship with the LORD. But engaging in these worshipful activities while neglecting to behave righteously is hypocritical. This was the indictment of God against many of the Jews in Isaiah's day.

And it has been God's indictment against many down through the centuries. They "have a form of godliness, but deny the power thereof" (2 Ti.3:5). Their hearts are far from God, and their daily behavior does not conform to the commandments of God. The prophet Isaiah described how they act. Note the feeble behavior of hypocrites:

1) Some hypocrites complain to God that He has not noted their fasting or prayer, not met their needs or blessed them (v.3). When trials or crises arise, they seek the LORD for help, even to the point of fasting. But they think God appears disinterested in their needs and seems to be ignoring their prayers. Thus, they question God, asking why He had not heard their cries. What they are overlooking is the importance of simply obeying God, for God considers obedience even better than offerings and sacrifices (1 S.15:22).

2) Many hypocrites live selfishly (v.3). Using fasting as an example, they will set aside a day to fast, but instead of spending the day in prayer, they selfishly go about their regular daily routines and activities. Professing to be followers of the LORD, many people faithfully participate in religious services, rituals, and ceremonies. However, directly after the religious activity, they return to their selfish ways. They live as they want, indulging the flesh and becoming entangled with the sinful pleasures of the world. Ignoring the commandments of God, they seek to please themselves and do their own thing, regardless of what God says.

3) Other hypocrites are guilty of exploiting those who work under their supervision (v.3^c). One moment they proclaim to know the LORD, and the next they are like slave drivers who abuse the people working under them. In certain cases, they are even guilty of extortion, stealing from their workers or employees by paying them low wages or shorting them hours worked or wages paid. Cheating their workers and being overbearing in their demands, these hypocritical employers or managers forget the commandments of God (Col.4:1).

4) A number of hypocrites are divisive (v.4). The picture being painted by Scripture is tragic. Some were arguing and fighting even after fasting and as soon as they walked out of worship. Think how many families every week walk out of worship and quickly return to their divisive behavior, quarrelling and treating each other coldly. Despite living under the same roof, they shut one another out and live what amounts to separate lives. This is phony and insincere. Think also about church members who are divisive within the church, who fuel or initiate heated discussions that at times, regrettably, lead to a split within the church. This is hypocritical behavior at its worst.

5) Most, if not all, hypocrites expect God to bless them despite their sinful, wicked behavior (v.4). Nevertheless, God is very clear in this passage: "You cannot fast [pray, seek God] as you do today and expect your voice to be heard on high" (v.4 NIV). God will not bless hypocrites. He will not answer their prayers until they have confessed and repented of their sins. No matter how religious they are or how many good deeds they do, God will not accept people who continue to live wickedly and disobey His commandments.

6) Hypocrites are themselves deceived, for they think the LORD will accept their religious behavior (v.5^a). Again the example given is that of fasting, for fasting is considered above and beyond "normal" religious activity. And the picture is that of religious people, those who confess the LORD, attend worship services faithfully, and perform *good deeds*. But these people do even more. When difficult times come or a crisis arises, they set aside a day or more for fasting and seeking the LORD in prayer. They humble themselves, bow their heads, and even put on sackcloth and ashes. Because of their commitment to religion and their religious activity, they feel confident that the LORD will accept, bless, and look after them. But God is clear: as important as it is to attend church and do good deeds, these activities are not His first demand. What God demands is given in the next point (point 2).

Thought 1. Throughout the Holy Scriptures God has much to say about hypocrisy and false religion. Take note of just a few references:

> "*Ye* hypocrites, well did Esaias prophesy of you, saying, This people draweth nigh unto me with their mouth, and honoureth me with *their* lips; but their heart is far from me. But in vain they do worship me, teaching *for* doctrines the commandments of men" (Mt.15:7-9).
>
> "But woe unto you, scribes and Pharisees, hypocrites! for ye shut up the kingdom of heaven against men: for ye neither go in *yourselves,* neither suffer ye them that are entering to go in" (Mt.23:13; see vv.14-33).
>
> "Even so ye also outwardly appear righteous unto men, but within ye are full of hypocrisy and iniquity" (Mt.23:28).
>
> "But and if that evil servant shall say in his heart, My lord delayeth his coming; And shall begin to smite *his* fellowservants, and to eat and drink with the drunken; The lord of that servant shall come in a day when he looketh not for *him,* and in an hour that he is not aware of, And shall cut him asunder, and appoint *him* his portion with the hypocrites: there shall be weeping and gnashing of teeth" (Mt.24:48-51).
>
> "He answered and said unto them, Well hath Esaias prophesied of you hypocrites, as it is written, This people honoureth me with *their* lips, but their heart is far from me" (Mk.7:6).
>
> "And why call ye me, Lord, Lord, and do not the things which I say?" (Lu.6:46).
>
> "*Ye* hypocrites, ye can discern the face of the sky and of the earth; but how is it that ye do not discern this time? Yea, and why even of yourselves judge ye not what is right?" (Lu.12:56-57).
>
> "Thou therefore which teachest another, teachest thou not thyself? thou that preachest a man should not steal, dost thou steal? Thou that sayest a man should not commit adultery, dost thou commit adultery? thou that abhorrest idols, dost thou commit sacrilege?" (Ro.2:21-22; also see vv.17-29. see outline and notes—Ro.2:17-29 for more discussion).
>
> "Now I beseech you, brethren, mark them which cause divisions and offences contrary to the doctrine which ye have learned; and avoid them. For they that are such serve not our Lord Jesus Christ, but their own belly; and by good words and fair speeches deceive the hearts of the simple" (Ro.16:17-18).

"Now the Spirit speaketh expressly, that in the latter times some shall depart from the faith, giving heed to seducing spirits, and doctrines of devils; Speaking lies in hypocrisy; having their conscience seared with a hot iron" (1 Ti.4;1-2).

"Unto the pure all things *are* pure: but unto them that are defiled and unbelieving *is* nothing pure; but even their mind and conscience is defiled. They profess that they know God; but in works they deny *him,* being abominable, and disobedient, and unto every good work reprobate" (Tit.1:15-16).

"And they come unto thee as the people cometh, and they sit before thee as my people, and they hear thy words, but they will not do them: for with their mouth they show much love, *but* their heart goeth after their covetousness. And, lo, thou *art* unto them as a very lovely song of one that hath a pleasant voice, and can play well on an instrument: for they hear thy words, but they do them not" (Eze.33:31-32).

2 **(58:5ᵇ-7) Acceptance, by God, Requirements—Hypocrites, Duty of—Salvation, Steps to, Results of**: the specific behavior demanded by God is spelled out (v.5ᵇ-7). The prophet must explain God's demands as well as the phony behavior of hypocrites. Hypocrites must understand exactly what they must do to become *truly acceptable* to God. Five specific behaviors are discussed.

OUTLINE	SCRIPTURE	SCRIPTURE	OUTLINE

2. The specific behavior demanded by God
a. To be humble before God
b. To bow one's head: Pray
c. To obey the LORD: Make every day acceptable to God
d. To be just & fair to all
  1) Bring an end to the stream of injustice
  2) Set the oppressed free
e. To minister to the needy,
	5 Is it such a fast that I have chosen? a day for a man to afflict his soul? is it to bow down his head as a bulrush, and to spread sackcloth and ashes *under him?* wilt thou call this a fast, and an acceptable day to the LORD? 6 *Is* not this the fast that I have chosen? to loose the bands of wickedness, to undo	the heavy burdens, and to let the oppressed go free, and that ye break every yoke? 7 *Is it* not to deal thy bread to the hungry, and that thou bring the poor that are cast out to thy house? when thou seest the naked, that thou cover him; and that thou hide not thyself from thine own flesh?	Ga.6:10
			1) Must provide food, shelter, & clothing
			2) Must not turn away from a family member who genuinely needs help

a. Hypocrites must become humble (v.5). *Humbling oneself* or *afflicting one's soul* means to acknowledge the LORD and one's total dependence upon Him. It is not enough for people to set aside one day a week to seek the LORD through worship or fasting. God is to be acknowledged seven days a week. If people profess the LORD, they are to humble themselves before Him, acknowledging that He alone is to be worshipped and served. As LORD, He is to be obeyed. His holy commandments are to be kept. People are God's *subjects*, created for the very purpose of worshipping and serving Him. None of us have the right to act as though we were *lord*, living as we please and doing whatever we want. To the contrary, all people must walk humbly before the LORD day by day, acknowledging that He alone has the right to dictate how life is to be lived.

> "But Jesus called them *unto him,* and said, Suffer little children to come unto me, and forbid them not: for of such is the kingdom of God. Verily I say unto you, Whosoever shall not receive the kingdom of God as a little child shall in no wise enter therein" (Lu.18:16-17).
> "For godly sorrow [humility] worketh repentance to salvation not to be repented of: but the sorrow of the world worketh death" (2 Co.7:10).
> "The LORD *is* nigh unto them that are of a broken heart; and saveth such as be of a contrite spirit" (Ps.34:18).

b. Hypocrites must continually bow their heads, seeking and praying to the LORD (v.5). Again, it is not enough to set aside one day for fasting and prayer. True believers pray continually throughout the day, offering up praise to the LORD for His great salvation and blessings. Moreover, when they spend a daily time in worship (devotions) or sense the need to set aside a special time for seeking the LORD, they do it privately, in secret, without attracting attention. Understanding the richness of God's salvation and the preciousness of His fellowship, they have a very special place where they meet with the LORD in their daily devotions. Whether in a prayer garden, a private closet, or elsewhere, they fellowship and commune with the LORD on a daily basis as well as on special occasions. Communing and fellowshipping with the LORD are an ongoing, continuous experiences for believers. When their minds are not focused upon their work or another essential activity, they take moments here and there to acknowledge and praise their Savior. What a contrast between true believers and hypocrites!

> "Watch and pray, that ye enter not into temptation: the spirit indeed *is* willing, but the flesh *is* weak" (Mt.26:41).
> "Hitherto have ye asked nothing in my name: ask, and ye shall receive, that your joy may be full" (Jn.16:24).
> "Likewise the Spirit also helpeth our infirmities: for we know not what we should pray for as we ought: but the Spirit itself maketh intercession for us with groanings which cannot be uttered. And he that searcheth the hearts knoweth what *is* the mind of the Spirit, because he maketh intercession for the saints according to *the will of* God" (Ro.8:26-27).

"Praying always with all prayer and supplication in the Spirit, and watching thereunto with all perseverance and supplication for all saints" (Ep.6:18).
"Pray without ceasing" (1 Th.5:17).

c. Hypocrites must make every day acceptable to the LORD by obeying Him (v.5ᶜ). Seeking to make one day a week pleasing to God is not enough, not to the LORD. Every day is to belong to the LORD. Every day is to be a day of prayer, a day of seeking His guidance and protection. God is not interested in people just one day a week. God loves and cares about what happens to us all the time—seven days a week, twenty-four hours a day. He also cares about what we do every moment of every hour of every day. Obeying God is a continual demand. It is never optional. We cannot choose which of the commandments we want to obey and when we want to obey them. God's commandments are to be the pattern of our lives, determining how we behave and conduct ourselves. A day becomes acceptable to God when we follow His holy commandments and live righteous and pure lives.

"Not every one that saith unto me, Lord, Lord, shall enter into the kingdom of heaven; but he that doeth the will of my Father which is in heaven. Many will say to me in that day, Lord, Lord, have we not prophesied in thy name? and in thy name have cast out devils? and in thy name done many wonderful works? And then will I profess unto them, I never knew you: depart from me, ye that work iniquity" (Mt.7:21-23).
"He that hath my commandments, and keepeth them, he it is that loveth me: and he that loveth me shall be loved of my Father, and I will love him, and will manifest myself to him" (Jn.14:21).
"Jesus answered and said unto him, If a man love me, he will keep my words: and my Father will love him, and we will come unto him, and make our abode with him" (Jn.14:23).
"They profess that they know God; but in works they deny *him*, being abominable, and disobedient, and unto every good work reprobate" (Tit.1:16).

d. Hypocrites must be *just* in their dealings with everyone (v.6). To God, a true fast is living an honorable and equitable life, treating others as we wish to be treated (Mt.7:12; Lu.6:31). The chains of unrighteousness and injustice must be broken. Every yoke of bondage must be removed. Any control or restraint that subjects or enslaves must be loosened, untied. The oppressed and exploited must be set free. Mercy must be shown to all who suffer and are burdened. It is only the merciful who will be blessed by God. Only the merciful will receive the mercy of God (Mt.5:7). Think about people down through history and in everyday life who oppress other people (dictators, world leaders, criminals, employers, next door neighbors, even family members). Yet many of them profess to know the LORD and are faithful in their worship and religious activities. "Hypocrites," God says. "Cry aloud! Shout it aloud!" They are hypocrites. Unacceptable. Even though they worship God and go to church, when they manipulate or mistreat others in any way, they are hypocrites. No matter what they proclaim or what religious activity they engage in, they are unacceptable to God.

"Therefore all things whatsoever ye would that men should do to you, do ye even so to them: for this is the law and the prophets" (Mt.7:12).
"Thou shalt love thy neighbour as thyself" (Mt.22:39).
"This is my commandment, That ye love one another, as I have loved you" (Jn.15:12).
"*Let* love be without dissimulation [hypocrisy]. Abhor that which is evil; cleave to that which is good" (Ro.12:9).
"*Be* kindly affectioned one to another with brotherly love; in honour preferring one another" (Ro.12:10).
"Charity suffereth long, *and* is kind; charity envieth not; charity vaunteth not itself, is not puffed up" (1 Co.13:4).
"And be ye kind one to another, tenderhearted, forgiving one another, even as God for Christ's sake hath forgiven you" (Ep.4:32).
"Put on therefore, as the elect of God, holy and beloved, bowels of mercies, kindness, humbleness of mind, meekness, longsuffering" (Col.3:12).
"Thou shalt not oppress an hired servant *that is* poor and needy, *whether he be* of thy brethren, or of thy strangers that *are* in thy land within thy gates" (De.24:14).
"He that oppresseth the poor reproacheth his Maker: but he that honoureth him hath mercy on the poor" (Pr.14:31).

e. Hypocrites must minister to the needy (v.7). The only behavior acceptable to God is feeding the hungry, providing shelter for the homeless, and clothing the poor (Ga.6:10). Turning a blind eye to the needs of others is clearly disgraceful. Furthermore, a person must not turn away from helping a family member who truly needs help. Note this fact: the LORD is talking not only about making a gift to meet the needs of the poor but also about *sharing* one's own food, shelter, and clothing if needed.

"And Jesus answering said, A certain *man* went down from Jerusalem to Jericho, and fell among thieves, which stripped him of his raiment, and wounded *him*, and departed, leaving *him* half dead. And by chance there came down a certain priest that way: and when he saw him, he passed by on the other side. And likewise a Levite, when he was at the place, came and looked *on him*, and passed by on the other side. But a certain Samaritan, as he journeyed, came where he was: and when he saw him, he had compassion *on him*, And went to *him*, and bound up his wounds, pouring in oil and wine, and set him on his own beast, and brought him to an inn, and took care of him. And on the morrow when he departed, he took out two pence, and gave *them* to the host, and said unto him, Take care of him; and whatsoever thou spendest more, when I come again, I will repay thee. Which now of these three, thinkest thou, was neighbour unto him that fell among the thieves?" (Lu.10:30-36).

"He saith to him again the second time, Simon, *son* of Jonas, lovest thou me? He saith unto him, Yea, Lord; thou knowest that I love thee. He saith unto him, Feed my sheep" (Jn.21:16).

"How God anointed Jesus of Nazareth with the Holy Ghost and with power: who went about doing good, and healing all that were oppressed of the devil; for God was with him" (Ac.10:38).

"Love worketh no ill to his neighbour: therefore love *is* the fulfilling of the law" (Ro.13:10).

"Brethren, if a man be overtaken in a fault, ye which are spiritual, restore such an one in the spirit of meekness; considering thyself, lest thou also be tempted. Bear ye one another's burdens, and so fulfil the law of Christ" (Ga.6:1-2).

"And let us not be weary in well doing: for in due season we shall reap, if we faint not. As we have therefore opportunity, let us do good unto all *men*, especially unto them who are of the household of faith" (Ga.6:9-10).

"Pure religion and undefiled before God and the Father is this, To visit the fatherless and widows in their affliction, *and* to keep himself unspotted from the world" (Js.1:27).

---

3 (58:8-12) **Righteousness, Results of, Sevenfold—Hypocrites, Repentant, Results—Repentance, Results of**: the hypocrite must be challenged with the results of righteous behavior (vv.8-12). God makes some wonderful promises to the hypocrite who will repent and do the specific behavior He has spelled out above. Seven wonderful promises are given:

OUTLINE	SCRIPTURE	SCRIPTURE	OUTLINE
3. The results of righteous behavior: God's promises a. Light & healing: Salvation b. Righteousness & protection: Assured by God's glory c. Answered prayer: After doing away with oppression, pointing the finger, & malicious talk d. Light: Will be a strong witness & beacon in the dark to those in need	8 Then shall thy light break forth as the morning, and thine health shall spring forth speedily: and thy righteousness shall go before thee; the glory of the LORD shall be thy rereward. 9 Then shalt thou call, and the LORD shall answer; thou shalt cry, and he shall say, Here I *am*. If thou take away from the midst of thee the yoke, the putting forth of the finger, and speaking vanity; 10 And *if* thou draw out thy soul to the hungry, and satisfy the afflicted soul; then	shall thy light rise in obscurity, and thy darkness *be* as the noonday: 11 And the LORD shall guide thee continually, and satisfy thy soul in drought, and make fat thy bones: and thou shalt be like a watered garden, and like a spring of water, whose waters fail not. 12 And *they that shall be* of thee shall build the old waste places: thou shalt raise up the foundations of many generations; and thou shalt be called, The repairer of the breach, The restorer of paths to dwell in.	e. God's guidance f. Abundant provision & strength to meet every need g. An honorable name 1) Will rebuild ancient ruins: Both ruined lives & property 2) Will be called *The Repairer of the Breach* (Broken Walls)

a. Hypocrites who repent will receive *light and healing* from the LORD. This refers to salvation, the light that broke forth and the healing that was provided with the coming of Christ, the promised Messiah (v.8).

"In him was life; and the life was the light of men" (Jn.1:4).

"Then spake Jesus again unto them, saying, I am the light of the world: he that followeth me shall not walk in darkness, but shall have the light of life" (Jn.8:12).

"For God, who commanded the light to shine out of darkness, hath shined in our hearts, to *give* the light of the knowledge of the glory of God in the face of Jesus Christ" (2 Co.4:6).

"Wherefore he saith, Awake thou that sleepest, and arise from the dead, and Christ shall give thee light" (Ep.5:14).

b. Hypocrites who repent will receive the righteousness and protection of God (v.8[b]). Righteousness is the result of salvation. Once people turn to the LORD, God covers them with His own righteousness. As a result, they appear righteous in His eyes. Amazing! In addition, they are guaranteed the presence and protection of the LORD.

"For I say unto you, That except your righteousness shall exceed *the righteousness* of the scribes and Pharisees [hypocritical religionists], ye shall in no case enter into the kingdom of heaven" (Mt.5:20).

"For he hath made him *to be* sin for us, who knew no sin; that we might be made the righteousness of God in him" (2 Co.5:21).

"*Let your* conversation [conduct, behavior] *be* without covetousness; *and be* content with such things as ye have: for he hath said, I will never leave thee, nor forsake thee. So that we may boldly say, The Lord *is* my helper, and I will not fear what man shall do unto me" (He.13:5-6).

"For the eyes of the LORD run to and fro throughout the whole earth, to show himself strong in the behalf of *them* whose heart *is* perfect toward him. Herein thou hast done foolishly: therefore from henceforth thou shalt have wars" (2 Chr.16:9).

"The angel of the LORD encampeth round about them that fear him, and delivereth them" (Ps.34:7).

"Fear thou not; for I *am* with thee: be not dismayed; for I *am* thy God: I will strengthen thee; yea, I will help thee; yea, I will uphold thee with the right hand of my righteousness" (Is.41:10).

"Fear not: for I have redeemed thee, I have called *thee* by thy name; thou *art* mine. When thou passest through the waters, I *will be* with thee; and through the rivers, they shall not overflow thee: when thou walkest through the fire, thou shalt not be burned; neither shall the flame kindle upon thee" (Is.43:1-2).

c. Hypocrites who repent will have their prayers answered. When they call upon the LORD, He promises to hear and answer. But hypocrites must turn absolutely away from their oppression and mistreatment of others. They must also stop pointing fingers at people and engaging in wicked talk such as malicious gossip and profanity.

"And I say unto you, Ask, and it shall be given you; seek, and ye shall find; knock, and it shall be opened unto you" (Lu.11:9).

"And whatsoever ye shall ask in my name, that will I do, that the Father may be glorified in the Son. If ye shall ask any thing in my name, I will do *it*" (Jn.14:13-14).

"If ye abide in me, and my words abide in you, ye shall ask what ye will, and it shall be done unto you" (Jn.15:7).

"And whatsoever we ask, we receive of him, because we keep his commandments, and do those things that are pleasing in his sight. And this is his commandment, That we should believe on the name of his Son Jesus Christ, and love one another, as he gave us commandment" (1 Jn.3:22-23).

d. Hypocrites who repent will become a light, a strong witness to people in their dark hour of personal need (v.10). When true believers minister to those in need, all the darkness and gloom surrounding their lives will be swept away by the light of their witness.

"Ye are the light of the world. A city that is set on an hill cannot be hid" (Mt.5:14).

"For ye were sometimes darkness, but now *are ye* light in the Lord: walk as children of light: (For the fruit of the Spirit is in all goodness and righteousness and truth;) Proving what is acceptable unto the Lord. And have no fellowship with the unfruitful works of darkness, but rather reprove *them*" (Ep.5:8-11).

"Do all things without murmurings and disputings: That ye may be blameless and harmless, the sons of God, without rebuke, in the midst of a crooked and perverse nation, among whom ye shine as lights in the world; Holding forth the word of life; that I may rejoice in the day of Christ, that I have not run in vain, neither laboured in vain" (Ph.2:14-16).

e. Hypocrites who repent will receive God's guidance and strength (v.11ᵃ). And God promises that His guidance will be *permanent*. He will faithfully direct those who have truly repented and who turn to Him in faith and obedience.

"Howbeit when he, the Spirit of truth, is come, he will guide you into all truth: for he shall not speak of himself; but whatsoever he shall hear, *that* shall he speak: and he will show you things to come" (Jn.16:13).

"The meek will he guide in judgment: and the meek will he teach his way" (Ps.25:9).

"For this God *is* our God for ever and ever: he will be our guide *even* unto death" (Ps.48:14).

"Thou shalt guide me with thy counsel, and afterward receive me *to* glory" (Ps.73:24).

f. Hypocrites who repent will receive the provision and strength of the LORD to meet every need (v.11). In fact, God will give them *abundant* provision and strength. Even in the drought of a sun-scorched land, the LORD will provide whatever believers need to strengthen them as they walk through trials and hardships. The reference to a well-watered spring that never fails indicates that God will provide for every need, both physical and spiritual.

"But my God shall supply all your need according to his riches in glory by Christ Jesus" (Ph.4:19).

"Wherefore in all things it behoved him to be made like unto *his* brethren, that he might be a merciful and faithful high priest in things *pertaining* to God, to make reconciliation for the sins of the people. For in that he himself hath suffered being tempted, he is able to succour them that are tempted" (He.2:17-18).

"For we have not an high priest which cannot be touched with the feeling of our infirmities; but was in all points tempted like as *we are,* yet without sin. Let us therefore come boldly unto the throne of grace, that we may obtain mercy, and find grace to help in time of need" (He.4:15-16).

"Casting all your care upon him; for he careth for you" (1 Pe.5:7).

"The eternal God *is thy* refuge, and underneath *are* the everlasting arms: and he shall thrust out the enemy from before thee; and shall say, Destroy *them*" (De.33:27).

"The LORD *is* my shepherd; I shall not want. He maketh me to lie down in green pastures: he leadeth me beside the still waters. He restoreth my soul: he leadeth me in the paths of righteousness for his name's sake. Yea, though I walk through the valley of the shadow of death, I will fear no evil: for thou *art* with me; thy rod and thy staff they comfort me. Thou preparest a table before me in the presence of mine enemies: thou anointest my head with oil; my cup runneth over. Surely goodness and mercy shall follow me all the days of my life: and I will dwell in the house of the LORD for ever" (Ps.23:1-6).

"*Oh* how great *is* thy goodness, which thou hast laid up for them that fear thee; *which* thou hast wrought for them that trust in thee before the sons of men!" (Ps.31:19).

"Fear thou not; for I *am* with thee: be not dismayed; for I *am* thy God: I will strengthen thee; yea, I will help thee; yea, I will uphold thee with the right hand of my righteousness" (Is.41:10).

"And *even to your* old age I *am* he; and *even* to hoar hairs will I carry *you:* I have made, and I will bear; even I will carry, and will deliver *you*" (Is.46:4).

g. Hypocrites who repent will receive an honorable name (v.12). Although this is a direct reference to the Israelites, it is applicable to every generation of believers. Isaiah predicted that when the Babylonian exiles were set free and returned to Judah, the nation would still be lying in ruins due to the Babylonian invasion. It would therefore be necessary for the exiles to rebuild their nation. While carrying on the construction of the city, the Israelites would be called the *Repairer of the Breach,* or the *Restorer of Streets to Dwell In.* That is, they would receive honorable mention as a people who were committed to the reconstruction of their nation. So it is with all hypocrites, with all people who repent and turn to the LORD. Immediately upon receiving God's salvation, new believers begin to rebuild the ruins of their lives. They become *Repairers* of the broken walls and lives that their sins have destroyed. They begin to rebuild their paths and lives with the structure of righteousness.

"In him was life; and the life was the light of men" (Jn.1:4).

"Then spake Jesus again unto them, saying, I am the light of the world: he that followeth me shall not walk in darkness, but shall have the light of life" (Jn.8:12).

"If any man serve me, let him follow me; and where I am, there shall also my servant be: if any man serve me, him will *my* Father honour" (Jn.12:26).

"For God, who commanded the light to shine out of darkness, hath shined in our hearts, to *give* the light of the knowledge of the glory of God in the face of Jesus Christ" (2 Co.4:6).

"Wherefore he saith, Awake thou that sleepest, and arise from the dead, and Christ shall give thee light" (Ep.5:14).

"Him that overcometh will I make a pillar in the temple of my God, and he shall go no more out: and I will write upon him the name of my God, and the name of the city of my God, *which is* new Jerusalem, which cometh down out of heaven from my God: and *I will write upon him* my new name" (Re.3:12).

"He shall call upon me, and I will answer him: I *will be* with him in trouble; I will deliver him, and honour him" (Ps.91:15).

"And the Gentiles shall see thy righteousness, and all kings thy glory: and thou shalt be called by a new name, which the mouth of the LORD shall name" (Is.62:2).

4 (58:13-14) **Hypocrite, Duty—Sabbath, Duty—Worship, Duty—LORD's Day, Duty**: hypocrites must know the importance of keeping the Sabbath day holy (vv.13-14). They must not break the Sabbath by doing as they please. Rather, they must keep the day holy by setting it apart as a day of worship and rest (Ex.20:8-11). The Sabbath was intended to be a day when people took delight in the LORD, honoring His Name and His law (Holy Word). The purpose for the Sabbath was not to do one's own thing, but to worship and honor the LORD. No business transactions were to take place on the Sabbath. People were not even to engage in idle, useless talk. The focus was to be upon the LORD and His Word. Three wonderful promises were given to those who kept the Sabbath day holy:

⇒ They would be filled with the joy of the LORD.

⇒ They would ride or be victorious over the high places or enemies of the earth and receive great honor from the LORD.

⇒ They would receive a full share of the inheritance promised to Jacob, the promised land itself (a symbol of heaven).

OUTLINE	SCRIPTURE	SCRIPTURE	OUTLINE

4. The importance of keeping the Sabbath day holy
a. God's commandment
  1) Must not break the Sabbath, doing as you please
  2) Must make the day a delight
  3) Must not engage in idle, useless talk
	13 If thou turn away thy foot from the sabbath, *from* doing thy pleasure on my holy day; and call the sabbath a delight, the holy of the LORD, honourable; and shalt honour him, not doing thine own ways, nor finding thine own pleasure, nor speaking *thine*	*own* words:
		14 Then shalt thou delight thyself in the LORD; and I will cause thee to ride upon the high places of the earth, and feed thee with the heritage of Jacob thy father: for the mouth of the LORD hath spoken *it.*
			b. God's promises
			  1) Joy in the LORD
			  2) Great honor: Will ride or be victorious over the high places or enemies of the earth
			  3) A full share of the inheritance promised to Jacob (the promised land)

Thought 1. Keeping the LORD's Day is the clear commandment of God. God recognizes man's need for both spiritual and physical renewal. Thus spiritual nourishment and physical rest are essential. Without worship, man's spirit

dries up; and without rest, man's body breaks down. Listen to what God's Holy Word says about being faithful in weekly worship with other believers.

"And he came to Nazareth, where he had been brought up: and, as his custom was, he went into the synagogue on the sabbath day, and stood up for to read" (Lu.4:16).

"And upon the first *day* of the week, when the disciples came together to break bread, Paul preached unto them, ready to depart on the morrow; and continued his speech until midnight" (Ac.20:7).

"Now concerning the collection for the saints, as I have given order to the churches of Galatia, even so do ye. Upon the first *day* of the week let every one of you lay by him in store, as *God* hath prospered him, that there be no gatherings when I come" (1 Co.16:1-2).

"Not forsaking the assembling of ourselves together, as the manner of some *is;* but exhorting *one another:* and so much the more, as ye see the day approaching" (He.10:25).

"Remember the sabbath day, to keep it holy. Six days shalt thou labour, and do all thy work: But the seventh day *is* the sabbath of the LORD thy God: *in it* thou shalt not do any work, thou, nor thy son, nor thy daughter, thy manservant, nor thy maidservant, nor thy cattle, nor thy stranger that *is* within thy gates: For *in* six days the LORD made heaven and earth, the sea, and all that in them *is,* and rested the seventh day: wherefore the LORD blessed the sabbath day, and hallowed it" (Ex.20:8-11).

CHAPTER 59

H. The Savior's Message to the Wicked: Guilty of Sin & Separated from God, 59:1-21

1. The problem of sin
  a. God could save the wicked & hear their prayers

  b. God is separated from the wicked
    1) He has to turn His holy face away
    2) He cannot answer them

2. The sinful behavior of the wicked
  a. Abuse, violence, & murder
  b. Lies, gossip, & slander

  c. Injustice, dishonesty, & false testimony
  d. Conceiving plots & carrying out evil acts

  e. Maliciousness & hatred: They are poisonous & deadly like snakes & spiders

  f. Deception: They attempt to conceal or disguise their sins but their attempts are no more than cobwebs—easily seen through by God
  g. Evil works & violent acts

  h. Rushing to the pleasure of sin
  i. Thoughtlessly killing innocent people
  j. Evil thoughts
  k. Destructive behavior
  l. Restless & unjust behavior: A lack of peace

  m. Making crooked paths: Leading others astray, away from peace—becoming a stumbling block

3. The impact of sin on society
  a. Lawlessness: A people who know little justice
  b. Disappointment, darkness, gloom, despair, hopelessness

  c. Spiritual blindness
    1) A groping for support & direction: Like a blind man
    2) A life just like the dead: No spiritual life
  d. Anger & moaning or suffering
  e. Desperation: They looked for

Behold, the LORD'S hand is not shortened, that it cannot save; neither his ear heavy, that it cannot hear:
2 But your iniquities have separated between you and your God, and your sins have hid *his* face from you, that he will not hear.
3 For your hands are defiled with blood, and your fingers with iniquity; your lips have spoken lies, your tongue hath muttered perverseness.
4 None calleth for justice, nor *any* pleadeth for truth: they trust in vanity, and speak lies; they conceive mischief, and bring forth iniquity.
5 They hatch cockatrice' eggs, and weave the spider's web: he that eateth of their eggs dieth, and that which is crushed breaketh out into a viper.
6 Their webs shall not become garments, neither shall they cover themselves with their works: their works *are* works of iniquity, and the act of violence *is* in their hands.
7 Their feet run to evil, and they make haste to shed innocent blood: their thoughts *are* thoughts of iniquity; wasting and destruction *are* in their paths.
8 The way of peace they know not; and *there is* no judgment in their goings: they have made them crooked paths: whosoever goeth therein shall not know peace.
9 Therefore is judgment far from us, neither doth justice overtake us: we wait for light, but behold obscurity; for brightness, *but* we walk in darkness.
10 We grope for the wall like the blind, and we grope as if *we had* no eyes: we stumble at noonday as in the night; *we are* in desolate places as dead *men.*
11 We roar all like bears, and mourn sore like doves: we look for judgment, but

there is none; for salvation, *but* it is far off from us.
12 For our transgressions are multiplied before thee, and our sins testify against us: for our transgressions *are* with us; and *as for* our iniquities, we know them;
13 In transgressing and lying against the LORD, and departing away from our God, speaking oppression and revolt, conceiving and uttering from the heart words of falsehood.
14 And judgment is turned away backward, and justice standeth afar off: for truth is fallen in the street, and equity cannot enter.
15 Yea, truth faileth; and he *that* departeth from evil maketh himself a prey: and the LORD saw *it,* and it displeased him that *there was* no judgment.
16 And he saw that *there was* no man, and wondered that *there was* no intercessor: therefore his arm brought salvation unto him; and his righteousness, it sustained him.
17 For he put on righteousness as a breastplate, and an helmet of salvation upon his head; and he put on the garments of vengeance *for* clothing, and was clad with zeal as a cloke.
18 According to *their* deeds, accordingly he will repay, fury to his adversaries, recompence to his enemies; to the islands he will repay recompence.
19 So shall they fear the name of the LORD from the west, and his glory from the rising of the sun. When the enemy shall come in like a flood, the Spirit of the LORD shall lift up a standard against him.
20 And the Redeemer shall come to Zion, and unto them that turn from transgression in Jacob, saith the LORD.
21 As for me, this *is* my covenant with them, saith the LORD; My spirit that *is* upon thee, and my words which I have put in thy mouth, shall not depart out of thy mouth, nor out of the mouth of thy seed, nor out of the mouth of thy seed's seed, saith the LORD, from henceforth and for ever.

justice & deliverance, but their search was futile

4. The need for confession of sins: Offered as a prayer by Isaiah
  a. They must confess their many sins: Acknowledge they were sinners
  b. They must confess their rebellion, their turning away from the LORD
  c. They must confess their oppressive behavior & lies

  d. They must confess their unjust, unrighteous, dishonest behavior: The total absence of integrity & truth

  e. They must confess their persecution of the righteous: The lack of justice in the land

5. The sad truth about the wicked earth
  a. The LORD scanned the earth for an intercessor: He found no one
  b. The LORD Himself set out to intercede, save His people

6. The judgment of the wicked
  a. God's preparation: He clothed Himself…
    1) In righteousness & salvation
    2) In vengeance & zeal

  b. God's judgment
    1) He will execute perfect justice: Repay exactly what is due
    2) He will judge all enemies, all the earth (islands)

7. The wonderful promise of salvation & glory: A picture of the Messiah's kingdom
  a. The people will respect the LORD's name & honor His glory

  b. The Redeemer will come to Zion (Jerusalem): To bring God's glory to earth for all who repent
  c. The Redeemer will fill the repentant with His Spirit & His Words

DIVISION VI

THE PROPHECIES OF THE GREAT DELIVERER: THE SUFFERING SERVANT OF GOD, THE SAVIOR OF THE WORLD, 49:1–59:21

H. The Savior's Message to the Wicked: Guilty of Sin and Separated from God, 59:1-21

(59:1-21) **Introduction**: the breakup of a loving relationship is a tragic and heartrending experience. When two people genuinely love each other, their being apart causes them deep pain and suffering. Their hearts long for the companionship of the person they love. But what is most damaging, even devastating, is when one of the partners ceases to love the other, becoming hostile, and severing the relationship. Unbearable pain usually surges through the heart of the rejected partner. Unfaithfulness—whether caused by disloyalty, betrayal, breach of trust, deceitfulness, infidelity, or treachery—oftentimes enters the picture. Few experiences cause as much anguish as *rejected love* and *broken trust*. Just imagine the pain and heartbreak God endures *every* day as a result of people's rejection and unfaithfulness! A broken relationship with God is the subject of the present passage. The entire world has become guilty of wickedness, and sin has separated the human race from God. This is, *The Savior's Message to the Wicked: Guilty of Sin and Separated from God*, 59:1-21.

1. The problem of sin (vv.1-2).
2. The sinful behavior of the wicked (vv.3-8).
3. The impact of sin on society (vv.9-11).
4. Their confession needed for sins: offered as a prayer by Isaiah (vv.12-15).
5. The sad truth about the wicked earth (v.16).
6. The judgment of the wicked (vv.17-18).
7. The wonderful promise of salvation and glory: a picture of the Messiah's kingdom (vv.19-21).

[1] (59:1-2) **Wickedness, Results, Separation from God—Sin, Results, Separation from God—Evil, Results, Separation from God—Separation, from God, Caused by—Prayer, Unanswered, Caused by—God, Separation from, Caused by—Salvation, Missed by, the Wicked—Tragedy, Missing Salvation—Message, of God, to the Wicked—Face, of God, Hid**: the wicked of the world have a problem of terrible and disastrous proportions: their sins have separated them from God. The Israelites were perplexed because God had not delivered them from their hardships and distress. Apparently they had been crying out in prayer for some time, seeking the LORD's help. But no help had been forthcoming. They simply could not understand why, so God sent His prophet Isaiah to explain.

a. First, the people needed to understand one unmistakable fact: God could save them. He could hear and answer their prayers. His arm (power) was never too short to reach out to help His people. He had the power to embrace them and deliver them from any hardship, difficulty, circumstance, or enemy. Moreover, His ear was not deaf. It was very sensitive and alert. God always heard every word spoken by them. Moreover, He was as ready and willing as ever to hear the prayers of His people. And He would immediately act to save them, but for one problem: sin.

b. Sin is a barrier that separates people from God (v.2). The wicked are *separated, alienated* from God due to their sins. When people lie, steal, or abuse and oppress others, God has to turn His face away from them because of their terrible behavior. Why? Because God is holy. He dwells in perfect righteousness, and He loves, cares for, and has deep concern for every human being. He longs for everyone to know the fullness of love, joy, and peace. Consequently, He will not tolerate wickedness or the mistreatment of others by any means, be it thievery, immorality, greed, covetousness, or any other oppressive acts. When people sin, they choose to live apart from God. For that reason, God turns His face away and will not answer their prayers. No matter how religious people may be or how strongly they profess to trust God, their wicked behavior alienates them from God, and He will not respond to their pleas. Furthermore the wicked will reap exactly what they have sown—oppression and mistreatment by their enemies.

OUTLINE	SCRIPTURE	SCRIPTURE	OUTLINE
1. The problem of sin	Behold, the LORD'S hand is	separated between you and	wicked
a. God could save the wicked & hear their prayers	not shortened, that it cannot save; neither his ear heavy, that it cannot hear:	your God, and your sins have hid *his* face from you, that he will not	1) He has to turn His holy face away
b. God is separated from the	2 But your iniquities have	hear.	2) He cannot answer them

"Ye ask, and receive not, because ye ask amiss, that ye may consume *it* upon your lusts" (Js.4:3).

"I denounce unto you this day, that ye shall surely perish, *and that* ye shall not prolong *your* days upon the land, whither thou passest over Jordan to go to possess it" (De.30:18).

"If I regard iniquity in my heart, the Lord will not hear *me*" (Ps.66:18).

"Because I have called, and ye refused; I have stretched out my hand, and no man regarded; But ye have set at nought all my counsel, and would none of my reproof: I also will laugh at your calamity; I will mock when your fear cometh; When your fear cometh as desolation, and your destruction cometh as a whirlwind; when distress and anguish cometh upon you. Then shall they call upon me, but I will not answer; they shall seek me early, but they shall not find me: For that they hated knowledge, and did not choose the fear of the LORD: They would none of my counsel: they despised all my reproof. Therefore shall they eat of the fruit of their own way, and be filled with their own devices" (Pr.1:24-31).

"Whoso stoppeth his ears at the cry of the poor, he also shall cry himself, but shall not be heard" (Pr.21:13).

"He that turneth away his ear from hearing the law, even his prayer *shall be* abomination" (Pr.28:9).

"And when ye spread forth your hands, I will hide mine eyes from you: yea, when ye make many prayers, I will not hear: your hands are full of blood" (Is.1:15).

"And *there is* none that calleth upon thy name, that stirreth up himself to take hold of thee: for thou hast hid thy face from us, and hast consumed us, because of our iniquities" (Is.64:7).

"And the heathen shall know that the house of Israel went into captivity for their iniquity: because they trespassed against me, therefore hid I my face from them, and gave them into the hand of their enemies: so fell they all by the sword" (Eze.39:23).

"They shall go with their flocks and with their herds to seek the LORD; but they shall not find *him*; he hath withdrawn himself from them" (Ho.5:6).

"Then shall they cry unto the LORD, but he will not hear them: he will even hide his face from them at that time, as they have behaved themselves ill in their doings" (Mi.3:4).

2 (59:3-8) **Sins, List of—Wickedness, Behavior of—Evil, Behavior of—Separation from God, Caused by—Alienation, from God, Caused by—World, Wickedness of, Described—Sin, Described, Thirteen Behaviors—Guilt, Caused by**: the wicked are guilty of the most terrible sins and evil. What follows shows and explains in far more detail why God must hide His face from the wicked. Thinking through this list of sinful behavior should arouse everyone's heart to combat all forms of wickedness. Wicked behavior damages lives, sometimes causing terrible pain, suffering, and even death. And wickedness always cuts the heart of God to the core, arousing His anger. Take just a moment and think about each of these wicked behaviors, all the misery, heartache, and anguish they cause:

⇒ People defile their hands through abuse, murder, and other acts of violence (v.3).
⇒ People speak lies, gossip, and other poison with lips that deceive (v.3).
⇒ People give false testimony, promoting injustice and dishonesty in the courts (v.4).
⇒ People scheme and carry out evil plots in homes, businesses, and elsewhere (Js.1:14-15; 4:1-2).
⇒ People act out of malice or hatred and become as deadly as snakes or spiders (v.5).
⇒ People deceive themselves and others with the intent to hide sin, forgetting that God sees through every deception (v.6).
⇒ People aggressively spread evil and violence, causing individuals, businesses, and even entire communities to fear for their lives and property.
⇒ People are reckless in their pursuit of fleshly, forbidden pleasures and increasingly more and more possessions, property, and wealth (v.7).
⇒ People kill senselessly, cheapening the value of life.
⇒ People flood the mind with evil thoughts—immoral, abusive, vengeful, covetous, greedy, selfish thoughts—that give rise to sinful, wicked behavior.
⇒ People are destructive, devastating both lives and property.
⇒ People act unjustly, upsetting the peace and cause chaos within the human heart and within society (v. 8).
⇒ People mislead others and become a stumbling block in life (v.8b).

OUTLINE	SCRIPTURE	SCRIPTURE	OUTLINE
2. The sinful behavior of the wicked a. Abuse, violence, & murder b. Lies, gossip, & slander	3 For your hands are defiled with blood, and your fingers with iniquity; your lips have spoken lies, your tongue hath muttered perverseness.	become garments, neither shall they cover themselves with their works: their works *are* works of iniquity, and the act of violence *is* in their hands.	conceal or disguise their sins, but their attempts are no more than cobwebs—easily seen through by God g. Evil works & violent acts
c. Injustice, dishonesty, & false testimony d. Conceiving plots & carrying out evil acts	4 None calleth for justice, nor *any* pleadeth for truth: they trust in vanity, and speak lies; they conceive mischief, and bring forth iniquity.	7 Their feet run to evil, and they make haste to shed innocent blood: their thoughts *are* thoughts of iniquity; wasting and destruction *are* in their paths.	h. Rushing to the pleasure of sin i. Thoughtlessly killing innocent people j. Evil thoughts k. Destructive behavior
e. Maliciousness & hatred: They are poisonous & deadly like snakes & spiders	5 They hatch cockatrice' eggs, and weave the spider's web: he that eateth of their eggs dieth, and that which is crushed breaketh out into a viper.	8 The way of peace they know not; and *there is* no judgment in their goings: they have made them crooked paths: whosoever goeth therein shall not know peace.	l. Restless & unjust behavior: A lack of peace m. Making crooked paths: Leading others astray, away from peace—becoming a stumbling block
f. Deception: They attempt to	6 Their webs shall not	in shall not know peace.	

Thought 1. A person who sincerely evaluates even this limited list of wicked behaviors can come to only one conclusion: sin is universal and we are all guilty of sin. The human heart is sinful and selfish beyond comprehension. Our only hope is in the mercy and compassion of the LORD.

"For from within, out of the heart of men, proceed evil thoughts, adulteries, fornications, murders, Thefts, covetousness, wickedness, deceit, lasciviousness, an evil eye, blasphemy, pride, foolishness: All these evil things come from within, and defile the man" (Mk.7:21-23).

"For all have sinned, and come short of the glory of God" (Ro.3:23).

"If we say that we have no sin, we deceive ourselves, and the truth is not in us" (1 Jn.1:8).

"And GOD saw that the wickedness of man *was* great in the earth, and *that* every imagination of the thoughts of his heart *was* only evil continually" (Ge.6:5).

"There is no man that sinneth not" (1 K.8:46).

"Have the workers of iniquity no knowledge? who eat up my people *as* they eat bread: they have not called upon God" (Ps.53:4).

"Who can say, I have made my heart clean, I am pure from my sin?" (Pr.20:9).

"All we like sheep have gone astray; we have turned every one to his own way; and the LORD hath laid on him the iniquity of us all" (Is.53:6).

"But we are all as an unclean *thing,* and all our righteousnesses *are* as filthy rags; and we all do fade as a leaf; and our iniquities, like the wind, have taken us away" (Is.64:6).

---

3 (59:9-11) **Society, Impact upon, by Sin—Sin, Results of, Upon Society—Wickedness, Results of, Fivefold—Evil, Results, Fivefold—Society, Results of Sin**: the wicked have a terrible and widespread impact on society. A quick glance at the sins above shows their horrible effects. So much evil is committed every day within every community that many people's hearts have become hardened to scenes of immorality, lawlessness, and violence. As a consequence, the news media and the public pay attention only to the most savage or unexpected acts of evil or violence. And unfortunately, as people become increasingly desensitized to the immorality and crime around them, society is slowly being consumed by the cancer of wickedness and sin. Note the impact of sin on society.

OUTLINE	SCRIPTURE	SCRIPTURE	OUTLINE

3. The impact of sin on society
a. Lawlessness: A people who know little justice
b. Disappointment, darkness, gloom, despair, hopelessness
c. Spiritual blindness
  1) A groping for support & direction: Like a
	9 Therefore is judgment far from us, neither doth justice overtake us: we wait for light, but behold obscurity; for brightness, *but* we walk in darkness. 10 We grope for the wall like the blind, and we grope as if *we had* no eyes: we stumble	at noonday as in the night; *we are* in desolate places as dead *men.* 11 We roar all like bears, and mourn sore like doves: we look for judgment, but *there is* none; for salvation, *but* it is far off from us.	blind man
			  2) A life just like the dead: No spiritual life
			d. Anger & moaning or suffering
			e. Desperation: They looked for justice & deliverance, but their search was futile

a. Wicked people bring lawlessness to society (v.9a). Lawless behavior such as stealing, assaulting, and killing disturbs the peace. Lawlessness is the force behind the sins of oppression, injustice, and unrighteousness. If rebellious and unmanageable people are given free rein, they soon take over communities and chaos and turmoil follow. Soon thereafter the stronger, more domineering individuals begin to control the communities and abuse the citizens. In Isaiah's day and throughout the years before the Babylonian captivity, many of the people were living wicked lives. Even when a godly ruler took the throne, most of the people continued in their lawless ways. As a result, little justice or righteousness could be found within society. Both the people and the courts were gripped by a spirit of injustice. The majority of people were mistreating their neighbors, leaving the minority to do what was right.

"For the wrath of God is revealed from heaven against all ungodliness and unrighteousness of men, who hold the truth in unrighteousness" (Ro.1:18).

"But glory, honour, and peace, to every man that worketh good, to the Jew first, and also to the Gentile: For there is no respect of persons with God. For as many as have sinned without law shall also perish without law: and as many as have sinned in the law shall be judged by the law; (For not the hearers of the law *are* just before God, but the doers of the law shall be justified. For when the Gentiles, which have not the law, do by nature the things contained in the law, these, having not the law, are a law unto themselves: Which shew the work of the law written in their hearts, their conscience also bearing witness, and *their* thoughts the mean while accusing or else excusing one another;) In the day when God shall judge the secrets of men by Jesus Christ according to my gospel. Behold, thou art called a Jew, and restest in the law, and makest thy boast of God, And knowest *his* will, and approvest the things that are more excellent, being instructed out of the law" (Ro.2:10-18).

"For neither they themselves who are circumcised keep the law; but desire to have you circumcised, that they may glory in your flesh" (Ga.6:13).

"But he that doeth wrong shall receive for the wrong which he hath done: and there is no respect of persons" (Col.3:25).

"In flaming fire taking vengeance on them that know not God, and that obey not the gospel of our Lord Jesus Christ: Who shall be punished with everlasting destruction from the presence of the Lord, and from the glory of his power; When he shall come to be glorified in his saints, and to be admired in all them that believe (because our testimony among you was believed) in that day. Wherefore also we pray always for you, that our God would count you worthy of *this* calling, and fulfil all the good pleasure of *his* goodness, and the work of faith with power: That the name of our Lord Jesus Christ may be glorified in you, and ye in him, according to the grace of our God and the Lord Jesus Christ" (2 Th.1:8-12).

"And shall receive the reward of unrighteousness, *as* they that count it pleasure to riot in the day-time. Spots *they are* and blemishes, sporting themselves with their own deceivings while they feast with you; Having eyes full of adultery, and that cannot cease from sin; beguiling unstable souls: an heart they have exercised with covetous practices; cursed children" (2 Pe.2:13-14).

"All unrighteousness is sin" (1 Jn.5:17).

"But we know that the law *is* good, if a man use it lawfully; Knowing this, that the law is not made for a righteous man, but for the lawless and disobedient, for the ungodly and for sinners, for unholy and profane, for murderers of fathers and murderers of mothers, for manslayers, For whoremongers, for them that defile themselves with mankind, for menstealers, for liars, for perjured persons, and if there be any other thing that is contrary to sound doctrine" (1 Ti.1:8-10).

"The wicked, through the pride of his countenance, will not seek *after God:* God *is* not in all his thoughts" (Ps.10:4).

"The transgression of the wicked saith within my heart, *that there is* no fear of God before his eyes" (Ps.36:1).

"An unjust man *is* an abomination to the just: and *he that is* upright in the way *is* abomination to the wicked" (Pr.29:27).

"And moreover I saw under the sun the place of judgment, *that* wickedness *was* there; and the place of righteousness, *that* iniquity *was* there" (Ecc.3:16).

b. Disappointment, despair, and hopelessness gripped society due to all the wicked, lawless behavior. The few moral and righteous people within the nation looked for a bright light, for some hope, but they saw only darkness. Not even a gleam of light appeared on the horizon. With the greater part of society walking in the darkness of sin, there was little hope for a just or righteous society. A spirit of gloom hung in the air. Personal freedom and the right to move about unhampered were both endangered. People had to be cautious and suspicious of others at all times in order to protect themselves. Doubt, uneasiness, restlessness, and fear gripped the people's hearts because of the wickedness and violence sweeping across the land.

"But if thine eye be evil, thy whole body shall be full of darkness. If therefore the light that is in thee be darkness, how great *is* that darkness!" (Mt.6:23).

"Let them alone: they be blind leaders of the blind. And if the blind lead the blind, both shall fall into the ditch" (Mt.15:14).

"And this is the condemnation, that light is come into the world, and men loved darkness rather than light, because their deeds were evil" (Jn.3:19).

"The night is far spent, the day is at hand: let us therefore cast off the works of darkness, and let us put on the armour of light" (Ro.13:12).

"That at that time ye were without Christ, being aliens from the commonwealth of Israel, and strangers from the covenants of promise, having no hope, and without God in the world: But now in Christ Jesus ye who sometimes were far off are made nigh by the blood of Christ" (Ep.2:12-13).

"If we say that we have fellowship with him, and walk in darkness, we lie, and do not the truth" (1 Jn.1:6).

"And in those days shall men seek death, and shall not find it; and shall desire to die, and death shall flee from them" (Re.9:6).

"And Moses spake so unto the children of Israel: but they hearkened not unto Moses for anguish of spirit, and for cruel bondage" (Ex.6:9).

"My days are swifter than a weaver's shuttle, and are spent without hope" (Jb.7:6).

"And where *is* now my hope? as for my hope, who shall see it?" (Jb.17:15).

"They know not, neither will they understand; they walk on in darkness: all the foundations of the earth are out of course" (Ps.82:5).

"The way of the wicked *is* as darkness: they know not at what they stumble" (Pr.4:19).

"But Zion said, The LORD hath forsaken me, and my Lord hath forgotten me" (Is.49:14).

"Wherefore their way shall be unto them as slippery *ways* in the darkness: they shall be driven on, and fall therein: for I will bring evil upon them, *even* the year of their visitation, saith the LORD" (Je.23:12).

"Then he said unto me, Son of man, these bones are the whole house of Israel: behold, they say, Our bones are dried, and our hope is lost: we are cut off for our parts" (Eze.37:11).

"I *am* the man *that* hath seen affliction by the rod of his wrath" (La.3:1).

c. Spiritual blindness is one of the major results of sin in society (v.10). When people forget God and become corrupt, they are like blind men trying to find their way in the dark. They stumble and grope about trying to hang on to something to keep from falling and injuring themselves. But being blind, they cannot even know if they are going in the right direction, much less protect themselves from harm. The spiritually blind can only hope to stumble along and stay on a road. Even so they are totally uncertain of what is ahead. In fact, their future is no more certain than that of the dead. They are *spiritually* blind, without God in this world, which means they are without hope. To be without God is to be left to plow through life all alone in the dark. To be without God is to be without a moral compass, without guidance and direction, without encouragement and hope.

"But if thine eye be evil, thy whole body shall be full of darkness. If therefore the light that is in thee be darkness, how great *is* that darkness!" (Mt.6:23).

"Let them alone: they be blind leaders of the blind. And if the blind lead the blind, both shall fall into the ditch" (Mt.15:14).

"But their minds were blinded: for until this day remaineth the same vail untaken away in the reading of the old testament; which *vail* is done away in Christ. But even unto this day, when Moses is read, the vail is upon their heart. Nevertheless when it shall turn to the Lord, the vail shall be taken away" (2 Co.3:14-16).

"In whom the god of this world hath blinded the minds of them which believe not, lest the light of the glorious gospel of Christ, who is the image of God, should shine unto them. For we preach not ourselves, but Christ Jesus the Lord; and ourselves your servants for Jesus' sake" (2 Co.4:4-5).

"This I say therefore, and testify in the Lord, that ye henceforth walk not as other Gentiles walk, in the vanity of their mind, Having the understanding darkened, being alienated from the life of God through the ignorance that is in them, because of the blindness of their heart: Who being past feeling have given themselves over unto lasciviousness, to work all uncleanness with greediness" (Ep.4:17-19).

"But he that hateth his brother is in darkness, and walketh in darkness, and knoweth not whither he goeth, because that darkness hath blinded his eyes" (1 Jn.2:11).

d. Sin always causes suffering in society leading to hostility or mourning (v.11a). When mistreated, many people retaliate in anger, seeking revenge. Isaiah said that a number of people were growling like bears in response to the injustices done them. Others moaned in their suffering, sounding like sorrowful doves. Wickedness is the source of immeasurable anguish and misery. Whether the infidelity of a husband, the assault and battery of a thief, the abuse of a child, or a false accusation—wicked behavior always harms someone, and in most cases many people.

e. Sinful behavior dooms people, both individually and as a society (v.11b). People may look for justice and deliverance, but if they continue in sin, their search will be futile. The testimony of Isaiah was that his generation looked for justice but found none. They looked for deliverance, but it was far, far away. Why? Because of the wickedness of the people. They treated others unjustly, so they suffered injustice. They refused to help the needy, so God refused to help them in their hour of need. What they had sowed, they reaped. So it is with every person in society. The life we sow is the life we will reap. If we sow wickedness, we will reap wickedness. If we sow rejection of God, we will reap God's rejection. If we choose to live apart from God, we will be separated from Him eternally. Wickedness dooms both people and society.

"O Jerusalem, Jerusalem, *thou* that killest the prophets, and stonest them which are sent unto thee, how often would I have gathered thy children together, even as a hen gathereth her chickens under *her* wings, and ye would not! Behold, your house is left unto you desolate" (Mt.23:37-38).

"And they made a calf in those days, and offered sacrifice unto the idol, and rejoiced in the works of their own hands. Then God turned, and gave them up to worship the host of heaven; as it is written in the book of the prophets, O ye house of Israel, have ye offered to me slain beasts and sacrifices *by the space of* forty years in the wilderness?" (Ac.7:41-42).

"For the invisible things of him from the creation of the world are clearly seen, being understood by the things that are made, *even* his eternal power and Godhead; so that they are without excuse: Because that, when they knew God, they glorified *him* not as God, neither were thankful; but became vain in their imaginations, and their foolish heart was darkened. Professing themselves to be wise, they became fools, And changed the glory of the uncorruptible God into an image made like to corruptible man, and to birds, and fourfooted beasts, and creeping things. Wherefore God also gave them up to uncleanness through the lusts of their own hearts, to dishonour their own bodies between themselves: Who changed the truth of God into a lie, and worshipped and served the creature more than the Creator, who is blessed for ever. Amen" (Ro.1:20-25).

"Be not deceived; God is not mocked: for whatsoever a man soweth, that shall he also reap" (Ga.6:7).

"And be not ye like your fathers, and like your brethren, which trespassed against the LORD God of their fathers, *who* therefore gave them up to desolation, as ye see" (2 Chr.30:7).

"So I gave them up unto their own hearts' lust: *and* they walked in their own counsels" (Ps.81:12).

"Then shall they call upon me, but I will not answer; they shall seek me early, but they shall not find me: For that they hated knowledge, and did not choose the fear of the LORD: They would none of my counsel: they despised all my reproof. Therefore shall they eat of the fruit of their own way, and be filled with their own devices. For the turning away of the simple shall slay them, and the prosperity of fools shall destroy them" (Pr.1:28-32).

---

4 (59:12-15) **Confession, of Sin, Essential—Sin, Confession of, Essential—Acknowledgment, of Sins, Essential— Rebellion, Remedy of, Confession—Oppression, Remedy of- Solution to, Confession—Evil, Solution to, Confession—Wickedness, Duty, to Confess**: the wicked have only one hope, and that is to confess their sins. Note that these few verses are a prayer that Isaiah himself offered up on behalf of the people. With a spirit of wickedness sweeping throughout the land and controlling society, confession before the LORD was desperately needed. The people needed to make five confessions:

⇒ They needed to confess their many sins (v.12). The three most common Hebrew words used for wicked behavior are used in this verse: *transgressions*, *sins,* and *iniquities.* People must acknowledge the fact that they are sinners who have committed many sins and come far, far short of God's glory.

⇒ They needed to confess their hypocrisy and their rebellion against the LORD. They had to admit that they had transgressed by turning away from the LORD after professing to be His followers (v.13).

⇒ They needed to confess their oppressive behavior and lies (v.13b).

⇒ They needed to confess their unrighteous and dishonest behavior (v.14). They had to acknowledge and repent of their lack of fairness, truth, and integrity in their lives.

⇒ They needed to confess their hypocrisy and their persecution of the righteous (v.15). Some who had turned away from their evil ways became prey to others. The wicked persecuted them. Note the LORD's response: He saw all of their wicked behavior and was very displeased, for there was no justice in society, including in the courts and government of the nation. The only hope for the wicked of that day or any generation is to confess their sins.

OUTLINE	SCRIPTURE	SCRIPTURE	OUTLINE
4. The need for confession of sins: Offered as a prayer by Isaiah a. They must confess their many sins: Acknowledge they were sinners b. They must confess their rebellion, their turning away from the LORD c. They must confess their oppressive behavior & lies	12 For our transgressions are multiplied before thee, and our sins testify against us: for our transgressions *are* with us; and *as for* our iniquities, we know them; 13 In transgressing and lying against the LORD, and departing away from our God, speaking oppression and revolt, conceiving and uttering from the heart words of	falsehood. 14 And judgment is turned away backward, and justice standeth afar off: for truth is fallen in the street, and equity cannot enter. 15 Yea, truth faileth; and he *that* departeth from evil maketh himself a prey: and the LORD saw *it,* and it displeased him that *there was* no judgment.	d. They must confess their unjust, unrighteous, dishonest behavior: The total absence of integrity & truth e. They must confess their persecution of the righteous: The lack of justice in the land

"Blessed *are* they that mourn: for they shall be comforted" (Mt.5:4).

"Repent therefore of this thy wickedness, and pray God, if perhaps the thought of thine heart may be forgiven thee" (Ac.8:22).

"If we confess our sins, he is faithful and just to forgive us *our* sins, and to cleanse us from all unrighteousness" (1 Jn.1:9).

"If my people, which are called by my name, shall humble themselves, and pray, and seek my face, and turn from their wicked ways; then will I hear from heaven, and will forgive their sin, and will heal their land" (2 Chr.7:14).

"Now therefore make confession unto the LORD God of your fathers, and do his pleasure: and separate yourselves from the people of the land, and from the strange wives" (Ezr.10:11).

"He that covereth his sins shall not prosper: but whoso confesseth and forsaketh *them* shall have mercy" (Pr.28:13).

"Let the wicked forsake his way, and the unrighteous man his thoughts: and let him return unto the LORD, and he will have mercy upon him; and to our God, for he will abundantly pardon" (Is.55:7).

"Only acknowledge thine iniquity, that thou hast transgressed against the LORD thy God, and hast scattered thy ways to the strangers under every green tree, and ye have not obeyed my voice, saith the LORD" (Je.3:13).

"Cast away from you all your transgressions, whereby ye have transgressed; and make you a new heart and a new spirit: for why will ye die, O house of Israel?" (Eze.18:31).

"Therefore also now, saith the LORD, turn ye *even* to me with all your heart, and with fasting, and with weeping, and with mourning" (Joel 2:12).

5 (59:16) **Intercessor, Lack of—Intercessor, No—Intercession, of the LORD—Salvation, Source, LORD's Intercession—God, Disappointment of, No Intercessor—Disappointment, of God—Salvation, Source—World, Tragedy of, No Intercessor—Prayer, Tragedy of, No Intercessor**: the wicked had to acknowledge the disturbing fact that there was no intercessor, no savior among men. The only Savior was the LORD Himself. In looking down upon earth at the wretched state of man, God saw an appalling picture. The whole earth was depraved, gripped by a spirit of wickedness. There was no intercessor, no one who could save it. Only God Himself could be the intercessor, the One to pay the penalty for sin and provide salvation for the people. For this reason the LORD stepped into the world to save the human race through His mighty power and righteousness. This He did through His Son, His Servant, the Lord Jesus Christ. Christ alone made intercession for the transgressions of all mankind (53:12).

OUTLINE	SCRIPTURE	SCRIPTURE	OUTLINE
5. The sad truth about the wicked earth a. The LORD scanned the earth for an intercessor: He found	16 And he saw that *there was* no man, and wondered that *there was* no intercessor: therefore	his arm brought salvation unto him; and his righteousness, it sustained him.	no one b. The LORD Himself set out to intercede, save His people

"Therefore will I divide him *a portion* with the great, and he shall divide the spoil with the strong; because he hath poured out his soul unto death: and he was numbered with the transgressors; and he bare the sin of many, and made intercession for the transgressors" (Is.53:12).

"Who *is* he that condemneth? *It is* Christ that died, yea rather, that is risen again, who is even at the right hand of God, who also maketh intercession for us" (Ro.8:34).

"Wherefore in all things it behoved him to be made like unto *his* brethren, that he might be a merciful and faithful high priest [intercessor] in things *pertaining* to God, to make reconciliation for the sins of the people" (He.2:17).

"Wherefore, holy brethren, partakers of the heavenly calling, consider the Apostle and High Priest of our profession, Christ Jesus" (He.3:1).

"Seeing then that we have a great high priest [intercessor], that is passed into the heavens, Jesus the Son of God, let us hold fast *our* profession. For we have not an high priest which cannot be touched with the feeling of our infirmities; but was in all points tempted like as *we are, yet* without sin" (He.4:14-15).

"For every high priest taken from among men is ordained for men in things *pertaining* to God, that he may offer both gifts and sacrifices for sins: Who can have compassion on the ignorant, and on them that are out of the way; for that he himself also is compassed with infirmity. And by reason hereof he ought, as for the people, so also for himself, to offer for sins. And no man taketh this honour unto himself, but he that is called of God, as *was* Aaron. So also Christ glorified not himself to be made an high priest; but he that said unto him, Thou art my Son, to day have I begotten thee" (He.5:1-5).

"Which *hope* we have as an anchor of the soul, both sure and stedfast, and which entereth into that within the veil; Whither the forerunner is for us entered, *even* Jesus, made an high priest for ever after the order of Melchisedec" (He.6:19-20).

"Wherefore he is able also to save them to the uttermost that come unto God by him, seeing he ever liveth to make intercession for them. For such an high priest became us, *who is* holy, harmless, undefiled, separate from sinners, and made higher than the heavens; Who needeth not daily, as those high priests, to offer up sacrifice, first for his own sins, and then for the people's: for this he did once, when he offered up himself" (He.7:25-27).

"But Christ being come an high priest of good things to come, by a greater and more perfect tabernacle, not made with hands, that is to say, not of this building; Neither by the blood of goats and calves, but by his own blood he entered in once into the holy place, having obtained eternal redemption *for us*. For if the blood of bulls and of goats, and the ashes of an heifer sprinkling the unclean, sanctifieth to the purifying of the flesh: How much more shall the blood of Christ, who through the eternal Spirit offered himself without spot to God, purge your conscience from dead works to serve the living God?" (He.9:11-14).

"And *having* an high priest over the house of God; Let us draw near with a true heart in full assurance of faith, having our hearts sprinkled from an evil conscience, and our bodies washed with pure water" (He.10:21-22).

6 (59:17-18) **Judgment, of Whom, the Wicked—Wicked, Judgment of—Judgment, Basis of—Judicial Judgment, Surety of**: the wicked will face the judgment of God. Note the dramatic scene of God's coming judgment. Like a well-armed soldier, the LORD will prepare Himself to execute judgment on earth. He will put on righteousness for a breastplate and salvation for a helmet. The *breastplate of righteousness* protects the heart. God's heart is set on justice. Thus, when He comes to judge, the basis of judgment will be righteousness. If people have lived righteously, they will not bear the judgment of God; but if they have lived unrighteously, they will suffer judgment. The *helmet of salvation* signifies that God will deliver the righteous before judgment falls on the earth. The helmet of salvation protects the head, the mind. In God's case, His mind is focused on salvation, the deliverance of His people and the world from wickedness. Therefore, He will save His people before His judgment falls upon the wicked.

God will also put on the clothing of vengeance and wrap Himself in a cloak of zeal in executing justice and judgment on earth. Throughout history, the LORD has insisted that vengeance belongs to Him. When He is ready, He will execute a just retribution against all the wicked who have defied, denied, and rejected Him as well as those who have cursed His holy name and persecuted His people. And He will do so with righteous fury. In the Day of Judgment, on a set day, God will execute perfect justice (v.18). All people will be paid exactly what is due them—nothing more and nothing less. No one will escape. All foes, even the *islands* (the distant lands of the earth) will receive full payment for their sinful behavior. All the earth will face God's wrath and judgment.

OUTLINE	SCRIPTURE	SCRIPTURE	OUTLINE

6. The judgment of the wicked
a. God's preparation: He clothed Himself...
   1) In righteousness & salvation
   2) In vengeance & zeal
	17 For he put on righteousness as a breastplate, and an helmet of salvation upon his head; and he put on the garments of vengeance *for* clothing, and was clad with zeal as a	cloke.
		18 According to *their* deeds, accordingly he will repay, fury to his adversaries, recompence to his enemies; to the islands he will repay recompence.
			b. God's judgment
			  1) He will execute perfect justice: Repay exactly what is due
			  2) He will judge all enemies, all the earth (islands)

"He that believeth on the Son hath everlasting life: and he that believeth not the Son shall not see life; but the wrath of God abideth on him" (Jn.3:36).

"For the wrath of God is revealed from heaven against all ungodliness and unrighteousness of men, who hold the truth in unrighteousness" (Ro.1:18).

"But unto them that are contentious, and do not obey the truth, but obey unrighteousness, indignation and wrath, Tribulation and anguish, upon every soul of man that doeth evil, of the Jew first, and also of the Gentile" (Ro.2:8-9).

"And not only so, but we glory in tribulations also: knowing that tribulation worketh patience; And patience, experience; and experience, hope: And hope maketh not ashamed; because the love of God is shed abroad in our hearts by the Holy Ghost which is given unto us. For when we were yet without strength, in due time Christ died for the ungodly" (Ro.5:3-6).

"For we must all appear before the judgment seat of Christ; that every one may receive the things done in his body, according to that he hath done, whether it be good or bad" (2 Co.5:10).

"And Enoch also, the seventh from Adam, prophesied of these, saying, Behold, the Lord cometh with ten thousands of his saints, To execute judgment upon all, and to convince all that are ungodly among them of all their ungodly deeds which they have ungodly committed, and of all their hard speeches which ungodly sinners have spoken against him" (Jude 1:14-15).

"Behold, I will cast her into a bed, and them that commit adultery with her into great tribulation, except they repent of their deeds. And I will kill her children with death; and all the churches shall know that I am he which searcheth the reins and hearts: and I will give unto every one of you according to your works" (Re.2:22-23).

"And I saw a great white throne, and him that sat on it, from whose face the earth and the heaven fled away; and there was found no place for them. And I saw the dead, small and great, stand before God; and the books were opened: and another book was opened, which is the book of life: and the dead were judged out of those things which were written in the books, according to their works. And the sea gave up the dead which were in it; and death and hell delivered up the dead which were in them: and they were judged every man according to their works. And death and hell were cast into the lake of fire. This is the second death. And whosoever was not found written in the book of life was cast into the lake of fire" (Re.20:11-15).

"Kiss the Son, lest he be angry, and ye perish from the way, when his wrath is kindled but a little. Blessed are all they that put their trust in him" (Ps.2:12).

"I the LORD search the heart, I try the reins, even to give every man according to his ways, and according to the fruit of his doings" (Je.17:10).

---

7 (59:19-21) **Promises, of Salvation and Glory—Glory, Promise of—Salvation, Prophecy Concerning—Messiah, Kingdom of, Prophecy Concerning—Prophecies, Concerning Messiah's Kingdom**: the wicked must pay attention to the wonderful promise of God, that of the coming Redeemer. The promised Messiah, the Lord Jesus Christ, is returning to earth. When He comes, He will set up God's kingdom right here on earth. In that day, people will come from all over the earth to honor His holy name, His splendor and magnificence. In addition, Christ's coming will flood the earth with the glory of God, so much glory that it will be like an ocean tide being driven across the earth by the breath of the LORD Himself. Note that the Redeemer will come to Zion, which means that He will set up His seat of government in Jerusalem (v.20). He will be coming to live with and govern those who have repented of their sins.

Note the wonderful covenant (agreement) the LORD makes with His people: in that day, He will fill the repentant with the fullness of His Spirit and His Word. And neither His Spirit nor His Word will ever depart from believers or any of their descendants who truly repent and receive the kingdom of God as their inheritance (v.21). All who repent of their sins and follow Him in righteousness will enter the Messiah's kingdom and experience the unbroken glory and presence of God.

OUTLINE	SCRIPTURE	SCRIPTURE	OUTLINE
7. **The wonderful promise of salvation & glory: A picture of the Messiah's kingdom** a. The people will respect the LORD's name & honor His glory b. The Redeemer will come to Zion (Jerusalem): To bring God's glory to earth for all who repent	19 So shall they fear the name of the LORD from the west, and his glory from the rising of the sun. When the enemy shall come in like a flood, the Spirit of the LORD shall lift up a standard against him. 20 And the Redeemer shall come to Zion, and unto them that turn from transgression in Jacob, saith the LORD.	21 As for me, this is my covenant with them, saith the LORD; My spirit that is upon thee, and my words which I have put in thy mouth, shall not depart out of thy mouth, nor out of the mouth of thy seed, nor out of the mouth of thy seed's seed, saith the LORD, from henceforth and for ever.	c. The Redeemer will fill the repentant with His Spirit & His Words

"Then shall the righteous shine forth as the sun in the kingdom of their Father. Who hath ears to hear, let him hear" (Mt.13:43).

"And Jesus said unto him, Verily I say unto thee, To day shalt thou be with me in paradise" (Lu.23:43).

"In my Father's house are many mansions: if *it were* not so, I would have told you. I go to prepare a place for you. And if I go and prepare a place for you, I will come again, and receive you unto myself; that where I am, *there* ye may be also" (Jn.14:2-3).

"Therefore by the deeds of the law there shall no flesh be justified in his sight: for by the law *is the* knowledge of sin. But now the righteousness of God without the law is manifested, being witnessed by the law and the prophets" (Ro.3:20-21).

"The Spirit itself beareth witness with our spirit, that we are the children of God: And if children, then heirs; heirs of God, and joint-heirs with Christ; if so be that we suffer with *him,* that we may be also glorified together" (Ro.8:16-17).

"For I reckon that the sufferings of this present time *are* not worthy *to be compared* with the glory which shall be revealed in us" (Ro.8:18).

"For our light affliction, which is but for a moment, worketh for us a far more exceeding *and* eternal weight of glory" (2 Co.4:17).

"When Christ, *who is* our life, shall appear, then shall ye also appear with him in glory" (Col.3:4).

"Therefore I endure all things for the elect's sakes, that they may also obtain the salvation which is in Christ Jesus with eternal glory" (2 Ti.2:10).

"The elders which are among you I exhort, who am also an elder, and a witness of the sufferings of Christ, and also a partaker of the glory that shall be revealed: Feed the flock of God which is among you, taking the oversight *thereof,* not by constraint, but willingly; not for filthy lucre, but of a ready mind; Neither as being lords over *God's* heritage, but being ensamples to the flock. And when the chief Shepherd shall appear, ye shall receive a crown of glory that fadeth not away" (1 Pe.5:1-4).

"After this I beheld, and, lo, a great multitude, which no man could number, of all nations, and kindreds, and people, and tongues, stood before the throne, and before the Lamb, clothed with white robes, and palms in their hands; And cried with a loud voice, saying, Salvation to our God which sitteth upon the throne, and unto the Lamb" (Re.7:9-10).

"And there shall be no night there; and they need no candle, neither light of the sun; for the Lord God giveth them light: and they shall reign for ever and ever" (Re.22:5).

"Thou shalt guide me with thy counsel, and afterward receive me *to* glory" (Ps.73:24).

DIVISION VII

THE PROPHECIES OF A GREAT AND
GLORIOUS FUTURE: 60:1–66:24

(60:1–66:24) **DIVISION OVERVIEW**: in this final division of the great book of *Isaiah*, these prophecies soar in the heights of God's promises. The reader quickly catches a spirit of the great and glorious future awaiting the true believer. All who sincerely follow the Lord soon learn to appreciate and treasure these chapters, for they stir within the believer a high level of expectation and hope.

In the last days of human history, the Messiah, Jesus Christ, will return to set up God's kingdom on earth. He will firmly establish the *seat of His government* in Jerusalem, which will become the glorious capital of the entire world. Peace, security, prosperity, and righteousness will then fill the earth, and true justice will be executed in a spirit of compassion (60:1-22). All this will be possible because of God's great gift of salvation, which has been made available through the Messiah, Jesus Christ (61:1–62:12).

However, the end times will also bring the great day of God's vengeance, the terrifying day known as Armageddon. Yet even as God executes final judgment on the wicked of the earth, He will shower mercy on those who have truly trusted Him, all who have followed in the steps of His righteousness (63:1–64:12). After Armageddon and the pouring out of God's mercy, the last days of human history will be followed immediately by the Millennium, the glorious one-thousand-year reign of Christ on the earth. Then God will create a new heavens and earth for His people in a magnificent consummation of history (65:1–66:24).

THE PROPHECIES OF A GREAT AND
GLORIOUS FUTURE: 60:1–66:24

A. The Future Glory of Jerusalem: A Picture of the Holy City During the Messiah's Kingdom on Earth—the Millennium, 60:1-22

B. The Gift of Salvation Through the Coming Savior, 61:1–62:12

C. The Great Day of God's Vengeance and Mercy: A Picture of Armageddon, 63:1–64:12

D. The Last Days of Human History (Part 1), 65:1-25

E. The Last Days of Human History (Part 2), 66:1-24

---

1. The Holy City will receive the light & the glory of God's presence (v.14): In Jesus Christ, Jn.8:12

a. The darkness presently covers the earth: Bondage, oppression, evil, disease, death

b. The Lord's glory will rise over the Holy City: To rescue it

c. The LORD's light, in the person of Jesus Christ, will draw all nations & kings to Jerusalem, Jn.8:12; Re.21:23
   1) All the Gentiles
   2) All the Jews: Sons & daughters of Israel

2. The Holy City will be the center of world trade & of worship

a. The center of world trade
   1) The commerce of the seas—the entire earth—will be centered in Jerusalem
   2) The products transported across the world by land will have their headquarters in Jerusalem

b. The center of worship
   1) The people of all nations will worship & praise the LORD
   2) The nations will present offerings to the LORD
      • He will accept their gifts
      • He will glorify, adorn His temple with their worship & offerings

c. The center & focus of the entire world
   1) The ships of the world—even from the most distant islands—will look to the LORD & Jerusalem
      • They will return the Jews to their land
      • They will honor the LORD, the Holy One of Israel
   2) The foreigners will rebuild

CHAPTER 60

VII. THE PROPHECIES OF A GREAT & GLORIOUS FUTURE, 60:1–66:24

A. The Future Glory of Jerusalem: A Picture of the Holy City During the Messiah's Kingdom on Earth—the Millennium, 60:1-22

Arise, shine; for thy light is come, and the glory of the LORD is risen upon thee.
2 For, behold, the darkness shall cover the earth, and gross darkness the people: but the LORD shall arise upon thee, and his glory shall be seen upon thee.
3 And the Gentiles shall come to thy light, and kings to the brightness of thy rising.
4 Lift up thine eyes round about, and see: all they gather themselves together, they come to thee: thy sons shall come from far, and thy daughters shall be nursed at thy side.
5 Then thou shalt see, and flow together, and thine heart shall fear, and be enlarged; because the abundance of the sea shall be converted unto thee, the forces of the Gentiles shall come unto thee.
6 The multitude of camels shall cover thee, the dromedaries of Midian and Ephah; all they from Sheba shall come: they shall bring gold and incense; and they shall show forth the praises of the LORD.
7 All the flocks of Kedar shall be gathered together unto thee, the rams of Nebaioth shall minister unto thee: they shall come up with acceptance on mine altar, and I will glorify the house of my glory.
8 Who are these that fly as a cloud, and as the doves to their windows?
9 Surely the isles shall wait for me, and the ships of Tarshish first, to bring thy sons from far, their silver and their gold with them, unto the name of the LORD thy God, and to the Holy One of Israel, because he hath glorified thee.
10 And the sons of strangers

shall build up thy walls, and their kings shall minister unto thee: for in my wrath I smote thee, but in my favour have I had mercy on thee.
11 Therefore thy gates shall be open continually; they shall not be shut day nor night; that men may bring unto thee the forces of the Gentiles, and that their kings may be brought.
12 For the nation and kingdom that will not serve thee shall perish; yea, those nations shall be utterly wasted.
13 The glory of Lebanon shall come unto thee, the fir tree, the pine tree, and the box together, to beautify the place of my sanctuary; and I will make the place of my feet glorious.
14 The sons also of them that afflicted thee shall come bending unto thee; and all they that despised thee shall bow themselves down at the soles of thy feet; and they shall call thee, The city of the LORD, The Zion of the Holy One of Israel.
15 Whereas thou hast been forsaken and hated, so that no man went through thee, I will make thee an eternal excellency, a joy of many generations.
16 Thou shalt also suck the milk of the Gentiles, and shalt suck the breast of kings: and thou shalt know that I the LORD am thy Saviour and thy Redeemer, the mighty One of Jacob.
17 For brass I will bring gold, and for iron I will bring silver, and for wood brass, and for stones iron: I will also make thy officers peace, and thine exactors righteousness.
18 Violence shall no more be heard in thy land, wasting nor destruction within thy borders; but thou shalt call thy walls Salvation, and thy gates Praise.
19 The sun shall be no more thy light by day; neither for brightness shall the moon give light unto thee: but the LORD shall be unto thee an everlasting light, and thy God thy glory.
20 Thy sun shall no more go down; neither shall thy moon withdraw itself: for the LORD shall be thine everlasting

Jerusalem
   • The rulers will serve Jerusalem
   • The LORD will show mercy

3. The Holy City will open the gates of salvation to all: The gates will never be closed

a. The purpose: So people can enter to worship & to bring their gifts—led by their rulers in triumphal procession

b. The people excluded: All who refuse to join those who serve the LORD

c. The place of worship: The temple
   1) A place of beauty: The glory of Lebanon's building materials
   2) A place of reverence: The LORD's presence

d. The worshippers
   1) The oppressors of God's people: Will bow in Jerusalem & confess the LORD
   2) The Israelites (true believers)

4. The Holy City will be the capital of the world, the center of the LORD's kingdom on earth

a. The city's fame: Will be the pride & joy of all

b. The city's maintenance: Will be sustained by the nations like a child being nursed

c. The city's ruler: Will be known as the LORD, the Savior, the Redeemer, the Mighty One

d. The city's beauty & wealth: Will be built by using the most striking & valuable materials

e. The city's government: Will execute peace & righteousness throughout the world

f. The city's society: Will have no criminals—no violence, lawlessness, or destruction

g. The city's defenses: Will be the salvation & the power of praise

h. The city's source of light
   1) Will no longer be the brightness of the sun or moon
   2) Will be the splendor & brilliance of God's glory
   3) Will be no night there

i. The city's perfection & joy: Will be no more sorrow or mourning—no more suffering, pain or death

j. The city's citizens: Will be the righteous 　1) They will inherit the promised land	light, and the days of thy mourning shall be ended. 21 Thy people also *shall be* all righteous: they shall inherit the land for ever, the branch of my planting, the	work of my hands, that I may be glorified. 22 A little one shall become a thousand, and a small one a strong nation: I the LORD will hasten it in his time.	2) They will be the people planted & looked after by the LORD: For His glory 3) They will be a mighty nation of believers

DIVISION VII

THE PROPHECIES OF A GREAT AND GLORIOUS FUTURE, 60:1–66:24

A.　The Future Glory of Jerusalem: A Picture of the Holy City During the Messiah's Kingdom on Earth—the Millennium, 60:1-22

(60:1-22) **Introduction**: among all the cities in the world, Jerusalem has one of the most interesting histories. Down through the centuries the city has been conquered time and again and left in utter ruin. No one living at the time of its destruction thought it would ever rise again. But it always has. It arose from the ashes of the Assyrian destruction, the Babylonian destruction, and the Roman destruction. Although it is the capital of only a small nation of people, the city seems to be indestructible. And its people have survived exiles, untold atrocities, and deliberate attempts to exterminate them from the face of the earth. Holocaust after holocaust has been launched against the Jewish people and their nation. For reasons sometimes unexplainable, certain nations and peoples down through history have despised and held the Jews in utter contempt. Nevertheless, these brave people have overcome and survived to raise Jerusalem and the nation from the ashes of total devastation. Interestingly, Jerusalem is considered to be the Holy City by three of the major religions of the world: Judaism (the Jews), Islam (the Muslims), and Christianity (the Christians).

The present Scripture is a prophecy concerning the future of Jerusalem. The day is coming when Jerusalem will be established as the capital of the world. At that time, the light and glory of God Himself will come to the Holy City and dwell there forever. All the nations of earth will be brought together in a worldwide government, and the seat of government will be in Jerusalem. The leaders will embark on a huge building project to make the city more spectacular than the world could ever imagine. And the LORD will govern the world from there. This is the prophecy concerning, *The Future Glory of Jerusalem: A Picture of the Holy City During the Messiah's Kingdom on Earth—the Millennium*, 60:1-22.

1. The Holy City will receive the light and the glory of God's presence (v.14): in Jesus Christ, Jn.8:12, (vv.1-4).
2. The Holy City will be the center of world trade and of worship (vv.5-10).
3. The Holy City will open the gates of salvation to all: the gates will never be closed (vv.11-14).
4. The Holy City will be the capital of the world, the center of the LORD's kingdom on earth (vv.14b-22).

1 (60:1-4) **Glory, of God, in Messiah's Kingdom—Kingdom, of Messiah, Glory of—Jerusalem, New, Prophecy Concerning, God's Glory—Messiah, Kingdom of, Citizens of—Light, of God—Jesus Christ, Light of, in New Jerusalem—Light, of Christ, Draws All People—Prophecy, Concerning New Jerusalem, Glory of—Prophecy, Concerning Messiah's Kingdom, Glory of**: the Holy City is destined to receive the light and glory of God's presence. At the close of the previous chapter, God predicted the coming of the Redeemer, the Messiah, to Zion (59:20). Now God paints a picture of the world's future, looking to the time when the Messiah will have already come. Remember that Jesus Christ is the "light of the world" (Jn.8:12). Here, Isaiah says that Christ Himself will be the very light of Jerusalem. The blazing glory of His presence and holiness will reflect so much light that Jerusalem will not need the light of the sun (Re.21:23). Now note what the prophet is saying: "Your light [the Messiah and Redeemer, the Lord Jesus Christ] has come, and the glory of the LORD [in the person of Christ] is shining upon you" (v.1). When the day arrives, nothing will stop His coming, for it is destined by God. The glorious return of the LORD to set up God's kingdom on earth will take place. Presently darkness covers the entire earth, holding it in the grip of...

- Sin and evil
- immorality and violence
- bondage and enslavement
- sorrow and despair
- injustice and oppression
- war and destruction

A thick, black veil has wrapped itself around the world. But there is wonderful news. The Lord is going to return. Imagine the scene! The day will come when His blazing glory will suddenly appear over the Holy City (v.2). He is coming as the Redeemer (59:20) to rescue His people from the darkness of the earth, from all wickedness, disease, and death. God's kingdom will be established in the full glory and light of His Person, and His glory and light will bring perfection to earth. In God's kingdom there will be no sin, disease, accidents, or death. There will no longer be tears of sorrow, not when the Lord Jesus Christ returns to set up God's kingdom on earth.

The LORD's glory and light will also draw all nations and kingdoms to Jerusalem (vv.3-4). All Gentiles and all Jews will be attracted there. They will travel to see the LORD, the implication being for the purpose of worship. Note that the Gentile nations will bring the scattered sons and daughters of Jerusalem, the Jews, with them.

Note one other fact: true believers are instructed to "arise, shine, for your light has come" (v.1). They are to be strong witnesses, reflecting the light of Christ's salvation. Even before He returns to earth, true believers should be taking the message of Jesus Christ to all the nations of the world. Citizens and rulers alike should be streaming to the salvation and light of the Lord Jesus Christ. All believers should "arise, shine."

OUTLINE	SCRIPTURE	SCRIPTURE	OUTLINE
1. **The Holy City will receive the light & the glory of God's presence (v.14): In Jesus Christ, Jn.8:12** a. The darkness presently covers the earth: Bondage, oppression, evil, disease, death b. The Lord's glory will rise over the Holy City: To rescue it c. The LORD's light, in the per-	Arise, shine; for thy light is come, and the glory of the LORD is risen upon thee. 2 For, behold, the darkness shall cover the earth, and gross darkness the people: but the LORD shall arise upon thee, and his glory shall be seen upon thee. 3 And the Gentiles shall	come to thy light, and kings to the brightness of thy rising. 4 Lift up thine eyes round about, and see: all they gather themselves together, they come to thee: thy sons shall come from far, and thy daughters shall be nursed at *thy* side.	son of Jesus Christ, will draw all nations & kings to Jerusalem, Jn.8:12; Re.21:23 1) All the Gentiles 2) All the Jews: Sons & daughters of Israel

Thought 1. Jesus Christ is the light of the world, the light that will bring salvation and glory to Jerusalem.

"In him was life; and the life was the light of men" (Jn.1:4).

"Then spake Jesus again unto them, saying, I am the light of the world: he that followeth me shall not walk in darkness, but shall have the light of life" (Jn.8:12).

"Then Jesus said unto them, Yet a little while is the light with you. Walk while ye have the light, lest darkness come upon you: for he that walketh in darkness knoweth not whither he goeth" (Jn.12:35).

"For God, who commanded the light to shine out of darkness, hath shined in our hearts, to *give* the light of the knowledge of the glory of God in the face of Jesus Christ" (2 Co.4:6).

"Wherefore he saith, Awake thou that sleepest, and arise from the dead, and Christ shall give thee light" (Ep.5:14).

"And the city had no need of the sun, neither of the moon, to shine in it: for the glory of God did lighten it, and the Lamb *is* the light thereof" (Re.21:23).

"The people that walked in darkness have seen a great light: they that dwell in the land of the shadow of death, upon them hath the light shined" (Is.9:2).

Thought 2. Believers are to reflect the light of the LORD through their lives. They are to let their *lights* shine, bearing strong witness to the Lord's salvation.

"Ye are the light of the world. A city that is set on an hill cannot be hid. Neither do men light a candle, and put it under a bushel, but on a candlestick; and it giveth light unto all that are in the house. Let your light so shine before men, that they may see your good works, and glorify your Father which is in heaven" (Mt.5:14-16).

"For so hath the Lord commanded us, *saying*, I have set thee to be a light of the Gentiles, that thou shouldest be for salvation unto the ends of the earth" (Ac.13:47).

"For ye were sometimes darkness, but now *are ye* light in the Lord: walk as children of light: (For the fruit of the Spirit is in all goodness and righteousness and truth;) Proving what is acceptable unto the Lord. And have no fellowship with the unfruitful works of darkness, but rather reprove *them*" (Ep.5:8-11).

"Do all things without murmurings and disputings: That ye may be blameless and harmless, the sons of God, without rebuke, in the midst of a crooked and perverse nation, among whom ye shine as lights in the world; Holding forth the word of life; that I may rejoice in the day of Christ, that I have not run in vain, neither laboured in vain" (Ph.2:14-16).

"Ye are all the children of light, and the children of the day: we are not of the night, nor of darkness. Therefore let us not sleep, as *do* others; but let us watch and be sober. For they that sleep sleep in the night; and they that be drunken are drunken in the night. But let us, who are of the day, be sober, putting on the breastplate of faith and love; and for an helmet, the hope of salvation" (1 Th.5:5-8).

2 (60:5-10) **Prophecy, Concerning Jerusalem, World Capital—Worship, Prophecy Concerning, in Messiah's Kingdom—Jerusalem, Prophecy Concerning, Worship Center; Economic Center**: the Holy City will be the center world trade and of worship. When the Messiah, the Lord Jesus Christ, sets up God's kingdom on earth, Jerusalem will become the economic and financial capital of the world (v.5). It will be the center of all commerce shipped by sea from all parts of the world. In addition, the Holy City will be the center of all trade in products transported over land. The latest method of transportation will carry goods around the world, just as caravans of camels and other animals transported the products of ancient history (v.6). The world's financial system will operate under the leadership of the LORD of glory, Christ Jesus Himself. The implication is that the world will know economic prosperity. No one will be homeless, unclothed, or hungry. Everyone will prosper under the world leadership of the Messiah.

Equally important, Jerusalem will become the center of worldwide worship (vv.6-7). People of every nation will worship and praise the LORD together. All people will present their offerings to the LORD, and He will accept their gifts.

Using the gifts to adorn His temple, He will be honored and glorified through their praise. Jesus Christ will be acknowledged as the true Messiah, the Savior and Redeemer of the human race.

In that day, Jerusalem will become the focus of the entire world (vv.8-10). Everyone, even the people in the islands, the distant parts of the world, will look to the LORD and the Holy City. The ships of Tarshish will travel to the nations of the world to secure their gifts to the LORD and to bring the Jews back to the promised land (v.9). Through the gifts of wealth and the return of His people, the LORD will be honored as the Holy One of Israel. Note also the wonderful promise to God's people: they will be endowed with the glory or splendor of the LORD (v.9c).

One of the reasons so many foreigners will travel to Jerusalem will be to rebuild the capital (v.10). When the city is established as the financial center of the world, businesses from far and near will construct their headquarters or administrative offices there. The sheer number and enormity of building projects in Jerusalem, along with their subsidiary businesses and services needed worldwide, simply explode the imagination. Under the leadership of the Messiah, the Lord Jesus Christ, the light and glory of God will come to Jerusalem. The ancient city will be the capital of the world, the center of the world's economic and financial institutions, as well as the center of worldwide worship.

Note how the LORD closes the prophecy of these verses. Due to the terrible sins of His people, God had executed His wrath, His judgment against them. But ultimately He would show them mercy and compassion.

OUTLINE	SCRIPTURE	SCRIPTURE	OUTLINE
2. The Holy City will be the center of world trade & of worship a. The center of world trade 1) The commerce of the seas—the entire earth—will be centered in Jerusalem 2) The products transported across the world by land will have their headquarters in Jerusalem b. The center of worship 1) The people of all nations will worship & praise the LORD 2) The nations will present offerings to the LORD • He will accept their gifts • He will glorify, adorn	5 Then thou shalt see, and flow together, and thine heart shall fear, and be enlarged; because the abundance of the sea shall be converted unto thee, the forces of the Gentiles shall come unto thee. 6 The multitude of camels shall cover thee, the dromedaries of Midian and Ephah; all they from Sheba shall come: they shall bring gold and incense; and they shall show forth the praises of the LORD. 7 All the flocks of Kedar shall be gathered together unto thee, the rams of Nebaioth shall minister unto thee: they shall come up with ac-	ceptance on mine altar, and I will glorify the house of my glory. 8 Who are these that fly as a cloud, and as the doves to their windows? 9 Surely the isles shall wait for me, and the ships of Tarshish first, to bring thy sons from far, their silver and their gold with them, unto the name of the LORD thy God, and to the Holy One of Israel, because he hath glorified thee. 10 And the sons of strangers shall build up thy walls, and their kings shall minister unto thee: for in my wrath I smote thee, but in my favour have I had mercy on thee.	His temple with their worship & offerings c. The center & focus of the entire world 1) The ships of the world—even from the most distant islands—will look to the LORD & Jerusalem • They will return the Jews to their land • They will honor the LORD, the Holy One of Israel 2) The foreigners will rebuild Jerusalem • The rulers will serve Jerusalem • The LORD will show mercy

Thought 1. Today is the day of God's mercy, the day in which He will have compassion on us, whether Jew or Gentile. In the future, God is going to restore Israel because of His mercy. He has not forsaken the entire nation, for there are some who truly trust and believe in the Messiah, the Lord Jesus Christ. These believers, whether many or few, will be saved and restored to the favor of the LORD. In the end time, when Jesus Christ returns to set up God's kingdom on earth, many will at last recognize that Christ is the true Messiah. These people will then believe and turn to the LORD for salvation. Because God is merciful, He will accept them and allow them to enter the promised land of His kingdom. But even now there is wonderful news: God longs to restore any of us who have gone astray, or have denied or rejected Him. If we will repent of our unbelief and denial, turn away from our sins, and trust the LORD, He will have compassion upon us. Listen to what God's Holy Word says about His abundant mercy and favor:

"And his mercy is on them that fear him from generation to generation" (Lu.1:50).

"But God, who is rich in mercy, for his great love wherewith he loved us, Even when we were dead in sins, hath quickened us together with Christ, (by grace ye are saved;) And hath raised us up together, and made us sit together in heavenly places in Christ Jesus: That in the ages to come he might show the exceeding riches of his grace in his kindness toward us through Christ Jesus. For by grace are ye saved through faith; and that not of yourselves: it is the gift of God" (Ep.2:4-8).

"Not by works of righteousness which we have done, but according to his mercy he saved us, by the washing of regeneration, and renewing of the Holy Ghost; Which he shed on us abundantly through Jesus Christ our Saviour; That being justified by his grace, we should be made heirs according to the hope of eternal life" (Tit.3:5-7).

"Praise ye the LORD. O give thanks unto the LORD; for he is good: for his mercy endureth for ever" (Ps.106:1).

"The earth, O LORD, is full of thy mercy: teach me thy statutes" (Ps.119:64).

"I have seen his ways, and will heal him: I will lead him also, and restore comforts unto him and to his mourners" (Is.57:18).

"Return, ye backsliding children, and I will heal your backslidings. Behold, we come unto thee; for thou art the LORD our God" (Je.3:22).

"For I will restore health unto thee, and I will heal thee of thy wounds, saith the LORD; because they called thee an Outcast, *saying,* This *is* Zion, whom no man seeketh after" (Je.30:17).

"*It is of* the LORD'S mercies that we are not consumed, because his compassions fail not. *They are* new every morning: great *is* thy faithfulness" (La.3:22-23).

"I will heal their backsliding, I will love them freely: for mine anger is turned away from him" (Ho.14:4).

"And rend your heart, and not your garments, and turn unto the LORD your God: for he *is* gracious and merciful, slow to anger, and of great kindness, and repenteth him of the evil" (Joel 2:13).

"Who *is* a God like unto thee, that pardoneth iniquity, and passeth by the transgression of the remnant of his heritage? he retaineth not his anger for ever, because he delighteth *in* mercy" (Mi.7:18).

"He will turn again, he will have compassion upon us; he will subdue our iniquities; and thou wilt cast all their sins into the depths of the sea" (Mi.7:19).

3 (60:11-14) **Salvation, Door to, Open—Access, to the LORD—Salvation, Universal—Worship, Prophecy Concerning, in Messiah's Kingdom—Prophecies Concerning Messiah's Kingdom, Worship in—Jerusalem, Prophecy Concerning, Worship in Messiah's Kingdom**: the Holy City will open the gateway of salvation to everyone. The gates into the LORD's presence will never be closed and access to Him will be possible at all times (Re.21:25). Throughout history the gates of cities have always been closed at night. Businesses, shops, and homes have also been locked due to the spirit of sin and lawlessness that has swept over the earth. But when Christ returns to set up His kingdom of righteousness, there will be no need to lock the gates or doors. Peace and security will envelope the earth, and there will be no lawlessness, crime, or secret attack by enemies. Everyone will know the salvation of the LORD that rules Jerusalem and the earth. People led by their rulers in a triumphal procession will enter to worship and bring their gifts to the LORD (v.11). The idea seems to be that the leaders of nations will have appointed times for conferences or meetings with the LORD.

The only people excluded from the kingdom of God will be those who have refused to join God's people in serving the LORD (v. 12). When the LORD first returns to establish God's kingdom on earth, all who have refused to trust and serve Him will face His judgment. They will be refused entrance into God's kingdom, be removed from the earth, and perish. Remember why: because they rejected the LORD's light, His holy character and love, which now fill Jerusalem and the earth.

In the New Jerusalem, the temple will be a place of spectacular beauty. In the ancient world, Lebanon was known for having the most beautiful and costly building materials. For that reason, the glory of Lebanon, its luxurious building materials, will be used to construct the temple. The temple will also be a place of reverence, for the LORD will honor the temple with His presence and fill the temple with His glory.

Some of the worshippers in that day will actually be descendants of people who had once oppressed the Jews (v.14). No doubt there will also be descendants of people who formerly tormented true believers. But these descendants of past persecutors will bow in Jerusalem and confess the LORD. They will call Jerusalem the "City of the LORD, Zion of the Holy One of Israel." Joining the descendants of the LORD's former enemies will be the Israelites themselves, those who have truly trusted the LORD.

OUTLINE	SCRIPTURE	SCRIPTURE	OUTLINE
3. The Holy City will open the gates of salvation to all: The gates will never be closed a. The purpose: So people can enter to worship & to bring their gifts—led by their rulers in triumphal procession b. The people excluded: All who refuse to join those who serve the LORD c. The place of worship: The temple	11 Therefore thy gates shall be open continually; they shall not be shut day nor night; that *men* may bring unto thee the forces of the Gentiles, and *that* their kings *may be* brought. 12 For the nation and kingdom that will not serve thee shall perish; yea, *those* nations shall be utterly wasted. 13 The glory of Lebanon shall come unto thee, the fir	tree, the pine tree, and the box together, to beautify the place of my sanctuary; and I will make the place of my feet glorious. 14 The sons also of them that afflicted thee shall come bending unto thee; and all they that despised thee shall bow themselves down at the soles of thy feet; and they shall call thee, The city of the LORD, The Zion of the Holy One of Israel.	1) A place of beauty: The glory of Lebanon's building materials 2) A place of reverence: The LORD's presence d. The worshippers 1) The oppressors of God's people: Will bow in Jerusalem & confess the LORD 2) The Israelites (true believers)

Thought 1. The door of salvation is wide open. Today any person can approach the LORD and be accepted by Him. However, the day is coming when access to the LORD will be closed. In that day, God will execute judgment upon all the wicked and the unbelievers who have turned away from Him. Still, for now, access into God's presence is possible. Every human being can cross the threshold into God's presence and be accepted by Him. But note these facts:

(1) Access into God's presence is granted only if a person comes in Jesus' name.

"I am the door: by me if any man enter in, he shall be saved, and shall go in and out, and find pasture" (Jn.10:9).

"By whom also we have access by faith into this grace wherein we stand, and rejoice in hope of the glory of God" (Ro.5:2).

"For through him we both have access by one Spirit unto the Father" (Ep.2:18).

"In whom we have boldness and access with confidence by the faith of him" (Ep.3:12).

(2) Access into God's presence is granted only if a person recognizes and honors the truth, and Jesus Christ is *the truth*.

> "Jesus saith unto him, I am the way, the truth, and the life: no man cometh unto the Father, but by me" (Jn.14:6).
> "Open ye the gates, that the righteous nation which keepeth the truth may enter in" (Is.26:2).

(3) Access into God's presence is granted only if a person repents, turns away from sin, and follows the LORD.

> "Having therefore, brethren, boldness to enter into the holiest by the blood of Jesus, By a new and living way, which he hath consecrated for us, through the veil, that is to say, his flesh; And *having* an high priest over the house of God; Let us draw near with a true heart in full assurance of faith, having our hearts sprinkled from an evil conscience, and our bodies washed with pure water" (He.10:19-22).
> "He restoreth my soul: he leadeth me in the paths of righteousness for his name's sake. Yea, though I walk through the valley of the shadow of death, I will fear no evil: for thou *art* with me; thy rod and thy staff they comfort me" (Ps.23:3-4).

4 (60:14b-22) **Kingdom, of God, Prophecy Concerning, Discussed—Messiah, Kingdom, Discussed—Jerusalem, Prophecy Concerning, World's Capital—Jesus Christ, Kingdom of, Discussed—End Times, Prophecy Concerning, Messiah's Kingdom**: as mentioned above, the Holy City will be the capital of the world, the center of God's kingdom on earth. The entire world will look to Jerusalem because it will be the seat of government, the city where the very throne and power of God will govern the earth. A magnificent description is given of the city, a description that staggers the mind (see outline and notes—Re.21:9-23 for more discussion on the New Jerusalem):

OUTLINE	SCRIPTURE	SCRIPTURE	OUTLINE
4. The Holy City will be the capital of the world, the center of the LORD's kingdom on earth a. The city's fame: Will be the pride & joy of all	14 The sons also of them that afflicted thee shall come bending unto thee; and all they that despised thee shall bow themselves down at the soles of thy feet; and they shall call thee, The city of the LORD, The Zion of the Holy One of Israel. 15 Whereas thou hast been forsaken and hated, so that no man went through *thee,* I will make thee an eternal excellency, a joy of many generations.	18 Violence shall no more be heard in thy land, wasting nor destruction within thy borders; but thou shalt call thy walls Salvation, and thy gates Praise. 19 The sun shall be no more thy light by day; neither for brightness shall the moon give light unto thee: but the LORD shall be unto thee an everlasting light, and thy God thy glory.	f. The city's society: Will have no criminals—no violence, lawlessness, or destruction g. The city's defenses: Will be the salvation & the power of praise h. The city's source of light 1) Will no longer be the brightness of the sun or moon
b. The city's maintenance: Will be sustained by the nations like a child being nursed c. The city's ruler: Will be known as the LORD, the Savior, the Redeemer, the Mighty One d. The city's beauty & wealth: Will be built by using the most striking & valuable materials e. The city's government: Will execute peace & righteousness throughout the world	16 Thou shalt also suck the milk of the Gentiles, and shalt suck the breast of kings: and thou shalt know that I the LORD *am* thy Saviour and thy Redeemer, the mighty One of Jacob. 17 For brass I will bring gold, and for iron I will bring silver, and for wood brass, and for stones iron: I will also make thy officers peace, and thine exactors righteousness.	20 Thy sun shall no more go down; neither shall thy moon withdraw itself: for the LORD shall be thine everlasting light, and the days of thy mourning shall be ended. 21 Thy people also *shall be* all righteous: they shall inherit the land for ever, the branch of my planting, the work of my hands, that I may be glorified. 22 A little one shall become a thousand, and a small one a strong nation: I the LORD will hasten it in his time.	2) Will be the splendor & brilliance of God's glory 3) Will be no night there i. The city's perfection & joy: Will be no more sorrow or mourning—no more suffering, pain or death j. The city's citizens: Will be the righteous 1) They will inherit the promised land 2) They will be the people planted & looked after by the LORD: For His glory 3) They will be a mighty nation of believers

a. In contrast to Jerusalem's history, the city will be the pride and joy of the entire world (v.15). Through the centuries Jerusalem has been maligned, hated, attacked, and destroyed time and again. People have hated the Jews, so much so that they have sworn continued hostility toward both the people and the nation. Various individuals or groups would not even travel through the nation or its capital. Moreover, each time Jerusalem was destroyed and her people exiled by invading armies, a significant number of Jewish exiles would not return even when given the opportunity. From the beginning of its history, Jerusalem has been despised and forsaken by the vast majority of people on earth. But the day is coming when the LORD Himself will establish the city as the spectacular capital of the world. In that day, Jerusalem will be the most prized possession of all the citizens of the earth.

b. The city's maintenance—its upkeep, provision, support—will come from the nations of the world (v.16a). All the nations will sustain the city as if it were a nursing child. They will love, nourish, and take care of the city for two reasons: because the light and glory of the LORD's presence will dwell there (vv.1-4) and because it is the seat of the world's government and economy.

c. The city's ruler will be the LORD Himself (v.16). Note the significance of this fact: all people will know that the LORD is their *Savior, Redeemer,* and *the Mighty One of Jacob.* All will know that Jesus Christ brought God's kingdom to earth, that He eliminated the darkness of sin and death that had held the world captive since the beginning of human history.

d. The beauty and wealth of the New Jerusalem will be absolutely breathtaking. The city will be built from the most stunning and valuable materials available. No corners will be cut in order to save money (v.17a).

e. The government of the New Jerusalem will bring peace and righteousness to earth. At long last, peace and justice will flood the earth and satisfy the soul's craving for freedom from wickedness and violence. There will be no more lawlessness—no wars, conflicts, terrorist acts, murders, assaults, abuse, or oppression. Neither will there be divisiveness between people, not even within families. It is nearly impossible to conceive of a world filled with peace and righteousness. Yet because Christ in perfection will govern the earth in perfection, a spirit of peace will rule over all.

f. Society will have no criminals (v.18). News commentators will no longer report on violence, lawless behavior, or destruction, for nowhere in the world will there be any evil taking place.

g. The city's defenses will be salvation and praise (v.18b). In that day, lust for power and wealth will no longer fill people's hearts. Instead, the joy of the LORD—freedom in Christ—will flood their hearts. As a result, there will be no conflict or war, no attempt to overthrow governments in order to seize power. There will be no need for military power or defenses. Salvation and praise will fill the Holy City and spread throughout the worldwide kingdom of God, providing assurance of safety for all.

h. The city's source of light will no longer be the brightness of the sun or the moon, but rather the splendor and brilliance of God's glory (v.19). This thought astonishes our finite minds. And it is totally impossible to envision such glory emanating from any being. Nevertheless, the blazing glory of the LORD's holiness and Person, brighter than the sun or moon, will provide all the light the city of Jerusalem needs.

i. The city's perfection and joy will spread across the face of the world (v.20). Of course, this will be due to the presence of the LORD Himself, for He alone can bring completion and fulfillment to all the citizens of the world. There will be no more sorrow or mourning, no more suffering, pain, or death on earth. Imagine such a world! Life in the LORD's kingdom will be utopia, perfection.

j. The citizens of the New Jerusalem will be the righteous, and they will inherit the promised land forever. Who are the righteous? They are the people planted and looked after by the LORD (vv.21-22). Note why He chose His people: to glorify His name and power. Through His work on earth, the LORD has demonstrated the splendor of His glory and the mighty power of His arm. This is clearly seen in His choice and care of Israel, as well as in the survival and growth of Israel's population in the face of the world's hostility.

Thought 1. The citizen's of God's kingdom will be the righteous. They alone will inherit the promised land. All the wonders and joys described in this Scripture will be given only to those who truly trust the LORD and obey His commandments. In addition to these, God gives many other wonderful promises to the righteous:

"**Therefore whosoever heareth these sayings of mine, and doeth them, I will liken him unto a wise man, which built his house upon a rock: And the rain descended, and the floods came, and the winds blew, and beat upon that house; and it fell not: for it was founded upon a rock. And every one that heareth these sayings of mine, and doeth them not, shall be likened unto a foolish man, which built his house upon the sand: And the rain descended, and the floods came, and the winds blew, and beat upon that house; and it fell: and great was the fall of it**" (Mt.7:24-27).

"**Then shall the righteous shine forth as the sun in the kingdom of their Father. Who hath ears to hear, let him hear**" (Mt.13:43).

"**Jesus answered and said unto him, If a man love me, he will keep my words: and my Father will love him, and we will come unto him, and make our abode with him**" (Jn.14:23).

"**If ye keep my commandments, ye shall abide in my love; even as I have kept my Father's commandments, and abide in his love**" (Jn.15:10).

"**But whoso looketh into the perfect law of liberty, and continueth** *therein,* **he being not a forgetful hearer, but a doer of the work, this man shall be blessed in his deed**" (Js.1:25).

"**Blessed** *are* **they that do his commandments, that they may have right to the tree of life, and may enter in through the gates into the city**" (Re.22:14).

"**Now therefore, if ye will obey my voice indeed, and keep my covenant, then ye shall be a peculiar treasure unto me above all people: for all the earth** *is* **mine**" (Ex.19:5).

"**O that there were such an heart in them, that they would fear me, and keep all my commandments always, that it might be well with them, and with their children for ever!**" (De.5:29).

"**He withdraweth not his eyes from the righteous: but with kings** *are they* **on the throne; yea, he doth establish them for ever, and they [seated] are exalted**" (Jb.36:7).

"**The eyes of the LORD** *are* **upon the righteous, and his ears** *are* **open unto their cry**" (Ps.34:15).

"**I have been young, and** *now* **am old; yet have I not seen the righteous forsaken, nor his seed begging bread**" (Ps.37:25).

"**The righteous shall flourish like the palm tree: he shall grow like a cedar in Lebanon**" (Ps.92:12).

"**Say ye to the righteous, that** *it shall be* **well** *with him:* **for they shall eat the fruit of their doings**" (Is.3:10).

CHAPTER 61

B. The Gift of Salvation Through the Coming Savior, 61:1–62:12

1. The promise of salvation through the coming Savior

a. The Savior's anointing: To be filled with God's Spirit

b. The Savior's mission
   1) To preach to the poor
   2) To heal the brokenhearted
   3) To proclaim freedom to those held captive
   4) To proclaim the year of God's salvation & the coming day of judgment
   5) To comfort all who mourn & grieve
   • Give them the clothing of beauty, gladness, joy, & praise
   • Give them a name, a testimony of righteousness: So that the Savior may be glorified

c. The Savior's kingdom & its blessings of salvation: A picture of life in His coming kingdom, 60:1-22
   1) A restored nation: God's people will rebuild all destroyed cities
   2) A position of authority: Others will serve under believers in Jerusalem
   3) A name of honor: They will be called priests of the LORD, ministers of God
   4) A nation that is the world's commercial center
   5) A double inheritance in the promised land

   6) A society free of criminals & lawlessness
   7) An everlasting covenant: A new & eternal relationship with God—through Christ, He.9:15-18; 10:1-18
   8) A strong honor before the world: All people will acknowledge God's blessings to Israel

The Spirit of the Lord GOD *is* upon me; because the LORD hath anointed me to preach good tidings unto the meek; he hath sent me to bind up the brokenhearted, to proclaim liberty to the captives, and the opening of the prison to *them that are* bound;

2 To proclaim the acceptable year of the LORD, and the day of vengeance of our God; to comfort all that mourn;

3 To appoint unto them that mourn in Zion, to give unto them beauty for ashes, the oil of joy for mourning, the garment of praise for the spirit of heaviness; that they might be called trees of righteousness, the planting of the LORD, that he might be glorified.

4 And they shall build the old wastes, they shall raise up the former desolations, and they shall repair the waste cities, the desolations of many generations.

5 And strangers shall stand and feed your flocks, and the sons of the alien *shall be* your plowmen and your vinedressers.

6 But ye shall be named the Priests of the LORD: *men* shall call you the Ministers of our God: ye shall eat the riches of the Gentiles, and in their glory shall ye boast yourselves.

7 For your shame *ye shall have* double; and *for* confusion they shall rejoice in their portion: therefore in their land they shall possess the double: everlasting joy shall be unto them.

8 For I the LORD love judgment, I hate robbery for burnt offering; and I will direct their work in truth, and I will make an everlasting covenant with them.

9 And their seed shall be known among the Gentiles, and their offspring among the people: all that see them shall acknowledge them, that they *are* the seed *which* the LORD hath blessed.

10 I will greatly rejoice in the LORD, my soul shall be joyful in my God; for he hath clothed me with the garments of salvation, he hath covered me with the robe of righteousness, as a bridegroom decketh *himself* with ornaments, and as a bride adorneth *herself* with her jewels.

11 For as the earth bringeth forth her bud, and as the garden causeth the things that are sown in it to spring forth; so the Lord GOD will cause righteousness and praise to spring forth before all the nations.

CHAPTER 62

For Zion's sake will I not hold my peace, and for Jerusalem's sake I will not rest, until the righteousness thereof go forth as brightness, and the salvation thereof as a lamp *that* burneth.

2 And the Gentiles shall see thy righteousness, and all kings thy glory: and thou shalt be called by a new name, which the mouth of the LORD shall name.

3 Thou shalt also be a crown of glory in the hand of the LORD, and a royal diadem in the hand of thy God.

4 Thou shalt no more be termed Forsaken; neither shall thy land any more be termed Desolate: but thou shalt be called Hephzibah, and thy land Beulah: for the LORD delighteth in thee, and thy land shall be married.

5 For *as* a young man marrieth a virgin, *so* shall thy sons marry thee: and *as* the bridegroom rejoiceth over the bride, *so* shall thy God rejoice over thee.

6 I have set watchmen upon thy walls, O Jerusalem, *which* shall never hold their peace day nor night: ye that make mention of the LORD, keep not silence,

7 And give him no rest, till he establish, and till he make Jerusalem a praise in the earth.

8 The LORD hath sworn by his right hand, and by the arm of his strength, Surely I will no more give thy corn *to be* meat for thine enemies; and the sons of the stranger shall

9) A nation filled with joy & rejoicing: All the citizens of Zion will praise God
   • Because the LORD has clothed them in salvation & righteousness

   • Because the LORD causes the seed of righteousness & praise to spring up in all nations

2. The assurance of salvation through the coming Savior

a. Salvation is assured because of the Lord's Word: He will not keep silent
   1) The Holy City's righteousness & salvation must shine forth
   • The nations must see & desire her righteousness
   • The city must be given a new name by the LORD: Undergo a complete change
   2) The Holy City will be a valuable possession to the LORD: Will be like a crown, a royal diadem
   3) The Holy City will no longer be called *Deserted* or *Desolate*: Will be renamed
   • Hephzibah: *My delight is in her*
   • Beulah: *Married One*
   4) The Holy City will be repossessed by believers: The LORD will rejoice just as a bridegroom rejoices over his bride

b. Salvation is assured because of the watchmen's (believers') proclamation: They must not be silent
   1) Believers must call on the LORD day and night
   2) Believers must give the LORD no rest until He fulfills His promises: Establishes Jerusalem

c. Salvation is assured because of the LORD's sworn oath, His strong promise
   1) His promise that Jerusalem will be restored & never again be invaded

by enemies	not drink thy wine, for the which thou hast laboured:	the people.	the highway" of salvation
2) His promise that the Jews will labor & worship in the promised land—*in peace*	9 But they that have gathered it shall eat it, and praise the LORD; and they that have brought it together shall drink it in the courts of my holiness.	11 Behold, the LORD hath proclaimed unto the end of the world, Say ye to the daughter of Zion, Behold, thy salvation cometh; behold, his reward *is* with him, and his work before him.	2) The LORD's proclamation to the whole world: "Your Savior comes! His reward is with Him"
d. Salvation is assured because of the LORD's worldwide summons & invitation 1) The Lord's summons: "Go... prepare the way...build	10 Go through, go through the gates; prepare ye the way of the people; cast up, cast up the highways; gather out the stones; lift up a standard for	12 And they shall call them, The holy people, The redeemed of the LORD: and thou shalt be called, Sought out, A city not forsaken.	3) The people who respond: The Holy People, the Redeemed of the LORD 4) The Holy City will be called *Sought after...*

DIVISION VII

THE PROPHECIES OF A GREAT AND GLORIOUS FUTURE, 60:1–66:24

B.   The Gift of Salvation Through the Coming Savior, 61:1–62:12

(60:1–62:12) **Introduction**: Have you ever needed to be rescued from a life-threatening situation? Car accident? Drowning? Disease? Some other crisis that could have easily snatched your life away? Even if you have not personally confronted death, most of us know someone who has.

When thinking about life-threatening situations, we must all face the crisis of sin in our lives. Whether or not we acknowledge the sin or deny it does not change the reality that sin will doom us to eternal death. We are all gripped by the hand of sin, held in bondage by its power. No matter how much we may try to keep from sinning, we discover that we still do wrong or come up short. We cannot achieve perfection, no matter how diligently we try. We are always coming short and failing to some degree. But even more tragic, we discover that we are gripped by death. No human being escapes death. The grave is inevitable.

But the wonderful message of the present Scripture is this: we can be saved. The wonderful gift of salvation has been offered to the human race. Salvation from sin and death can be ours. God sent the Savior, the Lord Jesus Christ, to provide redemption for us. It is this great message that Isaiah the prophet proclaimed.

Keep in mind that this prophecy was given over 700 years before Christ ever came into the world. We today can look back through human history to see how this prediction of the coming Savior was fulfilled in the Lord Jesus Christ. This is, *The Gift of Salvation Through the Coming Savior*, 61:1–62:12.

1. The promise of salvation through the coming Savior (61:1-11).
2. The assurance of salvation through the coming Savior (62:1-12).

1 (61:1-11) **Salvation, Source, Christ—Jesus Christ, Purpose, Prophecy Concerning—Prophecy, Concerning Christ, His Purpose—Brokenhearted, Solution, Christ—Bondage, Spiritual, Answer - Solution to, Christ—Grief, Deliverance from, by Christ—Poor in Spirit, Deliverance, by Christ—Captivity, Deliverance from, by Christ—Freedom, Proclamation of, by Christ—Jesus Christ, Anointing of, by God's Spirit—Holy Spirit, Anointing of, Jesus Christ—Blessings, in Messiah's Kingdom, Ninefold—Kingdom, of Messiah, Blessings in**: God gave the wonderful promise of salvation through the coming Savior. Amazingly, this prophecy was given over 700 years before Jesus Christ ever came to earth. Right after Jesus' baptism and wilderness temptation, the first thing He did was revisit His hometown of Nazareth. On the Sabbath He attended worship in the synagogue and personally stood up to read the Scripture, choosing part of this passage of Scripture to read (Is.61:1-2ᵃ). What happened at the conclusion of His reading was most dramatic, astounding the congregation. Listen to the account given by the gospel of *Luke*.

> **"And there was delivered unto him the book of the prophet Esaias. And when he had opened the book, he found the place where it was written, The Spirit of the Lord is upon me, because he hath anointed me to preach the gospel to the poor; he hath sent me to heal the brokenhearted, to preach deliverance to the captives, and recovering of sight to the blind, to set at liberty them that are bruised, To preach the acceptable year of the Lord. And he closed the book, and he gave *it* again to the minister, and sat down. And the eyes of all them that were in the synagogue were fastened on him. And he began to say unto them, This day is this scripture fulfilled in your ears" (Lu.4:17-21).**

Jesus Christ claimed to be the *Messiah*, the *Servant of the LORD*, the promised Savior of the world. Note how the predicted mission of the Savior was fulfilled by Jesus Christ just as the present Scripture and outline of Isaiah show:

OUTLINE	SCRIPTURE	SCRIPTURE	OUTLINE
1. The promise of salvation through the coming Savior	The Spirit of the Lord GOD *is* upon me; because the LORD	hath anointed me to preach good tidings unto the meek;	a. The Savior's anointing: To be filled with God's Spirit

OUTLINE	SCRIPTURE	SCRIPTURE	OUTLINE
b. The Savior's mission 1) To preach to the poor 2) To heal the brokenhearted 3) To proclaim freedom to those held captive 4) To proclaim the year of God's salvation & the coming day of judgment 5) To comfort all who mourn & grieve • Give them the clothing of beauty, gladness, joy, & praise • Give them a name, a testimony of righteousness: So that the Savior may be glorified c. The Savior's kingdom & its blessings of salvation: A picture of life in His coming kingdom, 60:1-22 1) A restored nation: God's people will rebuild all destroyed cities 2) A position of authority: Others will serve under believers in Jerusalem 3) A name of honor: They will be called priests of the LORD, ministers of God 4) A nation that is the world's commercial center 5) A double inheritance in the promised land	he hath sent me to bind up the brokenhearted, to proclaim liberty to the captives, and the opening of the prison to *them that are* bound; 2 To proclaim the acceptable year of the LORD, and the day of vengeance of our God; to comfort all that mourn; 3 To appoint unto them that mourn in Zion, to give unto them beauty for ashes, the oil of joy for mourning, the garment of praise for the spirit of heaviness; that they might be called trees of righteousness, the planting of the LORD, that he might be glorified. 4 And they shall build the old wastes, they shall raise up the former desolations, and they shall repair the waste cities, the desolations of many generations. 5 And strangers shall stand and feed your flocks, and the sons of the alien *shall be* your plowmen and your vinedressers. 6 But ye shall be named the Priests of the LORD: *men* shall call you the Ministers of our God: ye shall eat the riches of the Gentiles, and in their glory shall ye boast yourselves. 7 For your shame *ye shall*	*have* double; and *for* confusion they shall rejoice in their portion: therefore in their land they shall possess the double: everlasting joy shall be unto them. 8 For I the LORD love judgment, I hate robbery for burnt offering; and I will direct their work in truth, and I will make an everlasting covenant with them. 9 And their seed shall be known among the Gentiles, and their offspring among the people: all that see them shall acknowledge them, that they *are* the seed *which* the LORD hath blessed. 10 I will greatly rejoice in the LORD, my soul shall be joyful in my God; for he hath clothed me with the garments of salvation, he hath covered me with the robe of righteousness, as a bridegroom decketh *himself* with ornaments, and as a bride adorneth *herself* with her jewels. 11 For as the earth bringeth forth her bud, and as the garden causeth the things that are sown in it to spring forth; so the Lord GOD will cause righteousness and praise to spring forth before all the nations.	 6) A society free of criminals & lawlessness 7) An everlasting covenant: A new & eternal relationship with God—through Christ, He.9:15-18; 10:1-18 8) A strong honor before the world: All people will acknowledge God's blessings to Israel 9) A nation filled with joy & rejoicing: All the citizens of Zion will praise God • Because the LORD has clothed them in salvation & righteousness • Because the LORD causes the seed of righteousness & praise to spring up in all nations

a. The Savior was to be anointed by God's very own Spirit (v.1). All three persons of the Godhead or Trinity are mentioned here: the Spirit, the LORD (Jehovah, Yahweh), and the Messiah or Savior, the Lord Jesus Christ who so clearly fulfilled the mission spelled out in this passage. Over 700 years before Jesus came, it was predicted that God's very own Spirit would rest on the Messiah. By the fullness of God's Spirit, the Messiah would be equipped to fulfill His task. And the Holy Scriptures say that when Jesus Christ was baptized, the heavens were opened and the Spirit of God descended upon Him like a dove. The voice of God was heard, saying, "This is my beloved Son, in Whom I am well pleased" (Mt.3:16-17). Down through history the Spirit of God has always filled God's prophets and servants, but they were mere human beings. Therefore, the presence and power of the Spirit was always limited. But not so with the Messiah, the Savior. The very fullness of God Himself, the fullness of His Spirit, rested upon the Savior, the Lord Jesus Christ. As the New Testament says:

> **"For in Him dwelleth all the fulness of the Godhead bodily" (Col.2:9, KJV).**
> **"For in Christ all the fullness of the Deity lives in bodily form" (Col.2:9, NIV).**
> **"For in Him the entire fullness of God's nature dwells bodily (Col.2:9, HCSB).**
> **"For in Him the whole fullness of deity dwells bodily" (Col.2:9, RSV).**
> **"For in Christ the fullness of God lives in a human body" (Col.2:9, NLT).**
> **"For in Him dwells all the fullness of the Godhead bodily" (Col.2:9, NKJV).**
> **"For in Him all the fullness of deity dwells in bodily form" (Col.2:9, NASB).**

b. The Savior was to be sent into the world on a very special mission. Keep in mind that Isaiah was preaching to the people of his own day, doing all he could to give them hope in the midst of a troubling world. Focusing their attention on the future, he pointed them to the coming of the Messiah, for their only hope was in the Savior of the world. Only He could deliver them from the trials, temptations, evil, bondages, and death of this world. The Savior's mission was to include six very specific tasks:

1) The Savior's mission was to preach good news to the poor (v.1). The *poor* means not only poor in material possessions, but also poor *in spirit*. A person who is *poor in spirit* acknowledges his utter helplessness before God, his spiritual need. He knows that he is solely dependent upon God to meet his need. He acknowledges his inability to face life and eternity apart from God, recognizing that the real blessings of life and eternity come only from a right relationship with the LORD. A person *poor in spirit* is humble, acknowledging that he is no better, no

more superior than the next person—no matter what he may have achieved in this world (fame, fortune, power). His attitude toward others is not proud or haughty, not superior or overbearing. He acknowledges that every human being is a real person, a person who has a significant contribution to make to society and to the world. He approaches life with humility and appreciation, not as though life owes him, but as though he owes life. Christ came to preach the salvation of God to the *poor*, those who readily know they need to be saved. And to these God promised the kingdom of heaven.

> "Blessed *are* the poor in spirit: for theirs is the kingdom of heaven" (Mt.5:3).
> "Whosoever therefore shall humble himself as this little child, the same is greatest in the kingdom of heaven" (Mt.18:4).
> "Then shall the King say unto them on his right hand, Come, ye blessed of my Father, inherit the kingdom prepared for you from the foundation of the world: For I was an hungred, and ye gave me meat: I was thirsty, and ye gave me drink: I was a stranger, and ye took me in" (Mt.25:34-35).
> "For whosoever exalteth himself shall be abased; and he that humbleth himself shall be exalted" (Lu.14:11).
> "Hearken, my beloved brethren, Hath not God chosen the poor of this world rich in faith, and heirs of the kingdom which he hath promised to them that love him?" (Js.2:5).
> "But he giveth more grace. Wherefore he saith, God resisteth the proud, but giveth grace unto the humble" (Js.4:6).
> "Be clothed with humility: for God resisteth the proud, and giveth grace to the humble" (1 Pe.5:5).
> "For all those *things* hath mine hand made, and all those *things* have been, saith the LORD: but to this *man* will I look, *even* to *him that is* poor and of a contrite spirit, and trembleth at my word" (Is.66:2).

2) The Savior's mission was to heal the *brokenhearted* (v.1). Throughout every generation there are masses who are *brokenhearted*, just as there were during Isaiah's day. These people are...

- crushed with grief
- devastated by divorce
- overwhelmed with financial problems
- blemished by sin
- deserted by friends
- consumed with loneliness
- ravaged by disease
- enslaved to the world

A host of experiences cause all kinds of suffering for man. Indeed, internal and external pain can be so deep that they break the human heart. To heal and bind up the heart was one of the purposes for which God was to send the Messiah. Once Jesus Christ came into the world, He immediately began to heal the brokenhearted. And He continues His healing ministry even today. Any broken heart can be restored by the *touch* of Jesus Christ. He longs to bind up and heal the brokenhearted.

> "That it might be fulfilled which was spoken by Esaias the prophet, saying, Himself took our infirmities, and bare *our* sicknesses" (Mt.8:17).
> "And deliver them who through fear of death were all their lifetime subject to bondage. For verily he took not on *him the nature of* angels; but he took on *him* the seed of Abraham" (He.2:15-16).
> "For in that he himself hath suffered being tempted, he is able to succour them that are tempted" (He.2:18).
> "The LORD *is* nigh unto them that are of a broken heart; and saveth such as be of a contrite spirit" (Ps.34:18).
> "The sacrifices of God *are* a broken spirit: a broken and a contrite heart, O God, thou wilt not despise" (Ps.51:17).
> "Surely he hath borne our griefs, and carried our sorrows: yet we did esteem him stricken, smitten of God, and afflicted" (Is.53:4).

3) The Savior's mission was to proclaim freedom to those held captive (v.1). Of course, this was not a promise that all the criminals in the world would be set free from prison. Rather, the meaning refers to the two captivating forces from which people cannot escape: the forces of sin and death. Every human being sins and cannot help but sin. And every human being dies and cannot keep from dying. Thus the human race has been taken hostage by sin and death (Ro.3:23; 6:23; 7:14; He.9:27). But the Savior was to liberate or set free the human race from the bondages of sin and death. No human being has the energy, power, or ability to free him or herself. Only God can redeem people, deliver them from wickedness and death. This He has chosen to do through the Savior, the Lord Jesus Christ. God Himself has paid the ransom for man's release—the ransom of a life for a life. He gave the life of His Son so that every person might be set free from the slavery of sin and death. As a result, every captive can be redeemed through the blood of the Savior, the Lord Jesus Christ, who died for the sins of the human race.

> "For God so loved the world, that he gave his only begotten Son, that whosoever believeth in him should not perish, but have everlasting life" (Jn.3:16).
> "For all have sinned, and come short of the glory of God; Being justified freely by his grace through the redemption that is in Christ Jesus" (Ro.3:23-24).

"In whom we have redemption through his blood, the forgiveness of sins, according to the riches of his grace" (Ep.1:7).

"But is now made manifest by the appearing of our Saviour Jesus Christ, who hath abolished death, and hath brought life and immortality to light through the gospel" (2 Ti.1:10).

"Forasmuch then as the children are partakers of flesh and blood, he also himself likewise took part of the same; that through death he might destroy him that had the power of death, that is, the devil; And deliver them who through fear of death were all their lifetime subject to bondage" (He.2:14-15).

"Neither by the blood of goats and calves, but by his own blood he entered in once into the holy place, having obtained eternal redemption *for us*. For if the blood of bulls and of goats, and the ashes of an heifer sprinkling the unclean, sanctifieth to the purifying of the flesh: How much more shall the blood of Christ, who through the eternal Spirit offered himself without spot to God, purge your conscience from dead works to serve the living God?" (He.9:12-14).

"Forasmuch as ye know that ye were not redeemed with corruptible things, *as* silver and gold, from your vain conversation [conduct, behavior] *received* by tradition from your fathers; But with the precious blood of Christ, as of a lamb without blemish and without spot" (1 Pe.1:18-19).

4) The Savior's mission was to proclaim the year of God's salvation and the coming Day of Judgment (v.2). The *acceptable year* or the "year [time] of the LORD's favor" (NIV, NLT) actually means the era, the age of salvation. When the Messiah came into the world, He was to proclaim the glorious message of God's salvation. From the point of the Savior's coming to the end of human history, the marvelous testimony of man's liberation from sin and death and from the coming judgment would be declared. God's favor or wonderful grace was to be poured out upon people. And because of God's grace, people could now be saved. It was the task of the Messiah, Jesus Christ, to make known the grace and salvation of God for the human race. But it was also His task to make known the vengeance of God, for the Day of Judgment was coming. God was to execute vengeance against all who rejected the Messiah and His salvation. It was the God-given task of the Messiah to proclaim both salvation and judgment.

Thought 1. The mission of the Savior, the Lord Jesus Christ, was to proclaim the salvation of God.

"And he said unto them, I must preach the kingdom of God to other cities also: for therefore am I sent" (Lu.4:43).

"I am come to send fire on the earth; and what will I if it be already kindled?" (Lu.12:49).

"For the Son of man is come to seek and to save that which was lost" (Lu.19:10).

"For God sent not his Son into the world to condemn the world; but that the world through him might be saved" (Jn.3:17).

"I am come into this world, that they which see not might see; and that they which see might be made blind" (Jn.9:39).

"And if any man hear my words, and believe not, I judge him not: for I came not to judge the world, but to save the world" (Jn.12:47).

"This *is* a faithful saying, and worthy of all acceptation, that Christ Jesus came into the world to save sinners; of whom I am chief" (1 Ti.1:15).

Thought 2. The mission of Christ was to warn people of the coming judgment or vengeance of God.

"And now also the axe is laid unto the root of the trees: therefore every tree which bringeth not forth good fruit is hewn down, and cast into the fire" (Mt.3:10).

"And if thy right eye offend thee, pluck it out, and cast *it* from thee: for it is profitable for thee that one of thy members should perish, and not *that* thy whole body should be cast into hell. And if thy right hand offend thee, cut if off, and cast *it* from thee: for it is profitable for thee that one of thy members should perish, and not *that* thy whole body should be cast into hell" (Mt.5:29-30).

"Every tree that bringeth not forth good fruit is hewn down, and cast into the fire" (Mt.7:19).

"And fear not them which kill the body, but are not able to kill the soul: but rather fear him which is able to destroy both soul and body in hell" (Mt.10:28).

"And shall cast them into a furnace of fire: there shall be wailing and gnashing of teeth....And shall cast them into the furnace of fire: there shall be wailing and gnashing of teeth" (Mt.13:42, 50).

"Woe unto you, scribes and Pharisees, hypocrites! for ye compass sea and land to make one proselyte, and when he is made, ye make him twofold more the child of hell than yourselves....*Ye* serpents, *ye* generation of vipers, how can ye escape the damnation of hell?" (Mt.23:15, 33).

"Then shall he say also unto them on the left hand, Depart from me, ye cursed, into everlasting fire, prepared for the devil and his angels" (Mt.25:41).

"And now also the axe is laid unto the root of the trees: every tree therefore which bringeth not forth good fruit is hewn down, and cast into the fire" (Lu.3:9).

"And thou, Capernaum, which art exalted to heaven, shalt be thrust down to hell" (Lu.10:15).

"But I will forewarn you whom ye shall fear: Fear him, which after he hath killed hath power to cast into hell; yea, I say unto you, Fear him" (Lu.12:5).

"And in hell he lift up his eyes, being in torments, and seeth Abraham afar off, and Lazarus in his bosom. And he cried and said, Father Abraham, have mercy on me, and send Lazarus, that he

may dip the tip of his finger in water, and cool my tongue; for I am tormented in this flame" (Lu.16:23-24).

"He that believeth on the Son hath everlasting life: and he that believeth not the Son shall not see life; but the wrath of God abideth on him" (Jn.3:36).

5) The Savior's mission was to comfort all who mourned or grieved (v.2c-3). A person *mourns* due to being *bruised* physically, mentally, emotionally, psychologically, or spiritually. Mourning can be caused by such things as...

- disability
- injury
- disease
- pain
- financial hardship
- marital problems
- loss of a loved one
- unemployment

In essence, the Savior was to comfort all who were burdened under the weight of their suffering. When Jesus Christ came, He began to fulfill this wonderful promise. He reached out to console and reassure those who hurt. Even today He will comfort any who turn to Him in their pain and suffering. Moreover, the Savior gives two wonderful promises to those who are going through hard times and deep sorrow:

⇒ They will be given the clothing of beauty—gladness, joy, and praise—instead of the clothing of sackcloth and ashes.

> **"These things have I spoken unto you, that my joy might remain in you, and *that* your joy might be full"** (Jn.15:11).
> **"Hitherto have ye asked nothing in my name: ask, and ye shall receive, that your joy may be full"** (Jn.16:24).
> **"And now come I to thee; and these things I speak in the world, that they might have my joy fulfilled in themselves"** (Jn.17:13).
> **"For the kingdom of God is not meat and drink; but righteousness, and peace, and joy in the Holy Ghost"** (Ro.14:17).
> **"Wherefore seeing we also are compassed about with so great a cloud of witnesses, let us lay aside every weight, and the sin which doth so easily beset us, and let us run with patience the race that is set before us, Looking unto Jesus the author and finisher of *our* faith; who for the joy that was set before him endured the cross, despising the shame, and is set down at the right hand of the throne of God"** (He.12:1-2).

⇒ He will give them a name, a testimony of righteousness (v.3b).

> **"For the kingdom of God is not meat and drink; but righteousness, and peace, and joy in the Holy Ghost"** (Ro.14:17).
> **"For he hath made him *to be* sin for us, who knew no sin; that we might be made the righteousness of God in him"** (2 Co.5:21).
> **"Being filled with the fruits of righteousness, which are by Jesus Christ, unto the glory and praise of God"** (Ph.1:11).
> **"But ye *are* a chosen generation, a royal priesthood, an holy nation, a peculiar people; that ye should show forth the praises of him who hath called you out of darkness into his marvellous light"** (1 Pe.2:9).
> **"Him that overcometh will I make a pillar in the temple of my God, and he shall go no more out: and I will write upon him the name of my God, and the name of the city of my God, *which is* new Jerusalem, which cometh down out of heaven from my God: and *I will write upon him* my new name"** (Re.3:12).

c. The Savior's kingdom and its blessings of salvation were then pictured by Isaiah (vv.4-11). A graphic description is given of the Messiah's coming kingdom, just what life will be like when Christ returns to set up God's kingdom on earth. Nine wonderful blessings are mentioned (also see 60:1-22; 65:17-25; 66:1-24):

1) The nation of Israel will be restored (v.4). All the destroyed cities will be rebuilt, even cities that have been laying in ruins for generations. Note how general this statement is, suggesting that Christ's kingdom will bring about a restoration of all nations on earth. His kingdom will definitely include all nations of the world. This certainly suggests that all cities must be restored to provide the best living conditions possible for people, as well as the best working and environmental conditions. Remember that Christ will be establishing the Kingdom of God in all its perfection throughout the whole world.

2) Positions of authority and management will be given to God's people (v.5). They will receive rewards from the LORD, and one of these rewards will be an assignment of influence and supervision. Remember that Jesus Christ will rule from Jerusalem, the capital or seat of His government. This verse suggests that those living in Jerusalem will be the Lord's officials responsible for the government of the world. Foreigners will be tending the flocks, fields, and vineyards. This simply means that the nations and peoples throughout the rest of the world will be carrying on the day-to-day work of the economy. Foreigners will no longer oppress Jerusalem but, rather, serve the capital of the Messiah.

> **"Do ye not know that the saints shall judge the world? and if the world shall be judged by you, are ye unworthy to judge [oversee, manage] the smallest matters? Know ye not that we shall judge angels? how much more things that pertain to this life?"** (1 Co.6:2-3).

"Because thou hast kept the word of my patience, I also will keep thee from the hour of temptation, which shall come upon all the world, to try them that dwell upon the earth" (Re.3:10).

3) A very special name will be given to God's people, a name of honor (v.6ᵃ). God's people will be called priests of the LORD, ministers of God. Some commentators apply this to Jewish believers, but the blessing is certainly applicable to all God's people, as other Scriptures bear out:

"Ye also, as lively stones, are built up a spiritual house, an holy priesthood, to offer up spiritual sacrifices, acceptable to God by Jesus Christ" (1 Pe.2:5).
"But ye *are* a chosen generation, a royal priesthood, an holy nation, a peculiar people; that ye should show forth the praises of him who hath called you out of darkness into his marvellous light: Which in time past *were* not a people, but *are* now the people of God: which had not obtained mercy, but now have obtained mercy" (1 Pe.2:9-10).
"And hath made us kings and priests unto God and his Father; to him *be* glory and dominion for ever and ever. Amen" (Re.1:6).
"Blessed and holy *is* he that hath part in the first resurrection: on such the second death hath no power, but they shall be priests of God and of Christ, and shall reign with him a thousand years" (Re.20:6).

4) A very special blessing will be given to the Jews and their capital: Jerusalem will become the world's capital and worship center (v.6ᵇ). The wealth of the nations will pour into Jerusalem, and believers will praise the LORD for these riches.

5) A double inheritance in the promised land will be given to God's people (v.7). Down through the generations God's people had been disgraced by the oppressors of the world. But in the Messiah's kingdom they will rejoice due to receiving a double inheritance, a double portion of prosperity in the promised land. Believers should always remember the wonderful inheritance promised them by the LORD:

"In my Father's house are many mansions: if *it were* not so, I would have told you. I go to prepare a place for you. And if I go and prepare a place for you, I will come again, and receive you unto myself; that where I am, *there* ye may be also" (Jn.14:2-3).
"The Spirit itself beareth witness with our spirit, that we are the children of God: And if children, then heirs; heirs of God, and joint-heirs with Christ; if so be that we suffer with *him,* that we may be also glorified together" (Ro.8:16-17).
"For ye are all the children of God by faith in Christ Jesus. For as many of you as have been baptized into Christ have put on Christ. There is neither Jew nor Greek, there is neither bond nor free, there is neither male nor female: for ye are all one in Christ Jesus. And if ye *be* Christ's, then are ye Abraham's seed, and heirs according to the promise" (Ga.3:26-29).
"For our conversation [citizenship] is in heaven; from whence also we look for the Saviour, the Lord Jesus Christ: Who shall change our vile body, that it may be fashioned like unto his glorious body, according to the working whereby he is able even to subdue all things unto himself" (Ph.3:20-21).
"That being justified by his grace, we should be made heirs according to the hope of eternal life" (Tit.3:7).
"Blessed *be* the God and Father of our Lord Jesus Christ, which according to his abundant mercy hath begotten us again unto a lively hope by the resurrection of Jesus Christ from the dead, To an inheritance incorruptible, and undefiled, and that fadeth not away, reserved in heaven for you" (1 Pe.1:3-4).

6) Justice, peace, and security will rule in the Messiah's kingdom (v.8ᵃ). Society will be free of criminals, and there will be no lawlessness. An unbelievable transformation! Nevertheless, this is the wonderful promise of the LORD given to His people.

"Through the tender mercy of our God; whereby the dayspring from on high hath visited us, To give light to them that sit in darkness and *in* the shadow of death, to guide our feet into the way of peace" (Lu.1:78-79).
"And suddenly there was with the angel a multitude of the heavenly host praising God, and saying, Glory to God in the highest, and on earth peace, good will toward men" (Lu.2:13-14).
"Peace I leave with you, my peace I give unto you: not as the world giveth, give I unto you. Let not your heart be troubled, neither let it be afraid" (Jn.14:27).
"These things I have spoken unto you, that in me ye might have peace. In the world ye shall have tribulation: but be of good cheer; I have overcome the world" (Jn.16:33).
"But in every nation he that feareth him, and worketh righteousness, is accepted with him" (Ac.10:35).
"For to be carnally minded *is* death; but to be spiritually minded *is* life and peace. Because the carnal mind *is* enmity against God: for it is not subject to the law of God, neither indeed can be" (Ro.8:6-7).
"For the kingdom of God is not meat and drink; but righteousness, and peace, and joy in the Holy Ghost" (Ro.14:17).

7) The Messiah will establish an *everlasting covenant* with the people (v.8b). When Jesus Christ came to earth the first time, He established a new, eternal relationship with God. In the Messiah's kingdom, God's people will be filled with the Holy Spirit and the Word of God. His laws and commandments will be written on their hearts.

> "For this *is* the covenant that I will make with the house of Israel after those days, saith the Lord; I will put my laws into their mind, and write them in their hearts: and I will be to them a God, and they shall be to me a people" (He.8:10).
> "And for this cause he is the mediator of the new testament, that by means of death, for the redemption of the transgressions *that were* under the first testament, they which are called might receive the promise of eternal inheritance. For where a testament *is*, there must also of necessity be the death of the testator. For a testament *is* of force after men are dead: otherwise it is of no strength at all while the testator liveth. Whereupon neither the first *testament* was dedicated without blood" (He.9:15-18).
> "This *is* the covenant that I will make with them after those days, saith the Lord, I will put my laws into their hearts, and in their minds will I write them" (He.10:16).
> "Incline your ear, and come unto me: hear, and your soul shall live; and I will make an everlasting covenant with you, *even* the sure mercies of David" (Is.55:3).
> "As for me, this *is* my covenant with them, saith the LORD; My spirit that *is* upon thee, and my words which I have put in thy mouth, shall not depart out of thy mouth, nor out of the mouth of thy seed, nor out of the mouth of thy seed's seed, saith the LORD, from henceforth and for ever" (Is.59:21).
> "And I will make an everlasting covenant with them, that I will not turn away from them, to do them good; but I will put my fear in their hearts, that they shall not depart from me" (Je.32:40).

8) God's people will be honored before the world (v.9). All the world will acknowledge God's blessings to Israel, which was one of the promises given to Abraham (see outline and notes—Ge.12:1-3 for more discussion). Because of their righteous lives, all believers bear opposition from the world, ranging from minor ridicule over to brutality and martyrdom. But in the day of the Messiah's kingdom, all people will acknowledge God's blessings upon His people.

> "If any man serve me, let him follow me; and where I am, there shall also my servant be: if any man serve me, him will *my* Father honour" (Jn.12:26).
> "To him that overcometh will I grant to sit with me in my throne, even as I also overcame, and am set down with my Father in his throne" (Re.3:21).

9) The coming kingdom of the Messiah will bring great joy and rejoicing (vv.10-11). In these two verses, all the citizens of Zion are seen praising God for two reasons:
⇒ because the LORD had clothed them in salvation and righteousness
⇒ because the LORD causes the seed of righteousness and praise to spring up in all the nations of the world (v.11)

When a person comes to the Messiah for salvation, God clothes him in the righteousness of Christ. Bringing the joy of righteousness and salvation to the earth was the very purpose for the Savior's coming.

> "And when the king came in to see the guests, he saw there a man which had not on a wedding garment [a robe of righteousness]: And he saith unto him, Friend, how camest thou in hither not having a wedding garment? And he was speechless. Then said the king to the servants, Bind him hand and foot, and take him away, and cast *him* into outer darkness; there shall be weeping and gnashing of teeth" (Mt.22:11-13).
> "And the son said unto him, Father, I have sinned against heaven, and in thy sight, and am no more worthy to be called thy son. But the father said to his servants, Bring forth the best robe [of righteousness], and put *it* on him; and put a ring on his hand, and shoes on *his* feet: And bring hither the fatted calf, and kill *it;* and let us eat, and be merry: For this my son was dead, and is alive again; he was lost, and is found. And they began to be merry" (Lu.15:21-24).
> "For he hath made him *to be* sin for us, who knew no sin; that we might be made the righteousness of God in him" (2 Co.5:21).
> "And that ye put on the new man, which after God is created in righteousness and true holiness" (Ep.4:24).
> "I put on righteousness, and it clothed me: my judgment *was* as a robe and a diadem" (Jb.29:14).
> "And he answered and spake unto those that stood before him, saying, Take away the filthy garments from him. And unto him he said, Behold, I have caused thine iniquity to pass from thee, and I will clothe thee with change of raiment [a robe of righteousness]" (Zec.3:4).

2 (62:1-12) **Salvation, Assurance, Source—Word of God, Promises of, Assurance—Watchman, Duty, to Assure Believers—Ministers, Duty—Believers, Duty—Prayer, Duty—Cry - Crying, to the LORD—God, Work of, to Give Assurance—Invitation, of God—God, Proclamation, Concerning Christ—Jesus Christ, Work of, to Give**

Assurance: God gave the wonderful assurance of salvation through the coming Savior. With all the oppression, suffering, war, death, and evil in the world, believers often have a yearning for Christ to return They long for God's kingdom on earth. This yearning has been in the hearts of believers for centuries, yet Christ has not returned (2 Pe.3:3-10). God's kingdom has not yet come to earth. The prediction that the Jews will experience a great revival, that many will turn to the Lord Jesus has not happened. Neither has Jerusalem become the Holy City of God, a city that is truly righteous. Due to the promises still unfulfilled and all the wickedness and corruption in the world, there are always some believers who need to be reassured. Every human being experiences the need for assurance at some point in time. Even believers need to know that God is truly going to fulfill His promises of salvation. In these verses God gives to Jewish and Gentile believers four wonderful assurances of salvation.

OUTLINE	SCRIPTURE	SCRIPTURE	OUTLINE
2. The assurance of salvation through the coming Savior a. Salvation is assured because of the Lord's Word: He will not keep silent 1) The Holy City's righteousness & salvation must shine forth • The nations must see & desire her righteousness • The city must be given a new name by the LORD: Undergo a complete change 2) The Holy City will be a valuable possession to the LORD: Will be like a crown, a royal diadem 3) The Holy City will no longer be called *Deserted* or *Desolate*: Will be re-named • Hephzibah: *My delight is in her* • Beulah: *Married One* 4) The Holy City will be re-possessed by believers: The LORD will rejoice just as a bridegroom rejoices over his bride b. Salvation is assured because of the watchmen's (believers') proclamation: They must not be silent 1) Believers must call on the	For Zion's sake will I not hold my peace, and for Jerusalem's sake I will not rest, until the righteousness thereof go forth as brightness, and the salvation thereof as a lamp *that* burneth. 2 And the Gentiles shall see thy righteousness, and all kings thy glory: and thou shalt be called by a new name, which the mouth of the LORD shall name. 3 Thou shalt also be a crown of glory in the hand of the LORD, and a royal diadem in the hand of thy God. 4 Thou shalt no more be termed Forsaken; neither shall thy land any more be termed Desolate: but thou shalt be called Hephzi-bah, and thy land Beulah: for the LORD delighteth in thee, and thy land shall be married. 5 For *as* a young man marrieth a virgin, *so* shall thy sons marry thee: and *as* the bridegroom rejoiceth over the bride, *so* shall thy God rejoice over thee. 6 I have set watchmen upon thy walls, O Jerusalem, *which* shall never hold their peace day nor night: ye that make mention of the LORD, keep	not silence, 7 And give him no rest, till he establish, and till he make Jerusalem a praise in the earth. 8 The LORD hath sworn by his right hand, and by the arm of his strength, Surely I will no more give thy corn *to be* meat for thine enemies; and the sons of the stranger shall not drink thy wine, for the which thou hast laboured: 9 But they that have gathered it shall eat it, and praise the LORD; and they that have brought it together shall drink it in the courts of my holiness. 10 Go through, go through the gates; prepare ye the way of the people; cast up, cast up the highways; gather out the stones; lift up a standard for the people. 11 Behold, the LORD hath proclaimed unto the end of the world, Say ye to the daughter of Zion, Behold, thy salvation cometh; behold, his reward *is* with him, and his work before him. 12 And they shall call them, The holy people, The redeemed of the LORD: and thou shalt be called, Sought out, A city not forsaken.	LORD day and night 2) Believers must give the LORD no rest until He fulfills His promises: Establishes Jerusalem c. Salvation is assured because of the LORD's sworn oath, His strong promise 1) His promise that Jerusalem will be restored & never again be invaded by enemies 2) His promise that the Jews will labor & worship in the promised land—*in peace* d. Salvation is assured because of the LORD's worldwide summons & invitation 1) The Lord's summons: "Go…prepare the way…build the highway" of salvation 2) The LORD's proclamation to the whole world: "Your Savior comes! His reward is with Him" 3) The people who respond: The Holy People, the Redeemed of the LORD 4) The Holy City will be called *Sought after…*

a. Salvation is assured because of God's Word (vv.1-5). Down through the centuries, God worked through the Jews to bring salvation to the world. And He will continue to work out His salvation for the world. Under no circumstances will He *hold His peace* or *keep silent*. Four reasons are given why the salvation of the world must be brought to completion.

1) The righteousness and salvation of Jerusalem must shine forth like the dawn or like a blazing torch (vv.1-2). Of course, this is a reference to the Messiah's presence and rule being centered in Jerusalem. The glory of His righteousness and salvation must be honored by the nations. For this reason, the city will be given a new name, which means it will undergo a complete change.

2) The Holy City of Jerusalem will become the valuable possession of the LORD (v.3). It will be like a crown, a royal diadem held in the hand of God Himself.

3) The Holy City will no longer be called *Deserted* or *Desolate,* not in the day of the Messiah's kingdom. It will be renamed *Hephzibah*, which means *my delight is in her* (v.4). Moreover, the land of Judah will be renamed *Beulah*, which means *married one*. God will look upon the promised land as belonging to Him, a land and a people whom He would never cast away.

4) The Holy City will be repossessed by believers (v.5). And the LORD will rejoice over Jerusalem like a bridegroom rejoices over His bride.

God has determined that the Messiah will return to set up God's kingdom on earth. The seat of government will be Jerusalem, which will be established as the capital of the world. From there the righteousness and glory of God will shine forth throughout the whole world. When God's kingdom has been brought to completion, salvation will be completed. This wonderful promise is *assured*, guaranteed by God's Word.

b. Salvation is also assured because of the watchmen's proclamation (v.6). Who are the watchmen? In ancient history they were men who were assigned the task of guarding the city from a surprise attack. In the present passage, *watchmen* refer to both *prophets* and *righteous believers*. All righteous believers are to be *watchmen*, prayer warriors. True believers are to cry out day and night to the LORD, never being silent and never giving themselves rest. They are to cry out for God to fulfill His promises, establishing Jerusalem as the center of God's government on earth. Believers are to cry for the LORD to return to set up God's kingdom on earth.

c. Salvation is assured because of the LORD's sworn oath, His strong promise (vv.8-9). The LORD has sworn that Jerusalem will be restored and never again invaded by enemies (v.8). This will take place after Christ returns to set up God's kingdom on earth. No longer will the food and possessions for which the people have labored be stolen from them. Instead they will eat their own food and be allowed to freely worship in the promised land. Peace will reign throughout Jerusalem and the entire world during the Messiah's kingdom. The LORD's sworn oath guarantees the promise of peace.

d. Salvation is assured because of the LORD's worldwide summons and invitation (vv.10-12). What is the summons? The people are to "go...prepare the way...build the highway" of salvation, for the salvation of God—the Savior Himself— is soon coming. Preparations must be made. A special roadway needs to be built or an existing roadway upgraded to be ready for His arrival. All obstacles that would keep a person from receiving and welcoming the Savior must be removed. Along with that, a high-flying banner must be raised so all the nations will know of His coming.

Note that the proclamation of His coming is to be shouted out to the very ends of the earth: "Your Savior comes! His reward is with Him" (v.11). When the message of salvation is proclaimed, some people will respond and become true followers of the Savior. These true believers will be given a new name, the *Holy People*, the *Redeemed of the LORD* (v.12). And the Holy City of Jerusalem will be known as a city *Sought Out, a city no longer forsaken*.

Thought 1. God's summons is meant for the world today as much as it was in Isaiah's day. We must "Go...prepare the way...build the highway" of salvation, for the Lord Jesus Christ, the Savior of the world, has already come. In view of this, we must respond to the message, accept His wonderful salvation. God gives us great assurance about the certainty of salvation, the assurance that we will be saved from sin, death, and the judgment to come. If we will truly receive Christ as our Savior, He will flood us with a deep sense of...

• being forgiven our sins
• being accepted by God
• inheriting eternal life

"Being confident of this very thing, that he which hath begun a good work in you will perform *it* until the day of Jesus Christ" (Ph.1:6).

"For our gospel came not unto you in word only, but also in power, and in the Holy Ghost, and in much assurance; as ye know what manner of men we were among you for your sake" (1 Th.1:5).

"I am not ashamed: for I know whom I have believed, and am persuaded that he is able to keep that which I have committed unto him against that day" (2 Ti.1:12).

"And the Lord shall deliver me from every evil work, and will preserve *me* unto his heavenly kingdom: to whom *be* glory for ever and ever. Amen" (2 Ti.4:18).

"Let us draw near with a true heart in full assurance of faith, having our hearts sprinkled from an evil conscience, and our bodies washed with pure water. Let us hold fast the profession of *our* faith without wavering; (for he is faithful that promised;) And let us consider one another to provoke unto love and to good works: Not forsaking the assembling of ourselves together, as the manner of some *is*; but exhorting *one another*: and so much the more, as ye see the day approaching" (He.10:22-25).

"Who are kept by the power of God through faith unto salvation ready to be revealed in the last time" (1 Pe.1:5).

"My little children, these things write I unto you, that ye sin not. And if any man sin, we have an advocate with the Father, Jesus Christ the righteous: And he is the propitiation for our sins: and not for ours only, but also for *the sins of* the whole world. And hereby we do know that we know him, if we keep his commandments. He that saith, I know him, and keepeth not his commandments, is a liar, and the truth is not in him. But whoso keepeth his word, in him verily is the love of God perfected: hereby know we that we are in him" (1 Jn.2:1-5).

"My little children, let us not love in word, neither in tongue; but in deed and in truth. And hereby we know that we are of the truth, and shall assure our hearts before him" (1 Jn.3:18-19).

"Hereby know we that we dwell in him, and he in us, because he hath given us of his Spirit. And we have seen and do testify that the Father sent the Son *to be* the Saviour of the world. Whosoever shall confess that Jesus is the Son of God, God dwelleth in him, and he in God" (1 Jn.4:13-15).

"And this is the record, that God hath given to us eternal life, and this life is in his Son. He that hath the Son hath life; *and* he that hath not the Son of God hath not life. These things have I written unto you that believe on the name of the Son of God; that ye may know that ye have eternal life, and that ye may believe on the name of the Son of God. And this is the confidence that we have in him, that, if we ask any thing according to his will, he heareth us: And if we know that he hear us, whatsoever we ask, we know that we have the petitions that we desired of him" (1 Jn.5:11-15).

"Now unto him that is able to keep you from falling, and to present *you* faultless before the presence of his glory with exceeding joy, To the only wise God our Saviour, *be* glory and majesty, dominion and power, both now and ever. Amen" (Jude 24-25).

1. The great day of God's vengeance, 34:1-17; Re.19:1-21
   a. Who will be judged? Edom & its capital Bozrah—symbols of a world that rejects God, 3
   b. Who will execute judgment?
      1) He who comes in glory, strength, & righteousness: To save people
      2) He who has clothes stained red with blood: Christ, Jn.5:22; Re.14:17-20; 19:13
         • He will act alone: Not use nations & people as He had in past history
         • He personally will crush the wicked & the oppressors: Just as grapes are crushed in a winepress
   c. Why will He execute judgment?
      1) Because vengeance against evil & redemption for His people are in His heart
      2) Because He will find no one else who will step forth to help His people
         • His own arm (power) & wrath will save His people
         • His own arm (power) & wrath will crush the nations

2. The great mercy of God: Proves that He will execute judgment & redeem or save His people
   a. God's acts of love for His people down through history: To be praised for His unfailing acts of compassion
      1) God had chosen them to be His people: Trusted them to be true to Him
      2) God had become their Savior
         • Identified with their distress & sufferings
         • Saved, redeemed, & carried them through all the years
      3) God had disciplined them when they rebelled & grieved His Holy Spirit

CHAPTER 63

C. The Great Day of God's Vengeance & Mercy: A Picture of Armageddon, 63:1–64:12

Who *is* this that cometh from Edom, with dyed garments from Bozrah? this *that is* glorious in his apparel, travelling in the greatness of his strength? I that speak in righteousness, mighty to save.

2 Wherefore *art thou* red in thine apparel, and thy garments like him that treadeth in the winefat?

3 I have trodden the winepress alone; and of the people *there was* none with me: for I will tread them in mine anger, and trample them in my fury; and their blood shall be sprinkled upon my garments, and I will stain all my raiment.

4 For the day of vengeance *is* in mine heart, and the year of my redeemed is come.

5 And I looked, and *there was* none to help; and I wondered that *there was* none to uphold: therefore mine own arm brought salvation unto me; and my fury, it upheld me.

6 And I will tread down the people in mine anger, and make them drunk in my fury, and I will bring down their strength to the earth.

7 I will mention the lovingkindnesses of the LORD, *and* the praises of the LORD, according to all that the LORD hath bestowed on us, and the great goodness toward the house of Israel, which he hath bestowed on them according to his mercies, and according to the multitude of his lovingkindnesses.

8 For he said, Surely they *are* my people, children *that* will not lie: so he was their Saviour.

9 In all their affliction he was afflicted, and the angel of his presence saved them: in his love and in his pity he redeemed them; and he bare them, and carried them all the days of old.

10 But they rebelled, and vexed his holy Spirit: therefore he was turned to be their enemy, *and* he fought against them.

11 Then he remembered the days of old, Moses, *and* his people, *saying,* Where *is* he that brought them up out of the sea with the shepherd of his flock? where *is* he that put his holy Spirit within him?

12 That led *them* by the right hand of Moses with his glorious arm, dividing the water before them, to make himself an everlasting name?

13 That led them through the deep, as an horse in the wilderness, *that* they should not stumble?

14 As a beast goeth down into the valley, the Spirit of the LORD caused him to rest: so didst thou lead thy people, to make thyself a glorious name.

15 Look down from heaven, and behold from the habitation of thy holiness and of thy glory: where *is* thy zeal and thy strength, the sounding of thy bowels and of thy mercies toward me? are they restrained?

16 Doubtless thou *art* our father, though Abraham be ignorant of us, and Israel acknowledge us not: thou, O LORD, *art* our father, our redeemer; thy name *is* from everlasting.

17 O LORD, why hast thou made us to err from thy ways, *and* hardened our heart from thy fear? Return for thy servants' sake, the tribes of thine inheritance.

18 The people of thy holiness have possessed *it* but a little while: our adversaries have trodden down thy sanctuary.

19 We are *thine:* thou never barest rule over them; they were not called by thy name.

CHAPTER 64

Oh that thou wouldest rend the heavens, that thou wouldest come down, that the mountains might flow down at thy presence,

2 As *when* the melting fire burneth, the fire causeth the waters to boil, to make thy name known to thine adversaries, *that* the nations may

      4) God had used His discipline to stir them to repent & to remember His care: During the days of Moses
         • To remember God's gift of the great leader Moses
         • To remember God's giving them His Holy Spirit
         • To remember God's awesome power in dividing the Red Sea
         • To remember God's guidance in leading them & in keeping them from stumbling
         • To remember the spiritual & physical *rest* that God had given them in the promised land (Jos.23:1)
   b. God's purpose: To make sure His name is glorified

3. The great cry for deliverance
   a. A cry for God to look down: To hear & help His people
      1) Because God's zeal & strength as well as His mercy & compassion seemed to be withheld from them
      2) Because God was still their Father & Redeemer: Although Abraham & Jacob (Israel) would have disowned the present generation due to their sins
      3) Because they had turned away from God, hardened their hearts & no longer feared Him
      4) Because there were still some servants (true believers) among them
      5) Because their enemies had destroyed God's holy temple
      6) Because they were so sinful, it was as though they had never belonged to God

   b. A cry for God to come down: To display His power
      1) To come down to execute judgment: A picture of God's awesome power on Mt. Sinai, Ex.19:16-19
         • To make His name known to His enemies

276

• To cause the nations to tremble	tremble at thy presence! 3 When thou didst terrible things *which* we looked not for, thou camest down, the mountains flowed down at thy presence.	calleth upon thy name, that stirreth up himself to take hold of thee: for thou hast hid thy face from us, and hast consumed us, because of our iniquities.	God's mercy or forgiveness 5) Confessed God was forced to turn His face away from them: His holiness would not allow Him to look on their sins
2) To come down because He alone had proven He was God (since the world began) 3) To come down to help those who waited (believed) on God & willingly did what was right	4 For since the beginning of the world *men* have not heard, nor perceived by the ear, neither hath the eye seen, O God, beside thee, *what* he hath prepared for him that waiteth for him.	8 But now, O LORD, thou *art* our father; we *are* the clay, and thou our potter; and we all *are* the work of thy hand.	6) Confessed God was their Father: He was the Potter; they were the clay
c. A cry of confession 1) Confessed they were habitual sinners: They angered God & did not deserve to be saved	5 Thou meetest him that rejoiceth and worketh righteousness, *those that* remember thee in thy ways: behold, thou art wroth; for we have sinned: in those is continuance, and we shall be saved.	9 Be not wroth very sore, O LORD, neither remember iniquity for ever: behold, see, we beseech thee, we *are* all thy people. 10 Thy holy cities are a wilderness, Zion is a wilderness, Jerusalem a desolation.	d. A cry for forgiveness: Feared God would be so angry He would remember their sins forever 1) Because they were His people 2) Because their cities—even the Holy City Jerusalem—had been destroyed
2) Confessed they were unclean, impure, infected with sin: Their righteousness was no better than filthy rags	6 But we are all as an unclean *thing,* and all our righteousnesses *are* as filthy rags; and we all do fade as a leaf; and our iniquities, like the wind, have taken us away.	11 Our holy and our beautiful house, where our fathers praised thee, is burned up with fire: and all our pleasant things are laid waste.	3) Because the holy, beautiful temple had been burned & ruined
3) Confessed they were weak, unstable: They were like a shriveled up leaf 4) Confessed no one sought	7 And *there is* none that	12 Wilt thou refrain thyself for these *things,* O LORD? wilt thou hold thy peace, and afflict us very sore?	4) Because they desperately needed His deliverance: He must not keep silent, refuse to help

DIVISION VII

THE PROPHECIES OF A GREAT AND GLORIOUS FUTURE, 60:1–66:24

C.   The Great Day of God's Vengeance and Mercy: A Picture of Armageddon, 63:1–64:12

(63:1–64:12) **Introduction**: Armageddon is the last, decisive battle or war among the nations of the earth. Because it is known to be the last battle, a discussion of Armageddon arouses keen interest among many, in particular true Christian believers. Armageddon is where human history, under the government of human leaders, will end. Why then and there? Because at Armageddon the Lord Jesus Christ will return to earth. He will intervene and stop the madness of the human race. In that climactic day, all the wicked of this earth will face the blazing fire of God's holiness and be consumed, doomed to spend eternity in hell separated from Him. But the righteous of this earth will receive the mercy of God. They will be delivered and receive their eternal inheritance promised by God through the ages. This is, *The Great Day of God's Vengeance and Mercy: A Picture of Armageddon*, 63:1–64:12.
　　1. The great day of God's vengeance, (63:1-6).
　　2. The great mercy of God: proves that He will execute judgment and redeem or save His people (63:7-14).
　　3. The great cry for deliverance (63:15–64:12).

[1] (63:1-6) **Vengeance, of God, Day of—Prophecy, Concerning Armageddon, Discussed—Judgment, in Last Days, Discussed; Armageddon—End Times, Judgment Day, Armageddon—Jesus Christ, Agent of, Judgment**: the great day of God's vengeance, the day of Armageddon, is coming. Furthermore, it cannot be stopped. In fact, this prophecy by Isaiah is a picture of Christ returning from the battle of Armageddon. The battle has already taken place, and the nations of the world who have sought to destroy God's people have just been crushed by the LORD Himself. Isaiah's prophecy answers the major questions about Armageddon:

OUTLINE	SCRIPTURE	SCRIPTURE	OUTLINE
1. The great day of God's vengeance, 34:1-17; Re.19:1-21 a. Who will be judged? Edom & its capital Bozrah—symbols of a world that rejects God, 3 b. Who will execute judgment? 　1) He who comes in glory, strength, & righteousness: To save people	Who *is* this that cometh from Edom, with dyed garments from Bozrah? this *that is* glorious in his apparel, travelling in the greatness of his strength? I that speak in righteousness, mighty to save. 2 Wherefore *art thou* red in thine apparel, and thy gar-	ments like him that treadeth in the winefat? 3 I have trodden the winepress alone; and of the people *there was* none with me: for I will tread them in mine anger, and trample them in my fury; and their blood shall be sprinkled upon my garments, and I will stain all my rai-	2) He who has clothes stained red with blood: Christ, Jn.5:22; Re.14:17-20; 19:13 • He will act alone: Not use nations & people as He had in past history • He personally will crush the wicked & the oppressors: Just as grapes are crushed in a

277

OUTLINE	SCRIPTURE	SCRIPTURE	OUTLINE

winepress
c. Why will He execute judgment?
  1) Because vengeance against evil & redemption for His people are in His heart
  2) Because He will find no one else who will step forth to help His people
	ment.
	4 For the day of vengeance *is* in mine heart, and the year of my redeemed is come.
	5 And I looked, and *there was* none to help; and I wondered that *there was* none to
		uphold: therefore mine own arm brought salvation unto me; and my fury, it upheld me.
		6 And I will tread down the people in mine anger, and make them drunk in my fury, and I will bring down their strength to the earth.
			• His own arm (power) & wrath will save His people
			• His own arm (power) & wrath will crush the nations

a. Who will be judged? Edom and its capital Bozrah. These sites symbolize all the nations and strongholds in the world that reject God and persecute His people (vv.1, 3, 6). Edom was chosen as a representative of the wicked nations of the earth because its people had always been *bitter enemies* of the LORD and His people. An unyielding hostility and deep-seated animosity flowed through the veins of the Edomites. Thus they became a symbol of the nations who defied the LORD and mistreated His people. All nations—governments, leaders, citizens—who take a stand against the LORD and His people will face the hand of God's judgment. They will be destroyed in the future battle of Armageddon.

b. Who will execute judgment? The LORD Himself (vv.1-2). This is a clear reference to Jesus Christ. Christ is returning, coming back to earth a second time. When Christ came the first time, He came as a baby born in a manger. He came as the Savior to rescue people from their sins and from death, offering eternal life to all. But when Christ comes the second time, He will come as judge of the entire earth. He will come clothed in the majestic glory and awesome power of God Himself. Note that He identified Himself as the One who speaks "in righteousness, mighty to save" (v.1). His purpose for coming will be to execute justice on earth. Executing justice includes rewarding those who truly believe and have been faithful to the LORD as well as punishing those who have lived wicked lives. In the great day of God's vengeance, the Battle of Armageddon, He will demonstrate His mighty power to save His people from their oppressors.

Note that the LORD's clothes will be stained red with blood, looking like the clothing of a person who has been trampling the grapes of a wine press. The ancient winepress was usually a shallow pit with a hole at one end through which the juice flowed out into containers. As people trampled the grapes, juice would naturally splatter their clothing. The picture being clearly painted is that of the LORD's robe being completely covered with the blood of the wicked. Note that Christ Himself is speaking, declaring that He has trampled the nations under His foot. He makes two declarations:

⇒ In executing judgment, God acted alone (v.3). Unlike His practice in the past, He did not use nations or people to accomplish the punishment of the wicked. In the great day of vengeance, God will execute His wrath against all the wicked nations and peoples of this earth.

⇒ God will personally destroy the evil and oppressive people of the earth. He will crush them as grapes are crushed in a winepress.

c. Why will the LORD execute judgment (vv.4-6)? First, because two things are in His heart: vengeance against evil and redemption for His people (v.4). His very nature is that of holiness and love. His holiness demands the execution of righteousness or judgment, and His love demands that He redeem and save His people. The immoral, lawless, and violent of this earth must bear the consequences of their wicked behavior. They must pay the penalty for having broken God's law. Thus true justice must be executed against them. But redemption is also in the heart of God. Because of His perfect love, He will return to earth to save His people from the oppression of their enemies and from sin and death.

Second, in the last days of human history, God will find no one who can step forth to help His people (v.5). The day is coming when the vast majority of the world's population will oppress and seek to stamp out God's people. In that day the LORD's arm of power and His wrath will save His people. Raising His arm in might and fury, the LORD will crush the nations. Every evil nation of this earth will be made drunk with the wine of God's wrath, and their blood will be poured out on the ground (v.6; also see 29:5-8. See outline and notes—Re.14:14-20; 16:12-16; 19:11-21.)

Thought 1. The day of God's vengeance is coming. All the nations and peoples of this earth who have opposed God and persecuted His people will face the judgment of God's hand.

> **"He that believeth on the Son hath everlasting life: and he that believeth not the Son shall not see life; but the wrath of God abideth on him" (Jn.3:36).**
> **"For the wrath of God is revealed from heaven against all ungodliness and unrighteousness of men, who hold the truth in unrighteousness" (Ro.1:18).**
> **"But unto them that are contentious, and do not obey the truth, but obey unrighteousness, indignation and wrath, Tribulation and anguish, upon every soul of man that doeth evil, of the Jew first, and also of the Gentile" (Ro.2:8-9).**
> **"Dearly beloved, avenge not yourselves, but *rather* give place unto wrath: for it is written, Vengeance *is* mine; I will repay, saith the Lord" (Ro.12:19).**
> **"But fornication, and all uncleanness, or covetousness, let it not be once named among you, as becometh saints; Neither filthiness, nor foolish talking, nor jesting, which are not convenient: but rather giving of thanks. For this ye know, that no whoremonger, nor unclean person, nor covetous man, who is an idolater, hath any inheritance in the kingdom of Christ and of God. Let no man deceive you with vain words: for because of these things cometh the wrath of God upon the children of disobedience" (Ep.5:3-6).**
> **"But of the times and the seasons, brethren, ye have no need that I write unto you. For yourselves know perfectly that the day of the Lord so cometh as a thief in the night. For when they shall say,**

Peace and safety; then sudden destruction cometh upon them, as travail upon a woman with child; and they shall not escape" (1 Th.5:1-3).

"And to you who are troubled rest with us, when the Lord Jesus shall be revealed from heaven with his mighty angels, In flaming fire taking vengeance on them that know not God, and that obey not the gospel of our Lord Jesus Christ: Who shall be punished with everlasting destruction from the presence of the Lord, and from the glory of his power" (2 Th.1:7-9).

"Kiss the Son, lest he be angry, and ye perish *from* the way, when his wrath is kindled but a little. Blessed *are* all they that put their trust in him" (Ps.2:12).

"O LORD God, to whom vengeance belongeth; O God, to whom vengeance belongeth, show thyself" (Ps.94:1).

"And I will execute vengeance in anger and fury upon the heathen, such as they have not heard" (Mi.5:15).

"God *is* jealous, and the LORD revengeth; the LORD revengeth, and *is* furious; the LORD will take vengeance on his adversaries, and he reserveth *wrath* for his enemies" (Na.1:2).

2 (63:7-14) **Mercy, of God, Example—Discipline, of God, Example—Chastisement, of God, Example—Love, of God, Example**: the great mercy and love of God has been demonstrated down through history. Therefore God's people can rest assured, His day of redemption will come. As Isaiah just predicted, all the oppressors of God's people will be crushed and true believers will be redeemed by God's mighty hand. The LORD will save His people. A quick glance at the history of Israel shows His unfailing love for all who truly trust Him:

1) The LORD had chosen Abraham and his descendants to be His people. They were to be God's family, His sons and daughters who would be true to Him. But down through history Israel had gone astray time and again. Nevertheless, the LORD had always held out hope that they would not continue to disobey and break His holy commandments.

2) Seeking to hold His family together, the LORD had always stepped forth as their Savior (v.8b-9). Despite their *wayward lives* He had always identified with their distress and sufferings. He had saved, redeemed, and carried them through all the years, never failing to show His love and mercy.

3) When the people rebelled and grieved His Holy Spirit, God always disciplined them as a loving Father (v.10). Sometimes His hand of discipline had to be strong, so strong it appeared as though He was their enemy and was fighting against them. But contrary to appearance, He was merely disciplining His people, seeking to arouse them to correct their behavior.

4) The LORD had used His discipline to stir the people to repent and to remember His care in days of old (vv.11-14). Often His discipline was effective. His people remembered God's love and mercy down through the centuries. In particular, they remembered the days of Moses...

• when God gave them the great gift of a shepherd, a leader like Moses (v.11)

• when God gave His Holy Spirit to dwell among them (Nu.11:17, 25; also see Ex.31:3, 6; 35:30-35)

• when God's awesome power divided the Red Sea (v.12; Ex.14:21-29)

• when God guided and led them step by step, keeping them from stumbling as long as they followed His leadership (v.13)

• when God gave them both spiritual and physical *rest* in the promised land (Jos.23:1)

No greater demonstration of God's love could be given to the human race than His leadership of Israel down through the centuries. He poured His love out upon them in order to glorify His Name among the nations of the earth. By demonstrating His love and mighty power, some people were aroused to repent of their sins and to trust Him as their Savior. God's great acts of compassion in behalf of Israel prove that He will execute judgment and redeem or save His people.

OUTLINE	SCRIPTURE	SCRIPTURE	OUTLINE
2. The great mercy of God: Proves that He will execute judgment & redeem or save His people	7 I will mention the loving-kindnesses of the LORD, *and* the praises of the LORD, according to all that the LORD hath bestowed on us, and the great goodness toward the house of Israel, which he hath bestowed on them according to his mercies, and according to the multitude of his lovingkindnesses.	redeemed them; and he bare them, and carried them all the days of old.	• Saved, redeemed, & carried them through all the years
a. God's acts of love for His people down through history: Isaiah praises God for His unfailing acts of compassion		10 But they rebelled, and vexed his holy Spirit: therefore he was turned to be their enemy, *and* he fought against them.	3) God had disciplined them when they rebelled & grieved His Holy Spirit
		11 Then he remembered the days of old, Moses, *and* his people, *saying,* Where *is* he that brought them up out of the sea with the shepherd of his flock? where *is* he that put his holy Spirit within him?	4) God had used His discipline to stir them to repent & to remember His care: During the days of Moses
1) God had chosen them to be His people: Trusted them to be true to Him	8 For he said, Surely they *are* my people, children *that* will not lie: so he was their Saviour.		• To remember God's gift of the great leader Moses
2) God had become their Savior	9 In all their affliction he was afflicted, and the angel of his presence saved them: in his love and in his pity he	12 That led *them* by the right hand of Moses with his glorious arm, dividing the water	• To remember God's giving them His Holy Spirit
• Identified with their distress & sufferings			• To remember God's

279

OUTLINE	SCRIPTURE	SCRIPTURE	OUTLINE
awesome power in dividing the Red Sea • To remember God's guidance in leading them & in keeping them from stumbling	before them, to make himself an everlasting name? 13 That led them through the deep, as an horse in the wilderness, *that* they should not stumble?	14 As a beast goeth down into the valley, the Spirit of the LORD caused him to rest: so didst thou lead thy people, to make thyself a glorious name.	• To remember the spiritual & physical *rest* that God had given them in the promised land (Jos.23:1) b. God's purpose: To make sure His name is glorified

"And his mercy *is* on them that fear him from generation to generation" (Lu.1:50).

"For God so loved the world, that he gave his only begotten Son, that whosoever believeth in him should not perish, but have everlasting life. For God sent not his Son into the world to condemn the world; but that the world through him might be saved" (Jn.3:16-17).

"Or despisest thou the riches of his goodness and forbearance and longsuffering; not knowing that the goodness of God leadeth thee to repentance? But after thy hardness and impenitent heart treasurest up unto thyself wrath against the day of wrath and revelation of the righteous judgment of God; Who will render to every man according to his deeds: To them who by patient continuance in well doing seek for glory and honour and immortality, eternal life: But unto them that are contentious, and do not obey the truth, but obey unrighteousness, indignation and wrath, Tribulation and anguish, upon every soul of man that doeth evil, of the Jew first, and also of the Gentile; But glory, honour, and peace, to every man that worketh good, to the Jew first, and also to the Gentile" (Ro.2:4-10).

"But God commendeth his love toward us, in that, while we were yet sinners, Christ died for us. Much more then, being now justified by his blood, we shall be saved from wrath through him" (Ro.5:8-9).

"But God, who is rich in mercy, for his great love wherewith he loved us, Even when we were dead in sins, hath quickened us together with Christ, (by grace ye are saved;) And hath raised *us* up together, and made *us* sit together in heavenly *places* in Christ Jesus: That in the ages to come he might show the exceeding riches of his grace in *his* kindness toward us through Christ Jesus. For by grace are ye saved through faith; and that not of yourselves: *it is* the gift of God" (Ep.2:4-8).

"Not by works of righteousness which we have done, but according to his mercy he saved us, by the washing of regeneration, and renewing of the Holy Ghost; Which he shed on us abundantly through Jesus Christ our Saviour; That being justified by his grace, we should be made heirs according to the hope of eternal life" (Tit.3:5-7).

"Good and upright *is* the LORD: therefore will he teach sinners in the way" (Ps.25:8).

"He loveth righteousness and judgment: the earth is full of the goodness of the LORD" (Ps.33:5).

"Because thy lovingkindness *is* better than life, my lips shall praise thee" (Ps.63:3).

"But the mercy of the LORD *is* from everlasting to everlasting upon them that fear him, and his righteousness unto children's children" (Ps.103:17).

"Praise ye the LORD. O give thanks unto the LORD; for *he is* good: for his mercy *endureth* for ever" (Ps.106:1).

"Thou showest lovingkindness unto thousands, and recompensest the iniquity of the fathers into the bosom of their children after them: the Great, the Mighty God, the LORD of hosts, *is* his name" (Je.32:18).

"*It is of* the LORD'S mercies that we are not consumed, because his compassions fail not" (La.3:22).

"And I will betroth thee unto me for ever; yea, I will betroth thee unto me in righteousness, and in judgment, and in lovingkindness, and in mercies" (Ho.2:19).

"And rend your heart, and not your garments, and turn unto the LORD your God: for he *is* gracious and merciful, slow to anger, and of great kindness, and repenteth him of the evil" (Joel 2:13).

"Who *is* a God like unto thee, that pardoneth iniquity, and passeth by the transgression of the remnant of his heritage? he retaineth not his anger for ever, because he delighteth *in* mercy" (Mi.7:18).

"The LORD *is* good, a strong hold in the day of trouble; and he knoweth them that trust in him" (Na.1:7).

---

3 (63:15–64:12) **Deliverance, Duty, Seek After—Confession, Essential, Sixfold—Israel, Confession of—Israel, Cry of, for Deliverance, Fourfold—Deliverance, Cry for, Fourfold—Forgiveness, Cry for, Example—Deliverance, Needed, Six Reasons**: the cry of God's people for deliverance was great. But as is often the case, Isaiah's writings are applicable to all generations of believers. There has never been nor will there ever be a generation that does not need to cry out the appeals of these verses. Note that a fourfold cry was lifted up to the LORD:

OUTLINE	SCRIPTURE	SCRIPTURE	OUTLINE
3. The great cry for deliverance a. A cry for God to look down: To hear & help His people 1) Because God's zeal & strength as well as His	15 Look down from heaven, and behold from the habitation of thy holiness and of thy glory: where *is* thy zeal and thy strength, the sounding of	thy bowels and of thy mercies toward me? are they restrained? 16 Doubtless thou *art* our father, though Abraham be	mercy & compassion seemed to be withheld from them 2) Because God was still their Father & Redeemer:

OUTLINE	SCRIPTURE	SCRIPTURE	OUTLINE
Although Abraham & Jacob (Israel) would have disowned the present generation due to their sins 3) Because they had turned away from God, hardened their hearts & no longer feared Him 4) Because there were still some servants (true believers) among them 5) Because their enemies had destroyed God's holy temple 6) Because they were so sinful, it was as though they had never belonged to God	ignorant of us, and Israel acknowledge us not: thou, O LORD, *art* our father, our redeemer; thy name *is* from everlasting. 17 O LORD, why hast thou made us to err from thy ways, *and* hardened our heart from thy fear? Return for thy servants' sake, the tribes of thine inheritance. 18 The people of thy holiness have possessed *it* but a little while: our adversaries have trodden down thy sanctuary. 19 We are *thine:* thou never barest rule over them; they were not called by thy name.	hath prepared for him that waiteth for him. 5 Thou meetest him that rejoiceth and worketh righteousness, *those that* remember thee in thy ways: behold, thou art wroth; for we have sinned: in those is continuance, and we shall be saved. 6 But we are all as an unclean *thing,* and all our righteousnesses *are* as filthy rags; and we all do fade as a leaf; and our iniquities, like the wind, have taken us away. 7 And *there is* none that calleth upon thy name, that stirreth up himself to take hold of thee: for thou hast hid thy face from us, and hast consumed us, because of our iniquities.	c. A cry of confession 1) Confessed they were habitual sinners: They angered God & did not deserve to be saved 2) Confessed they were unclean, impure, infected with sin: Their righteousness was no better than filthy rags 3) Confessed they were weak, unstable: They were like a shriveled up leaf 4) Confessed no one sought God's mercy or forgiveness 5) Confessed God was forced to turn His face away from them: His holiness would not allow Him to look on their sins
b. A cry for God to come down: To display His power 1) To come down to execute judgment: A picture of God's awesome power on Mt. Sinai, Ex.19:16-19 • To make His name known to His enemies • To cause the nations to tremble 2) To come down because He alone had proven He was God (since the world began) 3) To come down to help those who waited (believed) on God & willingly did what was right	**CHAPTER 64** **O**h that thou wouldest rend the heavens, that thou wouldest come down, that the mountains might flow down at thy presence, 2 As *when* the melting fire burneth, the fire causeth the waters to boil, to make thy name known to thine adversaries, *that* the nations may tremble at thy presence! 3 When thou didst terrible things *which* we looked not for, thou camest down, the mountains flowed down at thy presence. 4 For since the beginning of the world *men* have not heard, nor perceived by the ear, neither hath the eye seen, O God, beside thee, *what* he	8 But now, O LORD, thou *art* our father; we *are* the clay, and thou our potter; and we all *are* the work of thy hand. 9 Be not wroth very sore, O LORD, neither remember iniquity for ever: behold, see, we beseech thee, we *are* all thy people. 10 Thy holy cities are a wilderness, Zion is a wilderness, Jerusalem a desolation. 11 Our holy and our beautiful house, where our fathers praised thee, is burned up with fire: and all our pleasant things are laid waste. 12 Wilt thou refrain thyself for these *things,* O LORD? wilt thou hold thy peace, and afflict us very sore?	6) Confessed God was their Father: He was the Potter; they were the clay d. A cry for forgiveness: Feared God would be so angry He would remember their sins forever 1) Because they were His people 2) Because their cities—even the Holy City Jerusalem—had been destroyed 3) Because the holy, beautiful temple had been burned & ruined 4) Because they desperately needed His deliverance: He must not keep silent, refuse to help

a. There was a cry for God to *look down,* to hear and help His people (vv.15-19). They needed His help as much as their forefathers had. Therefore they were begging the LORD to *look down,* to remember their hardships and distress in the same way He had remembered their forefathers. Appealing to the LORD, Isaiah listed six reasons why the people needed God's help:

1) The people needed God's help because His zeal and strength seemed to be withheld from them as well as His mercy and compassion (v.15). Simply stated, God seemed to be far away, off in the distance and untouchable. There was no evidence or sense of His presence among them. No acts of God's love, miracles, or works were taking place in their midst.

2) The people confessed they needed God's help because He was still their Father and Redeemer (v.16). Note the acknowledgement of the people: they knew that Abraham and Jacob (Israel) would disown them, the present generation, due to their sins. Acknowledging this fact is a clear indication that a true confession was being made.

3) The people cried out for help because they had turned away from God. In fact, their hearts had become so hardened they no longer *feared* the LORD (v.17). None of the people seemed to reverence the LORD, to esteem Him as the Creator, the sovereign LORD and Majesty of the universe. Neither did they fear the judgment, the holy wrath and vengeance of God.

4) The people cried out for God's help because they knew there were still some *servants,* that is, true believers, among them (v.17b). Not all Israelites were genuine and righteous followers of the LORD. But there were always a few sincere disciples who trusted the LORD with all their hearts and obeyed His holy commandments. Thus the cry is for God to help His people for the sake of these few. Moreover in considering the cry for deliverance, the LORD needed to take into account His promise to true believers, that He would always deliver them.

5) The people cried for God's help because their enemies had destroyed the LORD's holy temple (v.18). Of course, this refers to the future destruction of the temple by the Babylonians and then centuries later by the Romans. With the temple destroyed, it was as though the LORD was powerless to stop the nation's hostility against His people and their worship of the LORD. Therefore the LORD needed to arise to prove His power, for His very honor was at stake.

6) The people cried out to the LORD because of their own appalling sinfulness. It was as if they had never belonged to God (v.19). Their sins had separated them from God, alienated and cut them off from His presence, guidance, and blessings. All because they had broken the covenant between the LORD and themselves.

> **"But seek ye first the kingdom of God, and his righteousness; and all these things shall be added unto you" (Mt.6:33).**
>
> **"And I say unto you, Ask, and it shall be given you; seek, and ye shall find; knock, and it shall be opened unto you. For every one that asketh receiveth; and he that seeketh findeth; and to him that knocketh it shall be opened" (Lu.11:9-10).**
>
> **"But if from thence thou shalt seek the LORD thy God, thou shalt find** *him,* **if thou seek him with all thy heart and with all thy soul" (De.4:29).**
>
> **"Seek the LORD, and his strength: seek his face evermore" (Ps.105:4).**
>
> **"I love them that love me; and those that seek me early shall find me" (Pr.8:17).**
>
> **"Seek ye the LORD while he may be found, call ye upon him while he is near" (Is.55:6).**
>
> **"And ye shall seek me, and find** *me,* **when ye shall search for me with all your heart" (Je.29:13).**
>
> **"Sow to yourselves in righteousness, reap in mercy; break up your fallow ground: for** *it is* **time to seek the LORD, till he come and rain righteousness upon you" (Ho.10:12).**
>
> **"For thus saith the LORD unto the house of Israel, Seek ye me, and ye shall live" (Am.5:4).**
>
> **"Seek ye the LORD, all ye meek of the earth, which have wrought his judgment; seek righteousness, seek meekness: it may be ye shall be hid in the day of the LORD's anger" (Zep.2:3).**

b. There was a cry for God to *come down,* to display His power in behalf of the people (64:1-5a). First, the people cried for the LORD to *come down* to execute judgment (vv.1-3). To the people, the LORD seemed far away, far out beyond the heavens, completely out of reach. Thus they cried for Him to burst forth from the heavens to come to their aid. They desperately needed a demonstration of His awesome power, the kind of power that had been so evident on Mount Sinai (Ex.19:16-19). They needed the LORD to forcefully make His Name known to those who defied and opposed Him. The secular, godless nations needed to tremble before the LORD, just as the mountains had quaked when He appeared on Mount Sinai. A similar appearance—a dramatic, flaming, visible intervention by the LORD—is urgently needed today.

Second, the LORD needed to *come down* because He alone had proven He was God (v.4). Since the beginning of the world, no ear had ever heard nor eye ever seen any God other than the LORD Himself. There is only one true and living God, the LORD Himself (Jehovah, Yahweh).

Third, the LORD needed to *come down* to help those who had *waited* on Him. In other words, those who had waited truly believed in God and His promises and obeyed His holy commandments. It is a known fact that God helps those who willingly do what is right (vv.4b-5a). A righteous individual is one who follows the teachings of the LORD, His holy Word. In addition, the righteous know the promise of God that He will help or rescue those who truly *wait* on Him.

> **"And, being assembled together with** *them,* **commanded them that they should not depart from Jerusalem, but wait for the promise of the Father, which,** *saith he,* **ye have heard of me" (Ac.1:4).**
>
> **"I have waited for thy salvation, O LORD" (Ge.49:18).**
>
> **"Rest in the LORD, and wait patiently for him: fret not thyself because of him who prospereth in his way, because of the man who bringeth wicked devices to pass" (Ps.37:7).**
>
> **"I waited patiently for the LORD; and he inclined unto me, and heard my cry" (Ps.40:1).**
>
> **"I prevented [preceded] the dawning of the morning, and cried: I hoped in thy word" (Ps.119:147).**
>
> **"My soul** *waiteth* **for the Lord more than they that watch for the morning:** *I say, more than* **they that watch for the morning" (Ps.130:6).**
>
> **"And it shall be said in that day, Lo, this** *is* **our God; we have waited for him, and he will save us: this** *is* **the LORD; we have waited for him, we will be glad and rejoice in his salvation" (Is.25:9).**
>
> **"Yea, in the way of thy judgments, O LORD, have we waited for thee; the desire of** *our* **soul** *is* **to thy name, and to the remembrance of thee" (Is.26:8).**
>
> **"O LORD, be gracious unto us; we have waited for thee: be thou their arm every morning, our salvation also in the time of trouble" (Is.33:2).**

c. There was the cry of confession (vv.5b-8). God is able to rescue His people anytime, no matter how difficult the trial or hardship. But God will not save His people if they are continuing in sin, denying and rebelling against Him, disobeying His commandments and living wicked lives. Isaiah as well as the other righteous believers down through the centuries, knew this fact. Thus Isaiah made a confession of sin on behalf of the people, a confession that stands as a model for believers of all generations. Identifying himself with the people, Isaiah made six confessions:

1) Isaiah confessed that they were habitual sinners, that is a people who sinned over and over again. The idea is that sin had become a habit, ingrained in the very nature of the people. Sadly, when they needed to repent of their sins, they *continued* right on sinning, disobeying God's commandments. As a result, they did not deserve to be saved, neither could they expect to be rescued by God. The thought being conveyed is that of *total depravity,* being totally undeserving of God's salvation.

2) Isaiah confessed that they were infected with sin and were unclean, impure (v.6). In fact, their righteousness was no better than filthy rags. *Filthy rags* refers to dirty, contaminated cloth that has been wrapped on a cancerous or contagious sore on a person's body. It could also refer to a cloth used during a woman's menstrual period, which meant that she was ceremonially unclean under the law (Le.15:19-24; Eze.36:17). When measured against God's holy righteousness, a person's righteous acts are no better than *filthy rags* in God's sight. All human beings are infected with sin; therefore, they are all unclean, impure, corrupted in the sight of God. This image may be distasteful to some readers; nevertheless, it is the picture painted by Holy Scripture. A person's dislike of the description is nothing compared to the repulsion and loathing God feels toward sin.

3) Isaiah confessed that the people were weak, unstable (v.6). Like leaves that are blighted by disease or shriveled with age, so people are blighted by the disease of sin. As diseased leaves shrivel up and are driven by the wind to the ground, where they rot and return to the dust of the earth, so people shrivel up due to the disease of sin. They too fall to the ground where they decay and return to the dust of the earth. Human beings are so weak that they can expect to live for only a few decades.

4) Isaiah confessed that no one sought God's mercy and forgiveness (v.7). People were enjoying the pleasures of sin too much to be overly concerned about the LORD and His cause. Little if any thought was even given to the LORD and His demand for righteousness. For many people, sin and evil were outdated concepts, beliefs that belonged to the religion of antiquity or to their forefathers. They felt that sin and righteousness—what is right and what is wrong—were subjective issues, issues determined by each person for him or herself. What may be sin to one person is acceptable behavior to another. It was such *rationalizing,* such explaining away of the truth, that people used to justify their sinful behavior. Due to their flawed reasoning, the people were able to participate in the wicked behavior of idolatry practiced by their neighbors. Thus bad behavior was called good and sin was called righteousness in Isaiah's day. Regrettably, this same perverted thinking has only grown stronger down through the ages. As Isaiah confessed, no one sought God's mercy and forgiveness, for sin was no longer sin in the eyes of many. Immorality, covetousness, greed, and a plurality of religions were acceptable to the majority of the population.

5) Isaiah confessed that God was forced to turn His face away from the people (v.7ᵇ). God was left with no choice due to His holiness and the people's terrible sins. Sin separated, alienated the people from God. Giving them up to their sins, the people became more and more corrupted (see Ro.1:22-32). Hence their alienation was not due to the LORD, but rather to their horrible, detestable sins.

6) Isaiah confessed that God was their Father. He was the Potter; they were the clay, the work of His hand (v.8). For this reason, they owed Him their very lives. All they were and had was owed to the LORD. He was the Father, and they were the children. As children, they were duty-bound to obey their Father. His instructions were for their own good, to protect them and keep them safe. He longed to give them sound guidelines for living victorious lives and conquering all the trials that confronted them.

"Whosoever therefore shall confess me before men, him will I confess also before my Father which is in heaven. But whosoever shall deny me before men, him will I also deny before my Father which is in heaven" (Mt.10:32-33).

"Whosoever therefore shall be ashamed of me and of my words in this adulterous and sinful generation; of him also shall the Son of man be ashamed, when he cometh in the glory of his Father with the holy angels" (Mk.8:38).

"Also I say unto you, Whosoever shall confess me before men, him shall the Son of man also confess before the angels of God: But he that denieth me before men shall be denied before the angels of God" (Lu.12:8-9).

"That if thou shalt confess with thy mouth the Lord Jesus, and shalt believe in thine heart that God hath raised him from the dead, thou shalt be saved. For with the heart man believeth unto righteousness; and with the mouth confession is made unto salvation" (Ro.10:9-10).

"Let this mind be in you, which was also in Christ Jesus: Who, being in the form of God, thought it not robbery to be equal with God: But made himself of no reputation, and took upon him the form of a servant, and was made in the likeness of men: And being found in fashion as a man, he humbled himself, and became obedient unto death, even the death of the cross. Wherefore God also hath highly exalted him, and given him a name which is above every name: That at the name of Jesus every knee should bow, of *things* in heaven, and *things* in earth, and *things* under the earth; And *that* every tongue should confess that Jesus Christ *is* Lord, to the glory of God the Father" (Ph.2:5-11).

"If we confess our sins, he is faithful and just to forgive us *our* sins, and to cleanse us from all unrighteousness" (1 Jn.1:9).

"Who is a liar but he that denieth that Jesus is the Christ? He is antichrist, that denieth the Father and the Son. Whosoever denieth the Son, the same hath not the Father: *(but) he that acknowledgeth the Son hath the Father also*" (1 Jn.2:22-23).

"Whosoever shall confess that Jesus is the Son of God, God dwelleth in him, and he in God" (1 Jn.4:15).

"Now therefore make confession unto the LORD God of your fathers, and do his pleasure: and separate yourselves from the people of the land, and from the strange wives" (Ezr.10:11).

"He that covereth his sins shall not prosper: but whoso confesseth and forsaketh *them* shall have mercy" (Pr.28:13).

"Only acknowledge thine iniquity, that thou hast transgressed against the LORD thy God, and hast scattered thy ways to the strangers under every green tree, and ye have not obeyed my voice, saith the LORD" (Je.3:13).

d. There was the cry for forgiveness. Isaiah knew that many people would fear God's anger, that He would remember their sins forever (vv.9-12). Obviously, when this realization strikes a person, the person needs to go before the LORD, praying and seeking His forgiveness. Isaiah's prayer for Israel is a pattern for all believers of every generation.

1) Isaiah pleaded for forgiveness because the Israelites were God's people (v.9). Apparently, Isaiah was pleading for the whole nation, realizing that this was the longing of God's heart. God is longsuffering, not wanting any person to perish but rather for all to be saved. Therefore, Isaiah cried out for God not to remember their sins forever. They were the descendants of Abraham, the very people whom God had chosen to be His true followers.

2) Isaiah cried for forgiveness because the cities of Israel, including the Holy City of Jerusalem, had been destroyed by their enemies (v.10). Keep in mind that this is a prophecy, that the Babylonian invasion and destruction had not yet taken place when Isaiah wrote this. But through the inspiration of God's Spirit, God's prophet foresaw the coming destruction of the nation by the Babylonians. Thus the prophet offered up this prayer in behalf of the future exiles in Babylon, asking God to forgive their sins. He wanted God to forgive their sins and return them to the promised land so they could rebuild the nation.

3) Isaiah prayed for forgiveness because the holy, beautiful temple of God had been burned and ruined (v.11ª). In the future all that Israel treasured would lay in ruins due to the destruction carried out by their enemies. Again, the prophet wanted God to forgive the people's future sins so they could return to rebuild the temple and the other treasured sites of the nation.

4) Isaiah prayed for forgiveness because the people would desperately need the LORD's deliverance (v.12). In light of these four great cries, cries that included a genuine confession of sin and a request for forgiveness, how could God keep silent? Would He refuse to help His people in the future, punishing them beyond measure?

"I tell you, Nay: but, except ye repent, ye shall all likewise perish" (Lu.13:3).

"The God of our fathers raised up Jesus, whom ye slew and hanged on a tree. Him hath God exalted with his right hand *to be* a Prince and a Saviour, for to give repentance to Israel, and forgiveness of sins. And we are his witnesses of these things; and *so is* also the Holy Ghost, whom God hath given to them that obey him" (Ac.5:30-32).

"Repent therefore of this thy wickedness, and pray God, if perhaps the thought of thine heart may be forgiven thee" (Ac.8:22).

"In whom we have redemption through his blood, the forgiveness of sins, according to the riches of his grace" (Ep.1:7).

"If we confess our sins, he is faithful and just to forgive us *our* sins, and to cleanse us from all unrighteousness" (1 Jn.1:9).

"My little children, these things write I unto you, that ye sin not. And if any man sin, we have an advocate with the Father, Jesus Christ the righteous: And he is the propitiation for our sins: and not for ours only, but also for *the sins of* the whole world" (1 Jn.2:1-2).

"If my people, which are called by my name, shall humble themselves, and pray, and seek my face, and turn from their wicked ways; then will I hear from heaven, and will forgive their sin, and will heal their land" (2 Chr.7:14).

"Restore unto me the joy of thy salvation; and uphold me *with thy* free spirit" (Ps.51:12).

"But *there is* forgiveness with thee, that thou mayest be feared" (Ps.130:4).

"I, *even* I, *am* he that blotteth out thy transgressions for mine own sake, and will not remember thy sins" (Is.43:25).

"I have blotted out, as a thick cloud, thy transgressions, and, as a cloud, thy sins: return unto me; for I have redeemed thee" (Is.44:22).

"Let the wicked forsake his way, and the unrighteous man his thoughts: and let him return unto the LORD, and he will have mercy upon him; and to our God, for he will abundantly pardon" (Is.55:7).

"Return, ye backsliding children, *and* I will heal your backslidings. Behold, we come unto thee; for thou *art* the LORD our God" (Je.3:22).

"Cast away from you all your transgressions, whereby ye have transgressed; and make you a new heart and a new spirit: for why will ye die, O house of Israel?" (Eze.18:31).

"I will heal their backsliding, I will love them freely: for mine anger is turned away from him" (Ho.14:4).

"Who *is* a God like unto thee, that pardoneth iniquity, and passeth by the transgression of the remnant of his heritage? he retaineth not his anger for ever, because he delighteth *in* mercy" (Mi.7:18).

CHAPTER 65

D. The Last Days of Human History (Part 1),[DS1] 65:1-25

1. The *new era of salvation*

a. God's salvation now offered to the Gentiles, Ro.10:19-20
   1) Revealed to them: In Christ
   2) Offered by God Himself

b. God's indictment of the Israelites: Five major reasons
   1) They rejected God & His invitation: Walked in their own evil ways & thoughts, 53:6
   2) They turned to idols & false worship: Insulted God

   3) They turned to the world of the occult: Sought the spirits of the dead & ate forbidden food, 8:19; 29:4; 57:3; 66:3,17; Le.11:7
   4) They were prideful & self-righteous, hypocritical: A stench to God
   5) They excluded, shut people out from God: Failed to be God's witness

c. God's warning to those who reject Him
   1) He has a written record of sin
   2) He will execute perfect justice—full punishment for sin
   3) He will punish the sins of all generations: Because of their idolatry & false worship

d. God's redemption of a remnant of Jews: Assured by His Word
   1) He will not destroy all Jews: Just as men do not destroy the good grapes found in a cluster of bad ones
   2) He will save a remnant of Jews to possess His land, the promised land (a symbol of heaven)
      • They will be His servants

      • They will have fertile land for nourishment & rest: From the western to the eastern edges of the promised land

e. God's judgment upon those who turn away to worship the gods of Fortune (Good Luck) & Destiny: These two

I am sought of *them that* asked not *for me;* I am found of *them that* sought me not: I said, Behold me, behold me, unto a nation *that* was not called by my name.

2 I have spread out my hands all the day unto a rebellious people, which walketh in a way *that was* not good, after their own thoughts;

3 A people that provoketh me to anger continually to my face; that sacrificeth in gardens, and burneth incense upon altars of brick;

4 Which remain among the graves, and lodge in the monuments, which eat swine's flesh, and broth of abominable *things is in* their vessels;

5 Which say, Stand by thyself, come not near to me; for I am holier than thou. *These* are a smoke in my nose, a fire that burneth all the day.

6 Behold, it is written before me: I will not keep silence, but will recompense, even recompense into their bosom,

7 Your iniquities, and the iniquities of your fathers together, saith the LORD, which have burned incense upon the mountains, and blasphemed me upon the hills: therefore will I measure their former work into their bosom.

8 Thus saith the LORD, As the new wine is found in the cluster, and *one* saith, Destroy it not; for a blessing *is* in it: so will I do for my servants' sakes, that I may not destroy them all.

9 And I will bring forth a seed out of Jacob, and out of Judah an inheritor of my mountains: and mine elect shall inherit it, and my servants shall dwell there.

10 And Sharon shall be a fold of flocks, and the valley of Achor a place for the herds to lie down in, for my people that have sought me.

11 But ye *are* they that forsake the LORD, that forget my holy mountain, that prepare a table for that troop, and that

furnish the drink offering unto that number.

12 Therefore will I number you to the sword, and ye shall all bow down to the slaughter: because when I called, ye did not answer; when I spake, ye did not hear; but did evil before mine eyes, and did choose *that* wherein I delighted not.

13 Therefore thus saith the Lord GOD, Behold, my servants shall eat, but ye shall be hungry: behold, my servants shall drink, but ye shall be thirsty: behold, my servants shall rejoice, but ye shall be ashamed:

14 Behold, my servants shall sing for joy of heart, but ye shall cry for sorrow of heart, and shall howl for vexation of spirit.

15 And ye shall leave your name for a curse unto my chosen: for the Lord GOD shall slay thee, and call his servants by another name:

16 That he who blesseth himself in the earth shall bless himself in the God of truth; and he that sweareth in the earth shall swear by the God of truth; because the former troubles are forgotten, and because they are hid from mine eyes.

17 For, behold, I create new heavens and a new earth: and the former shall not be remembered, nor come into mind.

18 But be ye glad and rejoice for ever *in that* which I create: for, behold, I create Jerusalem a rejoicing, and her people a joy.

19 And I will rejoice in Jerusalem, and joy in my people: and the voice of weeping shall be no more heard in her, nor the voice of crying.

20 There shall be no more thence an infant of days, nor an old man that hath not filled his days: for the child shall die an hundred years old; but the sinner *being* an hundred years old shall be accursed.

21 And they shall build houses, and inhabit *them;* and they shall plant vineyards, and eat the fruit of them.

22 They shall not build, and another inhabit; they shall not

pagan gods were also known as *Troop & Number*
   1) Their fate: Death
   2) Their closed minds, stubborn wills
      • Would not listen

      • Continued to do evil

f. God's assigned destiny for the saved & the rejected

The Saved will...	*The Rejected will...*
Eat	Hunger
Drink	Thirst
Rejoice	Be sad, ashamed
Sing for joy	Cry out in agony & brokenness
Receive a new name or character	Be cursed to die (spiritual & eternal death)
Ask for blessings & take oaths only in the Name of the LORD	. . . . .
Live in perfection: No trouble or sorrow	. . . . .

2. The creation of a new heavens & earth, an eternal universe

a. The corrupt universe: Will no longer be remembered
b. The new Jerusalem: Will be created to be the center of joy (the capital of the eternal world)

c. The citizens
   1) Will be the joy of the LORD
   2) Will no longer weep or be sorrowful, 25:8
   3) Will not experience the power of death, 18, 19; 25:8
      • No longer will a baby die young or an adult early, 19
      • No person will fail to reach 100
      • Any person who fails to reach 100 will be considered under a curse, 25:7-8
   4) Will be assigned responsibility: Be engaged in meaningful work

   5) Will live & work in peace & security: Will enjoy the

fruit, production of their hands	plant, and another eat: for as the days of a tree *are* the days of my people, and mine elect shall long enjoy the work of their hands.	24 And it shall come to pass, that before they call, I will answer; and while they are yet speaking, I will hear.	7) Will have constant, unbroken communion with the LORD
6) Will live in a new, transformed, perfect world • Will be no wasted labor • Will be no children doomed to trouble, but only a blessed people	23 They shall not labour in vain, nor bring forth for trouble; for they *are* the seed of the blessed of the LORD, and their offspring with them.	25 The wolf and the lamb shall feed together, and the lion shall eat straw like the bullock: and dust *shall be* the serpent's meat. They shall not hurt nor destroy in all my holy mountain, saith the LORD.	d. The transformation of nature: Nothing will cause pain or destruction, 11:6-9 1) The wolf & the lamb will feed together 2) The snake will be harmless, Ro.8:19-20

DIVISION VII

THE PROPHECIES OF A GREAT AND GLORIOUS FUTURE, 60:1–66:24

B.   The Last Days of Human History (Part 1), 65:1-25

(65:1-25) **Introduction**: many people are serious in their pursuit to know the future or to see what the future holds for them. In fact, psychics, fortune-tellers, and astrologers have gained popularity through the years, not declined. Even in government, officials and other professionals do all they can to anticipate future events. They try to study every conceivable possibility and potential consequence when dealing with other nations and businesses. If they could just know or see future events, they might be able to prevent conflicts, economic slumps, and bad business dealings. If any individual could see the future consequences of his actions, imagine how radically he might change his behavior.

In the present Scripture, God allowed the prophet Isaiah to see into the future. What he foresaw was the most wonderful news imaginable. The LORD actually enabled the prophet to foresee the glorious consummation of human history. This consummation began when the Savior, Jesus Christ, came to earth. He launched a *new age* of human history. Isaiah foresaw both the coming age of salvation and the creation of a new heaven and earth, the eternal universe that has been promised by God and is yet to come. This is, *The Last Days of Human History (Part 1)*, 65:1-25.

    1. The *new era of salvation* (vv.1-16).
    2. The creation of new heavens and earth, an eternal universe (vv.17-25).

DEEPER STUDY # 1
(65:1-25) **Jesus Christ, Millennial Reign**: Because of the length of this Deeper Study, it is being placed at the end of this commentary, p.297.

☐1 (65:1-16) **Salvation – Era of, Offered to Everyone—Gentiles, Age of – Times of, Offered Salvation—Jews, Indictment Against, Fivefold—Israel, Indictment Against—Warning, to Whom, Rejecters—Israel, Remnant of, Assured—Judgment, Against Whom, False Worshippers—Gods, False, Names – Titles, Fortune and Destiny; Troop and Number—Destiny, of Whom, the Saved; the Rejected—Believers, Destiny of—Unbelievers, Destiny of—Age, of Salvation, Discussed—Era, of Salvation, Discussed**: in the latter days of human history, God would bring about a *new era of salvation*. Remember, this is a prophecy being predicted by Isaiah, but God is the spokesman. The LORD is speaking through Isaiah and sharing these facts about events yet to come, the wonderful hope that lay out in the future for true believers. A *new era of salvation* would come to earth. And the *new era* would not be launched by man but, rather, by God Himself. A dramatic intervention into human history would take place. God would reveal Himself to man in the person of His Son, Jesus Christ.

    a. God's salvation would be offered to the Gentiles as well as to the Jews (v.1; also see v.10; 15; Ro.10:19-20). Paul the apostle tells us that this verse applies to the Gentiles, to God's offer of salvation to them (Ro.10:19-20). Whereas the Jews had failed to be God's witnesses to the Gentiles, God Himself would intervene and share the good news of salvation with the whole world. He would intervene by revealing Himself through His Son, the Lord Jesus Christ. Where Israel had failed, Christ would succeed. Christ would become God's witness to the whole world, the very revelation of God Himself. Through Christ, the Gentiles would turn to the LORD. Although the Gentiles had never sought after the true and living God, the day was coming when they would seek Him. God would be found by people who had never sought Him before. But note why the Gentiles sought and found the LORD. It was not because of the witness of the Jews. They had failed to be God's witnesses to the other nations of the world. Rather, it was because of God's intervention into world history. God sent His Son Jesus Christ to be His witness to the whole world. Through Christ, God offers salvation to every human being, both Jew and Gentile. Note God's dramatic offer of Himself: "Behold Me, Behold Me" (KJV) or "Here am I, Here am I" (NIV). Christ came to earth to offer Himself and His wonderful salvation to the world. He launched the *new era of salvation*. Note the Scripture and outline:

OUTLINE	SCRIPTURE
1. The *new era of salvation*	I am sought of *them that* asked not *for me;* I am found of *them that* sought me not: I said, Behold me, behold me, unto a nation *that* was not called by my name.
a. God's salvation now offered to the Gentiles, Ro.10:19-20	
1) Revealed to them: In Christ	
2) Offered by God Himself	

"And all flesh shall see the salvation of God" (Lu.3:6).

"That if thou shalt confess with thy mouth the Lord Jesus, and shalt believe in thine heart that God hath raised him from the dead, thou shalt be saved. For with the heart man believeth unto righteousness; and with the mouth confession is made unto salvation. For the scripture saith, Whosoever believeth on him shall not be ashamed. For there is no difference between the Jew and the Greek: for the same Lord over all is rich unto all that call upon him. For whosoever shall call upon the name of the Lord shall be saved" (Ro.10:9-13).

"For this *is* good and acceptable in the sight of God our Saviour; Who will have all men to be saved, and to come unto the knowledge of the truth. For *there is* one God, and one mediator between God and men, the man Christ Jesus; Who gave himself a ransom for all, to be testified in due time" (1 Ti.2:3-6).

"For the grace of God that bringeth salvation hath appeared to all men, Teaching us that, denying ungodliness and worldly lusts, we should live soberly, righteously, and godly, in this present world; Looking for that blessed hope, and the glorious appearing of the great God and our Saviour Jesus Christ; Who gave himself for us, that he might redeem us from all iniquity, and purify unto himself a peculiar people, zealous of good works" (Tit.2;11-14).

"That the Gentiles should be fellowheirs, and of the same body, and partakers of his promise in Christ by the gospel" (Ep.3:6).

"The Lord is not slack concerning his promise, as some men count slackness; but is longsuffering to us-ward, not willing that any should perish, but that all should come to repentance" (2 Pe.3:9).

"The people that walked in darkness have seen a great light: they that dwell in the land of the shadow of death, upon them hath the light shined" (Is.9:2).

"And now, saith the LORD that formed me from the womb *to be* his servant, to bring Jacob again to him, Though Israel be not gathered, yet shall I be glorious in the eyes of the LORD, and my God shall be my strength. And he said, It is a light thing that thou shouldest be my servant to raise up the tribes of Jacob, and to restore the preserved of Israel: I will also give thee for a light to the Gentiles, that thou mayest be my salvation unto the end of the earth" (Is.49:5-6).

"Behold, I have given him *for* a witness to the people, a leader and commander to the people. Behold, thou shalt call a nation *that* thou knowest not, and nations *that* knew not thee shall run unto thee because of the LORD thy God, and for the Holy One of Israel; for he hath glorified thee" (Is.55:4-5).

"And the Gentiles shall come to thy light, and kings to the brightness of thy rising" (Is.60:3).

"And there was given him dominion, and glory, and a kingdom, that all people, nations, and languages, should serve him: his dominion *is* an everlasting dominion, which shall not pass away, and his kingdom *that* which shall not be destroyed" (Da.7:14).

"And I will sow her unto me in the earth; and I will have mercy upon her that had not obtained mercy; and I will say to *them which were* not my people, Thou *art* my people; and they shall say, *Thou art* my God" (Ho.2:23).

b. God's *new era of salvation* also included His strong indictment of the Israelites (vv.2-5). Remember that God had chosen Israel for four primary purposes:

⇒ to be His holy, righteous people, the people who obeyed His holy commandments and worshipped Him, the only living and true God
⇒ to be the people through whom He would send the Messiah, the Savior, into the world
⇒ to be the people through whom He would give His Word, the Holy Bible, to the world
⇒ to be His witnesses to the world, that He alone is God and that He alone can offer true salvation to the world

In choosing Israel to be His people, God was bestowing upon the Jews the most wonderful privilege. Through them He would send the Savior and His Word to the world. And these two purposes were irrevocable. God personally guaranteed that He would preserve the Jewish race down through the centuries so that He could send His Son and His Word to the world. But the responsibility for living righteous, holy lives and for being God's witnesses to the world—lay with the people themselves. It was their duty to obey God's commandments and to bear strong witness to the only living and true God. In these two purposes, the Israelites failed miserably. They failed because of five major sins. What follows are God's accusations against the Israelites:

OUTLINE	SCRIPTURE	SCRIPTURE	OUTLINE
b. God's indictment of the Israelites: Five major reasons 1) They rejected God & His invitation: Walked in their own evil ways & thoughts, 53:6 2) They turned to idols & false worship: Insulted God	2 I have spread out my hands all the day unto a rebellious people, which walketh in a way *that was* not good, after their own thoughts; 3 A people that provoketh me to anger continually to my face; that sacrificeth in gardens, and burneth incense upon altars of brick;	4 Which remain among the graves, and lodge in the monuments, which eat swine's flesh, and broth of abominable *things is in* their vessels; 5 Which say, Stand by thyself, come not near to me; for I am holier than thou. *These* are a smoke in my nose, a fire that burneth all the day.	3) They turned to the world of the occult: Sought the spirits of the dead & ate forbidden food, 8:19; 29:4; 57:3; 66:3,17; Le.11:7 4) They were prideful & self-righteous, hypocritical: A stench to God 5) They excluded, shut people out from God: Failed to be God's witness

1) The Israelites rejected God and His invitation of salvation (v.2). All day long God had stretched forth His hands in love, tenderly pleading for the Israelites to trust and follow Him. With a heart that longed for a personal, loving relationship with His chosen people, God continually sought after them. But they rejected the LORD and His appeals. Their hearts were obstinate, stubborn, stiff-necked against God. They chose to walk in their own wicked ways and evil thoughts, seeking to fulfill their lusts and sinful desires. Rejecting God, they turned away from Him and His commandments.

"The LORD shall send upon thee cursing, vexation, and rebuke, in all that thou settest thine hand unto for to do, until thou be destroyed, and until thou perish quickly; because of the wickedness of thy doings, whereby thou hast forsaken me" (De.28:20).

"And the LORD said unto Samuel, Hearken unto the voice of the people in all that they say unto thee: for they have not rejected thee, but they have rejected me, that I should not reign over them" (1 S.8:7).

"But my people would not hearken to my voice; and Israel would none of me. So I gave them up unto their own hearts' lust: *and* they walked in their own counsels. Oh that my people had hearkened unto me, *and* Israel had walked in my ways! I should soon have subdued their enemies, and turned my hand against their adversaries. The haters of the LORD should have submitted themselves unto him: but their time should have endured for ever. He should have fed them also with the finest of the wheat: and with honey out of the rock should I have satisfied thee" (Ps.81:11-16).

"Because I have called, and ye refused; I have stretched out my hand, and no man regarded; But ye have set at nought all my counsel, and would none of my reproof: I also will laugh at your calamity; I will mock when your fear cometh; When your fear cometh as desolation, and your destruction cometh as a whirlwind; when distress and anguish cometh upon you. Then shall they call upon me, but I will not answer; they shall seek me early, but they shall not find me: For that they hated knowledge, and did not choose the fear of the LORD: They would none of my counsel: they despised all my reproof. Therefore shall they eat of the fruit of their own way, and be filled with their own devices. For the turning away of the simple shall slay them, and the prosperity of fools shall destroy them. But whoso hearkeneth unto me shall dwell safely, and shall be quiet from fear of evil" (Pr.1:24-33).

"But thou hast not called upon me, O Jacob; but thou hast been weary of me, O Israel" (Is.43:22).

"Thou hast forsaken me, saith the LORD, thou art gone backward: therefore will I stretch out my hand against thee, and destroy thee; I am weary with repenting" (Je.15:6).

"O LORD, the hope of Israel, all that forsake thee shall be ashamed, *and* they that depart from me shall be written in the earth, because they have forsaken the LORD, the fountain of living waters" (Je.17:13).

2) The Israelites turned to idols and false worship (v.3). In seeking to establish relationships with their neighbors, many of them joined their neighbors in the worship of false gods. Whereas they should have remained true to the LORD, worshipping Him and Him alone, they instead worshipped the idols and false gods of their neighbors. In open defiance of God's clear commandment, they insulted the LORD. And they provoked Him to anger. Note that they continually provoked the LORD with this sin. They openly and shamelessly insulted Him over and over again.

"Professing themselves to be wise, they became fools, And changed the glory of the uncorruptible God into an image made like to corruptible man, and to birds, and fourfooted beasts, and creeping things" (Ro.1:22-23).

"Thou shalt have no other gods before me. Thou shalt not make unto thee any graven image, or any likeness *of any thing* that *is* in heaven above, or that *is* in the earth beneath, or that *is* in the water under the earth: Thou shalt not bow down thyself to them, nor serve them: for I the LORD thy God *am* a jealous God, visiting the iniquity of the fathers upon the children unto the third and fourth *generation* of them that hate me" (Ex.20:3-5).

"And he received *them* at their hand, and fashioned it with a graving tool, after he had made it a molten calf: and they said, These *be* thy gods, O Israel, which brought thee up out of the land of Egypt" (Ex.32:4).

"Ye shall make you no idols nor graven image, neither rear you up a standing image, neither shall ye set up *any* image of stone in your land, to bow down unto it: for I *am* the LORD your God" (Le.26:1).

"And they called the people unto the sacrifices of their gods: and the people did eat, and bowed down to their gods" (Nu.25:2).

"Take heed to yourselves, that your heart be not deceived, and ye turn aside, and serve other gods, and worship them" (De.11:16).

"And the children of Israel did evil in the sight of the LORD, and forgat the LORD their God, and served Baalim and the groves" (Jdg.3:7).

"For they served idols, whereof the LORD had said unto them, Ye shall not do this thing" (2 K.17:12).

"There shall no strange god be in thee; neither shalt thou worship any strange god" (Ps.81:9).

"I *am* the LORD: that *is* my name: and my glory will I not give to another, neither my praise to graven images" (Is.42:8).

3) The Israelites turned to the world of the occult, seeking the spirits of the dead and eating forbidden food (v.4; also see 8:19; 29:4; 57:3; 66:3, 17; Le.11:7). Their sitting in cemeteries suggests that some of the people were attempting to make contact with the spirits of their dead loved ones. And spending the nights in secret places suggests participation in occult practices. Throughout Scripture the world of the occult is condemned, and God's people are forbidden to participate in occult practices. A number of Israelites were even eating pork and other meats that were considered unclean and were clearly forbidden by the Law (see outlines and notes—Le.11:7; De.14:3-21 for more discussion).

"Now the works of the flesh are manifest, which are *these;* Adultery, fornication, uncleanness, lasciviousness, Idolatry, witchcraft....of the which I tell you before, as I have also told *you* in time past, that they which do such things shall not inherit the kingdom of God" (Ga.5:19-21).

"But the fearful, and unbelieving, and the abominable, and murderers, and whoremongers, and sorcerers, and idolaters, and all liars, shall have their part in the lake which burneth with fire and brimstone: which is the second death" (Re.21:8).

"When thou art come into the land which the LORD thy God giveth thee, thou shalt not learn to do after the abominations of those nations. There shall not be found among you *any one* that maketh his son or his daughter to pass through the fire, or that useth divination, *or* an observer of times, or an enchanter, or a witch, Or a charmer, or a consulter with familiar spirits, or a wizard, or a necromancer. For all that do these things *are* an abomination unto the LORD: and because of these abominations the LORD thy God doth drive them out from before thee. Thou shalt be perfect with the LORD thy God. For these nations, which thou shalt possess, hearkened unto observers of times, and unto diviners: but as for thee, the LORD thy God hath not suffered thee so *to do*" (De.18:9-14).

"And they caused their sons and their daughters to pass through the fire, and used divination and enchantments, and sold themselves to do evil in the sight of the LORD, to provoke him to anger" (2 K.17:17).

"But these two *things* shall come to thee in a moment in one day, the loss of children, and widowhood: they shall come upon thee in their perfection for the multitude of thy sorceries, *and* for the great abundance of thine enchantments" (Is.47:9).

"For the idols have spoken vanity, and the diviners have seen a lie, and have told false dreams; they comfort in vain: therefore they went their way as a flock, they were troubled, because *there was* no shepherd" (Zec.10:2).

"And I will come near to you to judgment; and I will be a swift witness against the sorcerers, and against the adulterers, and against false swearers, and against those that oppress the hireling in *his* wages, the widow, and the fatherless, and that turn aside the stranger *from his right,* and fear not me, saith the LORD of hosts" (Mal.3:5).

4) The Israelites were prideful, self-righteous, and hypocritical (v.5). Many became super-spiritual, feeling they were more righteous, and more acceptable to God than others. But in reality their profession was false. Although they claimed to be followers of the LORD, they were living disobedient lives by breaking God's commandments and participating in false worship. Thus they were insincere and deceitful, living out lies before the world. Note God's comment about the self-righteous and hypocritical: they are a stench in His nostrils, their behavior provokes His anger.

"And whosoever shall exalt himself shall be abased; and he that shall humble himself shall be exalted" (Mt.23:12).

"Even so ye also outwardly appear righteous unto men, but within ye are full of hypocrisy and iniquity" (Mt.23:28).

"But and if that evil servant shall say in his heart, My lord delayeth his coming; And shall begin to smite *his* fellowservants, and to eat and drink with the drunken; The lord of that servant shall come in a day when he looketh not for *him,* and in an hour that he is not aware of, And shall cut him asunder, and appoint *him* his portion with the hypocrites: there shall be weeping and gnashing of teeth" (Mt.24:48-51).

"Now the Spirit speaketh expressly, that in the latter times some shall depart from the faith, giving heed to seducing spirits, and doctrines of devils; Speaking lies in hypocrisy; having their conscience seared with a hot iron" (1 Ti.4:1-2).

"Unto the pure all things *are* pure: but unto them that are defiled and unbelieving *is* nothing pure; but even their mind and conscience is defiled. They profess that they know God; but in works they deny *him,* being abominable, and disobedient, and unto every good work reprobate" (Tit.1:15-16).

"Speak not thou in thine heart, after that the LORD thy God hath cast them out from before thee, saying, For my righteousness the LORD hath brought me in to possess this land: but for the wickedness of these nations the LORD doth drive them out from before thee" (De.9:4).

"Though thou exalt *thyself* as the eagle, and though thou set thy nest among the stars, thence will I bring thee down, saith the LORD" (Ob.4).

5) The Israelites excluded or shut people out from God (v.5b). Down through the centuries the Israelites failed to be God's witnesses to the world. They failed to be the righteous people who would take the message of the only living and true God to the world. This was one of the LORD's strongest indictments against the Israelites, for the message of salvation was always intended for the whole human race. Even when God called Abraham to be the

founder of the Jewish nation, He made this statement to Abraham: "In thee shall all families of the earth be blessed" (Ge.12:3). Abraham and his descendants were to take the blessings given them by God and share those blessings with everyone, no matter race, creed, or nationality. They were to be God's witnesses far and wide, proclaiming the wonderful message of salvation and sharing the Word of God with the world.

"And this gospel of the kingdom shall be preached in all the world for a witness unto all nations; and then shall the end come" (Mt.24:14).

"Go ye therefore, and teach all nations, baptizing them in the name of the Father, and of the Son, and of the Holy Ghost" (Mt.28:19).

"And he said unto them, Go ye into all the world, and preach the gospel to every creature" (Mk.16:15).

"And that repentance and remission of sins should be preached in his name among all nations, beginning at Jerusalem" (Lu.24:47).

"But ye shall receive power, after that the Holy Ghost is come upon you: and ye shall be witnesses unto me both in Jerusalem, and in all Judaea, and in Samaria, and unto the uttermost part of the earth" (Ac.1:8).

"Now the LORD had said unto Abram, Get thee out of thy country, and from thy kindred, and from thy father's house, unto a land that I will show thee: And I will make of thee a great nation, and I will bless thee, and make thy name great; and thou shalt be a blessing: And I will bless them that bless thee, and curse him that curseth thee: and in thee shall all families of the earth be blessed" (Ge.12:1-3).

c. God issued a strong warning to those who rejected Him (vv.6-7). He had recorded their sins and kept a written record of their misbehavior. Because God's judgment had not yet fallen, it may have seemed that sin had no consequences, as though people could get away with their sins. But this is far from the truth. There is a record of sin being kept, a record of all wicked deeds. God will not always keep silent, not always remain passive with the wicked who commit their sins brazenly before His very face. God will repay every sinner in full! Every person who continues to reject Him will be held accountable for his misbehavior and disobedience. Perfect justice will be carried out against the wicked of this generation as well as their forefathers and ancestors. And the punishment will be measured out in full upon those who continue in their evil ways and their worship of false gods.

OUTLINE	SCRIPTURE	SCRIPTURE	OUTLINE
c. God's warning to those who reject Him 1) He has a written record of sin 2) He will execute perfect justice—full punishment	6 Behold, *it is* written before me: I will not keep silence, but will recompense, even recompense into their bosom, 7 Your iniquities, and the iniquities of your fathers to-	gether, saith the LORD, which have burned incense upon the mountains, and blasphemed me upon the hills: therefore will I measure their former work into their bosom.	for sin 3) He will punish the sins of all generations: Because of their idolatry & false worship

"For the Son of man shall come in the glory of his Father with his angels; and then he shall reward every man according to his works" (Mt.16:27).

"For the wages of sin *is* death; but the gift of God *is* eternal life through Jesus Christ our Lord" (Ro.6:23).

"For if the word spoken by angels was stedfast, and every transgression and disobedience received a just recompence of reward; How shall we escape, if we neglect so great salvation; which at the first began to be spoken by the Lord, and was confirmed unto us by them that heard *him*" (He.2:2-3).

"The Lord knoweth how to deliver the godly out of temptations, and to reserve the unjust unto the day of judgment to be punished" (2 Pe.2:9).

"And [they] shall receive the reward of unrighteousness, *as* they that count it pleasure to riot in the daytime. Spots *they are* and blemishes, sporting themselves with their own deceivings while they feast with you; Having eyes full of adultery, and that cannot cease from sin; beguiling unstable souls: an heart they have exercised with covetous practices; cursed children" (2 Pe.2:13-14).

"And Enoch also, the seventh from Adam, prophesied of these, saying, Behold, the Lord cometh with ten thousands of his saints, To execute judgment upon all, and to convince all that are ungodly among them of all their ungodly deeds which they have ungodly committed, and of all their hard *speeches* which ungodly sinners have spoken against him" (Jude 1:14-15).

"And, behold, I come quickly; and my reward *is* with me, to give every man according as his work shall be" (Re.22:12).

"See, I have this day set thee over the nations and over the kingdoms, to root out, and to pull down, and to destroy, and to throw down, to build, and to plant" (Je.1:10).

d. God gave a wonderful promise to the Israelites regarding the *new era of salvation*: some Jews would be saved. A remnant would be redeemed (v.8). Note that this promise was spoken by the LORD Himself. It was His Word that assured the salvation of the remnant of Jews. Although many within the Israelite nation had lived wicked lives, there were still some righteous believers. The righteous would not be destroyed when the hand of God's judgment fell upon the vast majority of Jews. Just as men do not destroy an entire cluster of grapes when there are a few good found among the bad, so the LORD would save His righteous and faithful followers within the nation of Israel. They would be His *servants* (v.8), and they would possess the promised land (v.9). Keep in mind that the promised land is a symbol of heaven, the perfect world that will be created by the Messiah when He returns to set up God's kingdom on earth. The Jews would live from Sharon to the Valley of Achor, which were the western and eastern edges of the promised land (v.10). This rich inheritance would provide nourishment and rest for the remnant and their livestock.

OUTLINE	SCRIPTURE	SCRIPTURE	OUTLINE

d. God's redemption of a remnant of Jews: Assured by His Word
  1) He will not destroy all Jews: Just as men do not destroy the good grapes found in a cluster of bad ones
  2) He will save a remnant of Jews to possess His land,
	8 Thus saith the LORD, As the new wine is found in the cluster, and *one* saith, Destroy it not; for a blessing *is* in it: so will I do for my servants' sakes, that I may not destroy them all.
	9 And I will bring forth a seed out of Jacob, and
		out of Judah an inheritor of my mountains: and mine elect shall inherit it, and my servants shall dwell there.
		10 And Sharon shall be a fold of flocks, and the valley of Achor a place for the herds to lie down in, for my people that have sought me.
			the promised land (a symbol of heaven)
			• They will be His servants
			
			• They will have fertile land for nourishment & rest: From the western to the eastern edges of the promised land

"Esaias also crieth concerning Israel, Though the number of the children of Israel be as the sand of the sea, a remnant shall be saved" (Ro.9:27).

"Even so then at this present time also there is a remnant according to the election of grace" (Ro.11:5).

"These all died in faith, not having received the promises, but having seen them afar off, and were persuaded of *them,* and embraced *them,* and confessed that they were strangers and pilgrims on the earth. For they that say such things declare plainly that they seek a country. And truly, if they had been mindful of that *country* from whence they came out, they might have had opportunity to have returned. But now they desire a better *country,* that is, an heavenly: wherefore God is not ashamed to be called their God: for he hath prepared for them a city" (He.11:13-16).

"And I will gather the remnant of my flock out of all countries whither I have driven them, and will bring them again to their folds; and they shall be fruitful and increase. And I will set up shepherds over them which shall feed them: and they shall fear no more, nor be dismayed, neither shall they be lacking, saith the LORD. Behold, the days come, saith the LORD, that I will raise unto David a righteous Branch, and a King shall reign and prosper, and shall execute judgment and justice in the earth. In his days Judah shall be saved, and Israel shall dwell safely: and this *is* his name whereby he shall be called, THE LORD OUR RIGHTEOUSNESS. Therefore, behold, the days come, saith the LORD, that they shall no more say, The LORD liveth, which brought up the children of Israel out of the land of Egypt; But, The LORD liveth, which brought up and which led the seed of the house of Israel out of the north country, and from all countries whither I had driven them; and they shall dwell in their own land" (Je.23:3-8).

"At the same time, saith the LORD, will I be the God of all the families of Israel, and they shall be my people....For there shall be a day, *that* the watchmen upon the mount Ephraim shall cry, Arise ye, and let us go up to Zion unto the LORD our God. For thus saith the LORD; Sing with gladness for Jacob, and shout among the chief of the nations: publish ye, praise ye, and say, O LORD, save thy people, the remnant of Israel. Behold, I will bring them from the north country, and gather them from the coasts of the earth, *and* with them the blind and the lame, the woman with child and her that travaileth with child together: a great company shall return thither" (Je.31:1, 6-8).

e. While the righteous would be spared in the *new era of salvation,* God's judgment would fall on those who had turned away to worship the gods *Fortune* (Good Luck) and *Destiny* (vv.11-12). These two pagan gods were also known as *Troop* and *Number.* Wishing or hoping for *good luck* or *fortune* is as common today as it has been down through the ages. Many people even avoid doing things that are thought to bring *bad luck.* But as God's people walk through life, they are to trust the LORD for guidance, provision, and security. In fact, no person should trust in *good luck* or *good fortune.* So it is with *destiny.* A person's fate and future must be placed into the hands of the LORD not pinned to some false belief that looks to the stars or psychics or to a false god called *Destiny.* The LORD alone is the living and true God. Any other god is false and exists only in the minds of unbelievers. A person who places his fate in these false gods—whether people or things or ideas—is destined for judgment (v.12). Despite all the LORD's warnings through the years, many of the Israelites closed their minds. Sadly, in a spirit of stubbornness, they did not listen to the LORD's warnings. They continued in their evil ways, placing their hopes in *Good Luck* and *Destiny,* two empty, powerless, and lifeless gods that have been worshipped down through history.

OUTLINE	SCRIPTURE	SCRIPTURE	OUTLINE

e. God's judgment upon those who turn away to worship the gods of Fortune (Good Luck) & Destiny: These two pagan gods were also known as *Troop & Number*
  1) Their fate: Death
  2) Their closed minds, stub-
	11 But ye *are* they that forsake the LORD, that forget my holy mountain, that prepare a table for that troop, and that furnish the drink offering unto that number.
	12 Therefore will I number
		you to the sword, and ye shall all bow down to the slaughter: because when I called, ye did not answer; when I spake, ye did not hear; but did evil before mine eyes, and did choose *that* wherein I delighted not.	born wills
			• Would not listen
			
			• Continued to do evil

"Ye stiffnecked and uncircumcised in heart and ears, ye do always resist the Holy Ghost: as your fathers *did*, so *do* ye" (Ac.7:51).

"For the time will come when they will not endure sound doctrine; but after their own lusts shall they heap to themselves teachers, having itching ears; And they shall turn away *their* ears from the truth, and shall be turned unto fables" (2 Ti.4:3-4).

"Son of man, thou dwellest in the midst of a rebellious house, which have eyes to see, and see not; they have ears to hear, and hear not: for they *are* a rebellious house" (Eze.12:2).

"Be ye not as the horse, *or* as the mule, *which* have no understanding: whose mouth must be held in with bit and bridle, lest they come near unto thee. Many sorrows *shall be* to the wicked: but he that trusteth in the LORD, mercy shall compass him about" (Ps.32:9-10).

"Yet he sent prophets to them, to bring them again unto the LORD; and they testified against them: but they would not give ear" (2 Chr.24:19).

"Hearken unto me, ye stouthearted, that *are* far from righteousness" (Is.46:12).

"Because I knew that thou *art* obstinate, and thy neck *is* an iron sinew, and thy brow brass....*There is* no peace, saith the LORD, unto the wicked" (Is.48:4, 22).

"To whom shall I speak, and give warning, that they may hear? behold, their ear *is* uncircumcised, and they cannot hearken: behold, the word of the LORD is unto them a reproach; they have no delight in it" (Je.6:10).

"And they have turned unto me the back, and not the face: though I taught them, rising up early and teaching *them,* yet they have not hearkened to receive instruction" (Je.32:33).

"*As for* the word that thou hast spoken unto us in the name of the LORD, we will not hearken unto thee" (Je.44:16).

"But they refused to hearken, and pulled away the shoulder, and stopped their ears, that they should not hear" (Zec.7:11).

"If ye will not hear, and if ye will not lay *it* to heart, to give glory unto my name, saith the LORD of hosts, I will even send a curse upon you, and I will curse your blessings: yea, I have cursed them already, because ye do not lay *it* to heart" (Mal.2:2).

f. God has assigned two different destinies for those who are living in the *new era of salvation*. One destiny is for the saved and the other is for those who have rejected Him (vv.13-16). This is obviously looking ahead to the time when God's kingdom will be established on earth. Much of what is said in these verses is not suffered by those who reject Christ. Many of the wicked do prosper and have excellent health throughout their lives. And although the righteous receive the gifts listed here to a certain extent after being saved, they do not experience the fullness of the gifts until they go to be with the LORD eternally. The Scripture and outline clearly show the two lines of destiny that run parallel to each other, but the two are worlds apart.

OUTLINE		SCRIPTURE	SCRIPTURE	OUTLINE	
f. God's assigned destiny for the saved & the rejected		13 Therefore thus saith the Lord GOD, Behold, my servants shall eat, but ye shall be	name for a curse unto my chosen: for the Lord GOD shall slay thee, and call	name or character	die (spiritual & eternal death)
The Saved will...	*The Rejected will...*	hungry: behold, my servants shall drink, but ye shall be	his servants by another name:		
Eat	Hunger	thirsty: behold, my servants	16 That he who blesseth		
Drink	Thirst	shall rejoice, but ye shall be	himself in the earth shall	Ask for blessings & take	. . . . .
Rejoice	Be sad, ashamed	ashamed:	bless himself in the God of truth; and he that sweareth in	oaths only in the Name of	
Sing for joy	Cry out in agony & brokenness	14 Behold, my servants shall sing for joy of heart, but ye shall cry for sorrow of heart, and shall howl for vexation of spirit.	the earth shall swear by the God of truth; because the former troubles are forgotten, and because they are hid from	the LORD Live in perfection: No trouble or sorrow	. . . . .
Receive a new	Be cursed to	15 And ye shall leave your	mine eyes.		

1) The destiny of those who are truly saved includes the most wonderful blessings of God:
   ⇒ God's gracious provision of food, drink, and a spirit of rejoicing
   ⇒ hearts that sing for joy over the rich blessings of God
   ⇒ a new name, which means a new character of righteousness that is stirred by God's Spirit
   ⇒ a spirit that asks for blessings and takes oaths only in the Name of the LORD. The suggestion is that the person would no longer seek blessings and swear oaths by false gods. The person's spirit would be pure and righteous, wishing only to edify the LORD.
   ⇒ a perfect state of being in which there is no trouble or sorrow. All sin and evil are forgotten and hidden from God's eyes because Jesus Christ has brought God's kingdom to earth. Hence the earth itself—God's kingdom—is in a state of perfection.

   "But seek ye first the kingdom of God, and his righteousness; and all these things shall be added unto you" (Mt.6:33).
   "Then shall the King say unto them on his right hand, Come, ye blessed of my Father, inherit the kingdom prepared for you from the foundation of the world" (Mt.25:34).

"The thief cometh not, but for to steal, and to kill, and to destroy: I am come that they might have life, and that they might have *it* more abundantly" (Jn.10:10).

"In my Father's house are many mansions: if *it were* not so, I would have told you. I go to prepare a place for you. And if I go and prepare a place for you, I will come again, and receive you unto myself; that where I am, *there* ye may be also" (Jn.14:2-3).

"And God *is* able to make all grace abound toward you; that ye, always having all sufficiency in all *things,* may abound to every good work" (2 Co.9:8).

"For our conversation [citizenship] is in heaven; from whence also we look for the Saviour, the Lord Jesus Christ: Who shall change our vile body, that it may be fashioned like unto his glorious body, according to the working whereby he is able even to subdue all things unto himself" (Ph.3:20-21).

"But my God shall supply all your need according to his riches in glory by Christ Jesus" (Ph.4:19).

"When Christ, *who is* our life, shall appear, then shall ye also appear with him in glory" (Col.3:4).

"And the Lord shall deliver me from every evil work, and will preserve *me* unto his heavenly kingdom: to whom *be* glory for ever and ever. Amen" (2 Ti.4:18).

"Wherefore the rather, brethren, give diligence to make your calling and election sure: for if ye do these things, ye shall never fall: For so an entrance shall be ministered unto you abundantly into the everlasting kingdom of our Lord and Saviour Jesus Christ" (2 Pe.1:10-11).

"Thou hast also given me the shield of thy salvation: and thy right hand hath holden me up, and thy gentleness hath made me great" (Ps.18:35).

"*Oh* how great *is* thy goodness, which thou hast laid up for them that fear thee; *which* thou hast wrought for them that trust in thee before the sons of men!" (Ps.31:19).

"Fear thou not; for I *am* with thee: be not dismayed; for I *am* thy God: I will strengthen thee; yea, I will help thee; yea, I will uphold thee with the right hand of my righteousness" (Is.41:10).

"And *even* to *your* old age I *am* he; and *even* to hoar [gray] hairs will I carry *you:* I have made, and I will bear; even I will carry, and will deliver *you*" (Is.46:4).

2) The destiny of those who reject the LORD will be both tragic and terrifying:
⇒ They will suffer hunger and thirst.
⇒ They will be sad and ashamed (v.13).
⇒ They will cry out in agony from broken hearts and tormented spirits (v.14).
⇒ They will be cursed to die, which for the unbeliever is both physical and eternal death (v.15). Sadly, the name of the wicked will become a curse among the righteous because of the evil they have committed.

"And this is the condemnation, that light is come into the world, and men loved darkness rather than light, because their deeds were evil" (Jn.3:19).

"And as it is appointed unto men once to die, but after this the judgment" (He.9:27).

"The Lord knoweth how to deliver the godly out of temptations, and to reserve the unjust unto the day of judgment to be punished" (2 Pe.2:9).

"And Enoch also, the seventh from Adam, prophesied of these, saying, Behold, the Lord cometh with ten thousands of his saints, To execute judgment upon all, and to convince all that are ungodly among them of all their ungodly deeds which they have ungodly committed, and of all their hard *speeches* which ungodly sinners have spoken against him" (Jude 1:14-15).

"And I saw a great white throne, and him that sat on it, from whose face the earth and the heaven fled away; and there was found no place for them. And I saw the dead, small and great, stand before God; and the books were opened: and another book was opened, which is *the book* of life: and the dead were judged out of those things which were written in the books, according to their works. And the sea gave up the dead which were in it; and death and hell delivered up the dead which were in them: and they were judged every man according to their works. And death and hell were cast into the lake of fire. This is the second death. And whosoever was not found written in the book of life was cast into the lake of fire" (Re.20:11-15).

2 (65:17-25) **Heaven and Earth, New, Prophecy Concerning—Heaven, Creation of, New, Prophecy Concerning—Earth, New Creation, Prophecy Concerning—Universe, New Creation, Prophecy Concerning—Jerusalem, New, Prophecy Concerning; Citizens of—Heaven and Earth, New, Citizens of—Nature, Transformation of, Prophecy Concerning—Earth, Transformation, Prophecy Concerning**: the glorious consummation of history will involve the creation of a new heavens and earth. The entire universe will be recreated and made eternal. God clearly predicted this astounding fact:

OUTLINE	SCRIPTURE	SCRIPTURE	OUTLINE
2. The creation of a new heavens & earth, an eternal universe a. The corrupt universe: Will no longer be remembered	17 For, behold, I create new heavens and a new earth: and the former shall not be remembered, nor come into mind.	18 But be ye glad and rejoice for ever *in that* which I create: for, behold, I create Jerusalem a rejoicing, and her people a joy.	b. The new Jerusalem: Will be created to be the center of joy (the capital of the eternal world)

OUTLINE	SCRIPTURE	SCRIPTURE	OUTLINE

c. The citizens
  1) Will be the joy of the LORD
  2) Will no longer weep or be sorrowful, 25:8
  3) Will not experience the power of death, 18, 19; 25:8
    • No longer will a baby die young or an adult early, 19
    • No person will fail to reach 100
 	
    • Any person who fails to reach 100 will be considered under a curse, 25:7-8
  4) Will be assigned responsibility: Be engaged in meaningful work
	19 And I will rejoice in Jerusalem, and joy in my people: and the voice of weeping shall be no more heard in her, nor the voice of crying.
	20 There shall be no more thence an infant of days, nor an old man that hath not filled his days: for the child shall die an hundred years old; but the sinner *being* an hundred years old shall be accursed.
	21 And they shall build houses, and inhabit *them;* and they shall plant vineyards, and eat the fruit of them.
	22 They shall not build, and another inhabit; they shall not plant, and another eat: for as
		the days of a tree *are* the days of my people, and mine elect shall long enjoy the work of their hands.
		23 They shall not labour in vain, nor bring forth for trouble; for they *are* the seed of the blessed of the LORD, and their offspring with them.
		24 And it shall come to pass, that before they call, I will answer; and while they are yet speaking, I will hear.
		25 The wolf and the lamb shall feed together, and the lion shall eat straw like the bullock: and dust *shall be* the serpent's meat. They shall not hurt nor destroy in all my holy mountain, saith the LORD.
			5) Will live & work in peace & security: Will enjoy the fruit, production of their hands
			  6) Will live in a new, transformed, perfect world
			    • Will be no wasted labor
			    • Will be no children doomed to trouble, but only a blessed people
			  7) Will have constant, unbroken communion with the LORD
			d. The transformation of nature: Nothing will cause pain or destruction, 11:6-9
			  1) The wolf & the lamb will feed together
			  2) The snake will be harmless, Ro.8:19-20

a. God paints a glorious picture of the future, a picture where this corrupt universe will no longer exist (v.17). That God has the power to create a new heavens and a new earth is undeniable, for He created the first heaven and earth. However, note this wonderful fact: in the new heaven and earth there will be no destructive earthquakes, hurricanes, tornados, floods, or any other force of nature going awry, killing people, devastating lives, and destroying so much property and land. In addition, a new heavens and earth will mean the erasing of all bad experiences. As the verse says, all the past troubles of life will be forgotten and hidden from God's eyes. And it is clearly stated in verse seventeen that the citizens of the new world will not remember the horrible evil, sufferings, and troubles of the former world. Neither will these bad experiences even come to mind—not ever. All things will be new in the new world, including the lives of its citizens who are the true believers and followers of the LORD.

    "Therefore if any man *be* in Christ, *he is* a new creature: old things are passed away; behold, all things are become new" (2 Co.5:17).

    "And he that sat upon the throne said, Behold, I make all things new. And he said unto me, Write: for these words are true and faithful" (Re.21:5).

    "Behold, the former things are come to pass, and new things do I declare: before they spring forth I tell you of them" (Is.42:9).

    "Behold, I will do a new thing; now it shall spring forth; shall ye not know it? I will even make a way in the wilderness, *and* rivers in the desert" (Is.43:19).

    "Thou hast heard, see all this; and will not ye declare *it?* I have showed thee new things from this time, even hidden things, and thou didst not know them" (Is.48:6).

    "Because the former troubles are forgotten, and because they are hid from mine eyes. For, behold, I create new heavens and a new earth: and the former shall not be remembered, nor come into mind" (Is.65:16-17).

b. In the new creation there will be what Scripture calls the *new Jerusalem* (v.18). The Holy City will be recreated by God and established as the capital of His new world. Jerusalem will become a delight, a joy for the citizens of the new world (62:7; see outline and note—Re.21:2 for more discussion).

c. All the citizens of the new world will be God's people, those who have trusted Christ as their personal Savior. Thus, life in the new world will be entirely different from life in this present world. A totally fresh, exciting existence is pictured:

1) The citizens of the new world will be the joy of the LORD. Note that He calls them "My people" (v.19). God will take great delight in His people, rejoicing over them. Apparently, God is going to be revealing the *exceeding, incomparable riches of His grace* to His people throughout eternity (Ep.2:4-10; esp.v.7). In demonstrating these riches of His person and His grace expressed through Christ, God will stir a response of love, praise, and worship from His people. In this, God will take great delight.

    "But God, who is rich in mercy, for his great love wherewith he loved us, Even when we were dead in sins, hath quickened us together with Christ, (by grace ye are saved;) And hath raised *us* up together, and made *us* sit together in heavenly *places* in Christ Jesus: That in the ages to come he might show the exceeding riches of his grace in *his* kindness toward us through Christ Jesus" (Ep.2:4-7; note esp.v.7).

2) The citizens of God's new world will not weep or be sorrowful any more (v.19). All pain, suffering, distress, grief, and mourning will be gone. There will be no cause for crying, no cause to feel sad or unhappy or upset. No longer will there be evil or trouble in the world. Lawlessness, immorality, and violence will be totally eliminated. Imagine! Peace, security, love, joy, and health will be the continued experience of everyone within the new world.

"For the Lamb which is in the midst of the throne shall feed them, and shall lead them unto living fountains of waters: and God shall wipe away all tears from their eyes" (Re.7:17).

"And God shall wipe away all tears from their eyes; and there shall be no more death, neither sorrow, nor crying, neither shall there be any more pain: for the former things are passed away" (Re.21:4).

"He will swallow up death in victory; and the Lord GOD will wipe away tears from off all faces; and the rebuke of his people shall he take away from off all the earth: for the LORD hath spoken *it*" (Is.25:8).

"And the ransomed of the LORD shall return, and come to Zion with songs and everlasting joy upon their heads: they shall obtain joy and gladness, and sorrow and sighing shall flee away" (Is.35:10).

"Therefore the redeemed of the LORD shall return, and come with singing unto Zion; and everlasting joy *shall be* upon their head: they shall obtain gladness and joy; *and* sorrow and mourning shall flee away" (Is.51:11).

"Thy sun shall no more go down; neither shall thy moon withdraw itself: for the LORD shall be thine everlasting light, and the days of thy mourning shall be ended" (Is.60:20).

"Therefore they shall come and sing in the height of Zion, and shall flow together to the goodness of the LORD, for wheat, and for wine, and for oil, and for the young of the flock and of the herd: and their soul shall be as a watered garden; and they shall not sorrow any more at all" (Je.31:12).

3) The citizens of the new world will not experience the power of death over their lives (v.20; also see "rejoice forever," v.18; "weeping...no more," v.19; and 25:7-8). In the new world no one will die early, neither child nor adult. And no person will fail to reach the age of 100. If a person should die before reaching 100, he would be considered under a curse (20c).

Although most commentators feel this verse applies to the Millennial reign of Christ on earth, the interpretation does not seem to fit in the context of these verses. These verses seem to be dealing with the new heavens and earth, the eternal world that God is going to create in the future. It seems far better to interpret or understand the present verse dealing with death as a symbol or *metaphor*, which is a striking way to get a point across. A metaphor is simply a figure of speech in which one thing is stated as if it were another. Today, as in Isaiah's day, few people live to be 100. So the number *100* symbolizes or represents an unending life. Note that the citizens of the new world will "rejoice forever" (v.18) and "sorrow...no more" (v.19). If Isaiah was saying in verse twenty that people will die in the new world, then he would be contradicting verses eighteen and nineteen. Isaiah would also be contradicting his earlier statement that God will "swallow up death in victory" for the sake of His people, and that He "will wipe away tears from off all faces" (25:7-8). Note how the earlier Scripture (25:7-8) ties together the conquest of death with the wiping away of tears, just as they are tied together in the present Scripture. The conditions of the new world will be eternal and wonderful, so wonderful that if a sinner should live there (an impossibility) and fail to reach 100, he would be considered cursed. Perhaps this is the meaning of this statement or perhaps Isaiah was saying that if a sinner were to live in the new world and "escape detection for a century, the curse would still search him out and destroy him."[1] Another possible way to word what Isaiah is saying is this, "Within the perfect environment of the new world, 100 years would be a very short life. Within the perfect world even a sinner would be considered cursed if he lived only 100 years." Of course there will be no sinners in the new world, the new Jerusalem (15c). Death will have no more power over God's people, and sin with all of its temptations and entrapments will no longer fill people's hearts.

"For God so loved the world, that he gave his only begotten Son, that whosoever believeth in him should not perish, but have everlasting life" (Jn.3:16).

"He that believeth on the Son hath everlasting life: and he that believeth not the Son shall not see life; but the wrath of God abideth on him" (Jn.3:36).

"Verily, verily, I say unto you, If a man keep my saying, he shall never see death" (Jn.8:51).

"And whosoever liveth and believeth in me shall never die. Believest thou this?" (Jn.11:26).

"To them who by patient continuance in well doing seek for glory and honour and immortality, eternal life" (Ro.2:7).

"The last enemy *that* shall be destroyed *is* death" (1 Co.15:26).

"For our conversation [citizenship] is in heaven; from whence also we look for the Saviour, the Lord Jesus Christ: Who shall change our vile body, that it may be fashioned like unto his glorious body, according to the working whereby he is able even to subdue all things unto himself" (Ph.3:20-21).

"Who hath saved us, and called *us* with an holy calling, not according to our works, but according to his own purpose and grace, which was given us in Christ Jesus before the world began, But is now made manifest by the appearing of our Saviour Jesus Christ, who hath abolished death, and hath brought life and immortality to light through the gospel" (2 Ti.1:9-10).

"Forasmuch then as the children are partakers of flesh and blood, he also himself likewise took part of the same; that through death he might destroy him that had the power of death, that is, the devil; And deliver them who through fear of death were all their lifetime subject to bondage" (He.2:14-15).

---

[1] J. Alec Motyer. *Isaiah.* *"Tyndale Old Testament Commentaries."* (Downers Grove, IL: Inter-Varsity Press, 1999), p.399.

4) The citizens of the new world will be assigned responsibilities, be engaged in meaningful work (v.21). Note these two facts:

⇒ First, Jesus Christ taught that believers would be made rulers over many things.

"His lord said unto him, Well done, good and faithful servant; thou hast been faithful over a few things, I will make thee ruler over many things: enter thou into the joy of thy lord" (Mt.25:23).

"And the Lord said, Who then is that faithful and wise steward, whom *his* lord shall make ruler over his household, to give *them their* portion of meat in due season? Blessed *is* that servant, whom his lord when he cometh shall find so doing. Of a truth I say unto you, that he will make him ruler over all that he hath" (Lu.12:42-44).

"Ye are they which have continued with me in my temptations. And I appoint unto you a kingdom, as my Father hath appointed unto me" (Lu.22:28-29).

"And he said unto him, Well, thou good servant: because thou hast been faithful in a very little, have thou authority over ten cities....And he said likewise to him, Be thou also over five cities" (Lu.19:17, 19).

"And I saw thrones, and they sat upon them, and judgment was given unto them: and *I saw* the souls of them that were beheaded for the witness of Jesus, and for the word of God, and which had not worshipped the beast, neither his image, neither had received *his* mark upon their foreheads, or in their hands; and they lived and reigned with Christ a thousand years" (Re.20:4).

"And there shall be no night there; and they need no candle, neither light of the sun; for the Lord God giveth them light: and they shall reign for ever and ever" (Re.22:5).

⇒ Second, Scripture teaches that believers will judge or supervise the world and the angels (see outline and note—1 Pe.1:4 for more discussion of the work and inheritance to be assigned to the believer in eternity).

"Do ye not know that the saints shall judge the world?...Know ye not that we shall judge angels? how much more things that pertain to this life?" (1 Co.6:2-3).

5) The citizens of the new world will live and work in peace and security (v.22). No longer will they suffer the loss of their homes, farms, or businesses. No enemy will oppress or assault them, threaten their lives, or steal from them. For the LORD will establish peace and security throughout the new world. A person's days and life will be as stable and secure as the days and life of a healthy, strong, and towering tree.

"And suddenly there was with the angel a multitude of the heavenly host praising God, and saying, Glory to God in the highest, and on earth peace, good will toward men" (Lu.2:13-14).

"These things I have spoken unto you, that in me ye might have peace. In the world ye shall have tribulation: but be of good cheer; I have overcome the world" (Jn.16:33).

"For the kingdom of God is not meat and drink; but righteousness, and peace, and joy in the Holy Ghost" (Ro.14:17).

"But now in Christ Jesus ye who sometimes were far off are made nigh by the blood of Christ. For he is our peace, who hath made both one, and hath broken down the middle wall of partition *between us*" (Ep.2:13-14).

"And, having made peace through the blood of his cross, by him to reconcile all things unto himself; by him, *I say*, whether *they be* things in earth, or things in heaven" (Col.1:20).

"He maketh wars to cease unto the end of the earth; he breaketh the bow, and cutteth the spear in sunder; he burneth the chariot in the fire" (Ps.46:9).

"And he shall judge among the nations, and shall rebuke many people: and they shall beat their swords into plowshares, and their spears into pruninghooks: nation shall not lift up sword against nation, neither shall they learn war any more" (Is.2:4).

"And in that day will I make a covenant for them with the beasts of the field, and with the fowls of heaven, and *with* the creeping things of the ground: and I will break the bow and the sword and the battle out of the earth, and will make them to lie down safely" (Ho.2:18).

6) The citizens of the new world will live in a transformed, perfect world (v.23). No longer will there be inefficiency, wasted labor. Problems at work, disappointments and frustrations, pressure and distress, sorrow and failure—all the difficulties that crowd a person's life will be eliminated in the new world to be created by God. Neither will children be doomed to trouble, either physically or morally. There will be no lawless youth or gangs nor any adult criminals. The citizens of the new world and all their descendants will be a people blessed by the LORD.

"But we all, with open face beholding as in a glass the glory of the Lord, are changed into the same image from glory to glory, *even* as by the Spirit of the Lord" (2 Co.3:18).

"For the law made nothing perfect, but the bringing in of a better hope *did;* by the which we draw nigh unto God" (He.7:19).

"Whereby are given unto us exceeding great and precious promises: that by these ye might be partakers of the divine nature, having escaped the corruption that is in the world through lust" (2 Pe.1:4).

"But the day of the Lord will come as a thief in the night; in the which the heavens shall pass away with a great noise, and the elements shall melt with fervent heat, the earth also and the works that are therein shall be burned up. *Seeing* then *that* all these things shall be dissolved, what manner *of persons* ought ye to be in *all* holy conversation and godliness, Looking for and hasting unto the coming of the day of God, wherein the heavens being on fire shall be dissolved, and the elements shall melt with fervent heat? Nevertheless we, according to his promise, look for new heavens and a new earth, wherein dwelleth righteousness" (2 Pe.3:10-13).

"And I saw a new heaven and a new earth: for the first heaven and the first earth were passed away; and there was no more sea" (Re.21:1).

"For, behold, I create new heavens and a new earth: and the former shall not be remembered, nor come into mind" (Is.65:17).

"For as the new heavens and the new earth, which I will make, shall remain before me, saith the LORD, so shall your seed and your name remain" (Is.66:22).

"And it shall come to pass in the day that the LORD shall give thee rest from thy sorrow, and from thy fear, and from the hard bondage wherein thou wast made to serve" (Is.14:3).

"I know that, whatsoever God doeth, it shall be for ever: nothing can be put to it, nor any thing taken from it: and God doeth *it*, that *men* should fear before him" (Ecc.3:14).

"The remnant of Israel shall not do iniquity, nor speak lies; neither shall a deceitful tongue be found in their mouth: for they shall feed and lie down, and none shall make *them* afraid" (Zep.3:13).

"In that day it shall be said to Jerusalem, Fear thou not: *and to* Zion, Let not thine hands be slack" (Zep.3:16).

7) The citizens of the new world will have constant, unbroken fellowship and communion with the LORD (v.24). The relationship between the LORD and His people will be so close that even before a believer calls out to Him, He will answer, and as the believer speaks, the LORD will meet the need.

"If ye abide in me, and my words abide in you, ye shall ask what ye will, and it shall be done unto you" (Jn.15:7).

"For whom he did foreknow, he also did predestinate *to be* conformed to the image of his Son, that he might be the firstborn among many brethren" (Ro.8:29).

"Beloved, now are we the sons of God, and it doth not yet appear what we shall be: but we know that, when he shall appear, we shall be like him; for we shall see him as he is" (1 Jn.3:2).

"The LORD *is* nigh unto all them that call upon him, to all that call upon him in truth" (Ps.145:18).

d. When God creates the new world, nature itself will be transformed (v.25). Nothing on earth will cause pain or destruction (v.25; 11:6-9; 30:23-26; 65:25; Eze.34:25-39; Ho.2:20-22). A radical change will take place in the very nature of animals, transforming them from being wild and ferocious to being tame and peaceful. The wolf and the lamb will feed together as will the lion and the ox. Even the snake or serpent, a symbol of Satan, will be harmless and no longer feared by so many. However, the snake will continue to feed on the dust of the ground, as prophesied in Genesis 3:14-15.

"For I reckon that the sufferings of this present time *are* not worthy *to be compared* with the glory which shall be revealed in us. For the earnest expectation of the creature waiteth for the manifestation of the sons of God. For the creature was made subject to vanity, not willingly, but by reason of him who hath subjected *the same* in hope, Because the creature itself also shall be delivered from the bondage of corruption into the glorious liberty of the children of God. For we know that the whole creation groaneth and travaileth in pain together until now" (Ro.8:18-22).

"The wolf also shall dwell with the lamb, and the leopard shall lie down with the kid; and the calf and the young lion and the fatling together; and a little child shall lead them. And the cow and the bear shall feed; their young ones shall lie down together: and the lion shall eat straw like the ox. And the sucking child shall play on the hole of the asp, and the weaned child shall put his hand on the cockatrice' den" (Is.11:6-8).

DEEPER STUDY # 1

(65:1-25) Jesus Christ, Millennial Reign: the only Scripture that tells us how long the millennial reign of Christ will be is found in Revelation (Re.20:2, 3, 4, 5, 6, 7). Millennium simply means one thousand years or a period of one thousand years. It refers to the coming again of Jesus Christ to earth, some time in the future when He will be returning to reign over the nations and peoples of the earth.

⇒ Here is a quick Scripture reference to show what is meant.

"I saw in the night visions, and, behold, *one* like the Son of man came with the clouds of heaven, and came to the Ancient of days, and they brought him near before him. And there was given him dominion, and glory, and a kingdom, that all people, nations, and languages, should serve him: his dominion is an everlasting dominion, which shall not pass away, and his kingdom *that* which shall not be destroyed" (Da.7:13-14).

⇒ Peter definitely said that the Millennium was coming and that it referred to some future time.

"Repent ye therefore, and be converted, that your sins may be blotted out, when the times of refreshing shall come from the presence of the Lord; and he shall send Jesus Christ, which before was preached unto you: whom the heaven must receive until the times of restitution of all things, which God hath spoken by the mouth of all his holy prophets since the world began" (Ac.3:19-21).

Although this is the only mention of one thousand years, the coming of Jesus Christ to rule this earth is mentioned many, many times in Scripture. Many more verses will be given below, but this gives a quick glimpse as to what is meant by the Millennium. The Millennium simply means the rule of Jesus Christ over this earth, over all the nations and peoples of this earth for one thousand years. Why is a Millennium necessary? Why does Jesus Christ not just end everything when He comes back to earth? Why is He coming back and ruling over this earth for one thousand years? There are at least three reasons.

1. The earth must be ruled over by Christ in its present form. Why? Because the earth belongs to Christ; it belongs to Him by right. Jesus Christ created the world and man. But man gave the world to Satan. Man obeyed Satan instead of God. When he did, he brought evil to earth. Therefore, Jesus Christ has to reclaim the earth and bring righteousness to the earth, and He has to do it while the earth is in its present form. To destroy the earth would be giving up this earth and dooming it to destruction; it would mean that God failed with the present earth. Of course, God cannot fail. Therefore, the Lord Jesus Christ must reclaim this earth and rule over it before He moves the world and believers into the perfect world.

2. Why is the Millennium necessary? Because God has to fulfill all the promises to man that are in His Word. But why would God make such promises that could not be fulfilled in sinful man? God knew that man would fail and that the promises would not be able to be fulfilled. So why make the promises? Because God loves man, and He wants to bless man. God would rather create man and have a few who will believe in Him and bless them than not to create man and have no one to bless.

The point is this: in order to bless the few believers upon earth, in order to fulfill God's promises, Jesus Christ has to come back to this earth while it is in its present form. God made some wonderful and great promises all through the Scripture that have not yet been fulfilled, and they cannot be fulfilled without Christ Himself ruling and reigning and bringing them about. Therefore, He is coming back to complete the promises, coming back while the earth is still in its present form.

3. Why is the Millennium necessary? Because God is love, and He wants to see more and more people saved despite the terrible evil of past history and the horrible evil of the end time under the antichrist. God is still merciful. Therefore, in the Millennium God is going to give man the very presence of His Son in His majestic glory ruling and reigning from Jerusalem. God is going to give man his utopia upon earth: peace and prosperity—give man every opportunity in the world to receive Jesus Christ as Lord and Savior. The Millennium is necessary because of the love of God for man, a love that longs for more and more people to be saved.

Now, what will the Millennium be like? A good way to gain some understanding of the Millennium is to ask questions and then to answer the questions by giving Scriptural support. Any minister or lay believer can do the same study that we are doing. It is needed because of so many erroneous ideas going around about the Millennium. We give just a brief study so that the reader will have some idea of what the Millennium will be. Note four questions and points about the Millennium:

1. What are some verses that tell us that Christ is coming back in glory to rule and reign over the earth?

⇒ He will rule over and govern the nations.

"And he shall judge among the nations, and shall rebuke many people: and they shall beat their swords into plowshares, and their spears into pruninghooks: nation shall not lift up sword against nation, neither shall they learn war any more" (Is.2:4).

"Of the increase of *his* government and peace *there shall be* no end, upon the throne of David, and upon his kingdom, to order it, and to establish it with judgment and with justice from henceforth even for ever. The zeal of the LORD of hosts will perform this" (Is.9:7).

"Behold, I have given him *for* a witness to the people, a leader and commander to the people" (Is.55:4).

"For the kingdom *is* the LORD'S: and he *is* the governor among the nations" (Ps.22:28).

"O let the nations be glad and sing for joy: for thou shalt judge the people righteously, and govern the nations upon earth" (Ps.67:4).

⇒ He will rule and judge the ends of the earth.

"The adversaries of the LORD shall be broken to pieces; out of heaven shall he thunder upon them: the LORD shall judge the ends of the earth; and exalt the horn of his anointed" (1 S.2:10).

"He shall have dominion also from sea to sea, and from the river unto the ends of the earth" (Ps.72:8).

"And I will cut off the chariot from Ephraim, and the horse from Jerusalem, and the battle bow *shall be* cut off: and he shall speak peace unto the heathen: and his dominion shall be from sea *even* to sea, and from the river *even* to the ends of the earth" (Zec.9:10).

⇒ He is coming to rule the earth.

"Before the LORD: for he cometh, for he cometh to judge the earth: he shall judge the world with righteousness, and the people with his truth" (Ps.96:13).

"Before the LORD; for he cometh to judge the earth: with righteousness shall he judge the world, and the people with equity" (Ps.98:9).

⇒ He will be made higher than the kings of the earth.

"His name shall endure for ever: his name shall be continued as long as the sun: and *men* shall be blessed in him: all nations shall call him blessed" (Ps.72:17).
"Before the LORD; for he cometh to judge the earth: with righteousness shall he judge the world, and the people with equity" (Ps.98:9).

⇒ All nations will come and see His glory and every knee shall bow.

"I have sworn by myself, the word is gone out of my mouth *in* righteousness, and shall not return, That unto me every knee shall bow, every tongue shall swear" (Is.45:23).
"For I *know* their works and their thoughts: it shall come, that I will gather all nations and tongues; and they shall come, and see my glory" (Is.66:18).

⇒ He will be exalted over all rule and authority in this world and in the world to come.

"Far above all principality, and power, and might, and dominion, and every name that is named, not only in this world, but also in that which is to come" (Ep.1:21).

⇒ God will subject the world to come to Christ.

"For unto the angels hath he not put in subjection the world to come, whereof we speak. But one in a certain place testified, saying, What is man, that thou art mindful of him? or the son of man, that thou visitest him? Thou madest him a little lower than the angels; thou crownedst him with glory and honour, and didst set him over the works of thy hands: thou hast put all things in subjection under his feet. For in that he put all in subjection under him, he left nothing *that is* not put under him. But now we see not yet all things put under him" (He.2:5-8).

⇒ The kingdoms of the world become the kingdom of God.

"And the seventh angel sounded; and there were great voices in heaven, saying, The kingdoms of this world *are become* the kingdoms of our Lord, and of his Christ; and he shall reign for ever and ever" (Re.11:15).

⇒ Christ the Stone will fill and rule the whole earth.

"Then was the iron, the clay, the brass, the silver, and the gold, broken to pieces together, and became like the chaff of the summer threshing floors; and the wind carried them away, that no place was found for them: and the stone that smote the image became a great mountain, and filled the whole earth" (Da.2:35).

⇒ Christ alone has the right to the crown.

"I will overturn, overturn, overturn, it: and it shall be no *more*, until he come whose right it is; and I will give it *him*" (Eze.21:27).

⇒ Kings will bring gifts to Him and serve Him.

"The kings of Tarshish and of the isles shall bring presents: the kings of Sheba and Seba shall offer gifts. Yea, all kings shall fall down before him: all nations shall serve him" (Ps.72:10-11).

⇒ His enemies will be made His footstool.

"The Lord said unto my Lord, Sit thou on my right hand, till I make thine enemies thy footstool?" (Mt.22:44).
"Till I make thine enemies thy footstool" (Lu.20:43).
"But to which of the angels said he at any time, Sit on my right hand, until I make thine enemies thy footstool?" (He.1:13).
"From henceforth expecting till his enemies be made his footstool" (He.10:13).

⇒ The people will obey Him.

"The scepter shall not depart from Judah, nor a lawgiver from between his feet, until Shiloh come; and unto him *shall* the gathering of the people *be*" (Ge.49:10).

⇒ The people will gather and obey and serve Him.

"The scepter shall not depart from Judah, nor a lawgiver from between his feet, until Shiloh come; and unto him *shall* the gathering of the people *be*" (Ge.49:10).
"And there was given him dominion, and glory, and a kingdom, that all people, nations, and languages, should serve him: his dominion is an everlasting dominion, which shall not pass away, and his kingdom *that* which shall not be destroyed" (Da.7:14).

⇒ The people will glorify and fear Him.

"Therefore shall the strong people glorify thee, the city of the terrible nations shall fear thee" (Is.25:3).

⇒ He will be given the throne of David.

"He shall be great, and shall be called the Son of the Highest: and the Lord God shall give unto him the throne of his father David" (Lu.1:32).

⇒ He will rule in Zion (Jerusalem) upon His throne.

"Yet have I set my King upon my holy hill of Zion" (Ps.2:6).
"Even he shall build the temple of the LORD; and he shall sit and rule upon his throne; and he shall be a priest upon his throne: and the counsel of peace shall be between them both" (Zec.6:13).

⇒ Jerusalem will be the place of the Lord's throne.

"At that time they shall call Jerusalem the throne of the LORD; and all the nations shall be gathered unto it, to the name of the LORD, to Jerusalem: neither shall they walk any more after the imagination of their evil heart" (Je.3:17).
"Behold, the days come, saith the LORD, that the city shall be built to the LORD from the tower of Hananeel unto the gate of the corner. And the measuring line shall yet go forth over against it upon the hill Gareb, and shall compass about to Goath" (Je.31:38-39).
"It *was* round about eighteen thousand *measures*: and the name of the city from *that* day *shall be*, the LORD *is* there" (Eze.48:35).
"So shall ye know that I *am* the LORD your God dwelling in Zion, my holy mountain: then shall Jerusalem be holy, and there shall no strangers [unbelievers] pass through her any more" (Joel 3:17).
"Thus saith the LORD; I am returned unto Zion, and will dwell in the midst of Jerusalem: and Jerusalem shall be called a city of truth; and the mountain of the LORD of hosts the holy mountain" (Zec.8:3).

⇒ The kingdom of Israel will be the LORD's.

"And saviours shall come up on mount Zion to judge the mount of Esau; and the kingdom shall be the LORD's" (Obad.21).

⇒ The millennial kingdom will be centered in Jerusalem and the Shekinah glory will dwell there.

"And the LORD will create upon every dwelling place of mount Zion, and upon her assemblies, a cloud and smoke by day, and the shining of a flaming fire by night: for upon all the glory shall be a defence. And there *shall be* a tabernacle for a shadow in the daytime from the heat, and for a place of refuge, and for a covert from storm and from rain" (Is.4:5-6).
"At that time they shall call Jerusalem the throne of the LORD; and all the nations shall be gathered unto it, to the name of the LORD, to Jerusalem: neither shall they walk any more after the imagination of their evil heart" (Je.3:17).
"Behold, the days come, saith the LORD, that the city shall be built to the LORD from the tower of Hananeel unto the gate of the corner. And the measuring line shall yet go forth over against it upon the hill Gareb, and shall compass about to Goath" (Je.31:38-39).
"It *was* round about eighteen thousand *measures*: and the name of the city from *that* day *shall be*, the LORD *is* there" (Eze.48:35).
"So shall ye know that I *am* the LORD your God dwelling in Zion, my holy mountain: then shall Jerusalem be holy, and there shall no strangers [unbelievers] pass through her any more" (Joel 3:17).
"The LORD hath taken away thy judgments, he hath cast out thine enemy: the king of Israel, *even* the LORD, *is* in the midst of thee: thou shalt not see evil any more....The LORD thy God in the midst of thee is mighty; he will save, he will rejoice over thee with joy; he will rest in his love, he will joy over thee with singing" (Zep.3:15, 17).
"Thus saith the LORD; I am returned unto Zion, and will dwell in the midst of Jerusalem: and Jerusalem shall be called a city of truth; and the mountain of the LORD of hosts the holy mountain" (Zec.8:3).

⇒ He will bring peace and security to the world.

"And he shall judge among the nations, and shall rebuke many people: and they shall beat their swords into plowshares, and their spears into pruninghooks: nation shall not lift up sword against nation, neither shall they learn war any more" (Is.2:4).

"Of the increase of *his* government and peace *there shall be* no end, upon the throne of David, and upon his kingdom, to order it, and to establish it with judgment and with justice from henceforth even for ever. The zeal of the LORD of hosts will perform this" (Is.9:7).

"And the streets of the city shall be full of boys and girls playing in the streets thereof" (Zec.8:5).

"In that day, saith the LORD of hosts, shall ye call every man his neighbor under the vine and under the fig tree" (Zec.3:10).

"And he shall judge among many people, and rebuke strong nations afar off; and they shall beat their swords into plowshares, and their spears into pruninghooks: nation shall not lift up a sword against nation, neither shall they learn war any more" (Mic.4:3).

⇒ Christ will begin to reign right after the victory at Armageddon.

"And I heard as it were the voice of a great multitude, and as the voice of many waters, and as the voice of mighty thunderings, saying, Alleluia: for the Lord God omnipotent reigneth" (Re.19:6; see Re.19:11-21).

⇒ He, the seed of Abraham, will be given the land of Canaan forever.

"And the LORD appeared unto Abram, and said, Unto thy seed [Christ] will I give this land: and there builded he an altar unto the LORD, who appeared unto him" (Ge.12:7; see Ga.3:16).

"For all the land which thou seest, to thee will I give it, and to thy seed [Christ] for ever" (Ge.13:15).

"And I will give unto thee, and to thy seed [Christ] after thee, the land wherein thou art a stranger, all the land of Canaan, for an everlasting possession; and I will be their God" (Ge.17:8).

"The LORD God of heaven, which took me from my father's house, and from the land of my kindred, and which spake unto me, and that sware unto me, saying, Unto thy seed will I give this land; he shall send his angel before thee, and thou shalt take a wife unto my son from thence" (Ge.24:7).

"Sojourn in this land, and I will be with thee, and will bless thee; for unto thee, and unto thy seed [Christ], I will give all these countries, and I will perform the oath which I sware unto Abraham thy father; and I will make thy seed to multiply as the stars of heaven, and will give unto thy seed all these countries; and in thy seed shall all the nations of the earth be blessed" (Ge.26:3-4).

"And give thee the blessing of Abraham, to thee, and to thy seed with thee; that thou mayest inherit the land wherein thou art a stranger, which God gave unto Abraham....And, behold, the LORD stood above it, and said, I *am* the LORD God of Abraham thy father, and the God if Isaac: the land whereon thou liest, to thee will I give it, and to thy seed [Christ]" (Ge.28:4, 13; see Ga.3:16).

"And the land which I gave Abraham and Isaac, to thee I will give it, and to thy seed after thee will I give the land" (Ge.35:12).

"And said unto me, Behold, I will make thee fruitful, and multiply thee, and I will make of thee a multitude of people; and will give this land to thy seed after thee *for* an everlasting possession" (Ge.48:4).

⇒ The whole earth was given to Israel's seed [Christ] forever.

"Thou shalt keep therefore his statutes, and his commandments, which I command thee this day, that it may go well with thee, and with thy children after thee, and that thou mayest prolong *thy* days upon the earth, which the LORD thy God giveth thee, for ever" (De.4:40).

"For the promise, that he should be the heir of the world [the whole world], *was* not to Abraham, or to his seed [Christ], through the law, but through the righteousness of faith" (Ro.4:13).

⇒ The borders of Israel will be enlarged.

"Thus saith the Lord GOD; This *shall be* the border, whereby ye shall inherit the land according to the twelve tribes of Israel: Joseph *shall have two* portions. And ye shall inherit it, one as well as another: *concerning* the which I lifted up mine hand to give it unto your fathers: and this land shall fall unto you for inheritance. And this *shall be* the border of the land toward the north side, from the great sea, the way of Hethlon, as men go to Zedad; Hamath, Berothah, Sibraim, which *is* between the border of Damascus and the border of Hamath; Hazar-hatticon, which is by the coast of Hauran. And the border from the sea shall be Hazar-enan, the border of Damascus, and the north northward, and the border of Hamath. And *this is* the north side. And the east side ye shall measure from Hauran, and from Damascus, and from Gilead, and from the land of Israel by Jordan, from the border unto the east sea. And *this is* the east side. And the south side southward, from Tamar *even* to the waters of strife *in* Kadesh, the river to the great sea. And *this is* the south side southward. The west side also *shall be* the great sea from the border, till a man come over against Hamath. This *is* the west side. So shall ye divide this land unto you according to the tribes of Israel" (Eze.47:13-21).

"Now these *are* the names of the tribes. From the north end to the coast of the way of Hethlon, as one goeth to Hamath, Hazar-enan, the border of Damascus northward, to the coast of Hamath; for these are his sides east *and* west; a *portion for* Dan. And by the border of Dan, from the east side unto the west side, a *portion for* Asher. And by the border of Asher, from the east side even unto the west side, a *portion for* Naphtali. And by the border of Naphtali, from the east side unto the west side, a *portion for* Manasseh. And by the border of Manasseh, from the east side unto the west side, a *portion for* Ephraim. And by the border of Ephraim, from the east side even unto the west side, a *portion for* Reuben. And by the border of Reuben, from the east side unto the west side, a *portion for* Judah" (Eze.48:1-7).

"And for them, *even* for the priests, shall be *this* holy oblation; toward the north five and twenty thousand *in length,* and toward the west ten thousand in breadth, and toward the east ten thousand in breadth, and toward the south five and twenty thousand in length: and the sanctuary of the LORD shall be in the midst thereof. *It shall be* for the priests that are sanctified of the sons of Zadok; which have kept my charge, which went not astray when the children of Israel went astray, as the Levites went astray. And *this* oblation of the land that is offered shall be unto them a thing most holy by the border of the Levites. And over against the border of the priests the Levites *shall have* five and twenty thousand in length, and ten thousand in breadth: all the length *shall be* five and twenty thousand, and the breadth ten thousand. And they shall not sell of it, neither exchange, nor alienate the firstfruits of the land: for *it is* holy unto the LORD" (Eze.48:10-14).

"All the oblation *shall be* five and twenty thousand by five and twenty thousand: ye shall offer the holy oblation foursquare, with the possession of the city. And the residue *shall be* for the prince, on the one side and on the other of the holy oblation, and of the possession of the city, over against the five and twenty thousand of the oblation toward the east border, and westward over against the five and twenty thousand toward the west border, over against the portions for the prince: and it shall be the holy oblation; and the sanctuary of the house *shall be* in the midst thereof. Moreover from the possession of the Levites, and from the possession of the city, *being* in the midst *of that* which is the prince's, between the border of Judah and the border of Benjamin, shall be for the prince. As for the rest of the tribes, from the east side unto the west side, Benjamin *shall have* a *portion.* And by the border of Benjamin, from the east side unto the west side, Simeon *shall have* a *portion.* And by the border of Simeon, from the east side unto the west side, Issachar a *portion.* And by the border of Issachar, from the east side unto the west side, Zebulun a *portion.* And by the border of Zebulun, from the east side unto the west side, Gad a *portion.* And by the border of Gad, at the south side southward, the border shall be even from Tamar *unto* the waters of strife *in* Kadesh, *and* to the river toward the great sea. This *is* the land which ye shall divide by lot unto the tribes of Israel for inheritance, and these *are* their portions, saith the Lord GOD" (Eze.48:20-29).

⇒ The city of Jerusalem will be laid out by very exact measurements.

"And the five thousand, that are left in the breadth over against the five and twenty thousand, shall be a profane *place* for the city, for dwelling, and for suburbs: and the city shall be in the midst thereof. And these *shall be* the measures thereof; the north side four thousand and five hundred, and the south side four thousand and five hundred, and on the east side four thousand and five hundred, and the west side four thousand and five hundred. And the suburbs of the city shall be toward the north two hundred and fifty, and toward the south two hundred and fifty, and toward the east two hundred and fifty, and toward the west two hundred and fifty. And the residue in length over against the oblation of the holy *portion shall be* ten thousand eastward, and ten thousand westward: and it shall be over against the oblation of the holy *portion;* and the increase thereof shall be for food unto them that serve the city. And they that serve the city shall serve it out of all the tribes of Israel" (Eze.48:15-19).

"And these *are* the goings out of the city on the north side, four thousand and five hundred measures. And the gates of the city *shall be* after the names of the tribes of Israel: three gates northward; one gate of Reuben, one gate of Judah, one gate of Levi. And at the east side four thousand and five hundred: and three gates; and one gate of Joseph, one gate of Benjamin, one gate of Dan. And at the south side four thousand and five hundred measures: and three gates; one gate of Simeon, one gate of Issachar, one gate of Zebulun. At the west side four thousand and five hundred, *with* their three gates; one gate of Gad, one gate of Asher, one gate of Naphtali. *It was* round about eighteen thousand *measures:* and the name of the city from *that* day *shall be,* The LORD *is* there" (Eze.48:30-35).

2. Who is going to be in the Millennium? Only the servants of the LORD, those who truly believe and follow the LORD (Is.65:13-16. Also see outline and notes—Re.20:4, pt.1; 20:7-10 for more discussion).
3. What will life be like in the Millennium?
  a. Life in the Millennium will be blessed.
    ⇒ There will be a covenant or treaty of world-wide peace and security. Imagine one thousand years of peace and security.

"And I will give peace in the land, and ye shall lie down, and none shall make *you* afraid: and I will rid evil beasts out of the land, neither shall the sword go through your land" (Le.26:6).

"In his days Judah shall be saved, and Israel shall dwell safely: and this *is* his name whereby he shall be called, THE LORD OUR RIGHTEOUSNESS" (Je.23:6).

"And in that day will I make a covenant for them with the beasts of the field, and *with* the fowls of heaven, and with the creeping things of the ground: and I will break the bow and the sword and the battle out of the earth, and will make them to lie down safely" (Hos.2:18).

"And he shall judge among many people, and rebuke strong nations afar off; and they shall beat their swords into plowshares, and their spears into pruninghooks: nation shall not lift up a sword against nation, neither shall they learn war any more. But they shall sit every man under his vine and under his fig tree; and none shall make *them* afraid: for the mouth of the LORD of hosts hath spoken *it*" (Mic.4:3-4).

"For the mountains shall depart, and the hills be removed; but my kindness shall not depart from thee, neither shall the covenant of my peace be removed, saith the LORD that hath mercy on thee" (Is.54:10).

"Violence shall no more be heard in thy land, wasting nor destruction within thy borders; but thou shalt call thy walls Salvation, and thy gates Praise" (Is.60:18).

⇒ There will be no evil done by one nation against another nation.

"The remnant of Israel shall not do iniquity, nor speak lies; neither shall a deceitful tongue be found in their mouth: for they shall feed and lie down, and none shall make *them* afraid" (Zep.3:13).

"The LORD hath taken away thy judgments, he hath cast out thine enemy: the king of Israel, *even* the LORD, *is* in the midst of thee: thou shalt not see evil any more" (Zep.3:15).

⇒ There will be no sickness.

"And ye shall serve the LORD your God, and he shall bless thy bread, and thy water; and I will take sickness away from the midst of thee. There shall nothing cast their young, nor be barren, in thy land: the number of thy days I will fulfill" (Ex.23:25-26).

"Then the eyes of the blind shall be opened, and the ears of the deaf shall be unstopped. *Then* shall the lame *man* leap as a hart, and the tongue of the dumb sing: for in the wilderness shall waters break out, and streams in the desert" (Is.35:5-6).

⇒ There will be a fruitful human population: no more barrenness or miscarriages.

"There shall nothing cast their young, nor be barren, in thy land: the number of thy days I will fulfill" (Ex.23:26).

"For I will have respect unto you, and make you fruitful, and multiply you, and establish my covenant with you" (Le.26:9).

"Thou shalt be blessed above all people: there shall not be male or female barren among you, or among your cattle" (De.7:14).

"Blessed *shall be* the fruit of thy body, and the fruit of thy ground, and the fruit of thy cattle, the increase of thy kine [oxen, livestock], and the flocks of thy sheep....And the LORD shall make thee plenteous in goods, in the fruit of thy body, and in the fruit of thy cattle, and in the fruit of thy ground, in the land which the LORD sware unto thy fathers to give thee" (De.28:4, 11).

"Thou hast multiplied the nation, *and* not increased the joy: they joy before thee according to the joy in harvest, *and* as *men* rejoice when they divide the spoil" (Is.9:3).

⇒ There will be bread and water and the necessities of life for everyone on earth.

"Behold, the days come, saith the LORD, that the plowman shall overtake the reaper, and the treader of grapes him that soweth seed; and the mountains shall drop sweet wine, and all the hills shall melt. And I will bring again the captivity of my people of Israel, and they shall build the waste cities, and inhabit *them*, and they shall plant vineyards, and drink the wine thereof; they shall also make gardens, and eat the fruit of them" (Am.9:13-14).

"And ye shall serve the LORD your God, and he shall bless thy bread, and thy water; and I will take sickness away from the midst of thee" (Ex.23:25).

"Blessed *shall* be thy basket and thy store. Blessed *shalt* thou *be* when thou comest in, and blessed *shalt* thou *be* when thou goest out....The LORD shall command the blessing upon thee in thy storehouses, and in all that thou settest thine hand unto; and he shall bless thee in the land which the LORD thy God giveth thee....The LORD shall open unto thee his good treasure, the heaven to give the rain unto thy land in his season, and to bless all the work of thine hand: and thou shalt lend unto many nations, and thou shalt not borrow" (De.28:5-6, 8, 12).

"And the LORD thy God will make thee plenteous in every work of thine hand, in the fruit of thy body, and in the fruit of thy cattle, and in the fruit of thy land, for good: for the LORD will again rejoice over thee for good, as he rejoiced over thy fathers" (De.30:9).

"He shall come down like rain upon the mown grass: as showers *that* water the earth. In his days shall the righteous flourish; and abundance of peace so long as the moon endureth....There shall be an handful of corn in the earth upon the top of the mountains; the fruit thereof shall shake like Lebanon: and *they* of the city shall flourish like grass of the earth" (Ps.72:6-7, 16).

"In that day shall the branch of the LORD be beautiful and glorious, and the fruit of the earth *shall be* excellent and comely for them that are escaped of Israel" (Is.4:2).

"And I will make them and the places round about my hill a blessing; and I will cause the shower to come down in his season; there shall be showers of blessing. And the tree of the field shall yield her fruit, and the earth shall yield her increase, and they shall be safe in their land, and shall know that I *am* the LORD, when I have broken the bands of their yoke, and delivered them out of the hand of those that served themselves of them....And I will raise up for them a plant of renown, and they shall be no more consumed with hunger in the land, neither bear the shame of the heathen any more" (Eze.34:26-27, 29).

"And it shall come to pass in that day, I will hear, saith the LORD, I will hear the heavens, and they shall hear the earth; and the earth shall hear the corn, and the wine, and the oil; and they shall hear Jezreel" (Hos.2:21-22).

"And it shall come to pass in that day, *that* the mountains shall drop down new wine, and the hills shall flow with milk, and all the rivers of Judah shall flow with waters, and a fountain shall come forth of the house of the LORD, and shall water the valley of Shittim" (Joel 3:18).

"Behold, the days come, saith the LORD, that the plowman shall overtake the reaper, and the treader of grapes him that soweth seed; and the mountains shall drop sweet wine, and all the hills shall melt" (Am.9:13).

⇒ There will be food and rest for all and no fear of enemies or criminals.

"I will feed them in a good pasture, and upon the high mountains of Israel shall their fold be: there shall they lie in a good fold, and *in* a fat pasture shall they feed upon the mountains of Israel" (Eze.34:14).

"They shall feed and lie down, and none shall make *them* afraid" (Zep.3:13).

"In that day it shall be said to Jerusalem, Fear thou not: *and* to Zion, Let not thine hands be slack" (Zep.3:16).

"And it shall come to pass in the day that the LORD shall give thee rest from thy sorrow, and from thy fear, and from the hard bondage wherein thou wast made to serve" (Is.14:3).

"In righteousness shalt thou be established: thou shalt be far from oppression; for thou shalt not fear: and from terror: for it shall not come near thee" (Is.54:14).

⇒ There will be long and full life spans.

"There shall nothing cast their young, nor be barren, in thy land: the number of thy days I will fulfill" (Ex.23:26).

"He will swallow up death in victory; and the Lord GOD will wipe away tears from off all faces; and the rebuke of his people shall he take away from off all the earth: for the LORD hath spoken *it*" (Is.25:8).

"There shall be no more thence an infant of days, nor an old man that hath not filled his days: for the child shall die a hundred years old; but the sinner *being* a hundred years old shall be accursed" (Is.65:20).

"Thus saith the LORD of hosts; There shall yet old men and old women dwell in the streets of Jerusalem, and every man with his staff in his hand for very age" (Zec.8:4).

⇒ It will be a day of no tears, but of joy and praise.

"He will swallow up death in victory; and the Lord GOD will wipe away tears from off all faces; and the rebuke of his people shall he take away from off all the earth: for the LORD hath spoken *it*" (Is.25:8).

"And the ransomed of the LORD shall return, and come to Zion with songs and everlasting joy upon their heads: they shall obtain joy and gladness, and sorrow and sighing shall flee away" (Is.35:10).

"Therefore the redeemed of the LORD shall return, and come with singing unto Zion; and everlasting joy *shall be* upon their head: they shall obtain gladness and joy; *and* sorrow and mourning shall flee away" (Is.51:11).

"Sing, O daughter of Zion; shout, O Israel; be glad and rejoice with all the heart, O daughter of Jerusalem" (Zep.3:14).

"Now unto him that is able to keep you from falling, and to present *you* faultless before the presence of his glory with exceeding joy" (Jude 24).

"And in that day shall ye say, Praise the LORD, call upon his name, declare his doings among the people, make mention that his name is exalted" (Is.12:4).

⇒ Shame and guilt will be removed.

"In that day shalt thou not be ashamed for all thy doings, wherein thou hast transgressed against me: for then I will take away out of the midst of thee them that rejoice in thy pride, and thou shalt no more be haughty because of my holy mountain" (Zep.3:11).

"And ye shall eat in plenty, and be satisfied, and praise the name of the LORD your God, that hath dealt wondrously with you: and my people shall never be ashamed. And ye shall know that I *am* in the midst of Israel, and *that* I *am* the LORD your God, and none else: and my people shall never be ashamed" (Joel 2:26-27).

⇒ There will be recognition and honor and a healthy ego and emotions.

"Behold, at that time I will undo all that afflict thee: and I will save her that halteth, and gather her that was driven out; and I will get them praise and fame in every land where they have been put to shame. At that time will I bring you again, even in the time that I gather you: for I will make you a name and a praise among all people of the earth, when I turn back your captivity before your eyes, saith the LORD" (Zep.3:19-20).

⇒ Everyone will be a neighbor to everyone else.

"In that day, saith the LORD of hosts, shall ye call every man his neighbor under the vine and under the fig tree" (Zec.3:10).

⇒ There will no longer be any slavery.

"For it shall come to pass in that day, saith the LORD of hosts, that I will break his [the oppressor's] yoke from off thy neck, and will burst thy bonds, and strangers shall no more serve themselves of him. But they shall serve the LORD their God, and [the descendent, the Lord Jesus Christ of] David their king, whom I will raise up unto them" (Je.30:8-9).

⇒ People will be able to trust the LORD's strong arm.

"My righteousness is near; my salvation is gone forth, and mine arms shall judge the people; the isles shall wait upon me, and on mine arm shall they trust" (Is.51:5).

⇒ It will be a day of mercy.

"And in mercy shall the throne be established: and he shall sit upon it in truth in the tabernacle of David, judging, and seeking judgment, and hasting righteousness" (Is.16:5).

⇒ All things will be restored.

"Whom the heaven must receive until the times of restitution of all things, which God hath spoken by the mouth of all his holy prophets since the world began" (Ac.3:21).

⇒ Destroyed cities will be rebuilt. (Remember: most of the major cities of the world will have been destroyed.)

"And they shall build the old wastes, they shall raise up the former desolations, and they shall repair the waste cities, the desolations of many generations" (Is.61:4).
"And they shall build houses, and inhabit them; and they shall plant vineyards, and eat the fruit of them" (Is.65:21).
"Behold, the days come, saith the LORD, that the plowman shall overtake the reaper, and the treader of grapes him that soweth seed; and the mountains shall drop sweet wine, and all the hills shall melt. And I will bring again the captivity of my people of Israel, and they shall build the waste cities, and inhabit them; and they shall plant vineyards, and drink the wine thereof; they shall also make gardens, and eat the fruit of them" (Am.9:13-14).

⇒ All animals will live in peace. There will be no savagery.

"The wolf and the lamb shall feed together, and the lion shall eat straw like the bullock: and dust shall be the serpent's meat. They shall not hurt nor destroy in all my holy mountain, saith the LORD" (Is.65:25).

⇒ Israel will be established as a nation forever.

"Thus saith the LORD, which giveth the sun for a light by day, and the ordinances of the moon and of the stars for a light by night, which divideth the sea when the waves thereof roar; the LORD of hosts is his name: If those ordinances depart from before me, saith the LORD, then the seed of Israel also shall cease from being a nation before me for ever. Thus saith the LORD; If heaven above can be measured, and the foundations of the earth searched out beneath, I will also cast off all the seed of Israel for all that they have done, saith the LORD" (Je.31:35-37).

⇒ The Gentiles receive the inheritance and blessings of Israel.

"And it shall come to pass, that ye shall divide it by lot for an inheritance unto you, and to the strangers that sojourn among you, which shall beget children among you: and they shall be unto you as born in the country among the children of Israel; they shall have inheritance with you among the tribes of Israel. And it shall come to pass, that in what tribe the stranger sojourneth, there shall ye give him his inheritance, saith the Lord GOD" (Eze.47:22-23).

"The princes of the people [from all nations] are gathered together, *even* the people of the God of Abraham: for the shield of the earth *belong* unto God: he is greatly exalted" (Ps.47:9).

⇒ The feast of Tabernacles will be celebrated on a yearly basis.

"And it shall come to pass, *that* every one that is left of all the nations which came against Jerusalem shall even go up from year to year to worship the King, the LORD of hosts, and to keep the feast of tabernacles" (Zec.14:16; see Ex.23:16. See note—Jn.7:37 for discussion.)

b. Life in the Millennium will be governed by righteousness.
   ⇒ Christ is going to judge the earth with righteousness and truth.

"The God of Israel said, the Rock of Israel spake to me, He that ruleth over men *must be* just, ruling in the fear of God. And *he shall be* as the light of the morning, *when* the sun riseth, *even* a morning without clouds; *as* the tender grass *springing* out of the earth by clear shining after rain" (2 S.23:3-4).

"O let the nations be glad and sing for joy: for thou shalt judge the people righteously, and govern the nations upon earth" (Ps.67:4).

"Before the LORD: for he cometh, for he cometh to judge the earth: he shall judge the world with righteousness, and the people with his truth" (Ps.96:13).

"Before the LORD; for he cometh to judge the earth: with righteousness shall he judge the world, and the people with equity" (Ps.98:9).

"And in mercy shall the throne be established: and he shall sit upon it in truth in the tabernacle of David, judging, and seeking judgment, and hasting righteousness" (Is.16:5).

"Behold, the days come, saith the LORD, that I will raise unto David a righteous Branch, and a King shall reign and prosper, and shall execute judgment and justice in the earth" (Je.23:5).

"In those days, and at that time, will I cause the Branch of righteousness to grow up unto David; and he shall execute judgment and righteousness in the land" (Je.33:15).

⇒ Christ is going to appoint a kingdom to the apostles.

"And I appoint unto you a kingdom, as my Father hath appointed unto me" (Lu.22:29).

⇒ Christ will prevent evil from being done by one nation to another nation.

"The remnant of Israel shall not do iniquity, nor speak lies; neither shall a deceitful tongue be found in their mouth: for they shall feed and lie down, and none shall make *them* afraid" (Zep.3:13).

"The LORD hath taken away thy judgments, he hath cast out thine enemy: the king of Israel, *even* the LORD, *is* in the midst of thee: thou shalt not see evil [from any nation] any more" (Zep.3:15).

⇒ God's commandments will be kept by the nations. There will be national obedience.

"But I said, How shall I put thee among the children, and give thee a pleasant land, a goodly heritage of the hosts of nations? and I said, Thou shalt call me, My father; and shalt not turn away from me" (Je.3:19).

⇒ The citizens of Jerusalem will be called holy.

"And it shall come to pass, *that he that is* left in Zion, and *he that* remaineth in Jerusalem, shall be called holy, *even* every one that is written among the living in Jerusalem: when the Lord shall have washed away the filth of the daughters of Zion, and shall have purged the blood of Jerusalem from the midst thereof by the spirit of judgment, and by the spirit of burning" (Is.4:3-4).

⇒ Believers will call God "my Father."

"But I said, How shall I put thee among the children, and give thee a pleasant land, a goodly heritage of the hosts of nations? and I said, Thou shalt call me, My father; and shalt not turn away from me" (Je.3:19).

c. Life in the Millennium will be a life of true worship.
   ⇒ All nations and kings and people of the earth will worship Christ.

"All the ends of the world shall remember and turn unto the LORD: and all the kindreds of the nations shall worship before thee" (Ps.22:27).

"All the earth shall worship thee, and shall sing unto thee; they shall sing *to* thy name" (Ps.66:4).

"And he shall live, and to him shall be given of the gold of Sheba: prayer also shall be made for him continually; *and* daily shall he be praised" (Ps.72:15).

"All nations whom thou hast made shall come and worship before thee, O Lord; and shall glorify thy name" (Ps.86:9).

"So the heathen shall fear the name of the LORD, and all the kings of the earth thy glory....To declare the name of the LORD in Zion, and his praise in Jerusalem; when the people are gathered together, and the kingdoms, to serve the LORD" (Ps.102:15, 21-22).

"All the kings of the earth shall praise thee, O LORD, when they hear the words of thy mouth. Yea, they shall sing in the ways of the LORD: for great *is* the glory of the LORD" (Ps.138:4-5).

"And thou shalt swear, The LORD liveth, in truth, in judgment, and in righteousness; and the nations shall bless themselves in him, and in him shall they glory" (Je.4:2).

"Thus saith the LORD of hosts; In those days *it shall come to pass*, that ten men shall take hold out of all languages of the nations, even shall take hold of the skirt of him that is a Jew, saying, We will go with you: for we have heard *that* God *is* with you" (Zec.8:23).

⇒ All nations will seek instruction from Christ. Gentiles will become the multiplied seed of David and members of the priesthood of God's true people, the true Israel.

"But in the last days it shall come to pass, *that* the mountain of the house of the LORD shall be established in the top of the mountains, and it shall be exalted above the hills; and people shall flow unto it. And many nations shall come, and say, Come, and let us go up to the mountain of the LORD, and to the house of the God of Jacob; and he will teach us of his ways, and we will walk in his paths: for the law shall go forth of Zion, and the word of the LORD from Jerusalem" (Mic.4:1-2).

"And it shall come to pass in the last days, *that* the mountain of the LORD'S house shall be established in the top of the mountains, and shall be exalted above the hills; and all nations shall flow unto it. And many people shall go and say, Come ye, and let us go up to the mountain of the LORD, to the house of the God of Jacob; and he will teach us of his ways, and we will walk in his paths: for out of Zion shall go forth the law, and the word of the LORD from Jerusalem" (Is.2:2-3).

"Neither shall the priests the Levites [the tribe of the priesthood] want a man before me to offer burnt offerings, and to kindle meat offerings, and to do sacrifice continually....As the host of heaven cannot be numbered, neither the sand of the sea measured: so will I multiply the seed of David my servant, and the Levites [the priests] that minister unto me" (Je.33:18, 22).

"And I will also take of them [Gentiles] for priests *and* for Levites [the priesthood], saith the LORD" (Is.66:21).

⇒ There will be a covenant of peace between God and Israel, even the forgiveness of sin.

"And so all Israel shall be saved: as it is written, There shall come out of Sion the Deliverer, and shall turn away ungodliness from Jacob: For this is my covenant unto them, when I shall take away their sins" (Ro.11:26-27).

"I will seek that which was lost, and bring again that which was driven away, and will bind up *that which was* broken, and will strengthen that which was sick: but I will destroy the fat and the strong; I will feed them with judgment" (Eze.34:16).

"For the mountains shall depart, and the hills be removed; but my kindness shall not depart from thee, neither shall the covenant of my peace be removed, saith the LORD that hath mercy on thee" (Is.54:10).

⇒ All of God's people will be purified.

"And he shall sit *as* a refiner and purifier of silver: and he shall purify the sons of Levi [the priests], and purge them as gold and silver, that they may offer unto the LORD an offering in righteousness. Then shall the offering of Judah and Jerusalem be pleasant unto the LORD, as in the days of old, and as in former years" (Mal.3:3-4).

⇒ The nations will bless Christ and glory in Him.

"And thou shalt swear, The LORD liveth, in truth, in judgment, and in righteousness; and the nations shall bless themselves in him, and in him shall they glory" (Je.4:2).

"All the ends of the world shall remember and turn unto the LORD: and all the kindreds of the nations shall worship before thee" (Ps.22:27).

4. What are some verses that show that resurrected believers will rule and reign during the Millennium?
⇒ The kingdom and dominion of the world will be given to believers.

"And the kingdom and dominion, and the greatness of the kingdom under the whole heaven, shall be given to the people of the saints of the most High, whose kingdom *is* an everlasting kingdom, and all dominions shall serve and obey him" (Da.7:27).

⇒ The apostles will rule and reign over the twelve tribes of Israel.

"And Jesus said unto them, Verily I say unto you, That ye which have followed me, in the regeneration when the Son of man shall sit in the throne of his glory, ye also shall sit upon twelve thrones, judging the twelve tribes of Israel" (Mt.19:28).

"And he saith unto them, Ye shall drink indeed of my cup, and be baptized with the baptism that I am baptized with: but to sit on my right hand, and on my left, is not mine to give, but *it shall be given to them* for whom it is prepared of my Father" (Mt.20:23).

"I beheld till the thrones were cast down, and the Ancient of days did sit, whose garment *was* white as snow, and the hair of his head like the pure wool: his throne *was like* the fiery flame, *and* his wheels as burning fire....And the kingdom and dominion, and the greatness of the kingdom under the whole heaven, shall be given to the people of the saints of the most High, whose kingdom *is* an everlasting kingdom, and all dominions shall serve and obey him" (Da.7:9, 27).

⇒ God's people will be heirs of the world, of the whole world or universe.

"And to make thee high above all nations which he hath made, in praise, and in name, and in honor; and that thou mayest be a holy people unto the LORD thy God, as he hath spoken" (De.26:19).

"For the promise, that he should be heir of the world, *was* not to Abraham, or to his seed, through the law, but through the righteousness of faith" (Ro.4:13).

⇒ God's people will rule as princes.

"Behold, a king shall reign in righteousness, and princes shall rule in judgment" (Is.32:1).

⇒ All believers will rule and reign with Christ.

"And he that overcometh, and keepeth my works unto the end, to him will I give power over the nations: and he shall rule them with a rod of iron; as the vessels of a potter shall they be broken to shivers: even as I received of my Father" (Re.2:26-27).

"To him that overcometh will I grant to sit with me in my throne, even as I also overcame, and am set down with my Father in his throne" (Re.3:21).

"And hast made us unto our God kings and priests: and we shall reign on the earth" (Re.5:10).

"And I saw thrones, and they sat upon them, and judgment was given unto them: and I *saw* the souls of them that were beheaded for the witness of Jesus, and for the word of God, and which had not worshipped the beast, neither his image, neither had received *his* mark upon their foreheads, or in their hands; and they lived and reigned with Christ a thousand years....Blessed and holy *is* he that hath part in the first resurrection: on such the second death hath no power, but they shall be priests of God and of Christ, and shall reign with him a thousand years" (Re.20:4, 6).

"If we suffer, we shall also reign with *him*: if we deny *him*, he also will deny us" (2 Ti.2:12).

⇒ The LORD will set up shepherds (leaders) over His people.

"And I will set up shepherds over them which shall feed them: and they shall fear no more, nor be dismayed, neither shall they be lacking, saith the LORD" (Je.23:4).

⇒ God's people will judge or rule over angels. (This may not take place until the new heavens and earth are created.)

"Know ye not that we shall judge angels? how much more things that pertain to this life?" (1 Co.6:3).

⇒ God's people will be put in charge of all of Christ's possessions.

"Blessed *is* that servant, whom his lord when he cometh shall find so doing. Of a truth I say unto you, that ye will make him ruler over all that he hath" (Lu.12:43-44).

⇒ Believers will rule over unbelieving Jews.

"Behold, I will make them of the synagogue of Satan, which say they are Jews, and are not, but do lie; behold, I will make them to come and worship before thy feet, and to know that I have loved thee" (Re.3:9).

Remember: the believers will be in their resurrected bodies and people on earth in their earthly bodies. There will apparently be mingling between the two groups. What we must keep in mind is this: heaven and eternity are not as most people imagine them to be, that is, with spirits floating around on clouds or else spirits appearing as ghosts or gas-like substances. We will have bodies in heaven and eternity. In fact, we will have our present bodies with one difference: they will be perfected. This is the very purpose for the resurrection: to raise up the very elements of our bodies and perfect them to live eternally in the perfect environment of heaven and earth. Therefore, during the Millennium it will be just like it was when Christ fellowshipped with the disciples after His resurrection. He was in His resurrected body and the disciples were in their earthly bodies. During the Millennium, it will be a common thing for the resurrected Lord and resurrected believers to fellowship with people in their earthly bodies. All will have bodies, some earthly bodies and others heavenly, that is, perfected bodies. Remember: the Millennium will be a new age for the earth. Life upon earth will be entirely different from what it is now. As has been seen in the study above, when Jesus Christ returns to earth, His presence and power will change everything.

CHAPTER 66

E. The Last Days of Human History (Part 2), 66:1-24

1. The true temple of God
a. The true temple identified
   1) God dwells in heaven & earth
      • Because no building can contain the LORD
      • Because He is the Creator
   2) God dwells with the person who is submissive & who trembles at His Word: The person's body becomes God's temple, Je.31:33; 32:40; He.8:10; see 1 Co.3:16; 6:19-20
b. The worshippers rejected
   1) Those who walk their own way instead of obeying God's Word: Their worship is unacceptable
      • Is as the worship of murderers
      • Is as the worship of people who offer dogs or pigs to God
      • Is as the worship of people who idolize false gods
   2) The rejected worshippers' fate: Their judgment is harsh
      • Because they did not respond to God's call for repentance
      • Because they deliberately did evil & engaged in false worship
      • Because they persecuted those who trembled at God's Word
   3) The rejected worshippers' fate explained
      • Will be shamed
      • Will suffer God's vengeance: Jerusalem's fall to Babylon (586 B.C.); & Rome (A.D. 70); 1:6-10

2. The restored Jerusalem: The restoration of the city & of the Jews, 54:1-17
a. The city & nation will be reborn
   1) Reborn quickly, suddenly—within a day: More quickly than a mother who gives birth before her labor pains begin
   2) Reborn by the guarantee of God—His Word & His promise: He Himself will restore Israel, 49:18-21; 54:1-3

Thus saith the LORD, The heaven *is* my throne, and the earth *is* my footstool: where *is* the house that ye build unto me? and where *is* the place of my rest?

2 For all those *things* hath mine hand made, and all those *things* have been, saith the LORD: but to this *man* will I look, *even* to *him that is* poor and of a contrite spirit, and trembleth at my word.

3 He that killeth an ox *is as if* he slew a man; he that sacrificeth a lamb, *as if* he cut off a dog's neck; he that offereth an oblation, *as if he offered* swine's blood; he that burneth incense, *as if* he blessed an idol. Yea, they have chosen their own ways, and their soul delighteth in their abominations.

4 I also will choose their delusions, and will bring their fears upon them; because when I called, none did answer; when I spake, they did not hear: but they did evil before mine eyes, and chose *that* in which I delighted not.

5 Hear the word of the LORD, ye that tremble at his word; your brethren that hated you, that cast you out for my name's sake, said, Let the LORD be glorified: but he shall appear to your joy, and they shall be ashamed.

6 A voice of noise from the city, a voice from the temple, a voice of the LORD that rendereth recompence to his enemies.

7 Before she travailed, she brought forth; before her pain came, she was delivered of a man child.

8 Who hath heard such a thing? who hath seen such things? Shall the earth be made to bring forth in one day? *or* shall a nation be born at once? for as soon as Zion travailed, she brought forth her children.

9 Shall I bring to the birth, and not cause to bring forth? saith the LORD: shall I cause to bring forth, and shut *the womb?* saith thy God.

10 Rejoice ye with Jerusalem, and be glad with her, all ye that love her: rejoice for joy with her, all ye that mourn for her:

11 That ye may suck, and be satisfied with the breasts of her consolations; that ye may milk out, and be delighted with the abundance of her glory.

12 For thus saith the LORD, Behold, I will extend peace to her like a river, and the glory of the Gentiles like a flowing stream: then shall ye suck, ye shall be borne upon *her* sides, and be dandled upon *her* knees.

13 As one whom his mother comforteth, so will I comfort you; and ye shall be comforted in Jerusalem.

14 And when ye see *this,* your heart shall rejoice, and your bones shall flourish like an herb: and the hand of the LORD shall be known toward his servants, and *his* indignation toward his enemies.

15 For, behold, the LORD will come with fire, and with his chariots like a whirlwind, to render his anger with fury, and his rebuke with flames of fire.

16 For by fire and by his sword will the LORD plead with all flesh: and the slain of the LORD shall be many.

17 They that sanctify themselves, and purify themselves in the gardens behind one *tree* in the midst, eating swine's flesh, and the abomination, and the mouse, shall be consumed together, saith the LORD.

18 For I *know* their works and their thoughts: it shall come, that I will gather all nations and tongues; and they shall come, and see my glory.

19 And I will set a sign among them, and I will send those that escape of them unto the nations, *to* Tarshish, Pul, and Lud, that draw the bow, *to* Tubal, and Javan, *to* the isles afar off, that have not heard my fame, neither have seen my glory; and they shall declare my glory among the Gentiles.

20 And they shall bring all your brethren *for* an offering unto the LORD out of all nations upon horses, and in

b. The restored Jerusalem will be a cause for rejoicing
   1) Because she will nourish, comfort, & satisfy those who love her
   2) Because God will overflow Jerusalem with peace & prosperity: Make her the capital of the world
   3) Because her children will be provided & cared for by her
   4) Because God will comfort her children just as a mother comforts her child
   5) Because Jerusalem will stir joy & bring good health to God's people

3. The Day of the LORD, His terrifying judgment
a. The LORD is coming in a storm of fire
   1) To punish with the fury of His anger
   2) To rebuke with flames of fire
b. The LORD is coming to execute judgment upon all people: Many will be slain
   1) All who followed the abominable practices of idolatry & false worship: Will meet a terrible end
   2) All who were guilty of evil works & thoughts: Will appear before the LORD & witness His glory

4. The proclamation of God's glory worldwide
a. The LORD will set a sign before the world: Most likely the appearance of Christ at His Second Coming, Mt.24:30
b. The LORD will choose some Jews as ministers to share the message of God's glory with the world: Will become a great evangelistic force to reach the world
   1) They will bring the Gentiles—their spiritual brothers—to worship in Jerusalem

2) They will reap such a vast harvest of worshippers that every means of transportation available will have to be used	chariots, and in litters, and upon mules, and upon swift beasts, to my holy mountain Jerusalem, saith the LORD, as the children of Israel bring an offering in a clean vessel into the house of the LORD.	name remain. 23 And it shall come to pass, *that* from one new moon to another, and from one sabbath to another, shall all flesh come to worship before me, saith the LORD.	b. God's people—the only humans alive at the end—will bow & worship the LORD: Regularly, month to month & Sabbath to Sabbath
c. The LORD will choose some Gentile believers to be His ministers **5. The gift of eternal life in the new heavens & earth** a. God's people will have names & descendants that endure eternally	21 And I will also take of them for priests *and* for Levites, saith the LORD. 22 For as the new heavens and the new earth, which I will make, shall remain before me, saith the LORD, so shall your seed and your	24 And they shall go forth, and look upon the carcases of the men that have transgressed against me: for their worm shall not die, neither shall their fire be quenched; and they shall be an abhorring unto all flesh.	**6. The sad fate of the unrepentant** a. They will be dead (separated from God) & punished eternally in an unquenchable fire b. They will have a disgusting, repulsive legacy

DIVISION VII

THE PROPHECIES OF A GREAT AND GLORIOUS FUTURE, 60:1–66:24

E.   The Last Days of Human History (Part 2), 66:1-24

(66:1-24) **Introduction**: this chapter is the climax to the great book of *Isaiah*. Through the power of God's Spirit, Isaiah has been able to look through the portal of time to see the events of the future. As has been seen, the behavior of the human race repeats itself generation after generation. For this reason, the discipline of God and His hand of judgment have repeatedly fallen on the wicked people and nations of this earth. God is very patient, suffering a long time with the sinful person. But eventually the day comes when His hand of discipline and judgment must fall. However, as Isaiah looked into the corridor of the future, he saw not only the judgments of God but also saw the salvation of God, even the sufferings of the Messiah Himself. As he now closes the great prophecies given him by the LORD, he is able to see the glorious consummation of human history. He actually sees the events of the end time, the last days of the human race on earth. This is the exciting subject that closes the great book of *Isaiah*, *The Last Days of Human History (Part 2)*, 66:1-24.

1. The true temple of God (vv.1-6).
2. The restored Jerusalem: the restoration of the city and of the Jews, 54:1-17 (vv.7-14).
3. The Day of the LORD, His terrifying judgment (vv.15-18).
4. The proclamation of God's glory worldwide (vv.19-21).
5. The gift of eternal life in the new heavens and earth (vv.22-23).
6. The sad fate of the unrepentant (v.24).

1 (66:1-6) **Temple, Identified—God, Temple of—Worship, True—Humility, Essential—Contrition, Essential—Word of God, Duty—Acceptance, by God, Essential—Worship, Rejected; Unacceptable; Acceptable—Worship, False, Judgment of—Israel, Worship of, Rejected—Temple, True—Submission, to God, Essential—Believers, Body of, God's Temple—Body, of Believer**: in the last days of human history, the true temple of God will take center stage. These six verses show that very significant issues are involved when people worship the LORD.

OUTLINE	SCRIPTURE	SCRIPTURE	OUTLINE

1. The true temple of God
a. The true temple identified
1) God dwells in heaven & earth
  • Because no building can contain the LORD
  • Because He is the Creator
2) God dwells with the person who is submissive & who trembles at His Word: The person's body becomes God's temple, Je.31:33; 32:40; He.8:10; see 1 Co.3:16; 6:19-20
b. The worshippers rejected
1) Those who walk their own way instead of obeying God's Word: Their worship is unacceptable
	Thus saith the LORD, The heaven *is* my throne, and the earth *is* my footstool: where *is* the house that ye build unto me? and where *is* the place of my rest? 2 For all those *things* hath mine hand made, and all those *things* have been, saith the LORD: but to this *man* will I look, *even* to *him* that *is* poor and of a contrite spirit, and trembleth at my word. 3 He that killeth an ox *is as if* he slew a man; he that sacrificeth a lamb, *as if* he cut off a dog's neck; he that offereth an oblation, *as*	*if he offered* swine's blood; he that burneth incense, *as if* he blessed an idol. Yea, they have chosen their own ways, and their soul delighteth in their abominations. 4 I also will choose their delusions, and will bring their fears upon them; because when I called, none did answer; when I spake, they did not hear: but they did evil before mine eyes, and chose *that* in which I delighted not. 5 Hear the word of the LORD, ye that tremble at his word; your brethren that	• Is as the worship of murderers
			• Is as the worship of people who offer dogs or pigs to God
			• Is as the worship of people who idolize false gods
			2) The rejected worshippers' fate: Their judgment is harsh
			  • Because they did not respond to God's call for repentance
			  • Because they deliberately did evil & engaged in false worship
			  • Because they persecuted those who trembled at God's Word

311

OUTLINE	SCRIPTURE	SCRIPTURE	OUTLINE
3) The rejected worshippers' fate explained • Will be shamed • Will suffer God's vengeance: Jerusalem's fall to	hated you, that cast you out for my name's sake, said, Let the LORD be glorified: but he shall appear to your joy, and they shall be ashamed.	6　A voice of noise from the city, a voice from the temple, a voice of the LORD that rendereth recompence to his enemies.	Babylon (586 B.C.); & Rome (A.D. 70); 1:6-10

a. The true temple of God is identified (vv.1-2). Contrary to what many people think, God does not dwell in buildings. God is Spirit, and He is omnipresent. Omnipresent means that His presence is everywhere, even expanding out beyond the far reaches of the universe. Although the starry sky demonstrates the glory of God, it is nothing more than a throne for God. And the earth in all of its beauty and glory is nothing more than a footstool for Him. God dwells in another dimension of being, the spiritual dimension, which is the permanent world. The physical, material world in which we live is corruptible, deteriorating, and wasting away. But the spiritual dimension of being is permanent and eternal. God lives in the *spiritual dimension* or *spiritual world*. That world supercedes this world enormously. The vast expanse of God's person and presence is infinite—far, far beyond human comprehension. Note how the LORD stresses this fact: Is it not His hand that has created the universe, brought all things into being? The point is that God supercedes, is out beyond this physical, material universe. Even the universe itself cannot contain God's presence. How then can people expect the temple or any other building to be a house for His presence?

Down through the centuries of human history, the LORD did manifest His presence at various worship sites, such as the altars built by the patriarchs, the Tabernacle, the Temple built by Solomon, and succeeding temples built by others. The LORD had said that the Temple would be the place where His Name would dwell (1 K.8:29). And the LORD had appointed Solomon to build a House for His Name (2 S.7:13; 1 K.5:5; 8:18-19; 1 Chr.22:10). Within these and all other worship centers that are truly set apart for the worship of the LORD, God does manifest His presence through people's praise and worship. He does not ignore the Temple or any other worship center that is truly sanctified, set apart to His Name.

However, the Temple is not the focus of God's attention. Just because a temple has been constructed does not mean that God will manifest His presence in the building. He will grant a special sense of His presence only if the hearts of the worshippers belong to Him. It is not the building that pleases God. It is the heart of the worshipper. This is exactly what God says.

God dwells with the person who is submissive and who trembles at His Word (v.2). A submissive person is humbled and contrite before the LORD, which means that the person bows before the LORD, acknowledging the greatness of God as well as his own unworthiness and sin. Bowing before the LORD, the individual confesses and repents of his sins. After arising from his knees, the true worshipper goes about his daily affairs *trembling at God's Word*. This means that the person respects God's Word so much that he continually seeks to obey it. He shudders, quakes, even fears lest he disobey God's commandments. This is the worshipper God accepts. When this worshipper and others of like mind enter the temple, God manifests His presence among them. He grants a very special sense of His presence to such worshippers. In the last days of human history, the body of the true worshipper actually becomes the true temple of God. Amazingly, God's very own Spirit dwells within the true believer. The true temple of God is the believer who is submissive to God and who trembles at God's Word.

"Know ye not that ye are the temple of God, and *that* the Spirit of God dwelleth in you?" (1 Co.3:16).

"What? know ye not that your body is the temple of the Holy Ghost *which is* in you, which ye have of God, and ye are not your own? For ye are bought with a price: therefore glorify God in your body, and in your spirit, which are God's" (1 Co.6:19-20).

"For this *is* the covenant that I will make with the house of Israel after those days, saith the Lord; I will put my laws into their mind, and write them in their hearts: and I will be to them a God, and they shall be to me a people" (He.8:10).

"But this *shall be* the covenant that I will make with the house of Israel; After those days, saith the LORD, I will put my law in their inward parts, and write it in their hearts; and will be their God, and they shall be my people" (Je.31:33).

"And I will make an everlasting covenant with them, that I will not turn away from them, to do them good; but I will put my fear in their hearts, that they shall not depart from me" (Je.32:40).

b. Some worshippers are rejected by God (vv.3-6). Who? Any person who goes through the motions of worship but is not submissive to the LORD. Those who live as they wish instead of obeying God's Word will be rejected by God. If a person ignores or disobeys God's commandments, his worship is unacceptable (v.3). No matter how often he enters a temple (church) or approaches God in personal daily worship, his worship is unacceptable to God (v.3). In fact, what God says is shocking and unsettling. The worship of a person who approaches the LORD with an impure, disobedient heart...

• is as unacceptable as the worship of a murderer
• is as unacceptable as the worship of a person who offers a dog or pig to God
• is as unacceptable as the worship of a person who idolizes false gods

These comparisons are graphic, but they emphasize strikingly the importance of true worship. A person must approach God with a humble, contrite spirit, *trembling at His Word*. Only the worshipper who is obedient, keeping God's commandments and living a righteous life is acceptable to God. The worship of a person who fails to be submissive to God, who fails to tremble at His Word is an abomination to God. It is utterly detestable.

Thus, a harsh judgment is pronounced against those whose worship is rejected or unacceptable (vv.4-5). Three reasons are given for the severity of the judgment:

⇒ They did not respond to God's call for repentance.
⇒ They deliberately engaged in false worship, committing evil before God's very eyes, even while God was calling upon them to repent.

312

⇒ They persecuted true worshippers, those who did tremble at God's Word (v.5). As a result of the false worshippers' terrible sin, the hand of God's judgment will fall upon them (vv.5-6). They will be utterly shamed, suffering God's vengeance. Suddenly and without warning an uproar will arise from the city of Jerusalem and from the temple itself. All the commotion and turmoil will come from the sound of the battle when God destroys His enemies, the false worshippers.

Note how this prophecy is applicable to every generation. It was certainly fulfilled in the fall of Jerusalem to the Babylonians (586 B.C.) and to the Romans (A.D.70). But it will also be fulfilled when the LORD returns at His second coming. In that day, all the false worshippers and wicked of this earth will suffer the hand of God's judgment.

"And to you who are troubled rest with us, when the Lord Jesus shall be revealed from heaven with his mighty angels, In flaming fire taking vengeance on them that know not God, and that obey not the gospel of our Lord Jesus Christ" (2 Th.1:7-8)

"Wherefore, behold, I send unto you prophets, and wise men, and scribes: and *some* of them ye shall kill and crucify; and *some* of them shall ye scourge in your synagogues, and persecute *them* from city to city: That upon you may come all the righteous blood shed upon the earth, from the blood of righteous Abel unto the blood of Zacharias son of Barachias, whom ye slew between the temple and the altar" (Mt.23:34-35).

"For the wrath of God is revealed from heaven against all ungodliness and unrighteousness of men, who hold the truth in unrighteousness; Because that which may be known of God is manifest in them; for God hath showed *it* unto them. For the invisible things of him from the creation of the world are clearly seen, being understood by the things that are made, *even* his eternal power and Godhead; so that they are without excuse: Because that, when they knew God, they glorified *him* not as God, neither were thankful; but became vain in their imaginations, and their foolish heart was darkened. Professing themselves to be wise, they became fools, And changed the glory of the uncorruptible God into an image made like to corruptible man, and to birds, and fourfooted beasts, and creeping things. Wherefore God also gave them up to uncleanness through the lusts of their own hearts, to dishonour their own bodies between themselves: Who changed the truth of God into a lie, and worshipped and served the creature more than the Creator, who is blessed for ever. Amen" (Ro.1:18-25).

"Know ye not that the unrighteous shall not inherit the kingdom of God? Be not deceived: neither fornicators, nor idolaters, nor adulterers, nor effeminate, nor abusers of themselves with mankind, Nor thieves, nor covetous, nor drunkards, nor revilers, nor extortioners, shall inherit the kingdom of God" (1 Co.6:9-10).

"But fornication, and all uncleanness, or covetousness, let it not be once named among you, as becometh saints; Neither filthiness, nor foolish talking, nor jesting, which are not convenient: but rather giving of thanks. For this ye know, that no whoremonger, nor unclean person, nor covetous man, who is an idolater, hath any inheritance in the kingdom of Christ and of God. Let no man deceive you with vain words: for because of these things cometh the wrath of God upon the children of disobedience" (Ep.5:3-6).

"For we know him that hath said, Vengeance *belongeth* unto me, I will recompense, saith the Lord. And again, The Lord shall judge his people" (He.10:30).

"Thou shalt have no other gods before me. Thou shalt not make unto thee any graven image, or any likeness *of any thing* that *is* in heaven above, or that *is* in the earth beneath, or that *is* in the water under the earth: Thou shalt not bow down thyself to them, nor serve them: for I the LORD thy God *am* a jealous God, visiting the iniquity of the fathers upon the children unto the third and fourth *generation* of them that hate me" (Ex.20:3-5).

"Behold, *it is* written before me: I will not keep silence, but will recompense, even recompense into their bosom, Your iniquities, and the iniquities of your fathers together, saith the LORD, which have burned incense upon the mountains, and blasphemed me upon the hills: therefore will I measure their former work into their bosom" (Is.65:6-7).

"For the day of the LORD *is* near upon all the heathen: as thou hast done, it shall be done unto thee: thy reward shall return upon thine own head" (Ob.15).

Thought 1. Matthew Henry gives an excellent discussion on the true temple of God (vv.1-2) that is well worth quoting in its entirety:

The temple is slighted in comparison with a gracious soul, v.1, 2. The Jews in the prophet's time, and afterwards in Christ's time, gloried much in the temple and promised themselves great things from it. To humble them therefore, and to shake their vain confidence, both the prophets and Christ foretold the ruin of the temple, that God would leave it and then it would soon be desolate. After it was destroyed by the [Babylonians] it soon recovered itself and the ceremonial services were revived with it. But by the Romans it was made a perpetual desolation, and the ceremonial law was abolished with it. That the world might be prepared for this, they were often told, as here, of what little account the temple was with God.

1. That he did not need it. Heaven is the throne of his glory and government; there he sits, infinitely exalted in the highest dignity and dominion, above all blessing and praise. The earth is his footstool, on which he stands, overruling all the affairs of it according to his will. If God has so bright a throne, so large a footstool, where then is the house they can build unto God, that can be the residence of his glory, or where is the place of his rest? What satisfaction can the Eternal Mind take in a house made with men's hands? What occasion has he, as we have, for a house to repose himself in, who faints not neither is weary, who neither slumbers nor sleeps? Or, if he had occasion, he would not tell us (Ps.1, 12), for all these things hath his hand made, heaven and all its courts, earth and all its borders, and all the hosts of both. All these things have been, have had their beginning, by the power of God, who was happy from eternity before they were, and therefore could not be benefited by them. All these things are (so some read it); they still continue, upheld by the same power that made them; so that our goodness extends not to him. If he required a house for himself to dwell in, he would have made one himself when he made the world; and, if he had made one, it would have continued to this day...[but] he had no need of a temple made with hands.

2. That he would not heed it as he would a humble, penitent, gracious heart. He has a heaven and earth of his own making, and a temple of man's making. But he overlooks them all, that he may look with favour to him that is poor in spirit, humble and serious, self-abasing and self-denying, whose heart is truly contrite for sin, penitent for it, and in pain to get it pardoned, and who trembles at God's word, not as Felix did, with a transient qualm that was over when the sermon was done, but with an habitual awe of God's majesty and purity and an habitual dread of his justice and wrath. Such a heart is a living temple for God; he dwells there, and it is the place of his rest; it is like heaven and earth, his throne and his footstool.[1]

---

2 (66:7-14) **Jerusalem, Restoration of—Jews, Restoration of—Israel, Restoration of—History, Last Days of, Events During—Restoration, of Israel**: in the last days of human history, both the city of Jerusalem and the Jews will be restored to their nation, Israel. The nation will be reborn quickly, suddenly—within a day—more quickly than a mother who gives birth even before her labor pains begin (vv.7-8). God Himself guarantees the rebirth (v.9). And because He is the source and the giver of life, He will not fail to deliver Israel. The nation and its capital will both be restored (49:18-21; 54:1-3).

In that day, all Jerusalem will be a cause for great rejoicing among God's people (vv.10-14). All who love the LORD—including the righteous believers down through the centuries who had mourned the city's sufferings and destruction—will rejoice over Jerusalem. Five reasons are given for the overwhelming joy of God's people:

1) People will rejoice because Jerusalem will nourish, comfort, and satisfy those who love her (v.11). When Christ returns, He will rule from Jerusalem. And all the world will receive what it needs from Him. Looking to Him who reigns in Jerusalem, believers will have every need in life met by Christ.

2) People will rejoice because God will overflow Jerusalem with peace and prosperity (v.12). This peace will allow all nations to become economically prosperous with Jerusalem as the capital of the world, the seat of government where Christ rules. Jerusalem will become the financial center of the world, the center into which the wealth of all nations will flow.

3) People will rejoice because Jerusalem's children will be provided and cared for (v.12b). Obviously the children of Jerusalem will be the true believers and worshippers who enter the Messiah's kingdom when He returns to earth. Naturally, the LORD will take care of all His people, all the citizens of His kingdom.

4) People will rejoice because Jerusalem will comfort her children (v.13). Comfort will flow from the heart of the LORD, reaching out to all His people. Although Christ will be ruling from Jerusalem, His Spirit will move throughout the world and comfort all His people.

5) People will rejoice over Jerusalem because the city itself will stir joy and bring vigorous heath to the population. The very lives of people—their mental and physical health—will flourish like grass, for the hand of the LORD will rest upon His people.

OUTLINE	SCRIPTURE	SCRIPTURE	OUTLINE
2. The restored Jerusalem: The restoration of the city & of the Jews, 54:1-17	7 Before she travailed, she brought forth; before her pain came, she was delivered of a man child.	satisfied with the breasts of her consolations; that ye may milk out, and be delighted with the abundance of her glory.	comfort, & satisfy those who love her
a. The city & nation will be reborn 1) Reborn quickly, suddenly—within a day: More quickly than a mother who gives birth before her labor pains begin	8 Who hath heard such a thing? who hath seen such things? Shall the earth be made to bring forth in one day? *or* shall a nation be born at once? for as soon as Zion travailed, she brought forth her children.	12 For thus saith the LORD, Behold, I will extend peace to her like a river, and the glory of the Gentiles like a flowing stream: then shall ye suck, ye shall be borne upon *her* sides, and be dandled upon *her* knees.	2) Because God will overflow Jerusalem with peace & prosperity: Make her the capital of the world 3) Because her children will be provided & cared for by her
2) Reborn by the guarantee of God—His Word & His promise: He Himself will restore Israel, 49:18-21; 54:1-3 b. The restored Jerusalem will be a cause for rejoicing	9 Shall I bring to the birth, and not cause to bring forth? saith the LORD: shall I cause to bring forth, and shut *the womb?* saith thy God. 10 Rejoice ye with Jerusalem, and be glad with her, all ye that love her: rejoice for joy with her, all ye that mourn for her:	13 As one whom his mother comforteth, so will I comfort you; and ye shall be comforted in Jerusalem. 14 And when ye see *this,* your heart shall rejoice, and your bones shall flourish like an herb: and the hand of the LORD shall be known toward	4) Because God will comfort her children just as a mother comforts her child 5) Because Jerusalem will stir joy & bring good health to God's people
1) Because she will nourish,	11 That ye may suck, and be	his servants, and *his* indignation toward his enemies.	

---

1 Matthew Henry. *Matthew Henry's Commentary*, Vol.4, pp.388-389.

Thought 1. Jerusalem and the Jews will be restored to their nation, permanently restored. When Christ returns to set up His kingdom on earth, He will set up His seat of government in Jerusalem. The Holy City will be reborn, restored as though it had been given a new birth. Old Jerusalem will become a brand new city, completely rebuilt. And all Jews who have truly trusted the LORD will be returned to their nation, becoming citizens of God's kingdom on earth. Listen to this wonderful promise of God given to all Jewish believers:

"And I will restore thy judges as at the first, and thy counsellors as at the beginning: afterward thou shalt be called, The city of righteousness, the faithful city" (Is.1:26).

"And he shall set up an ensign for the nations, and shall assemble the outcasts of Israel, and gather together the dispersed of Judah from the four corners of the earth" (Is.11:12).

"Thus saith the Lord GOD, Behold, I will lift up mine hand to the Gentiles, and set up my standard to the people: and they shall bring thy sons in *their* arms, and thy daughters shall be carried upon *their* shoulders" (Is.49:22).

"And the sons of strangers shall build up thy walls, and their kings shall minister unto thee: for in my wrath I smote thee, but in my favour have I had mercy on thee" (Is.60:10).

"For in mine holy mountain, in the mountain of the height of Israel, saith the Lord GOD, there shall all the house of Israel, all of them in the land, serve me: there will I accept them, and there will I require your offerings, and the firstfruits of your oblations, with all your holy things" (Eze.20:40).

"Cry yet, saying, Thus saith the LORD of hosts; My cities through prosperity shall yet be spread abroad; and the LORD shall yet comfort Zion, and shall yet choose Jerusalem" (Zec.1:17).

"And I will strengthen the house of Judah, and I will save the house of Joseph, and I will bring them again to place them; for I have mercy upon them: and they shall be as though I had not cast them off: for I *am* the LORD their God, and will hear them" (Zec.10:6).

"And *men* shall dwell in it, and there shall be no more utter destruction; but Jerusalem shall be safely inhabited" (Zec.14:11).

"Then shall the offering of Judah and Jerusalem be pleasant unto the LORD, as in the days of old, and as in former years" (Mal.3:4).

3 (66:15-18) **Day of the LORD, Prophecy Concerning—Judgment, Described As, Day of the LORD—Judgment, Against Whom, Twofold**: the last days of human history will bring forth the Day of the LORD, the hour of His terrifying judgment. The LORD is coming in a storm of blazing fire. His chariots, His army of angels, will accompany Him with the destructive force of a violent tornado. The LORD is coming to punish the wicked with the full force of His anger and the flaming fire of His rebuke (v.15). When He comes, it will be to execute judgment upon all the wicked of the earth. They will all be punished with fire and with the sword of His mouth (vv.16-18). Only the righteous will enter the Messiah's kingdom. When Jesus Christ returns to earth, two classes of people will face His wrath and His judgment:

1) All who have followed the abominable practices of idolatry and false worship will suffer the terrifying judgment of God (v.17). These will meet a terrible end, because they engaged in the detestable practices of sorcery and the occult world.

2) All who are guilty of evil works and thoughts will also suffer the terrifying judgment of God (v.18). These allowed their thoughts and imaginations to dwell on the immoral, the lawless, and the violent instead of focusing their minds on things that are true, honest, just, pure, lovely, good, virtuous, and praiseworthy (Ph.4:8). By allowing their thoughts to linger on the forbidden, they eventually began participating in immoral and wicked deeds.

When Christ returns to earth, the sinners of this world will appear before the LORD to give an account for their behavior. They will see His glory and suffer the hand of His judgment.

OUTLINE	SCRIPTURE	SCRIPTURE	OUTLINE

3. The Day of the LORD, His terrifying judgment
a. The LORD is coming in a storm of fire
  1) To punish with the fury of His anger
  2) To rebuke with flames of fire
b. The LORD is coming to execute judgment upon all people: Many will be slain
  1) All who followed the
	15 For, behold, the LORD will come with fire, and with his chariots like a whirlwind, to render his anger with fury, and his rebuke with flames of fire.
	16 For by fire and by his sword will the LORD plead with all flesh: and the slain of the LORD shall be many.
	17 They that sanctify them-
		selves, and purify themselves in the gardens behind one *tree* in the midst, eating swine's flesh, and the abomination, and the mouse, shall be consumed together, saith the LORD.
		18 For I *know* their works and their thoughts: it shall come, that I will gather all nations and tongues; and they shall come, and see my glory.
			abominable practices of idolatry & false worship: Will meet a terrible end
			
			2) All who were guilty of evil works & thoughts: Will appear before the LORD & witness His glory

"For the Son of man shall come in the glory of his Father with his angels; and then he shall reward every man according to his works" (Mt.16:27).

"When the Son of man shall come in his glory, and all the holy angels with him, then shall he sit upon the throne of his glory: And before him shall be gathered all nations: and he shall separate them one from another, as a shepherd divideth *his* sheep from the goats: And he shall set the sheep on his right hand, but the goats on the left....Then shall he say also unto them on the left hand, Depart from me, ye cursed, into everlasting fire, prepared for the devil and his angels" (Mt.25:31-33, 41).

"Because he hath appointed a day, in the which he will judge the world in righteousness by *that* man whom he hath ordained; *whereof* he hath given assurance unto all *men*, in that he hath raised him from the dead" (Ac.17:31).

"And to you who are troubled rest with us, when the Lord Jesus shall be revealed from heaven with his mighty angels, In flaming fire taking vengeance on them that know not God, and that obey not the gospel of our Lord Jesus Christ" (2 Th.1:7-8).

"I charge *thee* therefore before God, and the Lord Jesus Christ, who shall judge the quick and the dead at his appearing and his kingdom" (2 Ti.4:1).

"And Enoch also, the seventh from Adam, prophesied of these, saying, Behold, the Lord cometh with ten thousands of his saints, To execute judgment upon all, and to convince all that are ungodly among them of all their ungodly deeds which they have ungodly committed, and of all their hard *speeches* which ungodly sinners have spoken against him" (Jude 14-15).

"Behold, he cometh with clouds; and every eye shall see him, and they *also* which pierced him: and all kindreds of the earth shall wail because of him. Even so, Amen" (Re.1:7).

"And, behold, I come quickly; and my reward *is* with me, to give every man according as his work shall be" (Re.22:12).

"Before the LORD: for he cometh, for he cometh to judge the earth: he shall judge the world with righteousness, and the people with his truth" (Ps.96:13).

4 (66:19-21) **End Time, Witnessing During; Missionaries During—Witnessing, Prophecy Concerning, in End Time—Missionaries, Prophecy Concerning, in End Time—Gentiles, Prophecy Concerning, in End Times**: when Christ returns, there will be a great proclamation of God's glory throughout the world. Note the reference to God's revealing *a sign* for the whole world to witness. Most likely this is the blazing appearance of Christ in the clouds at His Second Coming (Mt.24:30). When Christ returns, all the earth will clearly see His coming and acknowledge Him to be the Son of Man. The blazing light of His holiness—the great splendor and brightness of His glory—will be easily manifested throughout the entire universe at that time (see outline and note—Mt.24:30 for more discussion).

Once Christ has returned, a number of Jews will become ministers to share the message of *God's glory* with the world (vv.19-20). Isaiah naturally mentions several major countries of the known world at that time, but note also his reference to "the distant islands," This term, *distant islands,* refers to the outer reaches of the world. In other words, these Jewish ministers will blanket the earth with the message of God's glory. Their purpose will be to bring the Gentile believers, their spiritual brothers, to worship in Jerusalem (v.20). Their missionary efforts will reap such a vast harvest of worshippers that every means of transportation available will have to be used. Isaiah mentioned the method of transportation in His day, but whatever forms of transportation will be in use when Christ returns will be used. The picture being painted is that people from all nations of the earth will make periodic journeys to worship the LORD in Jerusalem. Stationed throughout the world in various locations will be Jewish ministers or representatives giving strong witness to God's glory and to His wonderful works performed in behalf of Israel. In addition to these representatives, there will be Gentile believers appointed as His ministers (v.21). Thus the LORD will have both Jewish and Gentile ministers scattered all over the world during the Messiah's kingdom on earth. Apparently their task will be to lead the people in worshipping the LORD and in giving strong testimony to His wonderful works in their lives.

Whatever the case, it appears that life during the Messiah's kingdom will be just what the term *eternal life* suggests. That is, eternal life will be life involving all the good activities of this present world, with two exceptions: life in the Messiah's kingdom will be both perfect and eternal. As people carry out their daily activities, they will be in constant communion with the LORD. And when they meet for joint worship with others, the LORD will have appointed ministers to lead them in worship, praising His glory and the wonderful works He has done in their behalf.

OUTLINE	SCRIPTURE	SCRIPTURE	OUTLINE
4. The proclamation of God's glory worldwide a. The LORD will set a sign before the world: Most likely the appearance of Christ at His Second Coming, Mt.24:30 b. The LORD will choose some Jews as ministers to share the message of God's glory with the world: Will become a great evangelistic force to reach the world 1) They will bring the Gen-	19 And I will set a sign among them, and I will send those that escape of them unto the nations, to Tarshish, Pul, and Lud, that draw the bow, *to* Tubal, and Javan, *to* the isles afar off, that have not heard my fame, neither have seen my glory; and they shall declare my glory among the Gentiles. 20 And they shall bring all	your brethren *for* an offering unto the LORD out of all nations upon horses, and in chariots, and in litters, and upon mules, and upon swift beasts, to my holy mountain Jerusalem, saith the LORD, as the children of Israel bring an offering in a clean vessel into the house of the LORD. 21 And I will also take of them for priests *and* for Levites, saith the LORD.	tiles—their spiritual brothers—to worship in Jerusalem 2) They will reap such a vast harvest of worshippers that every means of transportation available will have to be used c. The LORD will choose some Gentile believers to be His ministers

"Now the God of patience and consolation grant you to be likeminded one toward another according to Christ Jesus: That ye may with one mind *and* one mouth glorify God, even the Father of our Lord Jesus Christ" (Ro.15:5-6).

"What? know ye not that your body is the temple of the Holy Ghost *which is* in you, which ye have of God, and ye are not your own? For ye are bought with a price: therefore glorify God in your body, and in your spirit, which are God's" (1 Co.6:19-20).

"Giving thanks unto the Father, which hath made us meet to be partakers of the inheritance of the saints in light" (Col.1:12).

"By him [Christ] therefore let us offer the sacrifice of praise to God continually, that is, the fruit of *our* lips giving thanks to his name" (He.13:15).

"But ye *are* a chosen generation, a royal priesthood, an holy nation, a peculiar people; that ye should show forth the praises of him who hath called you out of darkness into his marvellous light" (1 Pe.2:9).

"Sing praises to the LORD, which dwelleth in Zion: declare among the people his doings" (Ps.9:11).

"Praise the LORD with harp: sing unto him with the psaltery *and* an instrument of ten strings" (Ps.33:2).

"Let the people praise thee, O God; let all the people praise thee" (Ps.67:3).

"Enter into his gates with thanksgiving, *and* into his courts with praise: be thankful unto him, *and* bless his name" (Ps.100:4).

"And let them sacrifice the sacrifices of thanksgiving, and declare his works with rejoicing" (Ps.107:22).

"Let them give glory unto the LORD, and declare his praise in the islands" (Is.42:12).

---

5 (66:22-23) **Eternal Life, Prophecy Concerning; Promised—Heavens and Earth, New, Prophecy Concerning, Guaranteed—Life, Eternal, Prophecy Concerning—Prophecy, Concerning Life Eternal; Concerning New Heavens and Earth—Worship, in Eternity, Predicted—Prophecies, Concerning Worship, in Eternity**: the last days of human history will usher in the wonderful gift of eternal life. At this point, the LORD's true followers will be the only members of the human race left. In this climactic end of history, God will create a new heavens and earth. And the new heavens and earth will be permanent, will never pass away. Neither will those who have truly trusted Christ and obeyed His commandments, living righteously. They will inherit eternal life and always be God's people. Their names and their descendants who have also trusted Christ will never disappear from God's presence. All the descendants of Abraham—all who have truly followed in his footsteps of faith—will live eternally before the LORD. They will live forever. From one New Moon to another and from one Sabbath to another, they will all worship the LORD on a regular basis. Worshipping Him both "in spirit and in truth" (Jn.4:24), they will bow before the LORD in praise and thanksgiving for all He has done for them.

OUTLINE	SCRIPTURE	SCRIPTURE	OUTLINE
5. The gift of eternal life in the new heavens & earth a. God's people will have names & descendants that endure eternally	22 For as the new heavens and the new earth, which I will make, shall remain before me, saith the LORD, so shall your seed and your name remain.	23 And it shall come to pass, *that* from one new moon to another, and from one sabbath to another, shall all flesh come to worship before me, saith the LORD.	b. God's people—the only humans alive at the end—will bow & worship the LORD: Regularly, month to month & Sabbath to Sabbath

"Then Peter said, Lo, we have left all, and followed thee. And he said unto them, Verily I say unto you, There is no man that hath left house, or parents, or brethren, or wife, or children, for the kingdom of God's sake, Who shall not receive manifold more in this present time, and in the world to come life everlasting" (Lu.18:28-30).

"And as Moses lifted up the serpent in the wilderness, even so must the Son of man be lifted up: That whosoever believeth in him should not perish, but have eternal life. For God so loved the world, that he gave his only begotten Son, that whosoever believeth in him should not perish, but have everlasting life" (Jn.3:14-16).

"He that believeth on the Son hath everlasting life: and he that believeth not the Son shall not see life; but the wrath of God abideth on him" (Jn.3:36).

"Say not ye, There are yet four months, and *then* cometh harvest? behold, I say unto you, Lift up your eyes, and look on the fields; for they are white already to harvest. And he that reapeth receiveth wages, and gathereth fruit unto life eternal: that both he that soweth and he that reapeth may rejoice together" (Jn.4:35-36).

"And I give unto them eternal life; and they shall never perish, neither shall any *man* pluck them out of my hand" (Jn.10:28).

"He that loveth his life shall lose it; and he that hateth his life in this world shall keep it unto life eternal" (Jn.12:25).

"And this is life eternal, that they might know thee the only true God, and Jesus Christ, whom thou hast sent" (Jn.17:3).

"To them who by patient continuance in well doing seek for glory and honour and immortality, eternal life" (Ro.2:7).

"But now being made free from sin, and become servants to God, ye have your fruit unto holiness, and the end everlasting life" (Ro.6:22).

"For he that soweth to his flesh shall of the flesh reap corruption; but he that soweth to the Spirit shall of the Spirit reap life everlasting" (Ga.6:8).

"Laying up in store for themselves a good foundation against the time to come, that they may lay hold on eternal life" (1 Ti.6:19).

"In hope of eternal life, which God, that cannot lie, promised before the world began" (Tit.1:2).

"And this is the promise that he hath promised us, *even* eternal life" (1 Jn.2:25).

"Keep yourselves in the love of God, looking for the mercy of our Lord Jesus Christ unto eternal life" (Jude 21).

"And many of them that sleep in the dust of the earth shall awake, some to everlasting life, and some to shame *and* everlasting contempt" (Da.12:2).

6 (66:24) **Unbelievers, Fate of—Unrepentant, Fate of—Wicked, Fate of—Sinners, Fate of—Lost, Fate of—Rebellious, Fate of—Transgressors, Fate of—Destiny, of Unbelievers—Punishment, of Unbelievers—Judgment, of Unbelievers—Hell, Inhabitants of—Fate, of Unbelievers**: in the last days of human history, the unrepentant will face a tragic and horribly fate. They will suffer *eternal death* and torment. Remember, *death* means to be separated. It does not mean to cease to exist. Physical death simply means that the soul is separated from the human body. Eternal death means that the soul is *eternally separated* from God's presence. Thus the sinners of the earth who fail to repent are doomed to be *eternally separated* from God. Note that they will suffer throughout all eternity: the worms that devour their dead bodies will never die, which suggests that their souls will suffer eternally. And the fire that burns them will never be quenched. What a frightening, graphic picture of hell! The unrepentant will leave behind a disgusting, repulsive legacy. The picture being painted here is that of the Valley of Hinnom that was located on the outskirts of Jerusalem. It was the garbage dump for the city, where the bodies of diseased or unclean corpses were sometimes burned. Christ used this picture to describe the sufferings of hell (Mk.9:43-48. Also see DEEPER STUDY #2—Mt.5:22; #3—Lu.16:23; #4—Lu.16:24 for more discussion.)

OUTLINE	SCRIPTURE	SCRIPTURE	OUTLINE
6. The sad fate of the unrepentant a. They will be dead (separated from God) & punished	24 And they shall go forth, and look upon the carcases of the men that have transgressed against me: for their	worm shall not die, neither shall their fire be quenched; and they shall be an abhorring unto all flesh.	eternally in an unquenchable fire b. They will have a disgusting, repulsive legacy

Thought 1. Eternal death means that the soul is *separated eternally* from God.

"But of the tree of the knowledge of good and evil, thou shalt not eat of it: for in the day that thou eatest thereof thou shalt surely die" (Ge.2:17).

"The soul that sinneth, it shall die. The son shall not bear the iniquity of the father, neither shall the father bear the iniquity of the son: the righteousness of the righteous shall be upon him, and the wickedness of the wicked shall be upon him" (Eze.18:20).

"For the wages of sin *is* death; but the gift of God *is* eternal life through Jesus Christ our Lord" (Ro.6:23).

"For to be carnally minded *is* death; but to be spiritually minded *is* life and peace" (Ro.8:6).

"But every man is tempted, when he is drawn away of his own lust, and enticed. Then when lust hath conceived, it bringeth forth sin: and sin, when it is finished, bringeth forth death" (Js.1:14-15).

"Let him know, that he which converteth the sinner from the error of his way shall save a soul from death, and shall hide a multitude of sins" (Js.5:20).

"But the fearful, and unbelieving, and the abominable, and murderers, and whoremongers, and sorcerers, and idolaters, and all liars, shall have their part in the lake which burneth with fire and brimstone: which is the second death" (Re.21:8).

Thought 2. The person who turns to the LORD, obeying His commandments and living a righteous life, will not face eternal death. But the unrepentant who refuses to turn away from his sins will suffer the just punishment for his or her evil behavior.

"And these shall go away into everlasting punishment: but the righteous into life eternal" (Mt.25:46).

"And to you who are troubled rest with us, when the Lord Jesus shall be revealed from heaven with his mighty angels, In flaming fire taking vengeance on them that know not God, and that obey not the gospel of our Lord Jesus Christ: Who shall be punished with everlasting destruction from the presence of the Lord, and from the glory of his power" (2 Th.1:7-9).

"The Lord knoweth how to deliver the godly out of temptations, and to reserve the unjust unto the day of judgment to be punished" (2 Pe.2:9).

Thought 3. The ungodly and unrighteous of this earth will spend eternity in a place Jesus Christ called hell.

"But I say unto you, That whosoever is angry with his brother without a cause shall be in danger of the judgment: and whosoever shall say to his brother, Raca, shall be in danger of the council: but whosoever shall say, Thou fool, shall be in danger of hell fire" (Mt.5:22).

"But I say unto you, That whosoever looketh on a woman to lust after her hath committed adultery with her already in his heart. And if thy right eye offend thee, pluck it out, and cast *it* from thee: for it is profitable for thee that one of thy members should perish, and not *that* thy whole body should be cast into hell" (Mt.5:28-29).

"And fear not them which kill the body, but are not able to kill the soul: but rather fear him which is able to destroy both soul and body in hell" (Mt.10:28).

"Wherefore if thy hand or thy foot offend thee, cut them off, and cast *them* from thee: it is better for thee to enter into life halt or maimed, rather than having two hands or two feet to be cast into everlasting fire. And if thine eye offend thee, pluck it out, and cast *it* from thee: it is better for thee to enter into life with one eye, rather than having two eyes to be cast into hell fire" (Mt.18:8-9).

"*Ye* serpents, *ye* generation of vipers, how can ye escape the damnation of hell?" (Mt.23:33).

"But I will forewarn you whom ye shall fear: Fear him, which after he hath killed hath power to cast into hell; yea, I say unto you, Fear him" (Lu.12:5).

Thought 4. Many other Scriptures teach that the ungodly and unrighteous will be doomed to hell.

"The Son of man shall send forth his angels, and they shall gather out of his kingdom all things that offend, and them which do iniquity; And shall cast them into a furnace of fire: there shall be wailing and gnashing of teeth" (Mt.13:41-42).

"And it came to pass, that the beggar died, and was carried by the angels into Abraham's bosom: the rich man also died, and was buried; And in hell he lift up his eyes, being in torments, and seeth Abraham afar off, and Lazarus in his bosom. And he cried and said, Father Abraham, have mercy on me, and send Lazarus, that he may dip the tip of his finger in water, and cool my tongue; for I am tormented in this flame" (Lu.16:22-24).

"For if God spared not the angels that sinned, but cast *them* down to hell, and delivered *them* into chains of darkness, to be reserved unto judgment; And spared not the old world, but saved Noah the eighth *person*, a preacher of righteousness, bringing in the flood upon the world of the ungodly....The Lord knoweth how to deliver the godly out of temptations, and to reserve the unjust unto the day of judgment to be punished" (2 Pe.2:4-5, 9).

"But the heavens and the earth, which are now, by the same word are kept in store, reserved unto fire against the day of judgment and perdition of ungodly men" (2 Pe.3:7).

"And the smoke of their torment ascendeth up for ever and ever: and they have no rest day nor night, who worship the beast and his image, and whosoever receiveth the mark of his name" (Re.14:11).

"And whosoever was not found written in the book of life was cast into the lake of fire" (Re.20:15).

"But the fearful, and unbelieving, and the abominable, and murderers, and whoremongers, and sorcerers, and idolaters, and all liars, shall have their part in the lake which burneth with fire and brimstone: which is the second death" (Re.21:8).

Thought 5. Several commentators close the great book of *Isaiah* with statements that are well worth quoting:
(1) *The Bible Knowledge Commentary* says this:

> This awesome way in which the majestic book of Isaiah concludes points to the need for unrepentant people to turn to the LORD, the only God, the Holy One of Israel.[2]

(2) In closing his comments on vv.22-24, H.C. Leupold says this:

> Peace eternal and death eternal! On this note the book of Isaiah comes to a close.[3]

(3) In his commentary *The Book of Isaiah*, John N. Oswalt says this:

> Thus Isaiah's great book comes to its end in ways not unlike those in which it began, with a reaffirmation of the great choice that lies before the human race: judgment or hope. But there is one great difference. The hope that the final chapters affirm is on the other side of judgment. Indeed, what they tell us is that since the Holy One of Israel is the Creator and the only God, even judgment can be turned to hope if we will let Him do it for us. No tragedy, no disaster, no fate that has befallen us because of our stubborn self-worship need be the final word for us while we yet breathe. This is the great good news of Isa. 52:13–53:12: God has entered into our judgment and taken it on Himself, and because of that he can declare that finally nothing can keep us from his love—except our own determination to persist in rebellion. This cosmos will be remade, and to all eternity it will ring with the praises of those who, though "walking in darkness have seen a great light" (9:1 [Eng2]), of those who live in that holy mountain where none will hurt or destroy (11:9; 65:25), of those from whom the shroud has been torn away forever (25:7).[4]

(4) In *The Preacher's Commentary on Isaiah*, David McKenna says this:

> Once Isaiah saw God's vision for the future, he never looked back. The progression of his prophecy from the current events of his lifetime, to the new exodus from Babylonian exile, followed by the coming of

2   John F. Walvoord and Roy B. Zuck, Editors. *The Bible Knowledge Commentary, Old Testament*, p.1121.
3   H.C. Leupold. *Exposition of Isaiah*, Vol.2, p.379.
4   John N.Oswalt. *The Book of Isaiah*, Chapters 40–66. "The New International Commentary on the Old Testament." (Grand Rapids, MI: Eerdmans Publishing Co., 1998), p.693.

the Messiah and the redemption of all nations gives us our marching orders. *Sounding again the double imperative for Israel and the redeemed of all generations to come, Isaiah urges us to leave the comfort and the splendor of our Jerusalems to become His servants in the world.*

> *Depart! Depart! Go out from there,*
> *Touch no unclean thing;*
> *Go out from the midst of her,*
> *Be clean,*
> *You who bear the vessels of the LORD.*

> *For you shall not go out with haste,*
> *Nor go by flight;*
> *For the LORD will go before you*
> *And the God of Israel will be your rear guard. (Is.52:11-12).* [5]

(5) The excellent commentator Matthew Henry says this:

> *Let the redeemed of the LORD with all humility, and not without a holy trembling, sing their triumphant songs.* [6]

---

5 David McKenna. *Isaiah 40–66. The Preacher's Commentary on Isaiah.* (Nashville, TN: Word Publishing, 1994, 2003), pp.665-666.
6 Matthew Henry. *Matthew Henry's Commentary*, Vol.4, p.397.

RESOURCES

ISAIAH

---

* A detailed listing of all the Prophets, their messages, and practical application can be found in the Resource Section of Isaiah Vol.1 and also as a separate supplement to *The Preacher's Sermon and Outline Bible*® entitled Old Testament Prophets, now available for a minimal cost.

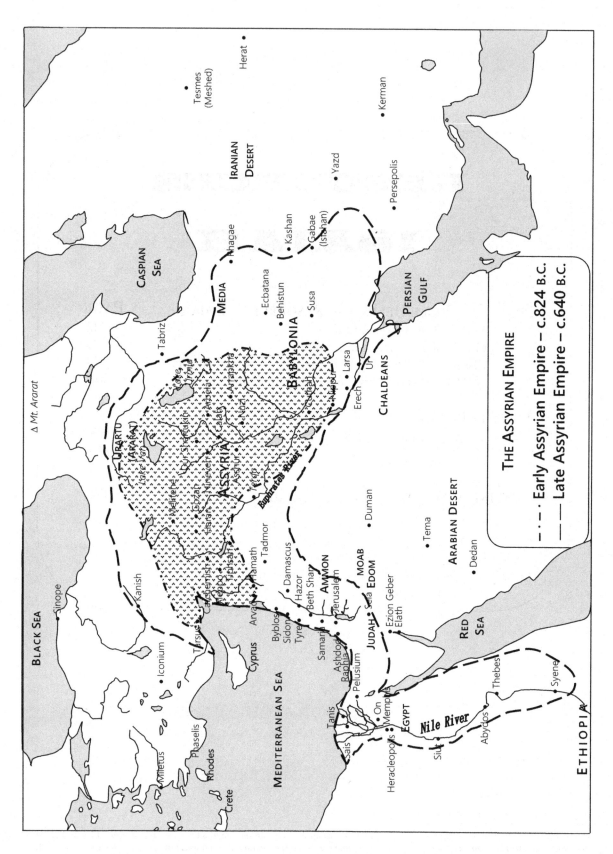

THE ASSYRIAN EMPIRE

- - - Early Assyrian Empire – c.824 B.C.
—— Late Assyrian Empire – c.640 B.C.

THE BABYLONIAN–MEDIAN EMPIRE

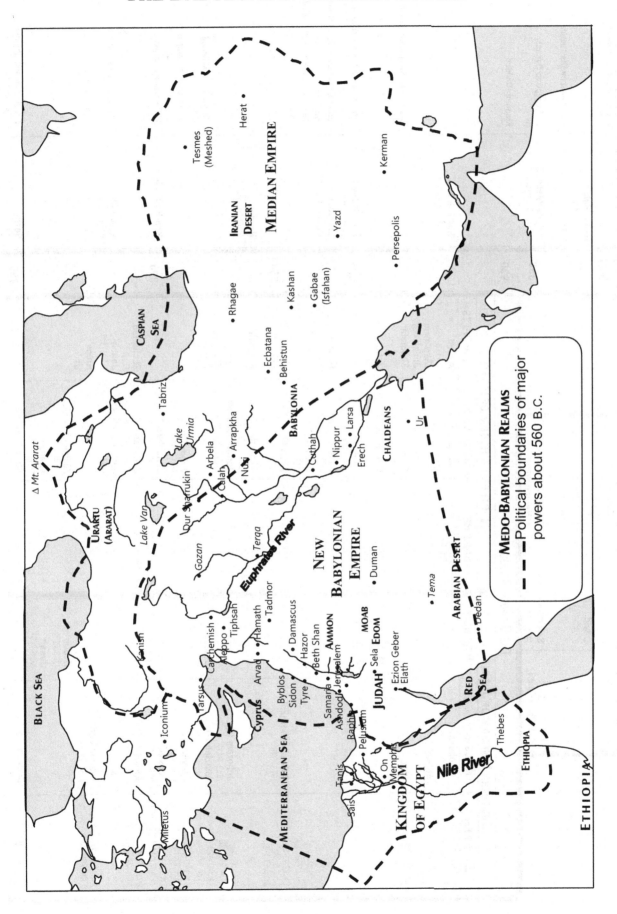

THE BABYLONIAN–MEDIAN EMPIRE

MEDIAN EMPIRE

Herat

Tesmes (Meshed)

Kerman

IRANIAN DESERT

Yazd

Persepolis

CASPIAN SEA

Rhagae

Kashan

Gabae (Isfahan)

Ecbatana

Behistun

Tabriz

Lake Irmia

BABYLONIA

Arrapkha

Larsa

Dur Sharrukin

Arbela

Nippur

CHALDEANS

Ur

Calah

Nuzi

Cuthah

Mt. Ararat

Erech

Lake Van

URARTU (ARARAT)

Gozan

Terqa

Euphrates River

NEW BABYLONIAN EMPIRE

Duman

Tema

ARABIAN DESERT

Dedan

Kanish

Carchemish

Tadmor

Aleppo

Tiphsah

Hamath

Damascus

Hazor

Beth Shan

AMMON

MOAB

Sela EDOM

BLACK SEA

Iconium

Tarsus

Cyprus

Arvad

Byblos

Sidon

Tyre

Samaria

Ashdod

Jerusalem

Raphia

JUDAH

Ezion Geber

Elath

RED SEA

MEDITERRANEAN SEA

Miletus

Pelusium

Tanis

On

Memphis

Sais

Thebes

ETHIOPIA

KINGDOM OF EGYPT

Nile River

ETHIOPIA

MEDO-BABYLONIAN REALMS
Political boundaries of major powers about 560 B.C.

323

TIMELINE OF KINGS, PROPHETS AND HISTORY*

THE UNITED KINGDOM

BIBLE REF.	KINGS (YEARS REIGNED)	PROPHETS
1 S.16:1-1 K.2:11; 1 Chr.11:1-30	David (40) (1011-971)	Samuel (1095-1015)
		Gad (1015-950)
		Asaph (1004)
1 K.2:12-11:43; 1 Chr.28:1-2 Chr.9:31	Solomon (40) (971-931)	Nathan (1003-931)
		Heman (971)

THE DIVIDED KINGDOM

SOUTHERN KINGDOM OF JUDAH

BIBLE REF.	KINGS (YEARS REIGNED)	PROPHETS
1 K.12:1-24; 14:21-31; 2 Chr.10:1-12:16	Rehoboam (17) (931-913)	
1 K.15:1-8; 2 Chr.12:16-14:1	Abijah (3) (913-911)	
1 K.15:9-24; 2 Chr.14:1-16:14	Asa (3) (911-870)	Iddo (910), Azariah (896)
1 K.22:41-50; 2 K.3:6-14; 2 Chr.17:1-21:1	Jehoshaphat (25) (873-848)	
2 K.8:16-24; 2 Chr.21:1-20	Jehoram (8) (853-841)	Obadiah (845)
2 K.8:25-29; 9:27-29; 2 Chr.22:1-10	Ahaziah (2) (841)	
2 K.11:1-16; 2 Chr.22:10-23:21	Athaliah (7) (841-835)	Joel (830)
2 K.11:17-12:21; 2 Chr.22:11-12; 24:1-27	Joash/Jehoash (40) (835-796)	
2 K.14:1-20; 2 Chr.24:27-25:28	Amaziah (29) (796-767)	
2 K.14:21-22; 15:1-7; 2 Chr.26:1-23	Azariah/Uzziah (52) (792-740)	Hosea (788-723), Jonah (780-765)
2 K.15:32-38; 2 Chr.26:23-27:9	Jotham (16) (750-731)	

NORTHERN KINGDOM OF ISRAEL

PROPHETS	KINGS (YEARS REIGNED)	BIBLE REF.
Ahijah (931-910), Man from Judah (930), Shemaiah (927)	Jeroboam I (22) (931-910)	1 K.12:1-24; 12:25-14:20; 2 Chr.10:1-16
	Nadab (2) (910-909)	1 K.15:25-31
Jehu (886)	Baasha (24) (909-886)	1 K.15:16-16:7; 2 Chr.16:1-6
	Elah (2) (886-885)	1 K.16:6-14
Hanani (870)	Zimri (7 days) (885)	1 K.16:9-20
	Omri (12) (885-874)	1 K.16:21-28
Elijah (860-845)	Ahab (22) (874-853)	1 K.16:28-22:40; 2 Chr.18:1-34
Micaiah (853)	Ahaziah (2) (853-852)	1 K.1:17; 3:1-8:15
Elisha (850-795), Eliezer (849-48)	Joram/Jehoram (12) (852-841)	1 K.22:49-51; 2 K.1:1-18; 2 Chr.20:35-37; 22:1-11
	Jehu (28) (841-814)	2 K.9:1-10:36; 2 Chr.22:7-9
	Jehoahaz (17) (814-798)	2 K.13:1-9
Zechariah (797)	Jehoash (16) (798-782)	2 K.13:9-25; 14:8-16
Jonah (780-765)	Jeroboam II (41) (793-753)	2 K.14:23-29
Amos (750)	Zechariah (6 mos) (753)	2 K.15:8-12
	Shallum (1 mo) (752)	2 K.15:13-15
	Menahem (10) (752-742)	2 K.15:16-22

DATE / FOREIGN KINGS / HISTORY

DATE BC	FOREIGN KINGS	WORLD EVENTS
1000	Ashur-Rabi II (1010-970) (Assyria), Hiram (1003-966) (Tyre)	David captures Jerusalem (1004); Foundation for the Temple (966)
950	Tiglath-Pileser II (960-935) (Assyria)	22nd Egyptian Dynasty (945)
930	Shishak I (945-924) (Egypt)	Kingdom Divided (930); Assyria makes peace with Babylon (915)
900	Ben-Hadad I (900) (Syria), Eth-Baal (887-856) (Sidon)	Jehoshaphat leads a revival (865); Elijah's contest with prophets of Baal (857); Elijah's mantle passed to Elisha (845)
850	Hazael (840) (Syria)	
800	Ben-Hadad II (798) (Syria), Ben-Hadad III (773) (Syria)	Carthage established (814); Joash repairs Temple (812); 23rd Egyptian dynasty (800); Olympic games begin (776); Rome founded (753)
750	Rezin (750) (Syria)	Babylonian and Chinese calendar (750)

The Divided Kingdom

Southern Kingdom of Judah			Northern Kingdom of Israel			Date BC	Foreign Kings	History / World Events
Bible Ref.	Kings (Years Reigned)	Prophets	Bible Ref.	Kings (Years Reigned)	Prophets			
			2 K.15:23–26	Pekahiah (2) (742–740)			Tiglath-Pil[n]eser III [or Pul] (745–727) *(Assyria)*	Assyria takes control of Northern Kingdom (745–627)
2 K.15:38–16:20; 2 Chr.27:9–27; Is.7:1–9:1	Ahaz (16) (735–715)	Isaiah (740–690)	2 K.15:27–31	Pekah (20) (752–732) (ruled only in Gilead) (752–740) (740–732) (ruled in Samaria)			Shalmaneser V (727–722) *(Assyria)*	Assyria invades Northern Israel (732)
		Micah (735–725) Oded (733)	2 K.17:1–23	Hoshea (9) 732–722			So (727–716) *(Egypt)* Sargon II (710–705) *(Assyria)*	Fall of Northern Kingdom (722)
2 K.18:1–20:21; 2 Chr.28:27–32:33; Pr.25:1; Is.36:1–39:8	Hezekiah (29) (729–686)					700	Sennacherib (705–681) *(Assyria)* Merodach-Baladan (721–710, 705–704) *(Assyria)*	Sennacherib defeats Egypt (701) Hezekiah's tunnel (701)
							Tirhakah (690–664) *(Egypt)*	185,000 Assyrians killed by God (701)
2 K.20:21–21:18; 2 Chr.32:33–33:20	Manasseh (55) (696–642)	Nahum (663–612)				650	Esarhaddon (681–669) *(Assyria)*	Sennacherib destroys Babylon (689)
2 K.21:18–26; 2 Chr.33:20–25	Amon (2) (642–640)						Nabopolassar (626–605) *(Assyria)*	Josiah's reform (621) Nineveh destroyed (612)
2 K.21:26–23:30; 2 Chr.33:25–35:27	Josiah (31) (640–609)	Zephaniah (640–609)					Neco (610–595) *(Egypt)*	Battle of Carchemish (605) 1st group of exiles from Judah taken to Babylon (605)
2 K.23:31–33; 2 Chr.36:1–4	Jehoaz/Jehoahaz (3 mos) (609)	Jeremiah (627–562)				600	Nebuchadnezzar II (605–562) *(Babylon)*	
2 K.23:34–24:7; 2 Chr.36:5–8	Jehoiakim (11) (608–598)	Habakkuk (615–598)						
2 K.24:8–17; 25:27–30; 2 Chr.36:8–10;	Jehoiachin (3 mos) (598–597)	Daniel (605–535)						2nd group of exiles from Judah taken to Babylon (597)
2 K.24:18–25:21; 2 Chr.36:10–14; Je.21:1–52:11	Zedekiah/Mattaniah (11) (597–586)	Ezekiel (593–571)						Fall of Judah—Third group of exiles from Judah taken to Babylon (586)
2 K.25:22–26; Je.40:5–41:18	Gedaliah (2 mos) (Appointed by Nebuchadnezzar) (586)					550	Evil-Merodach (562–560) *(Babylon)*	Fall of Babylon to Medo-Persian Empire (539)
							Cyrus II (559–530) *(Medo-Persia)* Belshazzar (552–539) *(Babylon)*	Cyrus II decrees that the Jews may return to the Holy Land (538) 1st exiles return to Holy Land with Zerubbabel (537)
		Haggai (520) Zechariah (520–518)				500	Darius I (521–486) *(Medo-Persia)*	1st Temple foundation laid (536) 2nd Temple foundation laid (520) Temple completed (516) Republic of Rome est. (509)
								2nd return under Ezra (458)
		Malachi (430)				450	Artaxerxes (465–425) *(Persia)*	3rd return under Nehemiah (445)

*Some dates are approximate.

Besides the Bible, the resources used for the Timeline are as follows:

[1] Archer, Gleason L. *Encyclopedia of Bible Difficulties.* (Grand Rapids, Michigan: Zondervan Publishing House), 1982.

[2] Freedman, David Noel, ed., et. al. *The Anchor Bible Dictionary.* (New York: Doubleday), 1992.

[3] Grun, Bernard. *The Timetables of History.* 3rd ed. (New York: Simon & Schuster), 1991.

[4] Kaiser, Walter C. *A History of Israel.* (Nashville, Tennessee: Broadman & Holman Publishers), 1998.

[5] Silverman, David P., ed. *Ancient Egypt.* (New York: Oxford University Press), 1997.

SACRED DAYS IN THE HEBREW CALENDAR
AND THEIR PROPHETIC SYMBOLISM

NAME OF FEAST OR EVENT	OLD TESTAMENT PURPOSE	NEW TESTAMENT SYMBOLISM	CALENDAR TIME	FARM SEASON (Crops/Weather)
The Festival of Passover	To remember God's judgment and deliverance from Egyptian bondage. (Le.23:6; Nu.9:5; Jos. 5:10; 2 K.23:22; 2 Chr.35:1)	A symbol of Christ our Passover who was sacrificed to deliver us from the judgment of God. (Mt.26:17; Lu.2:41; Lu.22:15; He.11:28)	*Hebrew Time*: The 1st Month [Abib or Nisan], 14th Day *Secular Equivalent*: March - April	Harvesting barley and flax; Later Spring rains***
The Festival of Unleavened Bread	To recall the need and urgency to leave Egypt (a symbol of the world). (Ex.12:17-18; Ex.13:6-7; Ex.23:15; Ex.34:18; Le.23:6; Nu.28:17; De.16:3; De.16:16; 2 Chr.8:13; 2 Chr.30:13)	A symbol of the urgency for God's people to escape the enslavement of the world and immediately begin their march to the promised land of heaven (Mt.26:17; Mk.14:1)	*Hebrew Time*: The 1st Month [Abib or Nisan], 15th thru the 21st Day *Secular Equivalent*: March - April	Harvesting barley and flax; Later Spring rains
The Festival of Firstfruits	To thank God for the crops, the first harvest of the season that sustained life. (Ex.34:22; Le. 23:10; Nu.28:26)	A symbol of Christ's resurrection and of the believers hope: Christ is the first of the harvest, the first to arise from the dead. (Ro.8:23; 1 Co.15:23)	*Hebrew Time*: The 1st Month [Abib or Nisan], 16th Day *Secular Equivalent*: March - April	Harvesting barley and flax; Later Spring rains
The Festival of Pentecost or Harvest or Weeks	To give thanks for the harvest and to dedicate one's life anew to God. This festival took place fifty days after the Festival of Firstfruits. (Ex.23:16; Ex.34:22; Le.23:16; Nu.28:26; De.16:10)	A symbol of Pentecost... • of the great harvest of souls • of people giving their lives to God • of the coming of the Holy Spirit and the birth of the church (Ac.2:1-47; Ac.20:16; 1 Co. 16:8)	*Hebrew Time*: The 3th Month [Sivan], the 6th Day *Secular Equivalent*: May - June	Wheat harvest; other crops—grapes and almonds begin to open
The Festival of Trumpets	To focus upon God, learning to trust God more and more and to proclaim the message of joy over the atonement or reconciliation with God. (Le.23:24; Nu.29:1; Neh.8:2)	A symbol of salvation and of the rapture, the glorious day when Christ will return and take believers—both the living and the dead—to be with Him forever.	*Hebrew Time*: 7th Month, [Ethanim or Tishri **], the 1st Day *Secular Equivalent* September - October	Plowing of the fields: Early autumn rains
The Day of Atonement	To focus upon the only way to approach God and be forgiven—through the shed blood of the atoning sacrifice. Celebrated yearly, it was a national day of repentance. (Ex.30:10; Le.16:30; Le.23:27; Nu.29:7)	A symbol of being reconciled with God through the atonement, through the substitute sacrifice of Christ. (He.9:7)	*Hebrew Time*: 7th Month, [Ethanim or Tishri **], the 10th Day *Secular Equivalent*: September - October	Plowing of the fields: Early autumn rains
The Feast of Tabernacles or Booths	To celebrate the wilderness wanderings when the people lived in tents on their way to the promised land and to thank God for the harvest. (Le.23:34, 39; Nu.29:12; De.16:13; 2 Chr.8:13; Ezr.3:4; Neh.8:14; Zec.14:16)	A symbol of the believer's march through this world to heaven, a symbol of how temporary our world is as believers march to heaven (Jn.7:2)	*Hebrew Time*: 7th Month, [Ethanim or Tishri **], the 15th through the 21st Day *Secular Equivalent*: September - October	Plowing of the fields: Early autumn rains
The Feast of Purim	To remember God's deliverance from Israel's enemies during the time of Esther. Purim was a time of sharing with one's neighbor and with the poor. (Est.9:18-32)	Not mentioned in the New Testament	*Hebrew Time*: The 12th Month [Adar *], the 14th & 15th Day *Secular Equivalent*: February - March	Blooming of almond trees; Harvesting of citrus fruit; the later rains begin.

*   Note: An additional month (Second Adar or Adar Sheni or Veadar) was added to the Hebrew calendar about every three years. This was how the lunar calendar corresponded to the solar year.

**   Hebrew names of the month that are not in the Bible are marked with two stars (**). These are known as "Post-exilic" names, from the period of history known as "The Babylonian Exile."

*** The idea for listing the Farm Seasons was stirred by the *NIV Study Bible*, Grand Rapids, MI: Zondervan Bible Publishers, 1985, pp.102-103.

OTHER SACRED DAYS IN THE HEBREW CALENDAR

NAME OF FEAST OR EVENT	OLD TESTAMENT PURPOSE	NEW TESTAMENT SYMBOLISM	CALENDAR TIME	FARM SEASON (Crops/ Weather)
The Sabbath Day	To have a day of rest and worship (Ex.20:8-11; Ex.31:12-17; Le.23:3; De.5:12-15)	The Sabbath is a symbol of the spiritual rest that God promises to those who believe and follow him. The Sabbath rest is a symbol of redemption, of God's deliverance from the heavy burdens and trials of this life. (Mt.12:1-14; Mt.28:1; Lu. 4:16; Jn.5:9; Ac.13:42; Col.2:16; He.4:1-11)	*Hebrew Time*: Celebrated on the seventh day of each week *Secular Equivalent*: Same as above	Not Applicable
The Sabbatical Year	The Sabbatical Year was celebrated every seven years. During the seventh year the land was given rest from agricultural use and debts were forgiven (Ex. 23:10-11; Le.25:1-7; De.15:1)	Not mentioned in the New Testament	*Hebrew Time*: Celebrated every seven years *Secular Equivalent*: Same as above	Not Applicable
The Year of Jubilee	The Year of Jubilee was celebrated at the end of every forty-ninth year on the Day of Atonement. On this special day, the trumpet would sound out the message of freedom to all the inhabitants of the land who had been held in bondage. In addition, all property was to be returned to the original owners who had been forced to sell because of poverty. This meant that all prices in the economy throughout the forty-nine years were to be fairly adjusted according to the closeness to The Year of Jubilee. (Le.25:8-17; Le. 27:17-24; Nu.36:4)	Not mentioned in the New Testament	*Hebrew Time*: Celebrated at the end of every forty-ninth year on the Day of Atonement. *Secular Equivalent*: Same as above	Not Applicable
The Sacred Assembly	To celebrate the end of the final feast. The sacred assembly was a day of sacrifice and then rest. (Le.23:36; Nu.29:35-38)	Not mentioned in the New Testament	*Hebrew Time:* The 7th Month [Ethanim or Tishri **], on the 22nd Day *Secular Equivalent:* September - October	Plowing of the fields; early autumn rains.

TYPES, SYMBOLS, AND PICTURES
THE BOOK OF ISAIAH
CHAPTERS 36–66

ALPHABETICAL OUTLINE

What is a biblical type or symbol? Simply put, a *biblical type* is a *foreshadowing* of what was to come at a later time in history. Through a person, place, or thing, a biblical type points toward a New Testament fulfillment.

In addition to biblical types, there are what we may call *biblical pictures*. A biblical picture is a lesson that we can see in the Scriptures *without distorting the truth*. The study of biblical types and pictures is a valuable tool in that it helps us apply the truth of the Scriptures in our lives. Scripture itself tells us this:

"Now all these things happened unto them for examples: and they are written for our admonition, upon whom the ends of the world are come" (1 Co.10:11).

"For whatsoever things were written aforetime were written for our learning, that we through patience and comfort of the scriptures might have hope" (Ro.15:4).

PERSON/PLACE/THING	SCRIPTURE, OUTLINE AND DISCUSSION
AMBASSADORS. *Sent ahead of a king. To announce his coming.* *A picture of preparing the way for the LORD.*	Is.40:3-5
BABYLON. **Defeat of.** *A picture of Christ's defeat of all those opposed to God*	Is.40:10
Nation of. *A symbol of the corrupt and immoral world.*	Is.48:14-16
Sudden destruction of. *A picture of judgment on the wicked in the last days.*	Is.47:9-11
CYRUS. *King of Persia. Liberator of Israel.* *A type of Christ.*	Is.45:1-13
EDOMITES. *A symbol of those who reject God.*	Is.63:1-6
Judgment upon. *A picture of Christ returning from the battle of Armageddon.*	Is.63:1-6
FLAX. *A picture of people who lack purpose and meaning in life.*	Is.42:3
GOD. *Arm of.* *A symbol of glorious power.*	Is.40:10
Power of. *To cause nations to submit.* *A picture of the Messiah's kingdom.*	Is.45:14-17
Summons by. *To the nations.* *A picture of future judgment.*	Is.41:1
Vengeance and mercy of. *Prophecy of.* *A picture of Armageddon.*	Is.63:1-64:12
HEZEKIAH. *Entertaining. Of ambassadors. From Babylon. A picture of pride.*	Is.39:1-8
ISRAEL. *Deliverance of.* *From captivity.* *A symbol of redemption.*	Is.48:12-22; 49:9; 51:3, 17
Fleeing. From the captivity of Babylon. A picture of spiritual separation.	Is.52:11-12
Freedom of. *From captivity.* *A picture of Christ setting people free from sin and death.*	Is.45:4-13
Restoration of. *A symbol of God's sovereignty.*	Is.48:20-22
JERUSALEM. *Restoration of.* *A picture of the Holy City during the Millennium.*	Is.60:1-22

PERSON/PLACE/THING	SCRIPTURE, OUTLINE AND DISCUSSION
JUDGMENT. *Upon the nations. Execution of. By King Cyrus of Persia*. A picture of Christ as Judge of the world.	Is.46:11
LAMB. *Led to slaughter*. A picture of Christ as the Lamb of God who takes away the sin of the world.	Is.53:10-12
OPPRESSOR. *Defeat of*. A picture of God's vengeance.	Is.47:1-5
PROMISED LAND. A type of heaven.	Is.43:5; 57:14; 58:13-14; 65:9-10
PROPHECY. *Of comfort and freedom*. A picture of believers being set free from the captivity of sin and death.	Is.40:1-48:22
SACKCLOTH. A symbol of repentance.	Is.37:1
SAVIOR. *Kingdom of. Prophecy of*. A picture of life in the Kingdom of Christ.	Is.60:1-22
SNAKE. A symbol of Satan.	Is.65:25
WICKED. *Mercy on. The promise of a glorious future*. A picture of Christ's kingdom on earth.	Is.54:11-17; 59:19-21

TYPES, SYMBOLS, AND PICTURES
THE BOOK OF ISAIAH
CHAPTERS 36–66

CHRONOLOGICAL OUTLINE

What is a biblical type or symbol? Simply put, a *biblical type* is a *foreshadowing* of what was to come at a later time in history. Through a person, place, or thing, a biblical type points toward a New Testament fulfillment.

In addition to biblical types, there are what we may call *biblical pictures*. A biblical picture is a lesson that we can see in the Scriptures *without distorting the truth*. The study of biblical types and pictures is a valuable tool in that it helps us apply the truth of the Scriptures in our lives. Scripture itself tells us this:

"Now all these things happened unto them for examples: and they are written for our admonition, upon whom the ends of the world are come" (1 Co.10:11).

"For whatsoever things were written aforetime were written for our learning, that we through patience and comfort of the scriptures might have hope" (Ro.15:4).

PERSON/PLACE/THING	SCRIPTURE, OUTLINE AND DISCUSSION
SACKCLOTH. *A symbol of repentance.*	Is.37:1
HEZEKIAH. *Entertaining. Of ambassadors. From Babylon. A picture of pride.*	Is.39:1-8
PROPHECY. *Of comfort and freedom. A picture of believers being set free from the captivity of sin and death.*	Is.40:1-48:22
AMBASSADORS. *Sent ahead of a king. To announce his coming. A picture of preparing the way for the LORD.*	Is.40:3-5
GOD. *Arm of. A symbol of glorious power.*	Is.40:10
BABYLON. *Defeat of. A picture of Christ's defeat of all those opposed to God and His people.*	Is.40:10
GOD. *Summons by. To the nations. A picture of future judgment.*	Is.41:1
FLAX. *A picture of people who lack purpose and meaning in life.*	Is.42:3
PROMISED *LAND. A type of heaven.*	Is.43:5; 57:14; 58:13-14; 65:9-10
CYRUS. *King of Persia. Liberator of Israel. A type of Christ.*	Is.45:1-13
ISRAEL. *Freedom of. From captivity. A picture of Christ setting people free from sin and death.*	Is.45:4-13
GOD. *Power of. To cause nations to submit. A picture of the Messiah's kingdom.*	Is.45:14-17
JUDGMENT. *Upon the nations. Execution of. By King Cyrus of Persia. A picture of Christ as Judge of the world.*	Is.46:11
OPPRESSOR. *Defeat of. A picture of God's vengeance.*	Is.47:1-5
BABYLON. *Sudden destruction of. A picture of judgment on the wicked in the last days.*	Is.47:9-11
ISRAEL. *Deliverance of. From captivity. A symbol of redemption.*	Is.48:12-22; 49:9; 51:3, 17
BABYLON. *Nation of. A symbol of the corrupt and immoral world.*	Is.48:14-16

PERSON/PLACE/THING	SCRIPTURE, OUTLINE AND DISCUSSION
ISRAEL. *Restoration of*. A symbol of God's sovereignty.	Is.48:20-22
Fleeing. **From the captivity of Babylon**. A picture of spiritual separation.	Is.52:11-12
LAMB. *Led to slaughter*. A picture of Christ as the Lamb of God who takes away the sin of the world.	Is.53:10-12
WICKED. *Mercy on*. **The promise of a glorious future**. A picture of Christ's kingdom on earth.	Is.54:11-17; 59:19-21
JERUSALEM. *Restoration of*. A picture of the Holy City during the Millennium.	Is.60:1-22
SAVIOR. *Kingdom of*. **Prophecy of**. A picture of life in the Kingdom of Christ.	Is.60:1-22
GOD. *Vengeance and mercy of*. **Prophecy of**. A picture of Armageddon.	Is.63:1-64:12
EDOMITES. A symbol of those who reject God.	Is.63:1-6
Judgment upon. A picture of Christ returning from the battle of Armageddon.	Is.63:1-6
SNAKE. *A symbol of Satan*.	Is.65:25

REMEMBER: When you look up a subject and turn to the Scripture reference, you have not just the Scripture but also an outline and a discussion (commentary) of the Scripture and subject.

This is one of the GREAT FEATURES of *The Preacher's Outline & Sermon Bible*®. Once you have all the volumes, you will have not only what all other Bible indexes give you, that is, a list of all the subjects and their Scripture references, but in addition you will have...

- an outline of every Scripture and subject in the Bible
- a discussion (commentary) on every Scripture and subject
- every subject supported by other Scripture, already written out or cross referenced

DISCOVER THE UNIQUE VALUE for yourself. Quickly glance below to the following subject of the Index. It is:

APOSTASY
Definitions. Listed and discussed. 54:1-17, Intro.
Problem of. Discussed. 54:1-17
Repentance of. Results.
  Deliverance from fear, shame and disgrace. 54:4
  Freedom and joy. 54:1-3
  Glorious future. 54:11-17
  Listed and discussed. 54:4, Thgt.1
  Reconciled to God. 54:5-10

Turn to the first reference. Glance at the Scripture and the outline, then read the commentary. You will immediately see the TREMENDOUS BENEFIT of the INDEX of *The Preacher's Outline & Sermon Bible*®.

OUTLINE AND SUBJECT INDEX

ACCEPTANCE (See **GOD**, Acceptance by)

ACCUSATIONS
Against God's people. By spiritual enemies. Discussed. 36:1-22, Thgt.1
Example. By Rab-Shakeh against King Hezekiah. 36:4-7

ADMONITION (See **BELIEVERS**, Duty; **WARNINGS**)

ADRAMMELECH
Deeds of. Murdered his father. 37:38
Son. Of Sennacherib. 37:38

ADULTERY
Problem of. Discussed. 57:3
Spiritual.
  Example. Judah. 57:3-5
  Meaning. To stray from commitment to God. 57:3

AGE, Messianic (See **MILLENNIUM**)

ALIENATION (See **GOD**, Separation from; **SIN**, Results)

AMBASSADORS
Example. Sent from Babylon to Hezekiah. 39:1-2
Sending of. Ahead of a king. A picture of preparing the way for the Lord. 40:3-5

ANSWER
To life's problems. Jesus Christ. 50:4-9
To Rab-Shakeh. By Hezekiah. He called on the LORD. 37:1-4

APOSTASY
Definitions. Listed and discussed. 54:1-17, Intro.
Problem of. Discussed. 54:1-17
Repentance of. Results.
  Deliverance from fear, shame and disgrace. 54:4
  Freedom and joy. 54:1-3
  Glorious future. 54:11-17
  Listed and discussed. 54:4, Thgt.1
  Reconciled to God. 54:5-10

APPEAL (See **SALVATION**, Invitation to)
By God.
  Calls people to salvation. 45:18-22
  To turn from worthless idols. 46:8-13
  To unbelievers. To accept salvation. 45:20-22
Example. Hezekiah a. to God for help against Assyria. 37:2-4
To God. Fact. Is the best thing to do in times of trial. 37:1-20

ARMAGEDDON
Battle of. Discussed. 63:1–64:12, Intro.
Prophecy about. 63:1–64:12

ARROGANCE (See **PRIDE**)

ASSURANCE
By God. (See **GOD**, Assurance by)
Of deliverance. By God.
  Example. God a. Hezekiah Judah would be delivered from the Assyrians. 37:1-13
To the believer. Promised by God. 37:1-13

ASSYRIA
Commander of.
  Accusations of. Against Hezekiah. 36:4-7
  Rab-Shakeh. 36:4, 11-13, 22, 37:4, 8
Deliverance from. Of Judah. By God.
  How. Slaughtered the Assyrian army. 37:36-38
  Promised. 37:21-35; 39:6
Invasion by.
  Of Israel. Conquered them before Isaiah's time. 36:1–37:8, Intro.
  Of Judah.
    Against Hezekiah. 36:1-22
    End of. By God's miraculous deliverance. 37:21-38
    Reason.
      Hezekiah refused to pay tribute. 36:1
      Thought that Judah was weakened by war. 36:1
Kings of.
  Esarhaddon. 37:38
  Sennacherib. 36:1
Rescue from. (See Deliverance from, above)
Threat of. To Judah. End of. 37:1–37:38

INDEX

COMPLACENCY (See SLOTH)

CONCEIT (See PRIDE)

CONDEMNATION (See JUDG-MENT)

CONFESSION, Of sin
By Isaiah. For the sins of the nation. 59:12-15; 64:5-8
Need for. Reasons. 59:12-15; 64:5-8

CONTRITION (See HUMILITY)

CONVICTION
Fact. Is a work of the Holy Spirit. 44:3-5, Thgt.1

CORRUPTION
Deliverance from. Need for. Discussed. 38:1–39:8, Intro.
In leadership. Warning against. 56:9–57:2

COVENANT
New. Instituted. By Christ. 42:9

COVETOUSNESS (See GREED)

CROSS (See JESUS CHRIST, Death of)

CRUCIFIXION (See JESUS CHRIST, Death of)

CUSH
Enemy. Of Assyria. 37:8-9
King of. Tirhakah. 37:9

CYRUS
Appointment. By God.
Purposes. Listed and discussed. 45:1-8
To execute judgment upon nations. 45:1-3
To free Israel. 45:4-5
King. Of Persia. 41:2-4
Prophecy about.
Agent of God to execute judgment on the nations. 41:2-7
Setting the Jewish exiles free. 44:28–45:3
Title. Anointed one. 45:1
Type. Of Christ. 45:1-13

DANGER
From enemies. (See ENEMIES)
Of pride.
Discussed. 39:1-8, Thgt.1
Pictured by Hezekiah. 39:1-8

DAY OF JUDGMENT (See ARMA-GEDDON; JUDGMENT; MIL-LENNIUM)

DAY OF THE LORD (See ARMA-GEDDON; JUDGMENT; MIL-LENNIUM)

DEATH, Spiritual (See CORRUP-TION)
Defined. Separated eternally from God. 66:24, Thgt.1
Fact.
Is caused by sin. 41:1-29, Intro.; 66:24
Is the fate of the wicked. 66:24
Final result. Hell. 66:24, Thgt.3, Thgt.4
Freedom from.
Discussed. 40:1-31, Intro.
Means. Repentance. 66:24, Thgt.2
Messages about. By Isaiah. 40:1–48:22

DECAY (See CORRUPTION)

DECISION
Demanded. By the Savior. To obey. 50:10-11
Of whom to trust. Fact. Is a d. everyone must make. 36:1-22, Thgt.1
To trust in the Lord. Fact. Needed by everyone. 36:1-22, Thgt. 1

DELIVERANCE
By God. (See FREEDOM; GOD, Deliverance by)
By the work of the suffering Savior. 49:1–59:21
Cry for. Fourfold. 63:15-19
Duty. To seek after. 63:15-19
From fear. Discussed. 51:916, Thgt.1
Need for. Six reasons. 64:5-8
Of Israel. (See ISRAEL, Deliverance of)
Of Judah. (See JUDAH, Deliverance of)
Seeking of. Example. Hezekiah sought God for d. from Assyria. 37:14-20
Source. The LORD. 51:9-16

DESPAIR (See HOPE)
Answer to. Prayer. 37:14-20, Thgt.1
Cause. Trials and temptation. 36:1–37:38, Intro.
Example. Judean leaders. Because of the Assyrian threat. 36:21-22
Mission to. Those weary and in d. By the Savior. 49:14-50:9
Sign of. Torn clothes. 36:21-22

DESPERATION (See DESPAIR)

DEVOTION (See WORSHIP)

DISEASE (See ILLNESS)

DISCIPLINE
Of Israel. Causes. 42:22-25
Purpose.
To draw us to God. 42:23-25
To stir us to repent. 63:11

DISCOURAGEMENT (See DES-PAIR)

DISGRACE (See SHAME)
DISOBEDIENCE (See HARD-HEARTED; REBELLION; SIN)

DISTRESS (See DESPAIR)

EARTH (See MILLENNIUM; WORLD)

EDOM
Judgment upon. A picture of Christ returning from Armageddon. 63:1-2
Symbol. Of those who reject God. 63:1-6

ELIAKIM
Servant. Of Hezekiah.
Envoy.
To Assyria. 36:3-22
To Isaiah. 37:2
Managed the household. 36:3, 37:2
Son. Of Hilkiah. 36:3, 22

EMPTINESS
Feelings of. Discussed. 40:1-31, Intro.

ENCOURAGEMENT
By God. (See GOD, Assurance by)
Fact. Is a need of every person. 40:1-31, Intro.
In Isaiah's sermons. 40:1-48:22
Source.
Greatest. God's promises and presence. 37:1-13, Thgt.1; 40:1-31, Intro.
The LORD. 43:1

END TIMES (See ARMAGEDDON; DAY OF THE LORD; JUDG-MENT; MILLENNIUM; WORLD, Judgment of)

ENDURANCE (See STEADFAST-NESS)

ENEMIES
Deliverance from. Fact. Is promised to the believer. 37:1-13, Thgt.1; 37:21-38, Thgt.1
Of Israel. (See ISRAEL, Enemies)
Of Judah. (See JUDAH, Enemies)
Spiritual. Works of. Threats and oppression. 36:1-22, Thgt.1

ETERNAL LIFE (See LIFE, Eternal)

ETHIOPIA (See CUSH)

EVIL (See JUDGMENT; SIN; WORLD, Evil of)
Listed. Of the oppressor. 47:6-8
Result. Provokes God. 47:8

INDEX

INDEX

Duty.
  Of every person. To prepare the way for s. 40:3-5
  Of the believer. To proclaim s. 40:9
  To seek God. 55:6-13
Fact.
  Is the free gift of God through the Savior, Jesus Christ. 55:1-5; 61:1-62:12
  Was very costly for the LORD. 55:1
Invitation to. By God.
  From the Savior. 55:1-56:8
  To come through His Son. 62:1-12, Thgt.1
  To eunuchs. 56:4
  To foreigners. 55:1; 56:3, 6-7; 65:1-16
  To the outcast. 55:8
Proclaimed. By Isaiah. 40:1-11
Promise of. 44:21-28, Thgt.1; 59:19-21; 61:1-11
Requirements for.
  Listed and discussed. 58:5-7
  Repentance. 40:1-5
Source. God
  His intercession. 59:16
  His mercy. 60:5-10
  His power. 38:1-39:8, Intro.; 45:18-25, Thgt.1
  His Son. Jesus Christ. 61:1-11
Time for. Right now. 60:5-10, Thgt.1; 60:11-14, Thgt.1
Witness of. In the life of the believer. Fact. Is a work of the Holy Spirit. 44:3-5, Thgt.1

SAVIOR (See **JESUS CHRIST**; **MESSIAH**)

SCRIPTURE (See **WORD OF GOD**)

SECURITY (See **BELIEVERS**, Promises to)

SEEKING
For deliverance. Example. Hezekiah s. God for help against Assyria. 37:14-20
The LORD. (See **GOD**, Seeking)

SELF-CENTEREDNESS
Example. Hezekiah. 39:5-8
Result. Desire for power. 45:1-25, Intro.

SELF-EXALTATION (See **BOASTING**; **PRIDE**)
Example. Sennacherib. About his military victories. 36:16-20; 37:10-13
Result. Judgment. 37:21-29

SELF-EXAMINATION
Duty. Of the righteous. To look back ahead and inward. 51:1-8

SELF-RELIANCE (See **PRIDE**; **SELF-SUFFICIENCY**)

SELF-SUFFICIENCY
Judgment of. Torment. 50:10-11

SENNACHERIB
Death of. Murdered by his own sons. 37:38
Invasion by. Of Judah. (See **ASSYRIA**, Invasion by)
Judgment of.
  Reason for. Blasphemy and pride. 37:23-25
  Song of. By Isaiah. 37:22-35
King. Of Assyria. 36:1
Sins of.
  Blasphemy. 37:23
  False worship. 37:38
  Pride. 37:23-25
Successor. Esarhaddon. 37:38
Wars of. Tactics. Against Jerusalem.
  Propaganda. 36:2-10
  Siege works. 36:1-22

SEPARATION
Pictured. By Israel fleeing from Babylon. 52:11-12
Spiritual. Duty to. Discussed. 52:11-12, Thgt.1

SERVANT (See **BELIEVERS**; **JESUS CHRIST**, Prophecy about)

SET FREE (See **FREEDOM**)

SHAME
Deliverance from. Promised.
  To Israel. 54:4
  To the repentant. 54:4
Suffering of. By the Messiah. 52:14; 53:2-4

SHEBNA
Envoy.
  To Assyria. 36:3-22
  To Isaiah. 37:2
Scribe. 36:3, 22, 37:2
Servant. To Hezekiah. 36:3-22

SHAREZER
Deeds of. Murdered his father. 37:38
Son. Of Sennacherib. 37:38

SICKNESS (See **ILLNESS**)

SIN (See **SALVATION**; **WORLD**, Evil of)
Confession of.
  Example. Isaiah. For Judah. 59:12-15; 64:5-8
  Need for. Reasons. 59:12-15; 64:5-8
Fact.
  Describes the behavior of the wicked. 59:3-8
  S. enslaves. 43:1, Thgt.1; 61:1-62:12, Intro.

S. is life-threatening. 61:1-62:12, Intro.
S. is universal. 59:3-8, Thgt.1.
Freedom from.
  Discussed. 40:1-31, Intro.
  Messages about. By Isaiah. 40:1-48:22
Impact of. On society. 59:9
Judgment of. Surety of.
  (See **JUDGMENT**, Surety of)
List of.
  Of Judah. 59:3-8
  Of oppressors. 47:6-8
Of Israel. (See **ISRAEL**, Sins of)
Penalty of.
  Is death. 53:4-6
  Payment for. (See Ransom for, Redemption from, below)
Problem of. 59:1-2
Ransom for. Discussed. 43:1-28, Intro.; 52:13-53:12, Intro.
Redemption from. Means.
  By the power of God. 38:1-39:8, Intro.; 45:18-25, Thgt.1
  By the shed blood of Jesus Christ. 43:1, Thgt.1; 44:21-28, Thgt.1; 52:13-53:12, Intro.
Results. (See also **JUDGMENT**)
  Guilt. 59:3-8
  Listed and discussed. 59:9-11
  Separates a person from God. 59:1-21
Witness about. Fact. Is a work of the Holy Spirit. 44:3-5, Thgt.1

SINNERS (See **UNBELIEVERS**; **WORLD**)

SLAVERY (See **BONDAGE**)
Problem of. Discussed. 48:1-22, Intro.
Spiritual. Freedom from.
  Available to those who trust in God. 48:1-22, Intro.
  God's plan for all. 48:1-22, Intro.

SLOTH
Dangers of. Discussed. 32:11-14
Warning against. 32:9-10

SOCIETY (See **WORLD**)
Leadership in. Need for. Discussed. 45:1-25, Intro.
Impact upon. Of sin. 59:9-11
Problems in.
  Answer to. Jesus Christ. 50:4-9
  Listed and discussed. 42:1-25, Intro.
  Oppression. 47:1-15, Intro.
  Slavery. 48:1-22, Intro.

SORCERY (See **OCCULT**)

SOUTHERN KINGDOM (See **JUDAH**)

SOVEREIGNTY (See **GOD**, Sovereignty of)

INDEX

INDEX

Promises in. Assurance of salvation
being made possible. 62:1-5
Prophecies in.
About the Messiah. 49:1-50:11;
52:13mjk–53:12; 61:1–62:12
Fulfillment of. Guaranteed by
God. 47:3-5
Spoken. By the Messiah. 49:2

WORKS, of God (See **GOD**, Works of)

WORLD (See **SOCIETY**; **UNBE-
LIEVERS**)
Destruction of. Pictured by the de-
feat of Babylon. 47:9-11
Evil of.
Discussed. 52:11-12, Thgt.1; 55:2
Pictured. By the evil nation of
Babylon. 48:14-16
Fact. God is greater than all the peo-
ple of the w. 40:22-24
History of.
Fact. Is controlled by God. 41:1-29
Last days of.
Events during. 66:7-14
Millennium. Discussed. 65:1-
25, DS#1

Judgment of.
Described. 66:15-18
Discussed. 66:1-24, Intro.
Pictured. By the defeat of Baby-
lon. 40:10
Witnessing during. In order to
save all who will. 66:19-21
New. Prophecy about. Guaranteed.
66:22-23
Problems in.
Answer to. Jesus Christ. 50:4-9
Is separated from God. 59:1-21
Listed and discussed. 42:1-25,
Intro.
Should arouse us to repent. 41:1-
7, Thgt.2
Separation from.
By the righteous. Discussed.
52:11-12, Thgt.1
God. Fact. Is the sad state of the
w. 59:1-21, Intro.
Tragedy of. No one to intercede for
sin. 59:16

WORLDLINESS (See **SIN**)

WORSHIP
False. (See **GODS, False**; **IDOLA-
TRY**)
Cause. Spiritual blindness and
stupidity. 44:15-20
Description of. 57:3-14

Example.
Judah. 57:3-5
Sennacherib. 37:38
Inadequacy. Discussed. 41:12-29;
47:12-15
Judgment of. 65:11-12; 66:3-6
Result. No help in time of trou-
ble. 46:1-2
Of God.
Example.
By Hezekiah. 37:16; 38:9-20
In the Messiah's kingdom.
66:21-23
Fact. We should only w. God.
41:12-29, Thgt.1
Failure to. Sin of. Example. Isra-
el. 43:22-28
In eternity. 60:11-14; 66:21-23
Principles of. 66:1-6
Rejection of. Reasons. 66:3-6

WRATH OF GOD (See **ARMA-
GEDDON**; **JUDGMENT**; **MIL-
LENNIUM**)

YAHWEH (See **GOD**)

ZION (See **JERUSALEM**)

LEADERSHIP MINISTRIES WORLDWIDE

PURPOSE STATEMENT

LEADERSHIP MINISTRIES WORLDWIDE exists to equip ministers, teachers, and laypersons in their understanding, preaching, and teaching of God's Word by publishing and distributing worldwide *The Preacher's Outline & Sermon Bible*® and derivative works to reach & disciple all people for Jesus Christ.

MISSION STATEMENT

1. To make the Bible so understandable – its truth so clear and plain – that men and women everywhere, whether teacher or student, preacher or hearer, can grasp its message and receive Jesus Christ as Savior, and…

2. To place the Bible in the hands of all who will preach and teach God's Holy Word, verse by verse, precept by precept, regardless of the individual's ability to purchase it.

The Preacher's Outline & Sermon Bible and derivative works have been given to LMW as LMW Resources for printing and distribution worldwide at/below cost, by those who remain anonymous. One fact, however, is as true today as it was in the time of Christ:

THE GOSPEL IS FREE, BUT THE COST OF TAKING IT IS NOT

LMW depends on the generous gifts of believers with a heart for Him and a love for the lost. They help pay for the printing, translating, and distributing of LMW Resources into the hands of God's servants worldwide, who will present the Gospel message with clarity, authority, and understanding beyond their own.

LMW was incorporated in the state of Tennessee in July 1992 and received IRS 501 (c)(3) non-profit status in March 1994. LMW is an international, nondenominational mission organization. All proceeds from USA sales, along with donations from donor partners, go directly to underwrite translation and distribution projects of LMW Resources to preachers, church and lay leaders, and Bible students around the world.

LMW Resources

This material, like similar works, has come from imperfect man and is thus susceptible to human error. We are nevertheless grateful to God for both calling us and empowering us through His Holy Spirit to undertake this task. Because of His goodness and grace, *The Preacher's Outline & Sermon Bible*® New Testament and the Old Testament volumes have been completed.

LMW Resources include *The Minister's Personal Handbook, The Believer's Personal Handbook,* and other helpful resources available in printed form as well as electronically on various digital platforms.

God has given the strength and stamina to bring us this far. Our confidence is that as we keep our eyes on Him and remain grounded in the undeniable truths of the Word, we will continue to produce other helpful resources for God's dear servants to use in their Bible study and discipleship.

We offer this material, first, to Him in whose name we labor and serve and for whose glory it has been produced and, second, to everyone everywhere who studies, preaches, and teaches the Word.

Our daily prayer is that each volume will lead thousands, millions, yes even billions, into a better understanding of the Holy Scriptures and a fuller knowledge of Jesus Christ the Incarnate Word, of whom the Scriptures so faithfully testify.

You will be pleased to know that Leadership Ministries Worldwide partners with Christian organizations, printers, and mission groups around the world to make LMW Resources available and affordable in many countries and foreign languages. It is our goal that *every* leader around the world, both clergy and lay, will be able to understand God's holy Word and present God's message with more clarity, authority, and understanding—all beyond his or her own power.

Leadership Ministries Worldwide
1928 Central Avenue • Chattanooga, TN 37408
1(800) 987-8790
Email: info@lmw.org
lmw.org

LEADERSHIP MINISTRIES WORLDWIDE

Product Listing

THE PREACHER'S OUTLINE & SERMON BIBLE® (POSB)   *Available in KJV (44 vols) & NIV (40 vols)*

OLD TESTAMENT

- Genesis I: Chs. 1–11
- Genesis II: Chs. 12–50
- Exodus I: Chs. 1–18
- Exodus II: Chs. 19–40
- Leviticus
- Numbers
- Deuteronomy
- Joshua
- Judges, Ruth
- 1 Samuel
- 2 Samuel
- 1 Kings
- 2 Kings
- 1 Chronicles
- 2 Chronicles
- Ezra, Nehemiah, Esther
- Job

- Psalms I: Chs. 1-41
- Psalms II: Chs. 42-106
- Psalms III: Chs. 107-150
- Proverbs
- Ecclesiastes, Song of Solomon
- Isaiah I: Chs. 1-35
- Isaiah II: Chs. 36-66
- Jeremiah I: Chs. 1-29
- Jeremiah II: Chs. 30-52, Lamentations
- Ezekiel
- Daniel, Hosea Joel, Amos, Obadiah, Jonah, Micah, Nahum
- Habakkuk, Zephaniah, Haggai, Zechariah, Malachi

NEW TESTAMENT

- Matthew I: Chs. 1–15
- Matthew II: Chs. 16-28
- Mark
- Luke
- John
- Acts
- Romans
- 1 & 2 Corinthians
- Galatians, Ephesians, Philippians, Colossians
- 1 & 2 Thessalonians, 1 & 2 Timothy, Titus, Philemon
- Hebrews, James
- 1 & 2 Peter, 1, 2, & 3 John, Jude
- Revelation
- Master Outline & Subject Index

Handbooks

- **What the Bible Says to the Believer** —
  The Believer's Personal Handbook
  11 Chapters. – Over 500 Subjects, 300 Promises, & 400 Verses Expounded - Gift leatherette or paperback options

- **What the Bible Says to the Minister** —
  The Minister's Personal Handbook
  12 Chapters. - 127 Subjects - 400 Verses Expounded - Gift leatherette or paperback options

- **What the Bible Says to the Business Leader**—The Business Leader's Personal Handbook
  12 Chapters – Over 100 topics plus hundreds of scriptural values for conducting business in a 21st-century world — Paperback

- **What the Bible Says About Series** —
  Various Subjects

everyWORD

Scripture, Outline, Commentary of the Gospels with ESV Scripture

- everyWORD: Matthew 1–16:12
- everyWORD: Matthew 16:13–28:20
- everyWORD: Mark
- everyWORD: Luke 1–13:21
- everyWORD: Luke 13:22–24:53
- everyWORD: John

- **The Teacher's Outline & Study Bible™** - Various New Testament Books
  Complete 30 - 45 minute lessons – with illustrations and discussion questions
- *Practical Illustrations — Companion to the POSB Arranged by topic and Scripture reference*
- *LMW Resources on various digital platforms Learn more on our website at lmw.org*
- *Contact for resources in other languages*

Contact Us

LEADERSHIP MINISTRIES WORLDWIDE
1928 Central Avenue • Chattanooga, TN 37408
1(800) 987-8790 • E-mail - info@lmw.org
Order online at lmw.org

Made in the USA
Columbia, SC
31 January 2025